6495

In this magisterial account of the life and work of St Anselm, Sir Richard Southern provides a study in depth of one of the most fascinating minds in Christian history.

St Anselm brings together all the elements of a man whose intensely concentrated search for God filled all the phases and aspects of his life and work. The study covers Anselm's development in prayer, friendship, philosophy and theology, and theological controversy; in his position as archbishop, in his work for the monastic community in Canterbury; in his relations with his disciples and transmitters of his teaching; in the records of his sermons and informal talk; and finally in his relations with his biographer.

Southern argues that Anselm belonged to a different world from the Scholastics of whom he is traditionally held to be the first. The tension of dialectic was quite foreign to Anselm's method of solitary and peaceful contemplation: his thought grew by drawing out the meaning in concepts, not by confrontation of opposites. Although the world he belonged to was essentially monastic, nothing in Anselm's thinking was simply ordinary or typical to his age. In Southern's words: 'He touched the thought, the piety and the politics of the time at every important point; and whatever he touched looked different afterwards.' Despite the austerity of his life and thought, friendship was central to both.

SAINT ANSELM

A PORTRAIT IN A LANDSCAPE

SAINT ANSELM

A PORTRAIT IN A LANDSCAPE

R. W. SOUTHERN

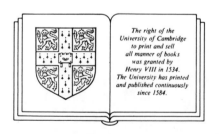

The right of the
University of Cambridge
to print and sell
all manner of books
was granted by
Henry VIII in 1534.
The University has printed
and published continuously
since 1584.

CAMBRIDGE UNIVERSITY PRESS

CAMBRIDGE
NEW YORK   PORT CHESTER
MELBOURNE   SYDNEY

Published by the Press Syndicate of the University of Cambridge
The Pitt Building, Trumpington Street, Cambridge CB2 1RP
40 West 20th Street, New York, NY 10011, USA
10 Stamford Road, Oakleigh, Melbourne 3166, Australia

First published 1990

Printed in Great Britain at the University Press, Cambridge

British Library cataloguing in publication data
Southern, R. W. (Richard William), 1912–
Saint Anselm.
1. Benedictines. Anselm, Saint
I. Title
271′.1′024

Library of Congress cataloguing in publication data
Southern R. W. (Richard William), 1912–
Saint Anselm: a portrait in a landscape/R.W. Southern.
p. cm.
Bibliography
Includes index.
ISBN 0 521 36262 8
1. Anselm, Saint, Archbishop of Canterbury, 1033–1109.
2. Christian saints – England – Biography. I. Title
BX4700.A58S59 1990
282′,092–dc20 89–7237 CIP
[B]

ISBN 0 521 362628 hardback

SE

To my wife

CONTENTS

Preface   xv
Abbreviations and short titles   xix
Chronology of Anselm's life, works, and canonization   xxvii

PART I FROM BIRTH TO REBIRTH, 1033–1070   1

1 ESCAPE FROM CONFINEMENT   3
    I Family and local background   3
   II Flight to the North   11

2 THE YEAR OF DECISION   14
    I The meeting of Anselm and Lanfranc   14
   II The impact of papal policy   19
  III Lanfranc's visit to Rome   25
   IV Anselm's apprenticeship   29
    V Notes on intellectual activity at Bec, 1050–1060   32
         1 The text of Nicholas II's letter to Lanfranc   32
         2 The development of Lanfranc's *Commentary
              on St Paul*   33
         3 Lanfranc's marginal symbols   35

3 ANSELM AND LANFRANC   39
    I Lanfranc's contribution to Anselm's future   39
         1 Lanfranc as teacher   39
         2 Lanfranc as disputant   43
              i The use of grammatical tools   46
             ii The use of dialectical tools   47
                  Substance and *Accidents*   47
                  Equipollent propositions   50
         3 Lanfranc as book-collector   53
   II Anselm's recognition of his debt   59
  III Anselm's *De Grammatico*   62
   IV The parting of the ways   65

CONTENTS

4   THE YEARS OF SILENCE   67
      I   Private and corporate disciplines   67
     II   The influence of the Bible   69
    III   The influence of St Augustine   71
            1 Stylistic similarities   73
            2 The discipline of meditation   77
            3 Similarities and contrasts   80
            4 Different times: different outlooks   82

PART II THE RADIANT YEARS, 1070–1093

5   ANSELM'S NEW START   91
      I   Prayers and Meditations   91
     II   The devotional background   93
    III   The Anselmian transformation   99
     IV   A new direction in medieval devotion   106
      V   Anselm's last phase   109

6   THE GREAT 'MEDITATIONS'   113
      I   Anselm's first peak   113
     II   The Monologion   118
            1 Talk among friends   118
            2 An example of meditation   120
            3 Faith and Reason   123
            4 Faith and understanding   125
    III   The Proslogion   127
            1 A supplement to the Monologion   127
            2 Meditating on the word 'God'   129
            3 Presuppositions of Anselm's argument   132
            4 Principles of meditation   134

7   THE NATURE AND IMPORTANCE OF FRIENDSHIP   138
      I   Anselm's letters of friendship   138
     II   The traditional pattern of friendship   139
    III   The new romantic ideal   141
     IV   The Anselmian experience   143
      V   The question of homosexuality   148
     VI   The symbolism of the kiss   153
    VII   The theology of friendship   155
   VIII   Friendship and the kingdom of Heaven   161

CONTENTS

8   AN UNWELCOME BUT ENLARGING WORLD   166
    I   Theology and the world   167
        1 Worldly liberty   167
        2 Spiritual liberty   171
        3 An outsider's attack   174
    II Anselm faces the world   181
        1 The benefactors of Bec   181
        2 The reluctant archbishop   186

PART III A MONASTIC VIEW IN A DEVELOPING
WORLD, 1093–1109   195

9   ANSELM AND THE HUMAN CONDITION   197
    I   Sources of a new dispute   197
        1 The Jews   198
        2 The Schools   202
    II   The outline of Anselm's argument   205
        1 The problem   206
        2 The necessity of a solution   206
        3 The solution   206
    III The rights of the Devil   207
    IV   Man alone with God   211
    V   Freedom, obedience, and punishment   216
    VI   Feudal imagery and universal order   221

10 'RELEASE MY SOUL FROM THIS SLAVERY'   228
    I   The new archbishop   228
        1 The background   228
        2 Lanfranc's legacy   230
        3 The Investiture dispute   232
    II   The framework of archiepiscopal life   234
        1 The precepts of Gregory the Great   234
        2 Anselm's assistants   238
    III Conflicting evidence   247
        1 Eadmer's records and recollections   247
        2 Anselm's letters   249

11 A NEW ARCHBISHOP'S PROBLEMS OF OBEDIENCE   254
    I   What is the law?   254
    II Problems of monastic obedience   259
        1 King Malcolm's daughter   260
        2 King Harold's daughter   262

III Problems of divided obedience   264
  1 in becoming an archbishop   265
  2 in choosing a pope   268
  3 in defending the Canterbury lands   270
  4 in holding an ecclesiastical Council   272
  5 in consulting the pope   274

12 THE LIBERTY OF THE CHURCH   277
  I Two views of liberty   277
  II The fruits of exile   278
    1 The anathemas of 1099   280
    2 The influence of Hugh, archbishop of Lyons   285
  III Anselm, Henry I, and the liberty of the Church   289
    1 Anselm misses a political opportunity   291
    2 The problem unfold   294
    3 Anselm reverts to essentials   298
    4 The inevitable compromise   302
  IV Final reflections   304

13 THE LIBERTY OF A MONASTIC COMMUNITY   308
  I Organization under Lanfranc   308
  II Anselm's liberating influence   315
  III Anselmian liberty   321

14 AN OLD LIBERTY: THE PRIMACY OF CANTERBURY   330
  I Principles of primacy   330
  II The privileges of primacy   335
    1 Legatine authority   335
    2 Territorial extension   337
      Wales   337
      Ireland   338
      Northern England and Scotland   339
  III The struggle with York   340
  IV Primacy in action   347
  V Was Canterbury's claim to primacy founded   352
    on forgery?
    1 Lanfranc's words in 1072   354
    2 The situation between 1072 and 1120   357
    3 The last resort: forgery   359

PART IV THE HARVEST OF FRIENDS AND
DISCIPLES   365

15 ANSELM'S EARLIEST THEOLOGICAL DISCIPLES   367
    I   Anselm's circle at Canterbury   367
    II Elaborators of Anselm's thoughts   371
        1 Gilbert Crispin, abbot of Westminster   371
        2 Ralph, prior of Rochester and abbot of Battle 372
        3 Honorius Augustodunensis   376

16 THE COLLECTORS OF ANSELM'S WORDS AND
    LETTERS   382
    I   Reporters of conversations and sermons   382
        1 Eadmer as reporter   384
            i   Eadmer's reports of Anselm's talk   384
            ii Eadmer's reports of Anselm's sermons 385
        2 Alexander's reports   389
        3 The reporter of Anselm's parables   390
    II The collectors of Anselm's letters   394
        1 General problems of letter collecting   396
        2 Two central manuscripts   398
        3 The importance of William of Malmesbury's 400
           initiative
        4 The final collections of Canterbury and Bec 402

17 EADMER AND ANSELM   404
    I   The development of a disciple   404
        1 The happy years   404
        2 The fall   410
        3 Patching up the past   414
        4 The road to disaster   416
        5 The years of recovery   418
    II Eadmer's *Anselm*: from intimate portrait to   422
        saint's *Life*
        1 The intimate portrait   422
        2 The saint's *Life*   426
    III In Anselm's footsteps   428
        1 The area of successful imitation   428
        2 Eadmer's *Prayers and Meditations*   430
            i   *On the excellence of the Blessed   430
                Virgin Mary*
            ii An appeal to St Peter   431

iii Eadmer's Guardian Angel 432
iv Eadmer on the Immaculate Conception 432

18 A BACKWARD GLANCE 437
   I Anselm in his time: between two worlds 437
  II The unity of Anselm's life and thought 443
 III Anselm no humanist 447
 IV Anselm and eternity 452

APPENDIX
Towards a history of Anselm's letters 459
   I The main manuscripts 459
  II The problems and their importance 460
 III Anselm's letters as prior and abbot of Bec 461
    1 The contents of **N** 464
    2 Pre-archiepiscopal letters in **V** 464
    3 Pre-archiepiscopal letters in **L** 465
 IV Anselm's archiepiscopal correspondence 466
    1 Preserving the letters 466
    2 The manner of their preservation 466
    3 Collecting the letters into volumes 468
      i Did Anselm make a volume of his archiepiscopal letters? 468
      ii How were the existing collections made? 469
    4 The collectors of the letters 470
      i Eadmer, 1109–1115 470
      ii William of Malmesbury, 1120–23 470
      iii The great Canterbury collection: **L**, *c* 1123–1130 473
      iv The great Bec collection: **V**, *c* 1125 476
  V The transmission of the collection 479
 VI Summary 480

Index 483

PREFACE

This book began as a second edition of my earlier work, *St Anselm and his Biographer*, and my initial intention was simply to make a few corrections and additions which would take account of work done during the twenty-five years since it first appeared. But I soon found that in one way this went too far, and in others not far enough: too far, in that I felt incapable of taking into account all that has appeared in the past thirty years of relevance to the subject; not far enough, in that Anselm is not a subject to be once thought of and then dismissed except for the correction or addition of a few details.

He has been in my thoughts in varying degrees of intensity ever since 1934 when his letters of friendship first attracted me as the revelation of a remarkable personality. This led me to spend several months in the Bibliothèque Nationale collating manuscripts with the intention of making an edition of his letters. I abandoned this plan when I discovered that Dom Schmitt intended to include them in his edition of Anselm's *Works*, and turned to other subjects. But Anselm remained a recurrent theme of lectures on Anselm and his friends, which led to an edition of Eadmer's *Vita Anselmi* and to *Anselm and his Biographer* in 1963.

I was always dissatisfied with the latter. Its plan was confused by attempting to combine a fuller introduction to the *Vita Anselmi* than could be accommodated in my edition with a new *Life* of Anselm. These subjects are only imperfectly related to each other. Yet Eadmer's records are so important for our knowledge of Anselm that he and his biographer cannot be separated; and this remark applies also, though in smaller measure, to the other reporters of Anselm's words. There is no perfect solution to this problem, but in re-thinking the whole subject I have tried to give Eadmer and the other reporters their due place while keeping Anselm more fully and consistently at the centre.

Anselm is so complicated a personality that I cannot but feel the imperfections of the chapters which follow. But there must be an end to all things. Even in 1963, the work had already been thirty years in the making; and now, after nearly another thirty years, it still presents itself as work in progress. I have tried to see Anselm as a whole and to avoid simplifying him, and in doing this I have freely taken from the earlier book whatever I wanted and rejected the rest, sometimes with regret.

Among other themes, Anselm's ideal and practice of friendship remains an important clue to the general character of his life and work. It needs to be understood as an expression of a religious ideal shared by all those who were his teachers, his pupils, and his actual or hoped-for companions in the monastic life. For members of this extensive group, he expressed a warmth of affection which recent scholars have not hesitated to call homosexual. Whether, and in what sense, this word can appropriately be used is a question which I have discussed so far as seemed necessary for understanding him. But, under a somewhat sugary surface, the real meaning of friendship for him is an austere sharing of a common monastic discipline. His relations with other people within, or on the threshold of, the monastic life, are central to his life's activity, and his search for God is at the centre of everything in his life from his arrival at Bec in 1059 to his death in 1109.

To understand this, we need to understand his *Prayers* and *Meditations*, and his doctrine of freedom and Redemption, as well as his attitude to the government of the Church and of the world. Only when we have understood all this, can we begin to understand him as a man as well as a monk, theologian and archbishop. His whole life is full of tensions and unexpected unities, and I cannot hope to have succeeded in conveying the unity of experience and outlook which underlies all these complexities. I can only say that I have tried to bring these threads together.

No idea can be pursued for fifty-five years without many necessary excursions into subjects only slightly or not at all related to it. This diversity has brought some benefits and some weaknesses, of which the latter will perhaps be more apparent than the former. Preparing an edition of Eadmer's *Life* of St Anselm, and then collaborating with Dom Schmitt in editing the reports of Anselm's talk and the unfinished fragments of his writings, have been the most fruitful of these excursions. A spurious letter promoting the observance of the Immaculate Conception, which caught my attention while collating the manuscripts of Anselm's letters in 1934, ultimately bore fruit in tracing its complicated association with Anselm's disciples and his influence on them. Most recently, that early period of work on the manuscripts of Anselm's letters got a new importance when it was necessary to consider some recent attempts to depict Anselm as a manipulator of his collection of letters for political purposes.

Altogether, therefore, some of my earliest work has unexpectedly taken a more central place in the interpretation of his life than seemed at all likely when I wrote the earlier form of this book thirty years ago. With all these complexities, it has been more difficult than ever to bring the varied aspects of his life and influence together into a coherent whole. At best, what I present here can be no more than a provisional interpretation of one of the most complex and fascinating characters in Christian history.

The many articles by Dom André Wilmart announcing his discoveries of the manuscripts of Anselm's works provided the most powerful impetus to my earliest work. Dom Schmitt's edition was important as providing the first texts which took account of Wilmart's discoveries, with the addition of many of his own. Of more recent work, Dr G. R. Evans's Anselm *Concordance* has been of the greatest help; and the works of Professor Sally Vaughn and Dr Walter Fröhlich have been a frequent stimulus to further thought. Dr Pierre Chaplais and Professor Donald Matthew helped me to understand several points in the letter of Pope Nicholas II to Lanfranc, which I print in Chapter 2; Professor William Kneale has once again enlightened me on several of the problems dealt with in Chapter 3; Dr Margaret Gibson's work has been an essential help in the same chapter; Dr Martin Brett has helped me on the matters dealt with in Chapter 14; Dr Geoffrey Nuttall suggested improvements in Chapter 18. Finally, Dr Adrian Ballentyne corrected my enumeration of letters and Professor Rodney Thomson drew my attention to several problems in the Appendix, and Dr Peter Meadows made the diagram on p. 458. My debt to these scholars and many others over the years is very great and I can now repay them only with my sincere thanks. But I must not burden them with my errors, for I have not always followed their advice.

I also owe a great debt to the officers of the Cambridge University Press, and especially to Frances Brown, for their patience and skill in coping with and correcting a text which has shown a remarkable propensity for fluidity.

I have left to the last my chief debt, which is to my wife, who –

besides correcting many errors – has been responsible for the unending process of machining necessary for bringing the book to completion. The earlier form of this work was dedicated to her; and now with even greater emphasis and gratitude, is also this, its latest and last.

ABBREVIATIONS AND SHORT TITLES

Biblical references are by chapter and verse (e.g. Romans i, 6)
c circa (approximate dates)
c.(cc.) chapter number(s)
col(s). column number(s) in Migne's *Patrologia*

MANUSCRIPTS

for individual MSS and their *sigla*, see Index; locations
are abbreviated as follows:

BL	British Library, London
Bodl.	Bodleian Library, Oxford
Bnl	Bibliothèque Nationale, Paris, MS latin
CCCC	Corpus Christi College, Cambridge
Lamb.	Lambeth Palace Library, London
TCC	Trinity College, Cambridge
Vat.	Vatican Library

PRINTED WORKS

AA. SS. OSB. J. Mabillon, *Acta Sanctorum Ordinis Sancti Benedicti*, 9 vols.,
 1668–1701, Paris
AHDLMA Archives d'histoire doctrinaire et littéraire du moyen âge
Anglia Sacra Henry Wharton, *Anglia Sacra sive Collectio historiarum . . . de
 archiepiscopis et episcopis Angliae*, 2 vols., London, 1691
ASC Anglo-Saxon Chronicle (a convenient translation by G. N. Garmonsway
 will be found in the Everyman Library)
Baeumker, 1914 *Das Inevitabile des Honorius Augustodunensis*, ed. F. Baeu-
 mker, *BGPTMA*, xiii
Barlow, 1983 Frank Barlow, *William Rufus*, London
Baudot, 1989 Marcel Baudot, 'Les prieurés du Bec-Hellouin', in *Les Amis du
 Bec-Hellouin*, 86, 1989, pp. 5–15, with excellent maps
Becker, 1885 Gustav Becker, *Catalogi Bibliothecarum antiqui*, Bonn

Bede, *Hist. Eccl.* Bede, *Ecclesiastical History of the English People*, ed. B. Colgrave and R. A. B. Mynors, Oxford, 1969

Bestul, 1977 T. H. Bestul, 'St Anselm and the continuity of Anglo-Saxon devotional traditions', *Annuale médiévale*, 21, pp. 167–70

1978 'A collection of Anselm's Prayers in BL MS Cotton Vespasian D.xxvi, *Medium Aevum*, Oxford, 47, pp.1–5

BGPTMA Beiträge zur Geschichte der Philosophie u. Theologie des Mittelalters: Texte u. Untersuchungen, begründet von C. Baeumker, Münster

Bibl. Hag. Lat. Bibliotheca hagiographica latina antiquae et mediae aetatis ed. Socii Bollandiani (2 vols. 1891–1901; Suppl. 1911)

Biffi, 1988 Inos Biffi, *Giovanni di Salisbury, Vita di Anselmo*, Milan

Biffi-Marabelli, 1988 Inos Biffi and C. Marabelli, *Anselmo d'Aosta, Opere*, i: Lettere, di priore e abbate del Bec, Milan

Birch W. de Gray Birch, *Cartularium Saxonicum*, 3 vols., London, 1885–93

Blumenkranz, 1956 B. Blumenkranz, ed. *Gilberti Crispini, Disputatio Iudaei et Christiani, Stromata patristica et mediaevalia*, iii, Utrecht

Böhmer, 1902 H. Böhmer, *Die Falschungen Lanfrancs*, Leipzig

Brett, 1975 Martin Brett, *The English Church under Henry I*, Oxford

Brooke, 1931 Z. N. Brooke, *The English Church and the Papacy from the Conquest to the Reign of John*, Cambridge

Brooks, 1984 Nicholas Brooks, *The Early History of the Church of Canterbury*, Leicester

Buttimer, 1939 C. H. Buttimer, ed., Hugh of St Victor, *Didascalicon de studio legendi*, Washington

Cantor, 1958 Norman F. Cantor, *Church, Kingship and Lay Investiture in England, 1089–1135*, Princeton

CC Corpus Christianorum, series latina, Turnhout, 1953–

CDH St Anselm, *Cur Deus Homo*, Schmitt ii, 38–133 (*references are to Book and Chapter*)

Charlesworth, 1965 M. J. Charlesworth, *St Anselm's* Proslogion, *transl. with introduction and commentary*, Oxford

Chibnall, 1956 Marjorie Chibnall, ed., John of Salisbury, *Historia Pontificalis*, Oxford

1959 Marjorie Chibnall, 'The relations of St Anselm with English dependencies of the abbey of Bec', *Spicilegium Beccense*, i, 521–50

1984 Marjorie Chibnall, *The World of Ordericus Vitalis*, Oxford (*see also*: Morgan; *Ordericus Vitalis*)

Concordance A Concordance to the Works of St Anselm, ed. G. R. Evans, 4 vols., New York

Councils, 1981 *Councils and Synods with Other Documents Relating to the English Church*, i, 871–1204, ed. D. Whitelock, M. Brett, and C. N. L. Brooke, 1981

CSEL Corpus Scriptorum ecclesiasticorum latinorum, Vienna

DA Deutsches Archiv für Geschichte des Mittelalters, (formerly *Neues Archiv*), 1937–

DCD St Augustine, *De Civitate Dei, PL*, 41

DCSD Lanfranc, *Liber de corpore et sanguine Domini, PL*, 150, cols. 404–42

DSC Berengarius Turonensis, *De Sacra Coena adversus Lanfrancum*, ed. A. F. et F. Th. Vischer, Berlin, 1824

DTC Dictionnaire de théologie catholique, ed. A. Vacant, E. Mangenot, and E. Amann, 1903–50, Paris

Douglas, 1964 D. C. Douglas, *William the Conqueror: the Norman Impact upon England*, London

EHR English Historical Review

Endres, 1906 J. A. Endres, *Honorius Augustodunensis: Beitrag zur Geschichte des geistigen Lebens im xii. Jahrhundert*, Kempten-Munich

Ep. (Epp.) St Anselm *Epistola (Epistolae)*. Two numbers are given: first that of Schmitt; second, that of *PL*, 158–9. If one of these numbers is omitted, the letter is omitted in either Schmitt or *PL*

Ep. De Incarn. Verbi St Anselm, *Epistola de Incarnatione Verbi*, Schmitt i, 281–290 (1st recension) ii, 3–41 (2nd recension)

Evans, 1978 G. R. Evans, *Anselm and Talking about God*, Oxford

1980 *Anselm and a New Generation*, Oxford

Fiske, 1961 F. Fiske, 'St Anselm and friendship', *Studia Monastica*, 3, pp. 259–90, Montserrat (Barcelona)

Flint, 1988 Valerie I. J. Flint, *Ideas in the Medieval West: Texts and their Context*, Variorum Reprints, London

Fröhlich, 1980 Walter Fröhlich, 'Die Entstehung der Briefsammlung Anselms von Canterbury', *Historisches Jahrbuch*, 100, 457–66

1983 'The letters omitted from Anselm's collection of letters', *Anglo-Norman Studies*, 6, *Proceedings of the Battle Conference*, 1983, (pr. 1984), 58–71

1984 'The genesis of Anselm's collection of letters', *American Benedictine Review*, 35, 249–66

Gibson, 1971 Margaret Gibson, 'Lanfranc's Commentary on the Pauline Epistles', and 'Lanfranc's Notes on Patristic texts', *JTS*, NS. 22, pp. 86–112, 435–50

1978 *Lanfranc of Bec*, Oxford

1979 *The Letters of Lanfranc, Archbishop of Canterbury*, ed. and translated by Helen Clover and Margaret Gibson, *Oxford Medieval Texts*

Gilbert Crispin, *Works The Works of Gilbert Crispin, Abbot of Westminster*, ed. A. S. Abulafia and G. R. Evans, *Auctores Britannici Medii Aevi*, viii, 1986

GP William of Malmesbury, *Gesta Pontificum*, ed. N. E. S. A. Hamilton 1870

GR William of Malmesbury, *Gesta Regum*, ed. W. Stubbs, 2 vols, *RS*, 1887–9

Gratian *Decretum Magistri Gratiani*, in *Corpus Iuris Canonici*, i, 1879, ed. E. Friedberg

Gregorii VII Registrum Das Register Gregors VII, ed. E. Caspar, *MGH Ep. Sel.* 1920

H and S i–iii A. W. Hadden and W. Stubbs, *Councils and Ecclesiastical*

Documents relating to Great Britain and Ireland, 3 vols, Oxford, 1869–71
HCY Historians of the Church of York and its Archbishops, ed. J. Raine, *RS*, 3 vols., 1879–94
Henry, 1964 D. P. Henry, *The De Grammatico of St Anselm*, Notre Dame
 1967 D. P. Henry, *The Logic of Saint Anselm*, Oxford
HJ Historisches Jahrbuch, Cologne
HN Eadmer, *Historia Novorum in Anglia*, ed. M. Rule, *RS*, 1884
HN, 1964 *Eadmer's History of Recent Events*, transl. by G. Bosanquet, London
Holtzmann, 1938 R. Holtzmann, *Zur Papstwahldekret von 1059*, *ZRG,KA*
Hopkins, 1972 Jasper Hopkins, *A Companion to the Study of St Anselm*, Minneapolis
 1974–6 J. Hopkins and H. Richardson, *Anselm of Canterbury*, (translations of all Anselm's treatises), 4 vols. Toronto and New York
Hugh the Chanter Hugh the Chanter, *History of the Church of York, 1066–1127*, ed. and transl. Charles Johnson, 1961, Edinburgh and Oxford
Hunt, 1943, 1950 R. W. Hunt, 'Studies on Priscian in the 12th century' *MARS*, 1, Pt 2, 1943, 194–231; 2, 1950, 1–56
In Pss St Augustine, *Enarrationes in Psalmos*, *PL*, 36–37
JWCI Journal of the Warburg and Courtauld Institutes
JTS Journal of Theological Studies
Ker, 1960 N. R. Ker, *English manuscripts in the Century after the Conquest*, Oxford
Kohlenberger, 1972 Helmut Kohlenberger, *Similitudo und Ratio: Überlegungen zur Methode bei Anselm von Canterbury*, Bonn
Knowles, 1940 David Knowles, *The Monastic Order in England, 943–1216*, Cambridge
Krause, 1960 Hans-Georg Krause, *Das Papstwahldekret von 1059 und seine Rolle im Investiturstreit, Studi Gregoriani*, vii, Rome
Lanfranc's Constitutions The Monastic Constitutions of Lanfranc, ed. D. Knowles, 1951, Edinburgh and Oxford
Leclercq, 1946 Jean Leclercq and J.P.Bonnes, *Un Maître de la vie spirituelle au xi siècle:Jean de Fécamp*, Paris
 1953 *Studia Anselmiana*, 2e série, xxxi: 'Ecrits spirituels d'Elmer de Cantorbéry', pp. 45–117; 'La lettre de Gilbert Crispin sur la vie monastique', pp. 118–23; 'Les lettres familières d'un moine du Bec', pp. 141–73
Lefèvre, 1954 Y. Lefèvre, *L'Elucidarium et les Lucidaires, Bibliothèque des écoles françaises d'Athènes et de Rome*, clxx
Levison, 1946 W. Levison, *England and the Continent in the Eighth Century*, Oxford
Leyser, 1984 Henrietta Leyser, *Hermits and the New Monasticism: A Study of Religious Communities in Western Europe, 1100–1150*, London
Liebermann, 1879 F. Liebermann, *Ungedrückte Anglo-Normannische Geschichtsquellen*, Strasburg

1886 'Anselm v. Canterbury u. Hugo von Lyon', *Hist. Aufsätze dem Andenken G. Waitz gewidmet*, pp. 156–203

Lottin, 1959 O. Lottin, *Psychologie et morale aux XIIe et XIIIe siècles*, 5: *L'école d'Anselme de Laon et de Guillaume de Champeaux*

Mabillon, *AA SS OSB* Jean Mabillon, *Acta Sanctorum Ordinis S. Benedicti*, 9 vols., 1668–1701, Paris

Macdonald, 1926 A. J. Macdonald, *Lanfranc: A Study of his Life, Works and Writing*, Oxford

McIntyre, 1954 J. McIntyre, *St Anselm and his Critics: A Reinterpretation of the Cur Deus Homo*, Edinburgh

McGuire, 1988 B. P. McGuire, *Friendship and Community: The Monastic Experience, 350–1250*, Kalamazoo

MARS Medieval and Renaissance Studies, ed. R. W. Hunt and R. Klibansky, 1–6, London, 1941–68

Matthew, 1962 Donald Matthew, *The Norman Monasteries and their English Possessions*, Oxford

Med. St Anselm, *Meditationes*, Schmitt, iii, 76–91

Memorials Memorials of St Anselm, ed. R. W. Southern and F. S. Schmitt, *Auctores Britannici Medii Aevi*, i, 1969.

Memorials of St Dunstan ed. W. Stubbs, *RS*, 1874

MGH, SS Monumenta Germaniae Historica, Scriptores in Folio

MGH, Ep. Sel. Monumenta Germaniae Historica, Epistolae Selectae

Michel, 1936 Anton Michel, *Papstwahl und Königsrecht: das Papstwahlkonkordat von 1059*, Munich

    1939 'Das Papstwahlpactum von 1059', *HJ*, 59, 291–351

Montclos, 1971 J. de Montclos, *Lanfranc et Bérenger, Spicilegium Sacrum Lovaniense*, xxxvii, Louvain-Paris

Monol. St Anselm, *Monologion*, Schmitt, i

Morgan, 1946 Marjorie Morgan, *The English Lands of the Abbey of Bec*, Oxford (see also Chibnall)

Or. St Anselm, *Orationes*, Schmitt, iii, 1–75

Ordericus Vitalis, i–vi Ordericus Vitalis, *The Ecclesiastical History*, ed. and transl. by Marjorie Chibnall, i–vi, *Oxford Medieval Texts* 1968–80

Pächt, 1956 Otto Pächt, 'The illustrations of Anselm's Prayers and Meditations', *JWCI*, 19, pp. 68–83

PUE Papsturkunden in England ed. W. Holtzmann, 3 vols., *Abhandlungen der Gesellschaft der Wissenschaften in Göttingen*, 1930–52

PL J. P. Migne, *Patrologia Latina*, 221 vols., Paris, 1844–64

Porée, 1901 A. A. Porée, *Histoire de l'abbaye du Bec*, 2 vols, Evreux

Prévité-Orton, 1912 C.W.Prévité-Orton, *The Early History of the House of Savoy, 1000–1233*, Cambridge

Prosl. St Anselm, *Proslogion*, Schmitt, i

RB Revue Bénédictine

Regesta Regesta Regum Anglo-Normannorum: i.1066–1100, ed. H. W. C.

Davis, 1913, Oxford; ii.1100–1135, ed. H. A. Cronne and R. H. C. Davis, 1968, Oxford

Regularis Concordia *Regularis Concordia Anglicae nationis monachorum et sanctimonialium*, ed. Thomas Symons, 1953, Edinburgh and Oxford

Reg. S. Ben. Regula S. Benedicti

R.Hist.S Royal Historical Society, London

Rivière, 1934 Jean Rivière, *Le Dogme de la Redemption au début du Moyen Âge, Bibliothèque Thomiste*, xix, Paris

   1936 'D'un singulière emprunt à S. Anselme chez Raoul de Laon', *Revue des sciences religieuses*, 16, pp. 344–6

Roques, 1963 René Roques, *Anselme de Canterbéry: Pourquoi Dieu s'est fait Homme, Sources chrétiennes*, 91, Paris

RS Rolls Series (Chronicles and Memorials of Great Britain and Ireland during the Middle Ages, published under the direction of the Master of the Rolls), 99 vols., London, 1858–96

RTAM Revue de théologie ancienne et médiévale

Salter, 1925 H. E. Salter, 'Two deeds about the Abbey of Bec', *EHR*, 40, 73–6

Schmitt i–vi F. S. Schmitt, ed. *S. Anselmi Opera Omnia*, i, Seckau, 1938; i (repr.)–vi, Edinburgh, 1946–61

   1932 *Zur Chronologie der Werke des hl. Anselm, RB*, 44, pp. 322–50

   1936 ed., *Ein neues unvollendetes Werk des hl. Anselm von Canterbury, BGPTMA*, xxiii, 3

   1939 *Cinq recensions de l'Epistola de Incarnatione Verbi de S. Anselme, RB*, 51, pp. 275–90

   1954 'Geschichte u. Beurteilung der früheren Anselmausgaben', *Studien u. Mitteilungen zur Geschichte des Benediktinerordens*, pp. 90–114

   1955 'Die unter Anselm veranstaltete Ausgabe seiner Werke u. Briefe: die Codices Bodley 271 u. Lambeth 59', *Scriptorium*, 9, pp. 64–75

Searle, 1980 Eleanor Searle, ed. and transl. *The Chronicle of Battle Abbey*, Oxford

Sharpe, 1985 Richard Sharpe, 'Two contemporary poems on St Anselm attributed to William of Chester', *RB*, 95, pp. 266–79

Southern, 1941 R. W. Southern, 'St Anselm and his English pupils', *MARS* 1, pp 3–34

   1948 'Lanfranc of Bec and Berengar of Tours', in *Studies in Medieval History presented to F. M. Powicke*, ed. R. W. Hunt, W. A. Pantin and R. W. Southern, Oxford, pp. 27–48

   1954 'St Anselm and Gilbert Crispin, Abbot of Westminster', *MARS* 3, pp. 78–115

   1958i 'The Canterbury forgeries' *EHR* 73, pp. 193–226

   1958ii 'The English origins of the Miracles of the Virgin', *MARS* 4, pp. 176–216

1963i *St Anselm and his Biographer*, Cambridge

1963ii ed. *The Life of St Anselm by Eadmer*, Oxford

1986 *Robert Grosseteste: The Growth of an English Mind in Medieval Europe*, Oxford

1988 'Sally Vaughn's Anselm: an examination of the foundations'; *Albion*, 20, pp. 181–204

H. M. Taylor, 1969 'The Anglo-Saxon cathedral church at Canterbury', *Archeological Journal*, 126, pp. 101–30, London

J. Taylor, 1961 Jerome Taylor ed. and transl. *The* Didascalicon *of Hugh of St Victor: A Medieval Guide to the Arts*, New York and London

Thomson, 1977 R. M. Thomson, ed., *The Life of Gundulf*, Toronto

1987 R. M. Thomson, ed., *William of Malmesbury*, Woodbridge

VA Eadmer, *Vita Anselmi*, *PL* 158, cols. 49–120; page refs. are to notes in Southern, 1963ii

Vaughn, 1987 Sally N. Vaughn, *Anselm of Bec and Robert of Meulan, the Innocence of the Dove and the Wisdom of the Serpent*, University of California Press

1988 'Anselm: saint and statesman', *Albion*, 20, 205–20

William of Jumièges Guillaume de Jumièges, *Gesta Normannorum ducum*, ed. J. Marx, Société de l'histoire de Normandie, 1914

Williamson, 1929 E. W. Williamson, ed., *The Letters of Osbert of Clare*, Oxford

Wilmart, 1923 *Le Recueil des Prières de St Anselme*, intro. by A. Wilmart, ed. A. Castel, *Collection Pax*, Paris

1924 'La tradition des prières de S. Anselme: Tables et Notes', *RB*, 36, pp. 52–71

1926 'La destinataire de la lettre de S. Anselme sur l'état et les vœux de religion', *RB*, 38, pp. 310–20

1928 'Une lettre inédite de S. Anselme à une moniale inconstante', *RB*, 40, pp. 319–32

1929 'Les prières envoyées par S. Anselme à la comtesse Mathilde en 1104', *RB*, 41, pp. 368–415

1931i 'La tradition des lettres de S. Anselme: lettres inédites de S. Anselme et ses correspondants', *RB*, 43, pp. 38–54

1931ii 'Les propres corrections de S. Anselme dans sa grande prière à la Vierge Marie', *RTAM*, 2, pp. 189–204

1931iii 'La tradition des grands ouvrages de S. Augustin', *Miscellanea Agostiniana*, ii, pp. 257–315, Rome

1932 *Auteurs spirituels et textes dévotes du moyen âge latin*, Paris

1935 'Edmeri Cantuariensis cantoris nova opuscula de sanctorum veneratione et observatione', *Revue des sciences religieuses*, 15, pp. 184–219, 354–79

1936 *Le manuel de prières de S. Jean Gualbert*, RB, 48, pp. 259–99

1940 'Precum Libelli quattuor aevi Karolini, prior pars', ed. A. Wilmart, *Ephemerides Liturgicae*, Rome

Woodcock, 1956 Audrey M. Woodcock, ed. *The Cartulary of St Gregory, Canterbury*, Camden third series, lxxxviii, R.Hist.S

ZRG, KA Zeitschrift der Savigny-Stiftung für Rechtsgeschichte: *Kanonistische Abteilung*, Weimar.

ADDENDUM

The edition of Berengar's work listed above (*DSC*), and used in the following pages, has now been superseded by the new edition of R. B. C. Huygens, Beringerius Turonensis, *Rescriptum contra Lanfrannum*, in *C.C. Continuatio Mediaevalis*, Turnhout, vol. 84, 1988. Since Huygens's edition, among its many other excellences, records Vischer's pagination on every page, the passages to which I refer can easily be found in the new edition and I have left my references unaltered.

CHRONOLOGY OF ANSELM'S LIFE, WORKS, AND CANONIZATION

1033	Born in Aosta
c 1047	First desire to become a monk, followed by relapse
c 1050	Death of his mother
1056	Leaves home after quarrelling with his father: crosses the Mont Cenis pass into the Rhône valley
1056–1059	Travels through Burgundy and France to Normandy
1059	Arrives at Bec: begins studying and teaching under Lanfranc
1060	Becomes a monk at Bec
1060–63	Probably writes *De Grammatico*
1063	Becomes prior of Bec on Lanfranc's removal to Caen
1070	Lanfranc becomes archbishop of Canterbury: Anselm's letters begin
1070–1075	Anselm's earliest *Prayers* and *Meditations*
1075–6	Writes *Monologion*
1077–8	Writes *Proslogion*
1078	September: elected abbot of Bec
1079	First visit to England: conversations with monks of Canterbury
1080	Second visit to England
1080–86	Writes *De Veritate*; *De Libertate Arbitrii*; *De Casu Diaboli*
1086	Third visit to England
1086–92	Starts collecting his letters; dispute with Roscelin
1092	Fourth visit to England; 7–8 September at Canterbury; September–October at Chester; October–?Dec/Feb: at Westminster with Gilbert Crispin
1093	6 March: at Gloucester, invested with archbishopric of Canterbury September: does homage to king for the lands of Canterbury 25 September: enthroned at Canterbury 4 December: consecrated at Canterbury
1094	February–March: with the king at Hastings Finishes *Epistola de Incarnatione Verbi*
1095	January–February: Disputes about recognition of Urban II

xxvii

February–March: King William secretly recognizes Urban II

Early May: unknown to Anselm, papal legate arrives with pallium

27 May: Anselm receives pallium at Canterbury

June–July: Anselm refuses to hold Council with legate without royal consent

1095–8   Writes *Cur Deus Homo*

1097   New disputes with king over knight service of Canterbury tenants

October: Anselm gets king's permission to go to Rome

25 October: Anselm's parting speech to monks of Canterbury

8 November: leaves England

23 December: arrives at Cluny with Eadmer and Baldwin Archbishop Hugh invites Anselm to stay at Lyons

1098   *c* 1 January–16 March: stays at Lyons

April: arrives at Rome

June–November: stays at Liberi near Capua: finishes *Cur Deus Homo*

3–10 November: defends Latin doctrine of the Holy Spirit at Council of Bari; returns to Rome with Urban II

1099   January–April: stays with pope in Rome

c April 25: hears decrees against investiture and clerical homage; leaves Rome next day

May 1099–August 1100: stays at Lyons with Archbishop Hugh; writes *De conceptu virginali et de peccato originali* and *Meditatio de humana Redemptione*

(July 29: death of Urban II; Aug 13: Paschal II elected pope)

1100   (2 August: death of King William II)

c 31 August: Anselm invited by Henry I to return to England 23 September: arrives at Dover

29 September: meets Henry I who demands a renewal of homage and the consecration of new bishops whom he had invested; Anselm refuses, quoting the papal decree of 1099 as his reason

11 November: performs marriage ceremony of Henry I and Matilda

1101   Invasion of England by Robert of Normandy; Anselm supports Henry

2 September: probably preaches Sermon on St Gregory's day

1102   *c* 29 September: holds primatial Council at Westminster Completes *De Processione Sancti Spiritus*

1103	27 April: leaves England to seek papal guidance on Investitures and Homage
	May–August: stays at Bec, with visit to Chartres
	October–November: at Rome
	November: meets Matilda of Tuscany at Piacenza
	December: arrives at Lyons; Henry I forbids him to return to England, and seizes Anselm's lands and revenues
	December 1103–May 1105: Anselm stays at Lyons and sets in motion procedure for excommunicating Henry I
1105	May: leaves Lyons to pronounce Henry's excommunication
	22 July: meets Henry I at L'Aigle: agreement reached on restitution of Canterbury lands; messengers sent to Rome to settle wider issues
1105	August–1106 August: stays a full year at Bec with visits to Rouen and Jumièges
1106	August: returns to England
1107	April: at royal court at Windsor; falls ill at Bury St Edmunds and stays till June
	1–3 August: Anselm absent from discussion between king and bishops at Westminster on the investiture dispute, but joins them when agreement has been reached
1107–8	Anselm completes his *De Concordia Praescientiae et Praedestinationis et Gratiae Dei cum Libero Arbitrio*
1108	28 May: Anselm holds his second primatial council in London
	July: falls ill at manor of Bosham, but recovers
1109	January–April: ill at Canterbury
	April 21: dies
1109–1114	Eadmer completes his *Vita Anselmi* and *Historia Novorum*
1122–25	Eadmer adds collection of miracles to his *Vita Anselmi*
1163	May: Archbishop Thomas Becket presents John of Salisbury's *Vita Anselmi* to Pope Alexander III at the Council at Tours with petition for Anselm's canonization; the pope remits the question to a council of English bishops. There is no record of a formal decision, but Anselm was henceforth included among the saints at Canterbury and elsewhere, and his body was translated to St Anselm's chapel in Canterbury cathedral.[1]

---

[1] For details of the results of the 1163 initiative and of later petitions to the pope for Anselm's canonization by King Henry VII in 1492–4, and by James III (the Old Pretender) in 1720, see Southern 1963, pp. 336–43; and Biffi, 1988, pp. 16–17; 137–8; and for the inclusion of Anselm among those regarded as doctors of the Church without any formal admission, see Prosperus de Lambertinis (later Pope Benedict XIV), *De servorum Dei Beatificatione et beatorum Canonizatione*, 1734–38, lib. iv, pars 2, c. xii, 9. The whole question of Anselm's canonization is complicated and inconclusive, as befits one who shrank from every new promotion.

PART I
FROM BIRTH TO REBIRTH, 1033–1070

CHAPTER I

ESCAPE FROM CONFINEMENT

I FAMILY AND LOCAL BACKGROUND

Anselm was born in 1033 in the Alpine town of Aosta, an ancient
Roman town, which then had many, and still has some, huge
Roman buildings – amphitheatre, Praesidium, triumphal arch,
walls and fortified gatehouses – gaunt witnesses to a great past
among the scattered remains of early medieval settlement. When it
was founded by the Emperor Augustus, after whom it was named,
it marked the frontier of Italy: it was the last town before crossing
the Alps. But in the eleventh century it was the southern outpost of
the kingdom of Burgundy. It was a matter of vital importance for
Anselm's future that it belonged to Burgundy and not to Lombardy: it looked northwards, and the connections of Anselm's
family on his mother's side were in the valley of the Rhône.

When he was born, the kingdom of Burgundy had recently
become an imperial possession under the Emperor Conrad II,
whose regime seemed to be entirely solid. Politically, Conrad was
the dominating figure in Europe. In the religious life, Odilo abbot
of Cluny, under whom Cluny came to stand for all that the western
world most admired in monasticism, had a similar position of
supremacy. By contrast, the pope, Benedict IX, was not a European
figure. He was a distinguished Roman aristocrat, about whom so
much evil was later believed that he put the name of Benedict out of
circulation among popes till the fourteenth century; but contemporaries were in happy ignorance of his posthumous ill-fame and
accepted him as part of the order of things without comment. In
Byzantium, the great reign of Basil II had recently ended. He had
extended the effective power of the Greek emperors from the
Dalmatian coast to the eastern boundary of modern Turkey, a
greater area of centralized government than anything known in
Europe before the rise of modern Russia; to all outward appearances, this victorious advance was still continuing in the earliest
years of Anselm's life.

3

When Anselm died seventy-six years later, all these landmarks had been moved. The Greek Empire was territorially only a shadow of its former self. At its southern boundaries were the western Crusading states. The maritime power of the Italian cities was beginning to dominate the Mediterranean. In the West, the successor of Conrad II, his great-grandson Henry V, was a hated tyrant whose ruthless energy and splendour could not conceal the antiquated nature of his power. By contrast, Paschal II, the successor of Pope Benedict IX, though himself a weak and vacillating man, governed an empire spiritual in nature but political in action, which was more powerful and more rapidly expanding, more loyal to its ruler and richer in resources for future development, than that which any western ruler including the ancient Roman emperors had ever commanded. And, in the sphere of religious life, by the time of Anselm's death, the monasteries of Cîteaux and the Chartreuse were already presenting a challenge to the supremacy of the Cluniac style of monasticism. By 1109 too the new masters of the schools, the founders of organized scholastic thought – Anselm of Laon, Abelard, Gilbert of Poitiers, William of Conches – were already active. In every aspect of life the western world was displaying an unprecedented range of new and world-changing activity.

It can scarcely be too strongly emphasized that the span of Anselm's life covered one of the most momentous periods of change in European history, comparable to the centuries of the Reformation or the Industrial Revolution. It is only against this background that his own balancing of the old and new, his mixture of political conservatism and intellectual and spiritual innovation, which are to be our chief objects of study in the following pages, can justly be measured. As a constellation of talent in different fields, Anselm, Gregory VII and William the Conqueror were the greatest men in Europe during this period. Anselm was slightly younger than the other two; he outlived William by twenty years and Gregory by twenty-four years, and he lived on to have the unexpected task of finding a path of survival between these mighty opposites. It was a task for which he was in no way prepared, and the perplexities into which it led him will concern us at a later stage in this story: for the present it is sufficient to mark its unexpectedness.

William and Gregory were men of action of a kind rare at any time, but almost unknown in the Middle Ages: they were creators

4

who dealt intuitively with confused situations, having little in precedent or business routine or learned construction to guide them. Gregory had an energy of purpose and clarity of vision in practical affairs of the highest order, probably unparalleled in the Middle Ages. William had an undaunted mastery of the problems of the secular world, unapproached in creative power by any other medieval ruler after Charlemagne. Anselm, who spent half his life in positions requiring business ability, never learnt to love business or to transact it with even tolerable efficiency. He had more opportunities than most men for observing the transformation of western Europe in his lifetime, but there is no sign that he saw himself in any way as an instigator, or even a supporter, of change. He sought no wide influence. He was at his best talking to a group of pupils, of whom not one made a lasting mark as a scholar of first-class importance. Yet in the long run, as one whose thoughts became part of the lives of others, Anselm out-distanced all his contemporaries. There is no side of the great change in the mind and imagination of Europe that began in his lifetime which he did not in some way touch or stimulate.

Like most men of his generation who made an original contribution to the world, he had himself struggled to be released from a cramping environment. William the Conqueror and Gregory VII too had seemed by birth and early circumstances to be destined to suffer the frustrations of men with minds greater than their situations; and Anselm's destiny seemed likely to consist of propping up a declining family fortune by ecclesiastical preferment with the help of a provincial education. It was against this future that he rebelled.

He showed no interest in law and rhetoric, which were the foundations of north Italian education and had a great future ahead of them in the schools and law-courts of northern Italy and in the government of the Church. Aosta was not a distinguished or growing town, but it had an abbey and a cathedral, and there is some reason to think that Anselm's family had destined him for a career which would have led to a canonry and perhaps to a bishopric.[1] But these opportunities in the local scene seem to have had no charm for him. He displays no affection for Aosta, and although he crossed the Alps four times in later life, he never

---

[1] Gilbert Crispin, *Works*, p. 204, in his *Vita Herluini* describes Anselm as a clerk of the church of Aosta, *clericus ecclesiae Augustensis*, and as one of Anselm's closest friends he was in a position to know.

revisited his native town. On the first occasion there were some practical reasons for this: the detour, though short, would have taken him into enemy country. But on his second journey, only age, weariness and indifference can account for his neglect. He escaped from this scene when he was a young man after quarrelling with his father, and he became in all essentials a man of northern France at the time when this area was first emerging as the pre-eminent force in the life of Europe.

Although Anselm did not talk about Aosta, he sometimes spoke of the impression which the mountains had made on him. Eadmer preserved a touching expression of his pleasure at finding himself in a mountain village in south Italy, where, 'exhilarated with the hope of future quiet', he exclaimed, 'Here I rest; here I stay.'[2] He felt at home. On another occasion he told Eadmer a story which shows that some of his later moral and intellectual dispositions were early developed. Above Aosta there are the glittering mountains of Jupiter, as they were called. Not unnaturally he imagined them to be the home of God. One night in a dream he climbed the mountain and came to the court of God. On its lower slopes, women were carelessly reaping the corn, and he resolved to accuse them to their Lord. Coming to the court of God, he found Him alone with His steward, the household being engaged on the harvest. He sat down at the Lord's feet, and was fed with white bread – not the black concoction of the countryside – which the steward brought him. And the next day, when he awoke, he confidently asserted that he had been in Heaven and had fed on the bread of God.[3]

There is nothing much here that could not have happened to anyone. But it evidently made a deep impression on Anselm, for he told the story to his biographer fifty or sixty years later. In a childish way it portrays the direction of his whole life – the clarity and simplicity of his objective, his horror of sin, his desire for the heights, a certain unquestioning literalness of outlook, are all there in old age as they had been in childhood. The hill of God stood before him in later life inviting a moral and intellectual ascent. He saw Heaven still in astonishingly physical terms, and with great clarity. Unbelief in any form puzzled him. Still less could he understand that men who believed should still disobey. He found it incredible that anyone could believe in God and put temporal advantage before the work of God. 'Are they not Christians?' he

[2] *VA* II, xxx.   [3] *VA* I, ii.

would say. 'If they are Christians, why should they break faith for any temporary gain? The thing is impossible.'[4] The truths which he grasped intellectually, he saw with the clarity of his childhood vision. He forgot that to others they might be no more than forms without content.

The ever-present mountains left their mark on him, but we must not exaggerate the peaceful seclusion of his early years. Aosta was a strategic point on one of the most important routes in Europe. The Great St Bernard, at the foot of which it lies, was one of the two main passes of the western Alps. Along this route pilgrims and merchants, and with them a steady stream of gossip and rumour, ceaselessly flowed. Anselm was well placed to know what was going on, and one of the stories of Rome in the time of Leo IX, which he later told his companions, must have reached him as a traveller's tale when he was a boy.[5]

As well as rumours, the valley attracted the conflicting ambitions of some of the most important rulers in Europe. The town of Aosta itself lay at the extreme south of the kingdom of Burgundy, where it marched with Lombardy. In the year before Anselm was born, the last independent king of Burgundy, of the line that had established itself on the ruins of the Carolingian Empire, had died. During the next six years, the king of Germany, Conrad II, succeeded in establishing his son and successor as king of Burgundy. From this time the valley of Aosta acknowledged the authority of the German king: but the real power had passed into the hands of the local nobility, not however into the hands of Anselm's family, which continued to show signs of declining fortune in his lifetime.

In later life he sometimes talked to Eadmer about his family. Unfortunately he did not say enough, or Eadmer did not record enough, to give us a clear impression of their position in the world; but we can learn something from Eadmer's report and from Anselm's letters. Anselm's mother, Ermenberga, was a native of Aosta; his father, a Lombard called Gundulf, had come to live in his wife's town, which seems to indicate that she was socially the more important of the two, perhaps an heiress.[6] Their only children were Anselm and his sister Richeza.[7] This much we can gather from Eadmer. But the most significant fact about the family's connec-

---

[4] *VA* II, xiv. [5] See Southern, 1958ii, pp. 213–16. [6] *VA* I, i.

[7] See *Ep.* 268 (iii, 67) where Anselm writes to Richeza: *ego enim sum unicus frater vester*. There may of course have been other brothers who died.

tions is supplied by one of Anselm's letters, written late in life to Humbert, Count of Savoy. In this letter Anselm addressed the count with fulsome respect, thanking him for his condescension in recognizing their consanguinity and declaring that 'my relatives rejoice to call themselves your vassals'.[8] This is little enough to go on, but it gives a clue to the position of Anselm's family in their native land.

First of all, Anselm's letter is to be read in the light of an important political fact about the counts of Savoy. When the kingdom of Burgundy came into the hands of the kings of Germany after the failure of the Carolingian royal house in 1032, it brought them very little authority. Here, as elsewhere, the real beneficiaries of the Carolingian decline were new local families. In the valley of Aosta, and in the whole troubled and contested area between Lyons and the upper Po valley, it was the ambitious house of Savoy which gradually gained the upper hand throughout the eleventh century. By amassing comital rights, episcopal nominations and monastic advocacies, and by building up chains of vassalage, it was slowly creating for itself an enduring political authority in the valley of the Rhône and the neighbouring Alps.[9] Anselm's family was related by both blood and vassalage to this great family.

How they were related remains obscure. But in the obscurity we can see a family which by its name invites attention. For a brief period at the beginning of the eleventh century a family, known to historians as the Anselmid family, competed with the House of Savoy for effective power in the dissolving kingdom of Burgundy. The progenitor of this rival to the house of Savoy was a certain Anselm, who died early in the eleventh century leaving three sons and a daughter: one son, who bore the family name of Anselm, was bishop of Aosta and died in 1026; another, Burchard, was archbishop of Vienne for about thirty years till his death in 1030; and a third, Ulric, was the chief official of his brother, the archbishop of Vienne. Their sister, Ancilia, married Count Humbert Whitehands, the ancestor of the Savoy dynasty.[10] The later fortunes of the Anselmid family are obscure, but it is clear that, while the family of Count Humbert Whitehands flourished and established its ascendancy through the whole district of the western Alpine passes, the Anselmid family failed to consolidate its

---

[8] *Ep.* 262 (iii, 65). [9] For the feudal struggle in this area, see Prévité-Orton, 1912.
[10] Prévité-Orton, pp. 10–11, 19–21, 27, 67–8.

advantages and came to nothing. We have here a striking picture of a branch of a great family in decline, reduced by lack of territorial inheritance to maintain itself by asserting its claims to non-hereditary ecclesiastical positions. While the Anselmid family sought to arrest its decline by clinging to ecclesiastical offices, the descendants of Count Humbert Whitehands and his Anselmid wife Ancilia throve, and laid hold on the former imperial and comital rights.

Exactly where Anselm's mother fitted into this complicated situation we cannot tell. We only know that she must have belonged to a decaying branch. Consequently Anselm, although he was an only son, seems to have become a clerk in the church of Aosta at an early age. It would appear therefore that he had no substantial inheritance to look forward to, and the little we know of other members of his family tells a similar story. When Anselm became an abbot, and still more an archbishop, various members of his family tried to derive some advantage from their kinsman's good fortune. A cousin, Folceraldus, who was already a monk elsewhere, made his way to Bec while Anselm was abbot, and tried to make Bec his permanent home, but Anselm refused to accept him unless his abbot agreed. This consent does not seem to have been given at once, but Folceraldus was very persistent. He turned up at Bec again after Anselm had gone to Canterbury, and Anselm commended him to the community.[11] Two other relatives, Haimo and Rainaldus, also visited Bec, and Anselm seems to have thought that they were promising recruits, for he tried hard to persuade them to become monks and stay with him. In this he failed, and they disappear from sight.[12]

Among these relatives, the most persistent claimant for Anselm's notice was Burgundius, the husband of his only sister. He showed signs of wanting to come to Canterbury, but Anselm warned him off in no uncertain terms.[13] Thwarted in this direction, Burgundius then prepared to go in the wake of the Crusaders to Jerusalem. Anselm encouraged this plan, but wrote to his sister, 'If your husband returns and wishes to come to me, I expressly forbid him to do so.'[14] Evidently Burgundius was not at all prosperous. He either did not return or died soon after his expedition, and this left Anselm with the problem of providing for his sister. He tried to

---

[11] *Epp.* 55 (i, 46), 56 (i, 47), 110 (ii, 20), 111 (ii, 21), 209 (iii, 25).
[12] *Ep.* 120 (ii, 28).   [13] *Ep.* 258 (iii, 63).   [14] *Epp.* 264 (iii, 66), 268 (iii, 67).

arrange for her to be received as a nun at the Cluniac house of Marcigny, and all seemed to be arranged when the abbot of Chiusa stepped in to forbid the arrangement.[15] What objection this great sub-Alpine monastery could have had is uncertain; but her only son had been a monk of Chiusa from childhood, and his monastery may have expected to succeed to the family property. In any event, the plan for providing for his sister broke down, and Anselm was reduced to supplying her wants as occasion arose.

For her son, he was able to do something more substantial. He visited the young man, who bore his own name, at the monastery of Chiusa on his way to Rome in 1098, and brought him back to England with him.[16] He was not a very bright young man. Anselm was still writing to him during his second exile, when he cannot have been less than twenty-five years old, urging him to practise writing every day, especially in prose, to prefer a plain and logical style to an obscure one, and to talk Latin whenever possible.[17]. This is good advice for anybody, but it is not the kind of advice Anselm was wont to give to those for whom he had the highest hopes. Nevertheless, the young Anselm was the only member of the family who rose to a modest eminence. He has a niche in general history as one of the earliest propagators of the Feast of the Immaculate Conception of the Blessed Virgin.[18] And for the last twenty-six years of his life he was abbot of Bury St Edmunds, a position which he owed entirely to the fame of his uncle.[19]

The family and local background which these scattered facts disclose is complicated and obscure, but they all suggest a position of insecurity and declining fortunes. Perhaps these family circumstances played a larger part in Anselm's development than we can now discover, and such facts as survive point to the tribulations of possessing a high lineage with a narrow fortune. If he had been wealthier and with an assured position he might have become a powerful baron in the Val d'Aosta, or at least a local bishop, and we would have had only a few charters to show that he had ever existed. Instead, torn by uncertainty and discontent, and fleeing from an uncertain future, he became one of the most important influences in this creative period of European history.

[15] *Ep.* 328 (iv, 114).   [16] *VA* II, xxix.
[17] *Ep.* 90 (iv, 31). Much the same advice is repeated in a later letter to him: *Ep.* 328 (iv, 114).
[18] For the influence of Anselm's pupils in propagating this feast, see below, pp. 432–6.
[19] For his career, see Southern 1958ii, pp. 90–1, 198–200; also Williamson, 1929, pp. 192–200.

11   FLIGHT TO THE NORTH

It was in about 1056 that Anselm broke loose from the restraints of his native town.[20] His mother, who had saved him from despair at a moment of break-down and to whom he was devoted, had died. With his father, he had nothing in common except mutual dislike and incompatibility. Eadmer does his best to make Anselm appear a humble and dutiful son, but we must be cautious in crediting the virtues ascribed to a young man who grows up to be a saint. We only know that Anselm quarrelled with his father and left home with very little preparation and with only the vaguest plan for his future. In earlier years he had felt an urge to become a monk; later he thought he might become a scholar. But these ambitions had come to nothing, and in 1056 he may have had no larger purpose than escape. The footsteps of a young man in this situation can scarcely be expected to follow any very rational plan, but he probably had a good immediate reason for the direction he took.

He crossed the Alps in great discomfort and some danger, but not by the shortest route northwards over the St Bernard Pass: he went south down the Val d'Aosta. In this direction the most obvious goal would have been some city in Lombardy with its schools and growing prosperity. But in Lombardy his only relations were his father's family, and they would be unlikely to help him. Members of his mother's family lived mainly across the Alps in the now fragmented kingdom of Burgundy, and they were his most likely means of support. If, as seems probable, the most important members of this family were to be found in the region of Lyons and Vienne, this would account for the fact that at some point in his journey down the Val d'Aosta he turned westwards over the Alps by the Mont Cenis Pass, which brought him into the valley of the Rhône, to Lyons and Vienne, where members of his mother's family were to be found. Support he must have found, for he could not have lived long on what he brought from his father's house.

It is impossible, from the few scraps of information preserved by his biographer, to give any detailed account of his itinerary thereafter. Eadmer reports that Anselm spent nearly three years partly in Burgundy and partly in France. The statement is admirably precise in its chronology. Geographically too it can be interpreted with fair precision: 'Burgundy', in the context in which

[20] For what follows, see *VA* I, v, and p. 7n.

Eadmer uses the word, almost certainly means the duchy of Burgundy which had recently become an appanage of the French royal family. It included Cluny, the most famous of all contemporary monasteries, and it is very likely that Anselm visited it and got his first view of its religious life as he came northwards. Certainly, when he came to decide his own future, he saw very clearly why Cluny would not suit him. Burgundy also had schools of some note at Auxerre, Autun, Nevers, and just beyond its boundary at Besançon. Anselm may have visited some of them. But they were not what he was seeking, and he cannot have spent long at any of them.

So from Burgundy he moved on into 'France', which then meant the area of the *langue d'oïl* in the valley of the Loire and further north. Here too there were schools of real fame, at Orleans, Tours, Angers, Chartres, and, most recently emerging, at Paris. It is inconceivable that Anselm should not have heard of them and of some of their masters. But even if he turned aside to any of them, he did not stay. They too were not what he was looking for. We do not hear of any place where he stayed until he came, of all unlikely places, to Avranches in the far west of Normandy: a cathedral city, doubtless with a school, but wholly unknown to fame, at the extreme limit of what was to him the civilized world.[21] Twenty years earlier another Italian, Lanfranc of Pavia, at the end of a more conventional *voyage scolaire*, had also finished up at the same place, and he had stayed and taught there with some success, until he grew tired of the whole thing and fled to Bec. We do not know where or what Anselm heard about his predecessor from northern Italy; but he may well have heard of Lanfranc at Avranches as a teacher with a romantic past, a fellow-countryman moreover, who had risen by this date to be the most distinguished personality in Normandy after the duke. Whatever it was that he heard, it sufficed to draw him to Bec. As it turned out, when he reached Bec, he had reached the end of his search. So we may stop at this point to ask what he was looking for.

At this stage, only a very general answer can be given, for Anselm himself had not yet discovered what he wanted. The one thing that seems clear from the recollections of his early life which he communicated to Eadmer, is that he was torn between a desire for

---

[21] The evidence that Anselm went to Avranches before going to Bec is slight, but it comes from a good source: it is one of the very early and apparently authoritative additions made at Bec to Eadmer's *Vita Anselmi*: see *VA* I, v, pp. xiv, 8.

intellectual eminence and religious dedication. Both these aims were being given new forms of expression in the middle years of the eleventh century, but they pulled in different directions. Intellectual ambition could best be satisfied in the growing schools of either northern France or northern Italy. In both these areas, and especially the former, there were masters with new skills and new materials in law, logic, rhetoric and grammar, who were beginning to attract students from distant parts of Europe. Anselm could have seen and heard a fair selection of these new masters in the course of his journey. But none of them moved him to stop. We can only conclude from this that the secular intellectual culture of their schools, with their organized classes and debates and their noisy urban environment, had no attraction for him.

On the other hand, religious dedication could best be satisfied at Cluny itself or in one of the increasingly numerous affiliated monasteries under its influence. Alternatively, a few small and still little-known communities were beginning to appear which were dedicated to a more contemplative, or charitable (in the sense of caring for the sick or poor) way of life. Most of the models for this latter kind of dedication were to be found in the neighbourhood of the Italian towns, and Anselm had been travelling in the wrong direction to find out more about settlements of this kind. As we shall see, he clearly sympathized with their aim; but his own account of his past in his earliest *Prayers* and *Meditations* suggests that he had by now abandoned the religious impulses of his early youth and did not know what he was looking for, which is not after all a very uncommon state of affairs. The conscious choice was to come later. Meanwhile he came to Bec – and to Lanfranc.

CHAPTER 2

THE YEAR OF DECISION

I THE MEETING OF ANSELM AND LANFRANC

It would be hard to find two more sharply contrasting characters than Lanfranc and Anselm: the one supremely able in a wide diversity of activities, as a lawyer, scholar, teacher, administrator, policy-maker, and disputant – outstandingly successful in all, but without any spark of original genius in any of them; the other presenting to any observant eye the marks of genius, in understanding the problems and natures of other people, in penetrating the recesses of problems in logic, theology, faith, but wholly lacking Lanfranc's ability in practical affairs, which would have made Lanfranc a very notable figure at any time. Anselm was all fire within; Lanfranc all energy of mind and activity.

Lanfranc had never known failure. He had been a conspicuous figure in the courts of the great legal city of Pavia before he was twenty-five. When he threw up this career, he became equally successful in the schools of the Loire valley. When he wearied of success in them, he gave the poor unknown monastic community at Bec prosperity and a European fame, while at the same time becoming the Duke of Normandy's chief adviser in religious matters, and taking a leading part in the downfall of his former scholastic friend Berengar. He was probably in his mid-fifties when Anselm came to him, and he had been a notable figure in the world for thirty years.

Anselm by contrast, aged twenty-six, had known nothing but failure. He had failed to make a mark in the little town of Aosta; he had left, not knowing what he wanted; he had seen nothing to excite him in the schools of France; he was a complete wash-out, and rather old to be in such a position. Lanfranc took him in hand, and in the course of a year he had given him a direction that would last his whole life. Within four years he had given him all the intellectual equipment necessary for his future. Nothing that he could give would have turned the introspective oddity of 1059 into a man of ability similar to his own; but by the time the two men parted in 1063, to meet again only at infrequent intervals, Anselm was set on a course of development so rich in its variety of achievements that the pages of this book can do no more than trace the outline of their varied shapes and content.

To understand this outline, it is necessary to take account, not only of the contribution that Lanfranc could make to Anselm's development, but also of the new circumstances at the moment of Anselm's arrival which presented an intellectual stimulus of great power.

It is almost certain that Anselm arrived at Bec in 1059, and quite certain that he arrived at a moment when the whole future of Normandy and England, and the position in the world of Lanfranc, the prior of Bec, were transformed by events of European-wide importance. Lanfranc's future, and consequently Anselm's too, were profoundly affected by the events of this year, both in their local consequences and in their wider effects. So the circumstances, as well as the personalities and natural endowments of the two men must be taken into account, if we are to understand Anselm's development.

We must begin with Lanfranc, for by Anselm's own admission, at the time of his arrival at Bec and for some years afterwards, Bec for him meant Lanfranc and nothing else. He arrived at Bec because, though he did not know what he wanted, he had heard of Lanfranc. When he got there, it was Lanfranc who started him on the course of religious and intellectual development which was to make him one of the outstanding figures in the history of Latin Christendom. He put himself entirely in Lanfranc's hands: 'So great was his influence over me' (he later confided to his biographer) 'and so greatly did I trust his judgement, that if he had told me to go into the forest above Bec and never come out, I would have done it without hesitation.'[1] Later observers, who know how greatly the two men differed in their temperaments and habits of thought, find it difficult to take this statement seriously. But as we shall see, even the possibility of retiring into the nearby forest and becoming a hermit was not a fantasy. It represented one of the real religious possibilities open to him. Twenty years earlier, Lanfranc

---

[1] For the date of his arrival at Bec, and for his account of Lanfranc's influence over him, see *VA* I, vii, and p. 12n.

himself had made just this choice – abortively, as it turned out – and it was one that Anselm was to consider seriously. We shall examine Anselm's choice in due course, but immediately it shows that they had more in common than appears on the surface. After all, they were both adventurers who had left, whether from surfeit of success or failure, the ancient cities of their birth to come to the outpost of the civilized world in Normandy. There was a streak of recklessness in them both, and their common background laid the foundation for an influence over him which, as Anselm consistently acknowledged, was immense.

Besides the obvious differences between the two men, which we can see more clearly than they could themselves, there is another reason why Lanfranc's influence has not been taken sufficiently seriously in the past. Until recently very little has been known, and still less understood, about Lanfranc's own contribution to contemporary thought. An important step in overcoming this obstacle has now been taken with the appearance of Margaret Gibson's surveys of his work, particularly on the Pauline Epistles. In what follows, I shall differ from several of her conclusions, but she has shown the way forward and I am greatly indebted to her.[2] But before going on to consider Lanfranc's scholarly work, the situation of Anselm himself and of Lanfranc at the moment of Anselm's arrival both require attention.

Although he was twenty-six when he arrived at Bec, Anselm still had almost everything to learn. His education had been limited by the circumstances of a small unintellectual town, by the meagre resources of his family, by a disastrous period of being taught by a tyrant who brought him to the verge of madness, by the death of his mother, the hostility of his father, and his uncertain future.[3] Even after his flight from Aosta, when he was in a countryside richly provided with schools and progressive masters, he seems not to have been sufficiently attracted by what he found to involve himself in the new methods of the schools. He arrived at Bec still a seeker after a new way of life, and it was in this mood that he gave himself up to Lanfranc's influence. At first sight, this self-abandonment may seem an act of quixotic enthusiasm, but there was no one in

---

[2] See Margaret Gibson, 1971 and 1978. The general argument of the following pages was briefly sketched in 'Lanfranc of Bec and Berengar of Tours', Southern, 1948; with the help of Dr Gibson's work, I now add many more details and a new emphasis.

[3] These details are in *VA* I, iii–iv. The account of his early experience with a tyrannical master was added in the recension of *VA* at Bec, pp. 172–3, and is certainly reflected in *VA* I, xxii.

Europe who by experience and achievement had a better claim than Lanfranc to guide his fellow-countryman in a strange land.

Consider only what Anselm would have known of him. First, he would have heard something about Lanfranc's scholastic reputation, and we happen to know a great deal about this, for it is a remarkable fact that although he went on to occupy very grand positions in the world, most of the reports about Lanfranc in European sources refer to his early fame before his arrival at Bec. The widespread stories of his legal precocity as a very young man at Pavia are so encrusted with legend that it is hard to distinguish the element of truth in them. Yet it is certain that they have a foundation of truth: his later knowledge of the Romanized law practised in northern Italy at this time alone would suffice to guarantee this.[4]

In addition, and much better attested, Anselm would have known something of Lanfranc's fame as a teacher of the liberal arts in France before he became a monk. The evidence on this is emphatic: 'He relit the light of the arts in the West'; 'God raised him up to be a guide and a light to lead the minds of the Latins to the study of the trivium and quadrivium, which had fallen into neglect and profound obscurity, and made him also a master and teacher of the Old and New Testament.' In similar vein, Hildebert of Tours wrote that Lanfranc 'had made his own all that philosophers and poets had said'. Several of his many eulogists picked out dialectic as the art which he had especially cultivated. To Sigebert of Gembloux, he was above all the *dialecticus* who 'expounded, summed up and clarified the *Epistles of St Paul* according to the laws of dialectic'. Similarly the monk of Bec who wrote the *Miracles of St Nicholas* described him as the scholar who 'repaired and renovated the art of dialectic in the West'; and William of Malmesbury, with his accustomed relish, described him as the man who had brought prosperity to Bec by opening a school from which he 'sent out his pupils into the world belching forth dialectic'. Some of this testimony is rhetorical; but we also have the precise statement of Pope Nicholas II, in a letter soon to be examined,

---

[4] F. Schulz gave me much help on this subject forty years ago. Despite the paucity of hard evidence, he pointed out that (to take only one example) Lanfranc's comment on I Timothy, v, 4: *in mundana lege 'parens parenti per gradum et parentelam' succedere iubetur*, shows clear evidence of his knowledge of Lombardic-Roman law. For further details, see Southern, 1948, p. 29n. It should be mentioned that the printed text of Lanfranc's comment (*PL* 150, col. 355) makes nonsense, and I have quoted from Vatican MS lat. 143, f. 142v.

which makes it clear that dialectic and rhetoric were the subjects for which he was still chiefly famous as late as 1059. Clearly dialectic was not popular with all these writers, but they all thought it had given Lanfranc his strongest claim to early fame.[5] In addition, early library catalogues contain dialectic works attributed to him which, if authentic, must have been written before he arrived at Bec.[6]

Anselm would probably have heard about Lanfranc's fame as soon as he reached Normandy. I have already mentioned the well-attested early addition to Eadmer's *Life* of Anselm which tells us that the last stage of his journey before he came to Bec ended at Avranches, and it seems certain that Lanfranc had taught there before he became a monk. It may have been a report of his teaching and his present importance in the counsels of the Duke of Normandy, which stimulated Anselm to go to Bec and see for himself. At all events, as soon as he got to Bec, he would have had evidence all around him of Lanfranc's vast contribution to the monastery's growing fame and vitality.

Besides these evidences of Lanfranc's energy and success, Anselm arrived at a moment when Bec suddenly acquired a new importance as a centre of intellectual controversy and activity in several different fields. His own future, and that of the duchy of Normandy, and in some degree the Church as a whole, all felt the impact of these events. This is a very large claim, and it needs to be substantiated. In doing this, I shall begin with the outermost circle of secular and ecclesiastical government and work inwards to Bec.

[5] For the sources and the weight to be attached to these judgements, see Southern, 1948, pp. 29–32; for the letter of Nicholas II, see the following section.

[6] For the lost works attributed to Lanfranc, see G. Becker, 1885, p. 130: *Questiones Lanfranci*, among the dialectical works belonging to an eleventh-century scholar called Bernard; and p. 150: *Lantfrancus de dialectica*, in the library at Toul before 1084. Gibson, 1978, pp. 42–3, 49, doubts whether these attributions can refer to our Lanfranc on the grounds that he still used the *De decem Categoriis* attributed to St Augustine, 'a text that is fundamentally irreconcilable with Boethian logic . . . if Lanfranc was still prepared to accept *De decem Categoriis*, it is almost impossible to see him as a pioneer in the *logica vetus*'. But there is no evidence that Lanfranc 'accepted' the logical teaching of Ps. Augustine *De decem Categoriis*. Like every other scholar of his time, he must have known this work, but the only evidence of his use of it comes from the following sentence in the collections of a late twelfth-century Canterbury monk: *Magister Lanfracus [sic] d(ixit), Nomen domini ineffabile, quia littere que quartum gradum tenent tres indicant esse primos aput quos ergo tante rei non est, nec vox esse potuit intellectum significans*. (For this passage, see Hunt, 1943, p. 208, and for an explanation, Gibson, 1978, loc. cit.) This sentence, whatever it may mean, lends no support to an adverse judgement on Lanfranc as a logician. Dr Gibson's emphasis on Lanfranc's grammatical expertise is well justified, but it points to the unity of the subjects of the trivium, not to a preference for grammar over logic.

II   THE IMPACT OF PAPAL POLICY

A new pope had been elected in the last days of 1058, and consecrated in January 1059. He began almost at once after his election to lay down lines of political and ecclesiastical development which altered the general development of papal government. Lanfranc was to play an important role in one part of this development, and Anselm probably arrived when he was in the full tide of his new importance. So we must first consider the pope and his problems before we can understand how Lanfranc fitted into their solution.

It may be remarked to begin with that the new pope chose a name which gives us some guidance as to his intentions: Nicholas II. The earlier Nicholas had been one of the most active defenders of papal authority in the Carolingian period, and the name announced the new pope's intention of following in his footsteps. In addition to the example of his namesake, the new pope also had before his eyes the example of the recent Pope Leo IX, who was the first pope for very many years to visit northern Europe: Nicholas intended to do likewise. But, though he planned to follow Leo in this respect, in another field he intended to break away from Leo's example. Leo had relied on the German emperor as a firm supporter both of his ecclesiastical policy and of his plans to restore papal territorial power in southern Italy. But for the present at least, there were two reasons why there was no future in that alliance for Nicholas II. The first was that Leo, depending on the support of the emperor, had engaged in war against the Norman invaders of southern Italy. In doing this, he had followed the conventional wisdom of the previous generation, which had seen the Norman invaders of the South as blood-thirsty intruders who needed to be checked if they could not be expelled. But even with a friendly emperor, this policy had been a failure. The papal army had been defeated by the Normans, and Leo himself had spent nearly a year in a Norman prison. So, from a purely political point of view, the old papal-imperial alliance was a dead letter, and a change was called for.

More important still, in his ecclesiastical policy Nicholas was working towards a new procedure for papal elections which would diminish, and prospectively virtually eliminate, imperial participation in papal elections. Moreover, this was only one part of a larger programme for excluding lay influence in several areas of ecclesiastical organization, especially in the nomination of bishops and other prelates, and in the ownership of churches and tithes. These were very daring plans, and to follow them in detail would take us far beyond the scope of our present theme.[7] But they had an immediate result in Nicholas's need for new allies. He appears to have been a man of great boldness and far-sighted political wisdom, and from his earliest days as pope, a switch of political alliance from the emperor to the hitherto abominated Normans would seem to have been in his mind. The general development of this new policy in the short reign of Nicholas II does not concern us here. But one of its manifestations is extremely relevant to our theme, and it may be introduced at once.

It is expressed in a letter addressed to Lanfranc, of which the only known copy was preserved by Lanfranc himself in his collection of Canon Law texts. More will need to be said later about the context of its preservation. For the moment we are concerned only with its message. It ran as follows:[8]

Bishop Nicholas, servant of the servants of God, to brother Lanfranc, greetings and apostolic benediction.

I would gladly, dearest brother, have your presence with me here to give advice on our ecclesiastical cares, in which, as we have heard, you have already given opportune help. [This is perhaps a reference to Lanfranc's assistance in the case against Berengar in 1050.] But since this may not easily be possible, we wish you to be fruitful to us and to the Roman Church in your present position. In this way the Roman Church will have the double advantage of your being both here and where you are. With this in mind, we are sending to you these well-beloved imperial and papal chaplains to be taught the arts of dialectic and rhetoric, in which – as we have heard – God has given you a special excellence. As soon as may be possible, let us see you and these pupils in Rome, unless, as may happen, we ourselves come to you.

We have heard that you are now fully occupied with the study of the Bible. If this is the case, we order you, in the name of St Peter and ourselves, to give us

---

[7] The whole subject of the papal electoral decree, and the changing policy of the popes towards the Normans of southern Italy from 1059 onwards, has been the subject of a very large and important literature since 1879, when the text and meaning of the papal electoral decree was first subjected to serious investigation. This literature reached its highest point of refinement with the contributions of Anton Michel, 1936, 1939; R. Holtzmann, 1938; H.-G. Krause, 1960. Michel and Krause argued for a diminution in the dramatic impact and intention of the electoral decree; Holtzmann for the opposite. So far as I know, none of these scholars or any others who have been concerned in this debate have considered the letter of Nicholas II, which I shall presently examine. If the interpretation of it which I shall offer is correct, it will tend to support the more dramatic view of the electoral decree and the policy which it made necessary.

[8] The commonly available text of this letter in *PL* 143, cols. 1,349–50, is defective in several details. Since no correct edition exists, I print it below, pp. 42–3.

your obedience in teaching the two chaplains those subjects for which we have sent them to you. We commit them to your charity to help them in every way. We have also heard – thanks be to God – that the Count [i.e. the Duke] our friend follows your advice in all things. May you so keep him that he may flourish in this world and in Christ. I have great confidence in him and in the counsel and companionship which he has with you. Let the talent which has been committed to you fructify among the clergy and your wild people, so that you may at last hear the words, 'Well done, thou good servant'. Amen.

Before examining the details of the letter, its general context must be understood. In the first place, it should be remembered that the Normans of southern Italy were still closely connected with Normandy, whence new recruits to Norman strength continued to arrive. It followed from this, as a by-product of the pope's new reliance on the support of the Normans of southern Italy, that friendly relations with Duke William were at least highly desirable.

But there was one outstanding obstacle to a *rapprochement* in this area: since 1050 Duke William had been living in a state of illicit marriage with Matilda, daughter of the count of Flanders, which had been condemned by Leo IX, and subsequently by the Church in Normandy. It had long been important for Duke William to bring this state of affairs to an end, but he too was in a difficulty. His marriage was of course political. It established a bond with the count of Flanders, with whom friendly relations were important to the duke for several reasons, and their importance was increasing. There is ample evidence that he was already planning to become Edward the Confessor's successor as king of England, and it was unlikely that this could be achieved without a struggle. But if there was to be a struggle, the support of the count of Flanders was essential for keeping one of William's frontiers quiet while he dealt with whatever problems might face him in grasping the English throne, and also for providing mercenaries for his army.

Then, quite apart from this military consideration, the duke needed papal support for his claim to the English throne; this could not be had until he had made peace with the papacy over his marriage with Matilda. The nature of the ecclesiastical obstacle is unclear; but the strength of ecclesiastical opposition to the marriage is well attested, and so far there had not been the slightest sign that Rome would relent.

On both sides, therefore, there were now strong reasons for bringing about a reconciliation, and it is in the light of this situation that the letter translated above needs to be read. It will be noticed that in his letter to Lanfranc the pope already speaks of Duke William as his friend – an indication either that the pope was ready to make peace with William over his marriage, or that peace had already been made.

The next question therefore is: at what date was the letter written? The contents make it clear that the pope had not yet met Lanfranc. Everything he says about him is from hearsay. So we must ask: when did Nicholas II and Lanfranc first meet? The time-honoured answer to this question, which I believe to be correct, is that they met at the Council in Rome after Easter 1059. Recently, a view has been put forward that Lanfranc was not at this Council, or at least not at that part of the Council's business which concerned the condemnation of the Eucharistic doctrine of Berengar of Tours. In the next section of this chapter I shall argue that this opinion is mistaken. But even if it is correct, everyone agrees that Lanfranc arrived very soon after the Council had finished its main business in May 1059 at latest, to negotiate the conditions on which Duke William obtained a dispensation legitimizing the duke of Normandy's marriage with Matilda. Consequently, on any showing, Lanfranc cannot have arrived in Rome much later than the end of April, and the letter cannot have been written after this date.

It must therefore have been one of Pope Nicholas's earliest letters as pope, and it provides remarkable confirmation of the importance which the pope attached to friendly relations with the duke of Normandy at the very moment when the duke of Normandy was equally anxious to have the support of the papacy. Indeed, it may well have been the arrival of this letter which alerted both the duke and Lanfranc, who was by now the duke's chief ecclesiastical adviser, that the moment had arrived when negotiations with the papacy about William's marriage could be undertaken with some hope of success.

With these circumstances in mind, we can now construct a rough chronology of the events of this year. From the time of his election in December 1058, Pope Nicholas must have been preparing the programme for his Easter Council, especially its main item which excluded the emperor from any part in papal elections. The moment was propitious for this dangerous innovation because the emperor was a child. Nevertheless, resistance to the papal decree was certain, and the Normans in southern Italy provided by far the readiest practical possibility of support against the imperial party and its allies in northern Italy. In these circumstances, it was only sensible for Nicholas to take all possible steps to cement friendly relations with the Normans both in southern Italy and in Normandy. So far as the pope's relations with the Normans of the south are concerned, we know that, after the Council which began its meetings in the Lateran church on 13 April, Nicholas II left Rome with a Norman army in May or June 1059, and spent the rest of the year shuttling between Rome and southern Italy. For the letter to have reached Lanfranc before this date, it must therefore have been written in January or, at the latest, February 1059.

If we now consider the letter itself in the light of this chronology, the pope's expressions of friendship and confidence made to the Norman duke despite his still unauthorized marriage indicate his anxiety for the duke's support. Second, the pope's accurate information about Lanfranc's changing scholarly interests and his place in William's counsels indicates that he had taken some trouble to inform himself about the situation in Normandy. Third, the importance which the pope attaches to Lanfranc's work as a master in rhetoric and logic, and his distinct coolness about Lanfranc's more recent switch to theology, reflects his need for men trained in the arts which were necessary in administration.

A minor point may also be noticed as evidence for the pope's personal intervention in the composition of this letter. This is the variable use of the singular and plural in the pope's references to himself and Lanfranc. When the pope speaks personally of his own feelings, he uses the singular; when he speaks officially of his actions or commands, the plural. Likewise, when he speaks of Lanfranc's official position and duties, he uses the plural; when of his studies, the singular. Admittedly, it is not possible to draw quite hard and fast boundaries between these two stances, but we find similar variations of address in Nicholas II's letters to Gervase, archbishop of Rheims, and in both cases these variations strongly suggest the pope himself had a hand in these letters. But it is also clear that although the pope knew so much about Lanfranc, they had not yet met, and what he knew, he knew only by report.

These friendly references may well have indicated both to William and to Lanfranc that, if ever there was to be a favourable moment for bringing the duke's matrimonial case to a satisfactory conclusion, this was it. From the duke's point of view time was getting short if he was to stabilize his position before the English throne became vacant. Once this was settled he could look forward to papal support when the time came for him to seize the English crown. Events were to show that papal support at the time of the Norman invasion of England was of the utmost importance for its success: so it was a correct appreciation of the situation on both sides which brought them together at this time. Both the duke and the pope were in a hurry. In view of this, it is entirely understandable that Lanfranc should have set out for Rome without delay.

His visit proved to be the turning point in Duke William's affairs and in Lanfranc's own career. It also brought him, accidentally it would seem, into the limelight as a leading opponent of Berengar at the Easter Council. Especially after the death of Cardinal Humbert in 1061, he alone could write the definitive answer to Berengar when he revoked the oath which he had been forced to take at the Easter Council.

This letter is a pivotal document in all these events, and if I am right in thinking that it provided the immediate stimulus for Lanfranc's visit to Rome, it had an important place also in the development of Anselm's career, for it led to Lanfranc's becoming the main upholder of the Eucharistic decision taken at the Roman Council in 1059, and to his being the chief agent of Duke William in carrying out the terms of the marriage agreement negotiated in Rome at the same time. Thus it brought about his removal, first to Caen in 1063, and then to Canterbury in 1070; and, perhaps most important of all for Anselm, it meant that he arrived at the moment when Bec was at the centre of important issues.

From several points of view, therefore, Nicholas II's letter has an important place in the unfolding of Anselm's career at Bec and later at Canterbury. Lanfranc obviously appreciated its general importance, for he preserved it in his volume of Canon Law in association with the very full collection of documents concerning the Council in Rome at Easter 1059.[9]

---

[9] For the general context of the letter in Lanfranc's collection of Canon Law, in Trinity College, Cambridge, MS B.16.44, see Brooke, 1931, 74–6. In addition, the following points should be noticed. At the end of the section of Conciliar decrees in his MS, Lanfranc has inserted the following documents: the encyclical letter of Nicholas II recording the decisions of the Easter Council of 1059 (*PL* 143, cols. 1,315–16); a further account of the pope's promulgation of the decisions of the Council (*PL* 143, cols. 1,314–15); the oath taken by Berengar with its concluding formula, *lecto et perlecto sponte subscripsi*; Nicholas II's letter to Lanfranc. In brief, therefore, Lanfranc put together a collection of documents relating to the Council, with the pope's personal letter to him in their midst.

III   LANFRANC'S VISIT TO ROME

Within two or three months of writing this letter, the pope held his first Council in Rome. Here three decrees were passed to give effect to the policy of excluding lay influence from the government of the Church. The first established an electoral procedure excluding the emperor and the local aristocracy from their traditional role in papal elections; the second prohibited lay possession of tithes and churches; the third, and most far-reaching of all, outlined the sternest measures so far taken to enforce celibacy on all clergy from the rank of deacon upwards. Thus the three main strands in papal policy for the next two generations, spanning the whole of Anselm's later career, were brought together in the Council of Easter 1059.[10]

The decree enforcing clerical celibacy was to have an especially important place in Anselm's conception of his responsibilities as archbishop. But for the moment, we are concerned less with the decrees of the Council than with decisions which were taken probably after the main business of the Council was concluded. These decisions were not mentioned in the circular letters which the pope dispatched to various parts of Europe announcing the results of the Council, but they had a profound influence on the lives of both Lanfranc and Anselm.

The first concerned the marriage of Duke William. No formal document on this matter has survived, but it is clear that whatever the canonical objections may have been, the duke was given a dispensation which legitimized his marriage on condition that he founded two religious houses, for men and women respectively. The main interest of this decision for Anselm's career is that Lanfranc, having been responsible for negotiating the settlement, became the first abbot of one of these new foundations at Caen and left Bec in 1063.[11] The immediate result of this was that Anselm became prior of Bec, saving him from the fate which in his unregenerate days he had feared, of living permanently in Lanfranc's shadow.

The second decision, probably also taken after the main business had been dealt with, was to have wider repercussions than any

---

[10] For these documents, see *PL* 143, cols. 1,314– 22.

[11] For the question of the duke's marriage, see Douglas, 1964, pp. 75–80; William of Jumièges, pp. 127–8, describes the marriage but does not mention the legal difficulties. These certainly existed, but their nature is unknown.

other. This was the condemnation of Berengar's doctrine of the Eucharist. Lanfranc's part in this is unclear. Although he had taken a leading part in the earlier condemnation of Berengar's doctrine at Vercelli in 1050, it is clear that Cardinal Humbert was in charge of the case against Berengar in 1059. The earliest explicit account of Lanfranc's participation in the condemnation comes from Miles Crispin, writing at Bec more than fifty years later. He reported that Lanfranc had gone to the Council for the double purpose of being present at Berengar's trial and of obtaining a dispensation for the duke's marriage.[12] It seems more likely in fact that he went to Rome solely to negotiate the terms of papal approval for Duke William's marriage, and happened only by chance to become involved in Berengar's condemnation. Nevertheless, despite its late date, Milo's testimony to Lanfranc's presence is borne out by several features in the documents relating to his involvement in the Eucharistic controversy.

In the first place, the words used by Lanfranc in describing Berengar's deportment at the Council seem to be those of an eye-witness:

When, with more reliance on your friends than on reason, you came to Rome in the time of Pope Nicholas, you did not defend your earlier opinion, but asked Pope Nicholas and his Council to give you in writing the formula which you should accept. This task was remitted to Bishop Humbert, and you accepted, read, confirmed and subscribed with your own hand.

And:

When your opinions had been examined and condemned by Pope Nicholas and the Council of a hundred and thirteen bishops, you bowed, though not with a humbled heart; you lit the fire; you threw the condemned books into it in the midst of the Council, swearing that you would henceforth hold the ancient doctrine . . .[13]

Then, too, so far as we know, it was only his participation in these events which laid on him the main responsibility for replying to Berengar after Cardinal Humbert, the author of the agreed formula, had died in 1061.

---

[12] *PL* 150, col. 37. After describing the proceedings against Berengar at the Council of Easter 1059, Milo continues with these words: *His enim gestis* [i.e. the proceedings against Berengar] *Lanfrancus interfuit, qui causae huius litis Romam venerat et ut ageret pro duce Normannorum et uxore eius apud apostolum, pro qua re, sicut diximus, illuc perrexerat.*   [13] *PL* 150, cols. 409B–C, 411D

Until recently, these facts and circumstances have been generally accepted as providing sufficient evidence for thinking that Lanfranc, who was responsible for conducting the business of the duke's marriage, was also present at the Eucharistic debate. The two cases cannot have been separated by more than a few weeks, or (more probably) days, and it would have been consistent with ordinary usage for both these matters to be dealt with immediately after the main business of the Council had been completed. Moreover, since neither Berengar's condemnation nor William's marriage is mentioned in the papal letters describing the decisions of the Council, it seems likely that they were both discussed after the main business of the Council was concluded. Lanfranc was certainly present for the marriage case; what reason is there for disputing his presence also at the Eucharistic discussion?

It is simply this. On one point there is a conflict of testimony between Berengar and Lanfranc. As we have seen in the first extract quoted above, Lanfranc asserted that Berengar had *signed* his acceptance of the conciliar formula with his own hand. In saying this, Lanfranc was stating what the words of the final document themselves declared to be the case. But, in replying to Lanfranc, Berengar later declared:

I did *not* sign the document which was presented to me, as was mendaciously reported to you. All that happened was that, in fear of instant death and without any expression of assent, I received that document into my own hands.[14]

On the basis of this evidence, Professor Montclos has argued that Lanfranc was not present at the Council, and Dr Gibson has accepted this verdict.[15] But, even if Berengar is right on the point to which he objects, it does not show that Lanfranc was not present during these proceedings: he may have been present at the discussion, but not at the final scene; or he may have been present at the final scene, but unable to see everything because of the confusion; or he may have thought he had missed something, for the document itself declares that Berengar had signed it: *Ego Berengarius . . . consentio . . . et ore et corde profiteor . . . lecto et*

---

[14] *DSC* pp. 25–26. Berengar's words are: *Manu, quod mendaciter ad te pervenit, non subscripsi, nam ut de consensu pronunciarem meo nullus exegit; tantum timore presentis iam mortis scriptum illud, absque ulla conscientia mea iam factum, manibus accepi.*

[15] Montclos, 1971 pp. 43–4; Gibson, 1978, p. 69.

perlecto sponte subscripsi. Anyone who has read accounts of the confusion on such occasions will know how difficult it was to be sure of the details. For example, we have two eye-witness accounts of the proceedings against Gilbert of Poitiers at the Council of Rheims in 1148, but it is still impossible to know precisely what happened.[16]

In brief, the balance of probability is still, as it always has been, in favour of Lanfranc's presence both at the negotiations over Duke William's marriage dispensation, and at the Eucharistic discussions. But, in either case, he returned to Bec from the scene of action bringing news of events which were to have profoundly important results for doctrine and ecclesiastical politics, as well as for himself personally and consequently for Anselm too.

Anselm arrived at Bec to observe the first impact of these events on a small monastic community which had suddenly become the centre of intense activity. Berengar's rapid renunciation of his acceptance of the Eucharistic formula gave Lanfranc the task of composing by far his most important theological work. The terms of the settlement of Duke William's marriage led to Lanfranc's removal from Bec to Caen in 1063, and finally to Canterbury in 1070. These changes had a profound influence on Anselm's future. But more important than any of them was the change which these months brought about in Anselm's environment, and the new duties which they imposed upon him.

He had come to Bec with no expectations of advancement: he arrived simply to learn. But he now found himself, for the first time in his life, in the midst of events and intellectual conflicts of great and lasting importance. What he had so far lacked in his life was that awakening of his mind which would bring all his faculties into play and change his life. The events of the year, in which Lanfranc had been so deeply concerned, meant that he arrived when Lanfranc and Bec had suddenly been placed at the centre of great changes in the political and intellectual map of Europe. This circumstance alone would have given a new edge to the intellectual life of the monastery.

In addition to this, Lanfranc now more than ever needed help in the school which had for nearly twenty years been the main source

---

[16] John of Salisbury was an eye-witness and left a vivid account of the proceedings in 1148 in his *Historia Pontificalis* (ed. Marjorie Chibnall, 1956; and R. L. Poole, Oxford, 1927, pp. xxxvi–xlvi, 16–27), but on several points he did not know what was happening. Eadmer's account of the Council in St Peter's in 1099 also shows that the confusion was so great that it was impossible to know what decisions had been taken. See below, pp. 280–1.

of Bec's prosperity. To understand Anselm's development from this point, it is necessary to understand what Lanfranc had so far achieved as a teacher, and how this affected Anselm's life. But before undertaking this quite formidable task, we must first briefly survey Anselm's first steps towards a full involvement in the monastic life.

IV ANSELM'S APPRENTICESHIP

Anselm probably arrived at Bec either during Lanfranc's absence, or shortly after his return from Rome. In the course of time he would hear much about the events of the Council, and the problem of defending its doctrinal statement on the Eucharist. But immediately it is unlikely that these subjects occupied much of his attention. He had come to Bec to experience a new way of life, and he would see all around him the evidence of Lanfranc's extra-ordinary success in raising a small, poor, and undistinguished monastic community to a state of some prosperity. Apart from the school for external pupils, the monastery had still only a modest reputation. The abbot was a man of engaging holiness, but of no noticeable ability; and, although the monastery was prosperous, it had not yet attracted many able young men to the monastic life: it was mainly filled with monks who had come as child oblates from neighbouring families.

For nearly twenty years, Lanfranc had been the main driving force at Bec, the main source of its growing prosperity, and the community's only scholar and teacher. Nearly everything that he had been able to do for the monastery was the result of his widely famed scholarship and teaching. He had opened a school for external pupils in order to relieve the poverty of the abbey, and it had succeeded beyond all expectation. Notable men in all parts of Europe, from the pope downwards, were glad to send their aspiring relatives to Lanfranc's school, not to become monks, but to learn grammar, rhetoric and logic, and to return to their native lands with these useful accomplishments. With the wealth which they brought, Lanfranc was able (not once but twice) to remove the monastery to larger and more salubrious sites, and to give it new buildings, new books, and a more elaborate way of life.[17] This

---

[17] Gilbert Crispin, in his *Vita Herluini; Works*, pp. 194–7, gives the best account of the original poverty of Bec and the dramatic improvement in its fortunes as a result of the success of Lanfranc's school. This account is supplemented by Miles Crispin, *Vita Lanfranci*, in *PL* 150, cols. 29–39.

might have seemed enough work for anyone; but to these local cares Lanfranc had now added wider responsibilities in Norman politics and, very soon, a new responsibility for doctrinal controversy.

To a man as overstretched as Lanfranc was in 1059, Anselm's arrival must have been a godsend. It must soon have been clear that he was capable of taking over much of Lanfranc's work of teaching pupils and correcting manuscripts; and Lanfranc had for the first time a brilliant and devoted pupil, eager to learn and formidable in argument, as well as an able assistant. As for Anselm, for the first time in his life, he was at the centre of purposeful activity. After years of aimless wandering, he was suddenly thrown into a scene of sustained effort in several fields – new buildings, new books, new debates, an exacting daily routine. We have his own word for it that his first months at Bec were a time of severe intellectual and physical strain. He later told Eadmer that he was exhausted by the efforts he was called upon to make. They were all the more exhausting because he did not know where they were leading him.[18]

The problem of his future soon began to worry him. He longed for intellectual fame, but this desire made him feel guilty. In reaction against this he recalled his childhood desire to be a monk. Naively he reflected that with no more labour than was now demanded of him, he might win a heavenly reward. It was thus, as he explained to Eadmer, that the monastic longings he had had as a child began again to stir within him. But how were they to be satisfied? He went over the varied possibilities in his mind. He might become a monk at Bec: but while Lanfranc remained, he would be a nobody. He might go to Cluny: but at Cluny the exhausting daily routine would leave him no time to think.[19]

---

[18] See *VA* I, v, p. 8, for Eadmer's account of Anselm's first year at Bec. The details can only have come from Anselm himself: *Occupatur die noctuque in litterarum studio, non solum quae volebat a Lanfranco legendo, sed et alios quae rogabatur studiose docendo. Propter quae studia, cum corpus vigiliis, frigore et inedia fatigaret, venit ei in mentem quia si aliquo monachus ut olim proposuerat esset, acriora quam patiebatur eum pati non oporteret.* For his correction of manuscripts, see *VA* I, viii, pp. 14–15: *Totus dies in dandis consiliis saepissime non sufficiebat, addebatur ad hoc pars maxima noctis. Praeterea libros qui ante id temporis nimis corrupti ubique terrarum erant nocte corrigebat.* For Anselm's confiding the details of his early life to Eadmer, see below, pp. 411–12.

[19] *VA* I, vi, pp. 10–11. Anselm seems to have been the first to react against the over-filled routine of Europe's most famous monastery. Fifty years later the criticism had become widespread, but by then Anselm's counsel was all for endurance: he looked back on his earlier view as the impatience of an untamed spirit with an unruly desire for fame.

Then there were other possibilities. He might become a hermit. There is much in his later writings to suggest that a life of solitary contemplation might have suited his natural inclinations better than the life of a monastic community. It was a pleasing prospect. Nothing is more characteristic of the time than the new light in which hermitages were beginning to be viewed: instead of being seen as battlefields in a savage war against demons and evil spirits, we begin to hear of the sweetness of solitude, the pleasing springs and refreshing breezes, and the unhindered communion with God which these surroundings afforded. Anselm fully shared these new aspirations, but such places and people were not yet to be found in northern France. So he turned to a fourth possibility: perhaps he would go back to his small family property, found a hospital, and dispense alms to the poor.[20]

These were the ideals which hovered before the eyes of Anselm as he tried to plan his life. They provide a preview of the future development of religious sensibility in Europe. But like many others who peer into the future, he found the choice too hard for him. The arguments were too finely balanced to lead to a decision. 'My will was not yet tamed', he said; and in a fit of self-disgust he left the choice to Lanfranc. Lanfranc in turn referred the matter to Maurilius, archbishop of Rouen. Maurilius, who was himself a monk, had recently advised a discontented member of his household called Gundulf to become a monk at Bec. Inevitably, he gave the same advice to Anselm. So Anselm joined Gundulf in his vocation at Bec, and Gundulf became his closest friend.

For Anselm, the initial crisis of conversion was now over. It was not a conversion of faith, as experienced by Augustine; nor was it yet a total conversion of mind and will as experienced by St Bernard in the next generation. As Anselm described the process to Eadmer, and as Eadmer reported it, it was a conversion in three stages over a number of years. First there was his meeting with Lanfranc in 1059. This immersed him in a routine of intellectual effort from which he derived a deeper satisfaction than any he had so far experienced, and it led to a first crisis of decision – what we may call a career crisis: should he become a monk, or a hermit, or run a hospital?

The problem proved too difficult for him, and he allowed himself to be guided by Lanfranc and Maurilius: he became a monk. This

---

[20] On these movements, see Leyser, 1984, and the literature there cited.

31

was the beginning of his 'conversion' in the only sense in which he (in common with his monastic contemporaries) came to use the term to mean simply the irrevocable adoption of the discipline of the Benedictine Rule. Within this total commitment there could indeed be minor perversities of the will, which disturbed without destroying the state of conversion; but there could be no turning back. What Anselm now undertook, and in later years never ceased to implore his friends also to undertake, was a total commitment of his will to the demands of the Rule. This long effort was to reshape his life and thought over the next decade. The immensity of the effort cannot be over-estimated; and even to understand the range of activity it demanded will require a prolonged inquiry in the next two chapters. It is only as a preliminary to this tremendous task that I here add some notes on a small part of the raw materials. They are an invitation to further inquiry rather than an answer to questions; but at least they will give some indication of the diversity of matter which confronted Anselm at the beginning of his conversion.

V   NOTES ON INTELLECTUAL ACTIVITY AT BEC, 1050–1060

1   The text of Nicholas II's letter to Lanfranc[21]

Nicolaus, episcopus servus servorum Dei, fratri Lanfranco, salutem et apostolicam benedictionem.

Satis desideratam vestram, carissime frater, libenter viderem presentiam, et in ecclesiasticis nostris curis libenter vestris recrearer consiliis, quem in Romanis et apostolicis servitiis satis opportunum audivimus. Sed quia tam facile nunc forsan fieri non potest, volumus ipsam vestram stationem nobis et Romanae matri ecclesiae esse fructuosam, ut ex fructu vestrae stationis cognoscatur et fructus desiderabilis adventus. Hos igitur nostrae dilectionis filios, imperatorios capellanos et nostros, dialectica et rhetorica arte caritati vestrae mittimus edocendos, ut sicut te, Deo gratias, singularem in hoc bivio audivimus, sic istos singulares tecum quam cito poteris Romae, vel forte cum apud vos cito venero, videamus.

Si vero divina, ut audivimus, pagina ab huiusmodi studio vos retinet, ex parte sancti Petri et nostra vobis precipimus, et ex vera obedientia illos edocendos vobis mandamus, quos ad hoc vestrae dilectioni mittimus, et vestre caritati in omnibus subveniendos relinquimus. Comitem autem vestrum amicum nostrum, quem vestris audivimus satis, Deo gratias, acquiescere consiliis, ita custodiatis ut hic et in Christo valere possit. Confido enim bene de

---

[21] As mentioned above, Lanfranc inserted this letter in his canonical collection, TCC MS B.16.44, p. 211. It has the marginal note: *Hanc epistolam accepit cum Becci monachus esset.*

illo, cuius concilium et conversationem vobiscum audio. In clero autem et fero illo populo, si potestis, fructificate, ut de talento vobis commisso mereamini tandem audire, 'Euge serve bone!' Amen.

2 The development of Lanfranc's Commentary on St Paul

In attempting to understand the intellectual 'workshop' in which Anselm's intellectual horizons were determined, it is important to understand the development of Lanfranc's mind, of which the most important features were reflected in his commentary on St Paul's Epistles. As is well known, this work survives in two main forms: first with only Lanfranc's elucidations of Paul's extremely tortuous arguments by analysing their grammatical, rhetorical, and logical structures, and second, with these explanations interspersed among extracts from the Fathers, which Dr Gibson has shown to have been culled from a Carolingian collection of extracts. Unlike Dr Gibson, however, I believe that these two stages follow each other in the order which represents Lanfranc's own personal development over a period of ten or twenty years as he developed from being a renowned master of the arts of the trivium, to being a scholar of wide patristic learning and grasp of theological problems.

As we have seen, this development is well attested, not least by the letter which Pope Nicholas II sent him in 1059, in which the change in Lanfranc's range of interests was mentioned as a matter of general report. The development of his commentary along the same lines would not only fit in with his personal history, but also it would very well explain the double nature of the material in the commentary, consisting on the one hand of grammatical and logical notes with Lanfranc's name attached to them; and, on the other hand, of extracts from the Fathers intermingled with Lanfranc's own grammatical-logical comments.

There is always an element of doubt about such *post factum* reconstructions. We may reach a fair degree of certainty by analysing the various strands after they have been intermingled. But in any evidence which comes from manuscripts at Bec or Canterbury, the early stages will probably have been 'contaminated' by later developments. We know, for example, that in the only copy of his work which Lanfranc left at Bec, his own comments were intermingled with the extracts from the Fathers.[22]

---

[22] See *Ep.* 66 (i, 57).

And this would be quite natural: we commonly destroy early drafts when they have been superseded by later ones.

Consequently, the best evidence for the early stages in a work will come from copies which were taken away from Bec by students who heard the lectures at an early date. In this way alone we can catch the process of development in the act. For example, in the parallel case of the development of Anselm's letter-collection, there are manuscripts which illustrate the state of development at two stages before the final collection emerged: MS **N** illustrates the state of affairs in 1092, and the group of MSS **MFD** performs a similar function in about 1121–23, before the final collection was achieved in 1125– 30 in **VCELP**.[23]

Records of lectures are among the most ephemeral of literary remains: the finished product generally ousts the intermediate records. Nevertheless, such records survive. Several years ago Bernhard Bischoff found a record of Hugh of St Victor's lectures at an early stage in their development, and it threw much new light on the proceedings of one of the great Parisian schools in the years around 1125–30. After this date, such records become more abundant; earlier, they are very scarce. But I think there is at least one manuscript which contains a record of Lanfranc's lectures as they were before they had been enlarged by the addition of theological extracts from the Fathers. In describing it, I must leave many technical details to scholars better equipped to deal with them than I am. But an outline of the nature, provenance and approximate date of the manuscript will suffice for our present purpose.

The manuscript is a composite volume, Berne Bibl. Publ. MS 334, in which folios 240 to 356 were originally a separate volume containing the Pauline Epistles in their normal sequence from Romans to Hebrews, followed by an *Epistola ad Laodicenses* at the end. The text is probably late tenth-century, and the eccentric last item suggests that it may have been a spare copy by the mid-eleventh century. At all events, it was used in a rough and ready way to accommodate Lanfranc's comments on the texts, which are scattered about the pages and often enclosed in exotic frames of varying sizes and shapes: in brief, the writer of the comments had an old, and probably out-of-date text of St Paul's Epistles with large margins in which he exercised his ingenuity in using the

---

[23] See below, pp. 458–81.

available empty spaces for Lanfranc's comments. His method of connecting the comments with the texts to which they referred seems to have developed as he progressed. At first, he put the comments in the margin or between the lines; then he began making little boxes for each comment with tendrils connecting each box with its appropriate text. Sometimes he would revert to his earlier style, or place both text and comment in the same frame, or devise symbols to connect the text with its appropriate comment. In brief, the appearance of the pages seems to put us in the presence of a student either making his notes during the lecture or writing them up afterwards.

More striking even than the appearance of the glosses is their irregularity: that is to say, some of the Epistles are very fully commented on, but these areas of dense comment are intermingled with areas in which comments are wholly or partially lacking, like the notes of any student who is prevented by illness, idleness or other avocations from attending all the lectures. If we examine the contents from this point of view, we find:

1 The whole of Romans and I Corinthians as far as chapter xv, 20, are fully commented on.
2 From this point to Ephesians iv, 30, there are no comments.
3 Then, from Ephesians iv, 31, to Hebrews ii, 5, there are fairly full comments.
4 Thereafter there are none.

If the comments are compared with the printed edition, it immediately appears that, where they are full, they contain most of the comments ascribed to Lanfranc in the printed text, together with a few unprinted comments of a similar kind, but with none of the Patristic quotations.

I cannot attempt to do more here than indicate the interest of this manuscript, and to suggest that records of Lanfranc's lectures exist, syphoned off by students and removed from the ambiance of Bec, which may tell us more than we know at present about the development of Lanfranc's lectures, and that the Berne manuscript seems to provide evidence of a stage in Lanfranc's lectures when he was wholly occupied with points of grammar, logic and rhetoric.

3 Lanfranc's wider influence: the copying of his marginal symbols.

The list which follows consists of scattered notes on MSS made many years ago. Imperfect though it is, I print it here simply as a guide to anyone who may wish to take the inquiry further. It may serve as a complement to the important article of Margaret Gibson (Gibson, 1971) on the circulation of Lanfranc's notes on Patristic texts.

Z. N. Brooke (1931, pp. 68–71) was the first to point out that Lanfranc's collection of Canon Law in Trinity College, Cambridge, MS B.16.44, contains many marginal signs, .a., or .A., which help to guide the reader to passages to which Lanfranc seems to have attached special importance. These *signa* are also found in many other Canterbury manuscripts, and they were copied into texts made for other monasteries, chiefly in England. The existence of these symbols in Lanfranc's canon law collection, which certainly belongs to his years at Bec and in several other manuscripts also associated with Bec, suggests that this system of annotation was started by Lanfranc while he was at Bec, and thereafter transferred to Canterbury. From each of these sources copies were made which carried these annotations far and wide in northern France and England among readers who perhaps had no idea of the source, or even the meaning of this convenient symbol.

Nevertheless, the fact that these annotations were copied, often very imperfectly, from one manuscript to another shows that they were held to have some degree of authority. And apart from any use which they may have had, they are a guide to the dissemination of texts which Lanfranc had caused to be transcribed in the first place for the libraries at Bec and Canterbury. That they deserve a really careful scrutiny as a whole is more than I can vouch for. But some of the annotation in the following texts certainly goes back to Lanfranc himself, and a study of them may throw light both on the subjects of his special interest, and on the diffusion of the collection of texts which he made at Bec, and later reproduced at Canterbury.

Any investigation of these marginalia must begin with Lanfranc's collection of Decretals and Councils. Brooke, 1931 listed the derivative MSS, so I shall here simply mention that one copy, Bnl 3865, perhaps made before Lanfranc became archbishop, contains several of his marginal .A.s. I append a list of volumes with theological texts which contain the same marginal symbol, .A. or .a.:

Ambrose,
On Luke: TCC B.3.9, from Christ Church, Canterbury; Bodl. e Mus. 27, from Bury St Edmunds;
De Virginibus: CCCC 274.

Augustine,
Confessions: TCC B.3.25, from Christ Church, Canterbury, CCCC 253, from St Augustine's, Canterbury;
Contra Faustum, Bodl. 135, from Exeter;
Enarrationes in Psalmis: BL Royal 5. D. 1–3, from Rochester; Durham, B ii, 13–14, from Durham; TCC B.5.26, from Christ Church, Canterbury; Bodl. e Mus. 7–8, from Bury St Edmunds.
Enchiridion, BL Royal 5 A xv, from Rochester;
Tractatus in Ioannis evangelium: TCC B.4.2, from Christ Church, Canterbury; Balliol College MS 6; Bodl. 301; Bodl. e Mus. 6, from Bury St Edmunds; CCCC 17.
Augustinian miscellany, I: Bnl 12211 (from Bec?); CUL Ff. 4. 32 from Christ Church, Canterbury.
Augustinian miscellany, II: Bnl 12230 (from Bec?).

Bede,
On Mark, Luke, and Catholic Epistles, Bodl. 217, from Christ Church, Canterbury;
De Temporibus CCCC 291, from St Augustine's, Canterbury;
De Tabernaculo, Bodl. 385, from Christ Church, Canterbury;
In Cant.: Bodl. 161, from Christ Church, Canterbury;
In epistolis catholicis, CCCC 62, from Rochester;
Expositio Actuum Apostolorum: Bodl. 160, from Christ Church, Canterbury.

Cassian,
Collationes, Alençon, 136, profusely annotated with **.A.** symbols and other notes; *Lanfrancus huc usque correxi* at end of text.

Eusebius,
Historia: CCCC 187, from Christ Church, Canterbury; CCCC 184, from Rochester.

Florus of Lyons,
In Epp. S. Pauli: Bodl. 317, from Christ Church, Canterbury.

Gregory,
Moralia in Job: BL Royal 6 C vi, from Rochester. *Registrum*: Durham B iii 9, from Durham.

37

To these theological texts, the following should be added as evidence of a continuing tradition of annotation at Bec:
Bnl 14146 (from Bec?): Quintilian, *Institutio Oratoris*; Bnl 16713: Letters and sermons of Ivo of Chartres, with a letter of Anselm's pupil Boso, when he was abbot of Bec.[24]

---

[24] I owe the description of the MSS in the Bibliothèque Nationale chiefly to N. R. Ker, who examined the Bec MSS in 1937, and to Mlle. Marthe Dulong, who examined them again for me in the summer of 1939. Ker reported that Bnl 12211 seemed indistinguishable from a Canterbury MS. May this slight note serve to recall the friendships of those years.

CHAPTER 3

ANSELM AND LANFRANC

I LANFRANC'S CONTRIBUTION TO ANSELM'S FUTURE

1 Lanfranc as teacher

At the time when he arrived at Bec, in about 1042, Lanfranc was already famous as a teacher of the liberal arts. When he became prior about three years later, he became reponsible for the daily discipline of the community, and for teaching the children who would become full members in due course. For these duties, he needed to add an expert knowledge of the Benedictine Rule and its highly developed Offices to his formidable scholarly equipment. But his main source of fame and usefulness to the community remained his command of the secular disciplines of dialectic and rhetoric. These were the subjects which drew pupils to Bec and made the monastery prosperous.[1] The need for skilled clerks in government was beginning to grow; and it was no doubt this need which caused Nicholas II, who had been elected pope with an ambitious programme of reform under papal leadership, to send his clerks to Lanfranc, and to urge him to continue to teach logic and rhetoric rather than theology. Many other rulers had a similar need. So the schools grew, Lanfranc's among them.

Despite this incentive, the central interest of Lanfranc's studies had in the last few years been changing to theology. He had shifted first to the careful examination of the grammatical, logical and rhetorical problems of St Paul's letters; then increasingly to doctrinal problems. This too was a development which was

---

[1] Gilbert Crispin, the earliest historian of Bec, is especially emphatic on the connection between the 'external' school and the prosperity of the monastery: *Accurrunt clerici, ducum filii, nominatissimi scholarum Latinitatis magistri. Laici potentes, alta nobilitate viri multi, pro ipsius amore multas eidem ecclesie terras contulere. Ditatur ilico Beccensis locus ornamentis, possessionibus, personis nobilibus et honestis. Interius religio atque eruditio multum accrescere, exterius rerum omnium necessariarum subministratio coepit ad plenum abundare.* (Gilbert Crispin, *Vita Herluini*, c. 62. *Works*, p. 197.)

beginning to become widespread, and Lanfranc's progression from the liberal arts to the Bible, and from the textual problems of the Bible to problems of theology, was a model for the future. It lies at the heart of the growth of scholastic thought; and, more immediately, at the heart of Anselm's development.

It may have been the growing demand for theology among his pupils which first prompted Lanfranc to undertake a *Commentary on the Epistles of St Paul*. But whatever its origin, it had probably been completed by 1059 when Anselm arrived at Bec. A near contemporary, Sigebert of Gembloux, describes the work thus:

Lanfranc expounded Paul the Apostle; and, wherever opportunity offered, he stated the premises, whether principal or secondary, and the conclusions of Paul's arguments in accordance with the rules of logic.[2]

This is a precise and complete description of Lanfranc's *Commentary* in what I believe to have been its earliest form.[3] In this form, without the interruption of Patristic excerpts, we find the grammatical tangles and notorious perplexities of St Paul's arguments smoothed away by a master-hand: 'This is the order of the argument' . . .; 'Here is the proof he is putting forward' . . .; 'Here, in his usual fashion, Paul proves his point by *dis*proving the opposite' . . .; 'Here he avoids arguing by way of syllogism, perhaps because he is afraid of being refuted, or because he thinks that faith arrived at by syllogism will be unprofitable' . . .; 'Here he argues from similarity of cases' . . .; 'here he argues from similar cases' . . .; 'Here he goes back to an earlier question' . . .; 'Here the gist of the argument is this' . . .; 'Here you might object . . .' and so on. Nothing can make the Pauline text easy, but whatever could be done by the grammatical, logical and rhetorical doctrine of the eleventh century to elucidate his extraordinarily convoluted arguments, Lanfranc did; and he pursued his task without faltering from beginning to end.

Unless I am mistaken, Lanfranc's *Commentary*, in its earliest state, consisted solely of notes on the structure of the sentences and arguments of the Epistles, with no attempt to bring together

---

[2] Sigebert of Gembloux, *Liber de eccl. scriptoribus*, PL 160, cols. 582–3: *Paulum apostolum exposuit Lanfrancus, et ubicumque opportunitas locorum occurrit, secundum leges dialecticae proponit, assumit, concludit.* The words *proponit, assumit, concludit*, are technical words of dialectic, repeatedly found, for example, in Gottschalk of Orbaix, *Opuscula theologica* ed. C. Lambot, *Spicilegium Sacrum Lovaniense*, xx, 1945, pp. 85, 101, 206–7, in connection with St Paul's arguments. It is possible that Lanfranc was inspired by Gottschalk's example.   [3] See above, pp. 33–5.

Patristic extracts to illustrate the sense. He treated the text as schoolmasters of all periods have treated classical authors, but as no one before him had treated the Bible. Of course, earlier commentators had seen that St Paul badly needed grammatical and logical explanations: Jerome, in particular, had remarked on Paul's tendency to state one premise of a syllogism and to leave the reader to provide the rest. As an example of this habit, he noted that, in the argument, 'If righteousness is through the law, Christ died in vain', Paul left the reader to supply the minor premise, 'But Christ did not die in vain', which led to the syllogistic conclusion: 'therefore righteousness is not of the law'.[4]

Remarks like this had been relished by scholars deeply dyed in the liberal arts long before Lanfranc. In particular, one of the most independent grammarians and theologians of the ninth century, Gottschalk of Orbaix, had noticed the need for a grammatical and logical commentary, and he had taken some tentative steps towards meeting this need. Lanfranc, therefore, was not breaking entirely new ground. But he stands out among commentators not only of his own but of any period, in providing a thorough and single-minded commentary on the words, sentences, and forms of argument used by St Paul.

I emphasize this aspect of Lanfranc's achievement because in trying to understand the intellectual atmosphere which Anselm found at Bec, it is important to recognize Lanfranc's relentless investigation of words and arguments in studying a major theological source. Anselm was to go much further and show a much more refined capacity for such investigations than Lanfranc; but he simply took many more steps along the same route.

The great difference is that, whereas we can still go to Anselm for enlightenment, no one will now find anything of value in Lanfranc's work. He spoke only for his own time, and in its earliest form the influence of his work was very short-lived. It was designed for his pupils, and it should be read with the classroom always in mind. Read thus, we can see how Lanfranc's bleak comments provided an impulse to argument. Each comment requires a close attention to the text, and several raise large issues. For instance, in explaining Romans, iii, 4, Lanfranc started an idea about the relation between Truth and Justice which re-emerged with notable clarity twenty years later in one of Anselm's mature works.

---

[4] For Jerome's observation, see his *Commentary on Galatians; PL* 26, cols. 346, 371–2.

The case deserves a moment's attention, for it shows how a luminous idea may have a humble birth. The Pauline text from which the problem arose is a troublesome one. On the surface, as often in St Paul, his argument seems to be a series of *non sequiturs*:

God is true, but every man a liar; as it is written, 'That thou mightest be justified in thy sayings and prevail when thou art judged'.

What can this mean? Lanfranc found a way through the tangle by identifying Truth with Justice. 'If this is understood', he declares, 'the sentence is a proof that God is Truth; for Truth is Justice expressed in words.'[5] This explanation is itself far from clear, and it can scarcely have been accepted without discussion. It requires as its major premise, 'God is just'; and as its minor, 'Truth is Justice-in-words', to give the conclusion, 'God is Truth'. Its main interest for us is that it is possible to trace this identification of Truth with Justice twenty-five years later in Anselm's *De Veritate*. Moreover, shortly before writing this work, on his first visit to Canterbury in 1079, Anselm had delighted the English monks by proving the sanctity of St Elphege on the same principle: Elphege, who died for justice, necessarily (he declared) died also for truth; therefore, he could justly be accounted a martyr.[6]

We may here be touching the very first impulse in Anselm's intellectual development: the most vital part of any teaching is the stimulus it provides for questions among the auditors. This is something which is suppressed in the surviving record, for generally only that portion survives which adds something to the stock of knowledge. What stimulated the pupils does not stimulate future scholars. Hence, the arguments and disagreements which enlivened lectures and influenced listeners have vanished. But a sympathetic eye can detect in Lanfranc's remarks the sources of new inspiration. Pupils did not come to Lanfranc from all over Europe to hear what they might have heard at home. His application of the art of dialectic to Biblical texts was new in the

---

[5] See *PL* 150, col. 115, for Lanfranc's comment on the words *ut iustificeris in sermonibus tuis* in Romans iii, 4: *iustitia enim sermonum est veritas*, (Truth is Justice in words). Conversely, Anselm later argued: Justice is Truth in action. For this, see below, pp. 172 and 316.

[6] Dr Gibson made this observation: see Gibson, 1978, p. 56. The relevant passages are, for Lanfranc, *PL* 150, col. 115; and for Anselm, *De Veritate*, c. xii. For a further link between Lanfranc and Anselm in their treatment of this theme, see Southern, 1948, pp. 42–3. For its application to St Elphege, see *VA* I, xxx.

1050s; by the end of the century it was common, as also was the practice of making a portable selection of Patristic texts to elucidate difficult Biblical passages. In this too, as we shall see, Lanfranc was an innovator: but at the beginning he specialized in introducing the liberal arts into Biblical exegesis.

When Lanfranc arrived at Bec in about 1040, it was a poorly endowed and unlearned community, and it cannot have had many books beyond those which he brought with him. But with Lanfranc as the driving force in the community, changes were rapid. His teaching and fame brought money with which books could be acquired, and he must soon have felt the need for more theological texts, from which he compiled two supplements to his *Commentary on St Paul*. The first of these supplements was gathered from Augustine, the second from a writer whom he believed to be Ambrose. Dr Gibson has examined these supplements, and has demonstrated that Lanfranc compiled both of them, not from the original texts, but by judicious selection from earlier anthologies. These supplements were therefore not the result of wide reading: they were the result of seeing a need and satisfying it as economically as possible. But as we shall see, there is also evidence that he was collecting major Patristic texts and reading them carefully.

By the time that Anselm arrived at Bec, it is likely that the library already contained at least the major works of Augustine, which were to have the greatest influence on his later development. To make this point clear, it is necessary to consider the evidence for Lanfranc's reading and the extent of the library he had built up at Bec. To do this, we must go back to the events of 1059 and examine the legacy of controversy which these events brought to Bec.

2 *Lanfranc as disputant*

At Easter 1059, Berengar had been forced to abjure his doctrine of the Eucharist and to assent to a doctrine of which Lanfranc later became the chief exponent. Berengar went back on his oath almost immediately, and the full weight of upholding the formula adopted at the Council fell on Lanfranc. There is no clear evidence for the date when Lanfranc wrote his reply. It was not sent to Berengar until Lanfranc had left Bec for Caen. Nevertheless, it is an elaborate work, quoting many Patristic authorities, and there are several indications that Lanfranc knew intimately the books from which these quotations were drawn. It was not the work of a moment; and the probability is that it was in preparation during the years from 1060 to 1063.[7]

It would be hard to over-estimate the importance for the future of the western Church of the Eucharistic doctrine as defined in 1059, and the concepts on which it was based. But we are here concerned only with Lanfranc's defence of the doctrine, and the influence of his work on Anselm's mind. From this point of view, the concepts are more important than the doctrine. On the doctrine it will suffice to say that the dispute was not, as was often alleged by Berengar's enemies at the time and has been frequently repeated ever since, about the real presence of the Body and Blood of Christ in the Eucharist. Both sides were agreed on this point.[8] The question was whether the presence was real and substantial in something like the Aristotelian sense of substance, as Lanfranc and the Council maintained, or real but not substantial in the Aristotelian sense, as Berengar maintained. If the first of these alternatives was accepted, the presence of a new substance on the altar entailed the destruction of the substance of the Bread, for two substances of this kind could not occupy the same area of space simultaneously. But if the second (the Berengarian) alternative was adopted, the question of exclusive spatial occupation did not arise: the material Bread and Wine could co-exist with the spiritual Body and Blood. Both sides claimed equal reality, but one side – that of Lanfranc – claimed a reality which was capable of some degree of explanation along the lines of Aristotle's *Categories*; the other side – that of Berengar – claimed that the reality existed in a manner

---

[7] Various dates have been suggested for the writing of Lanfranc's *De Corpore et Sanguine Domini*. In my view, Macdonald, 1926, p. 51, is right in thinking that it was mainly written *c* 1060–63. Montclos (pp. 196, 249) dates it 1063–68, mainly on the grounds that Lanfranc was abbot of Caen when he sent it to Berengar, and that Theodoric, a German pupil of Lanfranc, who wrote when Lanfranc was already at Caen, claims that it was he who urged Lanfranc to write it (*PL* 147, col. 334). But even if Theodoric's claim is correct, there is nothing in his statement to preclude his having been a pupil of Lanfranc's when he was still at Bec. Indeed this is most likely, for there is no evidence that Lanfranc continued his external school after leaving Bec.

[8] Berengar consistently maintained that he accepted the reality of the Body and Blood of Christ in the Eucharist: e.g. *Panem et Vinum per consecrationem converti in altari in verum Christi corpus et sanguinem, non mea, non tua, sed evangelica apostolicaque simul autenticarum scripturarum, quibus contraire fas non sit, est sententia. DSC*, p. 57; and see also pp. 56–7, 67–8.

known only to God, certainly not in any sense comparable with the primary substances of Aristotle.

The strength of the Lanfrancian position was that it made it possible to go some way towards explaining how the Eucharistic change took place: it took place by the replacement of one substance by another. The weakness of Berengar's position was that he could not explain what had happened: he could only resist the attempt to explain a revealed truth by adding explanatory words which were not (as he believed) authorized by Christ or the Fathers. He would not, he said, follow Lanfranc in adding to the true statement, *panis sacratus in altari est Corpus Christi*, the unauthorized word *substantialiter*.[9] Lanfranc felt no scruples about this addition. In making it, he was displaying an early symptom of the scholastic urge to use the sciences of the trivium and quadrivium to push back the frontiers of mystery and enlarge the area of intelligibility.

The use of the sciences of grammar and logic to clarify theological problems was to have many triumphs in the next two centuries, and the success of Lanfranc's argument was one of the first. Indeed, Berengar too used grammar and logic to support his position; but Lanfranc's explanation had the overwhelming advantage that it gave the fullest scope to the operations of the natural world. In doing this, he satisfied one of the most powerful urges of this period, and it was not an accident that, whereas Lanfranc's treatise circulated widely and was developed by half a dozen writers in his lifetime, Berengar's view remained virtually unknown except as reported by his enemies, and his final statement of his position has survived in only one manuscript, which was perhaps his own and only copy.[10] Without doubt, in this dispute Lanfranc had the mind of the immediate future on his side.

What influence did this have on Anselm? In view of the importance and notoriety of the debate, it is a striking fact that Anselm *never* mentioned the subject. Indeed, he never mentioned the Eucharist in any of his writings for the next forty years; even then, the words he used are consistent with either of the views

---

[9] These words are taken from the most moving of Berengar's expostulations against his enemies, printed by P. Meyvaert, 'Bérenger de Tours contre Alberic du Mont-Cassin', *RB*, 70, 1960, pp. 324–32.

[10] On the only surviving, and perhaps only ever, copy of his defence, see R. B. C. Huygens, 'À propos de Bérenger et son traité de l'Eucharistie', *RB*, 76, 1966, pp. 133–9.

developed in the dispute.[11] Several of Lanfranc's pupils rose up to defend their master's view of the matter, but not Anselm. His silence may only mean that he thought enough had been said. It might mean more – that he did not like Lanfranc's manner of handling it; or further still, that he did not agree with his conclusion. There is something that might be said in favour of all these possibilities. But whichever may be right, Lanfranc's involvement does not seem to have engaged his interest sufficiently to take part in the dispute. The mere fact that Anselm felt no urge to speak on the subject may be the first sign of a division between them. But it did not mean that he was uninterested in the methods and arguments used in the dispute. Far from it; there is, as we shall see, some reason to think that it was with these methods and arguments that his intellectual development began.[12]

With regard to these methods, two observations may be made. The first is that neither Lanfranc nor Berengar was a theologian by training. They were essentially and by general repute the most famous masters of the liberal arts of the day. They were both thoroughly skilled in grammar and dialectic – with this difference, that Berengar's preference would seem to have been for grammar, and Lanfranc's for dialectic. This difference is apparent in their rival methods of arguing about the Eucharist, which may be broadly distinguished as grammatical on Berengar's part, and dialectical on Lanfranc's. The point requires some elucidation if its limitations are to be understood correctly.

I   THE USE OF GRAMMATICAL TOOLS

Berengar's crucial argument was that the sentence *Hoc est corpus meum*, can only be intelligible and therefore valid, if the subject of the sentence 'Hoc', indicating the Bread, is preserved intact till the end of the sentence. Consequently, whatever 'Hoc' meant at the beginning of the sentence, it must still mean at the end. Otherwise, the sentence becomes meaningless.

A further argument in favour of this view was drawn from the

---

[11] *Oratio ad accipiendum corpus domini et sanguinem.* (Schmitt, iii, p. 10, *Or.* no. 3). This prayer is not among the earliest of Anselm's prayers. It appears to have been added between 1093 and 1100. See below, p. 111 for details of the growth of the collection and for the audience for which this prayer would have been written. Anselm's only other, and still later, words on the Eucharist were in reply to questions asked by Waleran, bishop of Nuremburg, about the use of unleavened bread. (Schmitt, ii, pp. 223–42.)   [12] See below, pp. 62–5.

grammatical doctrine that pronouns, being replacements for nouns, signify *substance*: in this case the substance of the Bread. Consequently, in the sentence *Hoc est corpus meum*, the subject is the substance of the Bread, and any change of substance in pronouncing the words of consecration would make the sentence meaningless.[13]

This was Berengar's argument as quoted by Lanfranc. And here it may be remarked that Anselm's argument about the existence of God, which he wrote twenty years later in his *Proslogion*, makes a similar claim: the statement that 'God does not exist' is strictly self-destructive, for by definition the subject, 'God', refers to a substance which exists *in re* as well as *in mente*. So the statement 'God does not exist' amounts to saying 'That which, in every possible sense of the word, exists does not exist'. This statement will require examination later.

II THE USE OF DIALECTICAL TOOLS

Substance and Accidents

In contrast to this grammatically based argument, Lanfranc's argument invokes the doctrine of one of the fundamental textbooks in dialectic. He explains the change which takes place in the consecration of the Bread and Wine in terms of the doctrine of substance and accidents as laid down in Aristotle's *Categories*.

To understand Lanfranc's position, we must begin by remembering that the formula which he was called upon to defend was brutally explicit. It declared that the Body of Christ is present in the Eucharist *sensualiter*; and that 'it is handled by the priest and broken and torn by the teeth of the faithful'.[14] These phrases were dropped in later definitions, but they were what Lanfranc had committed himself to defend. Their stark emphasis on the physical nature of the change has both a philosophical and a historical significance. Philosophically, the formula invites, and perhaps

---

[13] For detailed references, see Southern, 1948, pp. 43–6. Berengar's argument is stated in various slightly different ways in the course of the controversy. In its first appearance it has the form: *Non enim constare poterit affirmatio omnis, parte subruta.* (Lanfranc, *DCSD*, c. 8.)

[14] *Corpus et sanguinem . . . non solum sacramento, sed in veritate manibus sacerdotum tractari, frangi et fidelium dentibus atteri. PL* 150, col. 411. It should be noticed that the formula which follows in the Migne text, in which these words are omitted, is not part of Lanfranc's work: it is a later insertion reporting the formula agreed in 1079.

requires, an account of the Eucharistic change along the lines of the doctrine of substance presented in the recently discovered *Categories* of Aristotle. Historically it reflects a new consciousness of the laws of the physical world.

The combination of these two influences led to a shift in the balance of theological discussion. Increasingly, scholastic theory sought to clarify the physical events which accompany spiritual changes, whether in the consecration of bishops, or in the processes of penance, or, as here, in the Eucharist. The Eucharistic dispute was the first important symptom of this change of emphasis in European thought. Looked at from this point of view, Berengar was a conservative: for him, the problem of the Eucharist was not about a physical change, but about a change of a spiritual order. But for Lanfranc, the question of the nature of the physical change was, if not primary, at least unavoidable.

Broadly Lanfranc's answer was this: if the Body of Christ becomes *sensualiter* present on the altar, its substance must have replaced the substance of the Bread. The fact that the Bread still appears to be there is simply a divine mercy to spare the congregation the horror of seeing what is really there, though occasionally (as several reports testified) the mask dropped and pious eyes saw the very Flesh itself.

To support this position, Lanfranc made use of the account of the physical universe elaborated in Aristotle's *Categories*, which had first become known in the Latin West in the schools of northern France in the late tenth century. Its diffusion had been rapid: from northern France alone, copies of the tenth to eleventh centuries still survive from Mont St Michel, Chartres, and St Benoît-sur-Loire. Considering how few scholastic manuscripts of this period still survive, this diffusion suggests that it met a widely felt need. There was certainly a copy at Bec when Anselm wrote his *De Grammatico*, and Lanfranc must also have been familiar with it.[15]

So far as the Eucharistic dispute is concerned, the relevant doctrine of Aristotle's *Categories* is that the visible universe consists of a substratum of invisible primary substances of which the visible and tangible 'accidents' of colour, shape, position and so forth are the sensible evidence. Armed with this instrument of analysis, it was possible to give a perfectly coherent account of what happened

---

[15] For a list of surviving MSS, see *Categoriae vel Praedicamenta*, ed. L. Minio-Paluello, *Aristoteles Latinus*, i, 1961. The existence of a copy, and probably more than one copy, at Bec can be deduced from Anselm's work: see below, pp. 62–5.

at the Eucharist: the substance of Christ's Body replaces the invisible primary substance of the Bread on the altar, although (by divine mercy) the accidents remained unchanged.[16]

Lanfranc's account of the Eucharistic change is based on this Aristotelian doctrine of substance. Nevertheless he seems to have taken some pains to blur the connection between his account of the Eucharistic change and its Aristotelian source. How else can one account for the fact that, whereas the common Latin translation of Aristotle's *Categories* always translates *protai ousiai* as *primae substantiae* or *principales substantiae*, Lanfranc always speaks of them as *pristinae essentiae* or *principales essentiae*? In themselves Lanfranc's phrases are perfectly good translations of Aristotle's *protai ousiai*, but they are not the common ones, and we cannot avoid the impression that he was reluctant to have his doctrine too closely associated with Aristotle.

Nevertheless, we can be sure that Aristotle's *Categories* provided him with the model of the universe on which his explanation of the Eucharistic change was based. In the first place, the Aristotelian text alone provides the necessary structure of substance and accidents for a change of the kind required by Lanfranc. And, secondly, Lanfranc describes the universe as consisting of *principales et secundae essentiae*, which can be none other than the *primae et secundae substantiae* of Aristotle's *Categories*.[17]

Lanfranc therefore used Aristotelian concepts with a slightly modified vocabulary. Indeed, it was only by using the Aristotelian concept of substance that he could insist that Berengar, by denying a substantial change in the Eucharistic Bread and Wine, degraded

---

[16] An interesting recollection of Lanfranc's interest in the relations between substance and accidents was found by R. W. Hunt among glosses on Priscian in a twelfth-century Chartres manuscript: the compiler cites various views about the use of the verb 'sum': e.g. Master Guido thinks that 'sum' signifies action only when used of God, and is otherwise passive; but Lanfranc thinks it signifies action when used of substances, as in *Homo est*; but is passive when used of accidents, e.g. *Albedo est*. On this the compiler comments: *quod magister Wido inter deum et creaturas attendit, hoc Lanfrancus inter substantias et accidentia.* (*MARS*, 1, part 2, 1943, 224.)

[17] The essential passage in which this is made clear is *DCSD* c. 7, *PL* 150, col. 418: *Deus condidit res ipsas in principalibus ac secundis essentias, easque tam verarum quam falsarum propositionum causas esse disposuit.* The *principales* and *secundae essentiae* of this sentence can only be the *primae et secundae substantiae* of Aristotle's *Categories*. Consequently, the *principales essentiae* which undergo change in the Eucharist are the *primae substantiae* of the Bread and Wine. Montclos rejects this association of Lanfranc's formulas with those of Aristotle's *Categories*; but he offers no alternative explanation, and I have not been able to follow him in rejecting the explanation of Lanfranc's words which I gave in Southern, 1948, pp. 40–1.

the words of the Eucharist to a purely figurative level of meaning, despite Berengar's persistent denial of this consequence.[18]

It may reasonably be asked why, if Lanfranc was using Aristotelian categories, he should have wished to conceal his dependence on Aristotle. A definitive answer to this question cannot be given, but several possibilities may be suggested. First of all, in 1059, dialectic was still perilous ground in theology, and Lanfranc was a prudent man. He certainly would not have wished to associate himself with Berengar's provocative brandishing of the secular sciences in discussing sacred subjects. Besides, he may well have been reluctant to associate the substance of Christ's Body too definitely with the primary substances of Aristotle. Useful though they were, as giving an intelligible account of what happened to the substances of Bread and Wine in the Eucharist, he may have hesitated to use the language of the Arts too starkly in expounding the mystery of the Body of Christ.

He stood on the threshold of a great revolution in the terminology of theological discussion, and any sensible innovator had to proceed cautiously. Aristotle had never yet been quoted in any medieval theological discussion. Indeed, so far as is known, the first explicit reference to Aristotle in a theological work is in Anselm's *Cur Deus Homo*, nearly forty years later.[19] But the important fact remains that, despite these dangers and delays, Aristotle in Lanfranc's hands had silently made his first successful intervention in a theological debate of central importance. This association of the language of Aristotle with the problems of theology was soon to become a matter of course; but in the mid-eleventh century it still carried alarming overtones.

Equipollent Propositions

In his own highly individual way, Anselm was to go much further than Lanfranc in 'rationalizing' theology. But as we shall see, his theological method allowed him to do this almost unchallenged,

---

[18] Thus Lanfranc describes Berengar's position:*panem vinumque ... sine materiali mutatione in pristinis essentiis remanere ... panem vinumque essentialiter non mutari ... panem et vinum in principalibus essentiis permanere*. Against this Lanfranc insisted: *Credimus terrenas substantias ... converti in essentiam dominici carnis*; and *Confitetur ecclesia ... panem et vinum ... in substantiam carnis et sanguinis commutari*; *panem et vinum ... in substantiam carnis et sanguinis commutari*; (and still more emphatically) *commutari secundum interiorem essentiam*. For these passages in Lanfranc, see *PL* 150, cols. 415, 417, 418, 419, 420, 430. It should be noted in these passages that Lanfranc uses the words *essentia* and *substantia* interchangeably.

[19] See *CDH*, II, 17 (Schmitt, ii, p. 125)

and almost without offence. Lanfranc by contrast, still known in the wider world primarily as a dialectician and perhaps remembered as a former friend of Berengar, was always conscious of the need for caution. Unlike Berengar, he wished always to avoid the *appearance* of dialectical arrogance. He left it to Berengar to assert that 'to appeal to dialectic is to appeal to reason; and not to do so is to deny the image of God in man'.[20] Lanfranc took the humbler line:

> Even when the matter in dispute is such that it could most clearly be dealt with by the rules of dialectic, I prefer, so far as possible, to proceed by means of equipollent propositions, thus hiding my art lest I should seem to depend more on art than on the truth and authority of the holy Fathers.[21]

No two statements could better bring out the different tempers of Berengar and Lanfranc, or more neatly point the way forward to Anselm than those which I have just quoted. They show Berengar provocative and bold, Lanfranc cautious and somewhat disingenuous. We shall find that Anselm was bolder than either, but apparently unconscious of the problem which made his immediate predecessors take refuge either in over-loud assertions or in over-secretive innovation.

With regard to Lanfranc's statement, there is an obvious embarrassment in his attitude. When he speaks of *ars celans artem* he wants to appear humble; but 'concealing art' is generally, and rightly, regarded as the highest expression of an art, not as its renunciation. The 'equipollent propositions' by which Lanfranc hoped to avoid the appearance of dialectical arrogance are as much a branch of dialectic as the syllogistic arguments which he affects to renounce. So here once more we see Lanfranc hesitating to allow his dialectical skills to show.

Yet it would be a mistake to think that Lanfranc's self-depreciation is disingenuous. By *equipollency*, he meant something less rigorous than the strict parity of meaning demanded by logicians: he was satisfied with a general congruity of meaning. This is clear from the single example of equipollent propositions which he gives in analysing one of St Paul's arguments. In his first Epistle to the Corinthians, St Paul discourages marriage on the ground that he wants everyone to be without worldly cares. In

---

[20] See Berengar's *DSC*, p. 101, one of the few passages in the whole dispute to which the adjective 'noble' seems appropriate: whether right or wrong, Berengar here steps outside the world of polemic to give an impassioned account of what it means for human beings to be made in the image of God.

[21] *PL* 150, col. 417A.

summarizing the argument, Lanfranc says that 'to be married' and 'to have worldly cares' are equipollent propositions. Too true. Yet the two statements are not equipollent in the way that logicians use the word: the second is simply a common consequence of the first; it is not another way of saying the same thing. So Lanfranc is not using the word strictly in calling the two statements 'equipollent'.[22] There is a laxity in his use of this technical term of which Anselm could never have been guilty.

Lanfranc's use of the word 'equipollent' was imprecise, and this imprecision is deeply rooted in his mode of theological argument, especially in his use of supporting statements from the Fathers. We can see this very clearly in the torrent of Patristic authorities which he launched against Berengar. He may well be right in thinking that the general tendency of these authorities supported his position. But at best they offered the support of congruity, not of compelling logic. As Berengar pointed out, no Patristic statements strictly required the formula to which he had been forced to agree; the most that Lanfranc could reasonably claim was that they provided general support for it. So once more we find Lanfranc hesitating between two worlds of theological discourse. Just as, in his use of Aristotelian categories, he drew a veil over his source, so, in claiming Patristic support for his Eucharistic doctrine, he was appealing to general congruity, not to conclusive agreement.

To sum up so far: in order to understand the course of Anselm's development, it is necessary to understand that in coming to Bec in 1059, he became part of an intellectual scene full of debate and conflict, dominated by the overpowering presence of Lanfranc. An important part of this scene was occupied by rival methods of employing grammar and dialectic in theological argument – Lanfranc using Aristotelian concepts lightly disguised; Berengar violently asserting the general claims of dialectic, but basing his main argument on grammar. Both attitudes had much to offer an observer of genius, and both were used with much greater strictness in Anselm's later work.

Although it is necessary to emphasize Anselm's superiority in logical thought to either Berengar or Lanfranc, it must not be forgotten that they too were innovators in the use of recent logical and grammatical discoveries in theological discussion, and Anselm carried their work several steps further. Lanfranc was an innovator

---

[22] The Pauline text is I Corinthians vii, 29–31; for Lanfranc's use of the word equipollence in analysing the argument of this passage, see *PL* 150, col. 178.

who did not want to be branded as such. Anselm too used new tools to support truths both old and new. But he felt no need for concealment: he was (as we shall see) sufficiently securely anchored in Augustine to be confident about his orthodoxy. He aimed at giving new clarity to ancient truths; and though his methods were sometimes questioned, not least by Lanfranc, his personal orthodoxy was never doubted until a new breed of logicians, personified in Roscelin, tried to claim him as one of themselves.

The nature of that attack and the way he dealt with it will concern us when we come to the last phase of Anselm's development. For the moment, Anselm's submission to Lanfranc's influence in 1059 was total. By 1079 it had almost vanished. During the years between, we can trace it in a number of ways, and we shall try to follow in his footsteps as he learnt from Lanfranc and refined his methods.

But before we inquire into the ways in which Anselm used the methods of argument which he learnt from Lanfranc, we must survey the availability of the books on which everything was built. Without the books which Lanfranc had collected at Bec, Anselm's immediate scope for intellectual growth would have been much restricted. Despite the destruction of almost all of them, their range can be defined with some confidence. This must form the next subject for inquiry before proceeding to the use that Anselm made of the books which Lanfranc had collected at Bec.

3   Lanfranc as book-collector

Without books no intellectual inquiry can prosper. Anselm needed fewer than most people, but it was important that he should have the right ones, and Lanfranc had provided them at Bec. As everywhere, our inquiry is hampered by lack of surviving evidence: but the smallest details – even the negative ones – sometimes have a surprisingly important message.

Only one book has survived which was certainly at Bec during his years with Lanfranc. It is a book intimately connected with the growth of Lanfranc's mind and outlook. It survives as a splendid witness to his powers of selection and foresight, and of his understanding of the needs of the Church; and it is also a witness to the gap which separated him from Anselm. This book was Lanfranc's collection of Canon Law, made under his direction, with his marginal annotations and the addition of documents of special personal importance to him, such as the documents of the Council of Easter 1059 and the letter from Pope Nicholas II, which had perhaps provoked his presence at the Council. Rather surprisingly, he left the volume at Bec when he went to Caen. But when he became archbishop, he paid for it to be sent to Canterbury for his use, and it became an essential tool of his administration.

Significantly, Anselm seems scarcely to have looked at it. He quoted from it once, with notable absence of enthusiasm, while he was at Bec; but, almost incredibly, he never quoted from it while he was archbishop. So if it is a monument to Lanfranc's qualities, it is also a monument to the difference between the two men.[23]

This one surviving book, therefore, which is one of our best guides in exploring Lanfranc's mind, provides only a negative clue to Anselm's mind: it underlines the obvious in showing that he was very different from his master.

What can be said of the other books at Bec? In the absence of surviving volumes, the question has to be approached obliquely, and – as a general guide to Lanfranc's tastes in books – we may start with books which he was responsible for collecting at Canterbury. When he arrived as archbishop in 1070, he found few books which he thought suitable for a library. Many had been destroyed by the great fire three years before his arrival, and those which had survived gave him no very flattering idea of the scholarship of the pre-Conquest monastery. One of his first tasks was to restock the library, and his readiest source of supply was the library at Bec. Consequently, some evidence of Lanfranc's plan for the library at Canterbury, and inferentially for the library at Bec, has survived in Anselm's replies from Bec to Lanfranc's requests for copies of books in the library; and the extensive remains of the Canterbury library provide further evidence of Lanfranc's general plan in restocking the library.

The combination of these sources provides considerable evidence of Lanfranc's tastes and aims as a monastic library-builder. The most conspicuous feature of the surviving books is their centrality. They do not display the foibles of the bibliophile or the curiosity of the searcher for rare texts: they contain only the key

[23] TCC MS. B.16.44. For Lanfranc's use of the collection when he was archbishop, and for the evidence that he caused it to be widely distributed among the English dioceses, see Brooke, 1931, pp. 57–105. For Anselm's use of this manuscript at Bec, see *Ep*. 65 (i, 56), and below, p. 256. For the evidence that Anselm's only quotation from it while archbishop was borrowed from Gilbert Crispin, see Southern, 1954, pp. 89–91.

works of Latin Christendom, and the more closely they can be associated with Lanfranc, the more central they are.[24]

Lanfranc impressed his character on these books, partly by the fact that he chose them, but even more by the evidence that he had read them carefully. One symptom of this is their system of annotation, which I have described above, and which conveyed some faint outline of Lanfranc's interests by being copied from one exemplar to another as far afield as Durham and Exeter, but going back, in some cases demonstrably and in others with varying degrees of probability, to Bec or Canterbury originals.[25] Since the earliest known manuscript with this peculiar symbol is Lanfranc's collection of Canon Law, and they are most frequently exemplified in manuscripts which belonged to the Cathedral library at Canterbury, it is very likely that this distinctive mark of annotation goes back to Lanfranc himself. Further, since the Canon Law collection was made at Bec, and copies with the annotation were made while it was in Bec, the system of annotation evidently goes back to Lanfranc's years at Bec. Of course nothing can be certain in such matters, but when looked at in conjunction with the other evidence for Lanfranc's careful use of his books, shortly to be mentioned, it does not seem fanciful to see in these annotations one more symptom of the school-masterly patience, perseverance and solidity which marked everything that he did.

With this evidence of Lanfranc's library-building propensities in mind, we may now go back to Lanfranc's answer to Berengar on the Eucharist. Here we find evidence of a different kind, which amply confirms the evidence from Canterbury of Lanfranc's careful attention to his books. In this work, the quotations from the Fathers are numerous, but they do not come from a very wide assortment of authorities. Three quarters of them are from Augustine, and most of the remainder from Ambrose, with a sprinkling from Gregory

---

[24] For books sent from Bec to Canterbury, see Anselm *Epp.* 23, 25, 26, 66 (iv, 122; i, 19, 75): and for those provided for Bec from Canterbury, *Epp.* 39, 42, 43, 60 (i, 47, 50, 51, 69). All these letters were written between 1070 and 1078 – an indication of the priority attached by Lanfranc to building up the library. For further details, see below, pp. 311–13.

[25] The identity of plan between the libraries of Bec and Canterbury can be made out only in a fragmentary way, but the surviving pieces of evidence, in conjunction with the evidence for Lanfranc's reading habits mentioned below, are significant. See C. R. Dodwell, *The Canterbury School of Illumination, 1066–1200*, 1954, pp. 6–20, and Ker, 1961, pp. 25–31; M. R. James, *The Ancient Libraries of Canterbury and Dover*, 1903, pp. xxix–xxxv.

the Great, Leo, Jerome, and the collection of Canon Law already mentioned.

Quotations in themselves do not necessarily tell us much about an author's reading, for nothing is commoner in medieval – to say nothing of modern – authors than the habit of borrowing quotations from an unnamed predecessor. But there is one feature of Lanfranc's quotations which precludes this possibility: this is the careful accuracy with which he frequently notes the precise place of his quotation in the original texts from which they come. Not only this: he quite often gives some indication of the relation between one quotation and the next. The result is that his quotations are conspicuous for the occurrence of such phrases as, 'in book 3' (or '4' or whatever), or 'a little further on '; or 'towards the end of the first (or second, or third) part of the work'; 'in some copies this is expressed in other words'.[26] He evidently did not take quotations accompanied with words like these from the works of other writers. He took them from the original texts, and from copies of these texts which he knew intimately.

Still more striking, as symptomatic of his intimate knowledge of the texts, is the way he can cap Berengar's quotations with another from the same work, or challenge his interpretation of the author's intention by reference to the original context.[27] Only someone who knew his texts intimately could have done this, and it would have been hard to do unless the books had been immediately available for consultation.

Everywhere Lanfranc replies with admirable attention to the source and meaning of Berengar's quotations. He writes like a lawyer handling a difficult brief, answering his opponent point by point, authority by authority, argument by argument. If we want to

[26] Lanfranc's quotations are too numerous to list, but they can easily be found in *PL* 150, cols. 421–41. The following examples will sufficiently illustrate his manner of indicating the sources of his quotations. e.g. Augustine *On the Psalms: in prima expositionis Psalmorum parte . . . Item in eadem . . . in tertia eiusdem operis parte . . . in eadem . . . In Ps. 33 . . . et post aliqua . . . in Ps. 44 . . . in Ps. 65 . . . in Ps. 98, et paulo post, . . . et paucis intermissis . . .* etc. On Augustine's *De Doctrina Christiana: In quibusdam codicibus prefata sententia verbis aliis invenitur . . . In hoc opere nec huius propositionis nec alicuius eius similis aliquo in loco mentionem fecit.* On Augustine's *Ep. ad Bonifacium: In eo libro non magis loquebatur de hoc sacramento quam de ceteris.* These and similar phrases taken together show that Lanfranc had a formidably detailed knowledge of his books.

[27] See for example, *DSCD*, c. 12: Berengar has quoted Augustine *DCD*, and Lanfranc retorts: *Augustinus in libro De Civitate Dei non ita abrupte, ut tu dicis, sacramentum sacrum esse signum diffinivit. Nihil vero eo in loco de Corpore et Sanguine Domini loquebatur.*

see how the youthful Lanfranc might have gained his early reputation in the courts of Pavia, we cannot do better than read his Eucharistic treatise: whatever may be thought of it as a piece of theological reasoning, it is a masterly exhibition of forensic power, challenging his opponent text by text.

Of course, Lanfranc's familiarity with the exact place in the sources, and in the volumes containing these sources, does not *prove* that the works which he speaks of in this familiar way were in the library at Bec. But taken together with the evidence of his library-building at Canterbury and his book collecting at Bec, it seems very likely that they were there. It is difficult enough in these days of multiple copies and ease of borrowing to know texts intimately unless they are immediately available. It was much more difficult in the eleventh century when copies were few, and when, if they were not in the library, they had to be sought at a distance. Books in other libraries were hard to find; and if found, they were valuable and irreplaceable possessions, to be lent only with reluctance. The strong probability is that the volumes which Lanfranc knew so intimately were at Bec, available also to Anselm.

To put the matter in its most concrete form, I shall list those Patristic works which are quoted in such a way by Lanfranc in his Eucharistic treatise as to suggest familiarity with the actual volumes from which he quotes:

AUGUSTINE
On the Psalms; On St John's Gospel; On the City of God[28]*; On the Trinity; On Christian Doctrine; On the Sermon on the Mount; On Baptism; On instructing the young; Letters.*

AMBROSE
On the Sacraments; On the Mysteries; On Faith.

GREGORY THE GREAT
Dialogues.

LEO
Sermons; Letters.

JEROME
On Hosea; On St John's Gospel.

---

[28] In addition to Lanfranc's quotations from this work in his *DCSD*, see Gibson, 1971, pp. 435–50, for his widely circulated comments, of which one shows a close knowledge also of Plato's *Timaeus*.

In the twelfth century, these works formed the core of any well-equipped monastic or cathedral library, and they were to be found in many libraries throughout Europe; but it was not so easy to find them in the eleventh century. Collections like this did not come into existence without great exertions. If my inference that these works were available at Bec when Lanfranc was writing his Eucharistic treatise is correct, their presence can only be explained by his activity as a collector. Starting a monastic library with almost nothing, he must have collected them during the twenty years before 1063. This inference gains support when we find that he repeated the process at Canterbury after 1070.

If we descend from these heights to look at the quotations in detail, it emerges that by far the greater part of them come from those works of Augustine which were also the main influence in Anselm's development. I shall later discuss Augustine's influence on Anselm. For the present it will suffice to say that, if Anselm had had no other sources of inspiration than the Bible, the Rule of St Benedict, and Augustine's *De Trinitate, Confessions, De Civitate Dei*, and *Sermons on the Psalms*, he would have had all the inspiration he needed for everything of importance that he wrote. All these works, with one exception, are listed above among the works quoted by Lanfranc. The exception is Augustine's *Confessions*. But its omission from Lanfranc's quotations can be explained by its silence on the Eucharist; and there were so many copies in northern France in the eleventh century that it is hard to think it was not at Bec. Besides, it was one of the earliest works to be copied at Canterbury after 1070.[29]

The importance of these minute observations for our theme lies in the light they throw on the intellectual environment of Anselm's early monastic and scholarly career. When Nicholas II mentioned in his letter to Lanfranc in 1059 that he had heard of his switch from logic and rhetoric to theology, he was saying something which we have been able to trace in detail in the successive stages of Lanfranc's commentary on the Pauline Epistles. We can trace it further in greater detail in his Eucharistic treatise, and further still in the evidence for his library-building at Bec and Canterbury.

---

[29] For a survey of surviving MSS of Augustine's *Confessions*, see A. Wilmart, 1931iii, pp. 251–68. Wilmart lists fourteen from the eleventh century, including one from Jumièges. There are none from England before the Conquest, but there are two with Canterbury connections before 1100.

We may take it as reasonably certain that by 1063, when Lanfranc left Bec for Caen, his change from being the most accomplished dialectician of his time to being a well-equipped theologian had been completed. From Anselm's point of view, he could not have hit upon a happier combination: in dialectical skills and theological literature, Lanfranc had provided all that he needed. Anselm did not need many books. He needed to live with a few congenial texts, and make them his own. The necessary Patristic texts were all at Bec, together with Aristotle's *Categories*. These texts in Anselm's hands opened up wider intellectual horizons than Lanfranc's. We shall follow his footsteps as he progressed beyond his master; but before tackling this theme, and before the master is forgotten in the greater creations of his pupil, it will be well to attempt a summary of Anselm's debt to Lanfranc. This will lead to a brief account of a single work of Anselm's, which stands apart from all his others and may well have been his first by several years, written under the shadow of Lanfranc's presence. It allows us to compare the different use which the master and pupil could make of a single source. Before coming to it, we may deal first with his own conception of his debt to Lanfranc.

II   ANSELM'S RECOGNITION OF HIS DEBT

There are, and will always be, great gaps in our understanding of Anselm's intellectual and religious development, and we come upon one such gap at the very beginning. Despite his acknowledgement of an overwhelming debt to Lanfranc, which can easily be traced until the moment of his taking his monastic vows, it is very difficult to find any signs of it after this point. It was inevitable, given the great differences in their personalities and gifts, that the two men should have grown apart. But common sense, as well as the duty of obedience, suggests that the process of Anselm's emancipation must have been gradual. During the four years from 1059 to 1063, Lanfranc was at the height of his powers as adviser to Duke William, and as prior of Bec he was responsible for the training of new monks and for the school for external pupils; he was probably also engaged in writing his reply to Berengar. Anselm was a novice, Lanfranc's chief assistant in the school, and still with everything to learn about the religious life and the methods of theological inquiry. Have we any record of his thoughts during these years with Lanfranc?

59

Anselm is not an author who leaves many traces of his workshop in his finished works. But we may begin with a letter, less trivial than it appears at first sight. It was written to Lanfranc in about 1075 when they had been separated for about twelve years. It begins with a form of address which seems at first sight to tell us nothing:

To his lord and father, the reverend Archbishop Lanfranc, brother Anselm sends all that he is – *suus quod suus*.[30]

It is tempting to look on this as one of those extravagances which letter-writers employ as a mark of friendship. But then we notice that, in all his previous letters to Lanfranc, and *only* in these letters, he used the same phrase – until 1077. And then never again. What did it mean? And why did it cease to be used?

The second of these questions may be answered first. The first occasion when he failed to use it was when he had received Lanfranc's censorious comments on his *Monologion*. It would be stupid to think that he stopped using the phrase in a huff. But what cannot be doubted is that he now knew, and knew for the first time, that he and Lanfranc were no longer of the same mind. There was no open breach between them. Anselm replied to Lanfranc's criticisms with further recognition of his debt: he remained Lanfranc's 'servant in subjection, his son in affection, his disciple in doctrine'. Respect, reverence, gratitude – all these remained, but there was never again an expression of total identification with Lanfranc; the completeness of intellectual accord had been broken, and it was never restored.

So it seems that the phrase *suus quod suus* really had a meaning which no longer was appropriate. This is only one example of a characteristic of Anselm's writing which we shall find exemplified again and again: he uses phrases which seem extravagant, and closer inspection shows that he meant them in serious earnest. Sometimes we may wish he didn't; but we cannot understand his mind unless we take his words at their face value.

But, to continue with the letter we are examining. After the address, it goes on:

Just as the prophet Zechariah underlines the authority of his prophecy by repeating at the end of every verse, 'Thus saith the Lord', so – in order to put on

---

[30] *Ep.* 57 (i, 48). The phrase is also used in the following letters to Lanfranc: *Epp.* 23, 25, 27, 32, 49, 66 (i, 31, 33, 35, 40, 58, 69); but not in the later *Epp.* 72, 77, 89, 90, 103, 124 (i, 80, 86; ii, 1, 2, 13, 53); nor in the letter which is the Preface to the *Monologion*.

my words the stamp of the person to whom, and the spirit in which I speak – I always begin my letters with this inscription on their forehead: 'To my lord and father, from one who is his in everything.' In saying this, I do not claim to be able to 'paint the mighty cypress', but at least I have its image imprinted on my mind, and I express this before anything else.[31] I have so often written to you in this way that I must complain that you never write back to the person whom I know myself to be, but to some 'lord and father', whom I am not. If you are indeed writing to your servant and son, why do you upset our relationship, not exactly by a flat contradiction, but at least by a relative opposition? Let me beg you in future to send letters to me, and not someone who is not me.

There are two learned jokes here. The first is the reference to the painter who could paint nothing but a cypress and brought it into every painting whatever its subject. The mighty cypress here of course is Lanfranc, and Anselm disclaims any ability to reproduce him, but at least he always has his image in his mind.

The other joke refers to the two types of opposites, *opposita negatio* and *relativa oppositio*, discussed in chapter 10 of Aristotle's *Categories*, 'On Opposites'. The chapter carried a long commentary by Boethius, which provided much matter for debate in the schools of the eleventh and twelfth centuries about the ways in which things are distinguished from each other: by nature, by relationship, by having a positive or negative value, and so on. What Anselm is saying is that Lanfranc has made a logical error in the category of opposites which he has used in writing to Anselm as his 'father' when he is really his son.[32]

Twaddle, one is tempted to say. But, behind the banter, the letter has a clear message: it recognizes an abiding debt, and it indicates

---

[31] The 'mighty cypress' is a reference to Horace, *Ars Poetica*, lines 19–21; the phrase *in fronte pictum praeferant* with regard to his letters is perhaps an echo of Virgil, *Eclogue* 6, 22: *sanguineis frontem moris et tempora pingit*. Anselm's references to classical authors are very infrequent, but they are not the common tags, and they imply a ready familiarity with the main poets. For Horace and Virgil, see also *Ep.* 2 (i, 2); for Lucan, *Ep.* 115 (ii, 25); and *Cur Deus Homo*, II, xvi, for a possible recollection of Terence. For the importance of Horace, see below p. 236.

[32] See *PL* 64, cols. 264–83, for the section *On Opposites* in Aristotle's *Categories*, with the discussion by Boethius, which formed the basis of much discussion in the eleventh century. For the popularity of debate on this subject, see Abelard's Glosses on the *Categories* in *Peter Abelards Philosophische Schriften*, ed. B. Geyer, *BGPTMA*, xxi, 1933, p. 260. Comments on Aristotle's chapter *De Oppositis* took much room in early dialectical teaching, and different schools seem to have developed differing vocabularies; cf. the somewhat earlier Gerlandus, *Dialectica*, ed. L. M. de Rijk, 1959, pp. 108–9. No doubt this subject would have been discussed in the still earlier Lanfrancus, *De Dialectica*. At all events, Anselm's rather tiresome joke implies that both he and Lanfranc were very familiar with these distinctions.

the area of the debt in two quotations of which Lanfranc is expected to recognize the source and meaning. In these little jokes, there is a whole world of scholastic debate, with which both are assumed to be familiar. In the schools, 'Father' and 'Son' were the common examples of things which were opposites 'by relationship': he who was his father's son could not also be his father's father. So Anselm, who was Lanfranc's son, could not also be his father. A simple truth no doubt, but important in establishing the logical system within which discourse about the world could be carried on.

Of course it may be said that, since it was all a joke, it is not important. But that is a mistake. In the first place, jokes are not funny unless their point is understood on both sides without effort. When everything has to be explained, the result is tedium. But, more important, private jokes are powerful expressions of past intimacy and shared experience. Moreover, in this case the common background of knowledge which Anselm shared with Lanfranc, he owed to him; so his joke was at the same time a recognition of his debt. No doubt, he was evoking an image of a shared past which was becoming fainter as time wore on. Yet in reviving the image of their earlier studies he tells us something that is worth knowing: Anselm owed to Lanfranc, and shared with him, a grounding in the texts with which he expects them both to be familiar – above all Aristotle's *Categories*. This is important, not only because it was the work on which Lanfranc's doctrine of substance was based; but also because it is the solitary work on which Anselm himself wrote a commentary, which is in style and subject-matter unlike any other work he wrote, and substantially unlike any other medieval commentary. It is also the only work in which Anselm shows a detailed familiarity with Aristotle's *Categories*. This work is his *De Grammatico*, and if we want to evoke the shared past referred to in Anselm's letter, we may find it here.

III   ANSELM'S 'DE GRAMMATICO'[33]

In this work, Anselm devotes himself to the study in depth of the first section of Aristotle's *Categories*, which deals with the nature of 'substance'. As we have seen, this section of the work also provided

---

[33] The title which Anselm gave the work is: *Quomodo grammaticus sit substantia et qualitas*. He only once referred to it later, and then by its opening words, *De Grammatico*, and this became the generally received title.

the philosophical basis of Lanfranc's reply to Berengar. For Lanfranc's purpose it was sufficient to grasp the nature of primary substances and their accidents, and to apply this distinction to the Eucharistic change. But for Anselm, the distinction between substance and accidents, and between primary and secondary substances, are scarcely mentioned. Everything that interested him lay in the logical and linguistic puzzles which arise in the later chapters of the *Categories*. He wrote his *De Grammatico* as an introduction to these problems, but with a purpose quite different from Lanfranc's: Lanfranc was interested in applying the concept of substance to a particular situation; Anselm was interested in the acts of speech and judgement which are the subject-matter of all logic. His little commentary was intended to be an introduction to a much larger subject than the work on which it was based. As in every aspect of the difference between the two men, this too was only the symptom of a still greater contrast: Lanfranc's goals were always within immediate reach, while Anselm's always lay in the far distance, in the opening up of a method of inquiry about the whole structure of reality and our thoughts about it.

It is no part of my plan or competence to examine in detail the course of the argument of the *De Grammatico*. It will suffice to notice the indications of the development of Anselm's mind – in particular, its literary distinction, its logical finesse, and its movement towards a new theological method.

Already in its literary distinction we can recognize the makings of the later Anselm. His style is already fastidious, precise and clear, but he seems not yet to have developed a taste for assonance and rhyme. Moreover, the pupil who acts as interlocutor is very different from the pupils who ask questions and receive instruction in the later dialogues: the latter are always ready to listen and agree, but, in *De Grammatico*, the pupil is less respectful, less willing to accept the master's view of any question, almost truculent. Then too, in contrast to all Anselm's later works, the content and temper are wholly secular, unconnected with the cloister. It was written, as Anselm himself says, as an introduction to dialectic, and there are several indications in manner and subject-matter which suggest that it was made in the first place for pupils who were not monks. One cannot help thinking of the two chaplains whom Nicholas II had sent to Bec to learn dialectic, and emphatically not theology: such men as these may have been among his pupils. At least, the dialogue seems more suitable for the external school than for the cloister, and the pupils it addresses are not the quiet persuadable pupils who are under instruction in the later dialogues.

Anselm describes the work as an introduction to logic, and it is in fact just that: a very widely ranging discussion of logical problems, despite the apparent narrowness of the problem posed by its title, *How 'grammaticus' is both substance and quality*. This problem is no more than an opening gambit, introducing a series of logical questions about the way in which we speak of substances and their attributes, the roles of nouns and adjectives, of subjects and predicates, and the varied strength of entailments, whether necessary, possible, or impossible. In Anselm's hands, his introductory problem opens up new territories of the mind as he penetrates ever more deeply into the structure of words, sentences, and the external objects to which words and sentences refer. The great lesson that he impresses on his pupil is that he cannot advance unless he penetrates the surface of words and appearances to reach the reality to which they refer. In his next phase, Anselm will extend his inquiry beyond the forms of speech, even beyond the forms of reason, to contemplate the supreme reality of God. In this work, he took the first step in a journey which was to lead to the argument of the *Proslogion*.

One purpose of the treatise was to train the pupil in syllogistic reasoning, and the word syllogism recurs frequently. It is a word found nowhere else in Anselm's writings. No doubt several reasons for this could be given; one is that he never again wrote on formal logic. But it must also be said that though he often mentions syllogisms, his arguments seldom, if ever, have a syllogistic form. The reason for this is that even in this work, and still more in his later writings, his main aim is to probe more deeply into the problems of 'being', and the logical implications of 'possible', 'probable', 'impossible', 'necessary', and 'contradictory' relationships. His inquiry does not advance by syllogisms, but by definitions and by examining the forms of sentences. This combination of definition and analysis became habitual in his thoughts and writings, and *De Grammatico* prepared the way forward by investigations into the logical consequences of such phrases as *nullo modo . . . aliquo modo . . . quolibet modo . . .* ; and by examining statements such as: *Esse Grammatici non est esse hominis* or *Esse uniuscuiusque rei in definitione consistit.*[34]

---

[34] For the elaborate discussions in *De Grammatico*, in which these phrases are central points, see especially Schmitt, i, p. 149, lines 27–30; p. 151, lines 5–30; and pp. 152–3.

There is nothing in *De Grammatico* about the central concepts of Anselm's mature theological thought: nothing about *Rectitudo* in its two forms of Truth and Justice, which became the key to his understanding of the universe and of God's activity in his creation. *De Grammatico* is simply an investigation into the rules for analysing words and sentences. But, since words and sentences are mirrors of reality, their analysis is the first step towards an account of the ultimate reality.

It has always been very difficult to place the *De Grammatico* among Anselm's works, and it is impossible to speak with certainty. But its peculiarities of content and treatment would be most readily intelligible if it had been composed in the years between 1060 and 1063, when Anselm was Lanfranc's assistant in the external school at Bec, teaching the subjects which had brought pupils from distant parts of Europe.[35] It is Anselm's only commentary on an ancient text, his only work on a secular subject, the work in which he was nearest to Lanfranc, and the only one in which he draws extensively on Aristotle.

Anselm never mentioned Aristotle again in any of his works until, in his *Cur Deus Homo*, he recalled that Aristotle's *De Interpretatione* provided the starting point for discussion about the sense in which any future event could be said to be necessary. This passage cannot have been earlier than about 1095: but the explicit use of Aristotle was so slow in penetrating into theological debate after Lanfranc's cautious innovation that this mention of Aristotle in the *Cur Deus Homo* is said to be the first in any medieval theological work.

IV   THE PARTING OF THE WAYS

After 1078, Anselm knew that he and Lanfranc had parted company in some fundamental way. Lanfranc had become increasingly the great organizer, devoted to the pursuit of order in all things, but more capable of bringing order into practical affairs than into a theoretical system. Anselm by contrast had become the great creator of an ideal world of thought and interior experience. The force and coherence which Anselm could achieve in abstract

---

[35] As to the date of composition, we must not be deceived by Eadmer's placing it among the works which Anselm wrote between about 1080 and 1085: it is clear that he does this simply because Anselm referred to it in the company of these works, but with the proviso that they had been written at different periods. See Schmitt, i, p. 173.

thought, Lanfranc could fully achieve only in practical organization.

The two men never ceased to address each other with affection and respect. Anselm continued to speak of himself as Lanfranc's 'servant in subjection, his son in affection, his disciple in doctrine', but the days when these phrases had been living experiences were over. Nevertheless, they expressed a reality which was still effective in Anselm's practical life to the end. Lanfranc had brought him to the religious life, to the community at Bec, to Aristotle and Augustine – the only two men besides Lanfranc to whom he recognized an explicit obligation. Lanfranc had brought him also to a central point in the intellectual life of Europe. There was not much else that anyone could have done for him.

When Lanfranc died, there is good reason to think that Anselm wrote the long and eulogistic epitaph which has been preserved. He praised most fully Lanfranc's generosity, his austerity, his love of justice and mercy; he acknowledged the loss the Church had suffered by his death, and urged the reader to pray for his soul. But a single lifeless line served to describe Lanfranc the teacher.[36] No one owed more to Lanfranc's powers as a teacher, and we must regret that Anselm left no record of his main characteristics. By 1087, it may be that their ways had diverged too far for the debt of those distant days to be recalled.

---

[36] The epitaph is in *PL* 158, cols. 1,049–50. It is preserved only in Vat. MS. Reginensis 499, which is a very important collection of Lives of abbots etc. from Bec. It is almost certainly referred to by Ordericus Vitalis, iii, 309: *Beccensis autem Anselmus suprascriptam compatriotae sui memoriam heroico carmine volumini lacrymabiliter indidit*. Presumably Orderic intended to give the text of this epitaph in his *History*, as he did of many others, but for some reason failed to do so. The single line on Lanfranc as a teacher in the epitaph is: *Huius doctrinam pars maxima senserat orbis*.

CHAPTER 4

THE YEARS OF SILENCE

I PRIVATE AND CORPORATE DISCIPLINES

If Anselm's *De Grammatico* belongs to the years between 1060 and 1063, it will follow that for the next seven years he wrote nothing which he published to the world. This of course does not mean that he wrote no drafts of thoughts or arguments which appear in his later writings; but it does mean that he wrote nothing for readers outside the monastery. Apart from the daily Offices, his time was spent in meditation and prayer, in study, in teaching the young monks, and in looking after the religious life of the community. Gradually in the midst of these responsibilities he discovered his strength, above all his capacity to inspire young men with a strong desire for a religious life of great austerity and intellectual intensity. His favourite pupils were those, as he would say, whose wax was neither too soft to retain, nor too hard to receive, a lasting impression.[1] It was from such material that he formed the monks who became his disciples. The English parallel that springs to mind is Cardinal Newman, when he was a tutor in Oxford at the same age as Anselm. They both combined great austerity of life with intellectual brilliance, originality, and intense seriousness: a combination which had the same fascination for the young of the nineteenth as of the eleventh century.

The account of these years in Eadmer's biography was written thirty years later by one who had not been there; but it was based on Anselm's own reminiscences, and in its anecdotal fashion it is probably a correct record. Apart from the study of the Bible, the two features of this time which Eadmer especially emphasizes are his devoted friendships and his hallucinatory experiences. Both of these will require further examination, especially the former. The latter, whatever interpretation may be put upon them, are no doubt

---

[1] For the theory, see *VA* I, xi; and for the practice, *VA* I, x, xxii, xxix, xxxiv, pp. 6–17, 20–1, 37–9, 50, 60– 1. For further discussion, see below, pp. 446–7.

to be associated with lack of food and sleep in this phase of his life: but they are also indicative of the visionary direction of his thoughts.[2]

The only other details of his early years as prior which Anselm communicated to his biographer recalled his task of correcting manuscripts far into the night. Here at least he followed in Lanfranc's footsteps: but in every other way he followed a line of his own choosing – a life of semi-starvation, spiritual intensity, and concentration on the needs of his young pupils.

The external school, which had kept Bec in the world's eye in Lanfranc's day, withered away. But within the cloister the number of monks began to grow. By 1070, the average entry had risen from the two or three a year in Lanfranc's time, to twelve or more.[3] Whether this was due to more applicants, or more room (the new buildings initiated by Lanfranc had been finished after his departure and the new church was finally consecrated in 1072), or the magnetism of Anselm, it is impossible to say. Probably all three played their part, together with Anselm's indifference to limitations of resources. His housekeeping was always rather vague, as we know not only from Eadmer's report, but also from Anselm's own letters.[4] But despite some desperate moments, the community at Bec by 1070 was beginning to flourish as never before. Altogether, it is not surprising that he had had no time for writing.

Then there was a sudden change: in 1070 or thereabouts Anselm began to write with an eye to a wider public than any he had so far addressed. The immediate cause of the change was the removal to Canterbury of several monks of Bec with others whom Lanfranc had already taken with him to Caen in 1063. Lanfranc, who became archbishop in 1070, had a stern task ahead of him: he had to rebuild the monastic community at Canterbury from a state of ruin, and, more widely, as he saw his task, he had to rebuild the Church in a barbarous land from a state of decrepitude. No doubt he exagger-

---

[2] *VA* I, vii, x, pp. 12–13, 18.

[3] A fairly reliable estimate of the growth of the community at Bec is made possible by the survival of a list of monks in the order of their profession from the earliest days of the monastery, printed in Porée, 1901, ii, pp. 629–31. Most of the names are of unknown men, but the titles of those who became bishops or abbots have been added, as well as the moment when there was a change of abbots at Bec. As a result, the following figures may be accepted as fairly reliable: 1042–1060, 34 recruits; 1060–1078, 70 recruits; 1078–1093, 160 recruits. See also the chart in Gibson, 1978, p. 201.

[4] For Eadmer's report, see *VA* I, xxviii, pp. 46–8; and for the precarious state of the finances, caused partly at least by fecklessness on Anselm's part, see Anselm's letters to Lanfranc, nos. 89, 90 (ii, 1, 2).

ated the English barbarity, but this was how both he and Anselm saw the situation.[5] So the best men were taken, and Bec became a main source of necessary books and of inspiration. This brought a new element into Anselm's life. From this moment, he began to write letters, as well as *Prayers* and *Meditations* for those outside the community at Bec, and in a rather haphazard way he began to preserve what he wrote.[6] From these materials we get our first view of Anselm's development since the days when he was still under Lanfranc's tutelage. Together they provide a startlingly clear record of the first thoughts and experiences of the man who was to become one of the three most influential men in the century, and the one with the most enduring message.

His letters were the earliest writings which he and others began to preserve; and these were followed shortly afterwards by his *Prayers* and *Meditations*. The two were closely related, for most of his early letters were concerned with the spiritual life of individual monks and those associated with them. A few letters also carried recently written *Prayers* to their recipients. The rest were written to convey advice, support, warnings and instruction. It is in these letters and prayers that the development of his mind beyond the stage reached in the *De Grammatico* begins to be disclosed. The *Prayers* and letters are both so important that they must be the subject of separate discussions, but they both draw on a common body of reading and reflection on the Bible and on the works of Augustine. Much of his fundamental reading must have been done during these years of silence; so in preparation for the more detailed study of his writings, something must first be said about two new influences which pervade his later writings, and on which his writings are in varying degrees a commentary.

II   THE INFLUENCE OF THE BIBLE

The only work which Eadmer mentions as the subject of Anselm's deepest meditation after Lanfranc's departure from Bec is the Bible, and this report may well be based on Anselm's own account of his thoughts. Although there is scarcely a single explicit

---

[5] For Anselm's view of the English monks at Canterbury, *c* 1073 and 1077, see *Epp.* 35 (i, 27), 80 (i, 71) where he describes the English monks of Canterbury as *barbari*. Although the word refers immediately to the unintelligible English language, it also has a cultural implication.

[6] See below, pp. 394–403, 458–81, for an account of the preservation of his letters.

quotation from the Bible in the whole of Anselm's works, his prose is filled with Biblical echoes. Fr Schmitt in his edition made an index of them, and it runs to thirty quarto columns with references to almost every book of the Bible. Anselm certainly knew the text intimately, but in his use of it, as in almost everything else, he differed widely from Lanfranc, and indeed from most of his contemporaries.

Lanfranc seems always to have been conscious of the Bible as providing proof-texts in the works of the Fathers and in the vast compilations of illustrative extracts which he and his contemporaries had inherited from the Carolingian age. The main tasks for Biblical scholars, as Lanfranc saw them, were first to cut down the exorbitant length of illustrative material, while retaining extracts likely to be of value for contemporary use; and, second, to begin the careful analysis of Biblical concepts in order to clarify their meaning and eliminate apparent contradictions. Lanfranc was among the first to undertake these two tasks systematically, but Anselm did not follow his example. He was not a collector or arranger of material; he simply absorbed the Bible in his thought and language, and allowed his meditations to grow, as a river gathers strength from the springs from which it flows.

We shall see several examples of this in his later works. But as a preliminary step, we may note that the point of departure of his *Proslogion* was a meditation on the meaning of the first verse of Psalm 13: 'the *fool* hath said in his heart, there is no God'. Anselm's argument proceeds by his asking, what precisely does this mean? Why is it the peculiar characteristic of the *fool* to say this? Similarly Anselm's arguments in his *De Veritate, De Casu Diaboli* and *De Libertate Arbitrii*, may be regarded as extended meditations on the biblical texts, from which they flow.

In his *Vita Anselmi*, Eadmer has preserved the earliest example of Anselm's manner of wrestling with Biblical texts. These are his words, slightly abbreviated:

He had so much faith in the Holy Scriptures that he firmly believed that they contained nothing which deviated in any way from the truth. He put his whole mind to the task of seeing with the eye of reason those things which seemed to be hidden in the deepest obscurity. He was meditating on this, and trying to understand how the prophets could have seen past and future as if they were actually present; and he was giving all his energy to this question, eagerly seeking to understand it, and fixing his eyes on the walls around him, when all at once he saw the various monks going about their tasks in different parts of the monastery as if they were in his presence.[7]

However the experience described by Eadmer may be explained, we have here an example of the way in which he approached the study of the Bible as a meditative activity which led to extensive and fundamental inquiry. It was much more than an intellectual activity; it was an activity of his whole being, in which mental activity merged into vision. This must be borne in mind in considering all his meditations: the hallucinatory experience attached to this particular meditation is simply an extension of his ordinary mode of reaching out to the boundaries of knowledge.

III THE INFLUENCE OF ST AUGUSTINE

The other all-pervading influence on Anselm's thought, of which the origin must be sought in his silent years from 1063 to 1070, was Augustine. A thorough review of the relationship between the thought of Augustine and Anselm would be beyond my capacity and beyond the limits of this biographical study. But there are some fundamental affinities and dissimilarities which must be recognized in attempting to understand Anselm's modes of thought.

We may start with the occasion already referred to, when Anselm sent his *Monologion* to Lanfranc. As we have seen, this marked the moment when Anselm's intellectual separation from Lanfranc and his new independent identity first became apparent to both of them. Lanfranc's first reaction to the *Monologion* was to challenge Anselm to name his sources. Anselm's reply was comprehensive, but enigmatic: comprehensive in ascribing everything to Augustine; enigmatic in providing no detail at all to substantiate his claim. Anselm's answer ran as follows:

It was my intention throughout this disputation to assert nothing which could not be immediately defended either from canonical *Dicta* or from the words of St Augustine. And however often I look over what I have written, I cannot see that I have asserted anything that is not to be found there. Indeed, no reasoning of my own, however conclusive, would have persuaded me to have been the first to presume to say those things which you have copied from my work, nor several other things besides, if St Augustine had not already proved them in

[7] *VA* I, vii, pp. 12–13.

the great discussions in his *De Trinitate*. I found them argued at length in this work, and explained them briefly on his authority in my shorter chain of argument.[8]

This is a statement which Lanfranc can scarcely have found satisfactory. It answers none of the detailed points on which he had asked for enlightenment: it simply ignores them. It does nothing to provide that buttressing of the argument by authority which Lanfranc clearly desired, and which Lanfranc himself had provided to support his own argument on the Eucharist. What Lanfranc clearly wanted was a series of quotations from the Fathers, supporting detailed statements in the *Monologion*. But what Anselm provided was simply an overall assurance that everything he had written could be found either in *canonica dicta* or, and above all, in Augustine, and especially in his *De Trinitate*. With this Lanfranc had to be content.

We too must be content with this degree of enlightenment. Yet, like Lanfranc, we surely have some grounds for complaint. It is not even quite clear what he means by *canonica dicta*. Anselm did not use any similar phrase until much later in his career, and then he meant Canon Law. This cannot be the meaning here. The most likely explanation is that, following Augustine in his use of a similar phrase, he means scriptural texts and their authoritative inter-preters. As for his claim that everything he had written could be found in Augustine, this must have seemed to Lanfranc even less satisfactory, for Anselm quoted no single text to support his claim. Moreover, despite Fr Schmitt's painstaking search for comparable statements in Augustine, there is scarcely a sentence in Anselm which is quite clearly derived from a parallel passage. No doubt, as we shall see, the seeds of nearly everything he said are to be found in Augustine – but they are seeds, not flowers. Anselm was not a writer of *florilegia*: his flowers are always his own. So, however close he and Augustine may be in their general sense, their intimacy is that of – in the sense in which Anselm used the word – friends.

In one way we are better off than Lanfranc. He can only have been puzzled, perhaps hurt, by Anselm's cursory dismissal of his question. But we can find in Anselm's reply some essential clues to his incentives and methods of thought, which were not what

---

[8] *Ep.* 77 (i, 68). The letters, in which he used a phrase similar to *canonica dicta* are *Epp.* 206 (iii, 166), 427 (iii, 142), 442 (iii, 183), 443 (iii, 149). Augustine's use of similar words meaning the Bible and its interpreters are in *DCD*, xviii, 36; and this seems to be Anselm's meaning here.

Lanfranc wanted. Anselm's answer shows that he was too deeply immersed in Augustine to search for proof texts to support him. Just as he never uses the Bible to provide texts to *prove* his conclusions, but only to provide a starting point for his meditations, or a premonition of his conclusions, so it is with Augustine. He absorbed Augustine as he had absorbed the Bible: he made them both an integral part of his experience. This did not mean that he had no more to do than to repeat what he had learnt. Quite the opposite: his absorption of his sources left him free. He looked on himself as an explorer of territory opened up by the Bible and by its great expositor, Augustine. They provided the maps to the country over which he had to find his way under their guidance. He never challenged anything he found in them; but they left him free to find new experiences of the truths they contained, perhaps new proofs of their truth, certainly new ways of expressing their truths.

We shall find this constantly in Anselm: his immersion in Augustine, as in the Bible, gave him freedom. This was the fruit of his years of silence, and it explains why he could not provide details of his borrowings: they were too extensive, too freely and deeply ingrained in his own thought and adapted to his own needs, to be capable of any exact enumeration as borrowings. He could not stop to disentangle his own words from those of Augustine. If we insist on knowing more, we must repeat his experience. We can find starting points and comparable phrases, but not exact quotations, and any attempt to find them puts us on the wrong track altogether. That is why he did not, and could not, provide what Lanfranc wanted. All that can be usefully done by way of general introduction is to list the symptoms of their deep congruities, and of the almost equally deep contrasts of thought and feeling between him and Augustine, which reflected their different personalities and historical situations.

1 Stylistic similarities

There is one Augustinian feature which is very prominent in Anselm's earliest writings, and becomes steadily less pronounced later: his carefully moulded, rhyming and antithetical sentences. Anselm is one of the most elegant latinists of the Middle Ages – one of the very few to whom the epithet 'elegant' can properly be attached. St Bernard was more powerful, John of Salisbury more classical, Lanfranc more robust; but Anselm in his early works is uniquely limpid, musical, and epigrammatic. One of the devices he used to obtain these effects was rhyme, which was one of the most frequently, and boringly, used of all the stylistic adornments commonly found in contemporary writers. But then no one else used rhyme as Anselm used it to reflect and emphasize his meaning.[9]

Other contemporary writers used rhymed prose simply as a literary artifice which contributes to the sound, but not to the sense. But in Anselm's prose his rhymes reinforce his argument: they are pointers to the meaning first, and adornments only by accident. The similarities of sound follow the construction of the sentence; the construction of the sentence follows the shape of the argument, and the shape of the argument reflects the balance of a universal order, which itself reflects the perfect symmetry of the whole Creation. The rhymes and assonances in Anselm's earliest writings recreate in miniature the tensions of the universe: the tensions between Sin and Righteousness, Creation and Re-Creation, Debt and Payment, Justice and Mercy, Eternal Misery and Blessedness.

The following sentences from one of his earliest Meditations will illustrate the way in which rhymes work to emphasize the sense. The sinner is seeking the help of the beloved disciple St John, and addresses him as follows:[10]

> Dilectissime discipule pietatis,
> cur negabis **abundans egenti**,
> **potens poscenti**,
> quod **nulli est noxium**
> et tot **bonis obnoxium**?
> Si enim **obsistunt optanti peccata sua**,
> Cur non potius **assistunt oranti merita tua**?
> An **peccata mea potentia sunt ad nocendum**,
> et **merita tua impotentia sunt ad subveniendum**?

Then, a little later, from his most elaborately articulated prayer written in about 1073, the following sentence will provide an example of similar congruities of sound and sense:[11]

---

[9] The remarks of K. Polheim, *Die lateinische Reimprosa*, Berlin, 1925, pp. 236, 422–3, on Augustine and Anselm are worth reading, but on Anselm they are flawed by his use of Prayers now known to be spurious.

[10] *Or.* 12, Schmitt, iii, p. 47: this was one of Anselm's earliest prayers which he sent to Adelaide in 1070–72. For the circumstances and date, see below, pp. 92–3, and *Ep.* 10 (iv, 121).

[11] *Or.* 7, Schmitt, iii, p. 22, and *Ep.* 28 (i, 20); written *c* 1074.

Deus igitur est **pater rerum creatarum,**
  et Maria **mater rerum recreatarum.**
  Deus est **pater constitutionis omnium,**
  et Maria est **mater restitutionis omnium.**
Deus enim **genuit illum per quem omnia sunt facta,**
  et Maria **peperit illum per quem cuncta sunt salvata.**
    Deus **genuit illum sine quo penitus nihil est,**
  et Maria **peperit illum sine quo nihil omnino bene est**

Unfortunately these assonances and rhythms seem to be untranslatable into English, but if the reader will ponder such contrasting phrases as *pater rerum creatarum* and *mater rerum recreatarum* their role will become evident: they concentrate the mind on the eternal congruities to which the similarities of sound draw attention. The rhyming contraries both provoke and are the result of meditation, and they cannot be understood unless the reader allows an experience of the tensions of the universe to flow in. This intermingling of reality and experience is the fruit of meditation. The nature of this meditation will be our next theme. For the present, we are concerned only with the question: under whose influence did Anselm arrive at this ideal of reproducing in his stylistic effects the joys of Heaven and the horrors of hell, and the uneasy balance of the human soul between these two extremes of joy and misery?

Here we must distinguish between the internal and external influences. No degree of external influence would have produced Anselm's carefully balanced sentences if his own mind had not provided the main driving power. Without doubt, he had the finest sensibility for words and sounds, and a strong conviction that human speech reflects the original ordering of the universe. From the first moment when he broke his silence, this correspondence between the ordering of words and the ordering of every part of Creation was one of his central principles. He chose his words, and settled their syntax and the order in which they were arranged, in order to display the congruity between words and the things they represent.

We may not like the result, but there can never be any doubt that the mind behind these sentences was fully in control of the argument, and intent on its most emphatic expression. There is nothing flaccid in his rhymes as there is in most of the rhymed prose of his contemporaries. The whole universe, even (so far as it is permissible to speak of it) the Being of God Himself, is in a state of tension between Justice and Mercy, Abasement and Glory. Every plus has its corresponding minus, every act of forgiveness requires its corresponding sacrifice, every debt its due payment. To give the balance of the universe as perfect an expression as human words permit, required a corresponding balance in the prose which sought to represent it. He who would write about these supreme realities has an obligation to express them as fully as language allows.

So much for the inner force which moulded Anselm's thoughts and their expression. But from whom did he learn to match his prose to his sense of universal equilibrium in this way? The answer is: almost certainly from Augustine. This discovery was made over a hundred years ago by the author of a Parisian thesis, who pointed out that Augustine used rhyme in his prose in a similar way, and for the same reason as Anselm.[12] Here is an example from Augustine in a sermon for Epiphany:

> **Eo nascente, superi novo honore claruerunt;**
> **quo moriente, inferi novo timore tremuerunt;**
> **quo resurgente, discipuli novo amore exarserunt;**
> **quo ascendente, caeli novo obsequio patuerunt.**[13]

Here, as in Anselm, the antithetical structure of the sentences, with their corresponding rhymes and stresses and similarities of words, are an expression of analogous tensions in the events which are being celebrated. Thus, the antithesis *nascente . . . moriente* is echoed in meaning as well as sound in the softer but still contrasting *resurgente . . . ascendente*. Likewise *honore claruerunt . . . timore tremuerunt*, respond to the contrasting *amore exarserunt . . . obsequio patuerunt*.

These devices of thought and speech in Augustine are mainly found in his sermons. But sermons were not, and could not be for Anselm as they were for Augustine, a central mode of communication. Anselm's central modes were meditation and prayer, and

---

[12] A. Regnier, *De la latinité des sermons de S. Augustin* , Paris, 1886. For a selection of Augustine's sermons illustrating his style, see Hans Lietzmann, *Ausgewählte Predigten*, ii, *Kleine Texte f. theologischen Vorlesungen und Übungen*, xiii, Bonn, 1905. E. Norden, *Die Antike Kunstprosa*, Leipzig, 1909, ii, 621–3, has valuable observations on Augustine's stylistic usage.

[13] *PL* 38, col. 995. The passage is quoted by Regnier among a wealth of similar assonances and contrasts of sound and meaning: it comes from Sermon 199, *De Temporibus*, *PL* 28, col. 1,028. Augustine's sermons for Christmastide, nos. 194–9, are especially rich in such contrasting rhymes and rhythms.

occasionally letters; and it is in these that we find most examples of his elaborate rhyming prose. In Augustine, the balanced rhymes and rhythms have rhetorical purpose in arresting the attention of an audience. In Anselm, they are symptoms of his sense of the congruity between words and the things they stand for. More generally, we may say that, in using these literary devices, Augustine made a poetry of persuasion, and Anselm a poetry of logical congruities and contrasts. They diminish in frequency as he gets older, perhaps because he got more careless or more busy, or because he placed increasing reliance on the force of his arguments irrespective of literary form. Whatever the reason for his later neglect of stylistic effects to which he had once attached great importance, the habits of thought which they reflected never changed. Besides providing a clue to his early development, they left a permanent mark on his theological thought in his desire to recreate in argument the eternal tensions of the universe, which the Redeemer resolved by his sacrifice on the Cross.

2 The discipline of meditation

The congruity of style between Augustine and Anselm is important only as reflecting a deeper congruity of mind and aim, which is also apparent in their modes of argument. Here too Augustine was both a model and an inspiration. He provided Anselm with a programme of meditation, which helped him to break away from the traditional Benedictine pattern of liturgical piety, and to create a new pattern of contemplative theological argument. Anselm was not the only one of his generation to feel the need for a more intense personal devotion; but under the influence of Augustine, he was able to give this new devotion a more powerful intellectual expression, and a more glowing representation in words, than any of his contemporaries. The only important aim in his life was the discovery of God; and the instrument of words as well as the procedure of meditation which he perfected for this purpose had already been outlined by Augustine.

Meditation for Augustine, and for Anselm following in his footsteps, is the mental activity which forms a bridge between knowledge of earthly objects and knowledge of the being and attributes of God. The programme of an ascent to God through a succession of mental activities, from images to cogitation, from cogitation to meditation, from meditation to contemplation, is

Augustine's. The whole sequence of activities brings the soul to the threshold of that eternal vision of God which is the goal of every rational nature.

The words I have just used, 'cogitation', 'meditation', 'contemplation', need further examination in the context of the programme of which they form the main stages. The programme may briefly be described as follows. If we exclude miraculous God-given knowledge such as that of the prophets, there are two sources of human knowledge: first, knowledge which comes from the senses; and, second, knowledge which comes from the mind's introspective knowledge of itself. From the senses there come images: these, when stored in the memory, are available for examination by the rational faculty of cogitation or meditation, which leads to knowledge of general substances such as Man, Animal, Rational Being. Unlike the new logicians who were just beginning to make their voices heard, Anselm had no doubt about the real existence of these general substances; indeed he thought that no one who doubted their existence had any claim to speak about God and the truths of the Christian religion. It is only because the senses give the mind access to these great realities beyond the range of the senses, that they have any place in the spiritual life. And further: since the senses have this mediating role in leading the mind from earthly things to the knowledge of God, they have an eternal place in Heaven. This is one of the more surprising features of Anselm's whole system, to which he gave a particular emphasis in his sermons.[14]

The examination of substances outside the mind is supplemented by a second route of knowledge, which proceeds from the intuitive self-knowledge of the mind, and leads by a similar process of cogitation to knowledge of immaterial substances such as Truth, Justice, Beauty, Virtue.

Finally, by the combination of these two branches of introspective and empirical knowledge, the mind begins its ascent to the knowledge of God, the supreme Essence, whose being can be only imperfectly contemplated in this life. Meditation may be described as embryonic contemplation, preparatory to the perfect contemplation of Heaven. Contemplation, therefore, which can alone be enjoyed by the purified spirits in Heaven, is the full fruition of meditation, which can be practised by purified spirits on earth.

---

[14] See below, pp. 385–6; and, for the various forms of his sermon on the Fourteen Beatitudes of Heaven, see *Memorials*, esp. pp. 31–4, 272–91.

Both Augustine and Anselm called the central activity of disciplined spirits in this life either *cogitatio* or *meditatio*. Generally, the two words are interchangeable; but there is one important difference between them. *Cogitatio* can be, and often is, concerned with worldly things and even with corrupt aims, whereas *meditatio* is solely concerned with pure reflection on the essences of things, whether knowable from the empirical data of the senses or from the intuitive knowledge of the mind. When directed towards a virtuous end, *cogitatio* is the same as *meditatio*, and it has as its aim the ascent of the mind to God, the supreme aim of all human life.[15] This kind of *cogitatio*, which is indistinguishable from *meditatio*, was the only kind of *cogitatio* in which Anselm willingly engaged. Hence his rather sketchy performance in practical administration, which requires *cogitatio* about the things of this world, from which after 1059 Anselm had turned away.

With regard to their goals, therefore, cogitation and meditation are distinguishable: cogitation can, but meditation cannot, serve corrupt ends. But with regard to their method they are identical. Their common data are images formed in the mind from the impressions of the senses, and concepts formed within the mind partly from its own self-knowledge and partly from sense-data; and their common tools are the rules of logic and grammar. These, for Anselm and Augustine alike, are the two fundamental instruments with which mankind was endowed at the Creation. It is by the possession of these tools and the ability to turn them to their true end of knowing God, that man fulfils the destiny laid upon him in being created in the image of God.

Anselm could have found all this in Augustine. To say that he did find it in Augustine is of course to go beyond the evidence, for Anselm (who alone could know) never wrote a history of his mind. But when we consider the similarities of speech and argument, and of assumptions and methods, together with Anselm's almost indignant claim that any reader of his great work of meditation, the *Monologion*, would recognize that it was all in Augustine, the line of descent seems clear enough. And we can also say with some assurance that the prolonged study of Augustine, which made this

---

[15] For *cogitatio/meditatio* in St Augustine, see *De Trinitate*, IX, iii; X, v, vii, viii, x; XIV, vi–viii; XV, xii–xvi; *Corpus Christianorum*, 50, 1968, i, pp. 295–6 , 320–9; ii, pp. 430–5, 490–501; *Confessiones*, VII, iv; VIII, v–vi; IX, ii; XIII, xi. See also R. G. Gassert, 'The meaning of *Cogitatio* in St Augustine', *The Modern Schoolman*, 25, 1948, 238–45; A. C. Pegis, 'The mind of St Augustine', *Medieval Studies*, 6, 1944, 1–61; F. Cayré, *La Contemplation Augustinienne*, Paris, 1927.

development possible, can only have taken place during his years of silence from 1063 to 1070.

The development which took place during these years was in large measure a process of absorbing the thought of Augustine, comparable to the absorption of Lanfranc during the previous four years. But these are crude words, which can do no more than indicate the major influences in Anselm's intellectual growth. What took place was not an appropriating of another man's ideas. It was a most subtle and rare process of assimilation in which Anselm's own personality grew as a result of the presence of these major influences in his life. But whereas everything in Anselm's personality promoted a continuing divergence from Lanfranc, nearly everything in him provoked a continuing propinquity to Augustine, offset by disparities almost equally great. To attempt a full survey of these complexities, such as is possible with Lanfranc, is beyond my capacity; but a few remarks may nevertheless be offered as guides to Anselm's future.

3 Similarities and contrasts

It will be well to begin with some fairly concrete instances of similarity of mind and aim. Among other shared characteristics, they both had the power of expressing general ideas in short and memorable phrases, often strikingly similar, but with differences which bear the stamp of two different personalities and environments. Consider, for example, the following from Augustine:

1 **Credite ut intelligas.** (*Serm.* 212, *PL* 35, col. 1,690)
2 **Intellectus merces est fidei.** (*In Joh. Ev.* xxix, 6)
3 **Omne peccatum est mendacium.** (*DCD*, xiv, 4)
4 **Da quod iubes et iube quod vis.** (*Conf.* x, 29)
5 **Deus ita cogitatur ut aliquid quo nihil melius sit.** (*DCD*, i, vii)

And these, from Anselm:

1 **Credo ut intelligam.** (*Prosl.* i)
2 **Fides quaerens intellectum:** (*Prosl. Proemium*)
3 **Omne peccatum est iniustitia.** (*Or.* 3)
4 **Da ut quantum iubes tantum te merear amare.** (*Or.* 2)
5 **Credimus te esse aliquid quo nihil maius cogitari potest.** (*Prosl.* i)

The similarities are obvious, and it is hard to think that Augustine's words were not in Anselm's mind as he wrote his own comparable phrases. But if we consider them carefully, they have differences which follow a consistent pattern. Anselm's words tend to be neater, more personal, more modest, than Augustine's. In Augustine there is a greater recognition of the grand scene of history, more sense of the outside world. It must also be said that many of Augustine's most justly famous remarks could never have been made by Anselm: Anselm's world was smaller, and small though it was, he knew less about it than Augustine knew of the world around him. Also, his self-knowledge, though it was searching, took a more restricted view of his personality than Augustine's. Augustine, with all his self-condemnation, could take an appreciative view of his own past; Anselm could only look back on his past with horror. However close he came to Augustine in his programme of meditation, Anselm had too agonizing a sense of the gap between Man and God ever to have linked them together as Augustine did in his lapidary prayer: 'May I know myself and Thee'.[16] Self-knowledge was valued by Anselm only as an incentive to self-rejection and a path to the knowledge of God. For Augustine too, self-knowledge was a path to knowledge of God; but the creature too had a value. Anselm could only find himself in despising himself; so, for him, self-knowledge ended in total humiliation, in 'loving to be treated with contempt'. For Augustine it ended in 'knowing myself and Thee'.

Comparable similarity and contrast are to be found in their manner of submission to the tradition of the Church. This submission conditioned all their thoughts, but with this difference: the Church was too unquestionably part of Anselm's life for him ever to have thought of its growth as a historical phenomenon, subject to all the strains and stresses of history. Nor could Anselm see his membership of the Church as the result of a personal struggle leading to final conviction contrary to all expectation, as Augustine did. For Anselm, the Church was the great stable, unchanging feature in his experience. Augustine, by contrast, could look back to a time when he had not belonged to the Church; he could realize that humanly speaking its claims as they had first been put forward by men of no learning or ability were absurd: 'It is incredible', he could say, 'that men so lacking in nobility, rank, experience and numbers, could so effectively have persuaded the

---

[16] Augustine, *Soliloquia*, II, i. 1; and cf. Anselm's 'Seven Steps of Humility', *Memorials*, p. 81, for which see below, p. 450.

world, and the learned world at that, of anything so incredible.'[17] Of course, in saying this, his purpose was to magnify the power of God, not to vilify the Christian message; but he had the historical sense which allowed him to judge the situation in human terms. Anselm had neither the sense of history, nor the recollection of a personal struggle for faith, to enable him to entertain such thoughts. Augustine had had to struggle to believe at all; Anselm's struggles were first to purify himself and then to practise and to clarify what he already believed.

Consequently, although from the moment when he first began to write Anselm's words and programme were wholly Augustinian, a closer inspection reveals some quite fundamental divergencies between the two men in their attitudes to the world, in the range and spirit of their theological inquiry, and in their personalities. When we look more closely at his individual works, we shall also find that Anselm brought to his Augustinian vision of the unity of all things in God a logical drive which was entirely his own: his programme was Augustinian, his operating system was Aristotelian. This led to his unique mixture of logical rigour with a vision of the unity of all existence in God.

4 Different times: different outlooks

The greatest of all the contrasts between Anselm and Augustine lay simply in the times in which they lived. In historical situation, Augustine stood, and felt himself to stand, at the culmination of a great non-Christian cultural tradition going back seven hundred years to Plato, and continuing through Cicero to the great schools of his own day. He had himself received the full force of this long tradition before he was a Christian, and he gladly accepted its fruits. He was fully aware that, by the rules of this tradition, Christianity was incredible, and that it was only by the grace of God that he had come to believe. But this contrast between the sciences of the world and the divine Revelation did not for Augustine diminish the value of the world's contribution to Truth. Nor did the incredibility, humanly speaking, of the Christian faith or the ignorance of the Christian witnesses, provide arguments against their message; on the contrary, they were a main reason for believing in its divine origin. But, within its limits, the pagan tradition was unassailable,

---

[17] *DCD*, xxii, 5: *Incredibile est, homines tam ignobiles, infimos, paucissimos, imperitos, rem tam incredibile tam efficaciter mundo, et in illo etiam doctis, persuadere potuisse.*

and its substantial achievement was not invalidated by God's miraculous intervention in history.

Augustine could speak with the full weight of two traditions behind him: the one fully human, the other fully divine. In Augustine, alongside the Christian saint, there was always the man of the great world. He constantly looked back over the historical scene, and he never ceased to reflect on the grand sweep of events which was visibly reaching a fatal climax before his eyes. He could accept it all as part of the divine plan for the glory of the Church, and equally he could look back over his own life and see a similar scene in miniature: his early life, his parents, his Platonism, his Manicheism, his conversion, the growth of his mind, the burden of his office as a Christian bishop: all of them are presented to the reader for appraisal, and to all of them except Manicheism he recognized his debt.

His gaze could sometimes be pitiless enough, as when, looking out over the smoking landscape which the Vandals were engaged in turning into a wilderness of carnage and destruction, he remembered the words of Plotinus, the pagan Platonist whom he had once revered, that it was after all only a scene of wood and stones falling down and mortals being mortal.[18] But even in this harsh dictum there is a note of acceptance: when everything was falling to pieces his sense of history and of his living in the presence of great events never deserted him. In the midst of it all, he felt secure, and he conveyed to countless readers the assurance of security in the life of the Church. The disasters in the world promoted the glory of God: the collapse of the City of this world was a step towards the City of God.

Anselm had inherited the same double tradition of pagan and Christian thought, but his relationship with both was quite different from Augustine's. The two streams came to him already reconciled and mutually supporting each other. He felt none of the tortured confusion of interlocking and mutually repelling elements through which Augustine had been able, by God's grace, to find his way to an assurance of Christian truth. Both forms of truth came to Anselm already fully assimilated, and he could not imagine that any reasonable man would wish to separate them. Moreover they both came to him, not as the two broad turbulent floods of events which

[18] See Possidius, *Vita Augustini*, xxviii, 12, (*PL* 32, col. 58; or ed. Pellegrino, 1955, p. 154). The passage which Augustine is said to have quoted comes from Plotinus, *Enneads*, i, 4. 7.

Augustine had experienced, but as two thin, clearly defined streams of life and teaching, each confined within its own recognizable limits: the pagan, but now Christianized, stream of the liberal arts in the schools; the Christian stream of doctrine now calmly flowing within the tradition of monastic life.

Augustine lived in the turbulence of the world, and he never forgot the long-drawn-out and agonizing struggle which had brought him to peace in the midst of the storm. Anselm had known much inner turbulence; but his choice of peace had been a moral, not an intellectual choice. He had put himself in Lanfranc's hands, and in principle the struggle was over. The decision was morally and physically hard, and required a great rejection of pleasures of the world; but it required no great intellectual decision.

It is not surprising, therefore, that Anselm shows no sense of the grand movements of historical development which Augustine shared with his contemporaries. This consciousness of participation in the great sweep of Imperial and Christian history, which Augustine more than anyone else in the ancient world had made his own, had continued in a diminished form, but still as an impressive experience, until the ninth century. As late as 850 the experience of the grandeur of the two traditions was still shared by the Carolingian rulers and their associates, both lay and ecclesiastical. But, after the death of the Emperor Henry III in 1056, there was very little grandeur left in the public life of western Europe: all the greatness that remained was in the Church, and it flowed along narrow channels, first in the practice of the monastic life, and more recently in a new ideal of Christendom reorganized under papal leadership. This new ideal had been given an impressive expression at the Roman council in 1059, the year of Anselm's arrival at Bec. But, as we shall see, it made little impression on him until the last years of his life, and even then in a very diluted form. It was only in the narrow stream of monastic life that safety lay.

So, at the age of twenty-seven, Anselm turned to the seclusion of an intensely conceived religious life, and the first result of this seclusion was a deeply searching programme of introspection. During the next hundred years introspection became a widely practised religious exercise, and it opened up new prospects of an enlarged individuality. But not for Anselm. In turning inwards he found no grounds for satisfaction. Self-abasement in the presence of God was the only appropriate human response. Apart from the bare scaffolding of rational argument pointing towards God, he found within himself only sin and insecurity. Anselmian introspection led to increased anxiety, not to an increased understanding of human powers. Anxiety was the constant refrain of his earliest spiritual writings:

> nimis peccator **anxius** confugio . . .
> ad te fugit **anxius** quem iniquitas fecit tam reum dei . . .
> **anxiatur** siti anima mea . . .
> **Anxiare** in me, spiritus meus, turbare in me, cor meum,
>   erumpe et clama, anima mea. . .
> **Anxius** itaque et tremens refugit ad te . . .
> aestuat et **anxiatur** desiderio tui . . .
> **anxius** de me et de mihi commissis . . .
> **anxius** intercessores quaero. . .[19]

The need first to intensify, and then to seek an escape from, anxiety was his primary message; and the ground for this well justified anxiety could be expressed in a single Biblical sentence: 'Many are called but few are chosen'. How few, he would add, we do not know; therefore no one is secure until he is certain that he is one of the very few of whose salvation we have no doubt: 'Whoever does not live as one of the few, let him correct his life or face the certainty of damnation.'[20] This fear was at the centre of some of his earliest letters, and he continued to repeat it at intervals for the next thirty years. It was a doctrine full of dread. He had grown up in a period when huge penances were imposed on sinners, which could only be discharged by those who either abandoned the world, or who, though living in the world, associated themselves with the monastic life.

Anselm's theological system helped to create a more hopeful outlook for sinners, but he did not himself share the new spirit of hope.[21] He could not escape from the expectation of widespread damnation; he could only try to persuade everyone to choose the narrowest path. There was no moderation, no sense of security in Anselm's thought. By contrast, Augustine, although no one was more aware of sin than he, had a sense of security which is never found in Anselm. Augustine knew that nothing is secure in this life,

---

[19] For these phrases, see *Prayers* 6, 8, 12, 13, 15, 16, 17, 18. (Schmitt, iii, pp. 15, 26, 49, 50, 63, 66, 68, 72)
[20] For this and similar warnings, see *Epp.* 2 (i, 2), 16 (i, 14), 51 (i, 43), 65 (i, 56), 167 (iii, 18), 184.   [21] See below, pp. 215–16, 447–52

but still he could say, 'Fear not; God is not deceived. Let the good be secure even in the midst of sinners.'[22] Nothing like this can be found in Anselm.

Anselm's world was much more contracted than that of Augustine; yet he felt less at ease in it. He thought as Augustine, but he developed these thoughts in ways which are more limited, more precise, more single-minded than Augustine's. These differences may be summed up in a single contrast between immensity and precision. Augustine is immense in both the world which he represents and the spirit in which he faces it. He had an awareness of the world, of time, of history, of the fate of nations, that Anselm almost entirely lacked. The whole of Anselm's life was spent in that relatively short period in European history when the grandeur of the ancient imperial ideal had shrunk to almost nothing and the new confidence of the West had not yet been established. This situation helps to explain why Anselm's introspective gaze, liberating though in the end it proved to be, led immediately to a deeper cry of horror. It was out of this horror that he initiated the discovery of the individual which, in the hands of its twelfth-century exponents, opened a view of new human potentialities and became the golden thread leading to the humanism of the later Middle Ages. For Anselm, liberation could only come from the steady recognition of human debasement and a total submission to the divine will.

These comparisons may appear to diminish the stature of Anselm. But what they diminish is rather the world in which he lived. As I have already remarked, the only men of his youth and middle age who faced the world with bold plans for the future were Duke William in Normandy and the group of papal organizers in Rome, among whom Gregory VII is the outstanding figure. Anselm did not plan for the world of the future: he thought and planned only for the souls of those who were willing to commit themselves to the rigours of a dedicated life. Within these rigours he found and proclaimed a sweetness and joy, which are the source of the charm that all felt who came near him.

Augustine is like an ocean, tempestuous, variegated, and with contradictory currents formed by the terrible stresses arising from the ruin of the ancient world. Anselm is a narrow channel, clear-cut, lucid, admitting no extraneous elements. He expressed his most anguished feelings with an artistry and a conciseness which he

---

[22] Augustine, *In Pss.* 25, ii, *PL* 36, col. 194.

had not learnt from Augustine. Precision was his aim and his gift. He had not the abounding flow of ideas of Augustine, who scatters his thoughts unsystematically and with a lavish hand: Anselm had a smaller supply, which he laid out to the best advantage.

The first impression Anselm's writings make is one of youthful briiliance and intensity. Yet they are the result of a long preparation and intense study. Apart from his *De Grammatico*, we have nothing that he wrote till he was nearly forty, and his greatest works came when he was either forty-five or over sixty years old. This is surprising. To judge from the example of those who are nearest to him in genius, his mind was of the kind that develops early. Clear, original thoughts of mathematical precision do not normally require laborious preparation: they come early or not at all. Similarly, the intense expressions of friendship in Anselm's early letters seem youthful and passionate; but they are the letters of middle age, heavily weighted with thought, enclosed within an ethereal atmosphere.

This contrast is also found in his theological writings. They are brilliant, and slight in bulk; but they too are the result of long preparation. Anselm's strength did not lie, as did that of earlier and later medieval theologians, in the mastery of a vast and intricate mass of materials. This must take time. Yet even Thomas Aquinas, and later Duns Scotus, who wrote when the materials to be co-ordinated were most abundant, had already produced great works of comprehension, and the latter was dead, before they reached the age at which Anselm wrote the works by which he lives. But when they wrote, the path was broad and clear. When Anselm wrote, the goal was clear, but the intellectual way to it was still unexplored. The task which he set himself was, with very exiguous materials of the finest quality, to draw an initial sketch of the whole route.

PART II
THE RADIANT YEARS, 1070–1093

CHAPTER 5

ANSELM'S NEW START

I 'PRAYERS' AND 'MEDITATIONS'

Anselm's earliest writings after his years of silence were *Prayers* and *Meditations*, and letters. They set a new standard of intensity of expression in both these branches of self-expression. Although all the *Prayers* and several of the letters were apparently private revelations of his inmost thoughts and feelings, they were also intended to be useful to others. But, whereas the letters failed to find a receptive audience after his death despite the activity of his disciples in collecting them, his *Prayers* had a huge success.

In the later Middle Ages, they became the most influential and widely read of all his works. By then, however, they had become inextricably mixed up with the productions of imitators, and the imitations were largely responsible for their popularity, for they preserved Anselm's style of devotion in a form easier to digest than the genuine articles. Naturally there was a price to pay for performing this service: the imitations obscured the peculiar quality of Anselm's contribution until this century, when the dilution was at last detected.[1] It is only now, when the accumulation of spurious additions has been cleared away, that it has become possible to go back to the beginning and trace some part of the growth of Anselm's mind and outlook in the development of his *Prayers* and *Meditations*.

The first notice we have of the existence of Anselm's *Prayers* is in

---

[1] The great unraveller of the intricate web of MSS of the *Prayers* and *Meditations* was Dom A. Wilmart in a series of articles of which the most important are collected in his *Auteurs spirituels et textes dévots du moyen âge latin*, Paris, 1932. His first account of the state of the problem in 'Méditations et prières de S Anselme', tr. A. Castel, intr. A. Wilmart, *Collection Pax*, xi, Paris, 1923, should not be neglected. So far as the texts are concerned, the fruits of these studies are to be found in Schmitt, iii, pp. 3–91; but anyone who wishes to know how the *Prayers* and *Meditations* presented themselves to generations of readers from the twelfth century almost to the present day must go to the old editions, most conveniently presented in *PL* 158, cols. 710–1,016.

a letter which he wrote to Adelaide, a daughter of William the Conqueror, in about 1072.[2] Like many unmarried aristocratic women, Adelaide had devoted herself to a semi-monastic life, which alone could give such women the freedom and authority that their station in the world led them to expect. We must not think of them as women retiring into an obscure corner to weep and say their prayers. Recluses of high birth would have a household and a chaplain: what they sought was a dignified order for their lives. They had no wish, nor had they the necessary learning, to follow a full routine of regular monastic Offices: they needed something simpler, following the model of the regular religious life at a less demanding level. For this, it was natural for them to turn to a monastic adviser. The widowed Empress Agnes, an older contemporary of Adelaide, had recently received a scheme of prayers and readings from John, abbot of Fécamp. If Adelaide had known of this, she might have thought that it met all her needs, for it expressed, better than Anselm could do, a gentle and refined piety, a confidence in the saving grace of Christ, a mild rejection of the world, and a fervent desire for progress in devotion – exactly what a great lady retiring from the world might desire.[3] Anselm could produce nothing quite like this: behind his mildness of manner, he made exacting demands that few could meet. But he did his best to provide what Adelaide needed.

Adelaide, however, could have known nothing of the *Prayers* written for the Empress Agnes, who (even in her widowhood) lived in Rome or in the German royal court at the centre of political life, and could seek advice wherever she wished. Adelaide was a much less distinguished person, and she had retired to live in obscurity in the neighbourhood of Bec. In these circumstances, it was natural for her to turn to Anselm as the most easily accessible adviser. She did not in fact ask him to write any *Prayers* specially for her. What she asked him to make was a selection of verses from the Psalms for her use. This was a very common starting-point for any religiously inclined person who lacked the resources for a full routine of monastic Offices, and Anselm sent her a series of extracts of his own

---

[2] *Ep.* 10 (iv, 121). Anselm's letter addressed to Adelaide describes her as *domina venerabilis regia nobilitate*, which suffices to identify her with the daughter of William I, who, as Ordericus Vitalis v, 11 (Chibnall, iii, p. 114) relates, had adopted a religious life under the protection of Roger of Beaumont, the centre of whose barony lay in the valley of the Risle, near Bec.

[3] For John of Fécamp's collection, see Leclercq, 1946, esp. pp. 211–17.

choice.[4] But, without being asked, he added some compositions of his own which he thought might be helpful to her. His extracts from the Psalms have not survived, but the *Prayers* can be identified, for he described them in an accompanying letter.

In this letter, he told Adelaide that besides the *Flowers of Psalms* for which she had asked, he enclosed seven Prayers, which he described thus:

> I have added seven Prayers, of which the first is less a Prayer than a Meditation. In it, the soul of the sinner briefly examines itself; despises what it finds; is humbled by what it despises; in humiliation is smitten with terror of the Last Judgement, and breaks into tears and lamentation. Among the Prayers there are two to St Stephen and St Mary Magdalen, which – if received into the heart – will tend to an increase of love. There are seven in all, and I exhort you as your servant and friend of your soul, to offer them as a sacrifice of humility, fear, and love.[5]

Brief though it is, Anselm's description suffices to identify *Med.* 1 and *Or.* 13, 16 with certainty; and *Or.* 8, 9, 10, and 11 with a high degree of probability.[6] Thanks to this clue, we can attempt an initial outline of Anselm's first steps in developing a mode of private devotion, which opens a new chapter in medieval spirituality. All reconstruction must be tentative, for we are here entering an area of historical development of great complexity, which has not yet received the attention which it deserves. But a cautious assessment of Anselm's innovations, and of the light they throw on his own development, seems within our reach. For this purpose, we must first understand the historical background of such compositions, and then we may look at Anselm's compositions in the light of the devotional tradition in which he wrote.

II THE DEVOTIONAL BACKGROUND

For the background, we must begin with the Psalter, for this was the main instrument of all devotion, whether formal or informal.

---

[4] A well-known collection of sentences from the Psalms was attributed (falsely) to St Jerome. It made a suitable devotional work for a semi-literate recluse, and a few years later a copy of it was given to the ex-pirate and trader, Godric of Finchale, by his friends when he retired, *c* 1100, to lead a religious life in or near Carlisle. (*Vita S. Godrici*, ed. J. Stevenson, Surtees Society, Durham, 1847, c. 9) For an anthology of verses from the Psalms attributed to Bede, see Wilmart, 1940, pp. 143–59.

[5] *Ep.* 10 (iv, 121).

[6] For discussion, see Wilmart, 1923, pp. xxvi–xxvii; but he is certainly wrong in suggesting that the Prayer to St Nicholas (*Or.* 14) was one of this group, for (as we shall see) it was one of Anselm's latest additions to his *Prayers*.

The repetition of the whole Psalter once a week, and of several additional Psalms once a day, was the central feature of the monastic *Opus Dei*. Equally, the new and more informal additions to the monastic Offices largely consisted of the repetition of selected Psalms encased (like the main Offices) in a surrounding pattern of readings, chants, hymns, and collects appropriate to the day, season, or subject of devotion.

This growing monastic routine offered little that could be adapted to the use of the pious laity except the Psalms; and here there was little to do except to shorten them. But in addition to the regular Offices, individual monks also engaged in private prayer and meditation. Of strictly private prayer the Rule says very little; and as the Offices became longer and more elaborate during the tenth and eleventh centuries, there was no time within the monastic time-table for prolonged individual prayer. Of course there were always some monks – Anselm was one of them – who created opportunities for themselves, rising in the night and depriving themselves of sleep in order to pray. But they had no need to commit their prayers to writing, and we know nothing of their contents.

Meditation was a different matter. Unlike private prayer, meditation was required by the Rule. But in the sense in which the word was used in the Rule, meditation meant simply preparation for the corporate acts which lay ahead – preparing the lessons, learning the chants, training the children in the choir.[7] By the eleventh century, prolonged individual preparation was especially necessary, for the Offices had become highly complicated and exacting musical and verbal performances, which required the expert collaboration, and therefore careful practice, of the whole community. In addition to learning the words (for it must be remembered that in the long night Office the written words would be difficult to see), intelligent production also required understanding their meaning; and since the meaning was often elaborately allegorical, it could be reached only by studying commentaries and making a determined effort of comprehension. By the eleventh century, therefore, 'meditation', which the writer of the Rule had

---

[7] For the meaning of Meditation in the Rule of St Benedict, see *Regula S. Benedicti*, ed. B. Linderbauer, Metten, 1933, pp. 49, 228. Naturally, modern editions of the Rule, especially those devised for practical use, give a much more extended meaning to the word. See, for example, the American Benedictine edition, ed. T. Fry and others, Minnesota, 1981, pp. 446–8. But this was not part of the original intention.

probably envisaged as a straightforward business of learning by heart, had gradually become much more complicated and demanding than the writer of the Rule could have foreseen.

The detailed stages in this development are largely hidden from our eyes. But it is clear that by Anselm's day, Benedictine meditation had become a more varied exercise than simply preparing the readings and chants required for the daily Offices. Like many human activities, what had originally had a corporate purpose was becoming an independent exercise with a future of its own. Out of the corporate routine, three related activities had emerged, each requiring new forms of expertise: the musical and literary elaborations of the Offices needed musical skills of a high order; additional short Offices, of which the most widely used were devoted to the veneration of the Virgin Mary or the Holy Trinity, needed new hymns and chants, and new prayers and readings. Ordericus Vitalis, the most articulate and enthusiastic observer of the monastic scene in Normandy during Anselm's lifetime, provides many glimpses of these activities in his *Historia Ecclesiastica*.[8]

Most of these developments had taken place without regard to the needs of pious lay men and women. But there was much in the new short Offices of the monasteries that could be used both by individuals within the monastery and by literate recluses, especially women, outside. The second of these developments especially helped to promote that mutual interdependence between monasteries and their lay patrons which, as we shall see, occupied much of Anselm's time in his later years. The monasteries could not exist without their lay patrons; the lay patrons would lack one of their main props for civilized life, not to mention the hope of eternal salvation, without the monasteries. Everywhere, but especially in the rapidly developing society of Normandy, the landed aristocracy and the Benedictine monasteries lived in a complicated state of symbiosis, each contributing an enlargement of life to the other.

Among the contributions which the monasteries made to the families which supported them, the provision of private prayers for their use, whether in their private chapels or in some more retired way, already had a long history by the eleventh century. Two hundred and fifty years earlier, Charlemagne had asked Alcuin to make him a scheme of daily prayer; later, King Alfred had a manual

---

[8] For these activities, besides Ordericus's own work, see Chibnall, 1984.

of psalms and prayers which he always carried in his pocket. These prayer books, consisting of extracts from the Psalms intermingled with brief prayers, were the contribution of the Carolingian age to the personal religious life of the later Middle Ages. Like most things, they gradually became longer and more varied to suit the circumstances or the person for whom they were made, but the elements remained broadly the same. In essentials, they embodied the ideas of the time when Alcuin had recommended a regular course of private psalmody to his master, the Emperor Charlemagne:

In the Psalms, if you look carefully, you will find an intimacy of prayer, such as you could never have discovered without their help: you will find words for an intimate confession of your sins, and for a perfect supplication of the divine mercy. In the Psalms, too, you will find thanksgiving for all that befalls you. In the Psalms you confess your weakness and misery, and thereby call down God's mercy upon you. You will find every virtue in the Psalms, if God in his mercy will deign to reveal to you their secrets.[9]

Following this line of thought, the Psalms were the main source of private devotion for the laity as well as monastic communities during the two centuries before Anselm. But round this central core, there grew a large assortment of collects and prayers. The collects were necessarily short, but the Prayers, which often followed the main body of Psalms in the manuscripts, allowed more scope for development.

Among these developments, there was one of special importance. Earlier collections of prayers had been mainly addressed to God; but in the tenth and eleventh centuries an increasing proportion were addressed to the saints, and especially to the Virgin Mary, St John the Baptist, St Peter, St Paul, St Andrew, St Stephen and St Benedict.[10] It would be perhaps too crude an analogy to say that this dispersal of supernatural power provided a spiritual analogy to the growing fragmentation of authority in the Carolingian Empire among semi-independent principalities. But if cautiously applied, the analogy is not absurd: the political dispersal of sovereignty

---

[9] *PL* 101, cols. 465–6, and cf. 509–10. For King Alfred's Prayer Book, see Asser's *Life of King Alfred*, ed. W. H. Stevenson, Oxford, 1904, pp. 21, 73.

[10] A main body of texts in pre-Anselmian days, including the piece translated below, is printed in Joseph Bianchini, *Venerabilis J. M. Thomasii Opera*, 476–96, 518–39. For the manuscripts, see A. Wilmart 1929, 370–2; 1936, 283–4; to which Bodleian MS D'Orville 45, from the Cluniac abbey of Moissac, *c* 1067, discussed below, should be added.

followed the dispersal of territorial power among the officials of the Carolingian Empire; and the increasing dispersal of relics among the churches and monasteries of the period led to a comparable dispersal of supernatural sovereignty. Just as trade is said to follow the flag, it was natural that the possession of relics should have excited interest in the saints whose relics lay in each individual church, and that their lives and efficacy as agents of salvation in various types of dangers and temptations should have become objects of special study and hoped-for help wherever their relics were found.

Intermingled, therefore, with extracts from the Psalms, we find an increasing number of *Prayers* to the most popular saints of the time and region. These prayers followed a plan which is both simple and effective: some incidents in the life of the saint were picked out and applied to the needs of the worshipper. Thus St Peter's sin in his three-fold denial of Christ, and his loss of faith on the water of Galilee, were used to associate his sin with those of the suppliant, and to invoke the use of his power of loosing and binding on behalf of those of like frailty to his own. Take, for example, the common Carolingian prayer to St Peter. It was very brief, but it managed to compress this appeal to the common weaknesses of the saint and the sinner alike into a few words:

Most holy Peter, prince of the Apostles, my shepherd and provider, to whom power to bind and to loose has been given by your Master, loose me, I pray, from all the bonds of my iniquities, and intercede for me, that the Lord, your Master, may look on me, as he looked on you; and may save me from the deep waters of wickedness, who saved you from the waters of Galilee; and that he may drive out of me all that he hates, and give me all that pleases him for ever. Amen.

The essential message could scarcely be conveyed with greater brevity and simplicity. There is reason to think that Alcuin himself may have been the author of the group of prayers to which this one belongs. But whoever the author was, this and its associated prayers admirably exhibit the discipline and sobriety of Carolingian scholarship in contrast to the earlier prolixity of the Anglo-Irish tradition.[11] These texts without much alteration served the purposes of private devotion for over two hundred years.

---

[11] They may be contrasted with the collection of early Anglo-Irish prayers in A. B. Kuypers, *The Book of Cerne*, Cambridge, 1902, pp. 154–98.

It does not seem that these brief formulas had been much added to before about the middle of the eleventh century. Nothing, indeed, shows the conservatism of the preceding two centuries more clearly than the stability of forms of devotion which had no liturgical framework to ensure their permanence. For example, a mid-eleventh century collection of private prayers has survived from the Cluniac abbey of Moissac with an arrangement of Psalms and prayers, which go back in all essentials to the ninth century: Carolingian order and sobriety, we may say, had survived and met all common needs till the eleventh century. Books like this for the private devotions of monks or literate laymen seem to have been quite common by about 1050, and they might equally well have been made two hundred years earlier.[12]

But by this date, there were also signs of change: most conspicuously, the brevity of the past no longer satisfied, and a new urge for independent elaboration began to prevail. This is especially noticeable in the rapidly growing numbers of prayers to the Virgin Mary, and these prayers posed a new problem, which (as we shall see) was to cause Anselm some difficulty. The problem was this: the well-established method of addressing the saints by referring to the sins which they shared with the suppliant could not be applied to the Blessed Virgin, the sinless one. This led to a new kind of elaboration – the elaboration of praise, and glorification. Maurilius, the archbishop of Rouen, on whose advice Anselm became a monk, was one of the first to expand somewhat cautiously the old Carolingian prayer to Mary. The original text ran as follows:

Singular in merit, sole, unexampled, Mother and Virgin, Mary, whom the Lord preserved inviolate in mind and body, in order that thy body might be worthy to form the body of the Son of God, the price of our redemption: I beseech thee, by whom the whole world has been saved, most mercifully to intercede for me, soiled and filthy as I am with all my iniquities, so that I who am worthy only to receive eternal punishment for my sins, may be saved by thy merits, most glorious Virgin, and attain the everlasting kingdom, through Jesus Christ. Amen.[13]

Like the other prayers to the saints, this prayer satisfied the needs of private devotion for about two hundred years, and it is preserved in many manuscripts from the ninth to the eleventh century. Then

[12] The manuscript I have in mind is Bodleian MS D'Orville 45, written in about 1067.
[13] Wilmart, 1940, p. 140.

the urge for a more profound self-abasement, a more glowing exaltation of the powers and privileges of the Virgin, and perhaps too a simple desire for more words, ensured the supersession of this Carolingian prayer. To meet the demand for greater elaboration, Maurilius added a long development containing much personal emotion, without however adding to its theological content. The following phrases are a fair sample of these lengthy additions:

Unhappy man that I am, I have entirely lost the grace of innocence and holiness. Again and again I have violated the holy temple of God. But what am I doing, pouring out my obscenities into undefiled ears? I tremble, Lady, I tremble: my conscience accuses me; I am ashamed to appear before thee in my vile nakedness . . .[14]

The religious conscience of the time was developing a great partiality for prolonged outpourings. The danger that they would degenerate into meaningless vapourings is only too clear: they often did so. What was needed was someone who could speak this language of self-revelation with power, and add to it a new theological insight. Self revelation and theological insight were just the qualities which Anselm could contribute: he added the discipline of exact thought and the warmth of exuberant feeling to the religious impulses of his day.

Another important aspect of the new development was the growing importance of women among the devout readers for whom the new *Prayers* were written and among whom they circulated. Whereas the main patrons of religious writings in the ninth century seem to have been such outstanding rulers as Charlemagne, Charles the Bald, and King Alfred, the new patrons of monastic prayers were women like Adelaide and the Empress Agnes, and later the Countess Matilda, for whom Anselm made his most elaborate collection of *Prayers* and *Meditations*. I must leave it for others to decide how far the increase in emotional appeal and in the flow of words is connected with this shift of emphasis. There are many factors which will need to be taken into account in any full record of these changes, but enough has been said to provide the background for understanding Anselm's contribution to the scene.

III   THE ANSELMIAN TRANSFORMATION

Anselm began by observing the Carolingian pattern of private prayer in one respect at least, by attaching his prayers to a selection

---

[14] *PL* 158, col. 946; for authorship, see Wilmart, 1932, pp. 480–1.

of passages from the Psalms. But he did this at Adelaide's request, and his anthology from the Psalms formed no part of later collections of his *Prayers*. This itself was a break with the past: instead of his *Prayers* being a brief appendix to a substantial body of extracts from the Psalms, the emphasis was now exclusively on the additions. The preliminary selection from the Psalms, which he sent to Adelaide, was regarded by Anselm himself as dispensable: no single manuscript of his *Prayers* has preserved it.

Moreover, unlike earlier compilers of prayers, he did not see himself as an anonymous contributor to an already formed liturgical tradition, but as the creator of a distinctive work. From the beginning, his *Prayers* and *Meditations* circulated under his own name and in the body of his other works. However contaminated with spurious compositions they became, they are nearly always found with his name attached to them. Clearly, this was not an act of authorial hubris: quite the contrary; but it was a declaration of personal responsibility. The words were all expressive of self-abasement, but their emphasis was all on the individual.

This absence of anonymity, self-abasing though it was in intention, was an important innovation. All earlier medieval prayers circulated either anonymously, or under the patronage of some great ancient name. Anselm's are the first medieval compositions to circulate under the name of a contemporary author, and to be preserved in the corpus of his works. Far from being esteemed because they were part of an ancient deposit of liturgical texts, they were valued from the beginning because they had Anselm's name attached to them – falsely in many cases as we now know, but that was not Anselm's doing.

These external differences which separate Anselm's *Prayers* from those of the past are the first public symptom of the Anselmian transformation: we are no longer in a corporate, anonymous environment. The sinner stands alone before God. But the most important innovation was within, in the contents. Here Anselm made a break with the past which was no less decisive for being a leap in a direction in which there was already a movement forward. The leap took him and his readers into a new area of self-disclosure. A sufficient illustration both of the difference and the continuity can be found in the first sentences of his prayer to St Peter, comparing their style and content with the Carolingian prototype quoted above (p. 97). These are Anselm's words:

Holy and most benign Peter, faithful shepherd of the sheep of God, prince of the Apostles, prince of those greatest princes, binding and loosing what thou willest, making whole and raising up whom thou willest, giving the kingdom of Heaven to whomsoever thou willest: great Peter, great and endowed with so many and such great gifts, elevated by so many and such great dignities, behold, I the poorest and basest of *homunculi*, stand in miserable need of the help of thy kindly power. My mouth does not have words with which to express my need, nor has my heart such strength of devotion to reach thy so great height from its so great depth. Again and again I try to stir up my dull mind and to hold it back from the vanities which destroy it; but even when my mind has summoned up all its strength, it cannot break through the darkness of the torpor which the stains of sin have brought upon it. It cannot even continue long in its intention. Alas, most wretched, wretched man that I am, this is the truth: it is no pretence; it is so. Who will help the wretched being who can neither express tribulation in his words, nor find sorrow in his mind?[15]

There are many finer passages than this in Anselm's prayers, but this will suffice to illustrate the main types of innovation for which he was responsible.

First, there is the immense elaboration which weighs down every thought. It looks like verbosity; but closer inspection shows that each phrase evokes a clear image of a mental state of agonized introspection. This is the first and continuing symptom of all Anselm's early writing.

Then there is the systematic identification of Peter's prerogatives: *solvis quod vis, resuscitas quem vis, das regnum caelorum cui vis.* Peter's commanding position could not be expressed more strongly.

Finally, after all this and despite all the verbal elaboration, what he asks is carefully articulated and restrained: 'Pray for me, teach me, heal me.' If these phrases are examined carefully, it is seen that, just as the sinful will has a threefold aspect – the sin, the sinner, and the goal at which it falsely aims – so it needs a threefold operation for its salvation: remission of sins, the revivifying of the spirit, the rewarding of the purified soul.

We see here, therefore, as everywhere in Anselm's writings, a characteristic combination of extreme fervour of expression, systematic completeness, practical restraint. These are the marks of the Anselmian revolution, which we shall observe also in his treatment of friendship: warmth, even violence, of expression is

---

[15] *Or.* 9 (Schmitt, iii, p. 30).

accompanied by great precision of intention and severity of operation.

Nevertheless, although systematic rigour is to be found everywhere in Anselm's thought and practice, exuberance of expression is an essential feature of his moderation and plays an important part in his break with the past. For example, although the plan of Anselm's prayer follows the well-established Carolingian pattern of taking incidents from the saint's life and applying them to the sinner, Anselm enforces his message, not only in intensifying the guilt of the suppliant, but in not sparing the saint. For example, it was part of the tradition that, in approaching St Peter, the suppliant should recall the chief Apostle's denial of his Lord as well as his role as shepherd of the sheep: the denial gave the sinner his point of contact with the saint whose help he sought. But Anselm carried his elaboration both of the Apostle's sin and of the suppliant's own state to lengths which were new and shocking:

The sheep is sickening to death: his ulcers swell, his wounds are reopened and grow putrid. The wolves have tasted his blood. They are waiting for him to be cast away. Faithful shepherd, turn your eyes on him: see that he is one of yours. If he has strayed, nevertheless, *he* has not denied his Lord and shepherd. If, through the filth, you cannot recognize the face of one washed white in the fountain of Christ, at least you see that he confesses the name of Christ, who had thrice to ask *you* 'Lovest thou me?' before He said 'Feed my sheep'.[16]

What is the reason for this extremity of elaboration? Briefly, elaboration is required to excite the mind to understand the extremity of the sinner's state. If we consider the few words quoted above, what is most remarkable is the completeness of the range of situations to which they refer. The words require careful thought to be understood. Whereas in the comparable prayer of an earlier generation everything is immediately clear, in Anselm there is much that is too subtle, too complex and too personal to be understood without a close concentration which is possible only in the seclusion of an inner chamber. The environment of prayer has shifted decisively from the church to the chamber, and from communal effort to severe and lonely introspection: we have not only withdrawn from corporate worship into the privacy of the chamber; we have withdrawn into the secrecy of the soul. It was entirely consistent with this degree of retirement that Anselm

---

[16] *Or.* 9 (Schmitt, iii, p. 31)

should express, and require from the reader, a sustained mental effort to understand his words; and an even greater effort to participate in the extremity of his self-abasement. To this we must finally return when we survey his message as a whole.[17] Here it will suffice to say that he was no optimist.

He requires, therefore, this double exertion: a high degree of mental excitation necessary for realizing abstract states of being; and the deep personal abasement necessary for thinking of the self with disgust. Anselm strains every resource of language to express and stimulate in his reader both the mental excitation and humiliation necessary for the double activity of self-examination and abasement in the presence of holiness. Rhyme, assonance, antithesis, the frequent employment of parallel grammatical constructions and closely similar words to express opposing or complementary ideas – all these devices are very common in this *Prayer*, as in all his earliest *Prayers* and letters. The function of antithesis is also here clearly seen: it expresses the tug of war between good and evil in even the most minute particles of the universe; it stresses the way in which words imitate reality.

Then there is another important innovation in these *Prayers*. Anselm thought it necessary to explain that one of them was more a *Meditation* than a *Prayer*. On inspection, we find that the distinction is not clear-cut: all his *Prayers* have some element of meditation in them, and vice versa. We have already noticed that *cogitatio* and *meditatio* are different modes of the same mental operation; now we find that prayer and meditation likewise represent two closely related modes of mental effort. Indeed, their intermingling is a main feature of the Anselmian method.

Nevertheless, there is a difference between the *attitudes* of prayer and meditation. The *Prayers* are petitions to saints, and they press home their message by relating the sinner's condition and needs to the saint's experience and powers. The *Meditations* are inward-looking acts, in which the soul examines itself, and seeks God in humiliation and supplication.

In his earliest explanation of his method, he told Adelaide how to meditate; and the sentence in which he did this is filled with rhymes and assonances which (as I have already mentioned above) are devices for making words represent the situation which they describe. Here is his account of the stages of meditation:

[17] See below, pp. 450–1.

Se peccatoris anima breviter discutiat,
discutiendo despiciat,
despiciendo humiliet,
humiliando terrore ultimi iudicii concutiat,
concussa in gemitus et lacrimas erumpat.

Let the soul of the sinner examine itself,
despise what it finds,
be humbled by what it despises,
in humiliation be filled with terror of the Last Judgement,
and in terror burst into tears and lamentation.[18]

Here we have one of the two aims of introspection in Anselm's theology: horror of self. The second aim was already formulated, but not articulated in detail until five years later in the *Monologion* and *Proslogion*, where introspection has become a first step to the knowledge of God.

By nature, the goal is prior to the method, for Man was created in the image of God and the first aim of all meditation is to revive this obfuscated image. But in the state of sin, which is the present state of mankind, the penitential stage of horror at the deformation of the image of God in the soul must come first: only then can the reaching out to God begin.

The combination of these two activities, penitential self-abasement and the approach to a final state of contemplation through meditation, was the foundation of Anselm's spiritual life, as also of his mental operations. The combination is, therefore, the starting point of his theology: the ascent towards contemplation cannot begin until self-abasement has obliterated self-will. The *Prayers* are cries to the saints for help. But these cries too are controlled by introspection, and their aim is to lay before the saints the results of penitential self-knowledge. Nearly everything of permanent value in Anselm's later writings presupposes an initial introspection. In one direction, introspection leads to horror of self; in the other direction, it provides the knowledge of being which leads to knowledge of God. In his two great meditations, to which he finally gave the titles, *Monologion* and *Proslogion*, he proceeded to the knowledge of God. But in the earliest *Prayers* and *Meditations*, we are only at the first stage, when the soul is torn between terror and joy, with the former greatly predominating:

[18] *Ep.* 10 (iv, 121).

Anima mea, anima aerumnosa, anima inquam misera miseri homunculi, excute torporem tuum et discute peccatum et concute mentem tuam. Reduc ad cor enorme delictum et perduc de corde immanem rugitum. Intende, infelix, intende sceleris tui horrorem et protende horrificum terrorem et terrificum dolorem.[19]

My soul, my soul of lead, soul of a wretched *homunculus*, throw off your torpor, lay bare your sin, stir up your mind. Take to heart the enormity of your sin, and roar with anguish. Miserable man, weigh the horror of your evil, roar out your horrified terror and your terrified anguish.

These words come from the beginning of the most turbulent of Anselm's early writings, his *Deploratio virginitatis amissae per fornicationem*. This was not a piece which he sent to the daughter of William the Conqueror, but it may well be the earliest of his *Meditations*. The fornication or worse that it laments, its comparative theological immaturity, and its strong rhyming antithetical style all point to an early date. In temper, it is more reminiscent of the later Donne than of the later Anselm:

Horror! Horror! What do I see, where no order, but everlasting horror, dwells? Only a confusion of wailing, a tumult of gnashing of teeth, a confused volume of groans. Woe! Woe! Again and again, woe! woe! The sulphurous fire, the Tartarian flame, the billows of smoke, with what terrific roaring do I see you revolve! And you worms, living in the flames, what strange avidity of gnawing burns within you, whom even the fire of fires does not burn? You burning demons, roaring with ire, why are you so cruel to those who twist and turn among you? You torments of every kind, limited by justice, unlimited in suffering, will no limit, no remedy, no end ever quench you? Are these the ends, great God, prepared for fornicators and despisers of thy word, of whom I am one?[20]

These are not the words of a man whose mind had always been a placid mirror of sweetness and light. Whatever else may be thought of them, they are certainly the words of a man with great literary gifts, great originality in transforming traditional models, great sensibility, and an overwhelming sense of the grievousness of his sin.

Here, as in his expressions of friendship, which we must later examine, Anselm's words wholly discard the Carolingian sobriety which he helped to make obsolete. This sobriety had itself been a reaction against the eccentricities of the Irish and insular piety of an

---

[19] *Med.* II (Schmitt, iii, p. 80).   [20] Schmitt, iii, p. 82.

earlier age: it had been a recall to normality and centrality of expression and aim. Anselm's prayers marked the moment of rebound. They introduced into a tradition still mainly Carolingian a new note of personal anxiety, of passion, of elaboration and emotional extravagance; to which Anselm added precision of thought. The combination is wholly Anselmian, and it had its origin in his unusual combination of two different kinds of intensity, of feeling and of thought; and to intensity, he added clarity of thought and expression. The earliest prayers show as yet little sign of the exact and metaphysical mind which was soon to produce classics of Christian theology: but when his later works are read in the light of these earliest productions, we can see the origins of his theological system in an intense horror of sin operating on a mind of exceptional power and precision, with the same clarity of utterance running through everything he wrote. We shall see the first signs of his power of metaphysical analysis in the next group of prayers to St Mary. So, step by step, they lead to the great meditations to be examined in the next chapter.

IV   A NEW DIRECTION IN MEDIEVAL DEVOTION

Anselm's first collection of *Prayers*, which he sent to Adelaide in about 1072, has the interest which attaches to the appearance of a new star in the heavens, and it exhibits all the qualities of forceful expression and a fresh view of the state of the human soul necessary for giving a new impetus to devotional literature. Those which followed extend our knowledge of his personal development and enlarged the area of his influence. But three of them did much more than this: they marked an epoch in the development of medieval devotion to the Virgin Mary. These three, therefore, require fuller treatment than the others, and we are fortunate in being able to follow the stages in their production in unusual detail, for they came into existence with difficulty, and even some reluctance.

In retrospect, it is surprising that the earliest collection which he sent to Adelaide contained no prayer to the Virgin Mary. This gap evidently disappointed some of his friends, and it is surprising for several reasons. The first phase of the great expansion of Marian devotion in western Europe had already begun, and it was nowhere more conspicuous than in Normandy and England, particularly in monasteries dedicated, as Bec was, to St Mary. Moreover, much of Anselm's later reputation as a writer of *Prayers* was based on the belief that he was one of the most effective promoters of Marian devotion in the early stages of its medieval development. This belief was based partly on the mistaken association of his name with the doctrine of the Immaculate Conception and with a large number of prayers to the Virgin mistakenly attributed to him.[21] But it was also based on the group of three genuine prayers, theologically the most remarkable of all, which mark an important stage in Anselm's development.

Anselm himself told the story of their composition in a letter which he wrote, probably in 1073–4, to his friend Gundulf at Canterbury.[22] In this letter, he described how the initial impetus to write the Marian *Prayers* had come from one of the monks at Bec, who had urged him to fill this gap in his collection. He had hesitated to do this, and the request had to be made several times before he agreed to try. His first attempt, which was remarkably jejune and colourless by his standards, had failed to satisfy, and he was asked to try again. The second was somewhat better, but still the stream did not flow. Again he tried, and at his third attempt, the words came.

So here, from his own pen, we have a strange story of reluctance, repeated failure, and final success. In addition to his own account, we have manuscripts which preserve texts and drafts representing different stages on the road to success; and these show that the process of reaching a finally satisfactory text took even longer than Anselm's own account would lead us to expect. To put the matter briefly, the manuscripts show that it took Anselm at least twenty years to complete the formulas which finally satisfied him. The later changes are indeed very small, but none are negligible; and it is very astonishing that a writer, who generally knew his mind very clearly before he wrote, should have experienced such difficulty on a subject which was later to be especially associated with his name and influence – a subject moreover which, in its final result, turned out to be peculiarly suited to his sensibility.

---

[21] In the collection of *Prayers* which circulated under Anselm's name in the Middle Ages and until this century, no less than eighteen were addressed to the Virgin Mary (*PL* 158, cols. 942–68). Of these only the three which we are now to examine, were genuine. Further, and above all, various documents promoting the Feast of the Immaculate Conception also were wrongly attributed to him (*PL* 159, cols. 301–26). For further discussion on these points, see below, pp. 432–6.

[22] For Anselm's account of his three attempts to write a Marian *Prayer*, see *Ep* 28 (i, 20). He preserved all three, and in order of composition they are *Or*. 5, 6, 7, (Schmitt, iii, pp. 13–25). See the following note for the evidence that Anselm continued to refine his third attempt for several years.

There were probably several causes for Anselm's difficulties. In the first place, the subject did not lend itself to his normal method of concentrating on points of contact between the sinner and the saint to whom the prayer was addressed. As we have seen, it had long been clear that this method was inappropriate in praying to the Virgin Mary, who shared none of the sins of the suppliant. This was especially serious in Anselm's case because the whole pattern of his *Prayers* depended on the detailed, introspective self-humiliation of the sinner, which offered some points of contact with the saint.

Then there was another difficulty. The alternative approach lay in magnifying the virtues and privileges of the saint to whom prayer was addressed. But Anselm had already lavished on St Peter all the prerogatives of salvation available to any human being: 'You unbind what you wish; you bring to life whom you wish; you give the kingdom of Heaven to whomsoever you wish.' He had no similar stock of Biblically inspired phrases to apply to Mary; and, despite his talent for coining phrases which astonish the reader by their boldness, there was a fundamental caution in his innovations: he never went further than he could justify theologically, and it seems clear that, in the case of Mary, he was unsure how far he could go. As we shall see, in his Marian theology he distanced himself from those of his disciples who became early advocates of the doctrine of Mary's Immaculate Conception, for this seemed to be inconsistent with the theology of Redemption which he was slowly elaborating. So he seemed to be cut off both from the theme of the union of saint and sinner in a common frailty, and from a theologically acceptable foundation for his prayer.

He had not solved these problems at his second attempt, but it contained one boldly innovative phrase in which he described Mary as *mundi reconciliatrix*. It was a phrase which he never repeated. He may have thought that it said more than he meant: Christ alone was the reconciler of the world to God. But, even if this phrase may have been too strong, it opened the way to a new approach, and put him on the road to success. Instead of finding points of contact between saint and sinner, he now sought to express in language of the utmost brilliance and great originality the immensity of the distance separating the Mother of God from the rest of mankind. With this clue, the torrent of descriptive phrases, full of power and possibilities of growth, began to flow in this third attempt:

> Regina angelorum, domina mundi . . .
> Mater illuminationis cordis mei . . .

Nutrix salutis mentis meae . . .
Altrix reparationis carnis meae . . .
Aula universalis propitiationis . . .
Causa generalis reconciliationis . . .
Porta vitae, Ianua salutis, Femina per quam elementa renovantur,
inferna remediantur, daemones conculcantur, angeli
redintegrantur . . .

The list of epithets could be prolonged, for the fervent stream flowed apparently effortlessly. Some of these phrases already had a long history, but most of them were new coinage, and they pointed to the future. Although they were compatible with an entirely Christ-centred theology, they opened the way to a new exaltation of Mary, and they diminished the anguished abasement of the sinner. The brilliance of the Marian exaltation was accompanied, as in the Petrine prayer, by a striking sobriety in the sinner's requests: 'heal my infirmity . . . arouse my languor, cleanse my squalor'. The gap between the lavish superlatives employed to describe Mary's powers and the modesty of the personal plea, is very striking and touching.

Anselm was to continue for several years to make slight refinements in his final Marian *Prayer*, but in essence he had said everything at his third attempt, and he never wrote another on the same theme.[23] He was to inspire plenty of successors.

V ANSELM'S LAST PHASE

By about 1075, when these Marian prayers were completed in all but their final details, Anselm had written all the *Prayers* and *Meditations* that are important for the development of his devotional theology. We may therefore pause at this point to survey the scene thus far.

We have seen that at some time probably not long before 1070 he had started writing *Prayers* and *Meditations* which contained a review of his inner state, his corruptions, his despair of salvation, and his recourse to the saints for help in gaining access to God. His *Deploratio virginitatis male amissae* would seem to belong to this stage of his development, and at about the same time we may place

---

[23] The various stages in the development of the third prayer were first elucidated by Wilmart, 1931 ii, 189–204. But even Wilmart's minute investigations did not exhaust the number of revisions: St John's College, Oxford, MS 165, in addition to the final text, has a version which may be earlier than any of those described by Dom Wilmart,

those prayers, like that to John the Baptist, which are most heavily laden with the sense of sin and horror. Then, under pressure from monastic friends, he had attempted a prayer to St Mary. This raised theological problems about the economy of Redemption, which he solved so far as was necessary for his immediate needs. But even the final version of the prayer, successful though it was for its intended purpose, left several questions about the nature and origin of Mary's sinlessness unanswered.

It was not the purpose of his early *Prayers* and *Meditations* to solve theological problems. In them he sought only knowledge of himself and the aid of the saints. But this search disclosed two areas which earlier writers, even the greatest of them, had left obscure. The first of these concerned the nature of our knowledge of God; the second, the economy of Redemption. These were to be the two main areas of his later theological speculation.

His early prayers were his earliest explorations of an introspective theological method and a preparation for his mature theology. After about 1075, he continued to add new *Prayers* and one new *Meditation*, prompted by special circumstances or by the desire to make them more generally useful to a wider public. Some of the occasions which prompted him to add to his collection of prayers can be identified with some degree of assurance, and to complete the record they may be briefly mentioned.

First, an early addition to the collection was a *Prayer* or *Meditation* on the Cross. This devotion had a place in the monastic routine for Good Friday, and Anselm's *Prayer* may have been intended as a private meditation during the liturgical prostrations before the Cross on this day. It may possibly have been inspired by an incident which took place in 1082. In this year, Anselm presided over the translation of the body of St Honorine at the dependent priory of Bec at Conflans on the river Seine. During the ceremony, when a boat-load of pilgrims was in danger of being swamped, Anselm held up the saint's skull and blessed the endangered pilgrims 'in the name of the Holy Cross'. The danger passed and they were saved. Whether his *Prayer* was inspired by this incident is impossible to say; but it is certainly later than the *Prayers* which we have so far examined, and a date around 1082 would be consistent with the manuscript evidence.[24]

---

[24] *Or.* 4 (Schmitt, iii, pp. 11–12). It is added at the end of the earliest MS of the *Prayers* and *Meditations* from Troarn, *c* 1085. For the incident at Conflans, see Mabillon, *AA.SS. O.S.B.*, iv, ii, 527; and Gibson, 1978, p. 28, for a comment on it.

Another event associated with one of his prayers was the translation of a relic of St Nicholas of Bari to Bec in about 1090. Anselm's prayer to St Nicholas was clearly related to this event, for it is included in the liturgical dossier compiled for this ceremony. Nevertheless, its words are strangely inappropriate for the occasion.[25] We should have expected some account of a saint who was new in the West, and some rejoicing at the acquisition of his relic. But it is so impersonal that in some manuscripts it is addressed to St Martin, and in one it is called a *Meditation* addressed to God alone. Moreover, it is filled to a degree unparalleled among Anselm's later prayers with the horror of hell, the misery of sin, the burden of a hardened heart, the anger of God, the fear of damnation: an analysis of its language connects it decisively with the earliest group of *Prayers*. It is tempting to think that, having to produce something for the occasion, he hastily refurbished one of his earliest prayers. Whatever the reason, he seems to have been dissatisfied with it, for he was still thinking about it in 1092, when he wrote from England to Bec asking for it to be sent to him with other unfinished work. But there is no sign that he ever revised it.

All Anselm's later additions and rearrangements of the Prayers reflect his position as a public figure, writing for a wider circle of users. It was in this role that his most important addition to the collection was made in 1099, when he composed a new *Meditation* on Redemption summarizing the argument of his recently completed *Cur Deus Homo*.

Then, finally, between 1100 and 1104, he filled some conspicuous gaps in his Prayers by adding new *Prayers* 'to God' and 'for communicants at the Eucharist', together with a preface with advice for the instructed laity about the best way to use the collection. With these additions, which were all designed to make them more generally useful for devotional purposes, he sent the whole collection to Countess Matilda of Tuscany, whom he had met on his way northwards from Rome, in 1104.[26]

---

[25] For the texts associated with the arrival of the relic of St Nicholas at Bec, see *Bibl. Hag. Lat.* , no. 6207; Anselm's prayer is found in this setting in MS Evreux 96, (copied, as Wilmart believed, from the original at Bec) with the title, *Oratio seu potius Meditatio ad Deum et ad beatissimum confessorem Nicholaum*. The letter of 1092 asking the monks of Bec to send him the prayer to St Nicholas and other unfinished work is *Ep.* 147 (ii, 51), for which see below, pp. 186.

[26] For the collection sent to Countess Matilda, see Wilmart, 1932, pp. 162–72, and below, n. 27.

So far as Anselm was concerned, the Matildan collection completed the cycle of his *Prayers* and *Meditations*. It seems probable that the copy which he sent to Countess Matilda was embellished with splendid illuminations in the best Canterbury style. Unfortunately, the original manuscript has not survived, but we possess a copy which exhibits the whole collection in its final form.[27] He had come a long way since he had first begun to record his personal anguish and his first steps in recovery through prayer and meditation. By 1104, words that had first been written towards the end of his years of silence as expressions of his most intimate fears and hopes had finally emerged from the privacy in which they had originally been composed to become part of the common devotional property of the medieval world.

Thereafter the whole collection became very generally known throughout Europe. The last additions by Anselm, in their polished moderation and impersonality, gave a normality of spiritual experience to the collection, and the unauthorized additions of disciples and imitators carried the process of normalization several steps further. These additions began to be made within a few years of Anselm's death, and they hid for centuries the real nature of Anselm's passionate and personal devotion, and the close ties between these early compositions and his later theology. It is only now, when the distracting accumulation has been cleared away, that we can see the main line of his development running from his first letters of spiritual advice and his earliest *Prayers and Meditations* to his *Monologion* and *Proslogion*; and then, more impersonally and with a more comprehensive scope, to his *Cur Deus Homo*, and his final *Meditation on human Redemption*.

---

[27] The best copy of the collection sent to Countess Matilda is Admont Stiftsbibliothek, MS 289. For an account of the illustrations and their English background, see O. Pächt, 1956, 68–95. The most notable illuminations show Anselm distributing his prayers to his monks, and presenting them to Matilda, in the form of scrolls on which extracts or summaries are inscribed. This motif is found in several eleventh-century Canterbury manuscripts both before and after the Norman Conquest. For examples, see C. R. Dodwell, *The Canterbury School of Illumination, 1066–1200*, Cambridge, 1954, pp. 4–5, and Plates 2a and 2b, 3a and 3b, 12b. These similarities support Pächt's suggestion on artistic grounds that the manuscript at Admont is a copy of an illuminated original made by monks of Canterbury for presentation to Matilda.

CHAPTER 6

THE GREAT MEDITATIONS

I ANSELM'S FIRST PEAK

Until he became abbot in 1078, Anselm's life for nearly twenty years was one of monastic peace, disturbed only by the occasional enmities inseparable from the lives of men living in close proximity in a small community. His correspondence with friends at Canterbury and elsewhere, and the development of his *Prayers* and *Meditations* after their first turbulent phase, are witnesses to the peace which he had now achieved. The great Meditations on the nature of God, to which after much hesitation he gave the names *Monologion* and *Proslogion*, were the greatest products of this new peace. The only controversy was with the remarkable Gaunilo over the argument of the *Proslogion*, and it was conducted with such mutual regard and identity of purpose that it is hard to realize that a new philosophical issue had suddenly sprung into existence. Nothing could be more withdrawn from the storms and hostilities which, in politics, were rending the empire and papacy, and, in doctrine, were producing the violently opposed interpretations of the Eucharist, leading to the final condemnation of Berengar in 1079.

The peaceful record of Anselm's thoughts during this period was in some ways deceptive. Theology was not standing still, either in his own mind or in the outside world, and theological development would soon produce new clashes over a much wider field than the Eucharistic controversy. In the secular schools, a new system of theological inquiry was emerging, in which the task of smoothing away discords in the authoritative literature of the past had a primary role. Of course attempts to reconcile contradictions in earlier writers had been made at all times. But the masters of the schools made the methods for doing this their speciality; and they applied all the refinements of logical analysis to discover agreement in statements which at first sight seemed irreconcilable. But, though reconciliation was the aim, the result of increasing refinement was often to provoke fresh discord, which gave a sharper edge to all theological discussion.

These refinements and their consequent creation of opposing schools of thought, which are a marked feature of scholastic discussion in the early twelfth century, covered only a narrow field in the controversy between Lanfranc and Berengar. In the main, both contestants in that dispute had been content with a general congruity between their views and those of their authorities. But this contentment with a general congruity among authoritative texts could not long survive when clashes of opinion in the schools became more frequent, and when the areas of dispute became greatly enlarged. One of the great contributions of the new secular schools to intellectual inquiry was to make clashes of opinion on important subjects a normal part of the process of learning, in which conclusions were reached by systematically contrived confrontations.

This new method of teaching and reaching conclusions was ideally suited to the conditions of life in the secular schools, with their ever-shifting bodies of itinerant students and masters. It was a method which – reversing Anselm's order of priority – made sharpness of understanding rather than prolonged meditation a first requirement. The external school at Bec in Lanfranc's time to some extent reproduced the conditions of the secular schools, but it did not long survive his departure, and Anselm is unlikely to have regretted its disappearance. His world was both narrower and wider than Lanfranc's: narrower in being mainly concerned to enrich the monastic life of a stable community; wider in his freedom to meditate afresh on God, Sin, and Redemption, unburdened by the weight of contrasting authorities, and free from the disputes of the schools.

In this freedom, Anselm developed a method of his own, following the model of Augustine. Fundamentally, Anselm's was not a dialectical method, though he made full use of dialectic. There is never in his works a moment of poise between two opposites, with the final solution emerging from confrontation. He reached his conclusions in private, and used the literary device of debate, not to arrive at his conclusions, but to sharpen the formulation of his answers. Everywhere he aimed at precision of language, of argument, of definition: but only when prolonged meditation had already brought him to see the truth with instantaneous clarity.

Thereafter, his task as a teacher was gently and persistently to lead his pupil to accept the conclusion which he himself had already reached.

If ever Anselm had a moment of hesitation between two conflicting conclusions, we are not allowed to see it: in all his writings, he appears on the field already a victor, ready to explain, perhaps to demonstrate, but not to fight. He urged his pupils to speak their minds, to give their opinions on the conclusions which he put before them, to express their doubts, to draw their own conclusions – not indeed to learn from them, still less in order to modify his own conclusions, but to enable him to dissect their statements, clarify their points and correct their errors, and in this way to sharpen the presentation of his own argument. In Anselm's early works, the conclusion is implicit in his beginning, and the student contributes nothing to it. Consequently, none of the scholastic paraphernalia of *pro* and *contra* had any place in the elaboration of his conclusions. For him, the points about which the schools would argue had been settled before the argument began.

It may therefore, initially at least, seem strange that so much of his work was cast in the form of dialogue, which of all forms seems most to suggest the existence of opposing points of view. But the form is deceptive. When real enemies appeared – Roscelin in 1090, or the doctrine of the masters of Laon in 1094–5, or that of the Greeks in 1098 – he dropped the dialogue form.[1] He used dialogue only between friends, as Plato had used it, to draw out his meaning and to give liveliness to his argument. His dialogues did not recognize two rival possibilities embodied in the persons of two protagonists: they were a pedagogical device, not the symptom of a real division of opinion.

The dialogue was one of his favourite forms of composition. But, if my dating of the *De Grammatico* is correct, nearly two decades elapsed before he again used the dialogue form. Throughout the 1070s, besides letters, he wrote only *Prayers* and *Meditations*, and among the *Meditations* we must count his two extended inquiries into the nature of God, with which we are now concerned. The succession of dialogues during the next three decades provided further explanations of conclusions already reached, or of princi-

---

[1] It is true of course that his *Cur Deus Home*, in which he rejected the doctrine of the masters of Laon, is cast in dialogue form. But the rejected doctrine was not a matter for debate: the two disputants agreed at the start to reject it, and the main aim of the ensuing dialogue was to clarify the grounds of its rejection. See below, pp. 204–5.

ples already embodied, in his *Meditations*. But, whether in the form of *Meditation* or dialogue, the whole body of his writings for twenty years after 1070 developed from the introspective method of his *Prayers* and *Meditations*. No doubt, the logical structure and validity of the arguments put forward in the *Monologion* and *Proslogion* can be examined without regard to his method of reaching them. But to understand them in the context of his experience they must be viewed as they evolved from prayer and meditation. They had their origin in introspection, and their end in God:

Come now, little man, put aside your business for a while, take refuge for a little from your tumultuous thoughts; cast off your cares, and let your burdensome distractions wait. Take some leisure for God; rest awhile in Him. Enter into the chamber of your mind; put out everything except God and whatever helps you to seek Him; close the door and seek Him. Say now to God with all your heart: 'I seek thy face, O Lord, thy face do I seek.'[2]

But, however close their connection with his earlier *Prayers*, the treatises we are now to examine were intellectually much more ambitious than anything he had previously attempted. They place him at once in the front rank of theologians and philosophers, and despite all his deprecatory gestures, he knew this. The best evidence that he was aware of the originality of these works is the passage in which Eadmer describes them. Eadmer's words at this point have almost the authority of autobiography, for there can be no doubt Anselm was their source, and he probably read, and at first approved, what Eadmer had written. This is what Eadmer records:

He also wrote a little book which he called *Monologion* because in it he alone speaks and argues with himself. Here, putting aside all authority of Holy Scripture, he inquired and discovered by reason alone what God is; and he proved by invincible reasoning that God's nature is what true faith holds it to be, and moreover that it could not be other than it is. Then (after writing it) it came into his mind to try to prove by one single and short argument the things which are believed and preached about God – that he is eternal, unchangeable, omnipotent, omnipresent, incomprehensible, just, merciful, righteous, true, as well as Truth, Goodness, Justice and so on; and to show how all these qualities are united in him. And this, as he himself would say, gave him great trouble, partly because thinking about it took away his desire for food, drink

___

[2] *Prosl.*, c. 1. Note that the *method* is an expansion of Matthew vi, 6, *Intra in cubiculum tuum, et clauso ostio ora* etc. quoted above and in *Ep.* 16 (i, 14); the *aim* is laid down in Psalm xxvi, 8–9, *vultum tuum domine requiram*.

and sleep, and partly – and this was more grievous to him – because it disturbed the attention which he ought to have paid to Matins and to divine Office. When he was aware of this, and still could not entirely lay hold on what he sought, he supposed that this line of thought was a temptation of the devil, and he tried to banish it from his mind. But the more vehemently he tried to do this, the more these thoughts crowded in on him. Then suddenly one night during Matins, the grace of God shone on his heart, the whole matter became clear to his mind, and a great joy and jubilation filled his inmost being.[3]

This passage gives an account of the origin of two works: first, the *Monologion*; then the *Proslogion*, which came out of that moment of 'joy and jubilation' at Matins probably in 1077. It is especially important to notice the reason for his joy. He had already, in his *Monologion*, succeeded in showing that God necessarily had all those qualities that are ascribed to Him in Christian doctrine. But he had not shown that all of them are necessarily united in the being of God. To give a rough analogy, it was if in his *Monologion* he had shown that a machine did all the things that its inventor claimed, but he had not shown that it did them as a necessary consequence of its nature. Or, to put it another way, he had demonstrated the necessary existence of the properties of God, but not the necessary existence of the single Being in whom these properties cohered. This is what he aimed at doing in his *Proslogion*.

It is a simplification to say that the *Proslogion* aimed at proving the existence of God. What he sought to prove is that justice, goodness, and truth are necessarily united in a single Being, who by definition is God. And since justice, goodness, and truth exist, God cannot *not* exist. The joy of this conclusion came from its completeness and its finality: the finality of one who has swept the floor to find a coin which was lost, and has found it.

The two works, *Monologion* and *Proslogion*, both belong to the years between 1076 and 1078. They are closely related in subject-matter, also in method, for they are both meditations on God's being. But whereas the *Monologion* is concerned with the *qualities* of God and is closely dependent on Augustine's *De Trinitate*, the *Proslogion* is chiefly concerned with the *being* of God, and is only slightly dependent on Augustine.

There is also a notable difference in Anselm's intellectual posture in the two works. Although they both contain proofs which Anselm regards as wholly convincing, the *Monologion* is presented as a

[3] *VA* I, xix, pp. 29–30.

philosophical meditation based on Augustine, while the *Proslogion* is a meditation arising from prayer addressed to God.

The distinction is important. The *Monologion* was a highly original work in form, but in substance it had the authority of Augustine behind it. In it Anselm speaks with the confidence of a man with all the best cards in his hand, and a manual which instructs him how to play them. Hence in its opening words there is a youthful confidence, as if it were the easiest thing in the world to prove, even to those of mediocre intelligence, that those things which we believe about God are necessarily true.[4] But in the *Proslogion* he was on his own, and he stretched out to the furthest limits of his powers. At the end, he trembled with the awe of a new discovery. The *Proslogion* was his greatest achievement, but it could not have come into existence if the *Monologion* had not shown the way; and we too must approach them in this order.

II THE 'MONOLOGION'

i Talk among friends

The first words of the *Monologion* laid down a method of inquiry from which he never afterwards departed:

Some of my brethren have persistently asked me to give them an example of meditation, by writing down some thoughts on the divine essence and other related matters, which I have communicated to them in my regular *Colloquia*. They asked that nothing should be put forward on the authority of Scripture, and in this I have consulted their wishes, rather than my own capacity or the nature of the subject. They also asked that whatever conclusion was reached in the course of each investigation should be expressed in plain language with intelligible arguments and simple disputation, so that the necessary conclusions and clear truth of the matter would be clearly expressed. They also wished me not to leave any objections unanswered, however simple or even fatuous they might appear.[5]

These are three characteristics which are to be found in nearly all his later, as well as in these earliest works: an origin in talking – mostly Anselm's – and the questions arising therefrom; a method which excluded the quotation of authorities; and a determination to leave no objection unanswered.

---

[4] *Monol.*, c. 1: *Si quis . . . perplura, quae de deo sive de eius creatura necessarie credimus, aut non audiendo aut non credendo ignorat, puto quia ea ipsa ex magna parte, si vel mediocris ingenii est, potest ipse sibi saltem sola ratione persuadere.*   [5] *Monol.* Prol.

As to the first of these, nothing is more clear in the reports about Anselm than his need to develop his thoughts by talking. From the beginning of his recorded life till the end, he needed to talk to congenial listeners: Gundulf listened to him at Bec, Guibert of Nogent listened to him on his visits to Flay, Eadmer at Canterbury, and they all said the same thing – his talk was irresistible. Gundulf especially reported of their earliest days together at Bec that they had 'frequent talk, and much shedding of tears and mutual exhortation'; but 'Anselm spoke most while Gundulf wept'. Gundulf is also reported to have recalled a characteristic Anselmian remark: he complained that Gundulf 'sharpened his knife on Anselm's skin, but did not give him a chance to do likewise'.[6]

Everyone wanted him to talk, naturally and simply, leaving no difficulties unravelled. To Lanfranc, the whole theological method appeared misguided, freeing the subject from the authorities which were the proper guides both to the questions to be asked and the answers to be given. But the younger men were ready for free and natural debate: they laid down that nothing was to be taboo. It seems that, despite his disclaimer, the 'conditions' they laid down for the manner of argument were prompted at least as much by Anselm's own practice as by their desires. But in outlining this radical programme of inquiry, Anselm was not speaking as a searcher for new truths, but as a conservative, who reached old conclusions by new methods, encouraged by pupils whom he had himself inflamed with intellectual zest.

That the pupils were eager there is every reason to believe: they were not a literary fiction. In the course of time young men began to come to Bec for answers to their speculative difficulties: they all wanted old truths made intelligible. If we seek the earliest traces of his method, we may look back to the De Grammatico and to Anselm's early conversations reported by Gundulf during the years 1060 to 1063. But another fifteen years passed before Anselm ventured to write an independent work.

It was in 1076 or thereabouts that the first fruit of all this talk emerged. Anselm sent it to Lanfranc asking him, as if casually, to approve it or destroy it; and, if he approved it, to give it a name. The casualness was deceptive. Lanfranc did none of the things that Anselm desired: he did not approve it, he did not condemn it

---

[6] Thomson, 1977, p. 30. The Life of Gundulf quoted here was written by a contemporary monk of Rochester, who knew his subject.

outright, least of all did he suggest a name. Instead, he suggested changes which would have altered the whole nature of the work. Anselm did not follow these suggestions; nor did he destroy the work. He tried only to think of a name for the work, and this was not easy. At first he called it an 'Example of meditating about the substance of faith', *Exemplum meditandi de ratione fidei*, leaving it still anonymous. Then he called it a '*Monoloquium* on the substance of faith'. Finally he dropped the descriptive phrase, and – introducing a literary refinement after the fashion of the time – abandoned the hybrid *Monoloquium* in favour of the more elegant *Monologion*, and attached his own name to it.

It is one of the curiosities of the surviving evidence that though we know so little about the stages of its composition, the stages in finding a name for it are brilliantly illuminated, and the final decision about name and acknowledged authorship is pin-pointed in two surviving letters.[7] And so, with many hesitations, but also with a considerable degree of firmness, not to say obstinacy, this first treatise was launched into the world under his own name, and with a title that would not easily be forgotten.

2   An example of meditation

It was quite unlike any other contemporary treatise, and substan-tially unlike anything of any earlier period. The most striking characteristic which separated it from other contemporary writings was its entire lack of quotation of authorities. This went further than the omission of appeals to Biblical authority, which Anselm in his preface ascribed to the pressure of his pupils: at no point is there any reference to any earlier writer. Of course, beneath the surface, it was deeply impregnated both with the Bible and Augustine: but the reader had to find this out for himself. Obviously this was not an accident; it was a deliberately chosen method, which sets him apart from all his contemporaries. He must have known that his method was wholly different from that of the schools, in which the long process of organized accumulation, arrangement, and examination of sources had already begun. Anselm set his face against all this. He would not repeat other men's words or thoughts, unless he too had arrived at them in his own way.

---

[7] *Epp.* 100 (ii, 11), 109 (ii, 17), to Hugh, Archbishop of Lyons, the first in answer to Hugh's request for a copy of the work, the second altering the title. See below, p. 286.

In anyone else this total independence would have seemed provocative, and it is clear that this is what Lanfranc thought it was, or might be. But Lanfranc's criticism did not cause Anselm to budge an inch, and it is a tribute to his reputation that no one thought him dangerous. The only word of criticism came from Lanfranc, and, with every expression of respect, Anselm stood firm.

The examination of the philosophical cogency of this work and its successor must be left to philosophers. It is the concern of historians to examine their external form, the influences which helped to shape them, the materials, method of argument, the audience, and the future consequences of what is written.

With this programme in mind, we may begin with the title of the *Monologion*. At first, Anselm called it simply 'an example of meditating about the substance of faith', *De ratione fidei*. He soon dropped this phrase from the title of his work, but it is the best description of his whole theological method, and we may ask what it means.

I have discussed above the meaning of meditation in Anselm's system of thought, and it is only necessary to say here that, in his *Prayers* and *Meditations*, meditation was mainly an introspective activity with the aim of inspiring that contempt of self which is a necessary preliminary to an approach to God. Now, in his two major meditations he goes a step further. In these works, meditation turns from its purgative role to recognize in self-knowledge and in the mind's images of the external world the general essences in which all things have their being. In this process, the mind rises towards that contemplation of God, which can be approached but never achieved in this life. This upward movement, which would have been easy because unimpeded in the sinless state of Man, requires a long and painful discipline in Man's fallen state.

Different though they are in their aim and in the data on which they are based, the sin-disclosing introspection of the earlier meditations and the essence-detecting, God-directed, introspection of *Monologion* and *Proslogion* were the two sides of Anselm's scheme of meditation. Under the influence of Augustine, Anselm had made both these kinds of meditation his own: the first was the necessary preliminary to the second. But, whereas the first began with the recollection of past sins, the second began with the recall of the soul's intuitive knowledge of real essences, without which there can be no intellectual approach to God. If pressed, he could say as he did to Lanfranc, that it was all in Augustine, but he did not claim the authority of Augustine for his method, or for the way he used it. Augustine was the source; but the activity had to come from within, and it was self-authenticating, or it was nothing.

This raises two problems. The first concerns the relationship between meditation and reasoning; the second the relationship between the goal of meditation and the authoritative statements of the Church.

With regard to the first of these problems, a useful starting point may be found in the description of meditation given by Hugh of St Victor about half a century after the time when Anselm wrote his *Monologion*. These are Hugh's words:

Meditation is frequent and mature thought about the cause, origin, nature and usefulness of everything. It has its origin in careful reading, but it is bound by none of the rules or constraints of reading. It rejoices to run freely in an open space which offers free opportunity for contemplating the truth. It investigates and penetrates, now the causes, now the nature of things, until nothing is left doubtful or obscure. The *foundation* of doctrine, therefore, lies in reading; its *completion* in meditation.[8]

Hugh of St Victor wrote these words twenty years after Anselm's death, when they were a corrective to the already hardening rigidity of scholastic reasoning. That, no doubt, is why Hugh emphasized the freedom which meditation allowed. In this sense, Anselm's meditation also is free; but his method differs from Hugh's in two main ways:

First, Hugh of St Victor's meditation has its origin in the reading of an authoritative text – *lectio*. This is the method of the schools. But Anselm's meditation has its origin in the mind itself, in the concepts which arise from sense-impressions, and in those arising from self-knowledge.

Second, Anselm's meditation is more strictly controlled than Hugh's. Hugh delights 'in running freely in an open space'; Anselm follows the thread of an argument with the utmost rigour.

In the *Monologion*, which is the most rigorously planned of all his investigations, he often describes the process as an *indagatio*. This is a word scarcely used by Anselm outside this work. But it is fairly

---

[8] *Didascalicon*, iii, 10 (Buttimer, 1939, p. 59); and see the translation and notes in Taylor, 1961, pp. 214–15.

122

often found, for instance in Gregory the Great, to describe an unremitting investigation of a troublesome case. This precisely describes Anselm's meditation in the *Monologion*: he is conducting a rigorous inquiry which leaves no area unexplored; he is not sketching truths authenticated by authority; he is seeking conclusions which can stand on the argument alone.

This method raises the question of the relationship between the results of this introspective reasoning and the authoritative statements of the Christian faith. It might reasonably be thought that a thorough inquiry conducted according to the method of the *Monologion* must either make faith unnecessary, or provide some supplementary truths beyond the limits of the authoritative statements of the Faith. Were either of these consequences in Anselm's mind when he called the *Monologion* a meditation *de ratione fidei*? He never explained what he meant by this phrase, but he repeated it in his *Proslogion* and applied it also to his *Cur Deus Homo*. So we cannot be wrong in seeing it as his own brief description of his theological method, and the scope of inquiry indicated by this phrase requires investigation.

3 Faith and Reason

Anselm was only once forced, in his own defence, to give an explanation of his view of the relations between reason and faith. This was in about 1089, when Roscelin made serious imputations against his orthodoxy. No doubt in general Anselm hoped that his teaching would speak for itself, and he was reluctant to give explanations beyond what was strictly necessary; but on this occasion he was forced to speak, and he did so in these words:

Our faith is to be defended by reason against unbelievers, not against those who profess to rejoice in the name of Christians. From the latter, it may justly be demanded that they hold inviolate the pledges made for them in baptism . . . The Christian ought to progress through faith to understanding, and not through understanding to faith. Let him rejoice if he is able to attain understanding; if he cannot, let him revere what he cannot apprehend.[9]

This is an accurate statement of his position, but it needs some elaboration. In the first place, we may note that the question of an unbeliever who asks, 'How can I come to believe?' does not arise for Anselm. He had no experience of unbelief as Augustine had known

[9] *Ep.* 136 (ii, 41).

it; all his experience had been in a society of baptized Christians. In this society everyone had an obligation to believe, and if anyone asked 'How can I believe?' the only answer was, 'Do what your godparents have promised on your behalf; if the will is there, you can believe.' This would certainly have been Anselm's answer; but he would also have added that careful meditation on the content of faith by a competent inquirer will lead to reasons which are satisfying and true. The reasons will not go beyond the truths of faith; but the believer will come to understand more fully what the doctrinal statements of the Church mean. This understanding will add nothing to, and subtract nothing from, the adhesion of mind and will, to which the baptized person is irrevocably committed. But it will add a justifiable pleasure: a warmth of adhesion, one might say. And if we ask why this pleasure or warmth is both innocent and desirable, the answer is the same as that which justifies the pleasure of friendship: they are both premonitions of that fully developed humanity which the redeemed will enjoy in Heaven. But to this it must be added that neither friendship, as Anselm used the word, nor faith can be fully experienced without an intense discipline of life. This is the first condition for approaching an experience which can only fully be enjoyed in Heaven. The *Monologion* was intended as a guide for those willing to submit to this discipline.

Ostensibly, the *Monologion* was written for anyone who could understand the meaning of words and arguments. But, even for those mentally capable of making the effort to understand, a preliminary degree of 'spirituality', attainable only by self-discipline, was necessary for success: it was necessary to have subjected the flesh to the spirit to the extent of recognizing the real existence of those non-material substances which Aristotle called 'secondary', but which (as Anselm thought) had a higher degree of being than those which Aristotle called 'primary'. The recognition of this truth required a preliminary state of intellectual awareness – a casting off of the torpor of mind – for which Anselm had prayed in his earliest prayers. Until this first step had been taken, the serious business of meditation could not begin.

There are thus three stages in coming to know the truths displayed in the *Monologion*: first, an adhesion to the belief promised in baptism; second, a capacity for prolonged and careful thought; and third, a state of mental excitation following a renunciation of worldly desires. The first was required as a condition of life for all in the Christian society; the second was the requirement of the schools; third was the requirement of the monastic life.

Long before, in his *De Grammatico*, Anselm had insisted that understanding sentences meant understanding not simply the words, but the things and connections between them which the words implied. Similarly, he who aims at understanding the nature and works of God must be prepared to use reason in a way that permits appropriate thoughts to be entertained. This preparation is both mental and moral, and it is an essential preliminary for secure reasoning on these subjects because the image of God implanted in the human mind at the Creation has been deformed by sin, and can only be restored by repentance, prayer, and a purifying of the mind. For reasoning on these subjects, therefore, it is not enough to perform a plodding series of mechanical acts; it requires a kindling of the spirit, a throwing-off of the chains of the flesh, a rising above the world of material things, all of which are the fruits of a long process of purification. Hence it was not inappropriate that Anselm should use the same phrases of mental excitation in his philosophical discourses which he had used earlier in his Prayers, for it was only through prayer that he could reach the state at which reasoning on these subjects could be profitable.

These requirements, as we shall see, are most evident in the *Proslogion*, where prayer and philosophy are most intimately combined. But the *Proslogion* is an appendix to the earlier *Monologion* in which the data for philosophical inquiry have been displayed, and the necessary procedures for developing them brought into use. The data are the tenets of the Church. The procedures are the rules of grammar and logic. The combination of these data and procedures lead to the truth which is already known and guaranteed by the doctrine of the Church. So the conclusions of Reason and Faith are, and must be, identical. Yet both are necessary for anyone who wishes to make progress in this life towards understanding eternal truths only to be fully revealed hereafter.

4 Faith and understanding

What then is the meaning of 'understanding eternal truths'? It means that statements which are believed by faith are shown by reason to be coherent one with another, and therefore necessary for the system as a whole: what faith guarantees, reason clarifies. So, in setting out on his fundamental inquiries in both his *Monologion* and *Proslogion*, faith was the essential prerequisite; and at the beginning of the *Proslogion* he coined the phrase which better than any other describes the theological programme which had been his from the beginning: *Fides quaerens intellectum.*

Reason then may be seen as the appropriate activity for clarifying the contents of faith, just as arranging the contents of a house is the appropriate activity for turning a heap of *impedimenta* into furnished rooms. Equally, faith in the concepts of the mind is an expression of confidence in the operations of the mind. Hence, at the most primitive level, those who refuse to believe the reality of universals fail before they begin to think: they are the slaves of their corporeal images and refuse to use the apparatus of the mind to transcend them: they are like bats disputing with the eagle about the rays of the noonday sun.[10] The bats are the 'have-nots' disputing with the 'haves' about the reality of that which they do not possess. Similarly, those who doubt the real existence of universals do so because they lack, or have suppressed, the faculty necessary for ascending to the plane of rational truth, which is the plane of incorporeal essences and, therefore, of theological truth.

Indeed it is clear that, if the objects of reason are incorporeal essences of which the existence is first known through sense-impressions, some sort of act of faith is necessary before the processes of reason can begin at all. If anyone does not admit the existence of such essences, he lacks the power of understanding not only the truths of the Christian Church, but also the truth that sense-impressions have their origin in real essences. Inability to recognize the existence of general essences nullifies the operation of the faculty of reason in its most important inquiry. Anyone in this condition must keep silent, for he must either assert that the supreme essence does not exist – and this will land him in the fundamental error of asserting the non-existence of that which can be shown to be logically necessary – or he must assert that which he does not believe.

The argument of the *Monologion* had brought Anselm to this position. He did not think that reason had made faith unnecessary. Quite the contrary. In covering the same ground and holding the same conclusion, faith and reason each add something to the other.

[10] Anselm first used the image in the preliminary draft of his answer to Roscelin written in about 1090; see Schmitt, i, p. 284.

Faith adds the glory of self-abandonment to the statements of reason; reason adds the glory of systematic understanding to the statements of faith. Neither the nature nor the conclusions of faith are changed by reason, but the concepts of faith, in becoming clearer in the understanding, become more active in the soul, more systematically interrelated in the mind, more joyfully embraced. This is the whole aim of meditation: to lead the inquirer forward along the road towards the final beatitude of the immediate experience of the object of faith. Until this final beatitude is enjoyed, reason will continue to have a contribution to make to faith.

III   THE 'PROSLOGION'

I   *A supplement to the Monologion*

When Lanfranc failed either to approve or to give a name to the *Monologion*, Anselm's reaction shows that the author in him in some degree predominated over the monk. He neither altered nor destroyed the work.[11] Instead, he gave himself the task of consolidating the argument of the *Monologion* by formulating it in a way that was both simple and complete. The effort drove him almost to despair, but in the end he found what he was looking for. His new work not only displayed the same absence of all reference to authorities, which Lanfranc found offensive in the *Monologion*, but also, as a further potential cause of offence, it put forward an entirely new argument about the being of God.

When he wrote the *Monologion*, Anselm could at least claim that everything in it could be found in Augustine. He could not say this about the *Proslogion*. He wrote it under the impulse of an original insight, and it is on this work that his philosophical, as distinct from his theological, reputation will always chiefly rest. It was written in a state of philosophical excitement which (it is probably safe to say) had never before been experienced so intensely, and was probably never again to be repeated, in any Benedictine monastery. This excitement is chiefly to be associated with the first three chapters of the treatise in which the famous so-called ontological argument for the existence of God is set out. Although everything Anselm wrote is stamped with his personal quality, these chapters are in a special sense his own, for he knew that the proof they contain was his own discovery.

[11] For Anselm's reaction to Lanfranc's letter, see above, pp. 60, 119–20.

As I have already mentioned, this proof was not intended to be a proof of the *existence* of God, but a proof that the essences of Goodness, Truth, Justice, etc., which he had shown in the *Monologion* to be the necessary attributes of God, must cohere in a single Being, and that this Being, properly understood, cannot be thought of as non-existent. Underlying the 'proof', therefore, is the presupposition that whatever cannot be thought of as non-existent without internal contradiction, must exist. Whether true or false, this argument is the only general, non-technical philosophical argument discovered in the Middle Ages which has survived to excite the interest of philosophers who have no other interest in the period.

Nothing is more surprising than the way in which this proof has united, at least temporarily, men of the most diverse temperaments and outlooks – a tenuous link across vast seas of spiritual difference. Among recent philosophers none is further removed from Anselm in outlook, though perhaps not so far in qualities of mind, than Bertrand Russell, who has recorded

the precise moment, one day in 1894, as I was walking along Trinity Lane, when I saw in a flash (or thought I saw) that the ontological argument is valid. I had gone out to buy a tin of tobacco; on my way back, I suddenly threw it up in the air, and exclaimed as I caught it: 'Great Scott, the ontological argument is sound.'[12]

Leave out Trinity Lane, the tobacco, and the 'Great Scott' (evocations of an age more remote from us in spirit than the eleventh century) and substitute Bec, Matins, and *Deo Gratias*, and it was just so that the argument came to Anselm in 1078:

Behold, one night during Matins, the grace of God shone in his heart and the matter became clear to his understanding, filling his whole heart with immense joy and jubilation.[13]

We can well believe that the argument came, as Eadmer describes, in a flash of illumination after days or weeks of frustrated searchings and reluctant distraction in the midst of the daily Offices. Yet it did not come from nowhere. Its distant ancestor must be judged to be St Augustine, but only in a remote and ineffectual way. Its immediate parents are the grammar and logic of Anselm's day, but applied with an otherwise unknown subtlety.

[12] Bertrand Russell, 'My mental development', in P. A. Schilpp, *The Philosophy of Bertrand Russell*, Evanston and Chicago, 1944, p. 10.   [13] *VA* I, xix.

2   Meditating on the word 'God'

As we shall see, what Anselm needed for his argument was a definition of God on which he could build a logical structure of a peculiar kind. He did not find this in Augustine, whose language, despite its similarity to Anselm's in other respects, lacked the precision of the logician. He could find in Augustine:

God is not really known in the sound of these two syllables (*Deus*), but this sound, when it strikes the ears of all who know Latin, moves them to think of some most excellent and immortal nature . . . For when God is thought of, our thought tries to reach something than which nothing is better or more sublime.[14]

This statement of Augustine may well have have provided Anselm with a hint of what he needed: it directed attention to the *word* 'God', and it connected this *word* with a nature 'than which nothing is better or more sublime'. But, in itself, this was not sufficient for Anselm's purpose, for it is possible to imagine a Being than which nothing is better, without being required to believe that such a being exists.

Strangely enough, the formula which Anselm needed for his proof was lying in a most unlikely place. It occurs in Seneca's *Quaestiones Naturales*. There was a copy of this work at Bec in the twelfth century, and it may already have been there in Anselm's time. In it Seneca asks the question, 'What is God?' He answers: 'his magnitude is that than which **nothing greater can be thought**'.[15] Seneca used these words in a sense very different from Anselm: he was speaking of physical magnitude, and this was certainly not what Anselm intended. But the phrase he used was the very phrase that Anselm needed. Whether he found it in Seneca and gave it a new application, or coined it afresh, we shall probably never know. We only know that it provided him with the starting point he needed for his argument.

Armed with this definition, Anselm's argument ran thus: Take the Fool, who is described by the Psalmist as one who says in his heart 'there is no God', and ask him, 'What is God?' He must answer: God is 'something than which nothing greater can be

---

[14] Augustine, *De Doctrina Christiana* I, vii: *Deus. . .ita cogitatur ut aliquid quo nihil melius sit atque sublimius illa cogitatio conetur attingere.* (PL 34, col. 22)

[15] *L. Annaei Senecae Naturalium Quaestionum libri viii*, ed. Alfred Gercke, Stuttgart, 1907 (reprinted 1970), p. 5. (I am indebted to Schmitt, i, p. 102n. for the quotation) For the copy at Bec, see Becker 1885, p. 266.

thought'. If then he understands the meaning of words, even the Fool has this 'something than which nothing greater can be thought' in his mind (*in intellectu*). So 'that than which nothing greater can be thought' is in his mind. But then the Fool says that this existent in his mind does not exist outside his mind.

If the Fool is right, then 'that than which nothing greater can be thought' exists in his mind; but it does not exist outside his mind. But, in this case, it would be possible for him to think of another Being, also having the quality of being 'that than which nothing greater can be thought', which exists not only in his mind but also outside his mind. Such a Being would be 'greater' (in a manner to be explained presently) than a similar Being existing only in his mind. Therefore the Being existing only in his mind is not 'that than which nothing greater can be thought'. Consequently, this being is not God, for it does not satisfy the definition of 'God' as 'that than which nothing greater can be thought'. Only the Being who exists *outside* as well as *in* the mind satisfies this definition. Therefore God must exist, not only in the mind, but also outside the mind.

If this argument is sound, we can go a step farther. The argument has forced an intelligent listener to agree that God exists both in the mind and outside the mind. But many other things exist both in the mind and outside the mind: for instance, the pen I am holding exists both in my mind and outside my mind. It exists *in re* and *in intellectu*; but it does not *necessarily* exist *in re* because in exists *in mente*: there is no logical necessity for its existence, nor for the existence of any other external object that we can think of, except God. God is therefore unique, for of no other being but God can both these statements be made:

1 He exists both in the mind and outside the mind;
2 Since He exists in the mind, He *necessarily* exists outside the mind.

The Fool, who has denied that God exists in any sense of the word, is now reduced to a very pitiable state. He thought he understood the meaning of the word 'God', and of sentences like 'God does not exist'. But if the argument is valid, the predicate 'does not exist' contradicts the subject 'God', of whom non-existence cannot be predicated without contradiction. So the Fool has been using words without understanding the things to which they refer. This is a situation about which Anselm in his *De Grammatico* had warned the merest beginner in logic: it is not the use of the same *word* in the major and minor premises of a syllogism which binds the argument together, but the use of the same word with the same – in this case its only true – sense.[16] The Fool constructs sentences without understanding the meaning of the words he uses. Not only has he no understanding of things, but he does not even grasp the meaning of words in their basic grammatical and logical connections.

Reviewing now the steps in Anselm's argument, we can distinguish three stages of knowledge, of which the first two correspond to the activities of thought and understanding which constitute meditation, and the third to the state of contemplation which is the goal of meditation:

1 *Cogitatio*: the inquirer meditates on the meaning of words, the data of the senses, and the self-knowledge of the soul;
2 *Intellectus*: meditation has brought knowledge of the existence of general essences of which sense data and intuitions are the indicators;
3 *Sapientia*: the inquirer knows that there is a supremely existent Being and stands at the threshold of that contemplation which is the chief joy of eternity.

The Fool, being by definition *insipiens* denies that such a being exists. He lacks *sapientia*; but he has also been shown to lack understanding, *intellectus*, in failing to understand the substance denoted by the word 'God'. And, finally, he even lacks the power of *cogitatio* in failing to understand the word, 'God', which he had presumed to use. He must be silent like a beast.

Meanwhile, by meditation, the right-thinking person has risen from understanding the meaning of the word 'God', to understanding the thing ('a Being outside the mind'), for which the word ('God') stands: and, further, to understanding that God cannot not-exist. The inquirer has now touched the hem of the final stage of *sapientia*, which is the experience of God's being which lies beyond this earthly life. It has been necessary to express the well-known argument in this way in order to bring out its grammatical and logical foundations, and also its close association with Anselm's programme of meditation as the proper exercise of the religious mind. It is clear that though Anselm's argument is to be placed philosophically in the same class as that of Descartes, his presuppositions, his method of proceeding, and even his conclu-

---

[16] *De Grammatico* c. iv, Schmitt, i, pp. 148–9. Berengar had made a similar point with regard to the sentence *Hoc est corpus meum*: whatever *Hoc* was at the beginning of the sentence must still exist at its end for the sentence to have a meaning. See above, pp. 46–7.

sion is different from that of his successor. It is only in a careless way that Anselm's proof can be called a proof that God exists. In Anselm's view, the fact that it is possible to attach any meaning to the word 'God' is sufficient to show that God has *some* degree of existence. What the proof undertakes to show is, first, that God's existence is external to the mind; and second, that it is necessary for any coherent thought about the world; and third, that it is absolutely necessary in the sense that God cannot be thought of as non-existent without self-contradiction.

Whether the argument can be refuted is not for me to decide, but the fact that it has for so long continued to attract defenders as well as opponents suggests that the refutations are never quite complete, or that the argument – whether logically sound or not – has some hidden source of life. Instead of attempting either defence or refutation, we may simply ask what conditions would have to be satisfied for the argument, as Anselm states it, to be valid. In this way we may hope to discover something which, whether or not of any philosophical value, is of historical value for understanding the mind and presuppositions of Anselm.

3 Presuppositions of Anselm's argument

It is evident that there are three conditions which have to be satisfied before the argument, in the form in which Anselm develops it, can have any claim to validity.

1 When we say that something which exists in the mind *and* outside the mind is greater than something which exists only in the mind, we must be speaking of the same thing in both cases; otherwise the argument would simply collapse. Granted then their common identity, wherein does their difference in point of 'greatness' lie? It can only lie in a greater or lesser degree of 'being'. So, in this context, when we say that something is greater than something else, we must mean that it is 'greater' in having a greater degree of being; and that when it exists in the mind *and* in the external world, it has a greater degree of being than that which exists only in the mind. If this were not the case, then the criticism, which has been made from Anselm's day to the present, would clearly be justified: God *in intellectu et in re* would not be 'greater' than God existing only *in intellectu*, any more than £100 which exists both in mind and pocket is 'greater' than this amount only in

our thoughts. For the argument to work there must be degrees of being, such that 'being only in the mind' and 'being both in the mind and outside the mind' are related as lesser to greater.

2 That which exists in the mind and outside the mind, *and* cannot be thought of as not existing outside the mind, has a higher degree of being than that (for instance a tree) which exists outside the mind but can be thought of as not existing; and both these classes have a higher degree of being than that which exists only in the mind and not outside the mind.

Thus, there must be degrees of being, which, in descending order from God down to such creatures as centaurs, are:

1 Having existence in the mind and outside the mind, and being unthinkable as not having external existence. (God alone)
2 Having existence in the mind and outside the mind, but being thinkable as not existing outside the mind. (All created things)
3 Having existence in the mind, but no existence outside the mind. (Phantasms of all kinds)

The one thing which all these classes have in common is some degree of Being.

3 Finally, in the phrases 'God exists in the mind' and 'God exists outside the mind', the word 'God' must have the same meaning in both sentences. If this were not so, we should (despite the grammatical identity) be talking about different things in the two statements; and to arrange them in series, as if the second sentence referred to the same thing as the first, would be to fall into the simplest form of blunder arising from an identity of grammatical structure, against which Anselm had also warned his pupil in *De Grammatico*.

For Anselm, therefore, the three states of existence, 'in the mind', 'in the mind and outside the mind', 'in the mind and necessarily outside the mind' are strictly related as ascending powers in a scale of existence. But this progression is plausible only if there is a still higher degree of being, of which both the idea in a human mind and its existence outside the mind are lower powers; and this higher degree of being can only be in the mind of God himself. We know from the *Monologion* that this is in fact what Anselm thought: things have their highest degree of being in the mind of God; a lower degree of being in the natural world and in the mind of the observer; and the lowest degree of existence in the mind that imagines that which does not exist outside the mind.

This is of course a form of Platonism. There seems to be no proof that Anselm had read that part of Plato's *Timaeus* which alone was accessible in his day, and which was almost certainly in the library at Bec.[17] But, even if he had not read the *Timaeus*, he had imbibed the elements of Platonic thought from St Augustine. As we shall see in his dispute with Roscelin, he thought that any other kind of philosophy not only led to heresy, but was also indicative of hopeless intellectual blindness.

4 Principles of meditation

These considerations bring us back to the principles of Anselm's mode of meditation. The *Proslogion* is intended both as a meditation for the believer and a proof for the unbeliever. The proof for the unbeliever does not, as has sometimes been thought, depend upon the previous acceptance of certain theological truths, but it does depend on a previous acceptance of a concealed philosophical principle which commits the unbeliever to a view of knowledge which necessitates the existence of God. A proof which demands assent to its conclusion before it begins, in however subtle and roundabout a way, may be thought to be no proof at all unless the philosophical principle on which it is based is itself demonstrable or self-evident. As we later discover, Anselm thought that his principle was self-evident to any properly disciplined inquirer.

Whether Anselm was conscious of this condition attached to his argument when he wrote the *Proslogion* we cannot tell. He seems to have thought that the account of knowing which his argument presupposed was the only possible one; and since the unbeliever would not accept it and could produce no acceptable alternative, he thought he had effectively silenced him. This is a possible and – despite many difficulties of which Anselm could not have been aware – a consistent point of view. It is both internally consistent and consistent with the theological programme announced at the beginning of the argument: *Fides quaerens intellectum*. The argument returns, and must always return, to the faith from which it starts. But, as we have seen, the faith required for this argument is not the Christian faith, but a philosophical faith which Anselm

[17] See above, p. 57 n. 28, for the proof that the *Timaeus* with the commentary by Calcidius was well known to Lanfranc.

seems to have thought an essential pre-requisite for any coherent system of thought, and certainly a necessary requirement for anyone who would speak about God.

To most people all these preliminary conditions will appear unacceptable. In the common view, horses exist and unicorns do not exist; and it does not seem an adequate description of the difference between the existence of the one and the non-existence of the other to allege that both exist, but one more than the other.

Anselm's position on this point differed from that of a growing number of his contemporaries. Consequently, his argument was not destined to command any wide body of assent for a long time to come. It was not until the thirteenth century that his argument engaged the serious attention of theologians; and even then, despite the respect with which it was treated, the weight of opinion was against its validity.

Even among Anselm's immediate friends and disciples no one except Eadmer so much as mentions the argument. Of the others, Gilbert Crispin repeats the definition on which the argument is based, but he did not build upon it. We know that Lanfranc disapproved of the *Monologion*; we do not know what he thought of the *Proslogion*, but it is hard to think that – if he ever read it – he approved. In the immediate future, the peculiar mixture of linguistic analysis and Augustinian philosophy on which the argument as Anselm stated it was based, was replaced by newer methods, and by a different conception of the purpose and method of theological argument.

Yet, if Anselm's argument did not meet with acceptance, the two treatises *Monologion* and *Proslogion* made his name known far and wide. In 1085 he could no longer have spoken of himself as he did ten years earlier as a man unknown to the world. Within a year or two of their composition the two works were known not only in Normandy and in Canterbury, but at Poitiers, Tours, and Lyons, probably also in Rome.

Of all the arguments about the being of God, Anselm's is the most refined, and the least capable of a finally satisfactory statement or refutation. It draws its strength from an ambiguity, which appears to be an ambiguity in language, but is more deeply an ambiguity in human experience. If God exists, there must be a level of experience at which it is impossible to think of God as not existing. But at what level can this impossibility be made to appear? Must the demonstration await the experience of the Beatific Vision?

Or can it, at the very opposite extreme, be made out at the level of linguistic-logical analysis? The latter is what Anselm claimed for it.

Whether valid or not, the first three chapters of the *Proslogion* were the first piece of writing in which this problem was raised, and a solution proposed which will probably never be finally buried. Perhaps Descartes put it better, because more simply and with fewer philosophical presuppositions. He had the advantage which Anselm lacked of inheriting, if only to reject, a long scholastic philosophical tradition. The Augustinian and grammatical background of Anselm's thought, which made it possible for him to formulate the argument, also burdened it with limitations. But these pages of Anselm must be placed among the most deeply interesting pieces of reasoning of general interest ever written.

The early chapters of the *Proslogion* in which the argument was first expressed will never be read without excitement, nor thought about without appearing, however momentarily, to be persuasive. For the most extraordinary thing about the argument is that it loses nothing of its power, its freshness, or even in a curious way its persuasiveness, by being refuted. Even if the argument is valid, it is doubtful whether it would ever persuade an unbeliever to worship God. But in its subtlety, and in a certain ethereal quality which antagonizes men of robust common sense, it perfectly reflects the quality and mystery of Anselm's mind and personality.

The *Monologion* and *Proslogion* were the product of two remarkable years in Anselm's life, 1076–78, his last years as prior of Bec. In brilliance of philosophical originality he never rose to these heights again. For the next fifteen years, before he became archbishop of Canterbury, he was occupied in monastic administration and in the composition of four works which display his talent and originality, but could not in themselves have formed the basis of his reputation, as the *Monologion* and *Proslogion* standing by themselves could have done. During these years his reputation in the world slowly grew, and the number of his pupils was increased, largely by men who had become monks at Bec mainly because of his influence and presence. At the same time, his monastic peace was disturbed by necessary journeys to courts and synods, and tours of inspection of his lands in England. In the midst of these distractions, it is not surprising that Anselm wrote nothing which reached the level of these two works.

The years which followed the *Proslogion* brought also an enlargement of his experience and range of thought which prepared the way to his second peak twenty years later. But, before turning to this period of enlargement, there is another element in Anselm's experience during the 1070s which requires examination. His circle of friends was essential for the development of his theology. But friendship had a larger place in his life than this: it had a central role in holding together the whole body of believers in this world in preparation for their union with God in heaven. This is a subject which requires elucidation before going further.

CHAPTER 7

THE NATURE AND IMPORTANCE OF FRIENDSHIP

I ANSELM'S LETTERS OF FRIENDSHIP

Anselm's surviving letters contain the best evidence we have for several sides of his mind and personality. But though the same mind and personality run through them all, those which he wrote as prior and abbot of Bec during the years from 1070 to 1093 need to be somewhat sharply distinguished from the later letters written when he was archbishop. One reason for this is that many of the later letters are naturally concerned with matters of public policy, and they will have to be discussed in connection with his aims as archbishop. But there is also a change after 1093 even in those letters which, like most of the earlier ones, are principally concerned with advice and exhortation on monastic life. In general, they are more sober in expression. No doubt, age and increased responsibility largely account for the change; but there were also misunderstandings and disappointments which brought new constraints. These changes of subject matter and personal relationships will concern us later. Here we are concerned chiefly with the pre-1093 letters.

A main aim of these letters was to expound a most austere view of man's sinful state and the narrow path to salvation. But in association with this theme there is another which eclipses all others in vividness of expression. This is the theme of friendship. Anselm's expressions of friendship, and the experience on which these expressions were based, are so different from those of any contemporary writer, and they are expressed in terms which are so open to misunderstanding, that they require careful examination.

Before embarking on this examination, it will first be convenient to describe the letters from which we derive our knowledge of his experience. Before 1070, not a single letter of Anselm's has survived; but for the period between this date and his death in 1109, we have nearly four hundred.[1] Of these, about a hundred and forty were written in the years from 1070 to 1093, while he was at Bec. It was in these that he expressed most fully and – in a sense of the word which will require explanation – passionately, the nature of the friendships which were a central experience in his religious life. The proportion of his later letters devoted to this subject is much smaller; but even from this later period, it would be easy to make a collection of about thirty letters in which his ideal of friendship is reiterated, in a more restrained way than in those of his earlier years, but with the same underlying doctrine of friendship as an aid to, and in a certain sense a culmination of, the religious life. Even when the letters show a falling off in intensity of expression, there was no period in Anselm's religious life when friendship was merely a personal and, so to speak, optional occupation: it was a central experience, and it had a profound and eternal importance.

We shall not understand the meaning and originality of Anselm's view of friendship unless we first understand the tradition in which he and his contemporaries lived, and of which his experience was a development. Nor shall we understand the language in which he expressed his friendship, unless we make a clear distinction between the experience which he describes, and that described in similar words in the romantic literature of the twelfth and later centuries. As with every part of Anselm's intellectual and emotional system, the first step is to recognize the common ground which he shared with his contemporaries, and the extent to which he transformed it. Before examining his own writings, therefore, it is necessary to say something about the tradition of friendship which he inherited.

II THE TRADITIONAL PATTERN OF FRIENDSHIP

Like every other serious monastic student, Anselm would have read the *Collationes* of Cassian, and he would have imbibed from them a theory of friendship which broadly represented that of the ancient world.[2] According to this theory, there are three kinds of friendship. The first is based on the natural association of brothers, parents and children, husbands and wives; the second, on the relationship of groups with a common purpose, such as merchants, soldiers, or thieves, or any group which exists for an end which

---

[1] For further details, see below, pp. 248–53.
[2] Cassian, *Collationes*, xvi, *De Amicitia*, ed. Petschenig, *CSEL*, xiii, 1886, pp. 437–62.

requires the co-operation of others. The third is based on a union of souls in pursuit of a single noble and rational aim, in which the emphasis is not on practical success but on the sharing of a common ideal.

If we translate this ideal into terms appropriate to the life of religion, we can see that all these three forms of friendship are as necessary in the monastic life as in the world. First, there was the natural friendship of the members of the monastic community with their families in the surrounding countryside, whose gifts and child oblates maintained the monastery. Second, there was the functional friendship within the monastic community, which was necessary for the realization of its learned and liturgical aims. And third, there were personal friendships among individuals in the community, which were a stimulus to greater exertions in the spiritual life of study, prayer and meditation. All monks needed these three forms of friendship for carrying out their professed vows. But it is probably true to say that the third and most private form of friendship was not common, or even desirable, in the elaborately organized monastic communities of the eleventh century. Certainly it was not given a high place in monastic literature, and for good reason: the formation of intimate groups within the community would have broken the solidarity of the group in its intricate daily routine.

Yet it was precisely with this last and most intimate form of friendship that Anselm's letters were chiefly concerned. To say the very least, he gave intimate friendship a new emphasis in the corporate religious life. Also the manner in which he expressed this intimacy was strikingly original, and open to misunderstanding. Thus, although in principle the idea of intimate friendships was not new, the centrality which he gave them, and the fervour of his expressions in describing them, are new and need careful examination.

We have only to compare some contemporary expressions of friendship with Anselm's to recognize the difference. Lanfranc, for instance, could write to his 'dearest brother and friend' Thomas, archbishop of York, that

distance diminishes the mutual love only of those whose love is based on worldly gain or bodily pleasures. But those who are joined in a sincere and Christian love suffer no division through bodily absence or local separation.[3]

---

[3] Gibson, 1979, Letter 23. Dr Gibson draws attention to Lanfranc's probable source, Augustine, *Ep.* 147 (*CSEL*, xliv, 1904, pp. 317–18).

This is one of the platitudes of ancient friendship, and we, knowing the coolness and conflict between the two men, may think even this language exaggerated. But, though Lanfranc certainly had no passionate attachment to his fellow archbishop, there is no reason to think him insincere. He knew very well that they were both engaged in a great common task which required their collaboration, and he used words appropriate, not to his sentiments, but to their common purpose. Above all, friendship meant working together for a common end despite differences of temperament and faults of character.

In this same tradition, Lanfranc could go on to say with equal sincerity: 'those who are joined together in love are never separated, though one is in the east and the other in the west'. This also was one of the commonplaces of traditional friendship. Lanfranc certainly did not long for the presence of Archbishop Thomas, but he believed that their union in a common task transcended all local or personal differences. In the tradition in which Lanfranc wrote, friendship had nothing to do with sentiment, or even with the union of souls. The common purpose was everything, whatever the heart might say, or wherever the two persons might be.

A common purpose was also an essential foundation for Anselm's friendships. But in his sentiments, and in the terms in which he expressed them, he added a new intensity of emotion and personal communion which needs to be examined to discover whether his innovations are only decorative, or are symptomatic of a restructuring of the whole experience. This is the fundamental question we must ask.

But, before investigating these expressions, it will be useful to consider briefly some comparable novelties of expression which came to have a dominant role in European literature during the century after Anselm's death. In this later literature, some of the expressions which Anselm freely used are associated with an ideal of romantic love, and they are sufficiently similar to Anselm's expressions to create a *prima facie* impression that they belong to the same line of development.

III   THE NEW ROMANTIC IDEAL

We must begin with one characteristic of traditional friendship: it was between men only, and there were both practical and theoretical grounds for this. The practical ground was that nearly all important corporate activities, whether military or monastic, or more broadly ecclesiastical, were the preserve of men. In addition to this practical consideration, there was the theoretical principle, expressed by women as well as men, that men alone had, or were thought to have, the strength of mind and will necessary for great enterprises which friendships existed primarily to promote.

Into this tradition of male friendship, the newly idealized vision of romantic love between men and women began to find ever more elaborate and passionate forms of expression about a generation after Anselm's death. This is not the place to discuss the reasons for the astonishing success of this new ideal, to which a long literary tradition since the twelfth century has given a status in European literature above all other human relationships. It must suffice to say that it brought into the European tradition a concept of union between men and women which went beyond reason, beyond prudence, beyond all the ordinary goods of this world, and totally captivated the spirits of those whom it possessed.

Whereas traditional friendships had been valued precisely because they promoted corporate and rational activities, and could be expressed without, so to speak, shrieking, the shriek was the hall-mark of the romantic friendships of later twelfth-century literature. And with good reason, for it expressed pain in a simple and intense desire to possess the person of the beloved. In this new emotion there was no place for the corporate purpose of friendship. Rather, there was a jealous hostility or secrecy towards those outside the magic bonds of love. In this change of emphasis, the old rational aim of friendship was replaced by the pursuit of a personal passion within the soul of the lover, inexplicable, irrational, or at least beyond reason. The experience could only be described as one of being possessed by a spirit, perhaps demonic, perhaps divine, but certainly beyond rational calculation. The aim was not the achievement of any common purpose, but the achievement of a state of union which was itself felicity – an end in itself. Associated with this characteristic, there was an emphasis on joy – not duty; on mercy – not justice; on passion against reason. There was no question of fulfilling a function in social life; the only aim was to rise above the world of sense, and even of morals; to break through the bounds of reason.

Now there are some features in this romantic ideal which are also found in Anselm. His words have an emotive violence similar to that of the language of romance, and foreign to the language of traditional friendship. Although his friendships are still based on a common purpose, they also demand the pursuit of an ideal beyond this world: a passionate pursuit, one may say, of the love of God, which breaks through the ordinary bounds of reason and prudent behaviour, and which ultimately can come only to individuals who have abandoned everything for this final felicity.

It would not, therefore, be correct to say that Anselm was simply expressing the old ideal of friendship in more ardent terms. No doubt, on this subject, as on every other, Anselm remains conservative in intention, yet innovative, not only in language, but also in aim and conception. He introduced into the sober tradition of friendship a note of ecstasy, which is characteristic of romantic love. But his aim was not that of romance – the possession of a person: his aim was the fulfilment of a purpose. So here we seem to come back to the ancient ideal of friendship as an aid to the attainment of a practical ideal. But again there is a difference: Anselm's goal in friendship was not of this world even in its most exalted activities: it was nothing less than the kingdom of Heaven – the ultimate goal of all rational beings. So here, as everywhere, he stands uneasily between two worlds: the old world of rational friendship, and the new world of romance; between this world and the kingdom of Heaven; between tradition and innovation.

With these prefatory notes, we may turn to examine Anselm's words and ask what they meant.

IV   THE ANSELMIAN EXPERIENCE

Ecstasy, or at least extravagance, is the first symptom of Anselm's innovation. He throws to the winds the *gravitas* of earlier writers, and flings himself into the pursuit of something more vivid and all-consuming. He avoids the risk of the cold and lifeless urbanity which had characterized Lanfranc's expressions of friendship, by rushing to the opposite extreme of apparently boundless emotion. It is difficult to give his words a sense which is at once plausible and sensible.

To illustrate the problem, we may begin by extracting from his letters a few passages which most conspicuously challenge the classical ideal of friendship and most closely approach the new language of romance. They cover at least twenty-five years, from about 1071 to 1087, and the length of time is important. Whatever else they may be, they are not expressions of youthful ardour; they are carefully chosen words, in which the same ideas recur over a period of at least twenty-five years. For convenience of reference, I shall number my examples:

1 The first passage is taken from a letter written to Gundulf, who had become a monk at Bec at about the same time as Anselm. As I have already mentioned, he was about ten years older than Anselm and already a man of experience in the world before he became a monk. After three or four years at Bec, Lanfranc selected him as one of the chosen band whom he took with him to Caen in 1063; then, in 1070, he took him to Canterbury, and in 1077 he made him bishop of Rochester. So, in writing to Gundulf on several occasions between 1070 and 1087, Anselm was neither young himself, nor writing to a youth. During the whole of this period, Gundulf was a man of wide practical experience, one of Lanfranc's most trusted lieutenants. This is what Anselm wrote to him in one of his earliest letters:

When I sit down to write to you, oh soul most dear to my soul, when I sit down to write to you, I am uncertain how best to begin what I have to say. Everything I feel about you is sweet and pleasant to my heart; whatever I desire for you is the best that my mind can conceive. For such as I have seen you to be, I have loved, as you well know; and such as I now hear you to be, I desire, as God well knows. And so, wherever you go, my love follows you; and wherever I may be, my desire embraces you. Why then do you entreat me through your messengers, exhort me in your letters, and constrain me by your gifts, to *remember* you? 'If I do not remember thee, if I prefer not Gundulf among my chief friends, let my tongue cleave to the roof of my mouth.' For how should I forget thee? How could he, who is impressed on my heart like a seal on wax, be removed from my memory?[4]

2 The messenger who carried this letter to Gundulf to Canterbury also carried a letter to another monk, Henry, a man of very different stamp, but also a man of experience in the world who had been taken to Canterbury by Lanfranc. He was a man of more secular interests than either Anselm or Gundulf, not (for reasons which will shortly appear) a natural disciple of Anselm. Nevertheless, Anselm's letter to him uses similar language:

[4] *Ep.* 4 (i, 4). The words in inverted commas are borrowed with alterations from Psalm cxxxvi, 6, in the Vulgate: *Adhaereat lingua mea faucibus meis si non meminero tui; si non proposuero Jerusalem in principio laetitiae meae.* These Biblical echoes, which are so numerous everywhere in Anselm, should be remembered in interpreting these passages.

Most beloved . . . since I do not doubt that we both love the other equally, I am sure that each of us equally desires the other, for those whose minds are fused together in the fire of love, suffer equally if their bodies are separated by the place of their daily occupations . . .

Anselm continues in this strain for some time, and then refers to his letter to Gundulf quoted above:

In the letter I have written to Gundulf, you may substitute your name for his and take it as written also to you. Whatever love I have expressed for him and whatever I have asked of him, take equally to yourself – especially in praying for the soul of my most dear Osbern who has died; and again let me say that everything I have written to Gundulf applies equally to you.[5]

3 Slightly later, he wrote again to Gundulf:

Again and again, that common consciousness which I share with my other self [i.e. with Gundulf] urges me to send letters flying one after the other across the sea testifying to the state of my friendship. But what could my letters teach you that you do not already know? Enter into the chamber of your heart and consider the impression of your own love which you find there; from it you will recognize the love of your true friend.[6]

4 At about the same time, he writes to the abbot of a monastery which had among its tenants the widowed mother of Anselm's dead friend Osbern:

The immensity of mutual love has so fused together into one myself and the dead son of this poor widow, that I wish his mother to take me as her own son. Therefore, as his other self, I am not ashamed to beg for her as for my own mother.[7]

5 We may now skip several similar effusions and go on about ten years. Anselm is writing to Gilbert Crispin, one of his earliest pupils at Bec, who had left Bec at Lanfranc's behest to become abbot of Westminster:

If I were to describe the passion of our mutual love, I fear I should seem to those who do not know the truth to exaggerate. So I must subtract some part of the truth. But you know how great is the affection that we have experienced – eye to eye, kiss for kiss, embrace for embrace. I experience it all the more now when you, in whom I have had so much pleasure, are irretrievably separated from me. He who has abundance does not know what it is to want; he who

---

[5] *Ep.* 5 (i, 5).
[6] *Ep.* 16 (i, 14); and compare this expression with the first stage of meditation in *Monologion*, c. 49; *Proslogion*, c. 1.   [7] *Ep.* 11 (i, 9).

abounds in delicacies cannot imagine deprivation; likewise, those who enjoy friendship cannot feel the lassitude of the deserted soul. Therefore, since that which has been between us cannot sufficiently be described, and I am speaking to one who knows, I shall say no more, but let us recall our not-forgotten love when we were together eye to eye, exchanging kiss for kiss, embrace for embrace.[8]

Here then we have representative passages from letters written over a period of some fifteen years to men of differing talents and types, some young, some middle aged, some priors, abbots, or bishops, some whom he has never seen; but all of them monks or men whom he hopes will soon become monks. To all of them he writes words that are (to say the least) very different from those of Lanfranc, or of any other exponent of friendship as traditionally understood. It is hard to read them without embarrassment.

What are we to make of them? The sentiments, the kisses and embraces, the passionate sense of loss at separation, his desire for the presence of his friends; the immense joy at meeting; the need for a physical expression as well as a physical presence; all suggest a world of emotional intensity nearer to that of late twelfth-century romantic love than to traditional monastic friendship. If we consider only the sentiments and the words used in expressing them, we would have to say that the whole experience belongs to the ecstasy of romantic love, rather than to the world of rational associations for a common purpose.

Yet Anselm himself was wholly unconscious of any problem. He looked on these letters as important sources of monastic instruction for a wider audience, and he freely urged others than those to whom they had been written to read them. He himself seems to have started collecting them for a wider audience in the years shortly before he became archbishop of Canterbury, but whether from lack of time or some other cause, he never completed his task.[9] Nevertheless, it is clear that he did not look on even his most intimate expressions of friendship as private communications. He expected them to be taken, not so much as expressions of private emotion (though they were certainly also that), as demands for greater severity in religious dedication.

The contrast between the softness of the words and the sternness of their doctrine is so great that it demands an explanation if we are to understand Anselm's mind, and the first step towards an explanation is to put the passages which I have quoted into their

***

[8] *Ep.* 130 (ii, 26).   [9] See below, pp. 189n., 399, 461–4.

context. First, the softest words of friendship are associated with the harshest requirements of obedience and self-abnegation in a complete dedication to the monastic life. Naturally, this life was governed by a Rule; but for Anselm's friends something more than a corporate commitment was required – something approaching that intense search for God which he outlined as the programme of his *Proslogion*: 'Enter into the chamber of your mind; exclude everything except God . . . close the door and seek Him.' Progress in friendship followed a similar programme: 'Enter into the chamber of your heart, consider the nature of your true love, and you will recognize the true love of your friend.' This was his message to Gundulf, the closest of his friends, with whom he had taken his first steps in the search for God nearly twenty years earlier.[10]

Does this mean that the letters which glow with such unexpected passion can be appropriated by any reader who is in, or seeks, a similar state of devotion? The answer to this question is 'Yes'. It is evident both from the publicity which Anselm sought for these letters, and from the diversity of persons to whom he wrote them, and whom he asked to consider themselves equally as the recipients of his most ardent expressions of love, that these letters were not intended to convey private emotional attachments, still less forbidden yearnings. They were public statements about the rewards of the life dedicated to God. The fusion of souls, the shared knowledge which needs no further explanation, the symbols of an everlasting union which will be consummated in Heaven: all these are symptoms of the other-worldly context in which alone Anselmian friendship existed. Total dedication to God, which for Anselm meant unalterable dedication to the monastic life, was the one requirement for complete acceptance in the community of his friends: given this, it would seem that he could use the same expressions to anyone.

From this it followed that all his warmest expressions of friendship were reserved for those who either were sharers in his religious life or were about (as he hoped) to share it. If there is romance in these letters, it is the romance of a monastic *Pilgrim's Progress*. Nevertheless, a problem remains which has exercised recent scholars, and requires an answer: whatever else they may be, are these letters also expressions of homosexual love?

[10] *Proslogion*, c. 1; *Ep.* 16 (i, 14).

147

V   THE QUESTION OF HOMOSEXUALITY

A convenient starting point for answering this question is the book by John Boswell on medieval homosexuality.[11] The author has collected a mass of material with some important discussion, and (I must add) with misconceptions which vitiate many of his conclusions. But what he has collected, including some of the passages quoted above, deserves close attention.

To begin with his misconceptions. Boswell invariably speaks of homosexuality as a well-recognized physiological or psychological state, which finds its normal expression in a wide range of 'homosexual activities', extending indiscriminately, so far as I can judge, from kissing to sodomy; and he deals with the subject as if an attitude at least similar to this existed in the eleventh century. For example, he speaks of the period of Anselm's life as a time when 'homosexual acts were demoted from the position of unique enormity to which a few influential early fathers had promoted them and joined the ranks of common failings with which almost anyone could empathize'. Boswell then goes on to represent Anselm as being, in some measure at least, a representative of this movement, and as having 'prevented the promulgation of the first anti-gay legislation in England' – an intention which is about as far removed from Anselm's mind as the phrase which Boswell uses to describe it.[12]

The fact is, as will appear when this legislation is dealt with below, Anselm was an innovator in proposing detailed action against sodomy. Earlier prohibitions, which (despite Boswell's opinion) show no sign of falling off in the eleventh century, belong to the ancient tradition of the Penitentials, which laid down severe penances for every kind of sexual act except intercourse between married persons for the strict purpose of procreation, but provided no procedure for the enforcement of these penalties. Anselm's legislation, by contrast, was carefully framed to bring a limited range of common homosexual practices to the notice of parishioners in every parochial church with penalties attached. The only reason for Anselm's delay in promulgating this legislation was his

---

[11] John Boswell, *Christianity, Social Tolerance and Homosexuality: Gay People in Western Europe from the Beginning of the Christian Era to the Fourteenth Century*, Chicago, 1980.   [12] For these two passages, see Boswell, pp. 204, 218.

anxiety to get the support of his fellow bishops, who had well-justified doubts about the practicability of his far-reaching proposals on this and other matters.

Anselm's careful preparation of his legislation will be dealt with when we consider his policy as archbishop. What we are here concerned with is the meaning to be attached to the language which he used in writing the letters quoted above and several similar letters during the years before 1093. We may begin with the hugs and kisses, and ask: what have these to do with spiritual ends? Are they not obviously symptoms of something other than joy in common religious devotions? Are they not expressions of homosexual love?

In answering this last question, there are two preliminary remarks to be made. First, no one knew anything about, or had any interest in, innate homosexual tendencies: in so far as they were known to exist, they were seen simply as symptoms of the general sinfulness of mankind, which led to every kind of sin – lying, stealing, bearing false witness, adultery and all the other violations of the Ten Commandments. In dealing with these matters, legislators were concerned only with practical actions arising from these evil intentions: preachers and pastors were concerned with the intentions which produced these forbidden acts. With regard to intentions, the only good ones were those which aimed at fulfilling the aims for which mankind had been created, using the means that God had provided for these purposes.[13] All actions which ministered to these good purposes were themselves good unless contrary to the laws of God, nature, or authorized legislators, such as popes, Councils, or kings.

So far as sexual sins were concerned, the purpose of the penitential literature of the early Middle Ages had been to list all the forms of forbidden activity with suitable penances attached. Sodomy, as Boswell remarked, was only one among a large number of forbidden actions. Like adultery and every other grave sin, it was very common, but this does not imply tolerance, as Boswell suggests, still less a growing legislative tolerance. The multiplicity of sexual sins simply reflected the extent of human depravity, and the only relevant generalization which emerges from the penitential

---

[13] On this, see Anselm *Ep.* 414 (iii, 133), and the separately circulating section of this letter in *Memorials*, pp. 269–70, beg. *Omnis actio laudabilis sive reprehensibilis ex voluntate habet laudem vel reprehensionem. Ex voluntate namque est radix et principium omnium actionum quae sunt in nostra potestate. . .*

codes down to the eleventh century is that sodomy was treated on about the same level as copulation with animals.[14]

In short, the only commonly recognized form of homosexuality in the eleventh century was sodomy, and this was roughly equated with another form of unnatural sex, copulation with animals. As for Anselm's attitude, as archbishop he was notable for the severity of his condemnation of this sin and of any behaviour, such as long hair and effeminate clothes, which might encourage it.

This brings us back to the kisses and embraces and expressions of a very warm, perhaps 'passionate' desire for the company of beloved friends expressed in his letters. It is clear that Anselm regarded these expressions of love as having nothing in common with sodomy, or with the habits of dress such as long hair and effeminate clothes which were an inducement to sodomy. It is perhaps somewhat strange that he should not have thought that kisses came into a similar category as long hair or effeminate clothing, and I shall deal with this question in greater detail presently. Meanwhile, it must suffice to say that he found kisses as an expression of love between individuals within a religious community, and in pursuit of religious ends, entirely acceptable: he saw them as contributing to the spiritual end for which the monastic life existed.

As a preliminary step in understanding this, it may be remarked that, in all physical actions which have a spiritual end, there is a tension between the spiritual end and the earthly means, in the sense that the earthly means may promote desires inimical to their spiritual end. Even in the daily monastic Offices, for example, there

---

[14] As an illustration of a pre-Anselmian code of penances, see the section *De adulteriis et fornicationibus* in the fairly widely distributed *Libri duo de synodalibus causis et disciplina ecclesiatica* of Regino of Prüm, ed. F. G. A. Wasserschleben, Leipzig, 1840, pp. 251–317: on sodomy, see c. 255 (p. 313) *De sodomitis: Qui fornicatus fuerit sicut sodomitae, quidam iudicaverunt decem annos (poenitentiae), quidam septem; alii unus; pueri centum dies. Item: alii iudicaverunt, si consuetudine est, laicus annos quinque; clericus septem; subdiaconus et monachus, octo; diaconus decem; presbyter duodecim; episcopus quattuordecim poeniteat.* With this, compare the preceding chapter, *De quadrupedum fornicatione: Qui cum pecude peccat, quidam iudicant annos decem, quidam septem, quidam tres, quidam centum dies iuxta qualitatem personae poenitere.* A similar association of sodomy with animal copulation is found also in the *Decretum* of Burchard of Worms (*PL* 140, col. 925). Boswell thinks that the omission of sodomy from the stringent new code of clerical celibacy issued by the Roman Council of 1059 implies a degree of tolerance. But this is mistaken: the Council of 1059 had more urgent business on hand; and in any case, sodomy had been condemned by Leo IX at Rheims in 1049 (See Uta Renate Blumenthal, 'Eine neuer Text für das Reimser Konzil Leos IX (1049)', *DA*, 32, 1976, p. 32).

is a tension between the supernatural end of worship and the sensuous pleasure of the music. The latter, if exaggerated or distorted, may be positively dangerous to the soul, as syncopation in the chants was later reputed to be. So we may ask whether this may also be true of the physical expressions of friendship in Anselm's letters. That they were recognized as being pleasurable is not in doubt. The question is: was Anselm conscious that they might promote or obstruct their spiritual purposes, and what, if any, safeguards did he impose?

In answer to this question, it may first be remarked that Anselm saw the pleasures of friendship (as also the pleasure of music) as a foretaste of the pleasure to be experienced at a higher degree of excellence in Heaven. In so far as these pleasures were enjoyed with their final end in view, their foretaste was an incentive to perseverance. If this is kept in mind, there are three conditions which friendship and its outward expressions must satisfy to be acceptable in Anselmian terms.

First, monastic friendship can only exist fully between those whose wills are directed to a heavenly end.

Second, the warmest expressions of friendship can only exist as a sweetening influence in the rigours of the lives of those who have dedicated themselves to monastic discipline: they encourage those who are now struggling with cold, hunger and the mortifications of religious exercises by holding out a foretaste of the joys of Heaven.

Third, there must be strict limits to these pleasures on earth: they are instruments, not ends, in a prolonged struggle. They do not lessen the struggle, but they are, so to speak, the smile on the frowning face of Providence.[15]

When all this has been said, there still remains a question which lies at the root of Boswell's inquiry, and requires an answer: do Anselm's words in his letters of friendship imply that he had himself a homosexual orientation in the modern sense of the word? Within the framework I have described, the question is irrelevant, but it is not irrelevant in a historical inquiry, though it may be unanswerable. We can only say that it is quite possible that Anselm had such a predisposition. The account of his early years which he gave Eadmer tells us little in detail, but the history of his love for his mother and hostility to his father may be facts of some psychologi-

---

[15] For the place of friendship in the joys of Heaven, see *Memorials*, pp. 60–1; 186–7; 282.

cal importance. Equally, the intense effort of his early days at Bec suggests a revolt from the past rather than a simple change of direction; this is borne out by the violence of his early *Prayers* and by his *Meditation* on his lost virginity. Unless these are the products of a fevered imagination, they must be expressions of genuine horror at real sins in the past.

If we are entitled to see here a record of a severe personal struggle, we may also have a clue to the extremism of his later demands for a total self-abnegation from others, which go well beyond the limits of law or even perhaps of common sense. His immediate horror at the sodomy in William Rufus's court, his detailed legislation against this vice and its accompaniments of long hair and effeminate habits in his first Council in 1102, may suggest that these subjects touched a raw spot in his own past.[16] The letter in which he explained the need for such legislation is also illuminating:

> It must be recognized that this sin [of sodomy] has become so common that hardly anyone even blushes for it, and many, being ignorant of its enormity, have abandoned themselves to it . . . As for those priests who refuse to have their hair cut, they are not to enter the church. I do not order that, if they enter the church, they shall cease to be priests, but they are to be warned that they are acting against God, and incurring damnation.[17]

There are therefore several indications in Anselm's words and attitudes of an exaggerated sensitivity on this subject, which may point to a violent rejection of his past. The all-pervading contrast in Anselm's life and words between an extraordinary mildness, which the whole world recognized as a dominant trait in his character, and the quite unusual, and indeed unreasonable, harshness of his judgements on these topics may perhaps best be explained as reflections of a personal struggle of great severity.

Having said this, it must also be recognized that, in all his writings after his early *Prayers,* he spoke from a plateau of achieved certainty and clear vision which he thought that others could share. Out of

---

[16] See *HN*, pp. 123–5, for the difference between Lanfranc and Anselm on marriage after a tentative approach to monastic vows; and *Councils*, i, p. 619, for their different attitudes to married clergy.

[17] *Ep.* 257 (iii, 62). For legislative texts on sodomy in the period immediately after Anselm, see Ivo of Chartres, *Decretum* ix, 105–6 (*PL* 161, cols. 684–5) and Gratian (C. 32, q. 7, c. 13), both of them quoting Augustine *Confessions* iii, 8, in which he placed sodomy among the crimes against nature, *quae ubique et semper detestanda atque punienda sunt.* This was the fundamental text on the subject, which Anselm would have known.

the struggles of his years of discipleship and silence, there had come a spirit more at home in the kingdom of essences – or perhaps we may say more simply, more at home in the kingdom of Heaven – than in the ordering of the everyday world of mixed motives and turbulent desires. He could use the soft words of friendship as an instrument and pleasure of the religious life, because behind them there was a will shaped by a brutal effort of self-discipline, such as Lanfranc for example had never had to endure.

The confidence that he would not be misunderstood may have been shaken by misunderstandings about his motives at the time when he left Bec for Canterbury, and thereafter his words of friendship became more restrained. But it was only his language that he moderated; on the role of friendship in the religious life as an incentive and foretaste of its reward, he never changed.

VI   THE SYMBOLISM OF THE KISS

In all his reflections on the physical world, Anselm interprets physical acts as the expressions of a spiritual state; and the physical acts which he freely mentions – the kisses, hugs, and so on – are symbols of unity in spiritual endeavour. But, as with all his symbols, there is a physical reality which was also part of the eternal order. Anselm's reported words on the joys of Heaven are unambiguous on this point: the legitimate physical pleasures of this life will be infinitely multiplied in Heaven. It may almost be said that what is symbol in this life is reality in Heaven. This consideration gave all symbols an enhanced importance: their meaning and their pleasure too would be fully experienced only in eternity. It was this foretaste of eternity which gave dignity and meaning to all the symbolic acts with which corporate medieval life in all its departments was filled.

Kisses had a peculiar importance among these symbolic acts. They were the climax in sequences of actions in both monastic and secular life. In the corporate life of the monastery, the kiss was the crowning act in several sacramental sequences: in the profession of new monks; in the reconciling of penitents; in the election of new abbots; in the farewell to the dying; in the dedication of physical objects to the use of the community; in the consecration of altars; in the blessing of sacred vessels and garments; in the dedication of buildings.

In the secular world, the kiss had a similar role as the climax in acts of homage and fealty; in reconciling enemies; in restoring the harmony of lords and vassals who had been fighting each other. This public role of the kiss did not quickly disappear. Henry II's refusal to bestow the kiss of peace on Archbishop Thomas Becket played a notable, perhaps a decisive, part in the quarrel between them, and one of the most attractive incidents in the life of St Hugh of Lincoln was the mild ruse which caused Richard I to give him the kiss of peace, which brought their hostility to an end.

Then, at the most exalted level of all, the kiss expressed the union of the three Persons of the Trinity, the union of the saints, the union between God and man. At this level, the Song of Songs was the main authority for the symbolism of the kiss, and the first medieval Commentary on the Song of Songs in the West, written by a Norman monk, Robert of Tombelaine, who was one of Anselm's correspondents, explained the first verse, 'Let him kiss me with the kisses of his mouth', in words which tell the whole story, so far as it concerns us here:

The mouth of the spouse is the inspiration of Christ; the kiss of the mouth is the love of that inspiration. So the meaning is: 'may He who is above all things touch me with the sweetness of His inspiration'.[18]

This sentence completes the cycle of witnesses testifying that the kiss was both an individual and physical act, and a corporate and a mystical symbol. The expanding symbolism of the kiss marks a new phase in the spiritual development of western Europe, and Anselm's letters of friendship tell part of the story of the intermingling of a corporate and an individual experience.

Of course it would be absurd to suppose that because the act of kissing had an important role in political and monastic life, and in symbolic theology and in personal piety, it did not also exist as an expression of many different degrees of love and affection. It is not to be supposed that Anselm and Gilbert Crispin had this whole range of meanings in their minds as they exchanged kisses on parting. But like all expressions of love, they summed up a whole range of common experiences, and Anselm could mention them in letters intended for a wider public because his friendships with those with whom he shared the discipline of monastic life were part of an eternal reality, as real as the association of limbs in a single body, and as everlasting as the kingdom of Heaven.

[18] *PL* 150, col. 1,364.

VII   THE THEOLOGY OF FRIENDSHIP

In these expressions of friendship, we can see a familiar characteristic of Anselm's thought. He turns his mind to contemplate an ideal image, attaches himself to it with passionate intensity, and seeks its realization in individuals. The dignity of friendship lay in this: of all relationships in the natural world, friendship alone has a continued existence essentially unaltered in Heaven.[19] All other physical attributes are changed beyond all earthly measure in Heaven: friendship alone survives without essential alteration. It even penetrates the nature of God in the mutual love of the three Persons of the Trinity.

We are now in a position to define the nature of his innovation in his conception of friendship. He made friendship part of his *theological* programme: in place of the philosophical principle of friendship, which had satisfied Lanfranc, Anselm developed a theological principle of union of souls in worship, and finally in union with God. It is only in this context that one of the strangest of Anselm's expressions of friendship can be understood. He is writing to two young relatives who had arrived at Bec during his absence. He had probably never met them before, so the warmth of his expressions can come only from the mind. He writes:

My eyes long to see your faces most beloved; my arms stretch out to your embraces; my lips long for your kisses; whatever remains to me of life desires your company to make my soul's joy complete for the future . . . Oh, how my love burns in my marrow, how it labours to break forth and to express itself in words. But no words suffice, time and parchment alike are unable to allow me to express what I wish. Do you, good Jesus, say to our hearts that they should leave all and follow thee.[20]

Here then, until the final sentence, we have some of the expressions of desire, which may appear at first sight to be indistinguishable from passionate homosexual love. But then the last sentence introduces a new theme which opens up a different world:

In coming [to Bec in Anselm's absence] you have lit a spark; you have blown it into flame; and in this flame you have fused my soul with yours. If you now leave me, our joint soul will be torn apart, it can never again become two. So

[19] See *Memorials*, pp. 60–1: *Nona pars beatitudinis est amicitia*; and cf. pp. 186–7, 282.
[20] *Ep.* 120 (ii, 28).

155

you cannot now take yours back into the world. You must either remain here with it, or tear it apart. If you stay with it, we will be more than blood-relations; we will be spiritual partners. If you tear it apart, far from being blood-relations, you will be stained with carnal blood.[21]

Then he continues:

But God forbid that this should be the reason for your coming. Say to their hearts, good Jesus, that they should leave all and follow thee.

Here at last we get back to traditional language. But we are still left with the concept of a new joint soul dedicated to the practice of the religious life, which can be murdered, but if once dissolved cannot again be reconstituted as two souls. This joint soul created by fusion in a common monastic profession must be taken very seriously. It is not just a poetic image; it is a spiritual entity in the scale of being which (as we have seen in the *Proslogion*) ascends from the lowest and most shadowy existences to the being of God.

Souls fused together in monastic obedience to the Rule of St Benedict occupy a distinct place in that ascent. They were fused together by identity of profession. The language of fusion had no doubt been used figuratively by many writers on friendship, but Anselm saw it as an indissoluble union here and in Heaven. His words on this subject only make sense in the context of an ascent of the soul to God. That this is their context becomes clear when we notice the consistency of his expressions to those who followed the monastic life, even though they were scarcely at all, in the ordinary sense of the word, his 'friends'. So he could write to Henry, prior of Canterbury, to whom on a later occasion (as we shall see) he wrote a letter of grave remonstrance:

Those whose minds have been fused together by the fire of love not unnaturally find it grievous when distance separates their bodies.[22]

And he could write of Osbern, an English monk from Canterbury, whom Lanfranc had sent for discipline to Bec:

We cannot now be separated without tearing apart our joint soul and wounding our heart.[23]

This fusion of souls, and the *scissura animae* at parting, are recurring themes in the letters of Anselm at Bec. They are used about persons and in situations astonishingly various: persons whom he has never seen, or not seen for many years, have the same

[21] *Ep*. 120 (ii, 28).   [22] *Ep*. 5 (i, 5). For his later letter, see below, p. 168.
[23] *Ep*. 66 (i, 57) to Lanfranc.

treatment as those with whom he had long lived in intimacy. Physical presence and incompatibilities of temperament brought no disillusion, absence and distance no cooling. All that mattered was community of profession.

The peculiar ardour of Anselm's imaginative projection of his personal ties no doubt bred misunderstandings in those who did not understand that the fire was wholly spiritual, and that it was nourished by an incorporeal ideal. It was a product of an intensely realized theology of union in Christ: the unity of souls in friendship is an example and realization of unity in Christ. It was an experience offered to the most transient applicants within the monastic fold, and never more than when it was sought by a fugitive. One of the most curious of all his expressions of friendship was written on behalf of a certain Moses, a runaway monk and embezzler from Canterbury, who had taken refuge at Bec and wished to return to his monastery. Anselm sent him back with letters which described him as 'clothed from head to foot in the skin of your servant and brother Anselm':

If therefore I have at any time offended any of you, scourge the skin of Moses for my fault, and in him deprive my mouth of food. For I have commended my skin to my brother Moses for him to keep it carefully as his own. Do not spare it on this account; but remember it is *my* skin you are beating, and if you beat *my* skin for *his* fault, I shall require satisfaction from him; if you spare me I shall be thankful.[24]

This apparently wilfully complicated statement was not a joke intended to turn away wrath by raising a smile. Anselm's words express in perfect seriousness one consequence of the fusion of souls in friendship: it made possible the perfect substitution of one man for another, which on a cosmic scale dominated his doctrine of the Atonement. Indeed his theology and his doctrine of friendship alike presuppose the homogeneity of the human race and the ability of one man to stand in the place of another, united in will and profession. If his language appears fanciful and extravagant, it seems so because we do not share either his philosophical views or his spiritual intensity. There was nothing fanciful or sentimental about it – nothing at all of the pleasant sentimentalizing of Aelred of Rievaulx and his Cistercian friends, who a hundred years later lived at the other end of the great divide created by the romantic revolution.

[24] *Ep.* 140 (ii, 45).

Enough has been said to show that Anselm's surprising statements about friendship have nothing in common with the experience of romantic love, whether homosexual or heterosexual. Here, as so often, Anselm hovers, not between the old and the new, but on the wings of both old and new. In his intellectual intention, he is on the side of tradition; but in the vividness of his experience and the novelty of his language, he points to the future. He uses phrases which foreshadow the language of romantic love; but the system within which he employs these phrases has nothing in common with romantic love. His friendships, like his theological insights, are intellectual realities, passionately conceived and vividly expressed. It is tempting to say that for him a friend is less a person than an idea. But this misses an essential feature of his mind: his ideas are realities. Just as the ideal essences, which Aristotle called 'secondary substances', are the fundamental realities of the whole Creation in time and eternity, so they are the most vividly realized experiences of his life.

Not unnaturally, some of his friends did not realize this, and they were disappointed and indignant when they found that he was going after all to leave them to become archbishop of Canterbury. Hence the bitter sense of desertion which swept through the community of Bec on learning that, after all he had said and written, he was in fact leaving them, when he could have stayed. This is another story which must be examined when we come to it. It must suffice to say here that no protestations of Anselm could dispel the suspicion that his sentiments were less stable than he had claimed. In this his friends were mistaken; but the fact that they had this suspicion shows that his contemporaries were as puzzled by his words and the ideas which they expressed as we at first sight are.

The multiplicity of those who were invited to read what he had written, and apply it to themselves, should have been a warning that his passion was for an ideal which could only be realized in individual lives. But this too is an unsatisfactory statement of his position. We must rather envisage a system in which the particular is generalized, but loses nothing of its particularity in the process. This also we have observed in his most private prayers, which he willingly published to the world.

In brief, when he spoke in ecstatic terms about friendship, he was thinking of individuals, not primarily on earth, but in Heaven. When he was stricken with grief at the sight of a trapped animal, it was not primarily the creature before his eyes he was grieving for, but the souls of those beset by sin which its fate represented. This did not mean that the physical world or the individual were unimportant: quite the opposite. But they were important because they also represented eternity. Just as the Old Testament is about things that had really happened, but these things are important mainly for what they foreshadowed, so all events in the world – friendships among them – were important equally for what they were and for what they stood for. That is why he wished letters which superficially seem embarrassingly intimate to be read by readers other than their recipients: in speaking of friendship, he was making statements about eternity.

He continued to expand the range of his friendships to the end of his life, but it is noticeable that his tone changes. Whereas the letters of the twenty years before 1093 sparkle with ardent and unconventional expressions, there is only one later letter with similar warmth. Friendship continued to have the same meaning for him, but he wrote about it with greater restraint. Partly, no doubt, this was due to the growing range of his correspondence. All his early letters of ecstatic friendship in the common pursuit of religious fulfilment are to fellow-monks. Among his later letters, those which approach most nearly to the tone of the earlier letters are to women. In general their expressions are more subdued, and their message is about the need to persevere, rather than rejoicing in an assured triumph. In only one of them did the stream of fervent expression flow as it had in the earlier days, and the purpose of this was to recall to the monastic life the daughter of the last Anglo-Saxon king, who like so many others had been captivated by his talk, and in whom Anselm had found a friend whom he feared to lose.[25]

In these last years, he still retained his power of drawing to himself those who had embraced a monastic life. But it was as disciples rather than as intimate friends that they now appeared. The change reflects a parallel change in the subject-matter of his writings and in his circumstances. His world had become larger and more hostile; he had left corporate peace behind at Bec, and faced a sea of troubles both practical and speculative.

In one of the last letters which he wrote to the monks of Bec when he was leaving them to become archbishop of Canterbury, he commended friendship to them as the ideal he had always pursued

[25] For this case, see below, pp. 262–4.

during his years at Bec, and bade them follow his example. This was his last will and testament to the whole community:

In this my final petition, I call on you all not to allow the sweetness of your love towards me to grow cool. For even if I can no longer be present with you in body, I will never cease to remain with you in the love of my heart. Remember why I was always accustomed to acquire friends for the church of Bec. Make haste to follow my example by exercising the virtue of hospitality and showing kindness to all; and, when you have nothing else to offer, at least offer the grace of friendly words to all. Never think that you have enough friends. Bind everyone, both rich and poor, to you in loving fraternity, for the good of your church and the salvation of those whom you love.[26]

In these parting words to the monastic community, he extended to the whole neighbourhood the bond of spiritual friendship which had been the foundation of his monastic life. Friendship had been his theme for the past twenty years in writing to prospective monks of Bec and to monks in other communities. Now he committed to the monks of Bec the task of continuing this work.

His most ardent expressions of friendship had begun with those who had left Bec for Canterbury, and now, as he followed them, he left it to those who remained to spread beyond the walls of the monastery to the whole surrounding countryside that 'gluing together' in love, which had been a main theme in his religious life while he was at Bec. [27]

VIII   FRIENDSHIP AND THE KINGDOM OF HEAVEN

Anselm's final letter of advice to the community at Bec provides a suitable moment to review the whole subject of friendship and its place in Anselm's life.

To get the subject in perspective, we must go back to the start of his monastic life. His becoming a monk in 1060, though at the time it seemed an act rather of despair than of self-commitment, had brought a real conversion. Of his purposes before this date, we have only a few fragmentary recollections of muddle and (as Anselm saw

---

[26] *Ep.* 165 (iii, 16). Vaughn, 1987, pp. 11–13 and *passim*, has given this passage a political interpretation on which I have commented in *Albion*, 20, 1988, 188–91.

[27] Anselm had used the image of the conglutination of souls in mutual love in several of his early letters, in which he extended the image from the union of individuals in friendship to the binding together of angels and human souls with God in the kingdom of Heaven. See *Epp.* 11 (i, 9), 39 (i, 47), 55 (i, 64), 112 (ii, 22), 121 (ii ,39). He used this image for the last time in his two parting letters to the monks of Bec, *Epp.* 165 (ii, 16), 166 (iii, 17).

it) grave sin. His love for his mother, whom he lost in his youth, his early longing for some eternal beauty and happiness which he failed to find, his hostility to his father and his flight from home, and (if his meditation on the subject is to be trusted) a loss of virginity, were all deeply embedded in his consciousness. It was against this background that he rebelled in turning to Lanfranc, who was the instrument of his conversion to the monastic life.

Three years later, Lanfranc's removal to Caen separated them in more ways than one. Anselm's intellectual gifts as well as his personality quickly distinguished his outlook from that of Lanfranc. For Anselm, monastic conversion meant a systematic and total rejection of the world and the flesh, and an unremitting search for the reality which lies beyond the senses, and which is attainable only by rigorous mental and spiritual discipline. By about the age of forty, after some ten years of this discipline, his character, aims, and ideas had been fully formed. There is no sign that they changed in any important way after he first began to write for a wider public about 1070. Except in a few small details, he never changed his mind on any subject that he had written about.

His general view of Man's state, and of the steps which were necessary to remedy its deep abasement, was formidably stern. The texts to which he most readily referred for guiding others into the paths which he himself had followed, were these: 'Many are called but few are chosen'; 'he that despiseth small things shall fall little by little'; 'No man, having put his hand to the plough, and looking back, is fit for the kingdom of God'.[28] These texts required scrupulous, unremitting watchfulness and obedience, and threatened damnation to backsliders.

On these stern foundations his life was built. But everywhere he found a surprising alleviation. When every worldly aim has been renounced, and Man appears before God as a delinquent servant who has lost all claim to his Lord's rewards, there remains one pleasure which belongs to this world but survives in Heaven: this is the pleasure of friendship. This alone can safely be expressed in terms of the warmest and most abundant fervour.

In the context in which they appear, his fervent expressions of

---

[28] Matthew xxii, 14: *Epp.* 2, (i, 2); 51 (i, 43); 167 (iii, 18); 164. Ecclesiasticus, xix, 1: *Epp.* 183 (iv, 105); 185 (iii, 30); 203 (iii, 54); 230 (iv, 110); 231 (iii, 50); 403 (iii, 125); 450 (iii, 151). Luke ix, 65: *Epp.* 2 (i, 2); 17 (i, 15); 51 (i, 43); 101 (ii, 12); 162 (iii, 13); 418 (iii, 137).

friendship seem strangely out of place, but only because their eternal goal and the discipline required for reaching it are not understood. The expressions which he used were not struck off in the heat of the moment in response to a passing mood, still less as the expression of a physical passion. Like everything else that he wrote, they were carefully considered, and their intensity was directly related to a theological plan. The warmest expressions were reserved for those whose intentions were fixed upon a life of religious dedication. If men or women receded from this position through lukewarmness or indecision, or still further through dissatisfaction or disobedience, the superlatives ceased and the words of love and longing gave place to cooler words of formal respect; and finally, when the person addressed had been disobedient and rebellious, the cooler words gave place to admonition or plain rebuke. I have mentioned that Lanfranc's view of friendship was 'political' in the sense that it expressed union in the government of the Church. It can now be added that Anselm's view was also 'political', but the kingdom to which it related, and in which alone it had its consummation, was the kingdom of Heaven.

This is important for understanding Anselm's view of all human relationships, and even for understanding his politics. For Anselm, human friendship arises entirely from a communion of wills in the service of God, and the supreme expression of this communion in the Church is the monastic community. These communities, and these alone in his experience, were associations of those who had irrevocably sealed their intention of resigning themselves and everything they possessed into God's hands. The importance Anselm attached to an irreversibility of commitment can be illustrated from many of his letters. But his most dramatic account of the difference between a full and only partial commitment appears in the records of his informal teaching.

In one of his Similitudes he contrasts the owner of an orchard who gives up his produce year by year to his lord, with the owner who gives his lord orchard and produce alike once and for all. The final result is the same: the lord has all. But, in the first case, the tenant retains an annual power of choice; in the second, he makes a complete surrender once and for all.[29] The latter is the state of the monk, and this was the necessary condition for entry into the closest circle of Anselm's friends.

[29] See *Liber Anselmi de humanis moribus*, c. 84, *Similitudo inter monachum et arborem*, in *Memorials*, pp. 73–4; also *VA* I, xi, pp. 73–8, and the references given there.

Freedom came from total surrender to the monastic rule, and this alone gave full assurance of salvation. He wished all to make this choice. There is no reason to think that he would have shrunk from the consequence that if every one became a monk or a nun, the history of mankind would soon end: after all, this would happen anyhow as soon as the perfect number of the elect was completed, neither sooner nor later, and the sooner the better. Meanwhile, there was but a thin stream of salvation issuing from the mass of humanity.

Naturally, he recognized that the world would not in the foreseeable future be composed solely of monastic communities, and his friendships extended, though in diminishing degrees of warmth, to those outside. There were people in the world who, without taking monastic vows, dedicated themselves to the secular equivalent of monastic vows: justice, alms-giving and self-denial. Anselm urged the practice of these virtues on those whose duties tied them to the world. But he also urged that their service should be completed when possible by assuming the monastic garments and vows in the last hours of life.[30]

To be joined together in self-abandonment in the monastic life, whether in present reality or in intention, was the condition of admission into the inner circle of Anselm's friends. The love which bound them together was a reflection of the love which identified their wills with the will of God. For those outside this circle, he could feel sorrow, anxiety, pity, pastoral concern; he could (and did) explain in the most forceful terms what lay before them; he could encourage them to enter; but he could do no more. Those outside could be his friends, but not close friends. For those whose wills were divided from his, there was no basis for friendship.

If we now apply this model of circles of friendship to human society in general, it may seem to imply a very contracted view of life. The only aim to which Anselm had any deep and lasting commitment was that of binding together and enlarging dedicated groups of men and women in monasteries, or nunneries, and in groups associated with monasteries. Yet, limiting though this aim was in one sense, it also allowed a large degree of tolerance for the institutional forms of secular life. All human institutions, so far as

---

[30] See his advice to Matilda, countess of Tuscany, *Ep.* 325 (iv, 37): *Hoc tamen praesumo consulere ut, si certum mortis periculum interim (quod Deus avertat) senseritis imminere, prius vos omnino reddatis quam de hac vita exeatis; et ad hoc velum semper paratum secrete penes vos habeatis.*

they did not oppose the formation of the dedicated groups of God's people, were tolerable. Consequently, Anselm looked benignly on all existing institutions, above all those of feudal fidelity, which had a tendency to promote monastic life. All associations and authorities which enlarged the area of peace, justice and charity partook in some degree of the monastic purpose. Anselm had no quarrel with any of them, least of all with kings and barons, who were the greatest patrons of monasteries.

For Anselm, the model of all authority was the paternal authority of the abbot in his monastery, advising, commanding, informing, and labouring for the good of all members of the community. His ideal of authority was expressed in the opening words of the Benedictine Rule:

> Listen, my son, to the commands of the master, and open the ears of your heart to receive the counsel of your loving Father, so that by the labour of obedience you may return to Him from whom you have departed by the sloth of disobedience.

The words, 'I command' in varying combinations with 'beg', 'pray', 'advise', and 'counsel', are frequently associated in Anselm's letters.[31] The advice was paternal, mirroring the paternal authority of God, and the authority behind it was absolute, provided that the commands were rooted in the source which the Rule summarized: the Bible. He had lived with this combination of authority and paternal care for thirty-three years as a monk: he never abandoned it. Even as archbishop, he never gave up his right to advise and command the monks of Bec. This right was his for ever, and he exercised it quite openly in telling the monks whom they were to elect as his successor. When he became an archbishop, the paternal authority which he had exercised as abbot was extended to a much wider circle: first to the community at Christ Church, then to religious communities and to everyone in his province, and in the still wider area over which he claimed primatial authority. Naturally, in this process of expansion the intensity which had seemed appropriate in writing to half a dozen intimate pupils in earlier days cooled: but the doctrine remained unchanged.

In almost the last year of his life, he wrote to a nun, perhaps a daughter of his old friend the earl of Chester:

---

[31] For the combination of these and similar phrases, see *Epp.* 117 (ii, 19); 137 (ii, 42); 157 (iii, 2); 169 (not in *PL*); 188 (iii, 33); 290 (iv, 31); 309 (iv, 52).

I love you, and I love your soul as my own: that is to say, I love it in the measure in which, by deserving to enjoy God in this life, your soul will enjoy Him in the life to come. It is this that I love, and this that I desire for you. Wherefore, I urge and advise you as a dearest daughter, not to delight in secular things, because no one can love secular and eternal blessings simultaneously. Let all your conversation be in the cloister, not in the world. This world is nothing to you, nothing but dung, if you wish to be a nun and spouse of God . . . Do not visit your relatives, they do not need your advice, nor you theirs. Your way of life is cut off from theirs. Let all your desire be for God.[32]

This is the doctrine he had been teaching for nearly fifty years. It is here more soberly expressed than in his earlier letters, but the doctrine is as demanding as ever: his friendship required renunciation of the world, and it could only be fully bestowed when this condition was observed absolutely. He was not offering an experience of genial humanity, but a programme of the most exacting renunciation. It is strange that a doctrine fundamentally so demanding, and so far beyond ordinary expectations, should have been expressed in terms that made everyone feel that they were the sole objects of his intense regard.[33] This is the paradox of his personality: he was renowned for his mildness and affability to all, and yet the demands he made on those whom he loved were beyond the reach of almost all.

[32] *Ep.* 405 (iii, 127).
[33] See Guibert of Nogent *De vita sua*, i, c. 16, for evidence of this (*PL* 156, col. 874).

CHAPTER 8

AN UNWELCOME BUT ENLARGING WORLD

So far we have followed a very private life within a monastic community – a life more private, indeed, than the eleventh century ideal of monastic life made provision for. In his prayers and meditations, and in his letters of friendship and spiritual advice, Anselm had been a pioneer of a more intense interior religious life, and in his *Monologion* and *Proslogion* he had undertaken more protracted meditations than can be found in any earlier Benedictine writer. Then, in the year in which he completed his *Proslogion*, he succeeded Herluin as abbot of Bec. From this date, the privacy of his earlier life could no longer be maintained, and he began to emerge into a larger world. This change had several aspects: his new position necessarily brought with it responsibility for the property and administration of the abbey, and the need for extensive travel to visit its distant priories.[1] In the next twelve years, he visited England at least three and probably four times, and we have notices of other journeys within Normandy and beyond.[2]

In addition to his necessary business activities, his slowly growing fame brought letters and visitors to Bec in search of advice. Moreover, his own thoughts began to expand from meditations on sin and God to embrace problems of will and action. These problems were raised partly by monks at Bec or elsewhere, and

[1] There is an excellent survey of the new priories in and around the borders of Normandy in Baudot 1989; for the English priories, see Morgan, 1946, and Chibnall, 1959, pp. 521–50.
[2] According to Eadmer, (*VA* I, xxix), Anselm's first visit to England took place during his first year as abbot: i.e. in 1079. This visit was a landmark in Eadmer's life, and it seems unlikely that he would have been mistaken on this point. Moreover, there was probably some urgency for preliminary arrangements to be made for the projected new settlement of monks from Bec at St Neots in Huntingdonshire. Anselm's second recorded journey to England seems to have been in 1081, but we know about it only from a reference in a letter written during his next visit in 1086, in which he remarked on the fact that during both of his absences in England new recruits had arrived at Bec (*Ep.* 117, (ii, 19)). It seems likely that this short visit was also occasioned by the need to supervise the establishment of the new community at St Neots. In contrast to these visits in 1079 and 1081, his next visit in 1086 is abundantly documented in his letters. To judge from the number of letters surviving from this trip, it must have been a fairly

partly by the logic of his own developing system. The new external calls on his time were a distraction which he never ceased to deplore; but they also helped to provoke the enlargement which is conspicuous in all his later theological work. These are complicated themes, and for the sake of clarity, intertwined though they are, they must be dealt with separately. We may begin with his own theological development, and then go on to his contacts with the lay world.

I THEOLOGY AND THE WORLD

1 Worldly liberty

Broadly speaking, Anselm's first phase of independent development, beginning with his *Prayers* and *Meditations* and culminating in his *Monologion* and *Proslogion*, had been wholly concentrated on self-examination, rising through meditation towards the contemplation of God. The world outside this range of experience had scarcely impinged on his writings by 1079. But the new stage in his work from 1079 to 1092–93, which we are now to examine, shows an extension in two main directions: first, to problems of freedom, choice, power, and necessity, and the actions of people in the world; then in the next few years to the activity of God in the world, especially in the work of Redemption.

This extension in the area of his theological inquiry was necessary for the completion of his system of thought; but it was also provoked by his broadening contacts with the world outside the monastery. We can see something of both of these influences in two letters which have the common theme of liberty. The first was written in about 1072, the second in 1086; and they connect his earlier introspective period with the later more broadly based stage in his theological thought.

lengthy visit (*Epp.* 116–21). He stayed for some time with Gilbert Crispin at Westminster, but he did not on this occasion go to Canterbury. The probable purpose of this visit was to take stock of the widely spread estates and churches with which the small group of families affiliated to Bec had been enriching the monastery in recent years. They formed a clumsy bundle containing two small estates, several small parcels of land, some two dozen churches, and varied portions of tithes in fourteen counties stretching from Devon to Essex and from Hampshire to Oxfordshire. The result of this visit was a royal confirmation of the scattered possessions of Bec in England (Salter 1925). The purpose of the next visit in the autumn of 1092, apart from visiting the sick earl at Chester and supervising the constitution of his new monastery, was probably to obtain a confirmation of Bec's English possessions from the new king. Its consequences must be dealt with later (see pp. 187–94).

The first of these two letters contains his earliest mature statement about a problem of secular obligation.[3] It was written to Henry, an Italian monk whom Lanfranc had taken from Bec to Canterbury, whose sister had been reduced to bondage by some unspecified act of injustice. Henry was proposing to go to Italy to bring about her release, and the purpose of Anselm's letter was to beg him, by all the ties of friendship and all the bonds of a common monastic vocation, not to go.

Perhaps this was the right advice for one who had taken monastic vows. But quite apart from the decisive terms in which Anselm offered his opinion, there are two points to be noticed: Anselm was not Henry's monastic superior; Lanfranc, who was, seems to have taken a more lenient view of Henry's plan. Anyhow, Henry went, and Lanfranc made him prior of Canterbury shortly after his return. This is only one example among several, first of Anselm's tendency to intervene well beyond the limits of his official authority, in urging a strict interpretation of monastic vows; second, of his differing from Lanfranc in the strictness of his principles. For our present purpose, however, in tracing the growth of his mind, the interest of his intervention lies less in its circumstances, but rather in the fact that it provoked Anselm's first statement about liberty. It ran as follows:

To those who have fled from the world, what does it matter who serves whom in the world, or under what name? Is not *man born to labour as the sparks fly upward*? Does not almost everyone serve someone, whether under the name of lord or serf? And is not the slave a *freeman of the Lord*? So, if everyone labours and everyone serves, and the slave is a freeman of Christ, what does it matter, apart from pride, whether anyone is called slave or free?[4]

The incident illustrates two different views of the monastic life. Henry was evidently not one of those who in becoming a monk had renounced all earthly ties and all considerations of rank; and there are several signs that Lanfranc shared his point of view. But for Anselm this was a sign of half-heartedness in religion, which in a monk or anyone else showed a lack of seriousness in pursuing an aim which, once adopted, admitted of no degrees of commitment: it demanded everything.

The practical implications of this doctrine in political life must await later consideration; for the present we are concerned only

---

[3] *Ep.* 17 (i, 15).
[4] Ibid. For the passage quoted here, see Schmitt, iii, p. 123, lines 15–25.

with its theoretical implications. It is clear that liberty for Anselm had nothing in common with the liberty of being one's own master, or of choosing when to labour, for whom, and for what purpose, and in what way. In Anselm's view, these liberties were not liberty in any important sense. What then *is* liberty?

As an aid to answering this question, it will be useful first to examine the second letter, written some fifteen years later, in which the subject of liberty is treated from a different angle. This letter was written, not to a monk, but to a young Italian nobleman who had an even more urgent call to action. In his case, the call was not mainly to help a member of his family, but to rescue Christendom itself. The brother of this nobleman had joined one of the western expeditions to aid the Byzantine emperor against the Muslim armies which, having seized Jerusalem, were attacking the central areas of the empire in Asia Minor. At the time when Anselm wrote to him, probably after the Turkish victory at Manzikert in 1085, the situation had become desperate, and the young man to whom Anselm wrote had decided to join his brother in action instead of becoming a monk of Bec, as Anselm wished.[5]

Anselm, as we discover from this and other sources, had no sympathy with the Crusade either in its early expeditions in aid of the eastern Christians, or in its later papally inspired stage after 1095. For him, the important choice was quite simply between the heavenly Jerusalem, the true *vision of Peace* signified by the name Jerusalem, which was to be found in the monastic life, and the carnage of the earthly Jerusalem in this world, which under whatever name was nothing but a vision of destruction. Once again, for Anselm, the rational, religious, and for that matter the prudent, decision was to become a monk. This remained his view to the end of his life. He put the matter in a nutshell: 'Do not be ashamed of breaking the bonds of the vanity of this world: it is a privilege, not a dishonour, to reach out to the liberty of truth.'[6] Real liberty lay in choosing the self-effacement of monastic life. Enslavement lay in the honour of the world. He turns the ordinary notions of honour and liberty upside down, and proclaims that true liberty is to be found only in an apparent lack of liberty.

The doctrine of these two letters is the same; but their differences are important. In the first, Anselm was addressing a professed monk, and he simply insisted that the vows he had already taken cut

[5] *Ep.* 117 (ii, 19).   [6] Ibid. lines 55–6.

him off from the affairs of the world. It is true that he went on to speak in very derogatory terms of the cherished liberty of this world; but it might be urged that he was speaking to someone who had explicitly renounced this world, and therefore should have no interest in its liberty. But in the second letter, he was writing to a nobleman who was not a monk, whose brother was in extreme danger, and who was engaged in the defence of Christendom, which was soon to become (if it was not already) a fundamental aim of papal policy. In the first letter, therefore, he was insisting that a vow to renounce the world, which had already been taken, should be kept. In the second, he insisted that, though the vow had not been made, it had to be made if true liberty was to be found.

It would be quite mistaken to think that these expressions were coloured by rhetorical exaggeration. Anselm's language may be fervent, but it is never rhetorical: that is to say, he never used language to evoke an emotional response. If he used fervent language, it was because the heavenly Jerusalem, with its liberty of Truth and vision of Peace, exists in a blaze of light which requires appropriate language to express it.

These two letters say exactly what he thinks, and separated though they are by some fifteen years, the later letter expresses his abhorrence of the world even more forcibly than the earlier one. It is evident in both that he thinks that the liberty and honour of this world are, in the most literal sense, trash.

The consolidation of his earlier view in the second letter represents an important enlargement in Anselm's thinking, and it has important practical and political consequences. In his earlier works he had not spoken at all of liberty, except once in referring to that unrestricted corporeal freedom of activity which is enjoyed by the spirits in Paradise.[7] It would be impossible to push the physical world further from the centre of everyday life than this. And yet, since Heaven is the aim of all human endeavour, and since absolute corporeal freedom is one of the rewards of Heaven, it follows that the body and its delights are part of the ultimate reality for which human beings were created. But we can only be assured of this enjoyment in eternity by renunciation in this world. This is the theological paradox which will soon be more thoroughly explored in his *Cur Deus Homo*.

---

[7] In the *Proslogion*, c. 25, he speaks of liberty in Heaven as *libertas corporis cui nihil obsistere possit*. This was a theme which he developed on many occasions in his reported sermons. See *Memorials*, pp. 59, 277, 299.

This is one of the most distinctive antitheses in Anselm's system: no one could insist more violently on the supremacy of the spirit and the corruption of the flesh in this world, but equally no one could give physical powers, extended to their utmost limit, a more explicit existence in the eternal kingdom. In this fallen world he rejected completely the struggle for material power and the freedom which comes from power. But in his frequently repeated and variously preserved sermon on the joys of Heaven, he emphasized above everything the unrestricted physical power and freedom which are infinitely available and desirable in Heaven. It is clear that with all his belittling of physical liberty in this life, and with all the Platonic elements in his philosophical outlook, he is no Platonist: he does not think that the physical world is fundamentally unreal. On the contrary, it is part of the ultimate reality, but it is available for rational human enjoyment only when the temptation to misuse it has vanished.

In this life, the physical world offers nothing that a rational being should desire – except friendship and health. We have already examined his conception of friendship. Health is less important, but Anselm always showed a keen interest in medicine and in the symptoms of disease.[8] He never explained his interest, but he may have looked on disease as the equivalent in the physical world to evil in the spiritual: it was a negative quantity capable of, and requiring, correction by timely action. But dignities, position, wealth, 'freedom' in the conventional sense, were simple distractions from the road that leads to God, to be endured if coming unasked, and necessary for the common good, but on no account to be sought.

2   Spiritual liberty

Behind the problem of liberty of action in the world, which was raised in the two situations which elicited the letters described above, there lay the deeper problem of the true definition of free-will, which became a central theme in this period of his life. In pursuing this investigation, he entered, if not the political arena, at least the area of active life which impinges on politics, and he was never again to disentangle himself wholly from this involvement.

Despite the pressure of worldly business which occupied much more of his time as abbot than he found easily supportable, he

---

[8]   For his interest in medicine, see *Epp.* 32 (i, 24), 34 (i, 25), 36 (i, 28), 39 (i, 31), 43 (i, 35) 44 (i, 36), 60 (i, 51).

managed, probably between 1080 and 1085, to write three new works. They were all in the form of dialogues with one of his growing number of pupils, and their titles sufficiently indicate their main subjects: *De Veritate, De Libertate Arbitrii* and *De Casu Diaboli*. He describes all of them as 'pertaining to the study of Holy Scripture'. Formally, this is entirely accurate. They are all careful, prolonged, exhaustive examinations of the doctrine of some central Biblical texts, employing the full apparatus of logic and grammar; and the interpretation of these texts takes him into a new range of problems in which the relations between Liberty and Justice have a central place.[9]

The first of these treatises, *De Veritate*, is strictly a continuation of the argument of the *Monologion* and *Proslogion*, developing the theme already touched on by Lanfranc, that Truth is Rectitude in thought, just as Justice is Rectitude in action; or, as Anselm puts it with elegant precision: 'Truth is Rectitude as perceived by the mind; Justice is Rectitude as chosen for its own sake by the will.'[10]

The only point that needs to be mentioned here with regard to these definitions is that Anselm considers Justice as well as Truth only as internal acts, not as activities in the world of legal decisions or procedures. This is a common feature of all his investigations: even those activities most deeply entangled in practical life present themselves to him primarily as problems of being or intending, culminating in the supreme self-commitment of monastic vows. We have already seen this in his letters on personal servitude and the Crusade. Anselm translated both questions into a choice between following the way of this world and taking the path to the Heavenly kingdom as represented by monastic life. The only liberty he recognized was in the service of God, and the only full service of God that he recognized in this life was that form of dedication which has its expression in monastic vows. So far at least, law and politics had no place in his vocabulary. How far his position will alter under new pressures in his later years remains to be seen; but, in his years at Bec, it is hard to find any symptoms of this change, and much in his later life as archbishop becomes clearer if we remember that every practical question had for him a monastic orientation.

[9] The opening words of *De Veritate* refer to John xiv, 6; in *De Libertate Arbitrii*, the recurrent theme is *qui potest peccare, servus potest esse peccati, quoniam 'omnis qui fecit peccatum, servus est peccati'*, quoting John viii, 34; and in *De Casu Diaboli*, a quotation from I Corinthians iv, 7 (*Quid habes quod non accepisti?*) sets off the discussion.

[10] *De Veritate*, cc. 11, 12, pp. 191, 194.

To the casual observer this may seem to argue a very contracted view of human life. But what others saw as confinement, Anselm saw as enlargement: this world is very small; only eternity is great, and the monastery is the gateway to eternity. All his mind was set on enforcing this truth, which alone gave human life any real enlargement. Those who enlarged the world by magnifying the importance of its concerns filled their field of vision with vain things. What they thought great was only vanity masquerading as grandeur; what they saw as enlargement was only a bigger prison. The most important extension of Anselm's philosophy during the decade after his *Proslogion* was his working out of the implications of this way of looking on the world.

His *De Libertate Arbitrii* marked the beginning of this process. As always, his argument proceeded by way of definitions. The main question he set out to answer was this: If sin is servitude (John viii, 34), what is freedom? Of course, if sin is servitude, freedom can be nothing else than absence of sin. But this absence is not a negative quality: it is the power to do that which fulfils the nature of Man as a rational being. So long as a man is following the law of his nature – that is to say, so long as he is on the road to final beatitude – he is free. When he deviates from this road, he becomes unfree, and unfree in a double sense: unfree in having lost his way without a plan to guide him, and even more unfree in being unable, having no plan, or at least not the right plan, to find the right road. Though lost, he may still have an illusion of freedom because he has a choice between various possibilities. But since none of them can be the right road, his freedom is illusory, and his bondage deeper than he can understand.

Yet, if only Man will understand this, all is not lost. The Devil, having with full knowledge rejected Truth, was forever excluded from the right road. Human beings, who had erred through being deceived, were offered a road of return. The Devil had chosen servitude to his own will; Man had only chosen servitude to another's will, offered under false pretences as freedom. The Devil had unconditionally chosen to be unfree by being freed from God; Man had chosen an appearance of freedom which turned out to be servitude. Man's sin was less; but the lesson was the same in both cases: to choose servitude cannot be an exercise of freedom. To make the wrong choice cannot be freedom: freedom can only be the power always and only to make the right choice.

Freedom, therefore, as generally conceived, is illusory. A man who exercises his power to choose his own route without having the right plan, and thereby loses his way, has lost his freedom even before he has lost his way, for the certainty of error is implicit in the exercise of independent choice. In exercising his power of choice, Man takes his first step away from God into the slavery of human choice, which is the world. The man who is entangled in worldly pursuits has lost not only his freedom, but also the rationality whereby he can be free. But if he abandons the illusion of freedom and chooses obedience to God without reservation, he may yet be freed.

In contrast to the many-sided freedom which the world offers, or seems to offer to those whom it calls free, the freedom which Anselm offers to human beings in this world is extremely narrow. Indeed, it must be narrow; but there are two enlargements, minor indeed to the spiritual eye, but giving some comfort in this world. The first is that the benefits of monastic fraternity are offered to people of all grades of society far beyond the walls of the monasteries. The second lies in the diversity of monastic customs. Although a life of simple meditation would appear most suitable to Anselm's spirituality, he gradually developed a growing commitment to the elaborations of the contemporary Benedictine Rule. He discountenanced the move that many monks contemplated, and some carried out, of leaving their monasteries to adopt simpler forms of life. Diversity always puzzled him, but he accepted it because it existed both in monastic life and in ecclesiastical and secular organization. When asked his opinion on diversities in the administration of the sacraments, he could only say:

We have it on the authority of the Fathers that, so long as the unity of charity is preserved in the Catholic faith, diversities of administration are not harmful. If you ask why these diversities of custom should exist, I can only say that they arise from the diversities of human opinions, by which it comes about that what one judges more suitable, another finds less so.[11]

Anselm could never have thought diversity intrinsically good; but he came to accept it as part of the necessary ordering of the world. It was a concession to human weakness.

3   An outsider's attack

For nearly thirty years after his arrival at Bec, Anselm's religious and intellectual development had been entirely shaped by his

---

[11] *Epistola de Sacramentis Ecclesiae*, c. 1, Schmitt, ii, p. 240.

monastic environment and by the course of his own development in the monastic life. His study of the Bible and Augustine, his *Prayers* and *Meditations*, his talks with friends within the monastery, his continuing intimacy with those who had left Bec to go to Caen or Canterbury with Lanfranc, his correspondence with monks in other monasteries who sought his advice, had provided all the stimulus he needed for everything that he had written.

But in his very last years at Bec, he was obliged for the first time to reply to a potentially damaging criticism – all the more damaging because it associated him in an apparently friendly way with an unacceptable doctrine. It seems to have been in 1089 that Anselm heard that Roscelin, who was then a little-known but extremely pertinacious and dangerous master of one of the secular schools of Northern France, had been proclaiming to the world that both Lanfranc and Anselm held a view of the Trinity similar to his own. Since this view was blatantly heterodox, an answer was required, and Anselm did not find it easy to know how to answer.

Before going into further detail, the situation, so unprecedented in Anselm's experience, but often to recur in the future, requires some elucidation, for in one way or another it was symptomatic of Anselm's later years: after thirty years of peaceful monastic development, when all his problems arose within himself and the religious community, he was to have another twenty in which nearly all his problems came from sources outside the main stream of monastic life.

The two sources of these new problems were the secular schools and the new forms of organized ecclesiastical and secular government. Both of them were made possible and necessary as a result of the increasing wealth and growing population of western Europe. In Anselm's experience, Roscelin represented the first of these new forces, the Hildebrandine papacy the second. The latter must be left for discussion in connection with Anselm's work and outlook as archbishop; Roscelin may briefly be dealt with here.

It was in about 1089, that Anselm first heard that Roscelin had produced a logical consequence of the doctrine of the Trinity, for which he claimed the support of both Lanfranc and Anselm. What made his claim peculiarly embarrassing was that (as we shall see) there was a grain of truth in it; and Roscelin was not a man easy to meet in friendly discussion. Like many secular masters, he was a rolling stone. When Anselm first heard of him, he was a canon of Compiègne; then, by 1092 he was at Bayeux, perhaps as a canon of the cathedral. Thereafter, we find him at Tours, then at Loches and later in England, teaching and making himself hated by established authorities, but always finding students eager to listen to him. Long afterwards, still undefeated, he is found as a canon of Besançon. He taught Abelard; he corresponded with the earliest of the Oxford masters; he started Anselm on a new phase of his theological career. These facts are his chief monument. There are not many who have raised so conspicuous a monument on so little material. Masters like Roscelin were men whom neither official condemnation nor popular execration could silence. Whatever disasters befell, they could always find new students and new positions. Among all the new phenomena of this time, these largely unchronicled masters are among the most important – symptomatic of a new relationship between the world and the religious life. In studying Anselm's later years, it is necessary to have the contrast between him and this new breed of masters frequently in mind.

Roscelin made enemies wherever he went, but he was irrepressible, and he touched nothing that he did not exacerbate. Far more than either Berengar or Abelard, who – though they both brought execration and condemnation on their heads – were essentially sober and well-versed theologians, Roscelin was always a cause of dissension wherever he went. So far as his conflict with Anselm is concerned, his importance is that he was the first medieval master to bring the logical problem of the doctrine of the Trinity into the open. He asserted that the three Persons of the Trinity must either be so separate that they could (if convention allowed) be said to be three Gods; or so united that all three must have been incarnate in Christ. If this was correct – and it was not easy to see the flaw – either the doctrine of the Trinity required revision, or it had to be admitted that the doctrine of the Trinity defied the rules of logic. The first of these possibilities was inadmissible; the second was extremely unwelcome at a time when the whole drive of theology lay in the attempt to give a logically coherent and systematically complete account of the whole range of Christian doctrine. In brief, therefore, Roscelin introduced discussion on what was to be a major problem in theological discussion during the next hundred years; and he introduced the subject in the most provocative manner by associating with his expression of doubt the names of Lanfranc and Anselm.[12] So far as Lanfranc was concerned this

---

[12] *Ep.* 136 (ii, 41).

claim was not very plausible, and it was anyhow beyond the possibility of proof. But in Anselm's case, the claim had (as we shall see) some plausibility, and it was this that made it dangerous.

At first, Roscelin's claim came to Anselm only at second-hand and in a single sentence; but it required an answer because he spoke as if Anselm was his friend, or anyhow his supporter. It was the situation of Berengar and Lanfranc all over again, but on a doctrine more central, more clearly defined in Creeds and worship, and more difficult to explain.

Roscelin's attack was the first dangerous criticism Anselm had encountered. Lanfranc had criticized the absence of authoritative quotations in the *Monologion*; Gaunilo, more fundamentally, had criticized the principal argument of the *Proslogion*. But neither had challenged his conclusion, only his method. Roscelin claimed nothing less than Anselm's support for a heresy:

> If the three Persons in God are one thing, and not three things (like three angels or three souls having the same will and power), then both the Father and the Holy Spirit must have been incarnate with the Son.[13]

If this argument was sound, the converse would also follow: if *only* the Son became incarnate, then the three Persons must be three things – three Gods – and not one.

This kind of language needed a very firm reply, and a reply was not easy to formulate. Anselm wrote first to the bishop of Beauvais in 1089 simply affirming his assent to the statements of the Creeds, and asserting that it was the duty of all Christians to believe these statements, whether they understood them or not.[14] He also started to write a longer explanation, but having heard that Roscelin had dropped his allegations, he put his unfinished reply aside, no doubt with some relief.

Two or three years then passed without further trouble; but by the time of his visit to England in 1092, Anselm had heard that Roscelin had returned to the subject, and a reply was a matter of urgency. He sent to Bec for his unfinished answer, and at least five drafts of his reply have survived in English manuscript collections; but the winter ended without his having done much more than add some new sections to his still incomplete draft.[15]

So far as he had gone by the spring of 1093, his additions were not

---

[13] These are Roscelin's alleged words, quoted in *Ep. de Incarn. Verbi*, first recension (Schmitt, i, p. 282).　　[14] *Ep.* 136 (ii, 41).
[15] See Schmitt, i, pp. 281–290; ii, pp. 3–35; and Schmitt, 1939, pp. 277–90.

altogether happy. For instance, Roscelin had quoted him as saying that the Persons of the Trinity were to God what the qualities *albus, justus, grammaticus*, were to an individual man. In other words, that the relationship between the one God and three Persons was like that of Substance and Accidents: a wholly unacceptable position in orthodox Christian doctrine. In the first draft of his reply, Anselm did not deny that he had said this, but he attempted to justify this parallel by explaining the sense in which it was true:

> If 'albus', 'iustus', and 'grammaticus', are said of a certain man, for instance St Paul, they do not make many Pauls; similarly if 'Father, Son and Holy Ghost' are said of God, they do not make many Gods: *this*, I accept, this I believe, this I do not deny that I said.[16]

This was a brave admission, and, in the sense in which Anselm intended, it was not objectionable. But it opened the way to so many misunderstandings that Anselm suppressed this passage in his final version. Nevertheless, the discovery of the unfinished draft has shown that Roscelin was not quite reckless in mentioning Anselm as a possible supporter of his views. One of the consequences of Anselm's remark might reasonably seem to be that the Persons of the Trinity were comparable to 'qualities' in created beings; and, if this was true, it could lead to the conclusion that all three Persons of the Trinity became incarnate in Christ – the very thing that Roscelin asserted, and all orthodox teaching denied.

From the evidence of these drafts we can be sure that Anselm had not made much progress before his election as archbishop of Canterbury in March 1093. It is also clear that, for the first time in his life, he was not writing *con amore* as in all his earlier works, but under pressure from hostile forces. It was a new experience, and he evidently did not enjoy it. But, like others, he benefited from criticism however unwelcome, and finally he gave his argument a sharper edge.

For instance, he had always held that it was necessary to believe in order to understand; but in his final version he elaborated: 'He who does not believe,' he writes, 'cannot *experience*; and whoever does not *experience*, cannot understand.' He never elaborated the nature of this experience. Elsewhere he uses the verb *experior* fairly frequently of sense-experiences and experiences of love, friendship, kindness, and so on; but here he seems to refer to some inner

---

[16] *Ep. de Incarn. Verbi*, first recension (Schmitt, i, p. 283).

mystical experience of the truth of a doctrine which lies beyond the limits of rational explanation.[17]

This extension of his vocabulary may be associated with another. We know that he had always insisted on the real existence of general substances like 'Truth' or 'Man'. But now, for the first time explicitly, he goes on to insist that logicians who think that such substances have no existence outside the mind are incapable of talking about the divine nature.[18] This would mean that it is not only the fool, who says in his heart 'There is no God', who is incapable of talking about the being of God; the philosopher also, who thinks that 'whiteness' does not exist outside the mind, is also pronounced incapable of speaking about the nature of God. Whether this elaboration of his philosophy is already implicit in the *Proslogion*, I am not competent to say. But the fact that it was made explicit at this moment suggests that he had to dig deep into the principles of his speculative system to find a reply to Roscelin.

Anselm's *Epistola de Incarnatione Verbi*, which in its various forms, was laboriously hammered out over a period of three or four years, is certainly not one of his masterpieces. It was clearly written against the grain on a subject on which he would have preferred to remain silent. In all his previous works he had drawn on the richness of his developing sensibility and understanding. By contrast, the wilderness of half-finished drafts of his reply to Roscelin reveal some weaknesses and ambiguities, which had to be rather laboriously refined or excluded from the final work which Anselm sent to the pope. Nevertheless, it is a work which conveys an important message: at the time when he became archbishop, Anselm even at Bec was entering a world of confrontations. Even if he had stayed at Bec, he could no longer have continued to unfold a quietly growing wealth of spiritual experience. Roscelin's intervention forced Anselm to take notice of a new and rapidly growing form of intellectual life in the secular schools, which could not be excluded from the monasteries.

As he enlarged and remoulded this controversial work, Anselm was taking his first steps into a new world. Before he finished it, he had been overtaken by events which changed the course of his life, and he had been confronted by a new theological issue which led to the writing of his *Cur Deus Homo*. The central event which changed

---

[17] *Ep. de Incarn. Verbi*, first recension (Schmitt, i, p. 284), and repeated in all later recensions.   [18] Ibid. Schmitt, i, p. 285 and repeated in later recensions.

his life was having the archbishopric of Canterbury thrust upon him in March 1093. Whatever his own feelings may have been, this development gave him a new position in the world, even as an author. It was in the midst of these events that in the course of the next two years he at last finished his reply to Roscelin.

The changes in the audience which he addresses in his various intermediate recensions bear witness to the change in his position in the world. His earlier works had all been written for his pupils and monastic friends, and he could take their good will for granted. But now he had to think of a wider audience, and we can see his conception of this wider audience changing while he wrote his reply to Roscelin. In the earliest form of his reply, in his last months as abbot of Bec, he addressed his work to 'all lords, fathers, and brother-worshippers in the Catholic and Apostolic faith'. In the version which he completed after he had become archbishop, he abbreviated this grandiose address-list to the pope alone. The change symbolizes his new position: whereas in the past he had thought of himself as a member of the community, with a whole hierarchy of spiritual superiors, now he stands alone with only the pope as his spiritual superior.

Another change that took place while he wrote his reply was that he extended its subject-matter. He had intended merely to prove against Roscelin that only a single Person of the Trinity could be incarnate. But – although, as he says, it was no part of the original plan – he finally went a step further and introduced various considerations proving that, since only one Person in the Trinity *could* be incarnate, that Person must necessarily be the Son: otherwise there would be *two* Sons in the Holy Trinity, and this would be 'unbecoming'.[19] This extension may seem modest, and perhaps frivolous. But it is certainly neither. It introduced a theme which was to have a great future in theological debate, especially among Anselm's pupils, in developing the idea that God always does, and always *must* do, not only that which is logically necessary, but also that which is most 'fitting'.

Anselm later pursued the question of 'that which is fitting' in all its ramifications, and these intricate rationalizations may seem scarcely compatible with the high dignity of the subject. But, from

[19] Ibid. c. 10, Schmitt, ii, p. 25: *Nempe si spiritus sanctus incarnatus esset . . . essent duo filii in trinitate dei, filius scilicet dei et filius hominis*; and note the wealth of variant readings testifying to Anselm's difficulty in reaching a satisfactory formulation. For the most complete discussion of how 'that which is fitting' applies to God, see *CDH* I, c. 12; and for its Biblical origin, Hebrews ii, 10.

an Anselmian point of view, to think thus is a mistake: all his reasoning has the final purpose of showing that there is not, and cannot be, the slightest deficiency or imbalance either in God's nature, or in God's creation. This was the doctrine that he most fully worked out in his *Cur Deus Homo*, and it was to be taken up later by those of his pupils who were to become some of the earliest protagonists for the doctrine of the Immaculate Conception of the Virgin Mary. The principle that God did whatever was most 'fitting' became one of the hall-marks of the Anselmian school. It exhibited the perfection of God in a new light: everything that God does follows a perfect order that is not only perfect in its rationality, but also supremely beautiful. This theme also will be more fully developed in Anselm's *Cur Deus Homo*.

The appearance of these new themes in his answer to Roscelin illustrates the way in which this unwelcome intrusion from the secular schools opened up a new phase in Anselm's thought at the moment when he was at the beginning of a new phase in his practical life, and to these origins we must now turn.

II ANSELM FACES THE WORLD

I   The benefactors of Bec

In speaking of Anselm as prior, I have remarked that he was no Lanfranc; and in speaking of him as abbot, it is necessary to make the same remark with greater emphasis. Lanfranc only reached his full stature when he was in command: Anselm only in self-abnegation.

No one was more conscious than Anselm himself of his defects as an administrator.[20] Not indeed that he saw them as defects: in his view, whatever deflected a monk from worship, study, and meditation was only to be admitted so far as was necessary for the well-being of the monastic body; beyond this it was a temptation to be resisted. In times of shortage, his first instinct was to leave everything to God. If the community remained loyal to the ideal for which it was founded, God would provide. Eadmer in his biography of Anselm perfectly caught and recorded this funda-mental fact, and in so far as his later biographers, in a mistaken zeal for showing that he was no fool, have forgotten it, they have

[20] *VA* I, pp. 27–8; II, pp. 8, 12–15, are of fundamental importance for understanding his attitude to secular business; see also *HN*, pp. 32–5, 84–7; also *Epp.* 159 (iii, 10), 183 (iv, 105), 206 (iii, 166).

presented a warped picture of his acuteness. Never was a man more acute than Anselm, but not in the way of the world. He simply believed that God would not desert those who purified their lives, strengthened their faith, and trusted in Him. The result, as Eadmer portrayed it, was that there were some desperate moments for the community while Anselm was abbot, but in the nick of time something always turned up – perhaps a gift from Lanfranc, or an unexpected catch of fish.

Another characteristic attitude, which needs to be borne in mind for understanding Anselm's activity in the world, is his view of the place of monasteries in society. They were for him, as for most of the aristocracy of his time, central points of cohesion in the social order. They were the mother-churches, shrines, burial places, refuges in old age and adversity, for widely dispersed family and feudal groups. To Anselm, the monasteries were this, and a great deal more than this. They were in principle, intention, and possibility, the perfect form of Christian life, giving the best opportunity for the exercise of Christian virtues in a tumultuous world, and for eternal salvation hereafter. The duty of the laity, and their best hope of salvation, lay in their supporting monastic foundations, to which they could commit their children as oblates, their unmarried daughters as associates in piety, their wives as widows, and if possible themselves at the end of their lives as converts to the Rule. This congruity of interest between himself and the lay aristocracy helps to explain the remarkable hold that he had on the affection of violent and aggressive magnates, who, as Eadmer remarked, became mild and tame in his company.[21] He could combine extraordinary severity in judging the dedication required of monks in their struggle for salvation with a strange acquiescence in lay violence. Monks were the fighters, and their lay patrons the support troops in the drive for salvation. The former needed to be equipped and disciplined in the inner lives to perform their task; the latter needed in the first place to provide the resources and goodwill necessary for the monasteries. This community of interest formed the bond which held society together in this world and it offered some hope for all in eternity.

As abbot, his relations with the world chiefly presented them-

---

[21] For Anselm's personal magnetism, see especially *VA* II, 32. Also the obituary verses in *PL* 158, cols. 135–42, of which there is now a critical edition by R. Sharpe, 1985, 266–79, should not be neglected.

selves in the dual context of organizing offshoots of the monastery and offering counsel and aid to their benefactors. For both of these activities he was well fitted by temperament and social background. He thought his external duties a distraction from more important work, and he always insisted that the happiest time of his life was when he was prior with no duties outside the monastery. Old men in high positions can often say this kind of thing while relishing the pomp and dignity of later life. But Anselm's own words, and Eadmer's accounts of his resistance to each step of promotion beyond the priorate, express an abhorrence which must be judged to be either entirely genuine or unusually hypocritical. Eadmer reports that when Anselm was elected as abbot his fellow-monks asked him to omit all formal objections, and to agree to his election without further ado, but:

he threw himself down at full length before them all, and with tears and pitiable sobs begged and prayed them to have mercy and to allow him to remain free from so great a burden.[22]

It was his frequent assertion, reported by Eadmer, that if Archbishop Maurilius had not interposed his authority, he would never have agreed to his election as abbot. We shall see very similar scenes enacted when he became archbishop of Canterbury, and he had good reason for doubting his administrative ability, as one small example will show.

His predecessor Herluin, the founder of Bec, had been sick and feeble for several years before his death in August 1078; and after Lanfranc's departure in 1063 it seems that, despite the growth in numbers of monks and in general esteem, the administration of the monastery was at least infirm. Unlike Lanfranc during his years as prior, Anselm had not filled the administrative gap left by the abbot's incapacity. He had relied on Providence in every emergency, and it needed a gift of £20 from Lanfranc to keep the monastery going through the winter after Herluin's death. When spring came, Anselm wrote two letters of almost comic incompetence to Lanfranc, setting out the tribulations of his early months as abbot: the dearness of vegetables and oats; his improvident purchase of some land after Herluin's death; his attempt to save money by improvising a new seal from two pieces which did not match; his appropriation of money, which Lanfranc had sent for

---

[22] *VA* I, xxvi, p. 44.

more urgent needs, to make a new chalice; his frantic search for evidence for impending law-suits.[23]

According to Eadmer, life continued in this makeshift fashion for the next fifteen years, always on the verge of crisis, and always saved just in time.[24] Amazingly, the system worked. The abbey grew in numbers, in reputation, and in benefactions as never before. When he finally left Bec in 1093, Anselm could make the remarkable statement that 'many of you, indeed *almost all*, came to Bec because of me'; though he added, 'none of you became a monk for my sake, nor in hope of any reward from me'.[25] They had come to consult him, to hear him, to be with him, and, following his advice, they became monks. They were young men who had come of their own free will, and not, like most of the earlier monks, as child oblates. This was one of the signs of a new age, and with Anselm as abbot Bec particularly benefited from the change.

Despite this new trend, many probably still came as child oblates; and of those who came as mature men, not all came of their own volition. Notably, Lanfranc's nephew, who bore his name, had been received at his uncle's request. He was an ambitious young man who thought (perhaps not unnaturally) that his uncle's eminence entitled him to early promotion – an idea that Anselm abominated. The young Lanfranc was, as we shall see, to be a cause of great trouble to Anselm. But despite his failure in this case, there is plenty of evidence from many sources that Anselm had an extraordinary power of winning the love of people of all kinds. Members of the military aristocracy saw him as one of themselves, differing only in having the hand of God upon him, and he saw them as members of the extended family of Bec despite their sins.

The last quarter of the eleventh century was an important moment in the settling of these families into their new position in the world. After the tumults of the first decade after the Conquest, the minor aristocracy of Normandy was beginning to settle down in England, getting accustomed to the permanence of their vast, their almost unbelievable, good fortune. One of their first instinctive reactions to their new affluence was to enrich the religious houses which they had founded or supported as best they could in their less

---

[23] *Epp.* 89 (ii, 1), 90 (ii, 2); and, for his hand-to-mouth habits of administration, *VA* I, xxviii, pp. 46–8. For a different view of Anselm's capacities as an administrator, see Vaughn, 1987, pp. 58–67, and our exchange of views in *Albion*, 20, 1988, 181–220.

[24] See especially the expressive phrases in *VA* I, xxviii, p. 47, where there is a charming description of the nice balance between poverty and destitution at Bec in Anselm's days as abbot. [25] *Ep.* 156 (iii, 7) (Schmitt, iv, p. 22, lines 144–6).

prosperous days.[26] This could not happen immediately. During the first ten years after the Conquest, the Norman invaders were still struggling to establish their position among a hostile population, to define their rights against neighbouring magnates, and to safeguard these rights against the native English whom they had ousted.

This task was broadly accomplished by 1080. Before this date, Bec had felt the lack of the patronage of the great families which had enriched the monasteries of Jumièges, Fécamp, and St Evroul. Its main supporters were of second or third rank, like the Crispins and the counts of Brionne. So benefactions did not come easily. But, as England became more settled, Bec felt the benefit of a new flow of endowments, and these led to a remarkable change in its position in the world. In 1078, when Herluin died, it had no dependent priories; by 1093, it had three in France and one in England, with a second new abbey in course of foundation at Chester under Anselm's direction.

In the intervening years, gifts of English lands and revenues had been flowing in, creating problems for the future, but bringing some immediate prosperity. In time, these gifts would dissipate the energies of the foundation they were meant to nourish; but for the moment, prosperity and discipline could go hand in hand. They created a situation ideally suited to Anselm's genius. He might be an indifferent housekeeper, but he took a close and effective interest in organizing dependent priories. This was the kind of work he was good at: overseeing the discipline, and sharing the aspirations of their members. The care he took in choosing their priors established a tradition of succession which was an important factor in ensuring the long stability of Bec. The work proved to be very demanding, and Anselm complained about the pressure of business.[27] But he had found a sphere of work as an organizer of monastic communities, not too big for close contact with their head, not too grand for simplicity, capable of being carefully cultivated.

The record of his fifteen years as abbot after the completion of his *Proslogion* is one of persistent activity as a teacher of the religious life at every level of practice and intellectual inquiry. His three dialogues on *Truth*, *Free Will*, and the *Fall of the Devil*, and the steady growth in the number and organization of the dependent priories of Bec, alone would have sufficed to give him a niche in

[26] For the endowment of Norman monasteries in England after 1066, see D. Matthew, 1962, pp. 26–71.   [27] See *Epp.* 103 (ii, 13), 129 (ii, 35), 132 (ii, 38).

eleventh-century monastic and intellectual history. But in comparison with the works of his earlier years they mark a period of consolidation rather than of new thoughts, not unnatural in a man burdened with many duties.

Anselm himself seems to have felt that by 1092, in making his last visit to England as abbot, he was approaching the end of his creative work. One symptom of this was that, to occupy what he expected to be a few months of leisure, he asked the monks of Bec to send him his letters, which he had been trying to collect for several years, together with his Prayer to St Nicholas, which he had lately provided for the translation of a relic to Bec, and his unfinished and long deferred reply to Roscelin. Clearly he was hoping to correct or complete these works while waiting for the king to find time to deal with his business in England. In the event, he did not have time to do much, if any, work on his letters and *Prayers*, and he was still making alterations to his reply to Roscelin more than a year later when he had been consecrated as archbishop of Canterbury.

There was a symbolic appropriateness in his double struggle during these months to finish his reply to Roscelin and to avoid becoming archbishop: they both projected him forcibly into a new and unwelcome world of thought and action. We have considered the stages of his enforced reply to Roscelin, and we must now consider the steps which brought him to Canterbury.

2 The reluctant archbishop

In approaching the very strange circumstances in which Anselm became archbishop of Canterbury, the first question we encounter is how seriously his violently expressed resistance to the move is to be taken. We have already seen that Anselm reacted to his election as abbot with similar violence. On both these occasions the basis of his objection was similar: he wanted to pursue a meditative and teaching life without the distractions of secular business in which he had no interest, and for which he felt no competence. But on both occasions the pressure to accept was irresistible. In becoming abbot, he had had the call of a unanimous election, the command of his ecclesiastical superior, and the well-being of the Church. And, though he lamented the distractions of his life as abbot, he found his vocation in attracting an increasing flow of young men to Bec, in teaching them and forming their minds, and in organizing small communities attached to the monastery. The progression from his earlier more purely contemplative days to the busy days of monastic growth came easily and naturally, and he never regretted it.

The Canterbury case is more complicated, and the facts must be left to speak for themselves. But before we approach the facts, there is one insinuation that may be met without delay. It is sometimes suggested that Anselm's long stay in England, perhaps even his coming to England in the first place, was connected with his desire to become Lanfranc's successor. Rumours to this effect seem to have circulated from an early date. But there is one objection which weighs heavily against them. It is this: when he arrived in England in 1092, the archbishopric had been vacant for over three years, and it was entirely in the interests of the king to keep it vacant. He was engaged in protracted military operations in Scotland and Wales; and he had even greater plans for absorbing Normandy and extending its boundaries into Maine. For these operations, money was the first requirement, and the revenues of vacant bishoprics and abbeys provided a much needed replenishment for his campaigns.[28]

Moreover, from the king's point of view, the circumstances were extraordinarily favourable for his retaining control of ecclesiastical property. No pope was recognized in England, and there was no effective pressure from his barons or bishops to recognize either of the papal claimants, or to make appointments to the vacant bishoprics and abbacies. The bishops were nearly all the king's men. Rebellions among the aristocracy had been crushed. The vacancy at Canterbury could continue apparently indefinitely to the king's advantage. Even on the quite unsupported hypothesis that Anselm wanted the archbishopric, he can scarcely have supposed that, simply by hanging around in England, the king would have been moved to make him archbishop. With this preliminary remark, we may turn to the evidence.

The facts are few. Nearly all of them come from Eadmer, who wrote partly as an eye-witness, and partly as a reporter of what Anselm or others had told him. What he relates is that Anselm had two urgent reasons for coming to England in 1092. The first was to supervise the properties and priory of Bec in England. For this

---

[28] There is a careful account of Rufus's income from vacant bishoprics and abbacies in Barlow, 1983, pp. 134–62, with perhaps too little emphasis on the importance of this addition to Rufus's resources: in an emergency, relatively small additions to income can make a great difference, especially when they are capable of rigorous exploitation.

purpose, a visit was overdue. Six years had passed since Anselm's last visit, and a new king had come to the throne. Apart from the supervision of the properties and priories of Bec in England, a renewal of the royal confirmation of the abbey's English properties, which he had obtained from William I as a result of his previous visit, was highly desirable.

Then there was a second reason: Anselm's friend, Hugh earl of Chester, was ill and wanted to see him before he died, partly with a view to the foundation of a monastery at Chester under Anselm's supervision. Despite these calls, Anselm long refused to come, according to Eadmer, because he was afraid that people would think he was angling for the archbishopric. Eadmer also reports that it was the monks of Bec who insisted that Anselm should put an end to his delay and visit England on the business of the monastery. Anselm had gone to Boulogne in the late summer of 1092 to visit the Countess Ida, who was a patron of Bec, and the monks of Bec forbade him to return until he had gone to England. Under this pressure, he crossed the Channel and reached Canterbury on 7 September. Here he was greeted by the monks as their hoped-for archbishop; and, according to Eadmer, this caused him so much dismay that, despite the fact that the next day was the Feast of the Nativity of the Blessed Virgin, he left at dawn.[29] His immediate destination was Chester, but on the way he had to pass through London, and it was probably here that he first met William Rufus, though he transacted no business on that occasion.[30]

Then he went on to Chester, where he found that the earl had recovered, but there was much work to be done in organizing the new monastic foundation in a church which was still staffed with secular canons. Eadmer speaks of him spending 'many days' on this work, and this is borne out by the documents of the new monastery which prove that, before he became archbishop and presumably before he left Chester, he laid down the outline of a new community, with an abbot and customs, and perhaps some monks, from Bec.[31] When this was done, Anselm returned to London and

---

[29] *HN*, pp. 27–9; *VA* II, i.

[30] For Anselm's meeting with the king on his way to Chester, see *VA* II, i.

[31] For Anselm's active participation in the foundation of the new abbey at Chester, see the *Cartulary of St Werburgh's Abbey, Chester*, Chetham Society, NS, 79, 1920, ed. J. Tait, pp. 15–22, 38–9. The foundation charter is obviously a composite document made some time after the event, but its details are supported by a *Testimonium Anselmi archiepiscopi*, which records that he made the arrangements while he was still abbot of Bec.

settled down at Westminster with his friend and pupil, Abbot Gilbert Crispin. From Westminster, he wrote to the monks of Bec telling them that the king had deferred their business, and that he had no hope of returning before Lent 1093. It is hard to see why the king should not have dealt with Anselm's business at his Christmas court in London, but it is useless to speculate on the reasons, except to this extent: if, as seems plausible, Anselm wished to obtain new royal confirmation of the possessions of Bec in England, this would have required the presence at the royal court of all the donors, and this may not have been practicable by Christmas. At all events Anselm made no complaint, and simply asked the monks to send him the unfinished works which he hoped to complete while he was waiting.[32]

After writing this letter, except for his presence at the royal court at Christmas, which was perhaps held at Westminster, we hear nothing about Anselm's movements until 6 March 1093, when he was staying at an unnamed village in Gloucestershire. The king at this time was based on Gloucester, and Anselm's presence in the neighbourhood is entirely consistent with the date which, as he told the monks, had been assigned for the business of Bec. We do not know exactly where he was, but he may possibly have gone to one of the manors of Westminster Abbey, of which there were several in this part of the country, to await the meeting of the royal court.

At this point, Eadmer takes up his story again with a wealth of detail which suggests that he was an eye-witness. What he tells us is that in March 1093 the king suddenly fell ill while he was in Gloucestershire. He struggled back to the royal base at Gloucester, fully expecting to die. In this expectation, Anselm was sent for to administer the last rites: he arrived, heard the king's confession, and exacted a promise of amendment. The terms were written, sealed, and placed on the altar. Then the question of filling the vacant archbishopric arose, perhaps as one of the conditions of absolution, and the king at once named Anselm.

Chaos and consternation ensued: Anselm resisted with tears streaming down his face, his nose bleeding, protesting his

---

[32] *Ep. 147* (ii, 51). Vaughn, 1987, p. 125, dates this letter after Christmas 1092; but, since Anselm's words and his request for his letters, etc. imply that there will be a considerable interval before his return, the autumn of 1092 seems much more likely. If his messenger had left Westminster after Christmas, there would have been very little time to get on with the unfinished works from Bec before the beginning of Lent on 2 March 1093, which Anselm mentioned as the date by which he might himself have returned to Bec.

incapacity and predicting disaster; the king and bishops and his own clerks all harrying him to accept. The king attempted to press the pastoral staff into his clenched hand, and when he failed, the bishops forced open his fist and closed his fingers round the shaft. Anselm was then carried into church with the crozier thus held in his hand in the midst of acclamations, '*Vivat episcopus*' and '*Te Deum*', while he continued to cry out '*Nihil est quod facitis.*' So the long day ended in tears and confusion, but with Anselm, however reluctantly and certainly uncanonically, still in possession of the archiepiscopal crozier.[33] What the future would be no one knew. Or did Anselm know? That is the question.

Everything depends on the sincerity of Anselm's protestations, for which we have not only Eadmer's vivid account, but also Anselm's own repeated statements. If we believe him, we shall think that the whole prospect was abhorrent to him. If we do not believe him, and think that his words were a calculated reaction to a situation which in his heart he welcomed, then we must think that, with whatever mitigation, he persistently mis-stated the truth. There is really no half-way house between these two positions, for we do not rely only on Eadmer's account of events; we have Anselm's own solemn and repeated declarations to the monks of Bec, to the bishops of Evreux and Beauvais, and finally to the pope.[34]

What is not in question is that at the end of the day he had taken the first step towards becoming archbishop: the crozier had been pressed into his hand and he had been proclaimed archbishop. Nothing was yet irrevocable. There was still a long way to go before he would be fully installed as archbishop. But in what had been done so far, there were two surprising features.

The first is that though Anselm objected violently to becoming archbishop, he raised no objection to the manner of his nomination and investiture, though these proceedings were in at least two respects offensive to Canon Law:

1 He had not been elected by the monks or by any properly constituted ecclesiastical body. No doubt he could take the consent of the monks for granted, but it was precisely such a

[33] See *HN*, pp. 31–7, for all these details.
[34] For Anselm's declarations, see *Epp.* 148 (iii, 1), 156 (ii, 7), to the monks of Bec, 159 (iii, 11), to the bishop of Evreux, 160 (iii, 11), to the bishop of Beauvais, 206 (iii, 166) to Urban II, where he asks to be relieved *de vinculo tantae servitutis*, and restored to the *libertatem serviendi Deo*. For the alternative interpretation, see Vaughn, 1986, pp. 129–135.

casual assumption of consent that was offensive to the strict upholders of Canon Law. Anselm never mentioned the matter.

2 He had been bluntly nominated by the king, who had signified his will in the old-fashioned way by attempting to give him the pastoral staff. In this attempt, according to Eadmer, he had not succeeded. But Anselm's objection had not been, and never was, that the king was the wrong source both of decision and of staff. He resisted the bishops' attempts to give him the staff quite as vigorously as the king's, and during the next five years he raised no objection to consecrating bishops who had been similarly nominated and invested by the king, although the Lateran Council of 1078 had, in the clearest possible terms, condemned and excommunicated all those who took part in such proceedings.[35] Clearly Anselm knew nothing about the conciliar decision, and continued to know nothing about it for another six years. No one can blame his initial ignorance, though it is strange ignorance in an abbot of fifteen years' standing. What is even stranger is that he took no steps, either immediately or in the next few years, to fill this gap in his knowledge of recent or (for that matter) ancient Canon Law.

Then there is an even more surprising fact. Before agreeing to accept his nomination, Anselm sought the consent of his secular and ecclesiastical superiors in Normandy, that is to say, the duke and the archbishop of Rouen, and of the community at Bec. The duke duly agreed, and urged him to do what his brother wished; the archbishop agreed and ordered him to accept. But the monks of Bec were more difficult. Important voices were raised in objection. They objected that he had told them he would never leave them; also that he had taken an oath to serve them without limit. But above all there were clearly several in the community and others outside, perhaps inspired by members of the community, who distrusted his motives. The community at Bec wrote saying that they had held an inconclusive meeting, in which some had favoured, but others – and it would seem a majority – had refused permission, and they sent a deputation to explain their views.[36] In this way the correspondence dragged on for several months, and it was not until August that Anselm took the matter into his own hands, told them he was going, and gave them the name of the monk

---

[35] *Gregorii VII Registrum*, pp. 400–3: Decrees of the Council of November 1078, c. 8.
[36] *Ep.* 155 (iii, 6).

whom he had chosen as his successor and ordered them to elect in his place.

These details would not be worth recalling if they did not seem to lend support to the view that Anselm was less unworldly in his ambitions than he pretended. It might be thought that if a high proportion of the monks of Bec, who knew him best, had doubts about his motives, they are likely to have been right. By any standards, his nomination of his successor was high-handed, if not flatly unconstitutional.

With regard to his nomination of his successor, however, it is important to note that there was no clear direction in the Rule about the procedure for electing a new abbot when his predecessor was still alive. Anselm looked on himself as having a continuing responsibility for the future of the monastery. He may have been misguided, but there is nothing in the Rule to suggest that he was wrong.

As for the suspicions among the monks about Anselm's motives, there are two facts that need to be taken into account. First, the leader of the opposition at Bec was the younger Lanfranc, the nephew of the archbishop. He had always been difficult to manage; and, when he had been elected abbot of St Wandrille in about 1090, Anselm had refused to give his consent. So Lanfranc had stayed at Bec, sore in himself, and a cause of unrest in others. Moreover, it would seem that he was not the only one whose ambitions had been checked by Anselm. Anselm's horror of ambition as a motive in the monastic life had always been sharply expressed, and now the malcontents had a chance to hit back. Even those who were well disposed to Anselm may have found his acceptance of the archbishopric hard to understand, and his expressions of unalterable devotion to Bec hard to reconcile with his decision after all to go up higher. It was the price he had to pay for having been the main attraction for new recruits for the last twenty-five years.[37]

It is plain from these events that many critics of Anselm then, like several of his admirers now, have thought that his expressions of dismay and anguish, his tears and struggles, were no more than a conventional cover for the real truth that he wanted the archbishopric. There are certainly some strange and inexplicable features in the events leading up to his final agreement to accept the archbishopric, and they are capable of being interpreted in a

[37] For Anselm's refusal to allow the young Lanfranc to leave the community to become an abbot, see *Epp.* 137 (ii, 42); 138 (ii, 43).

number of different ways. In the end, our interpretation of his motives and the trustworthiness of his explanations must depend on our judgement of his character and aims as a whole, and a final verdict must be delayed until we have followed his later history as archbishop. But a preliminary judgement may be reached on the basis of the advice which he had given to others in similar circumstances in the past.

This was not the first time that Anselm had been required to think deeply about the circumstances in which a monk should consent to that 'promotion' in the world which no monk should seek, but which the good of the Church sometimes required. He had been consulted on this question on several occasions, and he had worked out a set of principles to be followed. These principles were: first, the nominee must genuinely wish *not* to be promoted; second, he must have done all he could to avoid it; third, the best advisers available must have urged acceptance of the bishopric. If these three conditions were met, acceptance was the right course.[38] In Anselm's case, there can be no doubt that they were fully met, and that the rules which he laid down for others required his acceptance.

Then, apart from the conditions for acccepting promotion which he had laid down for others, there were special considerations applicable in this case, in particular the state of the English Church, the probability of a long-continued vacancy if he refused, and the consequent decay of monastic discipline. On these grounds too, he could only accept. To have refused would have been an example of that spurious freedom which is slavery to self-will; to accept was an example of that freedom which he had defined ten years earlier as the renunciation of free choice.

A more serious problem arises with regard to his indifference to, or ignorance of, the canonical procedure for election and investiture, and the blemishes in the procedure of his own election. But this problem concerns, not his consent to election, but his attitude to canonical procedures, and this can best be discussed in examining his record as archbishop.[39]

Indeed all three problems of Anselm's behaviour in the matter of his election can only be solved in the light of his record as

---

[38] See *Epp.* 52 (iii, 115), 61 (i, 52), 78 (i, 69), 80 (i, 71), 88 (to Anselm quoting his own reservations about promotion), 106 (ii, 16), 137 (ii, 42), 144 (ii, 49), which are all concerned with this problem. It will be noticed that even when Anselm is writing to congratulate a friend on 'promotion', he always includes words about the sacrifice which promotion requires.   [39] See below, pp. 254–9.

archbishop. At the heart of all of them are the overwhelming problems of liberty and obedience, which are at the centre of the Christian universe and which were of special importance to Anselm as a monk who had renounced all exercise of self-will. Anselm's intellectual development had for several years been leading towards a confrontation with this great problem on a multiplicity of issues, which became more urgent and more diversified during his years as archbishop. It is to these problems that we must now turn, beginning with his treatment of the most fundamental of all problems of law and obedience – mankind's fundamental disobedience and God's response to it, which he dealt with in his *Cur Deus Homo* – and going on from this to examine the many varieties of the problem as they presented themselves in the course of his career as archbishop.

PART III

A MONASTIC VIEW IN A
DEVELOPING WORLD, 1093–1109

CHAPTER 9

ANSELM AND THE HUMAN CONDITION

I SOURCES OF A NEW DISPUTE

Even before he accepted the archbishopric in August 1093, the peace of Anselm's earlier days had gone for ever. Wherever he looked, there were controversies. Beside the growing clamour of politics, there were questions which were becoming very insistent. In writing against Roscelin he mentioned 'the many whom I feel to be struggling with this problem'. Similarly in his next work, the *Cur Deus Homo*, he refers to 'many, not only learned but even illiterate men, who ask this question and require an answer'.[1] This large army of questioners was no more imaginary than Roscelin himself. All the appearances are that the scope of theological inquiry had been greatly enlarged during the last decade, both in the range of the questions asked and the variety of people asking them. It would take us too far from our main subject to attempt to classify the very large social and intellectual changes which were responsible for this broadening area of debate.[2] But no account of the new stage in Anselm's development in the last decade of the eleventh century can omit the two main external influences which helped to produce the *Cur Deus Homo*, the greatest of his later works.

These influences came from two main sources: first, from the theological debates of the secular schools; and second, from the criticisms of Christian doctrine coming from the growing Jewish communities in western Europe. As abbot of Bec, Anselm had had some contact with the secular schools through those who came to him from the schools with their doubts, and sometimes stayed to become monks; and Roscelin's attempt to recruit him as a supporter of his views had also drawn his attention to some of the

---

[1] *Ep. de Incarn. Verbi*, c. 1, Schmitt, ii, p. 6; and *CDH* I, c. 1, Schmitt, ii, p. 48.
[2] I have attempted further elucidation of this question in my Gifford Lectures of 1970–71, 'The Rise of Scholastic Christendom', which I hope may one day appear in print.

opinions current in the schools. Now, in the winter of 1092–93, his old friend and pupil Gilbert Crispin, abbot of Westminster, was able to tell him about the criticisms of the Jews. The two together were largely responsible for his writing the *Cur Deus Homo*, and we may consider them in turn, beginning with the Jews.

I The Jews

We have already seen that when Anselm was settling down to spend a few quiet months at Westminster in the autumn of 1092 he had several pieces of work in hand. Meanwhile, Gilbert Crispin was engaged in a new controversy about the Incarnation, which had arisen from the arrival in London of some learned Jews from Mainz. He wrote an account of the argument and dedicated it to Anselm. During the months before, and even after, his nomination as archbishop of Canterbury, Anselm had much time on his hands: for the first time for thirty years he had no administrative responsibilities, and there is reason to think that among other matters he and Gilbert discussed this new controversy.[3]

The Jews whom Gilbert Crispin met in London had raised fundamental questions about the Incarnation: Why was it necessary? Was it possible? Was it not derogatory to the dignity and impassibility of God? Was it not idolatrous? Rabbis who raised these questions were the only learned, the only uncompromising opponents of Christianity in Europe. Dialectic might cause Roscelin to err on the Persons of the Trinity in relation to the Incarnation; but only the Jews were opposed to the possibility of divine Incarnation, and could support their position by learned arguments.

It might be thought that outcasts from Christian society as they were, treated as serfs of the king, living semi-outlawed and wholly despised in areas to which they were confined, they were too remote from ordinary life to be thought dangerous, or worthy of refutation by Christian apologists. But it is a remarkable example of the inefficacy of social ostracism in preventing the spread of ideas that this was not the case. Their ostracism was largely the result of fear, and one of the main fears at this time was about the number of reported conversions to Judaism. Probably the number was

---

[3] For a discussion of the stages in the development of Gilbert's work and their dates, see Gilbert Crispin, *Works*, pp. xxvii–xxx; and for some further details, Southern, 1954, pp. 81–8, and 1963, p. 91n.

exaggerated; but several notable people – a bishop of Bari among them – had been converted to Judaism, and the danger was magnified in common report. Christian apologists felt more embattled than the self-sufficiency and completeness of the Christian system of life and thought might suggest. The sense of being ill-prepared for repelling intellectual attacks was widespread. Even as late as the thirteenth century, after all the scholastic advances of the last two centuries, there was a widespread feeling that the enemies of Christendom were somehow better prepared for an intellectual duel than the Christians. Much more in the eleventh century, scholars in western Europe felt their insufficiency against enemies whose thoughts were almost unknown.

Creating enemies in order to refute them is a common didactic method. For instance, in the *Proslogion*, Anselm created a type of unbeliever who was probably imaginary. But there is nothing unreal about the enemies of his later works. In the *Epistola de Incarnatione Verbi*, Roscelin was a very real enemy, and behind him there lurked an indefinite array of questioners who derived some of their doubts from the schools. Similarly, the unbelievers whom Anselm mentions in his *Cur Deus Homo* were real, and of these the most formidable were the Jews. They were to be seen in increasing numbers in all the towns of northern Europe: they were already strong in Rouen, and they were rapidly becoming familiar in English towns also. They have been too much overlooked as a source of criticism and an incentive to inquiry among Christian theologians at this time.

There were two main targets of Jewish attack. The earliest and most basic was the allegorical exegesis of the Old Testament, which was essential for the Christian rejection of Judaic law. This was an ancient dispute on which nothing new could be said, and nothing old could convince the other side. This controversy could never die, since neither side had anything new to say, and there was always a thin trickle of candid Christians who thought it a confession of weakness to have to make words mean more than they said.[4] Indeed, in the twelfth century it appeared that a certain measure of Christian and Jewish collaboration in Old Testament exegesis was possible.

But in addition to this dispute a new line of Jewish attack was emerging, which touched on a subject dear to Anselm: the honour

---

[4] Beryl Smalley brought to light two such men, Andrew of St Victor and Herbert of Bosham, in *The Study of the Bible in the Middle Ages*, Oxford, 3rd edition, 1983, c. 4.

or dignity of God. The Jewish question was this: how can the Incarnation, with all its indignity of human misery, insult, and shameful death, be reconciled with God's supreme dignity and unchangeable stability? To the Jew, this affront to God's transcendent majesty was of immense importance. It was certainly not less important to Anselm, who is outstanding among theologians for the emphasis he lays on God's honour, arguing that the atrocity of all sin lay in the eternal dishonour which, in intention though not in reality, the sinner inflicts on God.

Honour is a word of complex meaning, as we shall see, but it certainly included the preservation of God's dignity against affront. It was essential, therefore, that the accusation of dishonouring God should be met; and nowhere was the dishonouring of God more conspicuous than in the supreme indignities of Christ's death. Consequently, although it was the Jews who raised the problem in its most acute form, Anselm was especially sensitive to the need for a more searching and satisfying explanation of these indignities than any so far put forward.

Of course Christians could, and did, say that it was the Jews, not the Christians, who had dishonoured God in the Crucifixion. But this did not answer the question: the indignity was not simply in intention, but in the real disgrace of Christ's humiliation, which the Christians hailed as the supreme glorification of God. This required an explanation, which was all the more urgent at a time when Christian art and piety were beginning to emphasize and make explicit with unprecedented realism the indignities and sufferings of Christ – at a time, moreover, when the concept of honour was becoming increasingly important in secular life. The Jewish criticism could not have come at a more sensitive moment.

Gilbert Crispin's debate with the London Jews brought the issue into the open, and there are several reasons for thinking that it was a lively issue at the time when Anselm went to stay with him in the autumn of 1092. In the first place, Gilbert's dedication to Anselm of his first recension of his account of the debate still calls him abbot of Bec. But in every later recension – and there are several – Anselm is addressed as archbishop of Canterbury. Clearly, therefore, the debate was a live issue in the autumn of 1092 when Anselm was staying with him, and Gilbert was still making alterations to the text. Moreover, Gilbert's work contains echoes of thoughts which are found in Anselm's *Cur Deus Homo*. But on the important question of the Devil's rights over mankind, Gilbert adopts the traditional view which Anselm's work refutes. In brief, it seems certain that Anselm had not yet worked out the solution to this problem which became the foundation of his *Cur Deus Homo*.

Even if we knew nothing about the close relationship between Anselm and Gilbert Crispin, there would still be strong reasons for thinking that the Jewish controversy was one of the incentives for writing the *Cur Deus Homo*. Anselm's description of the enemy against whom his work was written could only have referred to the Jews, who were, so far as we know, the only unbelievers who raised the objection to the Incarnation that it entailed the humiliation of God:

The unbelievers deride our simplicity, objecting that we do God an injury, and disgrace Him, when we assert that He descended to a woman's womb, was born of a woman, was nourished with milk and human food, and – not to mention many other things unbecoming to God, – suffered weariness, hunger, thirst, scourging, and death on the Cross among thieves.[5]

To Anselm, with his intense sense of the inviolable dignity of God, even the appearance of divine humiliation was a very serious matter. To be acceptable, it needed to be shown to be necessary and glorious as the only way in which a central purpose of the Creation – Man's salvation – could be achieved. If any other way had been possible, the objection of the unbeliever might have some force. But if it was the only way of achieving that for which the universe had been created, then, far from humiliating God, it showed only the lengths to which God was prepared to go for Man's salvation. Hence its glory. It stretched the love and power of God to the utmost limit, and it succeeded where nothing else would have served God's purpose.

Anselm was often blamed by his later critics for attempting to show that the Incarnation was *necessary*. The traditional Christian view was that God could have chosen other methods, but he chose this because he willed it. This might suffice as an explanation for Christians; but it was clearly inadequate as an answer to the Jewish complaint that the chosen method was an unnecessary outrage to the dignity of God. Moreover, it was not an answer that could satisfy Anselm's own requirement that all God's actions should preserve the order of the universe and the dignity of God. In seeking a proof of the necessity of the Incarnation, therefore, Anselm was seeking to satisfy both his own criterion of 'fittingness'

---

[5] *CDH* I, c. 3, Schmitt, ii, pp. 50–1.

and the requirements of the unbelievers against whom his argument was directed.[6]

The necessity of 'fittingness' in God's activity is the second of Anselm's original theological axioms. The first, which he had discovered in the *Proslogion*, is the necessity of God's existence, in the sense that God cannot be thought of as non-existent – can indeed only be thought of as existent in the highest degree. The second, which he discovered in his *Cur Deus Homo*, is that God's acts can only, whatever the appearances to the contrary, be thought of as displaying the highest possible degree of fittingness. As we shall see, the second of these axioms, besides providing the structure of *Cur Deus Homo*, also had a long history ahead of it, not least in stimulating some of his disciples to draw conclusions about the Immaculate Conception of Mary as an example of an action which can be deduced from its supreme 'fittingness'.

We must soon ask how he went about laying the foundations of this second axiom. But before asking this question there is another influence on Anselm's argument which must be briefly examined.

2 The Schools

We have already seen that the new arguments of the schools, as presented by Roscelin, influenced Anselm's development in the years between about 1088 and 1092. But Anselm was also exposed to scholastic influences nearer home by the presence at Bec of several young men who came to him from the schools to seek his advice. Most conspicuous among these was his pupil Boso. He had come to Anselm with his two brothers in about 1085, troubled with doubts. Anselm resolved them, and Boso stayed at Bec for the rest of his life. Of all Anselm's pupils he was the one with most aptitude for philosophy, and in about 1094 Anselm summoned him to Canterbury to help him with the writing of his *Cur Deus Homo*.[7] Apart from an interval in 1095, when he went to the Council of

---

[6] *CDH* I, cc. 3–6, are occupied with this initial argument against the objection of the unbelievers. For the formulation of this argument by the Jew in Gilbert Crispin's *Disputatio*, see *Works*, p. 27; and B. Blumenkranz, 1956, for references to earlier literature. For the importance which Anselm attached to 'fittingness' see *Prosl.*, c. 10, and *CDH* I, c. 12.

[7] See below, pp. 367–8, for Boso's place among Anselm's friends; and see his tribute to Boso in *De Conceptu Virginali et de originali peccato*, Schmitt, ii, p. 139: *librum* 'Cur Deus Homo' *tu maxime inter alios me impulisti ut ederem*. See also the *Vita Bosonis* in *PL*, 150, col. 725–6, for Boso's early life and ability, and for his mission on Anselm's behalf to the Council of Clermont in 1095.

Clermont as Anselm's representative, and had a serious illness which kept him abroad for several months, he seems to have stayed in England until Anselm's exile in 1097. Later, once more at Anselm's urgent request, the abbot of Bec released him again and Boso returned to England to be with Anselm during his last years. Quite simply Anselm needed him as a stimulus, and he played a more significant role in the *Cur Deus Homo* than any pupil in any other of Anselm's works.

The difference between Boso and the other pupils who took part in Anselm's theological dialogues is shown in two ways.

First, Boso alone is the only participant in his dialogues whom Anselm names; all others are nameless. More important, all other participants play only a very subordinate part in the development of the argument: they seek instruction, and make mistakes for Anselm to correct, but they make no positive contribution to the argument. Boso's part in the *Cur Deus Homo* is quite different: the central argument of the whole work, in its first formulation, is put into his mouth. This contribution, not to speak of several others, provides so marked a contrast to the role of other pupils in Anselm's dialogues that it requires an explanation.

Then we must remember that Boso had come to Anselm because he was troubled (as his biographer relates) with *perplexae quaestiones*, which he could neither solve nor forget. The secular schools were at this time the most fertile breeding ground for *perplexae quaestiones*, and Boso's main intervention in the *Cur Deus Homo* outlines at length, and then contradicts, an opinion which came straight from no less a school than that of Laon, and his briefly expressed objection becomes the main theme of the whole work. So here Boso's intervention introduces a new element into Anselm's work, coming neither from Augustine, nor from Aristotle, nor from monastic life, nor from his own meditation, nor from a criticism of his own work. It came from the most famous cathedral school of its time in northern France, arguably the school which did more to change the intellectual landscape of western Europe in the next fifty years than any other.

In Boso's intervention, Anselm was faced with an opinion of the most respected and responsible secular school of the day. Roscelin was something quite different: he was indeed a man of the secular schools, but he was not a representative figure, simply a maverick logician.

The thirty years since Anselm's arrival at Bec had seen a great increase in the fame and influence of secular – as contrasted with monastic – schools. Among the rest, the school attached to the cathedral of Laon had scarcely been heard of when Anselm came to Bec; but by 1090, its most celebrated master was beginning to have a European fame. His real name was Anseau, but, confusingly enough, he is generally known in later sources as Master Anselm. With the help of his brother Ralph, he taught at Laon during the whole of the period from about 1070 to 1120, and during this time he had a greater number of famous pupils than anyone else in Europe.[8]

We are not here concerned with the fame or contribution of Master Anselm's school to the growth of scholastic thought, but only with a single question and a single opinion, which played a central role in the argument of the *Cur Deus Homo*. As an aid to understanding the situation, it may simply be said that the main written products of the school of Laon were of two kinds: first, there were extensive glosses on the Bible, which after many transformations and additions came to be known as the *Glossa ordinaria*; and second, there were collections of short answers to miscellaneous questions, generally arising from biblical texts, which were discussed and summed up in a *Sententia* by one or other of the masters associated with the school, most often by Master Anselm himself, but sometimes by his brother Ralph, or William of Champeaux, who were also associated with his school.

Among the *Sententiae* of this school there is one attributed to Ralph, the brother of Master Anselm, which has the same title as Anselm's work – *Cur Deus Homo*. The argument it puts forward is that God became Man because Adam's sin had delivered mankind into the dominion of the Devil; and it was only by trapping the Devil into overstepping his authority, and subjecting a sinless man to the death which was the punishment for sin, that mankind could be rescued from the Devil's dominion. This sinless man was of course Christ. Leaving aside for the moment the logic and Christology of this position, it will suffice to say that Boso quotes the words and rejects the argument of this *Sententia* at the beginning of the *Cur Deus Homo*. Anselm then agrees with Boso's objection and develops its consequences at great length and with

---

[8] The best introduction to that part of Anselm of Laon's work with which we are here concerned, is Lottin, 1959, pp. 9–188. The passage of immediate interest for *Cur Deus Homo* is on pp. 185–6 (no. 232); cf. also pp. 44–7 (nos. 47–8). In what follows, in order to distinguish Anselm of Laon from St Anselm, I shall call the former *Master* Anselm.

immense subtlety and elaboration throughout the remainder of his work.[9]

In giving his pupil the role of making the initial breakthrough to the new doctrine which the *Cur Deus Homo* was written to establish, Anselm gave Boso a position which he conceded to no other pupil. If we also remember the primary role which Anselm ascribed to Boso in stimulating the composition of the work, we must conclude that he wished Boso to be given some credit for an important moment in his own theological development. Anselm had never before disagreed with a traditional doctrine, nor had he challenged an argument of one of the central schools of his day. In his earlier works, he had been original in method, but conservative in his conclusions. But in the *Cur Deus Homo* both method and conclusion were new. In undertaking to show with all his customary rigour that many great teachers had been wrong, he took a step beyond anything he had written in the past: consciously and deliberately he went against tradition.

II   THE OUTLINE OF ANSELM'S ARGUMENT

Although he was breaking new ground, we have only to look back over Anselm's earlier works to see that however important Boso may have been in drawing his attention to the argument about the Devil's rights, and exposing its weakness, Anselm was unlikely ever to have entertained such a proposition as that of the Devil having rights. His whole concept of sin meant that it could neither create nor convey rights, least of all for the Devil, whose supreme sin had made him irretrievably lower than the least created thing in the universe. Consequently, any theory of the Devil's rights as the cause of divine activity was excluded from the start. How then did Anselm explain the need for the Incarnation? Leaving aside digressions, the essential stages of his argument may be set out in three complementary sequences.

---

[9] The connection between the passage in *CDH* I, c. 7, and the *Sententia* of the school of Laon printed by Lottin, 1959, no. 232, was first noticed by J. Rivière, 1936, pp. 344–6. Rivière supposed that Radulfus was quoting *from CDH*, and not *vice versa*. But the doctrine which Radulfus supported was common to the whole school of Laon, as can be seen from several *Sententiae* printed by Lottin. So there was no need for him to seek it in a work in which it was refuted. By contrast, it is readily intelligible that Boso should quote a doctrine of a well-known contemporary school, express his own doubt about it, and ask Anselm to clarify the issue. For further details, see Southern 1963, pp. 357–61, and for the development of the doctrine, see Rivière 1934.

1 **The problem**

i Man was created by God for eternal blessedness.
ii This blessedness requires the perfect and voluntary sub-mission of Man's will to God. (Freedom is to love the limitations appropriate to one's being.)
iii But the whole human race has refused to make this submission (and has thus lost its freedom).
iv No member of the human race can restore the lost blessedness, because even perfect obedience cannot now make up for lack of obedience in the past.
v Therefore the created universe is deprived of its due harmony, and in the absence of external aid, the whole human race has irretrievably forfeited the blessedness for which it was created.

2 **The necessity of a solution**

i God's purpose in the creation of Man and the universe has been frustrated.
ii But it is impossible that the purpose of an omnipotent Being should be frustrated.
iii Therefore a means of redemption must exist.

3 **The solution**

i To restore the lost harmony and blessedness, an offering of obedience must be made, equal to or greater than all that has been lacking in the past.
ii Only Man, as the offender, *ought* to make this offering; but no man can do this, because he already owes to God all and more than all he has to offer.
iii Only God *can* make an offering which transcends the whole unpaid debt of past offences; but God ought not to make it, because the debt is Man's.
iv Since only Man ought to, and only God can, make this offering, it must be made by one who is both Man and God.
v Therefore a God-Man is necessary for the Redemption of the whole Creation.

This bare sketch can give no idea of the subtlety and power of Anselm's argument, but it will suffice to trace its rigour. It is also a necessary foundation for some remarks about the preconceptions and personal characteristics disclosed in Anselm's argument.

Even the outline of the argument presented above will show that it cannot claim the *a priori* certainty claimed for the argument of the *Proslogion*. Each stage presupposes established truths which Anselm, for all his determination to pursue every objection and answer every doubt, only partially elucidates. Moreover, there is a fundamental difficulty, already perceptible in the *Proslogion* and now more than ever disturbing: in speaking about the activity of God in relation to created beings, some of the words which must be used, like 'cannot' and 'ought not', seem to suggest a limit to God's omnipotence. What Anselm intends to suggest, but has no words which will accurately convey, is that there are some acts – such as acts of injustice – which would be a diminishing of God's absolute Being, and therefore must be excluded from consideration, not because of any limitation in God, but because of defects inherent in the acts themselves. To understand their meaning, the 'cannots' of human language have to be translated into the 'cans' of absolute Being, and we have no language for doing this. Consequently, since in our present condition we have no language capable of expressing the situation, any explanation must be provisional until a new language – the language of direct vision in Heaven – is available.

These problems of 'being able' and 'not being able', of 'owing' and 'not-owing', of 'being' and 'not-being', were to occupy Anselm increasingly in his later years, and their elaboration would take us beyond the scope of this study. Nevertheless, some aspects of the problem must be mentioned if Anselm's conception of the role of the *Deus-Homo* is to be placed in its historical setting.

III THE RIGHTS OF THE DEVIL

We must begin by recognizing the strength of the traditional view which Anselm overturned. The theory was that Adam and Eve, in following the Devil's counsel instead of God's command, had made themselves and their descendants outlaws from God, and subjects of the Devil in perpetuity. Their sin created a new social contract of the universe: so long as the Devil kept within the bounds of his jurisdiction, the arrangement freely entered into by the ancestors of the human race could not justly be overturned. The Devil had a just dominion so long as he kept within the limit of those over whom his jurisdiction extended. As soon as he unjustly extended the exercise of his jurisdiction to the sinless Christ, the condition on which he held a just dominion over the human race was broken. When this happened, He whom the Devil had unjustly condemned to die inherited the Devil's jurisdiction and, under whatever conditions He wished, He could restore mankind to the end for which the human race had been created.

The strength of this account was that it conformed to recognizable norms of justice in human society, and in doing this it satisfied an underlying desire for justice in the universe. Moreover, it emphasized the personal authority of Christ over the redeemed portion of mankind, and his right to lay down laws for those whom he would redeem. Further, it recognized the cosmic scale of Man's fall: he had fallen, after all, to the greatest enemy of God, and the recognition of the Devil's ensuing rights gave a certain dignity to the sinner, if not to sin.

Moreover, the justice of the process whereby the Devil's rights over mankind were destroyed, revealed God as the master strategist of the universe: He had outmanoeuvred the enemy on a cosmic scale. The contemplation of God's triumphant strategy satisfied imagination and piety alike. The shattered empire of the Devil remained visible to everyone in the calamities of nature and of ordinary life, but they were counterbalanced by the triumphs of the saints. And if this world-view contained a strong element of dualism, this also recommended it to an age which could easily associate the daily experiences of life with a cosmic battle between God and the Devil. Several of these sources of strength are emotional rather than strictly logical or religious, but they gave dignity to the struggle and could not be abandoned without loss.

When we contrast this traditional scene with the account given by Anselm, we shall see that, whatever superiority his account may have in logic or religious seriousness, the imaginative appeal of the older account was much more vivid and more easily accessible to ordinary people, and gave a more easily recognizable dignity to life, than Anselm's grim account of the human situation. To put the matter bluntly, everyone could appreciate that the treason involved in having renounced obedience to the Lord of the Universe in order to follow a rebel and traitor deserved endless punishment, which could most appropriately be remitted as a result of a heroic sacrifice by the Son of the rejected Lord. Here the ideals of the heroic age are most fully displayed. But if, as Anselm suggested, the Devil had no rights over mankind at all, new questions at once arose. The most important was the one which Abelard emphasized: Why could not God, like any good lord, simply pardon, on whatever condition seemed appropriate, those who repented? Why resort to the cruelty of subjecting his Son to a pitiless death? What, after all, was so terrible about the ordinary sins of ordinary people, who themselves were bidden to forgive sins, that made them incapable of receiving free forgiveness in return for love? In solving one problem, Anselm seemed to open up others more deep-seated than that which he had solved.

Reason and instinct alike recommended to most people the old view of Man's situation. Why did they find no sympathetic echo in Anselm? The simple answer is that he had too uncompromising and too unitary a view of God's dominion over the whole Creation to accept any view which diminished God's majesty in the smallest way. To allow the Devil, or any other rebel, a claim to justice against God was an unacceptable diminution of the divine majesty. Rebellion deserved nothing but punishment, and to have seduced the whole of mankind into rebellion only increased the punishment: it did not create an empire.

Anselm's elimination of the Devil from the process of Redemption satisfies every rational instinct, and the direct confrontation of God and Man in the work of Redemption gives mankind a new kind of dignity which will appeal to later generations. But Anselm did not clear out the Devil's rights to replace them with the Rights of Man. On the contrary, he cleared out the Devil to enforce more completely the submission of Man to God. For Anselm, the only human dignity consists in submission to God's will; and it is this alone, strenuously pursued, which will lead to union with God. And so we come back in the end to the monastic choice which for Anselm represented the supreme resignation of everything to God.

Besides these conflicting human reactions to his argument, Anselm's removal of the rights of the Devil from the cosmic scene also created a logical problem of formidable dimensions. In the old scheme of things, the three-cornered drama of God, Man and Devil corresponded to a readily intelligible situation in human affairs: Man, by an act of rebellion, owes a service to the Devil from which he cannot free himself; a deliverer, stronger than either, steps in and effects his discharge. This reproduces a situation which common sense and experience both pronounce to be possible. But if the Devil is eliminated, and if Man owes only to God a service which he cannot pay, the logical problem of Redemption seems insuperable.

Where there is only a debtor who cannot pay, and a creditor who cannot be paid, common sense and logic equally suggest that the creditor must for ever forgo his payment. He may punish or he may forgive, but he cannot be paid; and there is an air of subterfuge and unreality in any attempt to show that he can.

However successfully Anselm may deal with the problem which he created, his whole attempt is dogged by this suspicion of logical legerdemain. Abelard at once detected this, and like the majority of his contemporaries – though taking a different direction – he rejected Anselm's argument. Anselm must have known that he was aggravating his problem by removing the third party to the transaction, and then insisting more stringently than ever on the necessity and possibility of payment. He had destroyed a satisfying triangle of divine, demonic and human rights, and had left Man and God facing each other with no go-between to bridge the gap.

It may be said at once that the verdict of Anselm's immediate successors was against him. Even those – they were chiefly monks rather than schoolmen – who most appreciated the rest of his argument, were unwilling to abandon the rights of the Devil. In the schools the tendency was to ignore Anselm's argument altogether, insisting on those elements in the case which had been made familiar by the school of Laon. The only school of thought which whole-heartedly accepted the refutation of the traditional account of the Devil's rights was that of Abelard. But he and his followers drew from this refutation a conclusion which was the opposite of that which Anselm intended: since Man could make no payment to God, and God need make no payment to the Devil, the purpose of the Incarnation could not be that of making any payment at all. It could only be an act of love. As Abelard said:

We are justified in the blood of Christ and reconciled to God by this singular grace shown to us, in that his Son received our nature, and in this nature left us an example by word and deed of enduring until death. In doing this he so bound us to himself in love, that – being enflamed by so great a gift of divine grace – we will not fear to endure all things for His sake.[10]

This complicated sentence (I have simplified it), contains one of the great new ideas of the twelfth century: it asserted that the Incarnation was efficacious, not in satisfying the just claims of God or Devil, but in teaching by example the law of love. It left out the whole idea of compensation to God for human sin, and threw the

[10] *Commentaria in Ep. Pauli ad Romanos*, ed. E. M. Buytaert, *CC*, 1969, pp. 117–18 (*PL* 178, col. 836).

whole emphasis of the Incarnation on its capacity to revive Man's love for God. Abelard filled the gap left by the disappearance of the Devil's rights in the simplest possible way.

In all probability, Abelard's line of thought had its origin in Anselm's restatement of the problem, but nothing could have been more alien to the whole spirit of Anselm's theology than the conclusion which Abelard drew from the the problem as Anselm had restated it. Anselm had not cleared out the Devil to make more room for Man, or to diminish Man's debt to God. On the contrary, with fierce intensity, he magnified the debt in order to glorify God. If in so doing he diminished Man, that was a conclusion from which he did not shrink: his aim was to magnify God, not Man. Abelard's view stands as a protest against all the essential elements in Anselm's thought that we are now to examine.

If we exclude all the derogatory implications which have been read into it, there is some truth in the allegation that Anselm's solution of the problem is monastic and feudal in inspiration; as also in the claim that Abelard's opens a path into that new territory of religious humanism, which was discovered in the twelfth century. This new land, a land in which natural virtues have an increasingly prominent place, lies between the areas of courtly love and Carthusian contemplation, sharing with each of them a certain spontaneous joy of life. For spontaneous joy there was no place in Anselm's theology: for him, joy could come only in the discipline of meditation and religious friendship.

Bearing this in mind, we must now return to Anselm's problem and attempt to see further into the nature of his response.

IV   MAN ALONE WITH GOD

By removing the Devil from the picture, Anselm concentrated the widely scattered tensions of the old world-view into a simple relationship between God and Man, and it might seem that there was nothing to prevent God's free forgiveness of Man's sin. Since the Devil could claim no just dominion over Man, forgiveness no longer presented an affront to distributive justice. So we must begin with the question: why should not God extend forgiveness to Man under whatever conditions were appropriate, without the need for a Redeemer's death?

In the first place, of course, there was the obstacle that Christ had in fact already suffered to redeem mankind. If sin were freely forgiven, the Jewish criticism that Christianity unnecessarily exposed God to the pain and indignities of human life and death would have to be answered (if indeed it *could* be answered) in a way quite different from that of traditional doctrine. This was the problem to which Anselm's treatise was primarily directed: the gross indignities offered to God in Christ could only be justified if they were necessary for the rectification of the universe under the will of God.

But if – leaving aside the historical fact – the prior question is pressed, why God should not freely forgive Man's sin, Anselm has two answers. In the first place, free forgiveness would place the disobedient will on the same level as the obedient one. Indeed (and this is a characteristic touch) it would make the disobedient will more God-like than the obedient one, for the nature of disobedience (like God in this respect) is being subject to no law. If the disobedient will were to be blessed, sinners would be, as Satan promised Eve, truly God-like. Secondly, such forgiveness would do nothing to correct the disturbance of the order and beauty of the universe caused by sin. On the contrary, by condoning disorder, it would lead to an ever-widening area of anarchy in God's kingdom, and destroy the beauty of the universe.

Beauty is a new word in Anselm's theological vocabulary, which first comes into prominence in the *Cur Deus Homo*. In using it, he refers not to poetic or pictorial beauty, but to the beauty of a perfectly ordered universe.[11] In God's kingdom of perfect power and justice, the slightest uncorrected disorder mars the whole: it shows a deficiency either of justice – in the sense of failing to exhibit the true nature of God – or of power in the work of God. Either of these defects would be contrary to the divine nature. Perfect power, perfect justice, perfect order, perfect beauty: the combination of these qualities in the highest degree constitutes the perfection of the universe in reflecting the divine nature. The intensity of Anselm's insistence on the inviolability of this combination is one of the most remarkable features of the *Cur Deus Homo*. It explains why God 'cannot' (in the Anselmian sense) freely forgive sin by a mere act of mercy: it would destroy the beauty of the universe, and in doing this would degrade God the Creator, Man the creature, and the whole Creation.

But, common sense will still urge, since Man can offer nothing to

[11] The theme of *pulchritudo* and *ordo* is most fully elaborated in *CDH* I, c. 15 (Schmitt, ii, pp. 72–4).

merit forgiveness, it can come only from God's mercy. Unless mercy can prevail against justice, Man cannot be redeemed, and there's an end of it. And why not? The quality of mercy is to forgo what is just. Formulas can of course be found to rub away the sharp antithesis, to make justice mild and mercy rational, until the two are almost indistinguishable. In a sense this is what Anselm does. But there are two ways of doing this. The first is to gloss over contradictions with ambiguities; the second is to discover behind contradictory appearances the unitary law which governs them. In every situation, whether practical or theoretical, it was always Anselm's method to take the second of these two courses – sometimes with surprising results, both practical and theoretical. How far he succeeded in this aim, in this problem as in others, raises questions of very great difficulty, and all I can do is to display the circumstances, tools, and incentives of his attempt.

We may start with a passage in the *Proslogion* in which he sought to build a bridge between justice and mercy:

Certainly, if thou art merciful because thou art supremely good, and supremely good because thou art supremely just, then it follows that thou art merciful because thou art supremely just. Help me, O just and merciful God, whose light I seek, help me to understand what I say: 'thou art merciful because thou art just'.[12]

It was from this position that the solution to the main problem of the *Cur Deus Homo* was evolved. In the *Proslogion*, he had asserted that justice and mercy were different aspects of the same activity. In the *Cur Deus Homo* he attempted to give a convincing proof and illustration of this improbable conclusion. He did it in this way:

The rational order of the universe requires that sinful Man shall be everlastingly unblest. This is the way of justice. But the rational order of the universe also requires that Man shall be everlastingly blessed, for it was for this end that the universe was created. This is the way of mercy. But it is also the way of truth, for it is only by Man's achieving this blessedness that God's word in Creation could remain inviolable, and the end for which the universe was created could be achieved. There could be no going back on God's Word: He had spoken on each of the six days of Creation and seen that all was good: He had ordained the end – Man's blessedness; and that end must be achieved.

[12] *Prosl.*, c. 9 (Schmitt, i, p. 108).

213

Within the created order, therefore, there are two intertwined strands, justice and mercy, both deriving from God's rational plan of Creation. In being merciful, God is also just, not in the sense of rendering to each his due, for God owes nothing to anyone, but in the sense of achieving that perfect rectitude which displays the supreme goodness of God. Further, the blessedness which is the promised end of Man is logically prior to his damnation, which is the result of sin. In this sense, mercy is prior to distributive justice, and must prevail, for in relation to its end it is itself justice.

But here Anselm reaches an apparently inescapable conclusion which is the opposite of that which lately confronted him. From being impossible that sin should be forgiven, it now appears impossible that it should *not* be forgiven. How else can the original intention of the Creation be achieved? We seem to be forced back into a free forgiveness, not just for some, but for all. Moreover, there seems to be no obstacle to this. Since the offering made by Christ is greater than all the sins of the world, past, present or to come, there is no logical objection to a universal forgiveness for all. Why then should not the forgiveness earned by the God-Man be extended to all mankind?

Anselm was here in a considerable difficulty. God's plan required that Man should be saved. This may mean either 'the species Man' or 'all men'. According to the first meaning, God's plan would be fulfilled by the salvation of a single representative of the race. According to the second, the damnation of a single individual would frustrate the intention of the Creator. Of these two possible meanings Anselm seems logically to be committed only to the first, and this would agree with his general tendency to think of the species as more real than its individual components. But though the salvation of one man may conceivably satisfy the logical requirements of his system, this could scarcely satisfy the requirement of God's mercy, especially since there is no logical objection to the benefits of the Saviour's offering being extended to all whom he chooses.

Logic can go no further, and in default of logic, Anselm falls back on a feudal image. He likened the work of Redemption to the act of a king whose people had all, except one, been guilty of a crime worthy of death. But the one innocent man, besides earning his own salvation, offered to perform on behalf of others a service greater than the offence of all his fellow-subjects put together. The king accepted this service, and agreed to extend pardon to all who wished for it, on condition that they presented themselves in court on the day this unique service was performed; or, if they could not come on the very day itself, on another day at the lord's discretion. The only absolute requirement was voluntary attendance at court on conditions laid down by the lord.[13]

In this image it is noteworthy that Anselm attempts no logical explanation of the condition of attendance which the king imposes. Such acts of renewal of homage and fealty, either by whole communities or by men guilty of rebellion, were a familiar part of his world. They were not capable of a strictly logical justification, but he accepted such acts in practice, and he used them here to bridge the gap in his logic which would have either restricted salvation to one, or enlarged it to all.

With the help of this feudal illustration Anselm retreated from the alternatives of either a single or a universal salvation, and found refuge in salvation offered to those who performed some small but clearly defined service. This retreat from the two extremes left the door to salvation potentially very wide open. Anselm found biblical grounds for believing that the door was only ajar: 'Many are called, but few chosen' was one of the texts to which he most frequently appealed. So, as Anselm had written in one of his early letters of monastic instruction, 'you cannot be secure unless you are one of the very few'. This continued to be his message to the end.[14]

Anselm himself thought that any easy conditions were excluded. Nevertheless, his argument opened the door to a new phase of religious history and an easier future for believers. The old view of the warrior Redeemer was associated with a harshly limited prospect of salvation for the few. The warlike and resourceful God who had outwitted Satan was not easily to be bent to the milder ways of mercy. In the penitentials of the early medieval Church, actual sins could be atoned for only by immense penances and abundant alms. This is what we find still in Anselm's life-time: the recompenses which men were struggling to pay for their sins were very great, and for most people they were quite beyond any hope of fulfilment. In his own religious outlook, Anselm retained this stern, unbending attitude: few will be saved, he reiterated; and most of these will be monks, he implied, for they alone have achieved a complete surrender to God's will.

Yet, despite all his severity of outlook, the new possibility of a

---

[13] *CDH* II, c. 16 (Schmitt, ii, p. 118).
[14] See *Epp.* 2 (i, 2), 51 (i, 43), 167 (iii, 18), 184.

widespread Redemption refused to go away. An offering had been made, capable of obtaining remission 'of *all* the sins of men and angels'.[15] Why then should anyone be damned? With regard to the fallen angels, Anselm was quite clear that, although a sufficient price for their redemption had been paid, their redemption was prohibited by 'immutable reason'. But this objection did not apply to Man, and Anselm did not contradict Boso when he expressed his reaction to the whole argument: 'it seems to me that God will reject no man coming to him under this name' (of Christ).[16] Anselm had nothing to say to this. So he allowed the dialogue to end on a note which he could not himself echo.

It is a very striking fact that, just as he had allowed Boso to lay the foundation for his main argument at the start, so he allowed him the last note at its end. He did not endorse Boso's hope, but in leaving it he allowed it to stand as a sign of the approach of a new and more hopeful age.

V FREEDOM, OBEDIENCE, AND PUNISHMENT

The *Cur Deus Homo* opened a way to the more genial and relaxed religious attitudes of the later Middle Ages, which Anselm had no inclination to share. Despite the loopholes which his argument provided, the moral force of the work comes from his utter abhorrence of sin, even down to the smallest detail. He did not reject the rights of the Devil in order to make Man's yoke lighter, nor to give Man a wider scope for self-expression. For that whole range of thought which appeals to Man's creative instincts and sees the fulfilment of the divine purpose in the development of human knowledge or experience, Anselm had no use at all. Abelard was less relaxed on these subjects than is often thought; but compared with Anselm, he is a man of the new age. Although he too was a monk, and – despite his reputation – a serious one, the world was Abelard's natural habitat; whereas Anselm, even in the world, was resolutely monastic.

The foundation of monastic life is obedience, and Anselm embraced obedience with passionate intensity, as his reported conversations make clear. This obedience, in the words of the Rule, is to be 'neither fearful nor slothful nor languid nor murmuring nor

[15] *CDH* II, c. 21 (Schmitt, ii, p. 132). [16] *CDH* II, c. 19 (Schmitt, ii, p. 131).

partial'. Anselm spelt this out in detail in his letters.[17] In a word, his monastic commitment was total, because he believed that a total commitment was the only acceptable relationship between Man and God. This aspect of Anselm's thought is fundamental to the understanding of his practical life as well as his theology. In both it led to difficulties. Anselm was more successful in resolving theological than practical difficulties; but, whether successful or not, his starting point was a passionate urge to obey God, and the Benedictine Rule most fully expressed the nature of this obedience. The place of obedience in human life was first fixed in his early monastic letters, brought to completion in his systematic theology in the *Cur Deus Homo*, and tested in his public life as archbishop of Canterbury, to which we must soon turn.

Unless the rigidity of his argument is seen also as the expression of an intense experience, a good deal of the *Cur Deus Homo* will appear to be somewhat glacial. As always in Anselm, the intensely emotional appeal is inseparable from the most rigorous logic, as the following brief extract will illustrate:

Anselm: Let us grant that you have paid for sin all that you have mentioned – penitence, a humble and contrite heart, abstinence and bodily labours, compassion in giving and forgiving, and obedience. And let us ask whether all these things can suffice as satisfaction for the smallest sin, the slightest glance of the eye, contrary to the will of God.
Boso: If I had not heard you say this, I should have thought that simple compunction would have sufficed to wipe out such a sin as this.
Anselm: That is because you have not yet recognized the enormity of sin . . . But, not to protract the matter further, were it not better that the whole world, and whatever is that is not God, should perish and be reduced to nothingness, than that you should make one movement of the eye against the will of God?

This passage must surely have been the inspiration of a more famous passage in which Cardinal Newman expresses the same idea; and a comparison of the two passages is illuminating. This is Newman:

It were better for the sun and moon to drop from heaven, for the earth to fail, and for the many millions who are upon it to die of starvation in extremest agony, as far as temporal affliction goes, than that one soul, I will not say,

[17] *Reg. S. Ben.*, c. 5; the references in Anselm's letters abound, but the following will suffice to give a summary of his views: *Epp.* 73 (i, 64), 156 (iii, 7), 196 (iv, 109). The most significant passage in *CDH* is I, c. 9, but the whole work is a commentary on obedience.

should be lost, but should commit one single venial sin, should tell one wilful untruth, though it harmed no one, or steal one poor farthing without excuse.[18]

The tragic emotion is the same in both passages; but Newman's words have a rhetorical exaggeration, even (if one may say so) an absurdity, which is never found in Anselm. The contrast between the two passages illustrates a characteristic of Anselm which is easily overlooked: however extreme his statements, he never says more than he means, and he never means more than his argument requires. It was essential to his argument that the slightest sin – even a single glance of the eye against the will of God – should (negatively) be greater than the whole positive value of the universe apart from God. This is the necessary logical foundation for his argument that *any* movement of the disobedient will, however slight, disturbs the perfect order of God's Creation in a way that nothing within the system can correct. The correction can only come through the offering made by Christ on the Cross, which is of greater weight than all the sins of the world put together. This he could contemplate because, however appalling, it came from God's free gift. But he could not have contemplated the reversal of God's purpose for the universe and its destruction because of Man's sin. Even though mankind had nothing with which to atone for sin, God's purpose would prevail. His whole argument was a development of this fundamental perception.

It may be objected that his insistence on obedience as the fundamental rule of the universe destroys the higher privilege of freedom. Anselm's answer to this objection is similar to his resolution of the problem of justice and mercy: obedience and freedom are different aspects of the same condition. We have already examined the background and consequence of this definition:[19] freedom is not the power of choice between good and evil, but the power of steadfastly willing nothing contrary to the will of God, which comes from the loving acceptance of the limitations of created being. This and this alone is the freedom of rational beings. Anselm wholly rejects the common-sense view that the essential quality of freedom is an unfettered power of choice. In arriving at his own definition, he turns from the freedom of common sense and experience to the more remote and ethereal freedom of the

---

[18] *CDH*, I, c. 21; and Cardinal Newman, *Lectures on certain difficulties felt by Anglicans in submitting to the Catholic Church*, Dublin, 1857, p. 190.
[19] See above, pp. 169, 172–4.

sanctified will. Freedom of choice between Good and Evil is servitude in Anselm's system; inability to sin is perfect freedom, to be sought in this life but attained only in Heaven.

In his habitual way, Anselm expressed this conclusion in two ways: by definition and by a parable. The definitions were these: Of obedience: 'Simple and true obedience exists when a rational nature freely and without necessity preserves the will which it has received from God.' And of freedom: 'Freedom of the will is the power of preserving the rectitude of the will for its own sake.' Now since the 'will received from God' in the first definition is indistinguishable from the 'rectitude of the will' in the second, it follows that true obedience is indistinguishable from freedom. Moreover, since justice is the 'rectitude of the will preserved for its own sake', and freedom is the power of preserving this rectitude, it follows that freedom is the power of acting justly, and obedience is the free exercise of this power. Obedience is therefore the practical exercise of freedom in the preservation of justice.[20]

Anselm, in his customary way in his talk, expressed the same doctrine in a parable, which ran as follows:

A woman had several daughters and servants whom she placed under a mistress. The mistress gave them a single comprehensive command: they were not to leave the house. The daughters [the free] obeyed without cavil; the servants [the unfree] vainly sought pretexts for gaining exemption from the rule, and took the refusal of permission with varying degrees of ill-will, but with an equal lack of power to disobey.[21]

This was a situation frequently met with in monastic life, and Anselm often returned to the theme: those who sought freedom were the unfree, those who willingly submitted were free. Neither class could escape from the limitation imposed upon them. But the free embraced their limitation with joy; the unfree submitted with resentment. The external condition of both classes was the same, but only those who *desired* to stay at home were free. Hence the cloister, for those who retained an unalterable will to persevere, was the home of true freedom.

Anselm thus attempted to satisfy the claims of both freedom and

---

[20] *De Veritate*, c. 12 (Schmitt, i, pp. 191–6) is the most important source for the definitions which permanently fixed the relationship between Freedom, Rectitude, and Justice in Anselm's thought. Obedience, always prominent in the letters, only enters his systematic thinking in *CDH*, as mentioned above.

[21] *Memorials*, p. 75, cc. 85–7: *Similitudo inter matronam et divinam voluntatem.*

obedience, and to express the heinousness of the slightest deviation from the will of God. This heinousness, which Anselm demonstrated in argument and parable, is expressed eternally by God in the act of punishment. In Anselm's argument, God 'cannot' treat the disobedient will in the same way as the obedient will, because to do so would be to raise injustice above justice, and to destroy the order and beauty of the universe. This order and beauty have indeed been disturbed by sin; but not finally destroyed. It was the function of the Incarnation and Crucifixion to restore the broken harmony. It is clear how this was achieved in Anselm's scheme of things, by the payment of a price greater than the value of the whole Creation. But it is much more difficult to see what role was left for punishment once this price has been paid.

Boso pointed out this difficulty, and Anselm attempted to meet it in a chapter which has probably done more harm to his reputation than any other part of his works: here if anywhere is to be found the God, whom some of his critics have detected in the *Cur Deus Homo*, a royal tyrant jealous for his honour and finding in punishment a substitute for service. Little though this accords with the general tenor of Anselm's works, it must be admitted that there is room for misunderstanding at this point. If Anselm had been content to demonstrate that even after the Atonement, the disobedient will cannot be admitted to blessedness, criticism would have been silenced. But this alone did not satisfy his demand for an exquisite harmony of the universe. The mere exclusion of the sinner was not enough; even his replacement by another in order to complete the perfect number of souls – a concept dear to Anselm's sense of the numerical harmony of all things – was not enough. There still remained a shadow to be erased from the brightness of the whole. The shadow is faint but perceptible: Anselm has explained that the preservation of God's honour is an essential function of the divine justice. He has added that it is incapable of diminution by sin: nevertheless, since this is what the sinner has attempted, his attempt has left a shadow that must be wiped away. Anselm erases it by what may be called a congruity of opposites, reverting for once, in a way unusual at this stage in his career, to the verbal antitheses which had been a favourite mode of expression in earlier days. The sinner has refused his due and willing subjection: God exacts his unwilling subjection. The sinner has taken what is God's: God takes what is Man's – his blessedness. God has no use for what he has taken from Man, but the fact of taking it shows it is his, not Man's, and this fact God uses for his honour.[22]

I do not think it is possible entirely to obliterate the disagreeable impression of these last words, but there are two considerations which somewhat soften it. In the first place, we must do justice to the motive behind this argument: Anselm was not concerned with a pettifogging game of tit-for-tat, but with the task of reconciling the present sinful state of Man with the incorruptibility of the Divine glory, and with the perfect relationship of God and the created universe. This perfection was Anselm's only interest: the human point of view with its excuses and tenderness for rebels against just authority interested him not at all. Secondly, when he spoke of 'honour', he meant something different from the word in modern usage. He spoke not of that personal thing associated with a man's good opinion of himself and the good opinion of others, but of an order within the system which guarantees its stability. To understand this we must turn to a feature of Anselm's thought which has often been traduced: his feudal imagery.

VI FEUDAL IMAGERY AND UNIVERSAL ORDER

Anselm's feudal imagery is not likely at first sight to commend his thought to modern readers, and it has offered an easy target for indignation and ridicule. But before following this line of attack, we must be clear what we are criticizing. There are two problems. First, how important is the feudal imagery in Anselm's thought? And second, if it is important, what does it mean?

On the first question, Professor McIntyre has effectively answered the criticism that the argument of the *Cur Deus Homo* is irretrievably feudal.[23] Everything of importance in Anselm's argument can survive the removal of every trace of feudal imagery and the supposed contamination by elements of Germanic law. The power of the *Cur Deus Homo* does not come from its feudal imagery, but from its combination of religious insight and logical force. This is entirely true, and for the theologian it suffices to save the argument from the disrepute to which the mere mention of feudalism has sometimes been thought to relegate it. But for the historian, this answer does not go far enough. Even if the argument

---

[22] *CDH* I, cc. 13–15 (esp. 14).   [23] J. McIntyre, 1954.

can be stated without any feudal imagery, it is nevertheless also true that Anselm's thoughts about God and the universe were coloured by the social arrangements with which he was familiar. The formal argument can survive, but its temper is quite different if the contemporary imagery is removed; equally it is quite different if the monastic fervour is brushed aside.

The *Cur Deus Homo* was the product of a feudal and monastic world on the eve of a great transformation. With all its originality, and personal intensity of vision, it bears the marks of this rigorous and – if the word can be used without blame – repressive regime. Anselm's favourite image of the relations between God and Man was that of a lord and his vassals. The status of his dependants varies. Some are knights, some freemen, some serfs; but, whatever their position in the hierarchy, the emphasis is always on their subordination to the lord's will. As we have already seen, he thought the exact position of anyone in the hierarchy a matter of little importance: all, serfs and freemen, were subordinate to a higher authority, not least those at the top.[24]

This is the state of mankind: at the very beginning of history the great renunciation of due service had taken place which condemned all the successors of Adam to the loss of their inheritance. At great cost, the lord had paid the default in full. He had not only paid the original service; he had made it possible for future deficiencies to be paid – but under conditions, in appearance simple, yet in practice so arduous that only a few would in fact fulfil them.

The simplicity of the conditions lay in the demand for faith, submission, and repentance; no more was required. The difficulty lay chiefly in the need for a rigorous submission of the flesh to the law, and of the law to God: few are prepared to make this submission. Hence, despite all the resources thrown into the scale of salvation, few would be saved. The superiority of monks over other men lay in their more complete submission. The laity had all kept something back, even if that 'something' were no more than an *explicit* promise of total obedience.

In one of the striking similes which we owe to the reports of Anselm's conversation, the difference was expressed in the story of two tenants who each had a precious fruit tree. One of them annually gave his lord the fruit of the tree; the other gave once and for all the whole crop for ever. The first represented the incomplete

---

[24] See *Ep.* 17 (i, 15), and p. 168 above.

offering of the layman at his best, the second the surrender of the monk.[25]

Anselm expressed the same idea in another simile in which he compared the various states of life to a countryside strongly reminiscent of the feudal scenery of the eleventh century. At the centre there is a castle, and within the castle a keep; around the castle there is a town, and outside this the open country. Those who live in the open country are Jews and unbelievers: the enemy destroys them without difficulty. The faithful laity are the dwellers in the town: here the enemy breaks in without much difficulty, and they will be fortunate if they escape. The monks are those within the castle walls: they have many alarms, but they are safe so long as they remain inside and keep out of sight. When they hear that their relatives are being killed and wounded, they must not so much as look through the window for fear of the enemy's arrows. For example, as we have seen, they must not leave the monastery to maintain the worldly interests of their relatives, and no one on the threshold or within the monastery must be diverted by a Crusading appeal. Within the walls they will be safe, and therefore free, but not yet with that inalienable freedom which cannot be lost. That is reserved for the elite who are within the keep inside the castle walls: these are the angels in Heaven, immune alike from danger and alarm.[26]

These were the themes which Anselm reiterated again and again in his spoken words. They appear scarcely at all in his writings, but they contain the practical application of his grand concepts and were reported by his pupils. Even in the imperfect form in which they have been preserved their force is not lost. It is unlikely that many now will find this aspect of his thought attractive, and if we knew nothing else there would be something repellent in the ideal picture of a well-ordered world of disciplined tenantry so assiduously submissive to their lord. But these similes were intended to illuminate a single point, not to sketch an ideal society. In their context they carry only the single message of his stern, proud, and uncompromising refusal of easy comforts and consolations, and his rejection of facile excuses for human frailty. If Anselm paints the human scene in drab colours, it is not that he hates colour, but that

---

[25] *Memorials*, pp. 73–4, *Similitudo inter monachum et arborem.*

[26] *Memorials*, pp. 66–7, *Similitudo de regno et villa et castello et dungione*; and cf. *Ep.* 117 (ii, 19), discussed above, pp. 169–70.

all colours are drab beside the true glory. The submission to the lord's will which he demanded was not a cringing submission: it was submission to reason and rectitude, and offered an entrance into a perfect friendship with God and with all whose wills were as one with his.

At this supernatural level, the appearance of repression was only temporary: when the deluding passions had been conquered, the repression would be seen as freedom. Of course, this was not true of the repressions of feudal society. In practice Anselm accepted the oppressive social framework of his day because it was the only social order that he knew. He knew very well that lords, more often than not, were brutal, licentious, and violent. But they represented order. It would be idle to look for social criticism in his works. We may regret that God should appear in the guise of a lord castigating disobedient serfs, but this was the only appropriate image available to him. Despite its limitations, it gave pictorial vividness to his central idea of service due from Man to God, on which mankind had defaulted, and which could be made good only by God's doing it himself on behalf of his tenant.

In one of his feudal illustrations of the relative positions of angels, monks, and laymen, he likened God to a king with three kinds of tenants: those who held fiefs in return for a fixed service; those who served in the hope of regaining a lost inheritance forfeited by their parents; and those who served for wages with no hope of a permanent establishment. The first class was that of the angels, established for ever in an unassailable position of due service and reward. The second class were the monks, enduring hardships and buffetings in the hope of gaining a permanent inheritance, but assured of final reward if they stayed firm. The last class consisted of secular men, serving only for the present, with no hope in the future.[27] This illustration was addressed to the monks of Canterbury in October 1097. It was an important moment in Anselm's life. He was leaving England for his first exile, from which he perhaps scarcely expected, and certainly did not desire, to return. In the event it exposed him to many new influences, and brought him for the first time into the full tide of European affairs in which he would never be quite at ease. The *Cur Deus Homo* was almost finished, and his theological system was complete. He was speaking to his monks of the things that moved him most: the due service of man to God and the essential hopelessness of those who broke this

[27] *VA* II, xxi, pp. 93–7.

bond of service. Such men stood outside the law. For those who were prepared to suffer, the Incarnation had extended the limits of the original covenant to the extent of bringing them into the presence of God. It was an extension of unimaginable splendour; but it had strict conditions of service attached to it which he wished to emphasize.

The feudal and monastic illustrations, which he used then and on other occasions when he spoke to monastic communities, have been fully reported. Naturally there was little room for them in his formal treatises, but in the light of his reported illustrations we can now examine the conception of God's honour which (as we have seen) has an important place in the *Cur Deus Homo*. Here, as also in his reported words, the attempted violation of God's honour constitutes the essential sin of disobedience: 'He who does not render to God this due honour, takes from God what is His, and dishonours (*exhonorat*) God: and this is sin.'[28] Due honour is equated with the well-known secular *servitium debitum*: it is capable of being paid, withdrawn, restored. Satisfaction is required from Man as payment for the honour withheld from God, with an additional payment *secundum exhonorationis factam molestiam*. Supreme Justice requires the preservation of God's honour. Christ offers his life *ad honorem Dei*; and God uses the punishment of the sinner *ad honorem suum*.[29] The language could scarcely be more feudal, and the thought it expresses is only intelligible if the language is understood in a strictly contemporary sense. It will not do to understand God's 'honour' only in the general sense of reverence, as in the familiar hymn of Theodulf of Orleans: *Gloria laus et honor tibi sit, rex Christe redemptor.*

Something more than 'honour' in this general sense is required if Anselm's language is to be intelligible. The solidity of his concept of honour, its minute gradations and equivalents, and its reiteration at the most important moments of his argument, all suggest a social and ideological background quite different from our own or from that of St Augustine or St Thomas Aquinas. This background, which sets Anselm as far apart from Patristic as from modern, or even later medieval thought, is the complex of feudal relationships.

In the language of feudal tenure a man's honour was his *estate*. The central feature of this estate was his landed property. But it also embraced his due place in the hierarchy of authority, his family background, and his personal honour. The fundamental crime

[28] *CDH* I, c. 11 (Schmitt, ii, p. 68).   [29] *CDH* I, cc. 10, 14 (Schmitt, ii, pp. 66, 72).

against anyone was to attempt to diminish this complex of rights and status. The seriousness of the crime was quite independent of the rebel's immediate intentions or power to give effect to his intentions: it was his disloyalty, the loosening of the social bond, which made the outlaw. Conversely, it was the maintenance of the king's 'honour' which preserved his kingdom, of the baron's 'honour' which preserved his barony, and so on down the scale. 'Honour' was essentially a social bond which held all ranks of society in their due place. Slowly honour dissolved into something private and incommunicable, divorced from the language of politics. But that dissolution lay far in the future. The fate of this term kept pace with that of a parallel term, famous in Magna Carta as expressing the bundle of rights or possessions which safeguarded a man's status and position in society – his *contenementum*.[30] Slowly this term also went down the same road towards political insignificance, the road which ended in keeping a man 'in countenance' and saving his face. The descent in either case was from a term associated with the structure of society to one denoting private feeling and reputation.

Anselm's references to God's honour are to be interpreted in the earlier of these two contexts, which was that of his own day. God's honour is the complex of service and worship which the whole Creation, animate and inanimate, in Heaven and earth, owes to the Creator, and which preserves everything in its due place. Regarded in this way, God's honour is simply another word for the ordering of the universe in its due relationship to God. In withholding his service, a man is guilty of attempting to put himself in the place of the Creator. He fails; but in making this attempt, he excludes himself from, and to the extent of his power destroys, the order and beauty of the universe. His rebellion requires a counter-assertion of God's real possession of his honour, not to erase an injury to God, but to erase a blot on the universal order. To do this, God as Man makes good the damage; and God as Lord takes seisin of his honour once more. And so the whole *servitium debitum* of the universe is re-established, and God's 'honour' in its full extent is displayed in the restored order and beauty of the whole.

All this is capable of expression in entirely non-feudal language. But Anselm used the language of feudal relationships, not because he approved every aspect of them, but because they provided an

---

[30] See 'Magna Carta', 1215, c. 20 (W. Stubbs, *Select Charters and other illustrations of English Constitutional History*, 9th edition, Oxford, 1929, pp. 295– 6).

example of hierarchy, which both philosophically and morally he found most satisfying; and – contrary to what is often thought – he valued hierarchy as an expression of the rule of reason.

Those critics who have imagined Anselm's God as a jealous tyrant, greedy for recognition and honour, have failed to recognize that the feudal image, however unsatisfactory in some of its implications, stood for rationality prevailing against the inroads of self-will and chaos. The rationality of Anselm's theology is based on the principle that there is nothing arbitrary in God. God's nature and works alike express the perfect harmony of reason. All else flows from this: if it were not so, all theology would become guesswork. In the *Cur Deus Homo*, Anselm deduced the necessity of the Incarnation from the nature of God and the need to protect the rational beauty of the universe which He had created.

The feudal and monastic illustrations, which are widely distributed among his spoken words, and used deliberately in the *Cur Deus Homo*, illustrate this principle from the facts of everyday life. They are complementary expressions of Anselm's argument. Anselm uses feudal imagery because the feudal hierarchy provided an illustration of the order which he found in the universe. The connection works also in the other direction. When we come to consider his actions in the political field, it must not be forgotten that he found feudal obligations of homage and service an acceptable image of rational order. We may judge from this that he is not likely to find any difficulty in accommodating his ideal of ecclesiastical order to the existence of complicated feudal relationships. We shall find him more tolerant of these secular arrangements than the enthusiasts for a new ecclesiastical ordering of society. After reading his feudal words in the *Cur Deus Homo* on the eternal ordering of the universe, this tolerance will cause no surprise. But it added an unusual complexity to his position as archbishop.

CHAPTER 10

'RELEASE MY SOUL FROM THIS SLAVERY'[1]

I THE NEW ARCHBISHOP

1 The background

During the fifteen years before 1093, Anselm's world can legitimately be described as 'expanding', in the sense that his earlier concentration on the life of religious seclusion, meditation, discussion among monastic friends, and gradually developing breadth of theological interest, was enlarged by his responsibilities for monastic communities outside Bec, by necessary attendance at courts and ecclesiastical meetings, by advising men who either were, or were intending to become, monks, but who also were drawn towards intervention in the Crusade or other worldly activities, and finally by the first, and last, serious attack on his orthodoxy by Roscelin.

All these new activities interrupted Anselm's earlier deep concentration on the daily round of religious meditation and engagement in monastic offices within the cloister. He looked on all these questions from a monastic centre: he took the cloister to the world; he did not admit the world into the cloister. In this, as in most other ways, he presented a contrast to Lanfranc. Even as a monk, Lanfranc continued to be a man of the world, immensely experienced and able to deal with all its ramifications. Hence he could not help bringing the world into the cloister, because he was equally at ease in the world. He had after all been a distinguished figure in the world before he was a monk, whereas Anselm was a man with no goal until he became a monk; and then he wished to be nothing else.

---

[1] The phrase appears in Anselm's review of his first five years as archbishop, sent to Urban II after he left England in 1097. For the text and circumstances see *Ep.* 206 (iii, 166) and below, p. 279. See also *Ep.* 183 (iv, 105) to the abbess and nuns of Shaftesbury: *Tam male enim sum in archiepiscopatu ut certe, si sine culpa dicere possum, malim de hac vita exire quam sic vivere.*

Nevertheless, though Anselm's view of the world was monastically centred, the increasing distractions of these years were more than interruptions in a life severely monastic. They were symptoms of a growing world outside the cloister, in which Anselm was caught up and could not escape. He was not only an archbishop with, as he believed, the duty of ecclesiastical rule over the whole of the British Isles, as well as the duty of maintaining the lands and possessions of his church. He was engaged in endless controversies on matters that had no interest for him, except that they were imposed upon him by his duty of obedience to the Benedictine Rule, to the pope, and (somewhat surprisingly) to the king. And we are bound to ask: what did he make of it all? Did he bring to the scene any insight from his monastic discipline or theological thinking?

These are not easy questions to answer. Anselm never formulated any general principle about the relationship of the world to the Church, beyond expressing his abhorrence of the world from which he had escaped into the cloister nearly thirty-five years earlier. The world was the enemy of the spirit. Consequently the freedom of the world could in no circumstances be a freedom to be desired. But freedom was what his soul yearned for, and freedom meant the power of making in all circumstances the right choice and no other; and the only right choice he had so far been concerned to emphasize on all occasions was the choice of monastic obedience, or, at the very least, preparatory steps towards that end.

It is important to realize that this was not a restrictive choice. It still left great opportunities for growth within the monastic life: growth in meditation, in friendship and experience alongside like-minded members of the community; in artistic and intellectual creation; in liturgical innovations; in increasing knowledge of the way of salvation. The variety opened up by the right choice was much greater than that offered by the world. But the way to this variety of riches was always through the same narrow door. This had been his message for twenty years before he became archbishop, and it continued to be his main message.

But in the bewildering complexity of issues which faced him as archbishop, although he continued to urge the duty of obedience on all possible occasions, it was no longer a sufficient answer to all problems. As we shall see, he had no ready answer for most of the problems which faced him, and on many issues, he had not the equipment necessary for formulating satisfactory answers. It was only on monastic problems that he had always something arresting to say, though what he said was not often acceptable to those whom he addressed. He had had no wish to become an archbishop, and he was only really happy when he could escape the pressures of business. His friends thought he escaped too readily. But in the end, what he said and did during his sixteen years as archbishop made a great addition to his legacy to the future. That is the importance of these years: not what he did, but the record that he left behind him.

2 Lanfranc's legacy

There were three crises in Anselm's life, and in all of them Lanfranc provided the foundation on which Anselm built. First, in 1059, he effectively determined Anselm's monastic future. Then, in 1063, when Anselm succeeded him as prior of Bec, he had Lanfranc's conduct of business as a model. Finally, just thirty years later, Anselm inherited a complicated web of responsibilities at Canterbury, which had been largely shaped by Lanfranc.

So at each step, Lanfranc provided the material and shaped the responsibilities which Anselm inherited. Yet at each step Anselm developed his inheritance in new ways of his own devising. At his first step, Lanfranc had provided the intellectual tools, the methods of using them, and examples of their use; Anselm absorbed the materials, but used them in a new way. Then, in 1063, Lanfranc left a flourishing community at Bec; but Anselm never attempted to follow him as a teacher in an external school, nor an administrator, nor as a force in ecclesiastical politics. He devoted himself to the rigours of self-discipline and the formation of young recruits in the monastery, and the abbey flourished more than ever, with growing numbers, and new dependent priories. So far as we can see, growth was a physical symptom of Anselm's spiritual power. Everywhere, what Lanfranc had achieved by ability, Anselm continued by genius and holiness.

With this record of dependence and innovation, Anselm came to the third crisis of his life. The situation in which he was now placed was vastly more complicated than that to which he had been accustomed at Bec. He now had at least three distinct areas of responsibility. First, he was the head of a monastery with ancient traditions and large claims to lands and rights. Lanfranc had flouted most of the traditions, but had defended the lands and rights with skill and perseverance. Secondly, he was the second person in the kingdom after the king: a position which Lanfranc had filled with complete success in the confidence of almost total identity of views between himself and the king. And, third, in the ecclesiastical hierarchy, the pope was now his only superior. Here indeed, as we shall see, Lanfranc had left an anomalous position; but Anselm accepted it without demur. It was in relation to the monastic community that Anselm differed most markedly from Lanfranc. So far as the kingdom and the papacy were concerned, he brought a full adhesion to Lanfranc's point of view. But, as in both of his earlier moves, he brought an entirely different mode of operation and a quite different emphasis. Whereas Lanfranc knew how to move as a man of the world, Anselm moved only as a man of God.

Outside the monastery, Anselm was filled with dismay at all that he saw – the morals of the court, the rapacity of tenants, and the futility of discussions in the king's court about his proposals for religious reformation. Lanfranc had dealt with all these matters with masterly skill based on long experience of government, a natural aptitude for business, legal training and expertise, and plain power of command. Anselm had none of these assets. Yet, as in all his earlier offices, he showed unexpected sources of strength, not least in having no idea of compromise. Of policy in the ordinary sense of having a practical goal, and steadily working towards it by carefully prepared moves, he had none: in every problem he sought only truth and justice with the most disconcerting directness.

The consequence was that, for Anselm, his years as archbishop were a time of grief and affliction. When he wrote about the religious life, he still wrote with all his old fire and conviction. But there were very few political problems on which he both knew the right answer, and could persuade others to follow his advice. He continued to gather round him men and, in a more distant fashion, women, who loved to hear his words, who collected and preserved them, and shaped their lives by them. These people preserved the records of his words, which are the really lasting results of his years as archbishop.

We shall come to these things later. Meanwhile Anselm's great problem was to adapt his well-established and eagerly pursued role as a monastic guide and prophet to the vastly more complicated and miscellaneous array of problems which faced him as archbishop. Even before he became archbishop he had had the uncomfortable experience of being forced by external pressures to abandon his self-chosen limitations. In his monastic dialogues he had been in control of the issues raised; but he had no control over the issues raised by Roscelin, even less those raised by the Jews of London, and still less those raised by popes who were seeking a re-organization of the Church on lines which were quite different from those to which he was accustomed. The world was everywhere beginning to show itself as more complicated, and less monastically orientated, than the world in which he had grown up.

In that old world, he had been able to bring a sense of security to people at every level of society. His final precept to the monks of Bec, urging them to extend the bonds of friendship to people of all ranks in the whole countryside, expressed his ideal of a world centred on monastic foundations which offered the highest hopes of Heaven to all who supported them. But this monastically orientated world was already being replaced by a new ideal of a hierarchically ordered administration. It was in this development that the future of government lay, and here Lanfranc's more this-worldly outlook and greater practical ability had advantages which Anselm could never aspire to. With Lanfranc we can reasonably talk about an archiepiscopal policy, and we can trace the working out of this policy, not very fully, but consistently throughout his years as archbishop. With Anselm, the best we can do is to follow the different lines of activity in which he was involved, and try to trace the principles which activated him in crises which he seems seldom to have foreseen. In his actions as archbishop, he displayed the qualities which he had developed at Bec: a character at once other-worldly and shrewd, world-despairing and yet mild, pro-foundly subtle and yet simple in the affairs of this world. It would create a false impression to see a unity of policy where there is only the unity of holiness manifesting itself in several different areas. If we find it difficult to trace a single dominant theme running through his years as archbishop, it is not because he lacked a dominant theme, but because his theme was not capable of administrative organization.

3   The Investiture dispute

Historians are naturally apt to think that the most important incidents in Anselm's archiepiscopal years are related to the new ideal of a clerically controlled Church free from the trammels of lay interference. This ideal was beginning to bite deep into the structure of society during Anselm's years as archbishop, and in doing so it was beginning to transform western Christendom. As archbishop, Anselm stood in the midst of the opening moves in the great social and ecclesiastical revolution which made the ecclesiastical hierarchy the dominant force in European society during the next two hundred years. From the papal summit down to the holders of parochial benefices, the clergy became a force capable of laying down and imposing on the world at large the fundamental rules, not only of ecclesiastical discipline, but also of lay behaviour, in marriage and in the other sacraments of the Church, in the confession of sins, in the duty of ensuring the prevalence of orthodoxy, in the payment of tithes to the clergy, and in the provision of armed force to combat external or internal enemies of the faith.

This great change, which in the course of the twelfth and thirteenth centuries created a highly integrated and purposeful western European society, passed through several phases. The first and most important one, which made possible all those that came later, was the intense effort directed by relatively few men between about 1075 and 1125 to separate the clerical from the lay element in society, and to make the former the intellectual and administrative creators of a new European order. The first step in this development was the struggle to bring all the most important ecclesiastical appointments under clerical control. This, the so-called Investiture struggle, reached its height and achieved its highest degree of success during the years when Anselm was archbishop.

Social and ecclesiastical historians alike have rightly seen this development as one of the most important episodes in medieval European history. Consequently, there has naturally been a tendency to judge Anselm's archiepiscopate almost wholly in relation to this struggle. On a long-term view this is wholly defensible, provided that we do not read this perspective into the minds of the actors, and especially not into Anselm's mind. There were indeed a few far-sighted and energetic innovators who were aware of the large issues involved in the Investiture struggle. But Anselm was not one of them. Nor was he alone in this. Most members of the lay and ecclesiastical aristocracies of the time would have been surprised to hear that they were living in the midst of a great Investiture contest, and dumbfounded to learn that it was the most important event of their time.

If we look on the scene through the eyes of Anselm, we can see that he was wholly unaware of the Investiture issue until he had been archbishop for six years; and even then he learnt about it only by accident, and accepted its aim only as a by-product of his duty of personal obedience to the pope. It was the attitude of obedience which concerned him; not the aim of the orders which he most scrupulously obeyed. The subjects of contemporary discussion which concerned him most deeply, and stand out in his letters as archbishop with the clarity of deeply felt issues, are: monastic vows, personal religious observance, monastic discipline, and doctrinal purity. These are the subjects which fill his most deeply felt and most forcibly argued letters as archbishop, just as they had filled his letters as prior and abbot of Bec. To these issues, he had now to add the extremely complicated and contentious rights of his community at Canterbury, but his view of the world and of his responsibilities in it had not greatly changed as a result of his 'promotion'. He did not see it as part of his archiepiscopal duties to fight for a programme. So, before going further, we must first try to define more closely what he thought, or may have thought, his duties were; then to examine the instruments he had for performing these duties; and, finally, to distinguish the main sources of evidence for knowing what he did.

II   THE FRAMEWORK OF ARCHIEPISCOPAL LIFE

1   The precepts of Gregory the Great

Since Anselm never wrote about his duties systematically, it may seem useless to inquire what he thought they were. But there was a book on the subject which was to be found in almost every monastic and cathedral library, and it will at least be worth looking at as a possible guide. The book is Gregory the Great's *Regula Pastoralis*, and it was peculiarly relevant to Anselm's case, for Gregory was also a monk, writing in reply to a charge that he had tried to escape the burden of office by running away. Thus Gregory was addressing himself to just such a problem as Anselm's, justifying both his resistance and his acceptance.

Gregory's first theme was expressed in the famous phrase: 'The art of arts is the guidance of souls'; for this, he added, it is first necessary to know oneself. Both of these *dicta* had long been the foundation of Anselm's spiritual advice; and no change was needed in carrying out this same programme as archbishop. Then, also

234

according to Gregory, and fully borne out by Anselm's behaviour at all periods of his career, the prelate must beware of busying himself with too many distractions: he must concentrate on preaching and teaching; and on being, in Gregory's words, 'the equal of everyone in compassion, above everyone in contemplation'. Here too Anselm had long been carrying out these precepts, and no change was required when he became archbishop.

Another section of Gregory's instructions related to the conduct of secular affairs, including all matters of estate management, finance, and the business of the royal court. In these matters, the words of the *Pastoral Care* are peculiarly relevant to Anselm's behaviour as archbishop: 'secular business is sometimes to be tolerated out of compassion; but never sought for love'. Further, 'when the soul falls from its true self into the tumults of external occupations, it must seek to rise again through intense study'. And with regard to willingness to answer questions: 'If a pastor is asked spiritual questions, it is disgraceful if he has then to learn the answers . . . he must always be ready to give a reason for the hope that is in him.'[2]

When these extracts and many others like them are put together, they provide to a remarkable extent an outline of Anselm as archbishop. His opportunities for preaching were of course limited by his ignorance of the language of the people; but his friends have left many reports of sermons preached to monastic audiences; his letters are a large repository of spiritual advice to individuals and communities; and we have (as I shall suggest later) a report of one of his sermons, probably preached in French, but preserved in a Latin summary by Eadmer, at a royal Council at a critical moment at the beginning of Henry I's reign. In this sermon, Anselm said nothing about the urgent political problems of the time, but urged a revival of the ancient Anglo-Saxon celebration of the Ordination of St Gregory, to whom England owed its conversion.[3] If I am right in identifying Anselm as the preacher, we have here an example of his using a political crisis to point to Gregory the Great's work as the foundation on which political order was based.

If we find that preaching and giving pastoral advice play a more important part in Anselm's archiepiscopal concerns than any matters of business or politics, we shall only be discovering that he followed the precepts for pastors as laid down by Gregory the Great.

[2] *Regula Pastoralis*, II, v. PL 77, cols. 32–4.   [3] See below, pp. 386–8.

In addition to the requirements of pastoral care, Anselm would have been guided by the routine of business already established at Canterbury by Lanfranc: the routine of visitations, ordinations, consecrations of churches, hearing complaints, admonishing delinquent monks, nuns, bishops, and laity, hearing appeals from dioceses in the province of Canterbury. As an ever-present influence on Anselm's conduct, the record of Lanfranc's activity preserved in his correspondence must be given a prominent place. Above all, this record would have revealed the importance that Lanfranc attached to the primatial position of Canterbury, and the need for co-operation with the king in holding primatial councils.

It would be quite wrong to think that Anselm spent his whole time either quarrelling with the king or making plans for the future. In fact much of his time during his first five years as archbishop was spent in giving spiritual advice to many people, and in continuing his own theological work. During these years he gave final shape to his reply to Roscelin, a work which he had found great difficulty in completing, and he wrote almost the whole of the greatest and longest of his theological works – his *Cur Deus Homo*. In addition to these major works, he devoted more continuing effort to patching up his misunderstandings with the monks of Bec, and to giving advice on monastic life, than to forwarding any broader ecclesiastical designs. After 1093, no less than before, his main thoughts were concerned with the discipline of monastic life; and here his most urgent duty was to the church at Canterbury. In all these new obligations his message for others remained what it had been for the past thirty years: 'prefer the security of peace within the monastic walls to the perils of the world outside; stay steadfastly in port; do not risk your eternal safety among the shipwrecks and storms of the world'.[4]

This was the main gist of all Anselm's advice to those he loved best. Even as archbishop, this thought lay at the centre of his teaching: the world had no attraction for him. He would not, like Lanfranc, assume a commanding position in society. Where the world was concerned, he was by nature a resigner. He tried very long and hard to resign the archbishopric, as he had tried to resign

---

[4] This idea runs like a thread through his letters both before and after he became archbishop. See *Ep.* 161 (iii, 12); and cf. *Epp.* 37 (i, 29) and 140 (ii, 45). The image of tenaciously staying in port amid the storms of the world seems to be an echo of Horace, *Odes*, i, 14: *fortiter occupa portum*: cf. *Ep.* 414 (iii, 133): *mentem vestram, donec illae (perversae cogitationes) evanescant, fortiter occupate.*

every earlier promotion; but Pope Urban II kept him at his post as archbishop, just as Archbishop Maurilius had kept him to his post as prior and abbot. It is very easy to brush aside this resigning-trait in his character, but it is a mistake to do so. He was not a policy-maker, nor a man of affairs, but always and essentially a monk; almost, perhaps ideally, a hermit; always seeking liberty in obedience.

Since he could not conscientiously resign, he had to do his duty. But what was his duty? As he saw it, it was certainly not to fight the king. It was rather, in conjunction with the king, to do what he could to bring order and discipline into the English Church. The main way in which he and the king could collaborate in doing this was through his holding ecclesiastical councils with royal support, such as Lanfranc had held in 1072, 1075, 1078, 1080, and 1085. The tradition was well established: he only had to follow it. It carried with it no threat to the royal position – quite the opposite. It was a policy based on a doctrine of collaboration, and if William II had agreed to collaborate with Anselm, as his father had collaborated with Lanfranc, he and his brother after him would have had more successful reigns even from a worldly point of view.

Anselm long believed that Rufus would come round, and he might have done so: a Lanfrancian peace with the Church appealed to that loyalty to his father's memory which was the one piety which Rufus retained. Perhaps Rufus would have followed the example of his father if his constant need for money had not forced him into extortionate measures with the Church. We forget how threatened Rufus felt. He knew how easily his father's reign might have ended in disaster if King Cnut of Denmark had not been murdered in 1086 while preparing to invade England. He knew also how necessary the conquest of Normandy was to his own survival in England. He knew too how weak was his northern frontier. Anselm sympathized with him on all these issues more than historians have been apt to do. But, in the end, Anselm realized that Rufus would never collaborate with him. When he realized this, he had no other immediate thought than to resign, and to go to Rome with this hope.

But until he reached this decision, there were several tasks – some of them congenial – which he could undertake. In the first place, he could influence his fellow bishops, as he had been influencing people for the past thirty years. He seems to have succeeded with several of them: on Herbert Losinga at Norwich, on Osmund at

Salisbury, perhaps even on William at Durham, his influence was deep and lasting. In addition, he could look after the rights of his own church of Canterbury: as we shall see, he did this with remarkable energy and zeal. Further, as in earlier days, he could give advice to all who needed or asked for it: to monks or nuns who wished to leave, or had left, their monasteries; to bishops, abbots, monks, or nuns, who asked questions about theology, ecclesiastical practices, monastic life, or private morals. Perhaps nearest to his heart of all, he could repair the breach with the monks of Bec.

It was only in the area of broad ecclesiastical policy – the area in which historians expect to be able to allot him a place – that he did almost nothing. The tendency to think that his only important activity during these years was quarrelling with the king comes from the desire to see him doing *something* in the area of ecclesiastical politics. Just how this expectation first arose is a problem which will be discussed in the next chapter. Here I am concerned only to draw out the general lines and conditions of his work as archbishop, and as a first step we must look at the helpers whom he gathered round him.

2 Anselm's assistants

The range of business which an archbishop can deal with, and his manner of dealing with it, will largely depend on the staff at his disposal. Likewise, the qualifications of his staff will give some indication of the business which he thinks important. Naturally, this staff will not always be with him; what is important is that it should be available when needed.

Another important limitation on the business he can attend to will arise from his manner of life. Even as abbot of Bec, Anselm had spent much of his time travelling round the priories and attending courts and councils. But as archbishop he was seldom in the monastery of which he was (in Lanfranc's words) 'abbot and father'. In the course of his visitations, and even for the simple purpose of consuming the produce of his scattered estates, he had to keep moving, besides having to be present at the royal court at least two or three times a year. To these necessary travels in England, he added a total of seven years of exile in the course of his sixteen years as archbishop. During these peregrinations he had to conduct whatever business came to him from his diocese, his province, and the still wider area over which he claimed authority as primate.

For all these purposes he needed to travel with a staff. At a later date, a normal retinue for an archbishop would amount to about thirty or more mounted retainers of varied ranks, from legally and theologically trained household officials down to a miscellaneous assortment of cooks, ostlers, and domestic managers. Anselm's retinue was certainly much smaller, and we hear about it only by chance. Indeed, to read Eadmer's account of their travels, one might think that Anselm travelled round England on official business, and round the Continent during his exiles, with only a few humble companions. No doubt this is how they saw themselves, *nudi nudum Christum sequentes*, but their poverty must be understood in a rather special sense. Outsiders, including the king, did not see matters in this light. Anselm as archbishop had an annual income from land alone, distinct from the revenues of the monks, assessed in Domesday Book at almost exactly £1500, and his lay vassals had in addition £350 a year. Besides this, he had, like the monks, his spiritualities and other unspecified payments from his tenants. But even the revenue recorded in Domesday Book is sufficient to put him in the very highest class of barons, and to make him the head of a very large-scale business.

We may take it that, at least while he was in England, Anselm's retinue was fairly numerous. But it had one feature which distinguishes it from the households of all future archbishops with the possible exception of his immediate successor, Ralph d'Escures, who like himself was a Benedictine monk: he had not a single scholastically trained lawyer or theologian, nor even one of that numerous class of Masters of Arts who abounded in the households of all ecclesiastical, or even secular, magnates from the mid-twelfth century onwards.

This would have surprised his successors, who looked on the conduct of official business as their main occupation, and recruited for their households highly trained experts with a respectable scholastic record. An archbishop who wished to have such men in his service could not hope to find many monks with the right qualifications. Even Theobald, who had also been abbot of Bec before becoming archbishop from 1138 to 1160, had a chancellor, assisted by some six or eight clerks. Not one of them was a monk; some were famous, and several were men of high scholastic achievement, such as were capable of dealing with the steady stream of ecclesiastical business.

This trait, which was already clearly marked in Theobald's

household in the 1140s, was even more distinctly emphasized in the household of Theobald's successor, Thomas Becket, as the well-known list of his twenty *eruditi* makes clear. Without these men, he would never have been able to conduct the influential correspondence and propaganda which kept his dispute with Henry II alive during six years of exile. Once more, as with Theobald, not a single one of these experts was a monk.

For understanding Anselm's position, and above all for understanding his conception of his position, it is important to recognize that he had no staff of this kind. Nor is there any reason to believe that he would have thought such a staff appropriate or even tolerable. He was a monk before he was archbishop, and he was archbishop because he was a monk. As archbishop, his first and most important duty was to guide and rule the monastic body at Canterbury, and his next duty was to exercise those rights, and perform those duties, which had come down to him from the long monastic past of the Anglo-Saxon Church.

It is against this background that we have to understand his conduct as archbishop. Moreover, this was not a merely escapist attitude: he saw his monastic role as providing the best contribution he could make to the religious state of the whole country. In a later chapter we shall examine the historical background of the claims of the church of Canterbury which Anselm fully endorsed. But briefly it may be said here that in the view of history which the monks of Canterbury maintained, and which Anselm accepted, the conversion of England and the maintenance of Christianity through the perils of the last five centuries had depended on the healthy state of monastic life in the whole country. It was from the monasteries that the conversion of England had been achieved in the seventh century, and from the monasteries that the renewal of religion had come in the tenth century. It was from this same basis that the post-Conquest revival had come. This whole view was entirely congenial to Anselm: indeed it is hard to see how, with his background at Bec and his association with Lanfranc, he could have held any other. Far from wishing to change this situation, he gave it a special poignancy by added to it his own intense monastic experience.

Both from his own experience and from the tradition which he found at Canterbury, he saw the maintenance of monastic discipline as the first essential for the religious well-being of the whole country; for this purpose, the maintenance of a monastic routine in his own life and in that of his household was of the first importance. With these principles in mind, we may examine the men whom he had around him in his almost constant journeyings and in his exiles.

To begin with, when he arrived in England in September 1092 on the visit which brought him to the archbishopric, he had with him two monks of Bec on whom he chiefly relied in his business affairs. These were Baldwin and Eustace. He seems to have kept both of them with him at Canterbury: Eustace reappears only occasionally in later years, but Baldwin has an important place in the story of Anselm's life, and he requires a brief description.

In 1093 Baldwin was a man of about fifty. He had had a distinguished career as a layman before he became a monk of Bec in about 1085. As a young man he had been the man of affairs and chief agent of the bishop of Tournai in Flanders, and as early as 1072 he had taken part in an embassy sent by the count of Flanders to the Emperor Henry IV. At Bec, he was probably the most experienced man of business among the monks, and Anselm made him head of his household when he became archbishop.[5]

So far as we know, Baldwin had no scholastic training, but he was practical, decisive, domineering, not given to doubt. These characteristics come out in many details supplied by Eadmer. For instance, when Anselm was staying in a house next to one that caught fire, it was Baldwin who came to him and urged him to do something. Anselm asked what he could do. 'Go out and make the sign of the Cross in the face of the fire; perhaps God will ward it off', said Baldwin. Anselm grumbled, but he went out and did as Baldwin told him. He raised his hand, made the sign of the Cross: the fire went out.

Then again, during Anselm's first exile, when his movements were the subject of widespread rumours and he was often in danger of ambush, Baldwin was in command in all emergencies. When they were travelling incognito through the Alps, and the abbot of Aspres-sur-Buech told them that he had heard that the archbishop of Canterbury had been forced to turn back to Lyons, it was Baldwin who promptly replied: 'He has done well; but we alas are forced to go on in the service of God, and by the command of our

---

[5] The main source of our information about Baldwin's early life is Hermann of Tournai, *De Restauratione S. Martini Tornacensis, MGH, SS*, xiv, pp. 278–81. For the details mentioned in the following paragraphs about his activity in Anselm's household both as abbot and archbishop, see *HN*, pp. 67, 95, 171; *VA* II, xvi, xxiv, xxviii, lvii; and *Epp*. 124 (ii, 53), 151 (iii, 4), 338 (iv, 47), 339 (iv, 48), 349 (iv, 55), 462 (iv, 94).

spiritual superior.' A few days later they told the abbot of Susa that they were monks of Bec, and when he began asking about Abbot Anselm, it was Baldwin who answered: 'He has been carried off to an archbishopric in another kingdom.' 'So I have heard; but now tell me, how is he, is he well?' 'Honestly, I haven't seen him at Bec since he became archbishop', said the ever-ready Baldwin, 'but they say he is very well where he is.'

Besides being ready with repartee, he was a great seer of marvels. It was he, and not Eadmer, who saw a large hole in the boat which had brought them from England, and Eadmer duly reported it among Anselm's miracles. Baldwin loved to spread the fame of these wonders: when he visited his old place of employment at Tournai, he would hold forth about the things he had seen and heard in Anselm's company. Both William II and Henry I recognized his importance: the first by sending him into exile in order to embarrass Anselm, the second by asking that Baldwin should accompany his own messengers to Rome in 1105. In all the affairs of the archbishop – whether it was a fire that needed to be extinguished, or a miracle to be testified to, or an embassy to be conducted – Baldwin spoke with authority and acted with decision: an active, blunt and credulous man, and the only man of wide practical experience in Anselm's entire household. His experience had been gained, not in the schools or in ecclesiastical affairs, but in the lay world. Eadmer calls him the *provisor ac dispensator rerum Anselmi*, and elsewhere Anselm's *provisor et ordinator rerum*.[6] At first sight it might appear from these words that Baldwin held the position of dispenser, but it is characteristic of the lack of definition in these matters that Eadmer intends something much wider. He means simply that Baldwin was Anselm's factotum. A useful man indeed, but emphatically not a man whom later archbishops would have thought suitable as their main official.

If Baldwin's province was thus large, the rest of Anselm's clerical household was probably organized less with an eye to the efficient conduct of ecclesiastical business than the adequate observance of a liturgical and religious routine. This was Eadmer's province. Anselm must quickly have chosen him as a member of his household, for they were already together at Hastings in February 1094, and Eadmer may have been present at the royal court in March 1093 when Anselm was nominated as archbishop. Officially

---

[6] *HN*, pp. 386, 417; *VA* II, xxiv, lxvii.

he was the keeper of Anselm's chapel and its relics: with this he combined the less definite office of being at the archbishop's side and acting, as Anselm himself says, as 'the staff of his old age'. How far he acted in any definite way as the archbishop's secretary is not clear. He was an expert scribe, and it is likely that he sometimes wrote the archbishop's letters. He certainly copied the *Cur Deus Homo* as a present for Boso and the monks of Bec, and he shared all Anselm's travels until the end of his life.[7]

It does not seem that Eadmer was responsible for preserving and arranging copies of the archbishop's letters; for as we shall see, they were never so ill-preserved as when Eadmer's influence was strongest. It was not until 1101, after Eadmer had been Anselm's companion for seven years and had fallen into the background, that any consistent attempt was made to preserve the letters which Anselm wrote as archbishop. Eadmer's usefulness was of a different kind. He sat at the archbishop's feet, and besides keeping a private record of events, he made notes of some at least of Anselm's sermons. When Anselm's nerves were jangled with business, he provided the sedative of spiritual conversation. William of Malmesbury tells us that when Anselm became archbishop he asked the pope to provide him with someone by whose commands he could regulate his life, and Pope Urban nominated Eadmer. Thereupon, he adds, Anselm attached so much importance to Eadmer's commands that he would not so much as turn over in his bed, much less get up, unless Eadmer told him to do so. This is a typical piece of embroidery, but the general fact may well be true, as also may the single example of Eadmer's authority which William of Malmesbury gives: Anselm, who was most fearful of committing any sin, one day ate pickled eel, then recollecting himself he bitterly lamented that he had eaten raw flesh contrary to the Law. Eadmer, who was sitting beside him, said 'The salt has removed the rawness of the flesh', and Anselm replied, 'You have saved me from being tortured by the memory of sin.'[8]

There is reason to think that the relations between Anselm and Eadmer changed during the last nine years of Eadmer's life. Perhaps it was Anselm's fear that, contrary to his express command, Eadmer may have been continuing to write his

---

[7] See *HN*, p. 52 for Eadmer's presence at Hastings in February 1094, and below, pp. 409–14, for the remainder of Eadmer's career in Anselm's household.

[8] For these details, see *VA* II, xiii; William of Malmesbury, *GP*, p. 122; and for Eadmer's reports of Anselm's sermons, see below, pp. 385–8.

biography, which led to a change in their relationship. At first Anselm had encouraged him. He read what Eadmer had written and made some changes. Then remorse set in: presumably he thought that in his encouragement he had been guilty of the sin of pride. Whatever the precise reason, he ordered Eadmer to destroy what he had written, and Eadmer obeyed, but not before he had made a copy. After 1100, not only does the biography lose all its earlier freshness and fullness, but another monk of Christ Church is to be found performing some of the functions which seem to have been in Eadmer's hands before.

This newcomer was the monk Alexander, who had not accompanied Anselm in his first exile, but was one of his companions during the second. On one occasion we find him taking Eadmer's place in the chapel, and it is chiefly to him that we owe the surviving records of Anselm's sayings and sermons during his later years. In 1102 he accompanied Baldwin to Rome on the archbishop's behalf, and he acted as Anselm's messenger again in 1104. The better order in which Anselm's correspondence was kept after 1101 may have been due to his joining the household: in any case it is clear that Eadmer's position became more limited, while Alexander came to occupy a position second only to that of Baldwin. As a man he is obscure, and as a writer he is unpolished: he shows none of Eadmer's perception of significant detail. Nevertheless his collection of Anselm's sayings helped to give a wide circulation to an important part of Anselm's teaching. Characteristically, it is only by chance that we can be sure that he was responsible for making this collection; but despite his obscurity, there can be no doubt that he was an important man in Anselm's household in his later years.[9]

This exhausts the list of the regular members of Anselm's household whose names are known to us, with the important exception of Boso, who was less a member of the household than Anselm's closest intellectual companion in his later years. His role in Anselm's circle of friends and in the writing of *Cur Deus Homo* has already been examined: it only remains to add here that, after Anselm's return from his second exile, when his last phase of philosophical activity was beginning, Anselm paid a further tribute to the importance of his help, and his lack of philosophical resources in England, by asking for him to be sent once more from Bec to Canterbury 'because he would prefer to live with him in a

---

[9] For Alexander, see *HN*, p. 132; *Ep.* 325 (iv, 37); *Memorials*, pp. 19–30, 105–270; and below, pp. 389–94.

desert than without him in great abundance'.[10] Thus Boso was with him when he wrote his last treatise on predestination, grace, and free-will, and he stayed in England till Anselm's death. Boso was the self-effacing assistant in the production of Anselm's later works. Although he outlived Anselm by many years, as abbot of Bec, he left only one piece of writing, a letter, that can be confidently ascribed to him, unless (as seems possible) he was responsible for some fragments of *Anselmiana* for which no other author has been found.[11]

Both Anselm and Boso had had some experience of spiritual terror in their youth, from which Anselm had been saved by his mother, and Boso by Anselm.[12] They recognized in each other a common background of panic followed by peace, as well as an uncommon sharpness of mind. Curiously, neither Eadmer nor Alexander ever mentions Boso's presence in Anselm's company. It may be that he did not move round with the others, but stayed at Canterbury to read and think and take part in the monastic life, as he and Anselm had formerly done at Bec, and as Anselm would himself have liked to do.

We hear almost nothing about the lay side of Anselm's household, but it certainly existed, and its main components must have been as in other households: a steward or dapifer at its head, and under him a number of officials – butler, dispenser, chamberlain, seneschal, cook, usher, porter, and marshal, each with a distinct province of his own in hall, chamber, kitchen, or stable. Domesday Book gives the titles dapifer, constable, dispenser, and chamberlain to four of the archbishop's tenants. Some of these were men too important to have been constantly in attendance on the archbishop, but he could not have moved unless they had provided someone to perform their functions. When he went into exile, nearly all the lay officials were left behind in England to look after their own and the archbishop's interests, but Anselm took with him a few minor officials and servants like Adam, who appears by chance because he had a vision while he lay sleeping in the archbishop's chamber; Lambert, a little man who worked in the chamber and was saved from blindness by St Dunstan; Norman, a chaplain whose horse was miraculously cured; and an unnamed young man whose house was preserved from fire long after

---

[10] For this testimony, see *Vita Bosonis*, PL 150, col. 726.
[11] For his letter, see Bnl. 16,713, f. 160; for other *Anselmiana*, below pp. 402, 477.
[12] For these two incidents, see *VA* I, xxxiii, and pp. 172–3.

Anselm's death by the invocation of his name.[13] Without a miracle, the chances that their memory would be preserved were negligible.

Looking at Anselm's companions as a whole, they reflect the lack of experienced and able men available for the archbishop's service. Baldwin was an active man, but he was not qualified to give advice on ecclesiastical affairs. About Alexander we know too little to give a confident judgement, but nothing he has left suggests abilities or accomplishments out of the ordinary. Eadmer had great qualities as a man of feeling and observation, and as the transmitter of a complex tradition, but he had neither the width of experience nor the judgement to fit him for the conduct of business. This meant that Anselm had no one near him on whom he could rely for expert advice on matters of ecclesiastical law and administration. We shall find, as might be expected, that Anselm had considerable skill in working out from first principles the correct solution to practical ecclesiastical problems, but for the growing complexity of legal problems the lack of learned men in his household must already have been a serious impediment to the efficient conduct of business, and it would have been incomprehensible twenty or thirty years later. Similarly, in deciding the agenda and writing the decrees of his two Councils, there is no evidence that he could draw on the knowledge and experience of anyone but himself. We can see how much thought he applied to the problems and decisions of the Councils, and how closely the decisions are related to his unbending determination that the secular clergy should obey the decrees on celibacy. His conciliar decrees, like his theological works, reflect his own spirituality. They are deeply interesting for this reason, but their deep internal source helps to account for their immediate ineffectiveness.

There is no sign that Anselm recognized that his household was deficient in contemporary expertise. He seems to have taken no steps, which he could easily have done, to recruit new men from the schools. Almost necessarily they would not have been monks, and this may have been for him an insuperable objection. Later archbishops had no similar scruples, but Anselm was only happy with like-minded monks as his helpers. It is necessary to remember this when we turn to the questions which occupied his mind in carrying out his archiepiscopal duties.

[13] *VA* II, xlvii; *Memorials of St Dunstan*, p. 246.

III CONFLICTING EVIDENCE

I have discussed in the previous two sections the principles of action of an archbishop and the practical limitations, partly self-imposed, partly inherent in his situation, which determined the range of problems which Anselm was equipped to face. The general result of this discussion indicated that monastic and spiritual problems were likely to take first place in his thoughts, for they were the only problems which his advisers and his own preparation gave him the equipment to deal with. The emphasis which has often been given to his quarrelling with the king comes partly from the desire to see him doing something in the area of ecclesiastical politics, and partly from the misleading emphasis of Eadmer's *Historia Novorum*, which (as its name implies) was written to support a theory about the events of the time, which was certainly not in the minds of either Anselm or Eadmer in Rufus's reign. As a first step in correcting this distortion, we must first survey the sources which are available for Anselm's early years as archbishop and assess their reliability. There are three main bodies of material: Eadmer's *Historia Novorum* and his *Vita Anselmi*, and Anselm's own letters.

1 Eadmer's records and recollections

Superficially, the *Historia Novorum* seems to offer by far the greatest body of material. It is an incomparably detailed eye-witness account of all Anselm's dealings with the king, barons, and bishops during the years from 1093 until he went into exile in October 1097. After Anselm's return from exile in September 1100 until his death in 1109, its credentials are less good (for reasons later to be explained), but for the earlier years it is an account probably compiled from notes made on the spot, by an observant eye-witness who was closer to Anselm than anyone else – his confessor, a monk who understood his spiritual aims better than anyone, recording the words spoken and the actions taken in his presence. There is nothing like it for any other contemporary figure, and there are not many such records for any medieval character. As William of Malmesbury was the first to acknowledge, 'He expounds everything so clearly that all seems to happen under our very eyes.'[14]

---

[14] *GP*, p. 74.

Nothing can replace it. Why then can we not trust it? Partly because it does not offer, or pretend to offer, a complete account of Anselm's activities, and more important, because it is in some vital respects fundamentally misleading. Let us consider these two limitations separately.

Eadmer himself is the best witness to the limited scope of the *Historia Novorum*, for he wrote his *Vita Anselmi* to complete the picture by giving an account of Anselm's *Life and Conversation*. By the word 'conversation', he meant more than simply private talk, though he reports much of this: he meant everything connected with Anselm's intellectual and religious behaviour and manner of life; everything, in brief, at the centre of Anselm's life.[15] By contrast, the *Historia Novorum* concentrated on the theme set out in its title and preface: the study of the *New Things* that had come to pass in England since the Conquest – in particular the new rules about the homage and investiture of prelates, which (according to Eadmer's preface) had been introduced into England by William the Conqueror in defiance of the principles of ecclesiastical order. But this brings us to the second and more important reason for its unreliability.

Eadmer did not give final shape to his notes until after Anselm's death, and, when he did so, he distorted the whole picture of Anselm's early years to suggest an awareness of the incompatibility between the political structure of the Church in relation to the king, as practised by Lanfranc, and the law of the Church, of which Anselm at that time knew nothing. Consequently, anything in the *Historia Novorum* before 1100 which reports Anselm's consciousness of this theme bears the marks of retrospective reassessment.

This flaw in the *Historia Novorum* is to some extent corrected by the *Vita Anselmi*, which deserves more attention than it has received as a record of Anselm's permanent interests and thoughts. But by far the most important corrective is to be found in Anselm's letters, which record his contemporary thoughts on some matters described by Eadmer, and on several others of which Eadmer tells us nothing. But before we can thoroughly understand the evidence of the letters, it is necessary to know something about the manner of their preservation, for mistaken views on this question have led to a belief that Anselm preserved or destroyed his letters as an

[15] *VA, Praefatio.* The word *conversatio* was frequently used to describe monastic life as a whole; cf. the Biblical *Nostra conversatio in caelis est.* (Philippians, iii. 20.)

instrument of policy. The contents of some of the letters described below are so culpable from a high ecclesiastical point of view that a wily politician might indeed have tried to suppress them. But since they have survived, the attempted suppression was either fatuous or non-existent – in fact the latter, as the following considerations will suffice to show.[16]

2 Anselm's letters

Deplorably few letters from Anselm have survived for the years 1093 to 1100: only fifty-two – about the same as for the previous seven years. Moreover, about half of them have survived only because their recipients preserved them, not because Anselm kept copies which have survived. The general picture of Anselm's correspondence, at least until 1100, when greater order began to prevail, suggests simple lack of organization in his household, and what has been said above about his household gives no indication of any high degree of efficiency. There is good reason to think that Anselm's business habits did not change after he became archbishop, and, unless his personal records suffered some catastrophic loss – which is not impossible – we must think of his circumstances as being less adapted to the preservation of letters than in his earlier years as prior and abbot.

His lack of a body of trained clerical officials for the conduct of ecclesiastical business is a fact of central importance for understanding his actions and his limitations. In principle, he knew very well what he wanted: he wanted personal righteousness, the maintenance of monastic discipline, and the preservation of the rights of Canterbury. But he was not an organizer for the present, nor a planner for the future: he was a personal force in the lives of others. What he had been at Bec, he was at Canterbury.

This continuity of outlook is strongly reinforced when we examine the subject-matter of his archiepiscopal letters before 1100, to which the following figures will serve as a provisional guide: seventeen of the fifty-two surviving letters are concerned chiefly with matters of monastic vows and discipline; fifteen others with the affairs of Bec, in which Anselm continued to take a close

---

[16] For a review of the whole problem of the transmission of Anselm's letters, which becomes a crucial issue in view of the constructions which have been built on the supposition that Anselm himself directed the compilations of his letter-collection, see below, pp. 394–403, 458–81.

interest. Another six deal with friendship, three with problems of theology and Canon Law. Only six were even remotely connected with general problems of the kingdom, and these by no means support the view that Anselm had any clear political aim – certainly not one of hostility to royal power over the Church. They contain requests for prayers for the king, fears for his safety, praise for his energy, and a refusal of the legate's invitation to hold a council without the king's consent. Only one was in any sense hostile to the king, and that was the letter to Hugh, archbishop of Lyons, deploring the king's hostility without rancour. This letter is the only one which deals in a general way with the state of the Church, and it contained at least one phrase which must have startled its recipient:

> This is my thought: the king gave me the archbishopric as it was held by Archbishop Lanfranc till the end of his life; and now he takes away from the church and myself that which he himself gave to me, and which the archbishop my predecessor had so long held quietly.[17]

This placid use of a phrase, 'the king gave me the archbishopric', which was anathema to right-minded ecclesiastical reformers, cannot have failed to alert Archbishop Hugh that Anselm stood in need of instruction: with what results, we shall see later. But, whatever the result of Hugh's influence, it was not operative in the reign of William Rufus. In the period before 1100, the most striking feature of his letters is their silence on large political questions. They are about theology, prayer, monastic obedience, chastity, religious friendship. They all bear witness to the fact that Anselm was a man whose soul was filled with a desire for monastic peace, with a limitless concern for the souls of individuals, among whom the king held a high place. But he was not a politician.

To test this impression, we may begin with a small collection of letters which were not preserved by Anselm or his clerks, but by their local recipients in the diocese of Salisbury, or perhaps by the bishop of the diocese, who may have received copies. The collection consists of six letters written between 1094 and 1097, and they have the merit of preserving a record of Anselm's activity in a single small area over a short space of time.

The first was written shortly after Anselm and Rufus had parted company at Hastings in February 1094: the king going to

[17] *Ep.* 176 (iii, 24).

Normandy, Anselm to his manors in England.[18] According to Eadmer's account in his *Historia Novorum*, they parted in great anger after fierce dispute. It is surprising therefore to find that in these letters Anselm speaks of Rufus only in terms of friendship and admiration: he says nothing about any breach between them. The main purpose of his first letter was to tell the bishop that he had spoken to the king about a daughter of the king of Scotland, who after wearing the monastic habit at Wilton (in the diocese of Salisbury) had recently returned to secular life. With great simplicity, Anselm says that he had hesitated to raise the matter with the king, fearing that Rufus might have been a party to this transaction. But when he did so, and demanded that the girl should be forced to return to her monastery, he found that Rufus, 'like a good king', was entirely ready to co-operate. As a result of their agreement, Anselm instructed the bishop to use his episcopal authority to force her to return. We shall examine this case in more detail later; for the present, it will suffice to note Anselm's expressions of continuing faith in the king's good will at a time when the *Historia Novorum* speaks only of fierce enmity.

This observation is confirmed in the second of this little group of letters.[19] It too was written to the bishop of Salisbury, about a year after the first, probably in June 1095. Rufus had returned to England from Normandy in February, and once more Eadmer speaks of altercations between king and archbishop reaching new heights of bitterness and fury. Again, it is surprising to find that Anselm's letter speaks only of his concern for the king's safety from his enemies. He describes these enemies with indignation as men who hate the king for his prudence and energy, 'as bad men are apt to hate good ones'. He asks the bishop to have prayers said throughout his diocese for the king's safety, and he ends with the striking phrase: 'his prosperity is ours; our adversity is his'. It sounds like Mr Gladstone writing about Queen Victoria, except that Rufus seems never to have disliked Anselm personally, as Victoria disliked her prime minister. The comparison is not as absurd as it seems at first sight: Anselm's respect for kingship was as

---

[18] *Ep.* 177. This letter and the others in the same group were unknown until discovered and published by Wilmart, 1931i, pp. 38–54. For Eadmer's contrasting account, see *HN*, pp. 48–52.

[19] *Ep.* 190. For Eadmer's account of the worsening political situation in 1095, see *HN*, pp. 52–67.

warm as Gladstone's, and both men moved only reluctantly away from the ideals of their youth.

In all his thoughts at this time, Anselm seems unconscious of what may broadly be called the Hildebrandine programme for the Church. His desire was for royal co-operation, and he persisted in this course despite all Rufus's delays. He recognized that the safety of the kingdom had to come first. He even welcomed military vigour in a ruler, as we can see in another letter shortly after the one I have just quoted. In the summer of 1095 Rufus took his army northwards into Scotland. In his absence, he left Anselm with the duty of guarding the Channel ports. Anselm approved the king's vigour and took his duty very seriously – so seriously that he refused to be diverted from it to meet the papal legate who had brought his pallium from Rome.[20]

The next in our small group of letters comes from a time more than a year later, when according to the *Historia Novorum* the king and archbishop were in a state of irremediable hostility. Once more Anselm's letters tell another story. He wrote to the bishop of Salisbury, instructing him, in his own name and that of the king, to prevent the abbot of Cerne from carrying out a plan for taking his monks on the Crusade in a vessel already hired at the abbot's expense. It was a madcap scheme of a wild and wealthy abbot, but interesting as expressing the general enthusiasm for the Crusade, which was shared neither by Anselm nor the king. Anselm wrote to the bishop to tell him that he and the king had agreed that the monks were to be forced to stay at home, and that the king would look into the matter when he returned from Normandy.[21]

Once more, we find co-operation with the king the foundation of Anselm's policy for the well-being of the Church; and this comes out even more strongly in his relations with the papal legate who brought his pallium to England in 1095. We have already seen that Anselm refused to meet the legate because a meeting would interfere with the duty of defending the kingdom from invasion which the king had laid on him. For the same reason, he would not

---

[20] *Ep.* 191 (iii, 35).

[21] *Ep.* 195 (iii, 85) Schmitt dates the letter 1095; but it must be after the Council of Clermont, and during the king's absence in Normandy, September 1096–April 1097. Further, since the letter refers to an existing bishop of Worcester, it must either be before January 1095, when Bishop Wulfstan died, or after June 1096, when his successor, the royal clerk Samson, was appointed. Clearly it is not before 1095; therefore it must be after June 1096.

hold a Council in conjunction with the legate (although such a council was what he greatly desired) without the king's approval.

In this matter as in others, he recognized his need for the king's approval and help. He was prepared to wait a long time, and it was only when he saw that he would not get what he wanted, that he asked the king for permission to leave England to consult the pope. The modesty of the request is very striking. He would not go without permission, and when in the end he got it, he did not go to press his case against the king, but to try to resign his archbishopric.[22] He had no intention of using ecclesiastical sanctions to force the king to change his mind, nor did he wish to deprive him of any power that he claimed. On the one occasion when he threatened a king – not Rufus but Henry I – with excommunication, his purpose was strictly limited to the restoration of his archiepiscopal revenues. If Anselm was no Lanfranc, he was a thousand times less a Becket. Diminishing the king's power over the Church was not one of his aims; still less was increasing the power of papal legates. With regard to the first, for reasons which will be examined later, his attitude changed to a limited extent; with regard to the second, never.[23]

[22] See *Ep.* 206 (iii, 166) to Urban II: *haec est summa supplicationis meae, propter quam ad vos ire volebam, ut, sicut deum animae meae et animam meam deo desideratis, per paternam et apostolicam pietatem, quae cor vestrum inhabitat, animam meam de vinculo tantae servitutis absolvatis, eique libertatem serviendi deo in tranquillitate reddatis..* For Anselm's plea at the Council of Bari in October 1098 that Rufus should not be excommunicated, see *HN*, p. 107; and for his threat to excommunicate Henry I, see below, p. 300–1.
[23] See below, pp. 335–6.

CHAPTER II

A NEW ARCHBISHOP'S PROBLEMS OF OBEDIENCE

I WHAT IS THE LAW?

Everything in Anselm's life during the past thirty years had predisposed him to regard obedience as a fundamental rule of conduct for himself and others. But obedience to whom, and in what respect? In the stormy sea of English affairs these were not easy questions to answer.

Of course, he had no doubt that all monks owed obedience to the Rule and to their abbot. Further, all clergy owed obedience to their immediate superior, provided that he did not order anything contrary to the law of God. This proviso was fundamental, and we can find it expressed in two letters of this period on the preference to be given to the claim of monastic life over every other demand – a theme of central importance in his thought. These two letters were written in 1093 when Anselm was awaiting consecration as archbishop. One was addressed to the bishop of Paris, the other to the precentor of Paris. Their theme was simplicity itself: the precentor wished to become a monk; the bishop wished to retain him in the service of the cathedral. Anselm had no doubt where justice lay: 'No man having put his hand to the plough [that is to say, in this case, having committed himself to a monastic life] and looking back, is fit for the kingdom of Heaven.' In writing to the precentor, Anselm enforced this theme with all his old ardour:

Bishops preserve their authority only so long as they agree with Christ; they destroy their authority when they disagree with Christ. Every bishop who speaks with the voice of Christ, *is* Christ, and 'the sheep hear him, for they know his voice'. But note what follows in the Gospel: 'the sheep do not follow him whose voice they do not know'.[1]

---

[1] *Epp.* 161 (iii, 12), 162 (iii, 13). The extract quoted above comes from the second of these two letters, Schmitt, iv, p. 35.

It follows from this that the test of legitimate episcopal authority is that the bishop should speak with the voice of Christ. Any bishop who speaks otherwise loses his authority, at least on the issue on which he has spoken. Anselm's advice to the precentor was that he should resist his bishop; to the bishop, that he should change his mind.

That was Anselm's message in this case. But it has far-reaching consequences. The pope's authority is superior to that of any other bishop, but the same rule applies also to him. As abbot of Bec, Anselm had owed obedience to several superiors whose permission he had sought before accepting the archbishopric. Now, his only ecclesiastical superior was the pope. But the pope was far away, difficult of access, and when appealed to, he often spoke with an uncertain voice. Besides, there was no acknowledged pope in England in 1093, and Anselm showed surprisingly little insistence in urging the king to recognize the pope whom he himself had recognized in Normandy. He had no doubt that his own recognition of Urban II was irreversible; but he could not commit the kingdom of England to the choice which he had made in common with the rest of Normandy. He seems to have recognized – at least he did not dissent from the view – that so far as England was concerned, the choice lay with the king. If he made the wrong decision, Anselm would leave England and resign the archbishopric into the pope's hands. Anselm never ceased to urge him to decide, but he issued no ultimatum, and made no threats: he insisted only on fulfilling his personal responsibilities. His long reflection on the divine ordering of the universe did not extend to principles of political organization, and certainly not to opposition to the established order.

Then there was another problem. Anselm sought papal advice with the ardour of one who desired to obey a father, but his knowledge of papal decisions and of the development of papal policy could scarcely have been more meagre. Anselm's ignorance of the major decisions of papal councils in his own lifetime would be thought disgraceful in a modern candidate for historical honours. Even the decrees of the Council of Clermont in 1095, to which he sent Boso as his envoy, and from which through illness Boso did not immediately return, remained unknown to him and went unheeded in practice for several years. To a modern mind, accustomed to expect that important decisions will be communicated without delay to those whom they concern, such a lack of businesslike habits is almost incredible. But even the papal chancery, which alone had a system for preserving important letters, had no regular means of communicating decisions to those who were most affected by them. As we have seen, the decisions of the Roman Council of 1059, which were more widely distributed than almost any others in the century, never mentioned the decision about the Eucharist. So, in his lack of business-like habits, Anselm was only exhibiting a defect which ran through the whole system.

With his ignorance of decisions of the present went an even more comprehensive ignorance about decisions of the past. Lanfranc, who had a practical mind, had foreseen this need when he was still prior of Bec, and had put together a collection of Canon Law, which stood him in good stead as archbishop. He quoted from it frequently in his letters, and he was responsible for its wide dissemination in England. Lanfranc's collection of Canon Law was in the library at Canterbury, but there is no evidence that Anselm ever used it while he was archbishop. He had quoted from it once when he was prior of Bec, and the manuscript was still at Bec. But even in this one instance, the way in which he introduced his quotation showed how little he was in the habit of being guided by it. The question was a difficult one: he had been asked whether an unchaste priest should be allowed to resume his office after confessing his sin. In his reply, Anselm argued from general principles that this was permissible. But then, for the benefit, as he wrote, of those 'who would not be persuaded by any other argument than authority', he mentioned two texts of Popes Calixtus I and Gregory I, which supported the view which he had arrived at by reason. He took these quotations from Lanfranc's manuscript. But having in a somewhat cursory fashion quoted the authorities, he at once proceeded to the more congenial task of elaborating his argument, bringing forward considerations of individual psychology, the effect of various judgements on the penitent, and the necessity for prudence in the actions of confessors.[2]

This letter belonged to a time long before he became archbishop, but promotion did not change his mind. As archbishop, his only quotations from Lanfranc's collection of Canon Law seem to have

---

[2] *Ep.* 65 (i, 56). Anselm's reply belongs in spirit to the confessional manuals of the thirteenth century rather than to the legal compilations of his own time: like these later writers, and like Gregory the Great, he was interested in pastoral exposition, not in listing authorities.

been taken at second hand from a treatise of his friend Gilbert
Crispin; then too, as on the earlier occasion, his quotations were
introduced only to reinforce a conclusion which he had already
reached.[3]

We may infer from these two cases that Anselm set no great store
by an extensive knowledge of Canon Law, and that the test of valid
authority was agreement with the voice of Christ. So, in his
practical advice and activity, as in his theology, he relied on a
correct understanding of principles.

We can see him very clearly following this method in his only
other surviving letter on a question involving a reference to Canon
Law written in Rufus's reign.[4] It was written in reply to an inquiry
from an abbot, probably the abbot of Fécamp, who was engaged in
rebuilding his abbey church. The question was one which must
often have arisen in this period of extensive rebuilding: Did an altar
require to be reconsecrated after it had been moved?

Anselm's reply shows that there was no authoritative answer
available. He told the abbot of Fécamp that he had heard that there
was a letter of Pope Eugenius (obviously a corruption of Hyginus)
which had settled the question, but he had been unable to get any
information about this alleged source. He had pursued the question
when he was in Rome (in 1098 or 1100), and had spoken to Urban II
on the subject. The pope's opinion was that an altar once moved
should never again be used as an altar. Others who were present
held that the altar could be used again without any reconsecration,
after a simple ceremony of reconciliation. Faced with this conflict of
views, Anselm expressed his own view that, despite the pope's
opinion, the altar could be brought back into use after simple
reconsecration. He recognized that this was contrary to the opinion
of the pope and others at the papal court, but he put it forward as his

---

[3] See Southern, 1954, pp. 102–3, for the source of the Canon Law quotations in *Ep.* 162
(iii, 13). Anselm may well have been staying at Westminster when he wrote this letter
and its companion, *Ep.* 161 (iii, 12).

[4] *Ep.* iii, 159. Schmitt omitted this letter, although it is found in all earlier editions,
because he found no manuscript in which it appeared. Nevertheless, the letter
survives without the address, but with the rubric, *Sententia Anselmi archiepiscopi de
motione altaris*, in two twelfth-century manuscripts, Hereford Cathedral, O.1, vi, f.
43, and Oxford, Bodleian Library, Digby 158, (f. 91) from Hereford and Cirencester
respectively. The first editor, J. Picard, who included it in his edition of 1612,
presumably found it in a Parisian manuscript which has not yet been identified, but in
view of its independent survival and its historical consistency, there can be no real
doubt about its genuineness.

own: 'others certainly may have thought of it, but I received it from no one'. He thought it could serve until better advice was available.

Better advice, as it happened, was forthcoming without difficulty. The abbot of Fécamp put the same question to Ivo of Chartres, who produced the text of Pope Hyginus, misquoted by Anselm but available in the Canon Law collection of Burchard of Worms.[5] It supported Anselm's conclusion. So, after travelling half round Christendom, this small problem finally had an acceptable solution, and Anselm had been right after all, against the views of both pope and Curia.

The difficulty experienced by the abbot of Fécamp in getting a decision on this small point has both a general and a particular interest. In general, it illustrates the amateurish state of government at this time: there were as yet no doctors of Canon Law, no schools in which the subject was studied, no lectures, no centres of expert knowledge. It is indeed strange that Anselm never referred the question to Ivo, bishop of Chartres: he knew him as a friend, but not apparently as the greatest authority on Canon Law in northern Europe. He looked on the question as one which every prelate had to solve as best he could. This is what it was like to live in the pre-scholastic age. Anselm thought out the problem for himself, and then sought the opinion of the best authorities known to him. But these authorities raised as many problems as they solved. The pope was wrong; the Curia was wrong; Anselm's judgement was right but had no authority; the authority quoted by Ivo was certainly spurious, but it produced an acceptable result. A formal papal judgement on this point would have dispelled all doubts. But the pope was in the same position as everyone else in having no clear procedure for reaching a decision.

Not only was a papal judgement difficult to get, but there were some points on which Anselm was not prepared to abide by a papal judgement unreservedly. These were points concerning the rights and privileges of his own church of Canterbury. They complicated the whole problem of obedience in a quite remarkable way, and they took up a great deal of Anselm's time as archbishop. We shall have to consider some of the details of these matters later. For the present, it must suffice simply to note the importance which Anselm attached to local rights. He never explained his reasons; but

---

[5] See Ivo of Chartres, *Epp.* 72 and 80. *PL* 162, cols. 92 and 101. Ivo also included the passage from Burchard in his *Decretum*, iii, 13, 14 (*PL* 161, col. 202), whence it obtained a place in Gratian's *Decretum*, III, i. 19.

obedience to his consecration oath of fidelity to the church of Canterbury would have been one reason, and the desire for absolute stability in gifts to the saints another. These were timeless things, and he would not acquiesce in their alteration. In this same category, but with an even more urgent insistence, he placed the irreversibility of monastic commitment, even when it fell short of a formal vow.

It is easy now to see that the problem of papal authority was the one problem of outstanding importance among many minor questions raised in these letters. But this was not clear to contemporaries. For the abbot of Fécamp, the question of the use of old altars in his new church was a question of immediate concern for the life of his monastery. For Anselm, the problems of the inviolability of monastic vows transcended all others in the care he was prepared to devote to it. But on this and all other questions there were were enormous gaps in the knowledge necessary for coming to generally acceptable decisions. This situation may best be illustrated, so far as Anselm is concerned, by examining his interventions on the subject of monastic vows.

II   PROBLEMS OF MONASTIC OBEDIENCE

I have already mentioned that sixteen of Anselm's forty-eight surviving letters of the period 1093–7 were about the problems of monks or nuns – a far higher proportion than on any other subject. Of course, in one way, this comes as no surprise. The monastic life was the subject on which Anselm could speak with widely recognized authority and with the power of deep personal experience. Nevertheless, the contrast between his assurance on this subject, and the somewhat sketchy framework of his opinions on matters more central to his strictly archiepiscopal duties, reveals the continuity of his personal life in the midst of the upheavals of his new responsibilities. Once more, the contrast with Lanfranc, who assumed command with easy confidence, is striking. Even more remarkable is the contrast with Becket, whose new ecclesiastical *persona* provoked a personal conversion and a consistency of action of conspicuous grandeur. Anselm was not unchanged by his new office, but the change was slow and never deep.

The evidence for these remarks is to be found in a series of letters which are among the most revealing of his later years. As we have seen, ardent friendship and commitment to the monastic life were the most frequently intertwining subjects of his years at Bec. This combination is still to be found in his letters as archbishop, especially in his letters to small communities of nuns. Among them there are two letters which show more intimately than any others the intricate web of monastic commitment, personal relationships, and politics, in which as archbishop he was required to work.

1   King Malcolm's daughter

One of these letters has already been mentioned. It is his letter of March 1094 to the bishop of Salisbury, instructing him in the name of himself and the king to take action about the case of the daughter of the king of Scotland, who had left the nunnery at Wilton and who – as Anselm and King William had agreed – was to be forced to return. This letter was only the beginning of a case with a long history, and by piecing together a number of disjointed fragments of information we can obtain an unusually clear picture of the sequence of events and of Anselm's reactions to them. The subject of the letter was Matilda, the daughter of King Malcolm III of Scotland, who later became the wife of Henry I and queen of England. In 1094 however such a future would have seemed unthinkable. Matilda was then simply a runaway nun, and in Anselm's eyes, in danger of damnation.

A few facts about her will help to clarify the position. We do not know at what date Matilda had gone to Wilton, but probably she had come from Scotland as a young girl with her aunt Christina in 1086 to be educated at Wilton. By 1093, when the events I am about to describe took place, she was of marriageable age, about thirteen, and the question of her marriage had become a political issue of some importance. It is clear, moreover, from facts which later became public, that her father King Malcolm had never intended her for a monastic vocation. She was not exactly a refugee from the violence of invaders like many other Anglo-Saxon women, including one whose case we shall soon encounter: she was simply a woman of royal birth being educated in a monastery awaiting a suitable marriage.

The importance of the question of her marriage in 1093 arose from the policy of her father in seeking a general settlement of his relations with the new Norman kingdom of England. The marriage which he contemplated for Matilda was with one of the most powerful of the new barons of the Conqueror, Count Alan Rufus, lord of Richmond, who for twenty-five years had been the greatest man in the north of England and one of the most constant witnesses of English royal charters: a central character, therefore, in the government of England, but a potential menace in the semi-conquered North. The projected match, therefore, opened up vistas of great political opportunity, and perhaps even greater danger. The prospect of a marriage between his most important baron in the North and the daughter of the English king's most dangerous enemy across the still ambiguous northern border must have given Rufus considerable food for thought.

In the circumstances, it is not surprising that the marriage plan foundered. We do not know precisely on what grounds, but it had already broken down by August 1093, the date which had been fixed for the final settlement of differences between the kings of England and Scotland. Elaborate preparations had been made for a meeting between the two kings at Gloucester: King Malcolm was there at the appointed time, but Rufus refused to see him, and the two parted, in the Chronicler's words 'in great enmity'.[6]

One fact in the situation, which later emerged from the gossip of Baldwin, Anselm's man of business, was that on his way to the meeting at Gloucester, Rufus had visited Wilton. If Baldwin is to be trusted, this visit had serious consequences, for it was on this occasion that the abbess placed a monastic veil on Matilda's head, and when Rufus saw the veil, he went away.[7] The details of Baldwin's story are confused, but one possibility is that the abbess's action was prompted by Rufus as a way of making Matilda unmarriageable. This would account for Rufus's readiness to fall in with Anselm's demand that Matilda should be forced to return to her cloister, which (as we have seen) rather surprised Anselm. It would also account for the immediate breach between Rufus and Matilda's father, King Malcolm.

At all events, King Malcolm's immediate reaction to Rufus's refusal to see him at Gloucester was to go straight to Wilton, tear the veil off Matilda's head, and take her back to Scotland. Matilda later reported that as her father tore off her veil, he swore 'that he

---

[6] *ASC*, A.D. 1093.

[7] Baldwin's talk during a visit to his old monastery at Tournai (probably in 1101–2) was recorded by Hermann of Tournai in his *De Restauratione S. Martini Tornacensis*, MGH, SS, xiv, 278–81.

had destined me as a wife for Count Alan rather than for a community of nuns'. But the marriage plan for Matilda was now dead, and within a few months her father was killed in a border skirmish, and we hear no more of her for the next seven years.[8]

Whether Anselm in 1093 knew anything about these intricate political manoeuvres, we have no means of knowing. But it would have made no difference to his attitude to Matilda: for him – whatever the circumstances in which she had been removed – she was a runaway nun who should be forced to return to her convent. This is the grim side to his thought: the circumstances of her 'taking' the veil were, so far as we can see, irrelevant. Of course Rufus's ready compliance with Anselm's wishes, for which Anselm gave him so much credit, can now be seen to have been wholly political. So far as he was concerned, a great danger had been averted, and the matter was now closed, but it had a sequel which we may now follow.

2 King Harold's daughter

The projected marriage between Matilda and Count Alan Rufus was now a dead letter. But it had a tragic consequence. While visiting Wilton Abbey to see his prospective bride, Count Alan saw another lady who must have been about thirty years of age. Unlike Matilda, she was a genuine refugee from the Norman invaders, for she was a daughter of Harold, the last Anglo-Saxon king, who had taken refuge in the monastery. Her name was Gunhilda. Like Matilda, she had worn the veil, probably for several years; but she too had never taken religious vows. Her encounter with Count Alan led to a strange and passionate romance which is now known only from two of Anselm's letters.[9]

The situation disclosed in these two letters is hard to disentangle. The clear facts are that Gunhilda left the monastery with Count Alan Rufus, and lived with him very briefly as wife or mistress until his death, which followed almost immediately, probably on 4 August 1093. Why did Gunhilda not then return to her monastery? The answer which emerges from Anselm's second letter is that

---

[8] For her re-emergence in 1100 as the bride of King Henry I with Anselm's reluctant consent, see *HN*, pp. 121–6. For Anselm's lukewarm reception of her later expressions of devotion, see Southern 1963, pp. 190–3; cf. Vaughn 1987, pp. 76–7.

[9] The two letters are *Epp.* 168, 169 (Schmitt, iv, pp. 43–50). They never became part of the regular collection of Anselm's letters, and their transmission raises several unsolved problems (for which see Schmitt, iv, pp. 43, 46; and Wilmart, 1926, pp. 331–4; 1928, pp. 319–32).

Count Alan's brother and heir succeeded not only to his estates but also to Gunhilda. Why these important barons, in the face of ecclesiastical censure, and as an alternative to the important political alliance with the king of Scotland, should have preferred Harold's daughter is a mystery. All we know is that Gunhilda was a woman of great talent and charm, for – in addition to having fascinated two powerful barons – she had also established the closest friendship with Anselm of any woman known to us.

Anselm wrote to Gunhilda twice after she had left Wilton. He recognized that, although she had worn the veil for several years, she had never made her monastic profession. According to the rules established by Lanfranc for refugee inhabitants of nunneries who had fled from the Normans but had not taken monastic vows, Gunhilda was eligible for marriage. But in Anselm's eyes, her wearing of the veil bound her irretrievably to the monastic life: to draw back now was to take the road to damnation. The letters he wrote to her are more reminiscent of his earliest letters than anything else that he wrote as archbishop. They are full of his early mannerisms of style, and the eloquent fervour of personal attachment. It appears from them that at the time of their earlier meeting, presumably during his long visit to England in 1086, Gunhilda had been captivated by his talk, and he by her attachment:

Receive [he wrote], dearest and most longed-for daughter, receive these words to the honour of God and to your own great benefit as an admonition of your true lover. You once said that you wished to be ever with me so that you could enjoy an uninterrupted talk. You said it gave you great delight; and you afterwards wrote me a letter full of sweetness, in which I could see that you would not renounce the holy profession of which you then wore the habit. I hoped you would fulfil what you promised in God's name.

Gunhilda was the last person to whom he wrote in such terms of intimacy. Necessarily the letter makes painful reading. In its imagery it recalls his own *Deploratio virginitatis male amissae* of long ago:

You loved Count Alan Rufus, and he you. Where is he now? What has become of the lover whom you loved? Go now and lie with him in the bed where he now lies; gather his worms into your bosom; embrace his corpse; kiss his bare teeth from which the flesh has fallen. He does not now care for your love in which he delighted while he lived; and the flesh which you desired now rots.

Whatever may be thought of this – I have softened it in translation – there can be no denying its intense urgency and power.

Anselm was here on ground which he understood. He brushed aside all arguments of law, and concentrated on what was to him the central issue. He did not care whether or not Gunhilda had ever made her profession: she had worn the habit; she had seemed to understand what Anselm had said about the religious life. To turn back now from the monastic life, however it had been approached, was to turn back to a world of uncertainty and to face a future in which only damnation was assured. Every step away from the cloister was a step further from salvation – bad enough in any case, worst of all when it meant a turning from the spiritual embrace of Christ to an impure love.

Anselm never felt as strongly on any political question as he did on this. We know no more than his two letters tell us. The second of the two brothers also died soon after the events I have described, and it is probable that Gunhilda then returned to Wilton, for she was later remembered there with honour. Certainly by 1100 the whole episode had fallen into almost complete oblivion. Only the two letters of Anselm remain as the record of an extraordinary conflict between contradictory passions, in their own way as poignant as those of Abelard and Heloise twenty years later.

These problems of monastic life and discipline, his two works on theology, the daily routine of monastic offices, together with ecclesiastical problems of all kinds on which his advice or judgement was required, were probably his main occupations during these years. But they had no place in public life, and we hear nothing about them in the *Historia Novorum*, which is concerned with events to which we must now turn.

III PROBLEMS OF DIVIDED OBEDIENCE

Anselm's early years as archbishop present two features of special note. First, with regard to ecclesiastical policy, he shows no sign of familiarity with, or sympathy for, two of the most important aspects of Hildebrandine reform. These may very briefly be described as the exclusion of lay influence from the Church at all levels from papal elections down to the investiture of bishops and the ownership of churches, and the centralization of government by frequent papal councils and synods, and by the appointment of papal legates with superior jurisdiction over wide areas. Second, he shows an intense dislike of his new position, and a continuing desire to resign. As he wrote to Eulalia, abbess of Shaftesbury: 'I am so harassed in the archbishopric that if it were possible to do so without guilt, I would rather die than continue in it'.[10] There is every reason to think that he meant this quite literally.

The main source of his harassment was that, instead of the simple and dedicated obedience which he had paid to his monastic vows for over thirty years, he now had a confusion of claims on his attention. He had too many disputes on his hands which never produced the results that he desired. He continued to hope that he and the king could work together and, strangely enough, he seems to have had a great deal of personal sympathy with the king. But new barriers were built up at every step, so he continued to seek an opportunity to resign, if this could be done without disobedience to the will of God. Should this prove to be impossible, he had three aims: to complete in due order the steps necessary for becoming archbishop, to maintain undiminished the possessions and privileges of his church, and to hold a Council for the correction of discipline in the Church. All these aims raised a variety of difficulties. Anselm met them as best he could as they arose, and we may trace them step by step, less to recall the stages in an archbishop's promotion, than to understand the state of mind in which Anselm progressed from one stage to the next.

1 Problems in becoming an archbishop

The necessary steps in becoming archbishop, after election and investiture, were homage, enthronement, consecration, and the receipt of the pallium from the pope. Election and investiture had been accomplished in a confused way when the king nominated him and offered him the pastoral staff, round which the bishops pressed Anselm's resisting fingers. This had happened at what was thought to be the king's deathbed on 6 March 1093. The day left Anselm in possession of the pastoral staff, but there was still a long way to go before he was a fully consecrated archbishop. Some would have said that he had not taken even the first step, since he had been invested irregularly with his pastoral staff by the king. But he knew nothing about Gregory VII's comprehensive decree of 1078 against lay investiture. In any case, Eadmer could claim that since it was the

[10] *Ep.* 183 (iv, 105).

bishops who had clasped his fingers round the staff, Anselm had not received investiture from the king.[11] This problem, however, did not arise: knowing nothing about the decree, he continued throughout Rufus's reign to consecrate bishops who had received investiture from the king.

Of course, on any theory, the ceremony by which he had been invested conformed to no canonical rules of election or investiture, and it is astonishing – or rather, it would be astonishing in anyone with even a rudimentary knowledge of Canon Law – that among all his other objections, Anselm never mentioned the defective procedure as a reason for refusing the office. This itself is suggestive of his lack of interest in the formal rules of Canon Law: he thought of the essence, not the externals. His reasons for wishing to avoid becoming archbishop were based, not on ceremonies whether correct or incorrect, still less on his own desires, strong though these were against acceptance. His reasons were all based on his search for *Rectitudo* in mind and will, as he had sought it for the past thirty years. Essentially, this meant maintaining his own personal renunciation of the world, cultivating the presence of God in meditation and prayer, and maintaining that liberty which is found only in rectitude. He had formulated these principles on several occasions in the past, not least when monks had consulted him about accepting ecclesiastical promotion.[12]

Although the rectitude which he sought was personal rather than public, this did not mean that public rectitude, which had required that the vacancy at Canterbury should be filled as soon as possible, was excluded from consideration. But such rectitude could only come when the inner disposition was right. What is essential in considering all these matters is to see beyond the weeping, struggling figure to the austere searcher who had devoted his life to reaching precise definitions of Truth, Rectitude and Justice, and to living accordingly. He did not abandon the results of these strenuous efforts under the stress of emotion: through all the superficial symptoms of strong feeling, he was still seeking to follow the principle of life to which he was committed by his monastic vows. His desire for monastic peace, his obligations to Bec, his fear

---

[11] For the decree of 1078, see *Gregorii VII Registrum*, p. 403, 'Decreta in eadem synodo facta', no. 3. For Eadmer's account, see *HN*, p. 35; and for Eadmer's later claim, when he was re-interpreting events in retrospect, that Anselm was the first bishop since the Conquest not to have received investiture from the king, see *HN* pp. 1–2.

[12] See above, p. 193.

of the world, were all strong; but his intellectually formulated principles were stronger.

So, to revert to the events of 6 March 1093, his first step was to seek the approval of those to whom he was in varying ways subject as abbot of Bec – the archbishop of Rouen, the duke of Normandy, and the monks of Bec. Only the last demurred, and rightly or wrongly Anselm overrode the objectors, told the monks of Bec to elect as abbot the man whom he believed to be most fitted, and finally accepted the archbishopric. It only remained for him to make his departure from Bec as acceptable as possible to the monks and to himself, and to face the consequences.

It may easily be objected that if he had wished to avoid becoming archbishop he had simply to refuse. This of course is true. But it will be remembered that in Anselm's system only justice makes free, and in this case, justice meant giving Canterbury an archbishop. If Anselm had refused, the chances of another appointment being made in the foreseeable future were remote. But if he accepted, and then resigned the archbishopric into the hands of the pope, as he continued to wish to do, the responsibility for a new appointment would lie with the pope, and Anselm would 'justly' be free from a position which he hated. This is what he more than once declared to be his aim. In the end, since the pope refused to free him, he had no alternative but to continue in office. He had been forced to make the move 'from the safe haven of the monastery to the tumultuous and wreck-strewn storms of the world', against which he had so often cautioned others; and there was no release in sight.

Anselm was now ready for the remaining stages of his promotion: in September he did homage to the king and was invested with the lands of the archbishopric; on 25 September he was enthroned at Canterbury, and on 4 December 1093 he was consecrated at Canterbury. With regard to homage, it will suffice to say that there was as yet no papal decree against the homage of ecclesiastics to laymen; and Anselm certainly thought that there was no objection in principle. After the papal decree of 1099, which will be discussed in the next chapter, Eadmer tried to suppress the fact of Anselm's homage. But the evidence is incontrovertible, and Anselm based his later opposition to homage entirely on the decree of 1099.[13]

[13] For Anselm's homage, see *HN*, p. 41; later, in his Preface (p. 2) Eadmer implies that Anselm, in contrast to all his immediate predecessors, did not become 'the king's man', but this is just one example of the change in his point of view after 1100. For the

Apart from this decree, his view of Church government was strongly in favour of a working partnership between the king and the archbishop. With regard to his consecration, the only controversial question which it raised concerned his relationship with the archbishop of York who consecrated him, and this will be discussed below in the context of the Primacy.

2   Problems in choosing a pope

Among several other flaws in Anselm's election and investiture, there was one which neither Anselm nor anyone else mentioned at the time, but was later to be held against him by the papal legate: on a strict view, his election – in addition to all its other legal defects – had been schismatic, since the king and all the others who took part, with the sole exception of Anselm himself, were schismatics, for they had not recognized Urban II as the legitimate pope although he had now been pope for five years. Moreover, apart from this defect, the election could not be regarded as complete until he had received his pallium from the pope, and he would be liable to deposition unless he received it within a year of his consecration. But neither the king nor the bishops of England had recognized either of the rival candidates to the papacy. Until this happened, Anselm could not receive his pallium, and the legal limit for its reception would expire in December 1094. It did in fact run out, and still Anselm had not received the pallium which would give him full authority as archbishop.

The preliminary problem was that neither William I nor William Rufus had recognized any pope since the death of Gregory VII in 1085, and it was still doubtful whether England would follow Germany in recognizing Clement III, or France in recognizing Urban II. Anselm himself, as abbot of Bec, along with the rest of the kingdom of France, had already recognized Urban II, and he would not change his obedience. Nevertheless, he did not deny that so far as the kingdom of England was concerned, the decision between the two rivals lay with the king. There was a right decision and a wrong decision, but it was for the king to make it, and if the wrong one were made Anselm would leave the kingdom.

> evidence of Anselm's homage, see *Regesta*, i, nos. 336, 337, of September 1093 at Winchester; especially the dating clause of the latter: *hoc donum factum est crastina qua Anselmus archiepiscopus meus ligeus homo factus est.*

Rufus delayed his decision, but there was never any chance that he would recognize Clement III. The reason for this lay not in any assessment of the rival claims, but in his unwavering determination to bring Normandy under his rule. It would have been a very unnecessary aggravation of his difficulties to have two different mutually excommunicated popes in lands which he intended to unite once more. To drive the archbishop into exile for having recognized a pope accepted by all Normandy would have been an act of political folly. This being so, the famous final and belated discussion of the problem at Rockingham in February 1095 was largely a display of shadow-boxing.

For various reasons the king would have preferred to keep his hands free, but as soon as he realized that Anselm would not move from his position and might leave the country, he decided to recognize Urban II. He acted with his usual promptitude, and a papal legate had arrived in England with the pallium before Anselm even knew of the king's decision. Not for the last time, he discovered, as some of his successors were later to discover, that king and pope could easily combine to ignore the archbishop.

So the pallium had arrived. But this only brought new difficulties. The legate, Walter Cardinal-Archbishop of Albano, who brought the pallium, was an eminent man at the papal court, and he clearly had doubts about Anselm's reliability. For one thing, he made it a reproach that Anselm's 'election' had been the work of schismatics – a charge which Anselm coldly denied.[14] More important, the legate clearly hoped to use the occasion to bring England under closer papal control. He suggested that he and Anselm should meet to confer about the measures needed to restore discipline in the English Church. Anselm told him, in only formally polite language, that he knew as well as the legate what needed to be done. Moreover – and this must indeed have given the legate food for reflection – Anselm said he was too busy with the defence of the part of the country which the king had committed to his care, to have a meeting with the legate. To make things still worse, he added that it would in any case be quite useless for them to make plans without the king's approval, for nothing could be achieved without his collaboration. He could scarcely have packed into a single letter more matter offensive to the ideals of the reformed papacy.

---

[14] See *Ep.* 192 (iii, 36), for Anselm's rebuttal of the legate's charges; and *Ep.* 191 (iii, 35) for Anselm's refusal to co-operate with the legate in holding a Council.

3 Problems in defending the Canterbury lands

On Sunday 27 May 1095 Anselm received the pallium from the papal legate at Canterbury. Now at last, in addition to his own church and diocese, he was entitled to rule his province, which (as he believed) included the whole area of the British Isles. For the past two years, although he lacked the metropolitan powers of an archbishop, he had been fully responsible for maintaining the possessions and privileges of Christ Church, Canterbury. The question of his metropolitan privileges will require separate discussion, for they cast a long shadow over the whole of Anselm's life as archbishop. But immediately, the burden of the territorial and other material possessions of his church weighed upon him in a way that had never been evident at Bec under the relaxed rule of Duke Robert of Normandy.

In England, everything was different. Already in 1093 and 1094, before he received the pallium, he had had two acrimonious disputes about the services which he owed the king as one of the greatest territorial magnates of the kingdom, and it was a third territorial dispute in 1097 which finally made him resolve to leave England. We shall not have his own view of his archiepiscopal obligations in proper perspective unless we realize that local territorial disputes were much more likely to precipitate a final crisis than any ecclesiastical issue.

Why was this? Mainly because the defence of the territorial possessions of each individual church presented the clearest and most immediate duty of its head. As archbishop, Anselm had many duties connected with the discipline, orthodoxy, organization, and peace of his whole diocese and province, and more broadly for the whole *alter orbis* of Britain. He was intensely aware of the importance of these ecclesiastical duties, and he carried out consecrations, and gave advice or judgements on discipline as necessary.

On the all-important matter of holding a Council he was prepared to wait on the king's convenience for a long time: he was never one to underestimate the needs of secular government. But the possessions of the church of Canterbury were a different matter. They could be lost for ever by a single failure of vigilance. Truth, justice, charity itself demanded the rigorous safeguarding of property dedicated to God and the saints.

Anselm had no doubts about this. He had had similar, though

slighter, worries at Bec, not least during his first year as abbot, when he found himself immersed in lawsuits against those who claimed lands and tithes belonging to Bec for which no title deeds could be found. At that time he had been able to write to Lanfranc to ask if he remembered anything about these transactions.[15] But now he was on his own, without a friend at court. If he did not move promptly on all matters affecting the lands, dues, and privileges of his church, there was no Lanfranc to come to his aid.

The first crisis over the possessions of the church of Canterbury had occurred in August 1093. At this date the king demanded that the archbishop should confirm some military tenancies which he had created on the archbishop's lands during the vacancy. Probably Anselm would have been well advised to comply. It is true that the archbishop's lands were already overstocked with knights in relation to the military service due from them. But he had a very large estate, and in the administration of it he needed the support of the king and his courts. Anselm was to learn too late that a landowner had more to fear from grasping tenants beneath him than from the king above. But Anselm did not think in these terms. He had a deeply rooted fear of being personally responsible for any diminution at all in the lands committed to his care. As always, his thought was clear and decisive:

This is my thought: the king has given me the archbishopric as Lanfranc held it to the end of his life. Now he takes from me and the church what the archbishop and the church so long have held, and what he gave me. I am certain that the archbishopric will not be given to anyone after my death except as I hold it on the day of my death; and if another king succeeds to the kingdom in my lifetime, he will not allow me to hold anything which he does not find me holding on his accession.[16]

The argument was impeccable. Nothing could be willingly given up, and nothing once given up could be expected to be restored. The king had to acquiesce. He did not even, as Anselm hoped, refuse to accept his homage. Rufus's masterful power had, in practice, very severe limitations: but he did not forget an injury.

The next crisis followed almost immediately, and once more Anselm took a similarly personal view of his responsibilities. In 1094 the king was preparing for war in Normandy, and he required an 'aid' from his tenants-in-chief. It was an unjust war if ever there was one; but it is probably true to say that no one attempted to

---

[15] See *Ep.*. 89 (ii, 1); and above, pp. 183–4.   [16] *Ep.* 176 (iii, 24).

discriminate morally between the wars of secular lords at this period unless they affected the interests of the Church. Certainly Anselm was not troubled by doubts about Rufus's motives. But he was troubled about a possible imputation of simony if he, as a very recently appointed prelate, paid money to the king. In the event he made an offer of £500. This was enough to show that he did not object to the aid in principle; but it was not enough to satisfy the king, who refused his offer and demanded £1000. Anselm, glad to escape from the secular snares into a world he understood, refused the king's demand and gave his proffered £500 to the poor. This was charity on a princely scale, but politically it further exasperated the king, who would rather have taken £500 with ill-will than nothing at all.[17]

When the king next had to raise money for the duchy of Normandy in 1096, he seems to have been satisfied with Anselm's offer: at least we hear no complaint. But this time it was the monks of Canterbury who were offended, for Anselm took their plate to help him pay. He paid compensation to the monks by giving them ten years' revenue from an archiepiscopal estate worth £30 a year. This was quite a good bargain for the monks, but it did not silence all their criticisms. It was impossible to please everybody, but Anselm's conduct in these affairs must be judged to have caused the greatest amount of dissatisfaction to the largest number of people. Nevertheless, it must also be said that the new revenue at the monks' disposal served to hasten the building of the new choir of the cathedral, which (as we shall see) was one of the major achievements of Anselm's archiepiscopate.[18]

4 Problems in holding an ecclesiastical council

Leaving aside for the moment a final conflict over the estates of Canterbury, we may turn to Anselm's efforts to hold a council for the reform of morals and discipline throughout the land. He had told the legate in 1095 that he knew very well what needed to be done, but that he had no power to do what was necessary without the king's aid and consent. This was particularly true of the first essential step of holding a council. He had very early broached the subject to the king. Eadmer reports him in February 1094 as addressing the king in these terms:

[17] See *HN*, pp. 43–5.   [18] *HN*, p. 75.

Order, if you please, the ancient usage in the matter of Councils to be revived
... Let us try together, you with your royal power and I with my pontifical
authority, to make some ordinance which may be published throughout the
realm to the terror and discomfort of wrongdoers.[19]

There is independent evidence in Anselm's letters that these
reported words correctly represent his idea of the relations between
king and archbishop. In this he was only following in Lanfranc's
footsteps, and it is clear that he expected the king to exercise more
authority in ecclesiastical affairs than the more 'advanced' ecclesiastical theorists of his time thought tolerable. In the same vein he
wrote to the papal legate in 1095:

It cannot escape your prudence that you and I can do nothing unless it has been
suggested to the king, so that by his assent and aid our decrees can be put into
effect.[20]

We shall see that in writing this letter Anselm was concerned to
safeguard the privileges of Canterbury against the claims of
legatine authority; but he was also inspired by a traditional respect
for royal authority, and the common-sense view that in fact nothing
could be accomplished without help from the king and his officials.
In 1095, Anselm had not yet given up hope of working amicably
with the king. He was prepared to wait a long time to gain the king's
good will, and meanwhile to support the king in his enterprises. We
have seen that he personally undertook the defences of the south
coast when the king campaigned in the North, and that he wrote in
warm praise of the king's energy and practical wisdom, and ordered
prayers for his protection against the malice of evil men who hated
the king's good qualities. Clearly he was not an opponent of royal
authority, or of secular policies, or of the warlike activities that
these policies required, or even of Rufus himself. Despite his severe
view of the temptations of the world, his spirituality allowed a very
large place for the physical world and for the rights of those to
whom the administration of this world had been committed. It was
against self-will and worldly desires that he set his face; and these
could only be overcome by personal conversion. They could not be
overcome by altering the organization of the world. That seems to
have been his view in his first years as archbishop. Whether, and
how far, he changed in his later years must be examined in the next
chapter.

[19] *HN*, pp. 48–9.   [20] *Ep.* 191 (iii, 35).

Meanwhile, it will suffice to say that the next two years, from 1095 to 1097, were passed in peace and frustration. We know almost nothing of Anselm's activity during this period except that he consecrated two Irish and two English bishops. Only a handful of letters for these years have been preserved; fewer than for any similar period of his later life. The vacant abbacies remained vacant, and he could do nothing about them. He could hold no Council. The reason given by the king was the disturbed state of the kingdom which prevented his attending to ecclesiastical business. Anselm acquiesced in this explanation and waited for peace, but then, long after it had been apparent to others, it dawned on him that he must either do the job or give it up – preferably, so far as he was concerned, the latter. But first, he needed the advice of his only ecclesiastical superior, the pope.

5   Problems in consulting the pope

According to Eadmer, it was a small incident which opened Anselm's eyes to the true state of affairs, and made him realize that the king would in no circumstances allow him to take any action beyond the routine of his episcopal duties. Anselm had waited patiently – too patiently perhaps – for the king to complete his complicated military operations in northern England, in Wales, in Normandy, and finally in the summer of 1097 in Wales again. At the end of this campaign it looked at last as if the time of peace had come, when the Council for which Anselm had been pressing for the past four years could be held with royal support. But instead of giving his long-delayed consent, the king raised a new complaint about the quality of the knights Anselm had sent on the recent Welsh expedition. It was this that gave Anselm the hint that peace would not bring him freedom to exercise his episcopal functions. Anselm's conclusion was undoubtedly correct. Eadmer noticed Anselm's habit of trusting men long after others had seen their deceptions: but then at last he would recognize them for what they were. Even now, his reaction was very moderate. He did not threaten or storm. He simply asked permission to visit the pope to consult him about his troubles.

The unexpectedness of this request seems to have taken the king by surprise. There was some reason for his bewilderment, for Anselm does not seem to have desired or expected any practical result from this consultation except a possible release from his archbishopric. Once more, his lack of desire, his lack of policy in any ordinary sense of the word threw the king's counsels into confusion. But Anselm's request, like everything else in his life, was quite simple and direct: he needed advice from his only ecclesiastical superior. It was also entirely uncompromising. Having seen what he needed, nothing on earth would stop him until he got it. As a matter of course, the king refused permission; Anselm acquiesced, but he went on asking:

He has the power: he says what he pleases. If he refuses now, perhaps he will agree another time.[21]

To keep asking is not a very refined form of political action, but it is very wearing. Rufus was never to see Anselm again without the question being raised. In the end the reiteration became intolerable, and in October 1097 he let him go. He could, he thought, safely do so: Anselm was not an active enemy, and even if he had been, he could scarcely harm him now. Normandy was safely under his control until Duke Robert's return from the Crusade, should he ever return. Anselm's departure contributed nothing to the solution of his own problems; it only benefited the royal treasury, to which the archiepiscopal revenues were now added. To Anselm it meant freedom from an intolerable position.

Reviewing the contents of these letters, the reader will be prompted to exclaim: What a miscellany of fragments without a theme! And yet, on a mature view, do not all these fragments suggest the pressures of real life? And through them all does there not run a consistency of effort to strengthen the ties of monastic life, to bring back those in error, to wait patiently for better times, while occupying his time with theological work, with preaching and counselling the erring, for whom he displays an affectionate concern – even for the king. What is lacking, and what some at least of Anselm's contemporaries would have thought highly blameworthy, is the complete absence of awareness of the Hildebrandine programme of the liberty of the Church – that is to say, its freedom from lay interference under a centralized papal authority.

It is true that right at the end, in October 1097, when Anselm was on the point of leaving England, Eadmer reports him as saying to the Canterbury monks: 'I go willingly, trusting in God's mercy that my journey will do something for the liberty of the Church in future

---

[21] *HN*, pp. 79–80.

times.'[22] This is the first appearance of the phrase *libertas ecclesiae* in any written or reported words of Anselm. Its appearance in Anselm's later letters will require further discussion when we come to the next phase in Anselm's life. For the present, it must suffice to say that Eadmer's report brings into Rufus's reign a theme which is wholly lacking in Anselm's letters, and we must ask whether Eadmer is not, here as elsewhere, reading back into Rufus's reign the lessons which he and Anselm were to learn in the course of their joint exile.

[22] *VA* II, xxi, p. 93. For further discussion of the concept of *libertas ecclesiae*, see below, pp. 284–9.

CHAPTER 12

THE LIBERTY OF THE CHURCH

I TWO VIEWS OF LIBERTY

As we have seen, during the years from about 1080 to 1095, Anselm had given much thought to the problem of liberty, and had reached a definition of free will which left no room for that freedom of choice which is commonly regarded as its essential feature. He defined freedom of the will as the power of making, only and always, the right choice in accordance with the will of God. The foundation of this freedom is a loving acceptance of the creature's limitations within the created universe.

But while Anselm was engaged in these researches, another definition of liberty was emerging, chiefly in the circle of Gregory VII, which was destined to have growing influence during the next hundred years and beyond. This definition was summed up in the formula *libertas ecclesiae*, by which was understood the independence of the Church from all lay interference in ecclesiastical appointments, in the exercise of the Church's spiritual functions, in the administration of its temporal rights and properties, and in the immunity of clerical persons from secular jurisdiction.

These contrasting forms of liberty of the individual will and the corporate body, which we may call Anselmian and Gregorian, were of course not mutually exclusive. Nevertheless, they belonged to two different modes of thought. The Anselmian concept of liberty was concerned with the willing subordination of the individual to God; the Gregorian concept of liberty was concerned with giving a centrally organized clerical Church complete independence from secular control under papal direction. Its chief purpose was to ensure corporate independence for the entire ecclesiastical organization in relation to all other social organizations, such as the Empire, and all the kingdoms, baronies, fiefs, and urban communities, which were beginning to proliferate in western Europe. Understood in this sense, *libertas ecclesiae* expressed a concept which could be, and was, in varying degrees adopted by the other

277

groups within the whole complex of social organizations. Indeed, the future of European liberty is largely a development of this concept of liberty applied to many kinds of corporate body.

For our present purpose, however, it will suffice to note that this organizational liberty was being developed by Gregory VII and his most active supporters at the same time as Anselm, in relative isolation from ecclesiastical politics during his time at Bec, was developing his own contrasting other-worldly view of the real nature of individual liberty.

The most enthusiastic advocate of 'Gregorian' liberty during these years was Hugh, bishop of Die and later archbishop of Lyons, whom Anselm first met on his way to Rome in 1097, and with whom he spent the last eighteen months of his exile from May 1099 to August 1100. Before this visit, Anselm shows no signs of being influenced by the Gregorian concept of the *libertas ecclesiae*; after his visit, he both used the phrase and supported the policy which the phrase summed up – at least to some extent. We have, therefore, a problem on our hands. Before his exile, Anselm's whole emphasis was on a strict adherence to that other-worldly freedom which comes from subjecting all individual desires to the eternal order of the divine plan. In political matters, he had acquiesced in the practices which he found established in England, notably antagonistic though they were to the *libertas ecclesiae* in the Gregorian sense of this phrase. Then, during his three years in exile he came for the first time into close contact with the main exponents of the Gregorian ideal, and we must ask how far and in what circumstances he adopted the phraseology of the Gregorian reformers; then, whether he adopted the theoretical structure which their favourite phrase *libertas ecclesiae* expressed, or adopted the phrase for use only in exceptional circumstances and for special reasons. It may be said at once that these questions cannot be answered with complete certainty. There remains, and probably will always remain, an area of ambiguity, which itself is disturbing in someone of Anselm's normal lucidity and precision. But so far as an answer can be found, it must be sought in the influences to which he was exposed during his exile.

II THE FRUITS OF EXILE

Anselm left England in October 1097 and reached Cluny in time for Christmas. While he was there, he got an invitation from

Archbishop Hugh to go to Lyons, and from Lyons he wrote to the pope explaining his reasons for leaving England. In this letter, he briefly recorded Rufus's harassments of the lands and knights of Canterbury, his overturning of all good customs, and the absolute impossibility which he himself had found of doing anything useful for the Church, concluding with this plea:

This is the sum of my application for which I wished to come to you, that you will free my soul from the bonds of so great a servitude and restore its liberty of serving God in tranquillity . . . and then that you will apply your wisdom and apostolic authority in taking counsel for the good of the English Church.[1]

In this letter, we hear only of the liberty of his soul and what his soul's health required, which was nothing else than being freed from his office as archbishop. On receiving this letter, the pope summoned Anselm to Rome. He would have preferred to stay at Lyons, but he set out at once in mid-March, and arrived in Rome about the end of April 1098. Here he learnt that the pope would not release him from the archbishopric, but wished him to expound the Latin doctrine of the Procession of the Holy Spirit at a meeting with representatives of the Greek Church at Bari in October. Thereupon, Anselm went off to spend the summer months in the hill village of Liberi above Capua, and here he found a renewed peace of mind and spirit which he had not known since his days as prior of Bec. He put the finishing touches to his long-interrupted *Cur Deus Homo*, and he prepared his defence of the Latin doctrine of the Procession of the Holy Spirit. At the request of the inhabitants, he also opened up a well from which they draw water to this day, and his name is still commemorated in the village. He was in his element.[2]

Meanwhile the affairs of the English Church stood still. At the Council of Bari in October 1098, Anselm delivered the main speech, and – according to Eadmer – Urban II would have excommunicated the king at the Council, but Anselm pleaded for him.[3] Anselm then returned to Rome with the pope and stayed with

[1] *Ep.* 206 (iii, 166). For the stages of Anselm's journey and the text of the letter as reported by Eadmer, see *HN*, pp. 89–93.
[2] *VA* II, xxx–xxxi, pp. 106–9. It is a pleasure to recall with gratitude the hospitality of the parish priest of Liberi just forty years ago, walking over the sites described by Eadmer. The site of the well which now bears Anselm's name does not, however, correspond with Eadmer's description.
[3] *HN*, pp. 106–7. This incident raises certain difficulties of procedure, and it is possible that either Anselm or his biographer misunderstood what the pope was about to do. But it must be remembered that popes were not always as well acquainted with canonical procedure as modern scholars who have had time to study the subject.

him until Easter 1099, when he took part in another Council. At this Council, on the last day and perhaps without premeditation, Urban pronounced two anathemas which were to have a delayed but decisive influence on Anselm's later years. At the time, Anselm seems not to have been aware of the importance of the words which he heard, for he left Rome the next day without further discussion and returned to Lyons. Here, as at Liberi, he was happy, and we hear nothing of any initiative on his part to bring his exile to an end or to settle the issue – chiefly his frustrated desire to hold a council – which had precipitated his exile.

He preached, visited Cluny, went to Vienne, and in both places he had talks with the abbot or archbishop, of which records have survived. He was indefatigable in confirming all who came to him as he moved around the countryside, and in his moments of leisure he wrote the longest of his *Meditations* on the theme of *Cur Deus Homo*, and his *De Conceptu Virginali* as a sequel to this work. But what were his thoughts about his duties as archbishop? Did his view of these duties change? To answer these questions, we must consider first the papal anathemas at the Easter Council of 1099, and then the character of his host at Lyons, Archbishop Hugh.

1   *The anathemas of 1099*

Eadmer has left an exceptionally full account of the Easter Council at St Peter's in April 1099; and for reasons which will become apparent later, this was his last full-scale account of any great event in Anselm's life. He used the occasion to display to the full his talent for description. He describes how Anselm had returned with the pope from the Council of Bari, and had stayed with him until the end of April. Then he gives a detailed description of the great Council in St Peter's with which Anselm's visit ended.

The Council, as Eadmer describes it, was arranged round the tomb of St Peter, with Urban II and the cardinals (among whom Anselm had been placed in a seat of honour) sitting in the apse behind the altar, and the remainder of the Council spread out in front of them. It seems that, despite the Council, pilgrims continued to come and go to the tomb of St Peter, and this was not irrelevant, for the noise and disturbance prevented many from hearing what was said. This led the pope to commission the bishop of Lucca, who was endowed with a stentorian voice, to read out the decrees of the Council. This he did. But he was evidently a man of powerful passions, and in the middle of his reading he broke out into an angry protest at the Council's acquiescence in secular tyrannies in general, and at the lack of action in the case of Anselm in particular. He went on at great length on this subject, banging his pastoral staff on the floor and haranguing the assembly until the pope cried 'Enough', and the reading of the decrees was resumed. But before he finished, the bishop of Lucca – to Anselm's intense surprise – once more warned the pope that God would not forgive him if he forgot Anselm.

Various matters of detail were dealt with, and then the pope rose to pronounce his final excommunications. Perhaps he had been moved by the bishop of Lucca's protest, for among these anathemas he included two which seem not to have been discussed, but which were relevant to his protest. The first declared excommunicate all laymen who gave, and all clergy who received, lay investiture of churches or ecclesiastical offices, and any bishop who consecrated a clerk who had been thus invested. The second excommunicated all clergy who did homage to laymen for ecclesiastical possessions, as well as those who associated with them afterwards. The pope laid special and dramatic emphasis on the second of these anathemas, saying that it was intolerable that hands which touched the flesh of Christ in the Eucharist, should suffer the indignity and contamination of being subordinated to hands made bloody by daily violence and bloodshed.[4]

On this note the Council broke up, and Anselm left Rome the next day to return to Lyons. The abruptness of this conclusion to the proceedings suggests a way of doing business which must seem strange to any modern mind. Consider the circumstances: the pope had ended the Council with two final anathemas which were intimately connected with Anselm's situation. One of these anathemas was already fairly old: Gregory VII had already condemned lay investiture of clergy to spiritual offices in 1078. Anselm had known nothing about it when he became archbishop, and still apparently knew nothing about it when he left England in 1097.

It seems a reasonable conjecture that, if he had known about the decree, he would have acted on it, or at least given reasons for not acting on it. But it must not be thought that papal conciliar decrees which seem so clear-cut to the modern scholar, who sees them in all

[4] *HN*, p. 114.

the clarity of the printed page, had a similar force and clarity for contemporaries. It is clear, for instance, that the best canonist of northern Europe, Bishop Ivo of Chartres, knew the decree, yet thought that it was open to a broad tolerance in practice.[5]

These considerations will suffice to save Anselm from the charge of contumacious neglect of recent papal policy. But they will not save him from the charge of indifference to ecclesiastical politics. After hearing a terrible denunciation of practices in which he had willingly taken part in the past, we might have expected that he would have wished to have further clarifications before he left Rome, or that some plan of action would have been agreed. But not at all. Without time for more discussion, Anselm simply left Rome the next day, to spend the next fifteen months in total inactivity so far as his archbishopric was concerned. Nor is the subject referred to again until nearly two years later, when he surprised everyone by suddenly disclosing what he had heard at the Council and proposed to carry out fully in future.

From this whole picture of ignorance and inactivity, and of continuing dissent even where there was knowledge, we can only conclude that legislative acts were commonly accepted, even by those responsible for them, as expressions of hope or at best long-term intention, rather than as strictly enforceable legislative acts. Indeed, as we shall see, Gregory VII rebuked his too active agent Hugh, now archbishop of Lyons, for his officious energy in harrying the king of England to carry out papal decrees, without regard to the king's virtues which earned him a claim to forbearance.[6]

Finally, there is a third feature of these two anathemas of 1099, which needs to be mentioned: they have a semblance of coherence which is illusory. The anti-investiture decree, however great its symbolic importance, did little to diminish the power of lay rulers over ecclesiastical appointments. Lay investiture was symbolically objectionable as representing the quasi-sacerdotal position which had long been claimed by kings and emperors. But this quasi-sacerdotal character was no longer an important aid to the power of

---

[5] See especially Ivo of Chartres, *Ep.* 60, *PL* 163, cols. 70–5. There is of course a large literature on this subject and on the interpretation of this letter. But it will suffice here to draw attention to Ivo's declaration that since investiture by the king did not confer any sacramental power, he could not see how it was detrimental, provided that it had been preceded by canonical election.   [6] *Gregorii VII Registrum*, ix, 5, p. 579.

secular rulers. Everyone agreed that investiture by lay rulers conferred no spiritual power: it did no more than put a prelate in possession of the rights, lands, and secular dignities of his new office. The newly elected prelate still needed ecclesiastical consecration before he could exercise his pastoral functions. In these circumstances, Gregory's decree against lay investiture could be left to make its way forward by the momentum of events.

But the prohibition of homage by ecclesiastical tenants to lay rulers was quite another matter. Homage was not concerned with spiritual functions: it was concerned only with the tenure of land, and the act of homage was one of the main foundations of social organization. The abrupt cessation of homage without some alternative ceremony would have divided a kingdom into two distinct parts: those parts held by laymen, for which homage was owed to the king, and those parts held by clergy, for which homage was forbidden. This would have excluded the whole ecclesiastical section of landholding society from the ordinary complex of feudal relationships, and in doing this, it would have threatened the cohesion of a kingdom in a way that no earlier reforming decree had done.

No doubt there had long been extreme Gregorians who would have liked to abolish the homage of ecclesiastical landholders for ecclesiastical lands. But such enthusiasts were not numerous, and there were not many of them in the papal Curia. It soon became clear that almost everyone in the Curia was in favour of making a distinction between investiture and homage, forbidding that which no one strongly supported, and gradually abandoning that to which almost no one strongly objected.

As we shall find, this distinction lies at the root of Anselm's movements in his last years as archbishop. It was a distinction which he found extremely disturbing, not because of its political consequences, but because the introduction of such a distinction cut at the root of his ideal of obedience.

We shall not understand Anselm's last years unless his fundamentally unpolitical attitude to his duties is borne in mind. Hitherto, he himself had been involved without protest in both the 'intolerable' evils condemned by the pope in his presence in 1099. He had himself – however ambiguously – received investiture with his archbishopric from the king, and he had certainly consecrated bishops who had been thus invested. He had also done homage for his ecclesiastical lands. But after hearing their condemnation in 1099 he conformed rigidly to both parts of the condemnation, and nowhere expressed an opinion about their substance. He never discussed their principle. Before 1099 he had made no difficulty about acting in a contrary sense. Afterwards, he treated both prohibitions as absolute commands, leaving no room for discussion or negotiation: he embarrassed his friends, and even the pope, by the stiffness of his obedience. When the pope finally retreated, Anselm saw a possible injustice in forcing others to a similar retreat.

The situation illustrates Anselm's indifference to the compromises of practical affairs. Obedience to lawful authority and to religious vows had the highest place in his whole system of theology and in his personal, as well as corporate, religion. First and last he sought only the strictest fidelity to justice, rectitude and truth. This led him to insist that those who had, however tenuously, dedicated their lives to God in religious vows were bound by them beyond recall. This was a principle based on unshakeable authority.[7] He had no such rigid views about any matters of political policy. But when the word was spoken by one who had the authority to speak, and especially when spoken in his presence and with his implied assent, he obeyed without discussion or reservation. Unlike almost everyone in the papal Curia, unlike the pope himself, he did not understand the need for compromise; he saw no grounds for withdrawal or discussion; he took pleasure in obedience.

At this point, we return to Anselm's definition of liberty: its characteristic expression is obedience to the will of God, and, by extension, to God's representative on earth. In this sense, Anselm is an extreme papalist; but, like many other extreme papalists, he draws unwelcome boundaries when he sees papal initiatives overstepping boundaries of God's will – for instance, in overruling local rights, which have a heavenly sanction as gifts to the saints. This double obedience needs to be remembered throughout these years, for a double obedience is never free from the possibility of conflict.

With this warning note, we return to Anselm's association with Archbishop Hugh of Lyons, the chief agent of the Gregorian policy of *Libertas Ecclesiae*.

---

[7] For Anselm's insistence on the simple principle, 'No one putting his hand to the plough and looking back, is fit for the Kingdom of Heaven' (Luke ix, 62), see *Epp.* 17 (i, 15), 101 (ii, 12), 162 (iii, 13), and the cases described above, pp. 260–4.

2   The influence of Hugh, archbishop of Lyons

It is just a hundred years since Felix Liebermann first propounded the theory that Anselm's friendship with Archbishop Hugh of Lyons brought a new element into his life.[8] It was not a friendship of the kind that had been so frequent in Anselm's early life. Quite the opposite, it was an association of two men wholly different in character and outlook, brought together by the circumstances of Anselm's exile. For a long time, I was inclined to think that the contrast was too great for any important exchange of ideas, and that Liebermann's suggestion, despite its attraction, could not be taken very seriously. But a closer examination has convinced me that, alien though Hugh's thought was to the main stream of Anselm's, an influence of some importance can be traced.

Anselm had known Hugh as papal legate in France when he was abbot of Bec, but his close association with him came at a moment when he was in a very perplexing situation. He had just left the Council at which the new decrees had been pronounced. He was conscientiously obliged to obey them, despite his lack of sympathy with, or knowledge of, the principle behind them. Hugh was the most forceful advocate of the principle which the new papal decree embodied. What Anselm needed was not an intimate friendship, but an understanding of an external aim which he was bound to support. This is precisely what Hugh could provide, and we must examine both the contribution he could make, and the evidence for his having made it.

By his nature, Hugh was one of those able, intensely loyal, dedicated men whom great movements are apt to attract. He had implicit trust in the righteousness of the 'movement', and was eager to carry out the orders of its leader. As papal legate in France during the last quarter of the eleventh century, he was the most energetic agent of the new policy of active centralized papal control of the Church. It had been one of Gregory's first acts as pope to invest and consecrate him as bishop of Die, and to follow this up with a letter to the count of Die which contains a first draft of his later decree prohibiting the investiture of bishops by secular rulers.[9]

---

[8] Liebermann, 1886, pp. 156–203.

[9] Gregory VII's letter of 1074 to the count of Die announcing his consecration of Hugh as bishop of Die contains these words: *Nos . . . eum sollicite ammonuimus, ut . . . ecclesias sue parrochie non prius consecraret nec consecratas aliter divinum officium celebrare permitteret nisi prius absolute a laicorum manibus, sicut canonicum est, suo iuri et episcopali eius providentie redderentur.* (*Gregorii VII Registrum*, i, 69, pp. 99–100.)

In an important sense, Hugh may almost be looked on as the instigator of the Investiture decree of 1078, for he had gone to Rome for his episcopal consecration four years earlier in order to avoid contact with a secular ruler, who claimed the right both to nominate and to invest his nominee in his episcopal office. Hugh, therefore, had been an initiator of the new policy even before its official promulgation. Then, as papal legate during the years when Anselm was abbot of Bec, he had shown endless energy storming through France on visitations, and sending offenders scurrying to Rome. Anselm himself, together with the other abbots of Normandy, had earned one of Hugh's censures: in 1081, Hugh had summoned all the bishops and abbots of Normandy to a council at Saintes in Aquitaine. It was a vexatious summons, and none of them turned up. By way of retaliation, Hugh threatened them all with deposition, and received a severe rebuke from Gregory VII for his pains. Not for the first time, the legate had shown more enthusiasm for papal power than the pope.

The battle-cry of Hugh, probably borrowed from Gregory VII's letters and applied with the zeal of an enthusiast, was *Libertas Ecclesiae*. It was a phrase with many shades of meaning, but essentially in these years it came to refer to that freedom from lay intervention in ecclesiastical appointments and operations which it was Hugh's special mission to promote. At about the same time as he issued his threat of deposition to all the abbots of Normandy, he ordered Anselm to send him his *Monologion* and *Proslogion*, perhaps initially for censure, and it may have been through Hugh that Gregory VII knew Anselm's works.[10] In various ways, therefore, Anselm knew Hugh well enough by 1093 to reckon him among his friends. But there is no sign that Hugh had any influence on his thought before his long sojourn in Lyons from May 1099 to August 1100.

At the time of his arrival, the prohibitions of lay investiture and clerical homage must have been fresh in Anselm's mind, and it is unimaginable that he should not have discussed the whole question with one of the main agents of the new policy. We have no means of measuring the extent to which Anselm's outlook may already have been changed by his experiences at the papal Curia, but there are

---

[10] See *Ep.* 100 (ii, 11) for Anselm's sending to Hugh the writings which Hugh had ordered him to send (*de scriptis nostris quod iussistis*). See also *Ep.* 109 (ii, 17) to Hugh announcing his decision to change the titles of the two works to *Monologion* and *Proslogion*. Anselm's next letter to Hugh in 1094, *Ep.* 176, has been examined above, p. 271. For Gregory's knowledge of Anselm's works by about 1085, see *Ep.* 102 (ii, 31).

two points at which we can observe an alteration in his language during and after his stay at Lyons.

The first is this: Urban died in August 1099, and Paschal II was elected in his place. By the time the news reached Lyons, Anselm would have been Hugh's guest for about six months, and the letter which he wrote to the new pope shows a remarkable advance on the letter he had written to Urban II two years earlier. He no longer asked to be relieved of his archbishopric. He still shrank from returning to England, but for a reason quite different from his earlier fear of loss of tranquillity:

> I pray and implore you not to order me to return to England unless I can put the law and will of God and the papal decrees before the will of men, and unless the king restores to me the lands of the Church, and whatever he has taken from the archbishopric because of my coming to the apostolic see.[11]

In this statement of his position there is a new note. He seems to fear a compromise with the king, which will require his return under conditions which he would now find unacceptable. For the first time, too, he writes with some bitterness about the customs of William I and Lanfranc which he had hitherto accepted without demur:

> The king, under the pretence of rectitude, required me to assent to his arbitrary demands (*voluntatibus suis*), which are against the law and will of God. For he did not wish the pope to be recognized in England, or appealed to, nor was he willing that I should send him a letter or receive one from him, or obey his decrees, except by his command.

Here too Anselm is adopting some part at least of the vocabulary of the new ecclesiastical theorists in describing the situation which Rufus had taken over from his father. Seven years earlier Anselm had not seen the king's responsibility for order in the Church as an expression of self-will fighting against *Rectitudo*. Like Lanfranc he had welcomed royal co-operation, and had been prepared to wait a long time for it. All his actions – still more his inactivity – during the first years of his archiepiscopate were based on this idea of partnership. But he was now, and only now, moving towards the rejection of those mutual accommodations between king and Church, which the Hildebrandine party in the Church had been denouncing for twenty years.

It is hard to resist the conclusion that this new attitude was the result of the company in which the exiles had found themselves

[11] *Ep.* 210 (iii, 40).

from 1097 to 1100. How far Anselm had travelled along this road, and how much further he would still travel, are questions to which an answer must be sought in the reign of Henry I. But it is clear that Anselm in exile was beginning to see events, if not through Hildebrandine eyes, at least with shades of Hildebrandine colour.

The second symptom of change following his long residence at Lyons is this: in later years, but never earlier, Anselm occasionally used the phrase *Libertas Ecclesiae*, of which Hugh and Gregory VII had been the chief advocates for the last twenty years. Overall he used the phrase in nine letters between 1101 and 1106, always in relation to papal policy: they were written to the pope and cardinals, to Hugh of Lyons, to the count of Flanders, to the king of Jerusalem, to Henry I, and to the prior of Canterbury in describing the condition on which the pope had agreed to give absolution to the count of Meulan.[12] All of them were either accounts of measures taken by the pope, or – in the letters to the king of Jerusalem and the count of Flanders – recommendations of obedience to the papal policy.

The circumstances in which Anselm used the phrase *Libertas Ecclesiae* in these nine letters from 1101 to 1106 show that he knew that this phrase embodied the papal policy with which Hugh of Lyons had probably made him familiar, and which he was in duty bound to carry out in the matter of homage and investiture. But there are no signs that either the phrase or the policy which it expressed ever became part of his own thinking either about the Church as a whole or about his own duties as archbishop. The phrase represented a manner of thinking about the world very different from that which he had worked out in his own thinking about liberty as perfect obedience to the will of God: an obedience of a will so attuned to the source of order in the universe that there has ceased to be any constraint in obeying. This was the obedience

---

[12] The letters (with approximate dates in brackets) in which the phrase appears are: (**1101–2**) 235 (iv, 9) to Baldwin, king of Jerusalem; 248 (iv, 13) to Robert, count of Flanders; 280 (iii, 73), to Paschal II; (**1104**) 338 (iv, 47), to Paschal II; 339 (iv, 48), to two cardinals; (**1105**) 364 (iii, 110), to the prior and monks of Canterbury; 388 (iv, 73), to Paschal I; 389 (iii, 123), to Hugh of Lyons, (**1106**); 402 (iv, 82), to Henry I. As mentioned above, Eadmer says that Anselm used the phrase in his parting speech to the monks of Canterbury in 1097. If this is correct, my suggestion that Anselm first became familiar with the new meaning of the phrase during his exile would of course have to be abandoned; but I think it much more likely that, here as elsewhere, Eadmer is reading back into the period before their exile a policy which became known to them during their exile.

which remained the foundation of his spiritual experience and of his admonitions to others. There was only one narrrow channel in which these two rival concepts of liberty could be reconciled: the two papal decrees about homage and investitures, which he had himself heard, required his own complete obedience. He seems to have had no interest in the larger plans for the liberty of the Church from lay influence, of which these two matters were only a small instalment. But on the two matters on which his own personal obedience was required there was no room for compromise.

Corporate liberty, even of the most exalted kind, could never be for Anselm, as it was for Hugh of Lyons, the mainspring of his whole life. In all the most important affairs of life, liberty remained for him what it had been for the last thirty years, a state of will which could not depart from rectitude. It was an essential characteristic of the state of will which Anselm called 'free' that it was intransigeant in the pursuit of rectitude. But contrariwise it was an essential part of corporate liberty that it was open to negotiation. So here a paradoxical situation arose. The two items in the struggle for the liberty of the Church to which Anselm was committed were for him not negotiable either by himself or the successor of the pope who had declared lay investiture and clerical homage to be irreconcilable with the law of the Church. If this was the case, there could be no going back. More realistically, the papal Curia thought that when the full ideal was unattainable, it was better to be content with what could be salvaged than to be left empty-handed: the precise opposite of Anselm, who (as he told Queen Matilda) would as soon be deprived of everything as of a little – 'and I say this not for love of property, but for love of God's Justice'.[13] God's justice – if it was really God's – could not be changed. For Anselm, this was a stumbling block in any negotiation.

III   ANSELM, HENRY I, AND THE LIBERTY OF THE CHURCH

The news of Rufus's death reached Anselm about the end of August 1100, while he was paying a visit to the monastery of La Chaise-Dieu in Auvergne. It was soon followed by a pressing invitation from the new king to return to England, and Anselm set off without delay. Rufus had been killed on 2 August, whether by conspiracy or accident will never be resolved. His younger brother Henry had

[13] *Ep.* 321 (iii, 97).

been crowned king in London on 5 August by the archbishop of York, amid a flurry of promises of liberties and grants of lands designed to stabilize his position. Anselm reached Dover on 23 September and met Henry I at Salisbury a few days later.

The scene to which he returned was very different from the one he had left. In the first place, the personality of the new king made it quite certain that any dispute would be conducted in a new way. Despite the more favourable opinion of chroniclers, Henry's personality makes a more unpleasing impression than that of Rufus. He was equally licentious and avaricious; and in his early days, at least until family misfortune brought a pronounced strain of piety, his aims were equally secular. But he had more craft and policy, more capacity to wait, to present a good face to the world, and to advance step by step towards his goal. He was a man of great political sagacity and formidable resolution. As a younger son he had learnt to be content with small advantages when greater ones were not to be had; yet he had not lost the capacity for large designs or for rapid action when need arose. He was too much of a politician ever to outrage religious feelings as Rufus did, but his smooth words concealed a purpose very little different from that of Rufus. Indeed, in his immediate aim of regaining Normandy in order to retain England he had little choice: his survival depended on it.

At Rome too, the temper of papal government altered under Paschal II's indecisive leadership. We are only at the beginning of a change which became more conspicuous later. But already the symptoms which are inseparable from the growth of bureaucracy are there: the importance of the permanent officials grows, rules become more numerous, violent pronouncements rarer, negotiation more frequent, and power is gradually drawn away from the regions to the central government.

Anselm was to experience the effects of these changes: they tended consistently to weaken the position of local bishops and archbishops, especially those superior archbishops who claimed to rule an area larger than their province. Canterbury was one of the chief sufferers from this development, but at the moment of Anselm's return to England, his position could scarcely have been stronger. It was very uncertain whether Henry would be able to retain the crown he had seized. To consolidate his position he had given the baronage their first general charter of liberties, and he had promised generous payments to the count of Flanders for mercenaries. But his position was extremely weak. Only a few families supported him, the rest were either wavering or hostile. At best, it looked as though a period of baronial bargaining between the two rival candidates, such as we find in Stephen's reign, would develop; but it was more likely that Henry would disappear in the coming struggle. His elder brother Robert had returned from the Crusade almost at the moment when Anselm reached England: he was newly married, and therefore, for the moment, rich. He had a European reputation, military experience, and the means for commanding the service of knights. He alone could at once restore the unity of England and Normandy, which was important for many great families. Yet Anselm decided against him, and his decision, as was recognized at the time, turned the scale in Henry's favour.

Why did Anselm not support Robert? One can only suppose that he preferred an effective ruler, however unpleasant, to an ineffective one, however much recommended by his personal qualities. Why then did Anselm not make his support of Henry conditional on concessions for the liberty of the Church comparable to the charter of liberties which the baronage had obtained? The only possible answer is that Anselm was not a bargainer chaffering the half-acceptance of one set of principles against the half-acceptance of another. In worldly terms, he missed his opportunity, for he could almost certainly have obtained Henry's acceptance of the new papal decrees on investiture and homage if he had insisted, for at that moment Henry would have had to agree to anything to get his support. But he missed his chance, and spent the next seven years trying to catch up on his lost opportunity.

But here we must beware: to speak of lost opportunities and clear objectives introduces an element of political calculation into Anselm's motives which is quite foreign to him. He did not return to England as the advocate of a new political ideal, but as a man who was himself under a new obligation of obedience.

I   Anselm misses a political opportunity

Henry knew nothing about the new papal anathemas of which Anselm was the bearer, and he immediately required him first to renew the homage which he had done to Rufus, and then to consecrate his chancellor William Giffard to the bishopric of Winchester, with which he had invested him on his coronation day. Henry can have expected no difficulty. On that day he had also invested two new abbots, both sons of important magnates, who as it happened were friends of Anselm. To Robert, son of Hugh earl of Chester, he had given the abbey of Bury St Edmunds; and to Richard, son of Richard of Clare, the abbey of Ely.[14] These were mere fragments of the complex arrangements which he had made in order to secure his throne, and they were entirely necessary to Henry if he was to have sufficient support among those families – perilously few and divided in their allegiance – who alone could ensure his survival as king of England.

Anselm supported Henry, and he did not make his support conditional on Henry's acceptance of the new papal decrees. For those who credit Anselm with political perspicacity and a clear adhesion to the principles of Hildebrandine organization of the Church, this is very difficult to explain. He had before him the example of the barons of the kingdom who had taken the opportunity to extract from Henry far-reaching legal and financial concessions at the time of his coronation. These concessions, sealed and set out in a formal document, were notified to all bishops and sheriffs throughout the kingdom. They are a model of administrative efficiency in making known the terms on which Henry had received the support which allowed him to be crowned. Anselm arrived too late to make similar terms for the Church before the king's coronation; but Henry's position was still extremely insecure, and it was only Anselm's support which tipped the balance in his favour.

Besides having this example of baronial efficiency before his eyes, common sense might have suggested the importance of revealing at once the new conditions for ecclesiastical support which he had brought back from the Roman Council of 1099. Anselm did indeed refuse to renew the homage which he had done to Rufus; he further refused to consecrate the bishops whom Henry had invested with bishoprics. But he did not, like the barons, insist on the general principle of abandoning all lay investitures and all clerical homage. He refused only to renew his own homage or to recognize or consecrate bishops whom the king had invested. From this it would seem that that he had no objection to these practices in principle; his refusal was an act of personal obedience to decrees which he had heard, and by implication promised to obey.

[14] For Winchester, see *ASC* A. D. 1100; *Annales Monastici, RS.* ed. H. R. Luard, 1864–66, ii, 40–1; for Ely, *Liber Eliensis*, ed. E. O. Blake, *R.Hist.S. Camden 3rd Series*, xcii, 1962, p. 225; for Bury St Edmunds, Liebermann 1879, pp. 131–2, and *Memorials of St Edmund's Abbey, RS*, ed. T. Arnold, 1891, i, 353. For Anselm's relations with the families of the magnates concerned in these arrangements, see *VA* I, xviii, p. 27n.

Even this degree of recalcitrance put Henry in a difficulty. He could not afford to antagonize Anselm, but – with motives very similar to those which led Anselm to maintain the rights of his see as he had received them from his predecessors – he had no intention of abandoning any rights enjoyed by his father and brother. Henry's only plan at this moment was to play for time. He did not press for an immediate renewal of Anselm's homage; and William Giffard stopped calling himself bishop of Winchester. It was agreed, with Anselm's consent, to send messengers to Rome to discover whether the pope was inflexible: meanwhile Anselm was restored to his lands. In the summer of 1101, faced with Robert's landing in England and the immediate prospect of widespread desertion, Henry went so far as to promise a general obedience to the papal decrees, and it seems likely that Anselm's activity on his behalf, secured by this promise, turned the tide in his favour, and brought Duke Robert's invasion to a halt.

Meanwhile the king's messengers went to Rome to see if any compromise was possible. They were were due to return by Easter 1101, but they were conveniently delayed, and it was not until September that the result of their mission became known. The papal letter which they brought was uncompromising in principle, though noticeably vague in its terms.[15] By this time, however, the military crisis was over, and Henry abruptly demanded that Anselm should either comply with his wishes or leave the country. Ironically, it was his brother Robert, angered by Anselm's lack of support for his evidently just case, who counselled this truculent attitude.[16] But it was not now so easy to get rid of Anselm: he refused either to comply with Henry's demand or leave the country, and for the next few weeks he lived quietly on his manors. The archbishop of 1101, with a clear command which required his obedience, was a different man from the Anselm of 1097 who asked for nothing better than an opportunity for escape.

But although Anselm was different in some ways, in most ways he was unaltered. He looked upon himself as absolutely bound to obey the papal decree; but he was no crusader for the principle which it enshrined. During the first year after his return, when the royal position was in the balance, Henry would have had to give way

---

[15] *HN*, pp. 128–131; *Ep.* 216.

[16] *HN*, p. 131. Eadmer remarks that Henry's skill had now succeeded in uniting his own original supporters and those of Robert (including Robert himself) against Anselm.

if Anselm had insisted on his renouncing homage and investiture. Whether he would have kept any such agreement is another question, but his capacity for resistance would have been much reduced. But Anselm did not look on himself as an agent of papal policy: he was no Hugh of Lyons. He always understood that the papal decree imposed on himself an absolute personal obligation of obedience, but it did not give him a general responsibility for promoting the principle, or for enforcing the obedience of others. That was a matter for the pope.

There was, however, always one matter for which he had a personal responsibility which he could share with no one else. This was his responsibility for protecting the rights, lands, and privileges of the church of Canterbury. At his consecration, he had promised to maintain Canterbury's rights of every kind, from the primacy down to the smallest knight's fee, and we have seen that in Rufus's reign he allowed many, as we might think, greater matters to lie dormant while he fought for Canterbury's rights. In such matters, size was of no importance: obligation was everything. It is impossible to understand the events of Anselm's years as arch-bishop – and more particularly the events of the next few years – unless this distinction between his public duty of preserving rights for which his office made him responsible, and his personal duty of obeying commands which he had heard and by implication assented to, is borne in mind.

2   The problem unfolds

The initial crisis of the reign was succeeded by a period of prolonged negotiations. Despite their complexity, the main development can easily be summarized. It is clear that until April 1102 the pope was still insisting on the full observance of his predecessor's decrees. Paschal II's letters of this date, which reached England in August, contain an exact restatement of the papal position, forbidding both homage and investiture. To this statement Paschal added a series of directions to Anselm showing in detail how the decrees were to be applied to parochial churches and to ecclesiastical land held by lay service. These papal letters represent the high point in the campaign for a Church both spiritually and temporally independent of the lay ruler. Never again in Anselm's lifetime was the papal position to be stated so clearly and uncompromisingly.[17]

But the logic of the situation now began to assert itself. From this moment the idea of compromise began to gain ground, not with Anselm, but with those around him on all sides, and in the papal Curia itself. The admission that compromise was possible is the first sign that the confident period of Hildebrandine reform – the period of intense conviction and hope of complete success – was coming to an end, and was being replaced by the age of negotiation, undertaken by lawyers and administrators, differing in their briefs, but alike in their methods, and understanding each other very well.

In April 1102 the pope still spoke of homage and investiture in equally uncompromising terms, but by the end of the year a change of emphasis is observable. In December his reply to a new mission from the king and archbishop contained no mention of homage, and this omission was balanced by unusual violence in the condemnation of lay investiture:

What are the bishops doing in the Church if the hands of laymen confer the staff, the symbol of the pastor's office, and the ring, the symbol of faith? The honour of the Church is torn in pieces, the bonds of discipline are broken, the whole Christian religion is besmirched if we suffer lay arrogance to usurp that which we know to belong to priests alone. It is not for laymen to betray the Church, or for sons to defile their mother with adultery.[18]

Significantly, this is the very language which Urban II had used three years earlier with regard to homage by priests to laymen: the hands, he had declared, in which Christ's Body was made in the Eucharist were defiled by having been enclosed in the bloody hands of laymen. Paschal II now used similar terms about lay investiture, and the absence of any mention of homage in this letter is significant. The change of emphasis which is implied in this silence

---

[17] Epp. 222 (iii, 44), 223 (iii, 45). Despite the rigidity of these letters, the king's messengers reported a verbal concession by the pope, which the pope later denied. It is noticeable, and it may be significant, that there is one striking difference between the text of the papal letter, Ep. 222 (iii, 44) in Eadmer's HN, p. 135, and in the other manuscripts: Eadmer's text says that the Lateran Council of 1102 prohibited lay investiture, but omits any mention of clerical homage to laymen. As we shall see, the issue of homage was the one which was really damaging to secular government, and which the pope finally relinquished. Whether Eadmer was following a genuine text of the pope's letter in which this withdrawal was already foreshadowed, or omitted this clause in the light of later developments, cannot at present be determined.

[18] Ep. 281 (iii, 74). Anselm delayed opening this letter until he had left England. For his reason, see HN, pp. 148–9, and the following note.

is confirmed by the negotiations of the next few years: Pascal was clearly already preparing a withdrawal from the extreme position adopted by his predecessor.

In the event, the letter to Anselm containing the passionate phrases condemning lay investiture which have just been quoted, had no effect on the subsequent negotiations. He had a premonition that if he read it, he would find himself committed to an ever-widening circle of excommunications. As a pastor, he had no desire to reduce England to a spiritual wilderness. So he adopted the simple expedient of not opening it until it was beyond his power to act on it. He agreed to go to Rome himself to try to obtain an acceptable solution. Eadmer gives a curiously confused account of Anselm's motives at this time, but one thing stands out clearly: Anselm would not bring about the chaos in personal relationships and conflict of obligations which he might find himself obliged to precipitate if he read the letter. He left England on 27 April 1103; and when the opportunity for practical action had passed, he opened it.[19]

There was now no need to hurry. He passed the summer at Bec, and reached Rome in October to find that messengers from the king had also recently arrived. Anselm and the king's envoy had an inconclusive meeting with the pope, Anselm remaining silent while members of the Curia openly took the king's side. The pope seems to have confined himself to insisting on the prohibition of lay investiture.[20] After the meeting, Anselm left to return (as he thought) to England, carrying with him a letter from the pope to the king and queen. The king's messenger stayed in Rome for further talks.

The seeds of compromise were beginning to take root. Eadmer noticed the change and the presence in the Curia of those who now openly supported the royal cause. The king's messenger in Rome, William of Warelwast, was well equipped to encourage this movement. He may with good reason be regarded as the first of that long line of professional civil servants who did more than any others to make and destroy the medieval Church: they were professional administrators, equipped to forward the interests of government

[19] In judging this action of Anselm's, it should be remembered that recipients of letters did not regard the authority of the written word as being on the same level as words spoken in their presence. There were good reasons for making this distinction: the papal letters which Anselm received had been written several weeks earlier in ignorance of distant events, and the text itself was subject to corruption. See below (p. 298) for a similar liberty taken by Anselm with another letter.   [20] *HN*, p. 153.

not by main force but by negotiation amidst the intricate issues of law and theology; men of international standing, retaining the respect of their opponents, and not too hatefully or too personally involved in the cause which they were required to maintain. They expected to become bishops in due course, and they performed their episcopal duties with equal ability. William of Warelwast was such a man. He stayed on in Rome after Anselm left, and managed to procure letters from the pope to the king of a different tenor from those entrusted to Anselm.

To Eadmer, and to William of Malmesbury who enlarged and exaggerated Eadmer's words, the secret of his success was simple bribery, the common charge of disappointed litigants. But we can see that he had something more to work on than the Roman thirst for gold. It was by now becoming clear that the papal Curia was not solidly behind the more extreme form of papal policy inaugurated by Urban II. The pope himself was beginning to waver, and there are signs that he felt some embarrassment at abandoning the position of his predecessor and leaving Anselm isolated. One symptom of the pope's embarrassment is that for the first and last time he made a concession to Anselm on the subject of the primacy of Canterbury, which we must deal with later.[21]

Anselm left Rome in November 1103. The king's messenger caught up with him at Piacenza and they went together as far as Lyons. Here he showed Anselm the pope's letter to the king which he had obtained after Anselm's departure. In it the pope said nothing about homage, and argued temperately against lay investitures, minimizing their importance, and denying that he sought for himself any increase of authority or any diminution of the king's due power. The violent metaphors which formerly had been freely used were absent, and the letter contained a suggestion that it was Anselm himself who had been going too far:

If anyone [the context makes it clear that the 'anyone' referred to is Anselm himself] has behaved harshly towards you, which we do not believe, we shall be guided by your will, so far as we can and God allows, provided that you put aside investitures.[22]

Clearly the pope was prepared for compromise. When Anselm was shown this letter by the king's messenger, he quietly suppressed the papal letters to the king and queen which had been entrusted to him. As he told the pope, they would either not be read or be read

---

[21] See below, p. 342   [22] *Ep.* 305, (*HN*, p. 155).

with derision after the arrival of the later letter brought by William of Warelwast:

I have judged it unsuitable [wrote Anselm to the pope] to deliver the letters which you ordered me to give to the king and queen, for William has brought further letters from your Holiness and has been told that the letters which I carry were written at my dictation. I am certain, therefore, that the letters which I carry would be read with derision and contempt; for, as I hear, the king says that I am his sole adversary.[23]

3 Anselm reverts to essentials

Anselm was now in a very vexatious position. The papal letter which he was carrying to the king had been superseded by another, which spoke more mildly and suggested that Anselm himself had been a mischief-maker, and that a compromise agreement could be reached with good will on both sides. But in addition, when they reached Lyons, the king's messenger told Anselm that the king would not allow him to return to England unless he promised to observe the customs of the kingdom as they had been in the time of Rufus. This was a clear breach of the understanding on which he had come on a joint mission to the pope. It is likely that William of Warelwast revealed an even more outrageous decision: if Anselm did not return to England on the king's terms, the king would seize his lands and revenues. It was this last, clearly tyrannical, action which stirred Anselm to take the only countervailing measure open to him. His position was now exactly what it had been during his exile in Rufus's reign: he was without an income and reduced to dependence on the hospitality of Hugh of Lyons. He stayed on in Lyons – what else could he do? – and took the first step to excommunicate Henry if his lands and revenues were not restored. This was the most positive action he had yet taken in his conflicts with the king: even with Rufus he had not gone so far. But he was now acting in defence of the properties of Canterbury, a matter for which he alone was responsible. Nevertheless, excommunication required a lengthy procedure of three summonses and three refusals before being finally imposed. So for the moment nothing could be done beyond issuing a warning.

Meanwhile he settled down to another period of peace and exile. To his friends in England he seemed to be inactive. They thought

---

[23] *Ep.* 315 (iv, 46).

that he reconciled himself too easily to his position, and that he had developed a taste for exile as an escape from business. There was perhaps some truth in this. He would gladly have died or suffered hardship or privation for the truth; but endless wrangling and prevarication on both sides made him ill, and distracted him from the ends to which he had dedicated himself. To all complaints about his conduct he made the same answer: he was bound by the decree of 1099, which obliged him to withdraw from the communion of all who had taken part in ceremonies of investiture or homage. Therefore, he could not return to England, where his duties would force him into communion with those whose company he was forbidden to frequent:

Certainly I cannot expel them; to pray with them I do not dare. I ought not to withdraw my accustomed duty from the king, for the lord pope has granted him this, and has ordered me to perform it if I am present.[24]

He could do nothing but wait while the procedure which he had initiated for excommunicating the king if he refused to restore his rights and revenues crawled towards its conclusion. This was a lengthy business, and from December 1103 to April 1105 he contented himself with justifying his exile in the face of criticisms from his English friends. The king continued to send messengers and letters to Rome, with the purpose, as Anselm soon perceived, of ensuring still further delay. The king's letters to the pope during this period are all missing, but we have two from the pope to the king. They are conspicuous for their conciliatory terms: although they insist as firmly as ever on the prohibition of lay investiture, they make no mention of homage.

Then in the spring of 1105 Anselm received a letter from the pope telling him that sentence of excommunication had been passed on Robert of Meulan and other royal counsellors, but that sentence on the king was delayed because the messengers whom the king ought to have sent to Rome before Easter had not arrived.[25]

To one who had waited so long, this letter would scarcely have

[24] *Ep.* 311 (iii, 90).
[25] The date of the papal letter giving Anselm this information has caused a great deal of confusion. It is dated *vii Kal. Aprilis*, i.e. 26 March, and it refers to Easter as having recently passed without the arrival of the royal messengers. But in 1105 Easter was on 9 April. So, if the letter is correctly dated, the reference must be to the previous year, and would indicate that the pope had been waiting patiently for a whole year. But this is absurd. The most likely explanation is that the date *vii Kal. Aprilis* is a mistake for *vii Kal. Maii* – a relatively easy confusion since *vii Kal. Maii* is of course 25 April. At all events, Anselm received the papal letter about the middle of May, 1105.

indicated that the time had come for him to take vigorous action on his own. But Anselm had another reason for action: the procedure he had started eighteen months earlier for excommunicating the king if he did not return the lands and revenues of the archbishopric was drawing to its end. He had hoped that the pope himself would have excommunicated Henry at the same time as his chief accomplice; but since this was not to be, Anselm consulted Archbishop Hugh and decided to go ahead with his own excommunication. Eadmer's evidence is decisive on this point:

Thrice Anselm had sent letters to the king demanding the restitution of his revenues, and he had received no response, only bland delays. So he consulted the archbishop of Lyons, and set out for France.[26]

The purpose of his journey, which he revealed to the king's sister, Adela, countess of Blois, was to excommunicate the king, 'for the injury which he had done to God and himself for the last two years and more.'[27] Evidently Anselm judged that he could not make his excommunication of the king effective if he stayed in Lyons, and he must move nearer to the scene of action. The threat was sufficient to alarm the king's sister Adela, and she warned the king, who was now in the last stages of planning his final great attack on his brother's duchy of Normandy. To have added excommunication to his other problems would have been folly, and his reaction showed that, when speed was needed, he could act quickly. Adela fixed up a meeting between the king and archbishop, and in a few days everything was arranged. Anselm and the king met at Laigle on the frontier of Normandy on 22 July, and agreed that Anselm's revenues would be restored. The agreement went no further than this. It was sufficent for the king's purpose to avoid excommunication, but Anselm could could not yet return to England because 'not being willing [as Eadmer reports] in any way to violate his obedience to the pope' he could have no dealings with the king's excommunicated ministers. So he retired to Bec. Meanwhile, it was agreed that he and the king should send another joint mission to Rome to attempt to reach a final conclusion.[28]

Nothing could define more clearly the limits of what Anselm regarded as his personal responsibility than this agreement. It said nothing about investiture or homage: these were matters for the pope. As in 1100, Anselm was content with the return of his lands and revenues, and he withdrew his threat of excommunication as

[26] *HN*, p. 164.   [27] *HN*, p. 165.   [28] *HN*, p. 166.

soon as they were restored to him. Henry was in no hurry to go further. He was able to complete his conquest of his brother's duchy without interruption, and to imprison for life – perhaps to blind – the only member of his family who deserved the protection of the Church. Nothing is more unsavoury in all these transactions than the total abandonment of Duke Robert to his fate. It is one of many indications of the limits, not only of Anselm's notion of his own responsibility as archbishop, but of the concerns of the Church as a whole. All that Anselm demanded was that the essential basis for carrying out his duties as archbishop should remain inviolate. It is quite likely that to have attempted more would have done more harm than good: at all events, nothing more was attempted.

Modern scholars, conscious of the large issues involved in this struggle, have generally found this intrusion of the local and material interests of the church of Canterbury at a critical moment incomprehensible, and having their eyes fixed on the historically more important matters of investiture and homage, they have supposed that Anselm's eyes must also have been similarly directed. Hence they have linked Anselm's only positive action in the whole sequence of events with the progress of negotiations between the king and the pope. To fit Anselm's action into this context it has been necessary to suppose that he was outraged by the slow progress of papal action against the king, and was determined to do something to strengthen the pope's resolve.[29] This theory does indeed get some support from the way in which Eadmer concentrates his attention on the Investiture dispute during these years. But there are three considerations which tell decisively against it:

1 Anselm immediately dropped the threat of excommunication when the king returned his lands and revenues, and he made no conditions about the issue of homage or investiture beyond agreeing that he and the king should make a joint approach to the pope to hasten a settlement. Having reached this agreement, he allowed the king to take his time, and he did not even insist on returning to England, but remained at Bec until a settlement had been reached.

2 Although Anselm made it clear that he personally was bound to observe the papal decrees of 1099 until released by proper

---

[29] For a highly politicized account of Anselm's motives in these events, for which so far as Anselm is concerned I can find no justification in the evidence, see Vaughn, 1986, pp. 272–94.

authority, he remained neutral in all the negotiations between the king and pope. He seems to have thought that the pope ought to have maintained the decrees of his predecessor, but this was not a matter for him to decide.

3 With regard to Eadmer's emphasis on the negotiations between the king and the pope, it is important to remember that, although the material for the *Historia Novorum* down to 1100 was collected in Anselm's lifetime, the final text belongs to the years after Anselm's death.[30]

4   *The inevitable compromise*

Part of the understanding between Anselm and the king at Laigle in July 1105 was that a new joint mission should be sent to Rome to effect a settlement by Christmas. But Henry was in no hurry. His hands were very full with arrangements for his attack on Normandy, and there must also have been many discussions about the terms on which he would be willing to make peace with the papacy. Meanwhile he made every possible excuse for delay until Anselm's patience was almost exhausted. After all, although in possession of his revenues, he was still excluded from his archbishopric, and it is remarkable that he waited so patiently. It was not until early in 1106 that his and the king's messengers finally left for Rome. By this time the king had decided that he would be prepared to abandon investiture if he could keep the homage of prelates for their lay fees. He lost little or nothing by the concession and, as we have seen, the papal letters had for some time indicated the likelihood of such a solution being acceptable at Rome. Once this decision was taken there was no further need for delay. On 23 March 1106 Paschal II wrote to Anselm to announce in veiled words that a compromise had been reached:

God, in whose hands are the hearts of kings, has turned the king's heart to the obedience of the apostolic see; wherefore the pope has condescended to raise him up . . . No one can raise another unless he himself bends. Yet, even if he who bends seems to come near to falling over, he does not lose his state of rectitude.[31]

Such words as these prepare the reader for a retreat. It is nowhere stated that the ground which had been occupied was to be

---

[30] For the circumstances and consequences of this cleavage, see below, pp. 412–14.
[31] *Ep.* 397 (iv, 77).

abandoned, but that was the result. Anselm was made to appear to have been too rigid in his interpretation of the decree of 1099. The pope's letter continued:

We absolve you, venerable and dearest brother in Christ, from that prohibition, or as you believe excommunication, which you understand to have been pronounced by our predecessor of blessed memory, Pope Urban, against investitures and homages.

It is hard to think that Anselm did not feel some indignation on reading these words, which implied that he had read too much into Urban II's decree, and that Paschal had not himself been present when those words were spoken. But, however this may be, the pope proceeded to the practical consequences of the new state of affairs: those who had already received lay investiture, or done homage, or consecrated others who had received lay investiture, were absolved; for the future, those who received ecclesiastical preferment and did homage to the king could be consecrated, provided that they had not received investiture at the king's hands; and this was to continue until the heart of the king was softened by the rain of Anselm's preaching. Predictably, this last consequence never followed, so homage succeeded by consecration continued to be the rule, and the practical diminution of royal control over the episcopate was negligible.

Anselm found this retreat difficult to accept; after his own loyalty to the terms of the papal decree, the pope's vacillation and suggestion of over-reaction on Anselm's part must have been hard to swallow. But Hugh of Lyons counselled acceptance, and indeed there was little else to be done. The compromise brought a clearer distinction between the spiritual and temporal aspects of ecclesiastical office than ever before: it abolished lay intervention in conferring the symbols of ecclesiastical office, while conceding that the temporalities remained within the secular domain. Altogether, this was the conclusion which best corresponded to the practical realities of the day.

Nothing remained but to tie up the loose ends of the dispute. The pope's letter reached Anselm late in April 1106. All obstacles in the way of his return to England were now removed, and he set out in May. Illness overtook him and delayed him until August, but he was in England in September. The king's continued absence in Normandy prevented the public promulgation of the settlement for another year till August 1107, but the final settlement contained no surprises: it followed the terms of the papal letter of fifteen months earlier. Anselm was now, for the first time since his election as archbishop in 1093, free from any cause of dispute with the king, and the last year and a half of his life were spent in the peaceful routine of episcopal duties, disturbed only by the growing problem of the relations of Canterbury with York.

IV   FINAL REFLECTIONS

It is natural that these political events should have received most attention from historians: they concern the principles of social organization, the relations between the two chief governmental powers in society, and the materials are comparatively abundant. Indeed, largely owing to Eadmer, it is the *only* aspect of Anselm's work as archbishop for which the materials allow a consecutive story to be told. Further still, despite their gaps, Eadmer's *History* and Anselm's letters together allow a remarkably complete account of royal and papal negotiations and political vicissitudes to be given for these few years. Yet it was the least characteristic and least congenial part of Anselm's work, the area of life on which he had least to say. He felt no call to entangle himself in the ecclesiastical-political questions of his day. Indeed there is a sense in which the clarity of his spiritual and theological doctrines inhibited clarity on political issues by relegating them to a position of relative unimportance: they led Anselm to believe that the system of joint secular and ecclesiastical responsibility for the functioning of the Church was as acceptable as any other. He had long ago accepted the feudal organization of Church and baronage as an adequate way of organizing the world: the real questions of salvation lay in a quite different area of experience, and on these he spoke with the simple and clear authority of a personal vision and prolonged thought. On political questions it is remarkable how little he has to say. Eadmer has provided a striking picture of him at the meeting between the pope and William of Warelwast in 1103, sitting silent while the royal messenger held forth and the pope replied with words which were received with enthusiasm by the bystanders as a declaration that no layman could ever be a doorway into the Lord's sheepfold. Eadmer's explanation of Anselm's silence is interesting – indeed, he may have had it from Anselm himself:

He did not wish to say anything which might mislead others into thinking that any mortal man could be the door to the Church of God, apart from Christ, who has pronounced that He alone is the door of the sheepfold, through whom whoever enters is saved.[32]

There is a range of possible meanings that might be attached to these rather ambiguous words; but, if no mortal man could be the doorway into the Lord's sheepfold, it would scarcely matter from whom the bishop received the emblems of his office: the reality could come only from Christ. This in fact seems to have been at least very close to Anselm's view in all these matters. He would obey the papal command, but for himself the question in dispute was a matter of indifference. Did it really matter from whom a bishop had received the lands and symbols of his office so long as he was the representative of Christ to his flock?

There must always be a danger in interpreting an ambiguous text. But all Anselm's actions, both under Rufus and Henry I, suggest that he thought that too much importance was being attached to the disputed ceremonies, and that the real problems of religious life were at the level of personal attitudes and motives known in the last resort only to God. So far as the ceremonies of investiture were concerned, he himself had lived, and could live, with either the old or the new. His only concern was with the integrity of souls in obedience to the laws of God.

His scale of values was that of few men, and it is hard to point to any of his successors who carried on his work. Thomas Becket modelled himself on Anselm – in his exile, his inflexibility, his austerities. But Becket fought for a principle of his own choosing, the 'liberties' of the clerical order in the realm of law, organization, privileges, immunities and so forth. These were not Anselm's principles. The centre of his world, conceptually as well as in his personal life, was the monastic life. It alone provided him with an ideal of peace.

Recent historians of institutions have seen Anselm's period as archbishop as a turning point in the relations between England and the papacy. To a very limited extent, this is correct: the papal legislation, and above all the determination to enforce it, became a permanent part of papal policy during these years. But it is a mistake to see Anselm as an instigator of this process. Apart from his personal duty to observe the papal decrees of 1099, his responsibility was limited to his duty to defend the rights and properties of the church of Canterbury. These rights were very

---

[32] *HN*, p. 153.

extensive, but they were threatened by, rather than dependent on, recent papal legislation. It was not until thirty years after Anselm that Archbishop Theobald began to build up an administrative staff necessary for the dual organization of ecclesiastical and secular affairs along the lines which became familiar in the later Middle Ages. More seriously, it is quite unlikely that the actions of any single archbishop could greatly alter the course or speed of the re-alignment of secular and ecclesiastical power which was taking place at this time.

Anselm was certainly not a policy-maker. To the community at Canterbury he was a saintly but somewhat ineffective archbishop, who had let them down in the matter of the primacy of their church. How little reason they had for this view we shall soon discover. But Anselm may have shared their disappointment: the tasks for which he felt the full weight of personal responsibility were very harassing, and his success in performing them was open to serious doubt. In the first place it was his duty to preserve intact the lands and rights entrusted to his care. As to this, Eadmer gives strong hints that he failed to prevent the encroachments of powerful tenants, but the details of these aggressions are lost: they seem to have had no important effect on the general prosperity of the Church of Canterbury. His second task was to preserve and exercise the metropolitan authority of his see. He tried hard to do this, but he was fighting a losing battle here against the rising tide of papal authority.

Indeed, Anselm's greatness as an influence in the Christian world must rest almost entirely on his *Prayers and Meditations*, on his *Monologion, Proslogion*, and *Cur Deus Homo*, and on the sanctity which pervaded his whole life after his conversion in 1059–1063. He was not wise in the affairs of the world, nor did he wish to be: he simply challenged the normal assumptions of the world and gave his attention to eternal truths and individual souls.

Anselm seems to have treated Rufus with more generosity and trustfulness than he showed to Henry I. This can probably be explained by his greater experience of the unreliability of kings; perhaps also by a certain attractive openness in Rufus which the prudent and wily Henry lacked. But this contrast should not blind us to the fact that he could work with Henry to an extent that was impossible with Rufus. This difference is most noticeable in his ability to hold ecclesiastical Councils.

From his earliest days as archbishop, his desire to hold a Council had been his most frequently expressed aim – expressed in vain while Rufus reigned, but almost at once realized under Henry. Henry after all wished to collaborate in the work of the Church; Rufus wished only to make money from it.

In the years 1100 to 1102, Henry was in a much weaker position than Rufus to refuse any reasonable request of Anselm which did not infringe the royal rights, and Anselm, newly returned from contact with Hugh of Lyons, was equipped with knowledge of papal theory and practice to a much greater extent than in the years before his exile. But even without this greater leverage, it is highly unlikely that Henry would have made difficulties over Anselm's desire to revert to Lanfranc's policy of holding ecclesiastical Councils. In the main, Henry's personal objectives were not very different from Anselm's: he too wanted a well organized church, clergy who obeyed the rules of clerical life, and monasteries which met the needs of a feudal kingdom and baronage. Moreover, the vice of sodomy, which Anselm was especially harsh in denouncing in his conciliar decrees, was not one to which Henry's court, unlike Rufus's, was especially addicted. He had nothing to fear from a Council, and Anselm was able to hold two Councils in the last years of his life; the first of these in 1102 was certainly the high point in his activity as archbishop. It brought into play all his practical abilities; in planning the event, articulating a programme of reform, and in directing its implementation he showed qualities of mind and will which had no other outlet. Besides giving Anselm his only opportunity for showing his abilities in action, the Council of 1102 also gave him an opportunity for displaying his primatial ideal in practice.

In so far as Anselm had a policy as archbishop beyond the pastoral duties outlined in Gregory the Great's *Regula Pastoralis*, the defence of the Canterbury primacy formed its foundation and the legislation of his two primatial Councils were its crowning achievement. It was a policy with deep roots in the history of the monastic community at Canterbury, and to understand it we must first examine the development of this community, and then the ideal which it considered its chief adornment and obligation.

CHAPTER 13

THE LIBERTY OF A MONASTIC COMMUNITY

I   ORGANIZATION UNDER LANFRANC

No part of Anselm's position as archbishop was more distinctly Lanfranc's creation than the monastic community at Canterbury, of which the archbishop was also, in fact if not in name, the abbot. Of course, Lanfranc did not create this situation. The combination of bishopric and monastery was one of the main results of the tenth-century monastic revival, and it had tenuous threads going back to the seventh century. Lanfranc seems to have had no interest in the achievements of his tenth-century predecessors who had given the monks their rule of life. Still less was he interested in what he considered the barbarous traditions of the Anglo-Saxon Church which he found on his arrival. Nevertheless, though he deplored what he found, he maintained the monastic connection.

There is an initial paradox here of some importance for the future: the monastic life which he found at Canterbury appeared to him so decayed that it needed a new beginning, yet he did not sweep it away and establish an up-to-date archiepiscopal church served by a community of secular clerks, on the pattern of Rouen or Lyons or most other cathedral churches in Europe. By this date, the monastic organization of English bishoprics was becoming an anomaly, and in an increasingly active administrative Church it was often a nuisance. It is clear that many others – perhaps Lanfranc too – saw this. Whether he ever contemplated replacing the monks by secular canons, we do not know. But it seems clear that some people, perhaps the members of the monastery themselves, thought it was a serious possibility, and they took steps to ensure that neither Lanfranc nor anyone else would be able to carry out this sweeping measure of reform. The evidence that this fear existed is to be found in a letter which Pope Alexander II sent to Lanfranc not long after his arrival in England. It begins as follows:

Certain persons coming to the threshold of the Apostles from your part of the world have reported that some secular clerks, in association with laymen filled with diabolical intentions, are aiming at expelling the monks from Christ Church Canterbury, which is the metropolitan church of all Britain, in order to install secular clerks in their place. It is said that this nefarious plot is part of a general plan to expel monks from all the cathedral churches of Britain and replace them with secular clergy. On this matter, we ordered a search to be made concerning the privileges of churches, and there came into our hands a statute of our predecessor Gregory the Great concerning the English churches . . .

At this point, Alexander II quoted from Gregory's replies to the questions of the first archbishop, Augustine, of which the full text is in Bede. This text gave mild, but not authoritative, support to the existence of some kind of monastic establishment in the cathedral church. But then, much more to the point, the pope went on to say that there was also a letter from Pope Boniface IV to King Ethelbert, from which he quoted a passage laying down that the monastic community of the cathedral church was to be continued by all Augustine's successors. He therefore confirmed this constitution, and anathematized anyone who sought to destroy it.[1]

All scholars agree that the text of Boniface IV's letter which is quoted here was a forgery of the eleventh century, and something must be said about this later. For the present, all that need be noticed is that the purpose of Alexander's letter was to convey a distinct papal command to Lanfranc that the monastic community in his cathedral church was to be preserved.

The pope's letter to Lanfranc is known only from Eadmer's *Historia Novorum*, and, according to Eadmer, it was Lanfranc himself who had sent to Rome to ask for a confirmation of Boniface IV's privilege. But this is certainly not what Alexander's letter says. Without implying that Lanfranc was an enemy of the monks of the cathedral church, the whole drift of the pope's account of the incident suggests that the request for a confirmation of the monastic status of the cathedral had come from someone other than Lanfranc: from whom the request came he left entirely unclear. But he emphasized the trouble he had taken to go into the matter personally, even to the extent of ordering a search in the papal archives.

---

[1] For Alexander II's letter, see *HN*, pp. 19–21. For the text and MSS of Boniface IV's letter, see H and S, iii, pp. 65–6; Birch, i, p. 16; and Levison, 1946, pp. 202–4. For further discussion, see below, pp. 353–4.

So Lanfranc was left no choice: he had to retain the monastic community in his cathedral church, and we may ask what he found on his arrival, and what impression it made on him. On these points we are left in no doubt: he found mainly ruins, and what was not ruined, was in his eyes so corrupt that it needed a completely new start.

It was on this basis that he set about creating a new monastic life with all the force and organizational ability which he possessed. What he had already done at Bec and Caen, he would do at Canterbury: he rebuilt the cathedral church and monastic buildings; he fought pertinaciously and successfully to defend the ancient properties of the cathedral church against the rapacious invading nobility, who scoured the land for what they could pick up; he drew up a new code of monastic practice, and he introduced new men who would know how to implement it. No one else could have done this as well as Lanfranc with his orderly mind and power of decisive action. But, as for the monastic life which he found, he never learnt to love or even tolerate the mental, spiritual, and historical traditions which, in the midst of the ruins, the surviving community of monks treasured with the utmost tenacity.

Indeed, to a superficial eye, not much had survived which could be salvaged. At the end of 1067 there had been a great fire which had made nearly all the buildings unusable except the dormitory, the refectory, and enough of the cloister to make it possible for the monks to walk from one building to another without getting wet. The church was in ruins, and the monks had put up a temporary building over the main altar, where they gathered round the body of St Dunstan for their daily offices.[2] As for the library, the surviving books without a proper building to house them must have made a dismal appearance.

A more imaginative eye might have found, both in the surviving monastic customs and in the books, much of great interest and perhaps even of value for the monastic life. But Lanfranc seems not even to have noticed that the community still followed, however imperfectly, the order of monastic life which had been laid down for all English monasteries a hundred years earlier, of which two copies from the pre-Conquest library at Christ Church, Canterbury, still survive.[3] During the next few years he drew up a similar body of monastic observances for use in his cathedral church. In its own way, it too is a masterpiece of coherent legislation. But it is an

---

[2] See *Memorials of St Dunstan*, pp. 142, 231. [3] See *Regularis Concordia*, p. liv.

astonishing fact, a revelation both of his independent power of creating an ordered system and of his limitations of vision, that in this work he never once referred to the work of his predecessor. He borrowed nothing from it or any other local text, but introduced a new routine of life almost exclusively dependent on the latest developments at Cluny.[4]

Lanfranc's silence about existing practices has sometimes been interpreted as a sign that the old order had fallen into complete neglect by the time he arrived at Canterbury. Indeed in the circumstances in which he found the community there is likely to have been a good deal of disorder. But the chance survival of a record of a miracle on Easter Day not long before Lanfranc's arrival shows that the monks were still giving a dramatic representation of the three women at the tomb searching for the risen Lord as laid down in the *Regularis Concordia*. So something was surviving among the ruins.[5] And there were several other signs of life. For instance, the monastic school was still in existence, with quite a large body of masters and children in the choir.[6] Also, the members of the community preserved a considerable sense of grandeur, however misplaced, and an implacable devotion to their local saints. Even the ruined library still contained many texts which were witnesses to a local tradition of artistic skill, showing a consuming interest in miraculous happenings and that curious mixture of vernacular and Latin literacy which were all characteristic of late Anglo-Saxon culture.[7]

It is perhaps in the surviving pre-Conquest books more than anywhere that we can find a clue to Lanfranc's impatient determination to make a completely new start with the monastic life at Canterbury. Among all the books which have survived – and nearly seventy have now been identified – there is not a single volume of the basic works of Patristic theology or of recent scholastic learning, which (as we have seen) were conspicuous in the library at Bec, and were to be equally conspicuous at Canterbury after Lanfranc had restored the library. Moreover, in none of these surviving volumes is there any sign of interest or skill in the rapidly developing scholastic disciplines of northern France and Lorraine at this time.

Some of the gaps must be due to chance, but there is no mistaking

[4] For the sources, see *Lanfranc's Constitutions*, pp. xi–xiii.
[5] *Memorials of St Dunstan*, p. 231.   [6] Ibid. p. 229.
[7] For a learned and judicious account of the present state of knowledge about the library, see Brooks, 1984, pp. 266–78.

the insularity of interest which these volumes display. A high proportion of the oldest books are Gospel books or Psalters, several of them with vernacular glosses and translations testifying to a low level of Latinity ; testifying too to their close connection with the Anglo-Saxon dynasty in the gifts of such benefactors as King Athelstan. The whole scene represented by these extensive remains is determinedly backward-looking and insular. The hand of the past lies heavily on everything. It was a past that had almost nothing in common with the learned past which Lanfranc had made abundantly available at Bec, and which pointed the way to the future.

Indeed, it is not difficult to understand Lanfranc's impatience with all that he found at Canterbury. The interest which the remains of the Anglo-Saxon past arouse in a modern scholar is an interest in strange and beautiful survivals, in which Lanfranc could see nothing but corruption and lack of learning. And the passion with which the surviving English monks defended their past and resisted change must have seemed to him simply a final proof of mental and spiritual decay.

Our knowledge of all these sides of religious life at Canterbury at the time of the Conquest has had to be reconstructed by laborious scholarship, largely because Lanfranc turned a blind eye to every aspect of a native religious tradition. That so much has survived, despite Lanfranc's hostility, is due first to the tenacity of the surviving monks, and then to the encouragement given to them by Anselm. The contrast between the two men in this matter points to one last difference of outlook between them, to add to those already discussed.

For Lanfranc, all the signs of life which he saw around him when he arrived at Canterbury were in one way or another manifestations of deviation from the norms of contemporary learning and religious observance, and his main aim in all his activities, whether at Bec or at Canterbury, was to strengthen the central normality of any church for which he was responsible. He had achieved this at Bec in his teaching, in the books which he collected, and – in the larger world – in his Eucharistic argument. He saw it now as his mission to establish similar normality in a barbarous land.[8]

---

[8] His attitude is well summed up in a letter to Anselm: *Tot enim tribulationibus terra ipsa in qua sumus cotidie quatitur, tot adulteriis aliisque spurcitiis inquinatur, ut nullus fere hominum ordo sit qui vel animae suae consulat vel proficiendi in deum salutarem doctrinam saltem audire concupiscat. Ep.* 30 (i, 22) in Anselm's letters; no. 19 in Gibson, 1979.

Among the local peculiarities which needed to be swept away, the most important was the array of outlandish local saints' days and festivals in the Canterbury calendar. Here he touched one of the most sensitive spots in the religious life of the surviving Canterbury community. As Eadmer reported, there was nothing more precious to the older monks than the recollection of the saints and their miracles. Indeed, his account of their interests gives the impression – and perhaps gave the same impression to Lanfranc – that they were a lot of old gossips chattering about wonders and miracles and gifts of relics, when they should have been engaged on more serious religious observances, or on the studies laid down in the Rule. No doubt it was very vexatious to Lanfranc, especially since he doubted whether their so-called saints deserved this title at all.

Into this scene of gossip and legend, of curious artistry and strange wonders, Lanfranc brought a more modern mind, great administrative ability, and a clear, constructive, expert knowledge of the up-to-date learning of the schools and of the monastic life in its contemporary forms. He set about reshaping the Canterbury community with great vigour and clarity of aim. He made plans for, and carried out, a complete rebuilding of the cathedral church on the model of the church he had built at Caen. He rebuilt the library and began stocking it with the central texts of secular and religious learning which he had made available at Bec. His new body of monastic regulations brought the up-to-date practices of Cluny not only to Canterbury, but also to monasteries in all parts of England. Similarly the texts which he introduced into the Canterbury library are soon also found at Durham, Rochester, Exeter, and in other English libraries. There can be no doubt that he planned on a great scale.[9]

All this could not be done single-handed, and Lanfranc's most important innovation was to bring new men from Bec and Caen to occupy all the main offices in the monastery at Canterbury, and to be ready for promotion wherever they were needed. The new men whom he introduced were central to Lanfranc's plans. We have already encountered several of them in Anselm's letters. Henry, Arnost, and Gundulf were among the earliest of his correspondents. Of these, the first became prior of Canterbury and the other two became successive bishops of Rochester. Then, in addition, there were Maurice and Herluin from Bec; Vitalis, Roger, and

---

[9] See Brooke, 1931, pp. 231–5; and above, pp. 36–7.

Samuel from Caen; and, briefly, Gilbert Crispin, who became abbot of Westminster. Probably there were never more than eight or ten newcomers at Canterbury among a native community of perhaps thirty or forty Englishmen; but it was the privilege of the newcomers to command, and of the native monks to exercise their monastic vocation of obedience.

The English monks seem for some years to have been able to resist the discipline of Lanfranc. A few years after Lanfranc's arrival, Eadmer described the English monks as living the lives of earls rather than monks, 'in all worldly glory, with gold and silver, with changes of fine clothes and delicate food, not to speak of the various kinds of musical instruments in which they delighted, and the horses, dogs and hawks with which they sometimes took exercise'.[10] It is hard to know what to make of this. But, even when we have made allowance for the exaggerated impressions of a boy of fifteen, recollected many years later, it may be taken as evidence that Lanfranc and his handful of monks from Bec and Caen met not only with hostility, but also with a good deal of successful resistance.

What is certain is that the two parts of the community continued to the time of Lanfranc's death and beyond to face each other with unconcealed hostility. This was not an uncommon state of affairs: less than a quarter of a mile away, at St Augustine's, a similarly tense situation was working towards a violent conclusion. But at Christ Church the antipathies of the early years of Lanfranc's rule were ultimately, with whatever resentment and secret insubordination, reduced to more or less furtive disobedience. As Eadmer saw it, the turning point came in 1076, when Lanfranc was pressing on with the building of the new church, and had recently appointed Henry, his Italian fellow-countryman from Bec, as prior. At this moment an English member of the community went mad. The horrible sufferings and uproar which resulted are fully described by two independent observers, Osbern and Eadmer.[11] But it was Eadmer, with his keen eye for significant detail, who noted two points omitted by Osbern: he observed that, as the monks stood round the sufferer, each of the two groups spoke a language which the other could not understand; and also he remarked that things went more smoothly after this event. The new church was finished in the following year, and the completion of the conventual

---

[10] See *Memorials of St Dunstan*, pp. 237–8.
[11] *Memorials of St Dunstan*, pp. 149–51 (by Osbern), 234–8 (by Eadmer).

buildings must have brought a more stable and orderly life. But in addition to his constructive plans, Lanfranc also took steps to cut down the force of opposition to his changes by sending away 'for correction' one of the chief trouble-makers, a monk called Osbern. He sent him to Bec to learn obedience from Anselm.

II ANSELM'S LIBERATING INFLUENCE

Whatever Lanfranc's intentions may have been, the result was different from anything that he can have anticipated. Osbern, besides being filled with anger and resentment at Lanfranc's destruction of the native tradition, was an exceptionally talented man with a gift for music, liturgical composition, and writing.[12] When he got to Bec, Anselm at once spotted his quality, and he was soon sending back to Lanfranc a glowing account of Osbern's progress: he was 'growing daily in knowledge and serenity'; and the friendship between him and Anselm had become so close that they could not be separated without tearing their two souls apart. Here at once we recognize the language of Anselm's warmest and most demanding friendship. Perhaps even more significant for the future, Anselm also told Lanfranc that he had heard about Dunstan's rule of life for monks: would Lanfranc please send it to him? Would he also send a *Life* of Dunstan?[13] So it would seem that an essential fact which had escaped Lanfranc's notice had come out in Anselm's talks with Osbern. Anselm had not yet visited Canterbury, but he had got hold of the one thing necessary for understanding the members of the old monastic community: they wanted recognition of their saints and understanding of their tradition. Two other letters of Anselm during Osbern's disciplinary exile at Bec complete the story of their first meeting. In one, he told Lanfranc that Osbern was now at peace with the new masters at Canterbury; in another, he told the Italian prior Henry, in somewhat guarded language, that Osbern now recognized and repented of his fault, which Anselm ascribed to imprudence rather than pride. Finally he sent him back to Canterbury with warm commendations.

The friendship thus established between the most talented of the leaders of the rebellious English and the future archbishop of

[12] See William of Malmesbury's account of Osbern, *GR*, i, p. 166, ii, p. 389; *GP*, pp. 24–5, 33, 148–9.
[13] *Ep.* 39 (i, 31). For Anselm's later reports, see *Epp.* 66, 67 (i, 57, 58) and p. 157 above.

Canterbury had wide ramifications. Osbern returned to Canterbury, not to make peace by abandoning his efforts to get recognition for the despised saints, but to gain recognition for them by writing their biographies. He was the first of a new generation of writers who sought to repair the post-Conquest destruction of earlier pieties and observances by steady persistence in re-creating the past.

The next step in this development was Anselm's own visit to Canterbury in 1079. I have already mentioned the argument on this occasion which convinced Lanfranc that he had made a mistake in sweeping the former archbishop Elphege out of the ecclesiastical calendar. This incident, besides its theological interest, was also a landmark in the restoration of the Old English saints to the ecclesiastical calendar.[14]

It may be recalled that Lanfranc's doubt about the sanctity of Elphege arose from lack of information about the circumstances of his death. It was known that he had been archbishop of Canterbury between 1006 and 1012, and that he had been killed by the Danes for refusing to pay Danegeld. But there was no written record of his life or death, or of the reasons for his resistance; and there was no one in the community who still remembered him. Like so much that was sacred at Canterbury, it was all hearsay, and all the more violently adhered to on that account. In 1079, Lanfranc asked Anselm to give his opinion, and (as we know) he argued that since Elphege had certainly died in the effort to save his tenants from an unjust exaction, he had died for justice; and, if for justice, then also for truth, which is only justice in another mode. And, since he had died for truth, he was a martyr, for this was what martyrdom meant.[15]

To say that Lanfranc was convinced by this argument would be an understatement: he seems to have been simply overwhelmed by it. Perhaps he was moved by the recollection that the argument propounded by Anselm had its origin in his own comment on an intricate saying of St Paul about truth and justice being the same thing in different modes; perhaps too he felt some remorse at his impatient dismissal of so many of the saints venerated at Canterbury, when so clever a man as Anselm could take Elphege seriously.

---

[14] Although it is in need of correction on several points, the process of revival can still best be followed in E. Bishop and A. Gasquet, *The Bosworth Psalter*, London, 1908, pp. 32–2, 63–4.

[15] For this incident, see above, pp. 41–2, and *VA* I, xxx.

Whatever the reason, he reacted to Anselm's demonstration with almost extravagant zeal.

The proof of this is to be found in the calendar of saints' days for the Canterbury community which he had so offensively purged. He now not only re-introduced Elphege: he brought him back into his carefully limited and graded sequence of holy days at a very high level indeed, placing him among the *Festivitates quae magnifice celebrantur*, on a level with the Epiphany, the Purification and Annunciation, the Ascension, the Feast of St Gregory, and about half a dozen other main feasts of the Church year.[16] This was of course extremely generous, but he extended his generosity to no other local saint after the first archbishop St Augustine, whom he could never have excluded. Dunstan, the greatest of his predecessors after Augustine, was still omitted.

To maintain the dignity of his new position, Elphege needed to have a biography and a complement of musical compositions for his feast-day. For these Lanfranc turned to Osbern. The musical composition is lost; and this is a great loss, for according to William of Malmesbury, Osbern was the best musician of his day. But the biography which he wrote still survives.[17] It marks the beginning of the post-Conquest revival of Canterbury's past; more generally, Anselm's intervention in Osbern's career marked a turning point in saving the monastic and cultural tradition of pre-Conquest England, and the movement gathered impetus during the next half century.

Osbern's next service to the revival of the old observances after his return from Bec was to write the first coherent *Life* of Dunstan. Here, he was much better supplied with materials than for Elphege. He had two almost contemporary biographies and a wealth of oral tradition to draw on, and out of these materials he made a lively and dramatic portrait, full of sentiment and warmth, which easily outdistanced in popularity the biographies written by later writers who tried to do better. In the end Lanfranc made Osbern precentor of the cathedral, the first Englishman in the community after the Conquest to hold a position of responsibility. But Osbern never ceased to be a rebel in the cause of the past, and the battle for Anglo-Saxon antiquity was only half won at Lanfranc's death.

Lanfranc himself was only partly converted, and, even in his last days, he was still giving quantities of the bodies of his predecessors,

---

[16] See *Lanfranc's Constitutions*, p. 59.   [17] *Anglia Sacra*, ii, pp. 134–7.

which had filled the old church before the fire of 1067, to his new foundation of canons outside the walls of the city.[18] Moreover the prior, who was the effective day-to-day head of the community, was still Henry, who shared Lanfranc's doubts about the native saints. This last statement is no more than an inference, but it is based on an event recorded by Eadmer, which illustrates the state of affairs after Lanfranc's death, when Prior Henry was in full control of the community:

After the death of Lanfranc, while I was sitting one day in the cloister as usual, engaged on a book which I was writing, Osbern the precentor came to me, and sitting down he began to say, 'As you know, brother, father Lanfranc of happy memory ordered and allowed us to look into the shrines and reliquaries of this church to find out what relics were contained in them. But we did this only in part, for while we were carrying out his orders, we came on one reliquary bigger and apparently more precious than the rest. When we opened it, we found it entirely full, and we left it untouched. Now, in case we never find out what it contains (though I have a suspicion what it is), let us two go together and take the sacrists with us, and make a careful examination of the contents of the coffer.' I agreed, and without consulting the prior, we went together to the place.[19]

Clearly Osbern thought there was still much to do; he must have seen Anselm's succession to the archbishopric as a new hope for the Anglo-Saxon past, and he was greatly alarmed by Anselm's delay in accepting. He wrote twice to Anselm urging him to come quickly. Among all the letters in Anselm's letter collection written by others than himself, there are no others which display so much of the heightened emotion of friendship characteristic of Anselm's own letters, and they show Osbern's state of near despair at Anselm's long delay.[20]

After these two letters, we hear no more of Osbern, and we can only conclude that he died soon after Anselm's consecration. Meanwhile, however, Anselm had chosen a permanent companion from among the English monks, who could more than fill the gap left by Osbern. This was Eadmer, about whom much more will

[18] In his foundation charter Lanfranc gave to St Gregory's *plurimam partem de reliquiis sanctorum pontificum qui ante nos ecclesie Christi prefuere*. See Woodcock, 1956, p. 1.

[19] This account, written by Eadmer many years after the event he describes, was printed by Wilmart, 1935, pp. 367–9. The relics were those of St Ouen, and Eadmer goes on to say that while he was in exile with Anselm, after Osbern's death, the sacrist of the day renewed the search, and the relics were given a place of honour in the cathedral.

[20] *Epp.* 149 (iii, 2), 152 (iii, 5).

need to be said later. Meanwhile, it will suffice to notice the strangeness of Anselm's choice. Even before he was consecrated, and perhaps as soon as he was elected, at a moment when, by ordinary rules of prudence, he should have been thinking of equipping himself with all the forms of expert knowledge required by his new position, he chose one of the group of English monks to be his closest and most constant companion. His choice fell on Eadmer, a man indeed of unusual talent, but no practical ability. From this moment Eadmer was constantly with him.

So far as we know they had met only in 1079, when Eadmer was one of the young monks to whom Anselm talked during his first visit to Canterbury. Of all the monks of Canterbury, apart from Osbern, Eadmer most markedly represented all that Lanfranc had scrupled to authorize. His mind was the richest repository of the past: he had been a child oblate at Canterbury before the Conquest; he had heard all the gossip of the older monks as a child, and he remembered as an adult all that he had heard. The inspiration of his reports always moves in the narrow circle of subjects dear to the ecclesiastically minded Englishman of the eleventh century. They told of the movements of relics: the bringing of the relics of St Ouen to the court of King Edgar; of the king's gift of them to the monastery; of Queen Emma's gift of the arm of St Bartholomew; of the translation of the body of St Elphege; and so on. Such stories as these must have been common in all religious communities, but the constant recurrence of these themes in Eadmer's recollections leaves the impression that his thoughts, and those of the monks with whom he had lived since his infancy, were centred almost exclusively on their relics, and on the stories of the gifts, purchases, translations, and miracles associated with them. The air which he breathed was that of the famous treatise on the resting places of the old English saints, and of the days when, in Eadmer's words, 'it was the custom of the English to prefer the patronage of the saints to every worldly aid'.[21]

He remembered the old church, and from the description of it which he wrote in old age, it is possible to form a more complete picture of its internal arrangements than of any other pre-Conquest

---

[21] The main list of eighty-nine 'resting places' of saints predominantly of English origin in pre-Conquest England, was printed by F. Liebermann, *Die Heiligen Englands*, Hanover, 1889. There is an important study of its contents and later diffusion by D. W. Rollason, in *Anglo-Saxon England*, vii, 1978, 61–93.

church. He remembered where the saints had lain, and where the altars had stood; he remembered the old confusion of secular and ecclesiastical affairs, and the use of the south porch as the place where pleas were settled which could get no solution in hundred or shire or royal court. He recalled the ancient baptistery which stood at the east end of the church, where the bodies of the archbishops had lain, and where the trials by ordeal had taken place.

It was not until fifty years after the great fire which had swept it all away that Eadmer wrote this description of what he had seen as a small boy of about seven. In appearance everything had been altered since then, and – so far as looks went – much for the better, but nearly everything he cared about most was enshrined in these earliest recollections.[22]

This was the man whom Anselm chose as his closest companion on the strength of a meeting thirteen years earlier. It is useless to speculate why he chose him, rather than one of the monks of Bec or Caen who had been at Canterbury thoughout Lanfranc's tenure of the archbishopric. But the choice emphasizes three important features of Anselm's mind at the moment when he became archbishop.

First, the rapidity and certainty with which he chose those with whom he shared his thoughts. We have seen this rapidity on other occasions also in his earliest letters of friendship, but never before in circumstances where so much depended on the quality of those around him.

Second, his indifference to business proficiency as a qualification for his closest companions. This too has been conspicuous in all the areas of business which we have examined; but never before when when he was likely to be confronted with so much debate and such a variety of decisions.

Third, his sympathy for the traditions of the old Canterbury monks. This has already been illustrated from his dealings with Osbern, but never before when he himself was responsible for everything that happened. As often with Anselm, what may seem to be a merely personal, or even sentimental sympathy, also illustrates a deep-seated belief in the power of growth within a monastic community.

[22] See Eadmer, in Wilmart, 1935, pp. 365–6; also his *Vita S. Breguini, PL* 159, cols. 757–8; also, Osbern's *Historia de Translatione corporis S Elphegi*, in *Anglia Sacra*, ii, pp. 143–7.

III ANSELMIAN LIBERTY

In Anselm's choice of Eadmer as his constant companion, Osbern may have seen an assurance that his hopes for the revival of Canterbury's past might yet be fulfilled. But whatever Osbern may have hoped, Anselm's first letter to the community brought no promise of unbridled liberty:

Anselm, by the grace of God archbishop, to his dearest lords and sons Henry prior, Antony sub-prior, dom Ernulf and dom Osbern and other servants of God at Christ Church . . .

I hear that there are scandals and divisions among you, and that some of you refuse to be subject to the prior, and are doing many things without his knowledge which should be done only with his approval. Further, when rebuked by the prior, they refuse to submit to his judgement, and even go so far as to say that they are acting on my authority. This has led to factions and divisions among you, and I wish you to know that so long as the church is committed to my care I will in no circumstances permit or encourage any such insubordination.[23]

The prior to whom this was written was still the Italian, Henry, who had been appointed by Lanfranc almost thirty years earlier. Osbern as precentor also appears in the list of those to whom the letter was addressed. Moreover, it seems very likely that Anselm was referring to the search for relics conducted in secret by Osbern and Eadmer; and it is also likely that Anselm had heard of the search from Eadmer himself. What is quite clear is that after the death of Lanfranc the English monks felt free to assert themselves in ways that would have been impossible while Lanfranc lived. From their point of view they still had a long way to go in rescuing their past. Anselm's sophisticated reasoning had saved St Elphege. But behind him there was a large array of saints, customs, observances, and claims of one kind or another going back to a remote past. Even after Anselm's visit in 1079, Lanfranc had been prepared to consign the greater part of these local saints and customs to oblivion.[24] Nevertheless, the English monks of the community went on hoping to see the process reversed. They had grounds for thinking that they would have Anselm's support, and despite Anselm's strong words about insubordination in 1094, they were not disappointed.

[23] *Ep.* 182 (iii, 29).
[24] For example, *Lanfranc's Constitutions* do not mention the Feast of St Dunstan even among the feasts of the third rank.

The local tradition of devotion which Lanfranc had found deeply embedded in their corporate memory, and which the native-born monks had struggled – at first so unsuccessfully – to preserve, showed no sign of withering away. Rather the contrary, it was spreading to members of the community with no pre-Conquest memories. It lived in their minds, their thoughts, and their daily talk, and it was contagious.

But liberty to take action contrary to authority was not the kind of liberty that Anselm had come to Canterbury to promote. Liberty for Anselm never meant freedom of individual choice; in the monastic life it meant only freedom to follow the Rule within a local framework authoritatively laid down. This is apparent in all the advice he gave to discontented monks. He would allow no exceptions to this fundamental rule; but he did not exclude growth within a framework authoritatively established, and he could help to reshape the future through the men whom he chose as prior. His opportunity came in 1096. In this year, the Conqueror's memorial abbey of Battle had no abbot, and Anselm advised the king to appoint Prior Henry.[25]

A rigorist for ecclesiastical law would have found much to object to in this procedure. But, for Canterbury, it made possible the appointment of a new prior, and Anselm appointed Ernulf, who was one of Lanfranc's men, but of a very different stamp from his predecessor. Wherever he went, first as prior at Canterbury, then as abbot of Peterborough, and finally as bishop of Rochester, Ernulf was associated with the revival of an interest in pre-Conquest traditions – with the revival of Anglo-Saxon liturgical practices at Canterbury, with the collection of Old English laws at Rochester, and perhaps with the renewed interest in the Anglo-Saxon Chronicle at Peterborough.[26]

Having chosen Ernulf, Anselm allowed him to work in his own way. Perhaps he could do little else, but there is no mistaking the magnanimity of the spirit in which he wrote the following reply to one question which had been sent to him during his exile. He wrote:

[25] This is reported by the Battle Abbey chronicler (Searle, 1980, pp. 100–3), who also reports that Henry brought his own monks with him from Canterbury to advise him.

[26] There is a lucid summary of the evidence for Ernulf's interest in the Anglo-Saxon past by F. Liebermann in his 'Notes on the *Textus Roffensis*' in *Archeologia Cantiana: Transactions of the Kent Archeological Society*, 23, London, 1898, pp. 101–12. For Ernulf's association with the *Textus Roffensis*, see also *Early English Manuscripts in Facsimile*, vii, Copenhagen and Baltimore, 1957, ed. Peter Sawyer, pp. 18–19.

As for the celebration of those feasts about which you have asked me, I leave them to your disposition, and whatever you arrange, I confirm. Likewise with regard to the octave of the Nativity of St Mary, the Mother of God, which many of the brethren wish to observe because it is kept in other churches: do as seems best to you.[27]

With this freedom, much could happen which would have been impossible under Lanfranc. We are here at the beginning of a new phase in the restoration of old customs and the addition of new ones, which in a brief space of time greatly altered the liturgical arrangements laid down by Lanfranc. Meanwhile, Anselm played the part of a benevolent but distant superior dealing with complaints about the negligence of monastic officials, restraining the over-officious severity of the sub-prior, remonstrating with monks who wished to leave the monastery for something vaguely better, defending his own absence, and dealing in a casual way with a variety of business. But his main contribution to the development of the community came from his choice of priors, Ernulf first and then Conrad, both men with a sympathetic interest in the past, and leaving them to do their work without interference. He also – as a by-product of the grant he made to repay the monks for the loss of their plate following his aid to Rufus in 1095 – provided money for the rebuilding of the cathedral choir on a greatly enlarged scale.[28]

Ten years after Anselm's death, when the tide of criticism was running strongly against Anselm at Canterbury for his failure to obtain a secure basis for the primatial claims, Eadmer thought it his best praise that he had allowed the monks to manage their own affairs. We can see the results of this in both the internal and external affairs of the house. For instance, the single entry in the English annals of the monastery between 1100 and 1109 records the inspection of the body of St Elphege in 1105, and the discovery that it was incorrupt.[29] Anselm was at this time in exile, so it is clear that the monks, who now had a prior whom Anselm had appointed, were able to do publicly what the Anglo-Saxon enthusiasts had had to do surreptitiously before Anselm's arrival.

As the community increasingly took charge of its own affairs, and felt its corporate strength, Anselm's political struggles, like those of Archbishop Thomas Becket after him, only remotely affected it. The monastery was borne along on a buoyant prosperity which,

[27] *Ep.* 331 (iv, 41). [28] *HN*, p. 75. [29] Liebermann, 1879, p. 5.

while it may have contributed to the dissatisfactions and distractions felt by the few, drew most of its members together in a sense of their importance and independence, and hastened the disappearance of earlier divisions. The number of monks increased. According to Eadmer there were over sixty in about 1080, and a high proportion of them must have been Englishmen of the old foundation. By the end of Lanfranc's life the number is given by a later domestic chronicler as a hundred, and it was still rising. Probably it had reached its maximum of some 120 by about 1120.[30] In this large body, very few would have known the pre-Conquest church; and most of them would probably have been children of the new gentry in the neighbourhood of Canterbury, perhaps with parents of mixed Anglo-Norman origin. This was the stratum of society from which Eadmer had come before the arrival of the Normans, and it almost certainly continued to provide most of the monks after the Conquest also.

During Anselm's time as archbishop, a new spaciousness of life developed in the monastery. This is shown in several ways: in growing income, in the great new choir of the cathedral which was begun in Anselm's lifetime, in the proliferation of precious ornaments, the growth of the library, and the freedom with which the Anglo-Saxon past was incorporated into the liturgical and devotional life of the community. In every way the past, of which Anselm had been quite ignorant until Osbern was exiled to Bec in about 1076, was coming into its own.

One immediate result of growing numbers and growing prosperity was that Lanfranc's church very soon needed to be enlarged. Lanfranc had modelled his church on the one which he had built at Caen with its notably short and stubby choir. With the growing numbers of monks, this soon became inconveniently small. In a new burst of corporate energy, the choir was demolished in Anselm's day, and replaced by a structure in proportions and plan unlike any other in England at the time. It seems almost certain that the model for the new building was the recently completed church at Cluny, which Urban II had dedicated in 1095, and which Anselm and Eadmer had visited in 1099. The building which they saw then was a landmark in the development of monastic architecture in Europe in size, architectural design, and decoration; and the new building at Canterbury, begun under Anselm and

---

[30] The number of monks and the evidence are given in Knowles, 1940, p. 714.

completed in 1130, incorporated several important details from the design of the new church at Cluny. 'The like of it [according to William of Malmesbury] was not to be seen in England in its windows, the splendour of its marble pavements or the diversity of its paintings.'[31] This too may be reckoned one of the results of Anselm's exile. But, above all, this enlargement made provision for the revival of the local past which Lanfranc's building had rigorously excluded: on either side of the high altar were the altars of Dunstan and Elphege, and over the altar was a beam on which they stood flanking the figure of Christ in Majesty.[32]

Canterbury was certainly not moving in the direction of Cistercian austerity in Anselm's time. It is difficult now to imagine the splendour which the vast incrustation of ornaments must have presented to the eye by the time the church was complete. In this, as in his support for the elaboration of monastic customs, Anselm's expansiveness stands in striking contrast both to the intimacy and austerity of his personal devotion, and to the new trend towards simplicity and severity which this type of devotion stimulated among the Cistercians. There is of course no formal contradiction

---

[31] The chief feature, which seems to have been introduced at Canterbury from Cluny, is the double transept (see plan, p. 327), for which see A. W. Clapham, *English Romanesque Architecture after the Conquest*, Oxford, 1934, pp. 71, 74. For William of Malmesbury's judgement, see *GP*, p. 138. For the ornaments which the priors appointed by Anselm added, including five large bells which required the labours of sixty-three men to ring, and a cope woven with gold thread and adorned with a hundred and forty little silver-gilt bells interspersed with precious stones costing £100, see *Anglia Sacra*, i, p. 137. For further details, see Southern, 1963, p. 261n.

[32] The plans illustrating the development of the cathedral from 1066 to 1130 are reproduced (pp. 326–7) from Southern 1963, pp. 264–5, following the plans of R. Willis, *The Architectural History of Canterbury Cathedral*, London, 1845. I have left them unaltered, despite alterations in the plan of the Anglo-Saxon cathedral suggested by H. M. Taylor in his very thorough study of the evidence in 'The Anglo-Saxon Cathedral Church at Canterbury', *Archeological Journal*, 126, 1969, pp. 101–30; and in the plan of the East end of Lanfranc's cathedral suggested by Francis Woodman, *The Architectural History of Canterbury Cathedral*, London and Boston, 1981, p. 30. Their suggestions may well be right, but three reasons have persuaded me to leave my original plans unaltered. First, in the absence of physical remains, all the suggested reconstructions are hypothetical. Second, the various suggestions do not alter the main outline of the growth of the building, but only details, of which the position and plan of the Anglo-Saxon baptistery is the most important. Third, and most important, the new suggestions do not materially alter the siting of saints' bodies and altars, or the story of the re-emergence of the Anglo-Saxon saints from the obscurity to which Lanfranc had consigned them, which largely determined the growth of the plan during these years. I may add that Willis's book is still worth reading as a masterpiece of architectural history by a pioneer who not only understood architectural details, but also the broader purposes which provoked the sequence of architectural changes.

I. THE PRE-CONQUEST CHURCH

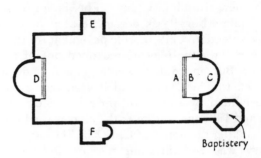

ALTARS WITH THE BODIES OF SAINTS AND ARCHBISHOPS ASSOCIATED WITH THEM

	Main Church		Crypt	
Altars	*Relics and tombs*		*Altars*	*Relics*
A. Matutinal altar	St. Dunstan			
B. Altar of Christ	Head of St. Swithin and other relics;			
	Abps. Elphege and Oda nearby.			
C. High Altar	St. Wilfrid		C. Altar	Head of St. Fursius
D. St. Mary	St. Austroberta			
E. St. Martin				
F. St. Gregory				

BAPISTERY: Here were the bodies of the Abps. from Cuthbert (740–60) onwards, with a few exceptions, of whom Oda, Elphege and Dunstan, who lay in the main church, were the chief. The precise site and shape of the building are conjectural.

II. LANFRANC'S CHURCH

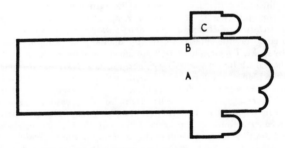

(The information about the arrangement of Lanfranc's church is very imperfect)

A. Altar of Holy Cross (over it, Lanfranc's Rood with figures of St. Mary and St. John; before it, the first burial places of Abps. Lanfranc and Anselm).

B. Altar of St. Mary.

C. Gallery with bodies of earlier archbishops.

III. ANSELM'S CHURCH

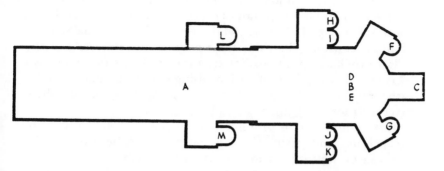

ALTARS WITH THE BODIES OF SAINTS AND ARCHBISHOPS AT THE TIME OF THE CONSECRATION IN 1130

Main Church		Crypt	
Altars	*Relics and Tombs*	*Altars*	*Relics and Tombs*
A. Holy Cross (Lanfranc's Rood)			
B. High Altar (over it, a beam with figures of Christ in Glory flanked by St. Dunstan and St. Elphege, and seven boxes of relics)		B. St. Mary	
C. Holy Trinity	St. Wilfred; Abps. Oda, Lanfranc[1] and Anselm[1]	C. 1. St. Augustine 2. St. John Baptist	Abp. Ethelred Abp. Eadsig
D. St. Elphege	St. Elphege		
E. St. Dunstan	St. Dunstan		
F. St. Andrew		F. Holy Innocents	
G. SS. Peter and Paul (later St. Anselm)		G. Archangel Gabriel	
H. St. Martin	Abps. Wilfrid and Living	H. St. Mary Magdalen	
I. St. Stephen	Abps. Ethelherd and Cuthbert	I. St. Nicholas	
J. St. John Evangelist	Abps. Ethelgar and Aelfric	J. St Paulinus	Abp. Sigeric
K. St. Gregory	Abps. Bregwine[2] and Plegmund[2]	K. 1. St. Ouen 2. St. Catherine	
L. (*above*) St. Blaise (*below*) St. Michael	Abps. Ethelhelm, Ethelnoth, Wulfhelm, Ceolnoth, Ralph		
M. (*above*) All Saints (*below*) St. Michael	St. Siburgis and Abp. Feologild		

Notes

[1] Translated to this place before 1125.   [2] Translated to this place in 1123.

Figure 1 The church at Canterbury, 1066–1130

in combining austerity of devotion with ebullience of architectural and internal decoration, but the combination illustrates the contrasts which we find in almost every area of Anselm's life. In the contrast between the austerity of his life and the emotional warmth of his friendships, between the rigour of his Prayers and the mildness of his disposition, between the eremitical strain in his own piety and his acceptance of the increasing wealth of ornament in his cathedral church, this most uncompromising of men stands where extremes meet, and embraces both.

The community as Anselm left it when he died was rich, prosperous, and assured of its position in the world. The annoyances, injustices, and setbacks from which it suffered seem small in retrospect, but they preyed on the minds of its members at the time. In one area especially the monks felt unjustly thwarted, and attributed a large part of their woes to Anselm. Oddly enough, it was an area about which he felt quite as strongly as the members of the monastic community. It concerned Canterbury's claim to primacy over the whole of the British Isles. Anselm fought for it with a tenacity which is only explicable if the whole scene which we have briefly surveyed is borne in mind: the primacy was the brightest of the dreams which the monks of Canterbury had inherited from their largely silent, ever-beckoning past, and on this question Anselm fell under the spell of the awe-inspiring tradition which he had helped to preserve. His violent defence of the primacy, though it was contrary to all the forward-looking governmental ideals and interests of the Church as a whole during his later years, is his nearest approach to a consistent political policy as archbishop.

In several ways his advocacy of the primacy reflects the tensions which run through Anselm's later career. He had come to Canterbury with a firmly established and clearly defined view of liberty as a state of the will wholly integrated with the will of God, seeking no escape from obedience, but finding freedom for the development of the soul in ever-deepening understanding of the divine nature, and ever-broadening assent to God's will. This had been his message to those in the world who thought that their duty might lie in saving a brother in the world, or a cause from destruction at the hands of the infidel. Even more decisively, it had been his message to monks or incipient monks who saw a duty in saving, as it might be, a sister from enslavement, or a call to take action in the world to prevent some evil. 'Seek the cloister'; 'stay safe in port': these were the precepts which he gave to those who desired true freedom.

But this freedom of the cloister was not static. In the company of like-minded friends in the community, advance was possible towards an increasing understanding of the substance of faith and of advance towards the vision of God. This freedom to advance was not a private matter. Its influence would be experienced throughout the whole monastic community, and beyond the cloister in the world. Intimate and inward looking though the Anselmian programme was in its origin, it was also a programme of growth for the whole community. Like a forest fire, it started from the individual and grew outwards until it enveloped the whole area of monastic patrons and friends and dependants. More than that: the web of monasteries provided an organizing principle for the whole society of Christendom. This had been the message of the monastic reform of the tenth century, which was being rapidly replaced by a new message of organization under papal direction, extending through dioceses and parishes until it finally reached the individual.

There can be no doubt that this new ideal was much better adapted to the intellectual and material developments in western Europe after 1050 than the old monastically oriented society of the earlier period. But in this respect Anselm belonged to the past, and one of the chief symptoms of this in his later years is the determination with which, against all the interests and policy of successive popes after Gregory VII, he argued the case, and fought for the principle of the primatial authority of Canterbury throughout the whole of the British Isles. The essential characteristics of this primacy which distinguished it from such primacies as that of Hamburg or Lyons were, first, that it was centred in a monastic community, and second, that its roots and its authorization went back (as Anselm was persuaded) to its original constitution in the seventh century. Its defence and enlargement in the new political circumstances of post-Conquest England represented a return to the aim of spreading Christian doctrine and discipline from a central monastic community. It claimed to have the authority of the past and the patronage of the saints in bringing to the world the fruits of monastic discipline and devotion. Anselm's struggle for this ideal had a central place in his pastoral conception of his archiepiscopal duties, and it requires a somewhat lengthy treatment if its place in his world-view is to be understood.

CHAPTER 14

AN OLD LIBERTY: THE PRIMACY OF CANTERBURY

I PRINCIPLES OF PRIMACY

Anselm's general habits of thought, which were essentially unitary, would lead us to expect him to be opposed, or at least indifferent, to local privileges. But this general expectation has already been shown to be misleading in his approach to the monastic life of the community at Canterbury. Unlike Lanfranc who aimed at creating a model community in accordance with the latest monastic thought without regard to local traditions, Anselm not only permitted, but welcomed, local habits of worship and models of sanctity, which Lanfranc had driven out with a strong arm.

In approaching the question of the primacy of Canterbury, we need once more to examine the roots of Anselm's support for a local claim which ran counter to one of the most powerful principles of papal policy at this time.

As a starting point, it is worth remembering that on the question of the sanctity of St Elphege, Anselm – unlike Lanfranc – was prepared to accept the testimony of the community with regard to the facts on which their veneration of the saint were based. What he provided were the principles. He reminded Lanfranc of their early agreement that justice and truth were the same thing in different modes. Consequently, if Elphege died for justice, even only in refusing to pay money demanded by Viking invaders, he died also for truth. In so doing, he earned all the privileges due to a martyr.

Anselm's procedure in this case reflects the principle on which his theology was built: he accepted the statements of faith of the whole Christian community, and set about finding explanations which satisfied the demands of reason. If his explanations were wrong, it made no difference to his faith; if they were right, they strengthened the community of believers against the attacks of critics, and added the pleasure of understanding to the duty of believing.

In the greatest matters, the universal testimony of the Church was the guarantee of truth. But in matters of local importance, he was prepared to accept the testimony of the local community: in this he was following the ancient practice of the Church with regard to canonization, which was replaced by a formal centralized procedure in the course of the next hundred years. Equally, Anselm accepted local monastic testimony as a sufficient basis for defending the possession of lands and privileges; and here he followed in Lanfranc's footsteps.

In brief, both Lanfranc and Anselm were living in a time when the ancient consensus of local testimony, which had sufficed in the past for most matters of faith and practice, was being subordinated to more formal legal and rational procedures. In the main, both of them belonged to the past, but Anselm was more conservative than Lanfranc. For Anselm, the voice of a local church, especially of a local monastic community, sufficed in most matters. Unlike the new Cistercian seekers for a simpler form of monastic life, Anselm – however much he shared a personal preference for simplicity – disapproved of a discontented search for something better than the present community provided. Indeed, his only idea of historical development was the process of adding to the number of the elect, which at a certain fixed target would bring history to an end. He does not seem to have thought that improvements in the world would hasten this process.

His main principle with regard to the past was that nothing once given to God or the saints could be restored to the kingdom of this world without injustice. This principle operated absolutely with regard to monastic vows, even in their most inchoate state. It operated also with regard to lands and rights that had once been given to God or the saints: the gift could never be withdrawn or diminished without sin. So far as Canterbury was concerned, the right of primacy over the whole of the British Isles was the greatest of all such gifts. It was not a right to be enjoyed as a source of revenue or worldly glory: it was to be guarded as a gift from the past, representing an eternal principle of order.

To descend from these heights to the commonplace, we have already seen that at the beginning of his time as abbot of Bec, Anselm had a problem about the rights of the abbey of Bec. Rival churches had claimed tithes and privileges which belonged to Bec. Unluckily, whether through carelessness or incompetence, no title deeds could be found, and he had to write to Lanfranc to beg his help.[1] The same happened at Canterbury, but on a much greater scale. Instead of contested tithes, he found himself the guardian of a rich, varied, and passionately cultivated tradition for which the documentary evidence was fragmentary, but the local testimony entirely firm. Despite the imperfections of the documents, he felt to the full his reponsibility to preserve and hand over intact to his successor all the rights, privileges, and possessions of which he was the divinely constituted guardian.

There was nothing merely theoretical in his duty to preserve these rights. Like every abbot or bishop, he was clothed in the *persona* of the saint to whom his church was dedicated or by whom it was founded. When the pope wrote to Anselm that 'we behold in you the venerable *persona* of St Augustine the Apostle of the English' this was more than a complimentary politeness.[2] It was – or was taken to be – a recognition of the important truth that the temporary holder of the office of archbishop stood in the place of, and was answerable to, St Augustine and the other saints of his church, and through them to God. From this it followed that whoever was archbishop of Canterbury inherited all the powers that Gregory had given to Augustine, just as the pope inherited all the powers that Christ had given to St Peter.[3] Anselm himself never quoted this analogy, but he went so far as to warn the pope that if he gave an adverse judgement in the dispute between Canterbury and York 'I would on no account remain in England; for I neither ought to, nor can allow the primacy of our church to be destroyed while I am alive.'[4]

In making this statement, Anselm was speaking both on his own behalf and on behalf of the monastic community. The sense of solidarity within the community was always the driving force

---

[1] *Ep.* 89 (ii, 1).   [2] *Ep.* 452 (iii, 153).
[3] See *HN*, p. 277. Eadmer is here summarizing the argument for the primacy sent to the pope by Archbishop Ralph in 1120, and he adds: 'Those who try to take from the successors of Augustine that power and dignity which St Gregory gave him, would, if they dared, deprive the successors of St Peter of the power and dignity which the just and holy Lord gave to Peter; for the Lord, in mentioning only Peter, spoke also of his successors, as did Gregory in mentioning only his disciple Augustine.' (*Qui ergo privare nituntur successores sancti Augustini potestate et dignitate quam ipsi Augustino concessit beatus Gregorius, privent si audent successores beati Petri potestate et dignitate quam ipsi Petro concessit sanctus et iustus dominus. Eodem enim modo quo Dominus locutus est aliis in apostolo suo Petro, locutus est Gregorius successoribus eius in discipulo suo Augustino.*) Compare also the threat made by the monks of Canterbury in the late twelfth century, that they would appeal to a higher tribunal if the pope gave judgement against them. See *Chronicles and Memorials of the Reign of Richard I*, ed. Stubbs, *RS*, ii, p. 63.
[4] This was Anselm's threat in *Ep.* 451 (iii, 152). See below, p. 343.

behind the primatial claims of Canterbury – indeed, behind all the claims to special rights and privileges which dogged the history of the Church for the next hundred years and more. It was the duty of the community to prod their prelate into action if necessary; it was his duty to share their determination. Anselm associated himself with their point of view whole-heartedly, though the community felt that he never did quite enough.

The primatial claim was the richest and rarest of the gifts of which the monks of Canterbury believed themselves to be the custodians. As befitted such a gift it represented a rich accumulation of the past from several sources. In the first place, the church of Canterbury inherited the pretensions of the Anglo-Saxon kings to a quasi-imperial authority over Britain and the adjacent islands. At the level of secular government, the Normans abandoned these grandiose pretensions, and relied simply on military conquest and settlement for the extension of the English kingdom. But the church of Canterbury had deeper roots, both in the kingdom of God and in the kingdom of England. It did not imitate the variability of the secular rulers who thought only of temporal gain. The claims of the monastic community were rooted in the kingdom of God. They were also rooted in the past and in the nature of things – in the past, through the gifts of land, relics, and rights which they had received at various times; in the nature of things through the physical separation of the British Isles from the rest of the world as an *alter orbis*.[5] Urban II himself paid homage to this point of view when he introduced Anselm to the Curia as 'one who is almost our equal, being as it were Pope and Patriarch of the *alter orbis*'.[6]

The tradition of an imperial unity of the British Isles was supported by statements in charters of pre-Conquest kings, in which the kings called themselves with varying degrees of circumlocution 'emperors of this British world'. There were ancient papal letters too, preserved by Bede, which granted the archbishop (in language less clear than later ages thought desirable, but still in words sufficient for men of good will) an ecclesiastical authority over the wide territories of the British Isles.[7]

There were several contemporary examples of similar patriarchal claims by the archbishops of Hamburg, Lyons, and Milan; Lanfranc may have been inspired by these examples when he

---

[5] On this, see C. Erdmann, *Forschungen zur politischen Ideenwelt des Frühmittelalters*, Berlin, 1951, pp. 8–11, 38–43.
[6] *VA* II, xxix and p. 105n.
[7] See Bede, *Hist. Eccl.* Bk. II, cc. viii, xviii.

vigorously supported the Canterbury claim to patriarchal authority over the whole of the British Isles. Such patriarchates represented a great design of Church government, which the Hildebrandine popes aimed at replacing with a centralized authority. But whatever else Anselm may have learnt from Hugh of Lyons, he did not learn to accept this extension of papal sovereignty at the expense of the church for which he was himself responsible. As archbishop, he accepted responsibility for spreading and enforcing Latin doctrine and Benedictine monastic discipline throughout the *alter orbis* of Britain. Lanfranc had seen this as his office, and Anselm saw it with even greater intensity. For both of them, the ecclesiastical primacy of Canterbury, in association with the extension of the kingdom of England, offered the hope of a permanent and disciplined future for the whole area of England, Scotland, Wales, and Ireland. In 1070, and even in 1093, the threat of an independent Scandinavian pagan kingdom in northern England was by no means dead. Fifty years later, everything looked different, but this was the situation which Lanfranc faced, and which Anselm inherited, and it is important to recognize that in these circumstances the primacy represented a practical instrument of unity.[8]

We shall later examine the documentary basis of their primatial claim. But for the present it will suffice to say that on this matter Lanfranc, no less than Anselm, would seem to have been content to rely on the tradition of the Canterbury monks, supported by documents which gave historical support to the testimony of the living word.[9] On this basis, it was Anselm's most consistent aim as archbishop to preserve and extend the primatial authority of Canterbury. In this matter, as on others where truth and justice

[8] For the threat of a separate Scandinavian kingdom north of the Humber in William I's reign, see F. M. Stenton, 'York in the eleventh century', *York Minster Historical Tracts*, 8, 1927. The report in *Hugh the Chanter*, p. 3, that in 1070 Lanfranc had urged Canterbury's primacy as a way of frustrating any attempt by a future Dane, Norwegian, or Scot to set up an independent kingdom of York with a king crowned by the archbishop of York, is probably mythical. But there was a real possibility of a separate Scandinavian kingdom of the North until the end of the century.

[9] For fuller details see below, pp. 352–64. A preference for the spoken testimony of living witnesses over the written word was not confined to monastic communities: it was also a principle of the schools. For example, Robert of Melun, referring to his own masters, Abelard and Hugh of St Victor, says that he had received their doctrine, *tanto fidelius tantoque verius* from their own mouths, and that this was preferable to receiving it from their writings, which were only an imperfect reflection of their intention: *Quid enim scriptura aliud est quam quaedam imago et obscura figura voluntatis ipsius scriptoris?* See *Oeuvres de Robert de Melun*, iii, *Sententiae*, (*Spicilegium sacrum Lovaniense: Études et Documents*, fasc. 21) ed. R. M. Martin, Louvain, 1947, p. 47.

were concerned, he knew no moderation. In such matters, moderation was only another name for sin. It may seem to modern eyes a very lop-sided assessment of his position that the primacy, together with the lands and other rights of Canterbury, should occupy so prominent place in his thoughts. But the eternal and temporal worlds met in the maintenance of rights given to the saints and committed to his guardianship. In this matter, as in that of monastic vows, there could be no compromise; and we must first understand what he wanted before we can judge the importance and practicability of his primatial claim.

II   THE PRIVILEGES OF PRIMACY

The privileges of primacy were three: first, the possession of permanent papal legatine authority in England; second, ecclesiastical jurisdiction over the whole of the British Isles; and third, the right to hold Councils and summon to meetings participants from this whole area. Anselm was concerned with all these aspects of primacy from the very beginning, and he held on tenaciously to them all so long as he lived. Indeed, if the test of statesmanship is the pursuit of a grand design for government, the primacy provides his only claim to this title. His activity on all three areas of primacy never faltered: we shall consider each of them in turn.

I   Legatine authority

As archbishop, Anselm claimed to be the pope's permanent legate in Britain. The claim seems to have been of recent origin, and it is not quite clear on what it was based apart from the general principle of primacy. Nevertheless, Anselm believed it to be well founded, and he certainly went further than Lanfranc, and was stiffer than Rufus and Henry I, in refusing to acknowledge any papal legate other than himself in England.

I have already mentioned Anselm's firm refusal to confer about the discipline of the English Church with the papal legate who brought his pallium. On that occasion he had a special reason – though an odd one – for his refusal: he was fully occupied with the duty of defence which had been entrusted to him by the king. Nevertheless, he also clearly implied that it was none of the legate's business. Beyond the immediate circumstances of this case, Anselm rejected, so far as England was concerned, the recent papal

335

practice of entrusting to specially appointed legates large areas within which they had authority over all archbishops and bishops. Archbishop Hugh of Lyons was the outstanding advocate and example of this policy in the last quarter of the eleventh century, and whatever influence he may have had on Anselm's later political vocabulary, he had none at all in this matter. Anselm continued to the end to be immovable in his opposition to papal legates in England. He had not come to Canterbury to dissipate the rights of his church. He made this clear in 1099, when he explained to the pope his objection to the sending of papal legates to any part of the kingdom of England:

I spoke to the pope about the Roman legation over the kingdom of England, which the men of this realm say has been held from ancient times until our own time by the church of Canterbury; and I showed him that it ought necessarily so to be, and could not be otherwise without damage to the Roman and English Church.[10]

In speaking of something being *necessarily* so and not otherwise, Anselm was using the language of his theological speculations, and he did not use the phrase lightly. In a practical context, there can be no doubt what it meant: it meant that the matter was not open to negotiation or alteration by any authority on earth.

This view did not commend itself to the pope. Following the model of the appointment of Hugh of Lyons as permanent papal legate in France, one of Paschal II's first acts as pope was to appoint Guy, archbishop of Vienne, as permanent papal legate in England. Eadmer reports that he visited England in this capacity in 1100 or 1101, but that no one received him. Whether this visit took place after Anselm's return to England in September 1100 is unclear, but Anselm left the pope in no doubt about his view of the matter, and the pope promised to send no legate with authority over Canterbury *during Anselm's lifetime*; but it is clear that he did not, and could not, accept the Canterbury claim made by Anselm, that he should never appoint a legate in England other than the archbishop himself.[11] Yet this remained Anselm's claim to the end, though it is clear that Anselm based his case, not on any documentary evidence, but on the consensus of the community of which he was the head.

[10] *Ep.* 214 (iv, 2), written to Paschal II in 1101, describing his words to Urban II in 1099.
[11] *HN*, p. 126; *Ep.* 222 (iii, 44). For the date of Guy of Vienne's visit, see Brett, 1975, pp. 35–6; and *Councils*, i, 655. The position of this visit in Eadmer's narrative suggests a date between 11 November 1100 (the date of the king's marriage) and Easter 1101.

2   *Territorial extension*

It was not only on the question of legatine authority that Anselm went further, and was more explicit, than Lanfranc. In extending the territorial limits of Canterbury's jurisdiction, he also made a notable advance. This was partly accidental: he became archbishop at a time when the expansive energies of the Norman conquerors were beginning to make an impression in Scotland, in Wales, and – very tentatively – in Ireland. The way for ecclesiastical expansion was prepared by conquest or marriage, and we must admire the consistency of effort with which, despite his other distractions, Anselm took advantage of the situation to press forward the authority of Canterbury in all areas. We shall consider each of them in the chronological order in which they came to Anselm's attention.

WALES

The first opportunity for exercising primatial authority in Wales had arisen during the vacancy at Canterbury shortly before Anselm became archbishop. It arose from the recent conquest of the northern coastal area as far as Anglesey by his friend Hugh, earl of Chester. To give ecclesiastical expression to this conquest, a˙ bishopric was established at Bangor in 1092. Hervey, a Breton, was appointed bishop, the first of a long series of members of the English royal court to be provided with a Welsh see: he was also the first bishop in Wales to come under the authority of an English archbishop. Since Canterbury was still vacant, he was consecrated by the archbishop of York, but this was an accident: all his successors came under Canterbury.

There were two other bishops in Wales at this time, at Llandaff and St Davids: both of them were Welshmen, and both adhered to the customs of the Celtic Church. One of Anselm's first actions during his first year as archbishop was to suspend them both.[12] This was the first time that an archbishop of Canterbury had taken disciplinary action against a Welsh bishop. The bishop of St Davids quickly made peace with Anselm and was restored. Thereafter Anselm gave him such aid as he could against the despoilers of his see among the Norman barons who had recently penetrated into southern Wales as far as Pembroke. Chief among

---

[12] *Ep.* 175 (iii, 23); *HN*, p. 72.

these was Arnulf of Montgomery, another friend of Anselm, and one of his earliest devotees after his death.[13] He may have been prepared to accept from Anselm a call for restraint which he would have taken from no one else.

The Welsh bishop of Llandaff seems never to have submitted, and it was not until 1107 that Anselm was able to consecrate a bishop thoroughly devoted to the interests of Canterbury. By the time of Anselm's death, therefore, the whole Church of Wales, which had never before been subject to Canterbury, was completely subordinated to the English primate. This was the most lasting expansion of the authority of Canterbury before the seventeenth century. Essentially, the position which Anselm established lasted till 1920, despite the heroic struggle of Gerald of Wales in the early thirteenth century to establish an archbishopric at St Davids.

IRELAND

Ireland was the next area in which Anselm took steps to establish the authority of Canterbury. Here he was following a precedent created by Lanfranc, who had already consecrated bishops of Dublin in 1074 and 1085. Anselm had no difficulty in consecrating their successor in 1096. What is remarkable about Ireland at this time is the lack of resistance to the authority of Canterbury: as a result, Anselm was able without controversy to extend the area within which the authority of Canterbury was effective. He was no less prompt here than he had been in Wales. Lanfranc's authority over the Irish Church had been confined to Dublin, but shortly after his consecration Anselm wrote generally to all the bishops in Ireland urging them to establish canonical discipline, concluding with the words:

If any question arises among you concerning episcopal consecrations or any other ecclesiastical business, or matters relating to our holy faith, which you cannot determine canonically, we urge you in the bonds of charity to bring it to our notice, so that you may receive counsel and comfort from us, and not fall under judgement as perverting the commandments of God.[14]

This is the gentlest of expressions of authority, but it could scarcely be firmer; and it fell on willing ears. Anselm had powerful friends in Ireland, and during his lifetime the ecclesiastical future of the country seemed to lie in his hands. In 1096, when everything in England was going badly with him, he consecrated two bishops, for

---

[13] *VA* II, lxix, and n.   [14] *Ep.* 198 (iv, 116).

Dublin and Waterford. The latter was the first Irish bishop outside Dublin to make profession of obedience to Canterbury; and Murchertach, the High King whose daughter married Anselm's friend Arnulf of Montgomery, promoted the extension of Canterbury's authority. To the bishops of Dublin and Waterford (and later of Limerick), Anselm wrote as a superior who could, when circumstances required, enforce his authority with discipline.[15]

For the moment everything seemed calm, but under the surface the whole situation was very unstable. Norse, Irish, and Norman elements were all competing for an advantage, and the future of the Canterbury claims, which seemed so bright in Anselm's lifetime, depended too much on obscure cross-currents of political ambition to be assured. Within half a century of Anselm's death the only traces of the once-active policy were to be found in the ecclesiastical calendar used by the church of Dublin, which had many peculiarities of Canterbury origin. The primacy had vanished with the setting up of four archbishoprics directly dependent on the pope. This development is one of many indications that the main obstacle to the Canterbury primacy was the growth of a unified legal and administrative system centred on Rome. All the evidence shows that Anselm would have resisted this development with all his power as an attack on the rights of Canterbury.

NORTHERN ENGLAND AND SCOTLAND

In Wales and Ireland, Anselm's claims met with no real opposition because there was, as yet, no rival organization to challenge them. The situation was very different on the northern frontier. Scotland, which he also claimed as part of his sphere of primatial authority, was cut off by the barrier of the province of York. The Scottish bishops of this period were normally consecrated by the archbishop of York, and there was no protest against this practice until 1120, when Anselm's disciple Eadmer, having received the bishopric of St Andrews, attempted to insist that he should be consecrated at

---

[15] *Epp.* 277 (iii, 27), 278 (iii, 72), 427 (iii, 142), 429 (iii, 143), 435 (iii, 147). For the relations between Canterbury and the Irish Church in the late eleventh and early twelfth century, see Aubrey Gwynn, 'The origins of the See of Dublin', *Irish Ecclesiastical Record*, 57, 1941, pp. 40– 55, 97–112; 'Lanfranc and the Irish Church', ibid. pp. 481–500; 58, 1941, 1–15; 'St. Anselm and the Irish Church', ibid. 59, 1942, pp. 1–14; 'The origins of the See of Waterford', ibid. pp. 289–96; 'Bishop Samuel of Dublin', ibid. 60, 1942, pp. 81–8. Fr. Gwynn, however, does not seem to me to attach enough weight to the consistency of the Canterbury claims under Lanfranc and Anselm.

Canterbury. That this was an ill-advised step is very clear to us, but Eadmer was only pressing a claim which he believed to be inherent in the original jurisdiction of Canterbury. Indeed, if the Canterbury claims were as well founded as Anselm believed, anything less than a general authority over the whole British Isles would have done a violence to the early history of the see as it was understood at Canterbury, and to the large geographical and historical conceptions which lay behind these claims.[16]

III   THE STRUGGLE WITH YORK

In order to exercise this authority, however, it was first necessary to settle the dispute with York, and it was on his handling of this issue that Anselm's reputation with the monks of Canterbury chiefly depended: they later compared him with Lanfranc to his disadvantage. The conventional view, then as now, was that Lanfranc had carried all before him in asserting the rights of Canterbury. Above all, in 1072 he had publicly defeated the archbishop of York, and obliged him to make a profession of obedience to Canterbury. By contrast Anselm appeared to have achieved nothing. This judgement was, and is, mistaken. It exaggerated the extent of Lanfranc's victory, and blamed Anselm for a failure which was inherent in the situation which he inherited.

Lanfranc's personal success in 1072 contained and concealed the roots of a permanent failure. In the first place, although he succeeded in getting an oath of obedience from Archbishop Thomas of York, Thomas could not bind his successors. Only a papal confirmation of the position as established in 1072 could have provided the basis for a permanent primatial authority. The limits of Lanfranc's success became apparent as soon as Anselm became archbishop. At his consecration by the archbishop of York, a dispute broke out about his title: was he to be consecrated as *Metropolitan* or as *Primate*?[17] For the moment it was immaterial;

---

[16] See Lanfranc's *Ep.* 47 (Gibson, 1979, p. 152), for an explicit claim that *totam hanc quam vocant Britannicam insulam unam unius nostrae ecclesiae constat esse parrochiam.* The whole letter contains a clear and well-documented account of the jurisdictional meaning of the primacy.

[17] Eadmer (*HN*, p. 42) says that the phrase in the consecration service which Archbishop Thomas objected to was *totius Britanniae metropolitana*, and that the phrase which he found acceptable was *totius Britanniae primas*; but it is hard to believe this, since the latter phrase is the one that the archbishops of Canterbury had consistently used, and the archbishops of York consistently objected to; and it is not easy to see

but it was symptomatic of the difficulties which would face the claims of Canterbury when they were opposed, not only by the canons and archbishops of York, but by the papal Curia, and – during Anselm's lifetime – also by the king.

Several years passed before the claim to authority over the archbishop of York was put to the test. Even when Archbishop Thomas died, he was succeeded by a new archbishop, Gerard, who was already bishop of Hereford, and as such had taken an oath of obedience to Anselm. So, while Gerard lived – and he did not die till 1108 – Anselm could believe that Gerard as archbishop was still bound by his oath of obedience as bishop. In these circumstances, a less dedicated man than Anselm would have let the matter rest, and hoped to end his days in peace. But Anselm never stopped trying to get an explicit recognition of Canterbury's claim from the pope. No messenger of his ever went to Rome in the early years of Henry I's reign without pressing for a papal confirmation of Canterbury's primacy. If the main business was investiture and homage, a subsidiary theme was the primacy. Indeed, in making this distinction between major and minor issues, we are conceding too much to the modern point of view. The issues appeared in different proportions at Rome and at Canterbury, but no one was inclined to minimize the importance of the Canterbury claim – and rightly, for the concession of a primacy such as Lanfranc and Anselm desired would have altered the future government of the medieval Church more than any concessions in the matter of investitures. With every inducement to satisfy Anselm – and Anselm did not hesitate to urge his sufferings on behalf of the papacy as a reason for conceding the claims of Canterbury – Paschal II was careful to concede nothing of lasting importance.

Anselm never stopped trying. Paschal II, who was slowly giving way on the question of homage, which Anselm looked on as settled,

how *primas* could be thought less objectionable than *metropolitana*. According to the York writer (see *Hugh the Chanter*, p. 8), the word objected to by York was *primas*, and the title which was finally agreed to and used in the service was *metropolitana Cantuariensis*. This would be acceptable to the archbishop of York, for he too was a metropolitan, and the title *metropolitana Cantuariensis* implied no superiority of Canterbury over York. It might just be acceptable to the monks of Canterbury because, for them, the metropolitan position of Canterbury included primatial authority over York. On several grounds therefore the account of the York writer is more likely to be correct. We have no means of knowing what Anselm thought on this occasion, for Eadmer reports that he took no part in the discussion. Certainly, in all his later words and actions, Anselm never ceased to express his conviction that he had primatial authority over York.

sweetened the pill by piecemeal concessions on the primacy. In April 1102, he confirmed the primacy personally to Anselm as his predecessors had held it. In November 1102, he explicitly ordered Gerard of York to swear obedience to Anselm. In November 1103, he extended this obedience to all future archbishops.[18] Here at last, as Anselm thought, was the long-desired breakthrough into an assured future. Anselm sent the letter to Canterbury at once for safe-keeping. But, alas, it was a chimera. Paschal's grant of 1103 certainly extended the primacy to Anselm's successors, but only so far as it had been 'enjoyed by Anselm's predecessors'. And, since the whole dispute was about what primacy, if any, these predecessors had enjoyed, the real issue was left – and was certainly intended by the pope to be left – wide open. If Anselm with so many claims to respect could not do better than this, there could be no hope except in forgery: this was to be the next step. But not in Anselm's lifetime.[19]

The privilege which Anselm had extracted from the pope in 1103, despite its inadequacy, was the high watermark in the Canterbury claim to primacy. It represented the only advance ever made towards perpetuity. In this it surpassed all that Lanfranc had been able to achieve even at the height of his influence in 1072. No other genuine document exists, nor (so far as the Canterbury monks could establish) ever had existed, which granted the primacy to the whole succession of archbishops. But it still remained to be determined what, if anything, it meant.

The current of informed opinion was now running ever more strongly against Lanfranc's conception of a British patriarchate. Anselm however never ceased to express himself in word and deed increasingly strongly in its favour: he persisted also in the Canterbury claim that the archbishop should be the pope's legate in England in perpetuity. In this too he failed: all he could get was a promise that no legate should come to England during his own lifetime.[20] He continued to urge Canterbury's supremacy over York, and in the general settlement of 1107, Archbishop Gerard promised at last to show him the same obedience as archbishop as he had owed as bishop of Hereford.[21] This promise, however, was expressed in no document; it had the character of an informal arrangement which had no binding force on the future; it was useless.

---

[18] For these papal letters, see *Epp*. 222 (iii, 44), 283 (iii, 131), 303 (iii, 169), 304.
[19] See below, pp. 352–63.   [20] *Ep*. 222 (iii, 44).   [21] *HN*, p. 187.

In all these arrangements, it is clear that the aim of everyone from the pope downwards was to keep Anselm happy during his lifetime, while retaining the power to make new arrangements for the more distant future after his death. The pope, the chapter at York, and (more reluctantly) the archbishop of York, were determined to defeat the Canterbury claim to which Anselm was committed. The king, anxious to pay Anselm back for disobliging him on investitures, was also determined to frustrate him. But Anselm still persisted, and the real test was bound to come when Archbishop Gerard died.

Gerard died on 21 May 1108. Within a week the king had nominated as his successor a member of one of the greatest royal administrative families in England, Thomas II, a nephew of the Thomas who had consecrated Anselm. Anselm made no objection either to the person appointed or to the manner of his appointment. But he exerted all his powers to bring Thomas to submit to Canterbury's primatial authority. The correspondence of Anselm's last year is filled with the subject, and no one can mistake the intensity of his feeling on the matter. He wrote to the pope, begging him not to send Thomas his pallium until he had sworn obedience to Canterbury, for if he once possessed his pallium, he would never make his submission. Foreseeing this, Anselm wrote in great agitation:

If this should happen, you may know that the Church of England will be torn asunder and brought to desolation – according to the word of the Lord that every kingdom divided against itself will be made desolate – and the vigour of the apostolic discipline will in no small measure be weakened. As for myself, I could on no account remain in England, for I neither ought to, nor can suffer the primacy of our Church to be destroyed in my lifetime.[22]

This shows that Anselm was quite as ready to face exile for the primacy as he had been for obedience to the pope. Indeed, they were both part of the same system, and they could not be separated. He saw the primacy as an essential part of 'apostolic discipline', that is to say, of the papal government of the Church. In method at least, there is here a complete identity between his theology and practical thinking: the supremacy of the ruler, whether of God in the universe, or the pope in the Church, implied the existence of order in all the details of the system. Strange as it may now seem, the primacy of Canterbury seemed to him an immovable feature which

[22] *Ep.* 451 (iii, 152).

343

guaranteed the firmness of the whole structure. He maintained this attitude to the end. In his last letter before his death, writing as *Anselmus archiepiscopus Cantuariensis et totius Britanniae primas*, with the full dignity of the primacy of all Britain, speaking on behalf of God himself (*loquens ex parte ipsius Dei*), he suspended Thomas from his priestly office until he renounced his rebellion against the church of Canterbury. A copy of this was sent to every bishop in England.[23]

Anselm died before Thomas's obedience was secured. After Anselm's death, this obedience was easily secured by the traditional combination of king and bishops. It must, indeed, have been clear to everyone that the claims of Canterbury could only be successful if they had the support of the king and the English bishops. This combination had been irresistible in 1072; it again proved its value in 1109 after Anselm's death. Under Rufus, the alliance of king and archbishop had been broken because the king was unmanageable; under Henry, it broke down because of Anselm's loyalty to the papal decree of 1099.

As the York writer noted, the king did not love Anselm after he had thwarted him in the matter of investitures. Henceforth he supported York until Anselm's death brought him back to his father's policy of supporting the unity of the Church under the southern see. By this time, however, it was too late to alter the general swing away from overlordships such as that claimed by Canterbury. If anything permanent were to be achieved, it should have been done under Rufus. Probably even by that time the whole policy was out of date; but it did not seem so to the monks of Canterbury, nor to Anselm himself.

The vision of a monastic cathedral of Canterbury with primatial authority over the whole of the British Isles, which had inspired Lanfranc, Anselm, and the community of Christ Church during these years, came to nothing. It broke up within a few years of Anselm's death under the impact of forces which were too strong for it. It is therefore easy to ignore Anselm's passionate fight for its success: but it is important for understanding the things he cared about. He believed in a monastically orientated Church, in which monastic communities served as centres of devotion and offered the hope of Redemption to a surrounding population of benefactors,

---

[23] *Epp.* 471, 472 (iii, 155).

friends and well-wishers of all ranks of society. He believed also that the monastic community at Canterbury with a primatial archbishop at its head was the source of order throughout the whole huge area of the archbishop's primatial authority; he thought too that this was part of an unchanging order of things, which should not be made the subject of political bargaining either with the pope or the king. In its way, it was a very practical ideal; but it was not an ideal with a future in western Europe.

The future lay with minds of a different type – minds which saw that government was a matter of administration, and not an attempt to reproduce on earth a pattern of things laid up in Heaven. Anselm aimed at the latter. Among Anselm's contemporary bishops, Samson, the aged bishop of Worcester, represented the former. He was of noble Norman birth, had studied at the school of Liège, and had been a clerk of William I in Lanfranc's time. He had seen the whole dispute between Canterbury and York from the beginning. Thomas I, archbishop of York from 1070 to 1100, was his brother; Thomas II, who became archbishop of York in 1108, was his son; and another son was bishop of Bayeux. Altogether, in his connections and his habits of thought, he was a bishop of the old school, of the time when secular and ecclesiastical affairs were totally intertwined. But he had the mind of an administrator.

Anselm evidently trusted him, and shortly before his death, he asked Samson's advice about the rights of Canterbury. Samson replied: 'If I truly knew what would be best both for you and us, I should not hesitate to tell you. But this I may say, that it seems unworthy of you that you should be too angry over this affair.'[24]

These few words of Bishop Samson make the whole affair a matter of business-like common sense, more in keeping with the way in which government was developing than with Anselm's grand and simple principles. Samson was the loyal suffragan of Canterbury, but he also expressed the views of the more secularly minded towards the dispute as a whole: it were well that York should submit, but it was undignified for the archbishop of Canterbury to urge his case with such unlimited fervour. Samson was a man of worldly tastes and habits: he was well connected, well educated, generous and rich. He was everything that the Hildebrandine Church abhorred, but he had virtues which won him the

[24] *Ep.* 465 (iv, 97).

warm friendship of Marbod, the talented bishop of Rennes, and of the greatest canonist of his day, Ivo of Chartres. His principles may have been those of the past, but his virtues were those of the new governments of Europe: common sense, ability, efficiency. They were not the virtues of the cloister. He probably had little understanding of the intensity of feeling about their rights and dignity which the communal life of the ancient monasteries engendered, and which Anselm shared. Indeed it requires a strong effort of historical imagination to understand this intensity.

Anselm carried into politics his search for an eternal order of truth and justice, unshakeable and subject to no alteration. Rights and properties going back to a remote and undocumented past appeared to him to have a sanction which no later enactment – not even by the pope – could alter. The eternal order which reflected the unchanging nature of God, and which found expression in the manner of God's Redemption of the world, was also expressed in the traditions of individual churches down to the smallest details. This is the lesson of the primatial dispute; and this is why Anselm was as intransigeant on this issue as on issues involving monastic vows: they were all reflections of an eternal order, unalterable.

Not far behind this overall vision of justice came his anxious consideration that the particular saints of each church, for whom the present community was only the trustee, would demand from their trustees a full account of their stewardship down to the most minute particulars. That which had once been given could never, without injustice and danger to souls, be alienated. Anselm himself remembered from his youth, and in old age told his companions, a story of a Roman judge in the time of Pope Leo IX, who was condemned to eternal punishment because he had incurred the hostility of saints Agnes and Laurence by depriving their churches in Rome of a garden and three houses respectively. The judge was only saved from this punishment by the intervention of St Praeiectus, whom he had honoured in his lifetime. Anselm and his companions took the story quite literally. With all his theological subtlety and insight into human behaviour he accepted the common views of the time in attributing to the saints in Heaven a concern for their worldly rights which, if they had not been part of an eternal order of the universe, would have disgraced a schoolboy.[25]

---

[25] For Anselm's story, see *Memorials*, pp. 249–53.

The grand vision of the position of Canterbury was reinforced by anxieties such as these. It was remembered long after Anselm's death that he had professed himself afraid to die, and to appear in the sight of God, until he had punished the archbishop of York for infringement of the jurisdiction of Canterbury.[26]

This attitude was kept alive by the strong sense of the permanence of human arrangements in the matter of property, which seems to us of all things the least permanent: gifts to the Church were made to last till the Day of Judgement, and many of the documents in the Canterbury archives invoked God and all his saints on the Day of Judgement to destroy those who violated their provisions. Such phrases were taken seriously. No clear distinction was made between the temporal and spiritual privileges of the Church; they all stood on the same level, enforced by the same sanctions, guaranteed by the same authority, reflecting the same divine ordering of the world. It was a world in which individual freedom in this world's affairs meant little; corporate continuance came before everything else. The ancient communities, at every level of their being, and in their virtues as well as their vices, were implacable custodians of what they imagined to be their rights. They remained so throughout their existence – the force of history and tradition was too strong to be resisted – but they gradually lost the sympathy of the world, which placed a higher value on convenience and common sense than on permanence and imposs-ible loyalties. It is this new spirit that Samson represents, while Anselm in this matter represents the old with an unparalleled intensity of conviction.

IV PRIMACY IN ACTION

So far we have considered primacy either as a manifestation of corporate tradition, or as a factor in Anselm's relations with the pope, the archbishop of York, and other interested parties who might for one reason or another support or oppose Anselm's claims. But there is another aspect of the primacy which has so far been only briefly mentioned. This is its function as part of the pastoral care attached to Anselm's office. Gregory's *Pastoral Care* said nothing about this aspect of a bishop's work for the good reason that jurisdictions such as that claimed by Canterbury did not exist in his

---

[26] John of Salisbury, *Vita Anselmi, PL* 199, col. 1,035; Biffi, 1988, p. 106. This is one of the few details in John of Salisbury's work which is not found in Eadmer.

day. But Anselm would have found much in Lanfranc's letters and practice to guide him. Quite apart from Lanfranc's example, the commonest of all images of authority, whether of the abbot with his monks, or the master with his pupils, or the king with his witan or barons, displayed the seated ruler presiding over them, dispensing justice and declaring doctrine. There is no reason to think that Anselm would have thought there was any contradiction between personal humility and the display of the greatness of his office: quite the contrary, humility and grandeur met in the exercise of his function as a ruler.

As we have seen, it was not until 1102 that he had the possibility of holding a council; but when the opportunity at last arrived, he applied all his talents and energies to the task. Acting in conjunction with the king so far as the details of the meeting were concerned, he prepared everything with great care. He made sure that lay magnates would be present, 'so that [as he wrote] whatever is decreed by the authority of the Council, shall be firmly supported by the joint care and solicitude of both clergy and laity'. But with regard to the substance of the decrees, he had no doubt that this was his responsibility. He wrote the decrees himself in advance, it would seem, of any discussion. Discussion might modify the details, or at most suggest new items, but the leadership was his.

His letters contain the clearest indication of his procedure and intentions. Writing to the archbishop of York after the Council, he told him he could send only the 'headings' (the *Capitula*) of the decrees because he did not wish to circulate the fuller texts until they had been approved by those who were present. Then, as a final step, he sent them to the pope for confirmation. Deliberation and determination are apparent in every step, and not least in his letters to bishops who wished to have discretion in relaxing some of the severity of the decrees. To those who wished to have this discretion, his message was always the same:

There must be no remission; we must carry the laity with us in the matters we have jointly agreed; if you are left without priests who are capable under the new regulations of saying Mass or of carrying the sacrament to the dying, or of hearing confession, you must use carefully selected monks, or (when permissible) clergy in lower orders; if we stand firm, we shall soon succeed.[27]

---

[27] For Anselm's 'message' to bishops who wished to soften the impact of the decrees, see Anselm's *Ep.* 254 (iv, 113) to Herbert, bishop of Thetford; to which may be added similar words in *Epp.* 256 (iv, 16) to the archbishop of York, and 257 (iii, 62) to the archdeacon of Canterbury. The relevant extracts for the Council of 1102, from *HN* and Anselm's letters, as well as related texts have been splendidly edited in *Councils,*

It is quite clear from several sources that general opinion among the bishops was in favour of relaxations for 'reasonable' causes, but Anselm resisted every appeal for moderation: for him no relaxation could be 'reasonable'.

So far as determination, careful preparation and foresight, as well as confidence of success and leadership, could go, Anselm provided all that was possible. Yet we can scarcely doubt that, in its practical effect, the Council of 1102 was a complete failure. Its decrees sank immediately into oblivion. There were several reasons for this lack of success. In the first place, the decrees were both numerous and varied in content, and it would have been extraordinarily difficult to supervise their implementation. But, more important, it is clear that on the most important matter of clerical celibacy, there was no body of support to justify Anselm's optimism about a rapid victory. Anselm was determined to make the clearest possible break with past practice: henceforth no priest or deacon was to be allowed, on any pretext whatsoever, to have a wife and continue to carry out his duties, and he had prepared an elaborate series of provisional arrangements to cope with the shortage of qualified priests under the new regulations. But when we remember that at least one bishop, Roger, bishop of Salisbury, was a married man, we can judge the likelihood of support in that diocese.

Anselm was prepared to insist on enforcement without qualification; but quite apart from Bishop Roger's case, it was most unlikely that he would have, or could have, the co-operation of the bishops in this. In the face of this major obstacle, the miscellany of other decrees – no archdeaconries to be farmed out, no priests to attend drinking-parties, no benefices to be sold, no monks to be godfathers, male hair-cuts to leave ears visible, sodomites to be excommunicated, etc. – could not have had much attention paid to them. In brief, it would seem that Anselm, like many reformers, had not reckoned with the solid weight of inertia on most matters, and positive dissent on others. He thought that by involving as many as possible in the formal decision-making, he was ensuring their support; but he forgot that his pleasure in obedience had been

---

1981, pp. 672–88. The meaning of *Capitula* in contrast to *expositiones* in Anselm's *Ep.* 253 (iv, 15), is elucidated by reference to Gregory VII's Council of 1078 (*Gregorii VII Registrum*, pp. 401–6), where the summaries (called *Capitula*) and the full texts are given separately. It is not quite clear whether the fuller texts which Anselm promised were ever written: several of the decrees seem to be preserved, and perhaps only ever existed, in the form of *capitula*. The confirmation by the pope is mentioned in *HN*, p. 141.

learnt the hard way of monastic conversion, and it was not shared by many – not even, when it came to the push, at Bec – much less in the world.

Anselm can scarcely have digested the lessons of this failure when he once more found himself unexpectedly in exile. His great Council had been held at Michaelmas 1102; by April of the following year he was once more abroad expecting a speedy return, but, as we have seen, he did not return until the end of 1106. By that date, he was an ailing man, and apart from his routine duties, his first tasks were to clear up the muddles of the last few years and re-establish an acceptable procedure for future episcopal elections, investitures, and acts of homage. There were no longer any grave differences of principle between him and the king, but there must have been many routine tasks after so long an absence, and these seem to have occupied the greater part of 1107.

When at last he could return to the plans he had left incomplete in 1102, he seems to have recognized that he had attempted too much. He held another Council in May 1108 on the same model as the last, with a similar representation of lay magnates, but on this occasion he concentrated entirely on the administrative problems arising from his earlier decree against clerical marriage. To judge from the very wide circulation of the decisions on these details, in contrast to the almost total lack of circulation of the earlier decrees, this concentration of effort was the right policy; but it took at least another two generations before the aim, which Anselm in 1102 had been confident could quickly be reached, was achieved.

It is no part of the intention of this survey to write the history of clerical celibacy. We are concerned only with the additional light which this part of Anselm's thought and action throws on the man himself, and here a number of features deserve attention. In the first place it is noticeable that the great theme of his two Councils was the same as that of the Roman Council of 1059, when the first effective legislation on clerical celibacy was initiated: it almost seems as if this subject had matured in his mind since that date; certainly his early *Deploratio virginitatis male amissae* suggests that he may have had cause for thought on this subject. Secondly, we see the noble simplicity of his mind in supposing that what the bishops and lay magnates had by their presence and silent consent accepted would at once be put into operation. Had he not himself acted thus after hearing the papal decree against lay investiture and clerical homage? And thirdly, with all his sympathy with people of every kind, uppermost in all his plans in 1102 was the simple thought that there could be no moderation in obeying God's law, and it would all be easy if people would only believe, and act accordingly. If there was a failure here, it lay in his inability to understand the position of those who, unlike himself and despite their faith, had no clear vision. He thought everything was easy to those who believed; and nothing would persuade him that it was not so. Hence, great pastor, preacher, and luminous expounder of the faith though he was, and moderate though his views were on most matters concerning the relations between the Church and secular society, his most cherished views were all doomed to failure from the start: they neither moved with the times, nor stood firm in the practical conveniences of the past. They reflected an ideal world to which he alone had the key.

I have dealt at length with these tedious and superficially unimportant details because they are the only area of activity in Anselm's years as archbishop in which a clear, persistent, and deeply felt course of action – such as can properly be described as a 'policy' – can be detected; and if we are to understand his mind, we must understand the importance which he attached to this issue. Further, it is necessary to understand the foundation on which he based his belief that the cause was a just one.

With regard to the foundation on which his advocacy of the primacy was based, it can be summed up by saying that he thought it was an integral part of the rights of the church committed to his care, testified to by the living members of the community and the tradition which they inherited. If we ask whether there were ancient documents which showed that the primacy went back to authoritative sources, the answer (as I shall argue later) is that there were documents which gave general support to the claim, sufficient to authenticate the living tradition of the community, but insufficient for use in a court of law. For their authentication, they required the experience of being in the situation in which they were part of the ordered life. This, it may be added, would be true of the Christian faith itself: it had to be accepted in life and faith before it could be argued about. Vast though the distance is which separates such a question as the primacy from the central truths of Christianity, there is a similarity in Anselm's approach to the greater and lesser questions.

351

V WAS CANTERBURY'S CLAIM TO PRIMACY FOUNDED ON
FORGERY?

The question of the 'Lanfranc forgeries' – that is, of the additions
made to nine papal letters addressed to archbishops of Canterbury
in order to provide clear papal authority for Canterbury's primacy –
hangs like a cloud over the primatial disputes of the years from 1072
to 1123; and it is important to seek such certainty as is to be obtained
on this question.[28] In particular, it is important to know as precisely
as possible what evidence satisfied Lanfranc and Anselm in
pursuing a policy which was opposed to papal policy, and to the
most forward-looking thinking on ecclesiastical government of
their time. Lanfranc and Anselm are to be distinguished here.
Lanfranc was an upright and able man, but perhaps not wholly
averse to the manipulations of worldly policy. But Anselm was
something more than this: he was the most rigorous thinker, and
the most severe appraiser of motives of his day; he abominated
worldly power, and – unless we believe his contemporary critics or
modern friends – he sought every excuse to avoid having to exercise
power himself. Yet in the matter of the primacy, which entailed the
most extensive ecclesiastical power in western Europe apart from
that of the papacy, he fought stubbornly from the beginning to the
end of his archiepiscopate against every papal or local obstacle to
the exercise of this power. It was an issue which was never absent: it
marred his day of consecration, and it was the subject of his last
letter. So the simple question whether the primatial claim
depended in any degree on forgery, is important for our assessment
of Lanfranc, but crucial for our assessment of Anselm.

The texts, which are generally agreed to have forged elements in
them, have been examined in detail by several scholars, and there
are only two preliminary remarks which need to be made.

First, no one doubts that papal letters from all the popes to whom
the forgeries are attributed existed at Canterbury in 1070 and much

---

[28] The fundamental study attributing them to Lanfranc and dating them 1070–72, is
Böhmer, 1902. Brooke, 1931, pp. 118– 28, agrees with Böhmer's date but deflects
responsibility from Lanfranc to the monks of Canterbury; Levison, 1946, pp. 199–
204, agrees, but concentrates on important observations about the sources and
methods of forgery; Gibson, 1978, pp. 231–7, also accepts an early date, but attributes
them to the monastic community and sees them as largely motivated by rivalry with St
Augustine's, Canterbury. The main proponents of a date c 1120 are Macdonald, 1926,
Appendix 1, and Southern 1958i.

earlier: they formed part of the quite substantial archival and literary remains which survived the fire of 1067. The only question is whether they existed in 1072 in their original form or in the contaminated form which they had in 1120, when their texts, as we know them, first come to light and are preserved in several copies.

Second, since any forger who makes additions to a genuine document will destroy the original to avoid detection, it must generally be impossible to know precisely the extent of forged elements in otherwise genuine documents. But here we have an unexpected aid: one of the forged Canterbury documents – a letter from Pope John XII to Archbishop Dunstan sending him his pallium – had been copied and had left Canterbury before the illicit addition was made. Consequently, in this one case, we know precisely the extent and aim of the addition, which reads thus:

> We fully confirm to you the primacy which has been exercised by your predecessors on behalf of the apostolic see, as fully as the blessed Augustine and his successors in your Church are known to have exercised it.[29]

Here then we have in a nutshell the substance of the whole primatial claim succinctly summarized; and when we find similar phrases in the documents of Popes Boniface V, Honorius I, Sergius I, and Gregory III, which came to light in 1120, we can say with a very high degree of probability that these sentences contain the main substance of the additions made to the documents in which they appear. The question which remains to be solved is: were these phrases added to existing documents in 1070–72 to support Lanfranc's claim to primacy over the whole area of the British Isles, or were they added as a last resort in 1120, when the claim which Lanfranc, Anselm and Archbishop Ralph had all supported was facing final and irrevocable defeat?

Since this is a controversial subject, on which the weight of scholarly opinion probably still supports Böhmer's thesis that the documents already existed in their contaminated form in 1072, and were used by Lanfranc in this form, it will perhaps help to clarify a complicated issue if I set out as bluntly as possible the reasons which seem to me to point decisively to 1120 as the date at which the forged additions were inserted into the texts.

We must begin by excluding from consideration the falsified privilege of Pope Boniface IV confirming the continuance of the monastic community in the cathedral church of Canterbury, which

---

[29] For the chance survival of the uncontaminated text, see Levison, 1946, p. 201n.

Alexander II quoted in his letter to Lanfranc in 1070. This has been dealt with above, and it stands on a quite different footing from the other forgeries in three important respects: first, it was never mentioned by Lanfranc; second, it was not concerned with the claim to primacy but solely with the survival of the monastic community at Canterbury, and this was never an issue after 1070; and, third, unlike the forgeries with which we are now concerned, it was actually submitted to Rome and approved. So it was a striking example of what was possible.[30]

We are, therefore, solely concerned with nine papal letters contaminated to a greater or lesser extent, predominantly with a view to providing explicit papal authority for the primacy of Canterbury over the whole area of Britain. The essential insertions will be found below, and we shall come to them in due course. Meanwhile, we may go back to the situation in 1072, and begin with some words of Lanfranc which provide the main evidence for the documents which existed at this date.

1   Lanfranc's words in 1072

In 1071, Lanfranc had gone to Rome for his archiepiscopal pallium. He took no documents with him, but he hoped to persuade Pope Alexander II to confirm Canterbury's primacy on general grounds of tradition. But the pope, who two years earlier had confirmed the forged privilege guaranteeing the existence of the monastic community at Canterbury, warily told him to have the matter of the primacy discussed in a provincial council in the presence of a papal legate. This was duly done, and in 1072 Lanfranc wrote an account of the proceedings to the pope, telling him that the whole question of Canterbury's primacy had been ventilated at two Councils, at Windsor and Winchester. He gave the pope an account of the evidence that had been brought forward, giving first place, and by far the greatest amount of space, to the testimony of Bede's *Ecclesiastical History*, which showed that the archbishops of Canterbury, acting on the authority of Pope Gregory I and his successors, had exercised general authority over the whole of the

---

[30] See above, pp. 308–9. Among the papal letters which Lanfranc mentioned in 1072 as the basis of the primatial claim is one of Pope Boniface: but he is here referring to the letter of Boniface V to Justus, Archbishop of Canterbury, of which an extract is quoted below (see p. 361), not to the letter of Boniface IV to King Ethelbert (see above, p. 309), which granted perpetual existence to the monastic community at the cathedral church of Canterbury and had no relevance for the primatial claim.

British Isles during the first hundred and forty years of its existence: they had consecrated bishops for all parts of the country, summoned councils, deposed unworthy bishops, and had been generally responsible for spreading Catholic discipline into Wales and Scotland.

Having recounted this history, Lanfranc mentioned that there were professions of obedience to Canterbury, all testifying to its primatial position. And lastly:

> As a final strength and support of the whole case, privileges and writings of your predecessors, Gregory, Boniface, Honorius, Vitalianus, Sergius, Gregory [III], Leo, and Leo [IX] written to the prelates of the church of Canterbury and the English kings at various times and for various reasons were brought forth.[31]

Here, then, at the end of Lanfranc's account of the proceedings which ratified the Canterbury primacy, is the sentence round which the whole controversy turns. The documents he mentions are those which now have in them the forged primatial passages, and the only question which arises is: were these passages already in them when Lanfranc wrote these words, or were they added later?

The main reason why scholars have thought that the forged passages conferring the primacy were already in the documents in 1072 is that, if they were not there, Lanfranc could not have said that these papal letters were the *ultimum robur* of his whole case. But, in fact, he does not quite say this. He says they are *ultimum quasi robur*. The word *quasi* here can mean anything or nothing. Dr Gibson ignores it and translates: 'as the corner stone of our entire case'; more cautiously, I translate: 'as a final strength'. The ambiguity, as I think, was what Lanfranc intended. We must remember that he had started his active life as a lawyer and as a student of rhetoric, and he is using a common figure of rhetoric, *hyperbole*, within carefully controlled limits. In plain English, he exaggerated a little – but not much. After all, even if the papal documents which he mentioned contained no statements about the primacy, the whole history of the archbishops' powers as described in Bede's *Ecclesiastical History*, which Lanfranc had recalled at length, rested on papal letters conferring the care of the whole

---

[31] *Ultimum quasi robur totiusque causae firmamentum prolata sunt antecessorum vestrorum Gregorii, Bonefacii, Honorii, Vitaliani, Sergii, item Gregorii, Leonis, item ultimi Leonis privilegia et scripta, quae Dorobernensis aecclesiae presulibus Anglorumque regibus aliis atque aliis temporibus variis de causis sunt data aut transmissae.* For the text of Lanfranc's letter, see Gibson, 1979, pp. 48–56.

country on Archbishop Augustine. Even if the surviving letters contained no explicit grant of perpetual primatial power, they were all written in general approval of this situation. Implicitly, if not explicitly, papal letters could with some truth be said to be *ultimum quasi robur* and *firmamentum* of the whole case.

We may agree that this is not wholly satisfactory. But now, look at the matter from the other side, and see how much less satisfactory the alternative explanation is. Supposing that the essential words conferring the primacy on all successive archbishops of Canterbury were in fact in the letters which Lanfranc mentioned, why did he go on at such length about the facts drawn from Bede, when a single quotation from one of the passages granting the primacy in perpetuity to the archbishops of Canterbury would have been worth all the rest of his argument put together? Why did he not quote the decisive passages which they contained? And why, having quoted one or more of these primatial passages, did he not produce them at Rome for confirmation? For this was what he needed, and knew he needed, more than anything.

To this question, the common answer is that he neither quoted the forged additions nor produced them at Rome, because he knew they were forgeries, and knew also that the forgery would be detected at once by a competent critic. But, in this case, we must suppose that he was both immoral and stupid: immoral in producing evidence which he knew to be forged, and stupid in not going further and producing the letters with their forged additions, for he would have known that a similar forgery supporting the monastic community at Canterbury had recently been submitted at Rome, and that it had been accepted and solemnly quoted to him by the pope as genuine.

If therefore the forgeries were in his hands, and he referred to them in his account to the pope without going further and quoting their contents and producing their texts, his conduct shows (to say the least) very muddled thinking on his part. By contrast, if the forged words were *not* in the documents, he could with pardonable exaggeration use the words *ultimum quasi robur*. But it would have been useless to produce the documents in Rome, for they contained no decisive evidence in favour of the primacy. Lanfranc could only hope that the papal Curia would come to recognize the substantial strength of this papally inspired practice of primacy going back to the seventh century. This hope turned out to be mistaken, but this was because of a new feature of the situation which was barely visible in 1072: the Hildebrandine vision of a unified administrative system of government under papal direction was the real enemy of the primacy, as we can see from the history of the next fifty years.

2 The situation between 1072 and 1120

These considerations apply equally to Lanfranc's two successors, Anselm and Ralph. They both spent a great deal of their time and energy maintaining the primatial claims of Canterbury, and neither ever mentioned the papal privileges in support of their claim. So either they knew only the uncontaminated documents, which did nothing to strengthen what they believed to be an already strong case, or they knew the documents in their contaminated form, but knew also that they were forged, and kept quiet about them. In whatever form they existed the documents continued to be known, for they were mentioned to Anselm by Osbern in 1093, and examined in the royal court in 1109 in the presence of at least one bishop who had been present also in 1072.[32]

There is no need to say more here about Anselm's primatial activity: he certainly thought that the evidence was sufficiently strong for him to make a most uncompromising claim to primatial authority over the whole of the British Isles, and it is quite clear that he did not think that the Canterbury claim to this position rested on a series of specific grants by popes after Gregory the Great. It rested on a grant of authority over the whole country by Gregory to the first archbishop, followed by a long history of the exercise of this authority from the seventh century onwards.

This situation emerges even more clearly when we come to Anselm's successor, Archbishop Ralph. He was abroad from 1115 to 1120, always with Eadmer as his constant companion, bitterly upholding, but with ever-diminishing hope of success, his claim to primatial authority over the archbishopric of York. Finally, in October 1119, the pope had taken the decisive step of consecrating the archbishop of York himself, without any reference to Canterbury's claim, and it was at last clear that unless some quite new influence could be brought to bear on the question, the primatial position of Canterbury as an active instrument of organization was finished.

[32] For 1093, see Osbern's letter to Anselm, *Ep.* 149 (iii, 2); and for the scrutiny in 1109, see *HN*, p. 208.

In these desperate circumstances in 1120, Archbishop Ralph wrote the most detailed account ever written on the subject of the primacy, explaining fully to the pope the basis of the Canterbury claim.[33] He went over the whole ground of Canterbury's history from the beginning, enforcing the one simple message that Gregory the Great and his successors had committed to Canterbury the task of introducing and upholding the Christian faith throughout the whole of the British Isles. He proved and illustrated from Bede that for the first hundred and forty years after its foundation as an archbishopric, Canterbury had held primatial authority over the whole country; then he went on to prove, though more sketchily, that this state of affairs had lasted without intermission until the Norman Conquest. It was only then that evil men had begun to disturb the ancient arrangements which had the stamp of Gregory's authority. The story he told was precisely the story that Lanfranc had told in 1072, with the single exception that he says nothing about the *ultimum quasi robur* of the whole case in the series of documents mentioned by Lanfranc. With this one exception, he said in many pages what Lanfranc had said in a few sentences. The central figure in his story is always Pope Gregory I. Ralph insisted that the Canterbury case was based on Gregory's actions and intentions, and on the weight that Gregory had attached to continuity of tradition. His recital of the history of the archbishops' exercise of authority over the whole of Britain over the centuries is punctuated by quotations from Gregory, proclaiming the claims of antiquity as a model for future conduct.

In considering Lanfranc's letter of 1072, we were faced with the question: Why did he not produce them at the papal court? Here the question is: why did not Ralph even mention them? It may be argued that they existed but had been forgotten. This was the explanation later given by the monks of Canterbury. But besides being improbable in itself, it can scarcely be true, for Eadmer had mentioned that they had been produced in the royal court after Anselm's death in 1109. Or it may be argued that the documents contained the forged additions, but Ralph was silent because he knew they were forgeries. But this will scarcely work, for it was precisely in this year, and perhaps as a result of the failure of Archbishop Ralph's letter to produce any effect at the papal court, that the Canterbury monks claimed that they had 'discovered' the

---

[33] The text is printed in *HCY*, ii, pp. 228–51.

long lost documents with all the essential primatial clauses in them. So we come back to the one explanation which resolves every difficulty: the 'discovery' made by the monks of Canterbury in 1120–21, as the canons of York at once realized, was the moment of their enlargement.

3   The last resort: forgery

To return to Archbishop Ralph's letter to Callixtus II. It must have been written after his return to England in January 1120, and probably not long after this date. The need for a final effort to arrest the decline of Canterbury's fortunes was urgent. In addition to the papal disregard of Canterbury's primatial claim over York, the monastic community suffered another grievous blow. There had long been bickerings between the monks of the cathedral church at Canterbury and the neighbouring monastery of St Augustine's just outside the city wall. As a general rule, the archbishop had sufficient political leverage to ensure success for his own monks in these dispute. But, in March 1120, the monks of St Augustine's obtained a papal privilege allowing them to ring their bells to their hearts' content, however much they annoyed their neighbours over the wall; more to the point, this privilege quoted four papal privileges of the seventh to tenth centuries, all of them forgeries and one of them a forgery either derived from, or the source of, the very privilege of Pope Boniface IV which Alexander II had quoted to Lanfranc in 1070.[34]

This was a combination of evils grievous to bear; and in these circumstances it is scarcely surprising that the monastic community of the cathedral church themselves took action, and instituted a search for papal privileges to uphold their failing fortunes. Archbishop Ralph's eloquent letter to the pope had had no effect; St Augustine's was throwing off the restraints that their neighbours had succeeded in imposing on them in the past; and York was poised for a final victory in the matter of the primacy. This is Eadmer's account of the steps they took in this emergency:

In these days [the time he is referring to is 1120] the anxiety of many stirred them to seek out the authorities and ancient privileges regarding the primacy which the church of Canterbury claims over the church of York . . . There was great anxiety among many to look into this; and, confiding in the justice of the

---

[34] *Papsturkunden in England*, i, nos. 10 and 11.

church of God, the hidden places of ancient cupboards and ancient Gospel books, which had been looked on only as ornaments in the house of God, were diligently searched. And behold, the desire for justice was not deprived of its result, for by God's guidance certain privileges were found, by which everything was given firm and apostolic authority.

What the searchers 'found' were the papal letters mentioned by Lanfranc in 1072, fortified with forged additions granting the primacy in perpetuity to the successors of the first archbishop of Canterbury. Nothing could have been more timely. They were just what their case needed, and for a few years these texts became the foundation of the Canterbury case. Eadmer inserted them at this point into his *Historia Novorum*. William of Malmesbury, who was collecting material for his histories at Canterbury at this time, put the news of their discovery into his *Gesta Regum*, and inserted the complete texts under the year 1072 into his slightly later *Gesta Pontificum*.[35] He is the first historian who purports to give us the texts which Lanfranc had quoted in 1072 – and, of course, they now contain the forged additions. Both he and Eadmer had written their *Histories* down to 1120 without mentioning these texts, and it was only from the Canterbury monks that William of Malmesbury now learnt that these were the texts quoted by Lanfranc fifty years earlier. In the next two or three years several copies of them were made; then they disappeared.

But not before they had been used. Indeed they were used almost at once. I have mentioned that it was the pope's consecration of Thurstan as archbishop of York without submission to Canterbury in October 1119, followed by the failure of Archbishop Ralph's letter to the pope stating the Canterbury case, which made stronger measures neccessary. This led to the 'search' for documents which produced the forgeries. So, when Thurstan arrived in England in 1121 with papal letters threatening with excommunication any who resisted his admission into England, the monks of Canterbury recited the primatial phrases from the newly enlarged documents and refrained from taking further action for the time being.

Eadmer had good reason for not telling us what happened to the forgeries after this. It was left to the York writer, Hugh the Chanter, to tell us that after Ralph died in 1122, his successor, William of Corbeil, took them to Rome in 1123 when he went to get his pallium. The canons of York, however, had known since 1121

---

[35] See *GR*, ii, pp. 346–53, for the new material which has come to light as he writes; and *GP*, pp. 46–62, for the full texts, independently transcribed also in *HN*, pp. 261–76.

that, in the words of their chronicler, 'the monks of Canterbury, like blacksmiths blowing up a nearly extinct fire, recently found, or invented, certain papal privileges about the dignity and primacy of the church of Canterbury'. So they too were at the papal Curia ready with their reply when the monks of Canterbury arrived. When the archbishop of Canterbury came before the pope for his pallium, the canons of York entangled the Canterbury monks in questions about the precise state in which they had found the privileges – whether they had seals attached to them, and so on. The Canterbury monks were unprepared for these questions, stumbled in their answers, and were laughed out of court. For practical purposes, the forgeries were never heard of again.[36]

It only remains to add that although I have no doubt that Hugh correctly identified the 'search' of the Canterbury monks with the process of forgery, it is quite possible, indeed probable, that at various times during the previous fifty years individual members of the community had made experiments in altering the documents to make them more effective. There may have been secret conclaves for this purpose. But it was only as a last resort in 1120 that the community committed itself to, and based its case upon, the expedient of introducing into existing documents the necessary phrases, which – if they had been there in the days of Lanfranc or Anselm – would have given their case a firm basis in papal documents. A brief list of these phrases which were in the documents in 1121 will show their relevance:

Boniface V: *ut in Dorobernia civitate* [i.e. Canterbury] *semper in posterum metropolitanus totius Brittanniae locus habeatur.*

Honorius I: *primatum omnium ecclesiarum Britanniae tibi Honorio tuisque successoribus in perpetuum obtinere concedimus.*

Sergius I: *a tempore ... Gregorii Romani pontificis nunc usque sua (Cantuariorum) ecclesia detinuit a nobis, immo a beato Petro apostolorum principe, primatum omnium ecclesiarum Britanniae.*

Gregory III: *tibi, Tatwine, Doroberniae civitate archiepiscope, tuisque successoribus legitimis, omnes ecclesias Britanniae earumque rectores subjicimus.*[37]

The men who inserted these phrases knew what they were doing, and they knew also that it was important not to overdo the subject of

---

[36] See *HN*, p. 291, and *Hugh the Chanter*, p. 105, for the reading of passages from the forgeries in 1121; and *Hugh the Chanter*, pp. 114–15, for the confrontation in Rome in 1123.

[37] For the context of these phrases in the documents of 1120, see *HN*, pp. 263, 264, 268, 269.

the primacy. We shall probably never know what went on behind the scenes when these phrases were added to the documents. But it so happens that we can compare the situation during the years 1070 to 1123 with a similar train of events at Canterbury just a hundred years later. A comparison of the two will throw light on the crisis of conscience on both occasions.

The next great archbishop after Anselm was Thomas Becket. The monks of his day, like those of Anselm's, believed that their archbishop had not tried hard enough to defend their rights. But the monks of the later date believed that Archbishop Becket had intended to confirm, but had been prevented by his death from confirming, their monastic privileges with regard to many matters such as their rights in the consecration of bishops, in the appointment and dismissal of monastic officers, in the distribution of chrism and holy oil for the whole province, in the receipt of various revenues from the Canterbury manors, and the prohibition of any future move of the archbishopric from Canterbury. All these matters are indeed of a lower order of magnitude than those which had been fought for under Lanfranc and Anselm. But they too were in danger of meeting the same fate, and for the same reason: the document safeguarding the rights of the monastic community, which St Thomas had intended to make, did not exist. Probably his supposed intention was a pure fiction of the monks' imagination, but the remembrance of a lost opportunity was a heavy burden for them as they watched their rights being pared away under successive kings and archbishops.

It would seem that they often thought of 'creating' the document which St Thomas, as they believed, had promised them. And in the end, the temptation was too great: at some date between 1232 and 1235, the prior and others conspired to make the document in the name of Archbishop Thomas Becket, which they believed was theirs by right. They persuaded one sympathetic new bishop, Robert Grosseteste, that one of their claims (that all new bishops in the province should be consecrated at Canterbury) was genuine, and that it had been confirmed by Gregory IX. But when the doctored document emerged into the public arena, the fraud was almost at once uncovered in a welter of confessions, counter-accusations, and scandal.

By 1235, the whole question of forgery stood on a new moral and legal footing, and the corporate ambitions of the monks fell to the ground in a blaze of scandal. Nevertheless, the case throws some light on the earlier situation. Here, as before, we see how claims which were thought to be just and well-attested in practice, were in danger of extinction from the lack of the documents which met the requirements of a new age. We see also how forgery was long resisted, then finally and fatally adopted as a last resort. This, I believe, is what had happened at Canterbury between 1070 and 1122, and more pathetically between 1170 and 1235. The two sequences testify to the importance which a monastic community attached to its corporate ideal, and the steps by which a final and fatal resort to forgery came to appear the only path to a just solution.[38]

The events of 1120 to 1123 marked the end of the primacy as Lanfranc and Anselm had conceived it. Thereafter, primacy sank into insignificant arguments about precedence. As a practical instrument of Church government, it had briefly revived a vision of a federated Church under papal leadership. Now it was replaced by an administrative, legal, and organizational unity, which first became possible in the twelfth century as a result of the development of the administrative, legal and scholastic instruments of government. More than anyone, Hildebrand had been the visionary force behind the new ideal. During the years from 1070 to 1109, when Lanfranc and Anselm were at Canterbury, the issue was still alive. By the time of Anselm's death the question was essentially settled and Anselm's successor Ralph was fighting in a hopeless cause: by the time of Ralph's death, the instruments of universal government had become sufficiently highly developed to make all that Lanfranc and Anselm had stood for in this aspect of their work a thing of the past. The forged additions to the papal letters were a short-lived and totally irrelevant instrument, a last-ditch measure for the defence of the primacy, which was already a lost cause.

It may seem a depressing conclusion to Anselm's struggle for the primacy that it should have ended in a futile resort to forgery. But this last resort of defeated men marks the transition from a system based on the traditions of the local community to reliance on legal

---

[38] The status and circumstances of the so-called *Magna Carta* of St Thomas for Canterbury were elucidated by C. R. Cheney, in a paper reprinted in his *Medieval Texts and Studies*, Oxford, 1973, pp. 78–110. I have given an account of the whole incident in the context of monastic dreams and ambitions, in *The Monks of Canterbury and the Murder of Archbishop Becket*, Canterbury, William Urry Memorial Trust, 1985.

and administrative procedures based on written records. In his manner of thought and sympathies, Anselm belonged to the first of these two periods, both with regard to the organization of the Church and the supremacy of the monastic foundations which had maintained the spiritual life of Europe for three or four hundred years. For the immediate future his influence contracted and was conspicuous only among the small group of monks who were his heirs in following his manner of prayer and meditation, and in collecting his works and his words. To them we now turn.

PART IV
THE HARVEST OF FRIENDS AND DISCIPLES

CHAPTER 15

ANSELM'S EARLIEST THEOLOGICAL
DISCIPLES

I   ANSELM'S CIRCLE AT CANTERBURY

We have already seen that Anselm had no one in his household who could give him legal or administrative help on the major aspects of ecclesiastical policy, and that there is no sign that he felt the need for help of this kind: his own insight into the principles raised by the problems with which he was faced served all his needs, and the members of his household were chiefly necessary to him for the maintenance of a monastic routine and for spiritual conversation. Those on whom he chiefly relied for support in these matters were, in his early years, Eadmer; in his later years, Alexander; and – when questions of real theological difficulty arose – Boso.

There can be no doubt that, if only for the contribution made to the argument of the *Cur Deus Homo*, Boso was by far the most necessary to Anselm for theological discussion. It only remains to add that after his return from his second exile, when his last phase of philosophical activity was beginning, Anselm paid a further tribute to the importance of his help by asking for him once more to come to him, 'because he would prefer to live with him in a desert than without him in great abundance'.[1] Thus Boso was with him when he wrote his last treatise on predestination, grace, and free-will, and he stayed in England till Anselm's death. Boso was the self-effacing catalyst in the production of Anselm's later works. Although he outlived Anselm by many years, as abbot of Bec, he left only a single piece of writing that can be confidently ascribed to him, together with some probable contributions to the preservation of Anselm's memory.[2]

Both Anselm and Boso had had some experience of spiritual terror in their youth, from which Anselm had been saved by his

[1] For this testimony, see *Vita Bosonis, PL* 150, col. 726.
[2] See above p. 245; and below pp. 402, 476.

mother, and Boso by Anselm.[3] They recognized in each other a common background of panic followed by peace, as well as an uncommon sharpness of mind. Curiously, neither Eadmer nor Alexander ever mentions Boso's presence in Anselm's company. It may be that he did not move round with the others, but stayed at Canterbury to read and think and take part in the monastic life, as he and Anselm had formerly done at Bec, and as Anselm would himself have liked to do always.

Among the other members of Anselm's household, only Eadmer and Alexander made any contribution either to the completion of Anselm's thought, or to its circulation. Their contributions will require detailed treatment later: for the present it will suffice to add that we know too little about Alexander to give a confident judgement about his intellectual powers, but nothing he has left suggests abilities or accomplishments out of the ordinary. As for Eadmer, his qualities will emerge when his works are examined. He was a man of feeling, with great powers as an observer, and as the transmitter of a complex tradition, but he absorbed only that part of Anselm's teaching which was compatible with, and could enrich, his English tradition. Although he was capable of giving a correct summary of Anselm's philosophical arguments, he was no philosopher. Considering that he enjoyed the company of one of the greatest of theologians over a period of fifteen years, it is remarkable how limited and insular he remained in his habits of thought. At Canterbury, as at Bec, Anselm found it easier to make disciples who revered him, than pupils who could carry on his work.

There are several reasons for this failure of intellectual communication. Anselm's methods demanded gifts of logical precision which are rare, and produced results which, luminous though they are, are too insubstantial for common use. He left nothing to be completed by the patient work of many hands. He needed to have around him men who could discuss and question. All his works, whether we look at their structure or at their origin and growth, demonstrate how much he needed the company of inquiring minds. But with the one possible exception of the argument of the *Cur Deus Homo*, he had no need of helpers in finding the solution to problems.

The contribution of Canterbury monks to the subjects in which Anselm excelled can be clearly defined: for the transmission of his

---

[3] For these two incidents, see *VA* II, xxxiii, and pp. 172–3.

spoken words, we are chiefly indebted to Eadmer and Alexander, to whom we owe our chief records of Anselm's life and conversation. Outside these definite limits the harvest is small. Among the younger monks, Elmer, who became prior in 1128, caught something of Anselm's style in his letters and meditations, but Anselm's influence never informed the whole community at Canterbury as it had at one time done at Bec. To most of the monks he must have remained a distant and shadowy figure, to be judged rather by the results of his work than experienced as a power in their lives.

Among the great teachers of the Middle Ages it is not easy to name one whose circle of pupils was as narrow as that of Anselm, or whose influence crept forward by such slow and imperceptible advances. His monastic profession and his own inclinations made the society of a small group of pupils, linked together in a common life, more congenial than the shifting population of students in the schools. But even in the Benedictine Order, there were teachers with a wider range of immediate influence. Contemporaries remarked on the slow growth of a reputation which shone so brightly in his immediate vicinity: 'Why', he was asked when he was forty, 'does the reputation of Lanfranc and Guitmund fly round the world more than yours?' 'Perhaps', he replied, with the elusiveness which characterized his early literary style, 'because any flower may imitate the colour of the rose without possessing its scent.'[4]

Twenty years later, when he became archbishop of Canterbury, his reputation had grown. His Prayers were becoming widely known in northern France and had reached Auvergne, England, and northern Italy; the *Proslogion* and *Monologion* were known in Lyons; and his name and good repute had reached Rome. But this does not amount to an intellectual influence such as Alcuin or Gerbert had exercised in the past, or the masters of Paris were to exercise in the immediate future. During his sixteen years as archbishop his name became known far and wide, but the number of his immediate pupils, and his means of influencing them, shrank rather than expanded.

In France especially, more energetic methods of teaching and disputation were replacing the colloquies on which Anselm's pupils had been nourished. Biblical, logical, grammatical commentaries,

---

[4] *Ep.* 20 (i, 16).

the compilation and arrangement of extracts, and the discussion of their points of difference – all these forms of intellectual activity proliferated in the schools and gradually invaded the monasteries, but they made no appeal to Anselm. The nearest he ever came to writing a commentary on an ancient text was in his *De Grammatico*, and it was, as I have argued above, his earliest and the least influential. Anselm did not inaugurate or advance a method of study suitable for the schools, and capable of being developed methodically by those who came after him. He stood aside from the intellectual fashions of his time.

The result was that his immediate pupils were a small body of followers with diverse interests and talents, linked only by their personal loyalty to Anselm. He had no major intellectual heir before Duns Scotus. Halfway to Scotus, Robert Grosseteste read and annotated his works, shared his philosophical principles, and was inspired by his *Cur Deus Homo*; but he was inspired to differ, and in the general character of his thought and actions he belonged to a different world from Anselm. Alexander of Hales, Bonaventure, and Thomas Aquinas had all read his works, probably in the collected editions which became widespread during the thirteenth century, but he was read rather as a classic than as an important influence in forming the thought of the century. As for Anselm's immediate pupils, they blossomed in his presence, learnt his tricks of phrase, and applied some of his characteristic arguments to new subjects, but their additions to the fabric, though interesting and sometimes important, are not large. To re-think Anselm's thoughts, as he had re-thought those of St Augustine, and to put them in a new and brilliant light, was beyond them. They could only reproduce, and in places develop, his ideas at a lower level of competence.

Yet it must also be said that his disciples at Canterbury did more to copy and transmit his works than the monks of Bec with their more limited resources could ever have done. Canterbury scribes and admirers were primarily responsible for the collection and transmission of his letters, and perhaps also of his *Prayers* and *Meditations*; and the great collected edition of his complete works which was made at Canterbury anticipated the manuscripts of his collected works which became common after the thirteenth century. So although Anselm remained more of an outsider at Canterbury than he had been at Bec, the monks of Canterbury preserved his works and the memory of his life more than the monks of Bec either did or could have done.

Probably Boso was the only pupil of Anselm who was capable of making an independent contribution to his theology, and his efforts were wholly expended in the help he gave in the composition of the *Cur Deus Homo* and *De Conceptu Virginali et de Originali Peccato*, in which Anselm acknowledged his help. Of the other pupils whose work shows distinct signs of his influence and some independence of development, there are four who deserve to be mentioned. The first of these is Eadmer, whose long years of close association with Anselm, the use he made of his opportunities, and his productivity as a monastic writer in fields untouched by Anselm, entitle him to a separate treatment. Of the others, Gilbert Crispin wrote one work of great distinction, which was one of the inspirations of Anselm's *Cur Deus Homo* and some small works which will be briefly discussed below; Rodulfus, or Ralph, monk of Rochester and later abbot of Battle, wrote meditations in the style of Anselm, which were long believed to be Anselm's work; and the third, Honorius Augustodunensis, showed a remarkable capacity for turning Anselm's thoughts, like those of several other men, into readable and popular works. They all deserve a brief record as reflections of Anselm in his own time.

II   ELABORATORS OF ANSELM'S THOUGHTS

1   Gilbert Crispin, abbot of Westminster

Gilbert Crispin's place among the closest of Anselm's early friends, and his important role in introducing Anselm to the disputes between Jews and Christians, which formed one of the inspirations of his *Cur Deus Homo*, have already been examined. Apart from Boso, he was probably the only one of Anselm's pupils with a gift for clear and coherent theological argument. The main evidence for this is a series of short works on fundamental problems of the Christian faith, especially the Trinity and the Incarnation, which were inspired by Anselm's methods and conclusions. To these must be added his two *Dialogues* between a Christian and a Jew, and between a Christian and a pagan philosopher. The first of these had a considerable circulation, and it is far superior to the generality of such treatises in the cogency of its argument and the humanity with which it treats the opponent of the Christian faith. The second is less successful, and shows that although Anselm imparted some of his philosophical conceptions to his friend, Gilbert was really more at home in Biblical exegesis, and in brief and clear theological expositions of central doctrines, than in the refinements of metaphysics and logic. He was an able writer, and at times he reproduced the flow of Anselmian argument with great clarity and vigour, but the final impression he leaves is of a man of sober judgement and solid learning rather than of any more brilliant gifts of intellect. He was the clearest expounder of Anselm's theological views, and his treatises were mainly an attempt to state them briefly and simply. He perhaps regarded himself as Anselm's theological executor, for in his *De Anima* he completed Anselm's work by writing on the subject which was in Anselm's mind at the time of his death.[5]

Gilbert had a considerable reputation for about fifty years, and then his works and name disappeared from view until modern times. Nevertheless, in the brief period when he was remembered, he was the only one of Anselm's pupils to make a reputation in the schools, at least to the extent of being mentioned as equal, and even as superior, to four of the best known scholastic theologians of the period – the brothers Anselm and Ralph of Laon, Gilbert the Universal, and Alberic the master of Rheims. It cannot however be said that we know of any works that would justify this contemporary reputation.

2 Ralph, prior of Rochester and abbot of Battle

The second of Anselm's theological followers has an important place as the most widely read writer of contemplative theological dialogues and meditations in a style which is clearly derived from

---

[5] On his death-bed, Anselm expressed a wish to live until he had finished writing on the origin of the soul, because (as he said) he did not know who would solve the problem after his death. Superficially this problem was much discussed in the school of Laon (See Lottin, 1959, pp. 119–20, 124, 244–5), but none there, so far as we know, discussed the problem of how, if each soul was newly created by God and was not transmitted from parent to child, Original Sin was inherited. Gilbert's treatise is chiefly concerned with this question, and – since it quotes Anselm's *CDH* and perhaps his later work *De Conceptu Virginali* – it must have been written either in the last years of Anselm's life or after his death. We may take it as probable that Gilbert wrote in the hope of answering the question which Anselm thought he could solve. But the last words of his treatise – *adhuc sub iudice lis est* – suggest that he had not succeeded. For Gilbert's reputation as a theologian a generation after his death, see John of Salisbury, *Historia Pontificalis*, c. 8 (ed. Chibnall, p. 19; ed. R. L. Poole, 1927, p. 20).

Anselm. Admittedly he owed his wide circulation to the mistaken attribution of his writings to Anselm, but they are not quite unworthy of their attribution. We know little about him except that he was one of the monks, probably originally from Bec, who went first to Caen and then came to England with Lanfranc. He became prior of Rochester when Anselm's closest friend Gundulf was bishop; then, in 1107, he became abbot of the Conqueror's new foundation at Battle, and died aged eighty-four in 1124. At the time of his death he had been a monk for sixty years. If his monastic career began at Bec, this would mean that he was probably the Rodulfus who appears as the tenth recruit after Anselm in the list of professions at Bec. The Battle annalist wrote a glowing eulogy when he died.[6]

He seems to have written all his surviving works before he left Rochester, and they had an uneven fortune. A single Rochester manuscript is the sole authority for some of them; others are known in only two manuscripts; another, on the monastic life, had a modest anonymous success. But by far the most successful was a group of prayers and meditations modelled on those of Anselm. Some of these became attached to Anselm's *Prayers* and *Meditations* at an early date, and circulated under Anselm's name throughout the Middle Ages, and in all editions of Anselm's works until that of Schmitt. They were the earliest of the many additions, which turned the small collection of Anselm's genuine Prayers into the very large collection which made Anselm's name known far and wide.[7] Once the discovery that they were not by Anselm was made, it became easy to see that they are more pedestrian and closer to conventional devotion than the genuine works of Anselm; but works which satisfied a very large public for several centuries clearly had qualities to which justice is not done when criticism is

[6] In Southern. 1941, pp. 14–19, 24–29, I mistakenly identified him as Ralph d'Escures, Anselm's successor as archbishop of Canterbury. I corrected this mistake in Southern, 1963, p. 206–7. For Ralph's career and writings, see *The Chronicle of Battle Abbey*, ed. E. Searle, Oxford, 1980, pp. 116, 118, 130, 132. For the Rodulfus in the Bec profession list, see Porée, 1901, ii, p. 629.

[7] The process of making additions to Anselm's collection of *Prayers* and *Meditations* to form the large collection which circulated from the thirteenth century onwards still requires further study. I would tentatively suggest that it began with the adaptation of portions of Ralph's *Meditations* to form what later became the sequence of additions to Anselm's collection: *Med.* 19 and 5; *Or.* 3; *Med.* 4; *Or.* 4 and 6; *Med.* 6; *Or.* 25–28 and 15. If this is correct, the first stage in this inflationary process may go back to the generation after Anselm's death, when Anselm's disciples were also collecting his letters. But whereas the letters had very few readers after the first generation, the collection of *Prayers* and *Meditations* met a widespread need, and the collection

made easy by the knowledge that they are not Anselm's. They were after all written for general use, and it is very likely that they met the needs of most readers better than Anselm's more elaborate and exhausting effusions.

The same general judgement may be passed on Ralph's philosophical works. In subject matter and literary form they were written under the immediate influence of Anselm's dialogues. The longest and most important of them were a sequence of discussions between *Nesciens* and *Sciens*, and between *Inquirens* and *Respondens*. These personifications in themselves indicate their Anselmian origin. They covered a much larger field of inquiry than Anselm's dialogues, necessarily at a much more superficial level, as a brief description of one of them will show.

The dialogue between *Nesciens* and *Sciens* starts with a sceptic who refuses to believe anything for which he has not the evidence of his eyes. The discussion gradually leads him to accept the evidence of his other senses, and then to acknowledge the existence of an invisible intelligence as a source of knowledge, and thence of a Supreme Intelligence and First Cause. The sequence is ably planned, but superficially treated. *Nesciens* is represented as being brought rather rapidly to a grateful acceptance of the whole range of Christian doctrine, but it is hard to think that a robust unbeliever would have succumbed so quickly. But once more it must be recognized that they were written to exercise the minds of believers, and not to convert unbelievers, who were unlikely ever to see them. In brief, Ralph's dialogues, like his prayers, were written for the comfort and mental exercise of readers who did not need to be converted, and to such readers they brought some of the qualities of Anselm's work in a form which they could appreciate.

This sequence of discussions is in some ways similar to Gilbert Crispin's dialogue between the Christian and the pagan: they both satisfied the growing need for a rational justification of the Christian faith, capable of meeting the objections which may occur to anyone. Ralph's treatment of the problems of faith covers a much wider range of topics than Gilbert's reply to the objections of his

continued to grow by the addition of spurious pieces until, by the fourteenth century, it had reached a total of about a hundred, of which only nineteen *Prayers* and three *Meditations* were genuine. The essential starting point for further work on this subject is still Wilmart, 1924, and 1932, pp. 173–201, 'Les méditations réunies sous le nom de saint Anselme'. For the growth of the collection in the twelfth century, see Bestul, 1977, and 1978.

learned Jew. But Gilbert was dealing with a genuine critic, while Ralph's unbeliever was imaginary.[8]

Both Gilbert and Ralph moved away from the systematic and penetrating analysis of major problems which were Anselm's permanent contribution to theological thought. Ralph drew on Anselm's stock; he did not add to it. He derived several of his arguments about the nothingness of sin, the true powerlessness implicit in the power to sin, the congruity of faith and reason, and the necessity of the Incarnation, from Anselm's works; but he was also an independent student of St Augustine, for whom he reserved his deepest veneration. So, without being an independent thinker, he was more than a mere imitator of Anselm.

Like Gilbert Crispin, he took as his main interlocutors those who claimed to stand outside the Christian faith. This was a radical departure from the practice of Anselm, who, arguing only with professed believers and aiming at extending their understanding of the system of their faith, finally reached a foundation on which, as he claimed, all rational argument had to be based. In aspiring to argue directly with unbelievers, both Ralph and Gilbert Crispin were showing their awareness of the wider and more hostile world with which Anselm came in contact only in his later years; but they required that their opponents should be easily satisfied, and it is easy to see now that their dialogues had no permanent importance. Yet in their own time, and for their mainly monastic readers for perhaps two generations, both Gilbert Crispin and Ralph were thoughtful and enlightened guides to the problems of Christian faith for articulate believers.

Both of them are also good examples of the Benedictine scholars and administrators who transformed the religious life of England in the half century after the Conquest. They were men who have left few records of their thought and scholarship outside the eulogies of local annalists, but the little collections of their treatises show that the new generation of scholar-administrators had reached a high standard of learning and rational meditation, and that Anselm played a considerable part in their education. Their thoughts were provoked and moulded by his, and they consciously echoed his methods. They themselves had no problems of faith to stimulate their thought. They had to invent problems in order to answer

---

[8] For a brief analysis, see Southern, 1941, pp. 14–19.

them, and they had only a very small audience for their thoughts. To expect such men to be original philosophers, or creators of new literary forms, is to expect something which only the strong force of native genius or the impact of deeply disturbing events could ever have effected.

3 Honorius Augustodunensis

There is one last developer of Anselm's thought who deserves to be mentioned. If it was the fate, and perhaps the choice, of Anselm's pupils to keep their personalities obscure, Honorius Augustodunensis showed a remarkable talent for egotistical camouflage. The enigma surrounding this prolific and popular writer is proverbial, and largely of his own making. He chose, like Ralph, to write many of his works anonymously, but he left a clear but misleading scent by giving a list of his own works at the end of his biographical dictionary of Christian writers, the *De Luminaribus Ecclesiae*, with his name: Honorius *Augustodunensis*. Nothing could be clearer: Honorius 'of Autun'. This was once the universally agreed explanation, and nearly everyone now agrees that it is wilfully misleading. What the right answer is has defied agreed conjecture, but no one can doubt his immense success.[9]

If we ask what else we know about him, it is clear that all his works were written in the first half of the twelfth century, that he had already produced a long list of works by 1125, and that by this date he was probably attached to the Irish community of St James at Regensburg, where he presumably stayed till the end of his life. At an early stage in his career, he spent some time in Canterbury and came under Anselm's influence.

This influence is clearly apparent in his earliest work, the

---

[9] The first serious modern study of Honorius was J. A. Endres, 1906. Since then both the man and his works have been extensively discussed, most recently and fully by V. I. J. Flint in numerous articles, collected and reprinted in Flint, 1988. The texts mentioned in the following pages are all in *PL* 172, but often in defective texts. For later and better editions of these works, see especially: *Imago Mundi*, ed. V. I. J. Flint, *AHDLMA*, 1982, pp. 7–153; *Das Inevitabile des Honorius Augustodunensis*, ed. F. Baeumker, *BGPTMA*, xiii, 1914; 'L'Elucidarium et les Lucidaires', ed. Y. Lefèvre, *Bibl. des écoles françaises d'Athènes et de Rome*, clxx, 1954, which, however, suffers severely from a failure to use manuscripts of English origin and does not mention the authorities quoted in the margins of the text, which appear to go back to the author. In Southern, 1963, pp. 215–6, I discuss the stages in his early career and give some reasons for thinking that he was of Irish origin, and that *Augustodunensis*, which certainly does not mean Autun, may be a cryptic reference to Cashel, the 'Hill of the Kings'.

Elucidarium. This work, a long dialogue between a Master and Pupil, achieved a very wide circulation as a popular survey of Christian doctrine, with many minute and curious answers to outlandish questions. It shows evidence of wide reading in a library well-stocked with the works of the Latin Fathers, and displays an unusual predilection for the works of the Irish scholar John Scot Erigena. Several of the manuscripts have the authorities named in the margin, and among them the name of Anselm makes a frequent appearance. These references show that Honorius was acquainted with the *Cur Deus Homo*, which (as we have seen) was mainly written in England between 1093 and 1097, but completed in Italy in 1098; and they also refer to passages which cannot be traced to Anselm's written works, but may derive from oral teaching.

In addition to these marginal references, Anselm's influence can be seen in some of the questions asked and the formulation of his answers. For instance, in the third book of the *Elucidarium*, he used Anselm's sermon on the Joys of Heaven to provide him with both questions and answers. As we shall see, both Eadmer and Alexander made reports of this sermon, which Anselm evidently repeated on several occasions, and Honorius may have had one of these reports, or he may himself have heard the sermon. In either case Canterbury is the most likely place for him to have got his information.

As a further link with Canterbury, the *Elucidarium*, or parts of it, were translated into Anglo-Saxon within a few years of its composition, and the translation also is closely associated either with Canterbury itself or with its sister monastery at Rochester.[10]

Similar influences and local connections can be traced in his other early works. The *Sigillum Sanctae Mariae*, his second work, drew heavily on a sermon of Anselm's friend and successor as archbishop, Ralph d'Escures, who was living in the ambiance of Canterbury for several years before he became bishop of Rochester in 1107, and finally archbishop of Canterbury in 1114. Further, Honorius's third work, a treatise on free will to which he gave the arresting title, *Inevitabile*, was extensively revised in the light of Anselm's last work, the *De Concordia Praescientiae et Praedestinationis et Gratiae Dei cum Libero Arbitrio*. Honorius's work belongs to the early years of the twelfth century, and Anselm's *De Concordia* was written in the neighbourhood of Canterbury in 1107-8. So

---

[10] See M. Förster in *An English Miscellany presented to Dr F. J. Furnivall*, Oxford, 1901, pp. 88-101, and *Archiv f. das Studium der neueren Sprachen*, 114, 1902, pp. 312-14.

there is a strong likelihood that Honorius was in touch with the monks of Canterbury when he made the revision of his *Inevitabile*.

Briefly, therefore, there are several pieces of evidence for Honorius's close connection with Canterbury, pointing to a prolonged visit between about 1100 and 1109. But by the time he wrote his next work – a collection of sermons for the Christian year called *Speculum Ecclesiae* – he was in a quite different environment and under new influences, and we know that he spent the last decades of his life between about 1120 and 1150 in Regensburg.

What emerges from these rapidly recorded details is that Honorius's *Elucidarium, Sigillum Sanctae Mariae*, and his *Inevitabile* in its final form, were written when Honorius was under the immediate influence of Anselm and his friends, probably after Anselm's return from his first exile. He must have kept in touch with Canterbury or with England for a few years after this date, for he had sufficient information about the doctrine of Anselm's last work –though he preserved only a very confused idea of its title – to enable him to make some corrections to his *Inevitabile* in accordance with Anselm's doctrine. But thereafter he lost touch with Canterbury and with England, and came under the influence of a new master, Rupert of Deutz: his ties with England were finally broken, and the German phase of his career began.

Honorius's career was very eccentric. But it has one characteristic in common with many others: he was an itinerant scholar seeking inspiration from well-known masters wherever they were to be found. 'Our' Anselm, as contrasted with his namesake at Laon, was not a master to whom such students normally came: the secular schools were their ordinary hunting grounds, for the masters of the schools had often no other source of income than the fees of itinerant students, and their teaching took the form of courses of lectures to which there was a beginning and an end. But 'our' Anselm taught only as an enhancement of monastic life, and his teaching required a long period of common life to make its influence felt. Then, further, in the circumstances of his life as archbishop, constantly on the move when he was not in exile, it was impossible for him to have disciples of the old kind, men whom he wished to make monks, not authors.

Honorius did not offer the kind of discipleship that Anselm required. He belonged either to an ancient tradition of itinerant scholar-monks, or to the new generation of scholars who sought masters wherever they could be found. It is hard to know which of these two traditions he represents, but he has no place in the old stability of Benedictine studies, to which Anselm with all his innovations of method belongs. Honorius had a restless instinct for seeking interesting men and places. He was only a cursory student of any master's works and thoughts: he was a magpie, not a philosopher. This will be clear to anyone who reads the *Elucidarium*: the astonishing assurance with which he answers questions of every possible kind assured him of long-lasting success as an author, but it gives no evidence of a philosophic temper. He takes information from all sides and presses it into service:

Disciple: How are the damned situated?

Master: They are hung head downwards, back to back, feet in the air, stretched in torment in all directions.

D: Do not the just lament when they see them thus punished ?

M: No. Even though a father sees his own son in torment, or a son his father, or a mother her daughter, or a husband his wife, or a wife her husband, they will not only not lament, but will find pleasure in the sight, as when we see fishes in a whirlpool.

D: Now I should like to hear about Antichrist.

M: Antichrist will be born in Babylon of a prostitute of the tribe of Dan. He will be filled with the Devil in his mother's womb, and brought up by malefactors in Khorassan.[11]

In such passages as these – and there are very many – Honorius is as far removed from Anselm as can easily be imagined. But this should not obscure the fact that he was a master of popular and vigorous exposition, which gave him many readers throughout the Middle Ages. He was a man of indefatigable energy, who could state clearly, judge confidently, and arrange systematically his very widely scattered materials. And, alongside the stream of factual information which he pours out in great abundance, there are questions and answers in which the influence of Anselm, if not profound, is clearly visible:

Disciple: How great was the sin of eating the apple?

Master: So great that the whole world could not suffice to atone for it.

D: Prove it.

M: Do you think it is right that man should obey the divine will?

D: Nothing juster: a rational creature should prefer the will of the Creator to everything else.

M: Therefore the will of God is greater than the whole world?

D: Certainly.

[11] *Elucidarium*, III, 4, 5, 10 (*PL* 172, cols. 1160–1, 1163.)

379

M: If God said to you 'Do not look back' and some one else said to you 'Look back, or the whole world will perish', would you think you should disobey God the Creator of all things in order to preserve the transitory world?
D: Certainly not.
M: Yet this is what Adam did: he looked back at the Devil's instigation and committed a sin greater than the whole world.
D: How was it greater?
M: Because he committed in this crime six criminal acts, in which he implicated the six ages of his posterity.[12]

In this argument Honorius interrupts his flow of often far-fetched information and adopts a style of theological dialogue in which Anselmian influence is apparent. His mention of the single glance of the eye contrary to the will of God, which is a sin 'greater' than everything in the created universe, is pure Anselm. It is derived from the same passage in the *Cur Deus Homo* which also inspired Newman:[13] and though Honorius's glib quotation has none of the intense emotion which the same thought inspired in Newman, he had for a moment caught something of the spirit of Anselm before reverting in his very next sentence to the cosmic speculations in which he delighted, and for which Anselm – except perhaps for the numerical symbolism which he enjoyed – had no use at all.

Clearly, Gilbert Crispin and Ralph were pupils of Anselm in a way in which Honorius was not. They had lived with him, following the same monastic routine, sharing the same thoughts and the same ideal of a monastically ordered world. Honorius belonged partly to an earlier age of wandering monks, ultimately seeking separation from the world in hermitages, partly to a new type of intellectual adventurer gathering the thoughts of masters wherever they were to be found. He naturally grew further away from Anselm at every later step, while Gilbert Crispin and Ralph were fixed in the same mould as Anselm. If they had been freed from administrative duties, both of them might have developed Anselm's thoughts in a more substantial way than they found possible. The pressure of administration, the responsibility for great estates, and the necessary engagement in political and legal responsibilities, absorbed the energies of those monks whom Lanfranc had taken to England and placed in positions of responsibility at Canterbury, Rochester, Westminster, and elsewhere. Several of them had been among Anselm's closest friends

[12] *Elucidarium*, I, 15 (*PL* 172, col. 1120).   [13] See above, pp. 217–18.

and disciples, but they had no leisure to make more than a small contribution to the literature of theology or prayer. By the time that Anselm was also drawn into this busy administrative world, he was too fully formed, and too aloof from the troubles of business, to change habits which he had built up over a period of over thirty years. His letters retain some of the earlier intensity of personal feeling, but he could no longer draw men to him and form their lives in peace, as he had been able to do at Bec.

CHAPTER 16

THE COLLECTORS OF ANSELM'S WORDS AND LETTERS

I REPORTERS OF CONVERSATIONS AND SERMONS

It was in talk that Anselm made his most powerful impression on his contemporaries. All his utterances, whether in Chapter or at table, in formal sermons or in remarks casually elicited, have a quality which reflects the meeting of the Benedictine and scholastic ages in a personality of exquisite charm and genius. They are a combination of old and new: of old, in the monastic setting and range of monastic topics: of new, in the penetrating analysis, the striking definitions, and the unfamiliar illustrations.

It was Anselm's talk which first excited the interest of the young Eadmer. When Anselm visited Canterbury in 1079, he talked about the monastic life 'in a way which had not been heard before this time'; he defended their martyr Elphege with arguments which would have seemed very far-fetched if their conclusion had not been so welcome. Above all, he drew aside some of the cleverer men and engaged them in discussion. This was Anselm's introduction to Canterbury, and there is plenty of evidence in Eadmer and elsewhere that wherever Anselm went, his talk left memories which were not easily effaced.

At about the same time as his first visit to Canterbury, Anselm also visited a small monastery near Beauvais, about fifty miles from Bec. It was on the road to one of the outlying priories of Bec, which Anselm probably visited as prior, and certainly later as abbot. In the course of his visit, a shy, troubled, intelligent young monk, who was just beginning to discover in the monastic library the works of Gregory the Great on Job and Ezekiel, came to him, and Anselm began to talk about the inner life, the laws of reason, and the study of the Bible. His remarks made a profound impression on the young man, which was deepened in several later visits and talks. The young man was Guibert, later abbot of Nogent, who wrote an autobiography in which he recalled the inspiration which he got from these talks.[1] Anselm gave him the feeling that he had come with no other purpose than to talk to him, and Guibert remembered these visits as the first important landmark in his intellectual awakening. Guibert in fact went on to other sources of inspiration, and in his later years he owed more to Anselm of Laon than to Anselm of Canterbury. Like others, he had moved with the times; but he never forgot what he had owed to the man who first aroused him to independent thought.

This is symptomatic. Anselm was more frequently remembered than followed. But the memory of his talk lasted long. The author of the *Life* of Lambert, abbot of St Bertin, gives several details of the discussions which Anselm had with the abbot as he passed through St Bertin during his first exile, and he increases Lambert's stature by attributing to him all the Anselmian ideas which he reports.[2] Likewise, the author of the *Life* of Abbot Hugh of Cluny breaks his rather monotonous recital to exclaim on the sweet discourse which passed between the abbot and Anselm, when he visited Cluny during his exile.[3] During the same exile, Anselm's talk at Vienne or in its neighbourhood has left its mark on the collection of the Miracles of St James of Compostela, associated with the archbishop of Vienne who became Pope Calixtus II.[4] At all periods of his life, and wherever he went, he talked, and others remembered what he had said.

These chance records disclose the wide extent of Anselm's reputation as a talker both in private conversation and in more formal discourses. But nothing is more difficult to convey to others. Of all the great forces which have formed the past, none has disappeared more effectively, or when recalled retains less of its once compelling force, than the power of the spoken word. This must be remembered as we rake over the embers.

Almost all of Anselm's talk would have disappeared if three monks at Canterbury, acting separately and reporting what they heard, had not undertaken the task of reporting Anselm's words. They were Eadmer, Alexander, and some third reporter who may be Boso. Even if we cannot bring the talk to life, we can at least know

---

[1] Guibert, *De Vita Sua*, Bk. I, c. 16; *PL* 156, col. 874. [2] *MGH, SS*, xv, 949.
[3] Gilo, *Vita S. Hugonis*, ed. A. L'Huillier, *Vie de St. Hugues, abbé de Cluny*, Solesmes, 1888, pp. 588–9. [4] See Southern 1958, pp. 188–90, 205–11.

the subjects about which Anselm talked, and some of the things he said about them, distinguishing the different habits of the three reporters.

I   Eadmer as reporter

I   EADMER'S REPORTS OF ANSELM'S TALK

Anyone who turns to the *Vita Anselmi* will at once be struck by the amount of natural and vivid talk which it contains. It is Eadmer's chief claim to fame as a biographer that he understood the importance of Anselm's talk and had the skill to reproduce it in a convincing and memorable way. Eadmer not only gives us words which seem to be those of Anselm, but he shows how they arose from the needs of the moment: how the hunted hare and the captive bird suggested parables of human life; how the parting speech to the monks of Canterbury provided an occasion for the allegory of the three classes of knights and the conditions of men in relation to God; how the troubles of the over-busy monk suggested the simile of the mill as an image of human life, and prompted the subtle distinction between acquiescence and obedience.[5]

Anselm's favourite time for such talk was at meals. In this he was somewhat stretching the Benedictine Rule. The Rule laid down, and common practice required, that a book should be read at meal-times, and the office of reader seems, at the archbishop's table, to have been performed by his cross-bearer. But it appears that Anselm often dispensed with his services: St Benedict allowed the superior to speak briefly for edification if he wished, and Anselm made generous use of this permission. If Eadmer is to be trusted – but he is not the only witness – it was only when no subject for edifying talk presented itself that Anselm sat back and listened to the reading. Thus it arose, as Eadmer says, that he heard almost daily Anselm's reflections on humility, patience, meekness, obedience, and other virtues, 'which would require another work to set down'.[6] What he gives is sufficient to make the reader regret that this 'other work' was not written. No one else was so well equipped as Eadmer to report Anselm's words, and when in the last years of Anselm's life – for a reason that will later appear – Eadmer's reports dry up, the life goes out of his work. There were others, however,

[5] *VA* II, vi, xviii, xix, xxi.   [6] *VA* II, ix.

who in some measure filled his place, and of these the chief appears to have been Alexander, who in several other respects took Eadmer's place in Anselm's last years.

11 EADMER'S REPORTS OF ANSELM'S SERMONS

Apart from the monastic colloquies which were the starting point of most of his works written at Bec, we know nothing of Anselm's sermons before he became archbishop. But from 1093 to 1100 Eadmer was an abundant reporter of Anselm's words, both in his *Historia Novorum* and his *Vita Anselmi*; in addition, he has left two full-length reports of sermons delivered on special occasions:

1 The first is a sermon on eternal life in which we have the fullest expression of Anselm's conviction that the physical attributes of life on earth are permanently and most fully experienced also in heaven. The occasion for Eadmer's report was that, after Anselm had preached at Cluny on a visit, probably in 1099–1100, one of the monks asked Eadmer to send him the full text. It appeared that Anselm had used no written text, and Eadmer had to reconstruct it from memory with Anselm's help. Later, Eadmer kept adding to it when he heard it on other occasions, and we can follow the additions in his own manuscript.[7]

There are two points of some importance to be made here. The first is that although some of the additions were certainly made after Anselm's death, Eadmer claimed that he had heard everything in the sermon from Anselm's own lips, and that – so far as the report had gone during Anselm's lifetime – Anselm had authorized it to be transcribed for posterity as his own. All these statements are probably true. But the impression which he conveys that the whole of the final text had been part of the original sermon at Cluny is certainly false, as the manuscript tradition clearly demonstrates. So here, as elsewhere, we have an example of Eadmer's carelessness about exact times: it was a matter of indifference to him that he ascribed to an occasion at Cluny words spoken on various occasions. We have already seen that he was probably guilty of a similar anachronism in his account of Anselm's parting words to the monks of Canterbury in 1097.

The second point of importance is that, in his own personal

---

[7] For the growth of the text, see *Memorials*, pp. 273–91; *PL* 159, cols. 587–606, has the final text.

copy of this sermon, it is not ascribed to Anselm at all, but appears simply as: *Scriptum quoddam de beatitudine perennis vitae*. This was certainly not an attempt to deceive readers as to the real author of the sermon, for Eadmer describes the circumstances of its delivery. He may indeed have taken some credit for putting it into literary shape, for Anselm had preached without a script. This small point will be important when we come to the next anonymous sermon.

So far as the sermon on eternal life was concerned, two independent versions spread widely throughout Europe from two different sources. Eadmer's report spread both from the copy which he sent to Cluny, and from the copy which he himself kept and continued to enlarge. But in addition to these versions by Eadmer, Anselm's later companion and reporter Alexander also wrote a report of the same or a very similar sermon, and this too circulated independently, and was finally printed under the name of Guigo of Chartreuse.[8] These small points would scarcely be worth mentioning if they did not throw light on the haphazard manner in which these central records of an important part of Anselm's teaching have been preserved. This has meant that they have never been given the importance they deserve in interpreting Anselm's thought as a whole.

2   In addition to this sermon, there is another on the feast of the Ordination of St Gregory, which has a very strong claim to be recognized as Anselm's. This sermon is known to us only from Eadmer's personal manuscript, where it also appears without any indication that Anselm was the author.[9] Indeed, I long thought that Eadmer must himself have been the author.[10] But, as we shall see, this is impossible, and there is a very high degree of probability that Anselm was the preacher.

The purpose of the sermon was to promote a renewed celebration of the feast of the Ordination of St Gregory, which had been observed in the Anglo-Saxon Church on 29 March. It seems to have been a purely English feast, expressing the deep attachment of the Old English Church to the originator of its organized faith; and it had been abandoned after the Conquest. Then, like some other rejects of Lanfranc, it reappears in

---

[8] *PL* 184, cols. 353–64. The tangled history of this literary blunder was first unravelled in Wilmart, 1935, pp. 248– 59.   [9] For the text, see Wilmart, 1935, pp. 207–19.
[10] See Southern 1941, p. 6.

England in the early twelfth century, but at a new date, 3 September, which was the date when Gregory became pope.[11] So here we have a case of a peculiar Anglo-Saxon feast, suppressed by Lanfranc, and re-introduced at a new, and more appropriate and convenient date in the early twelfth century.

The sermon which Eadmer preserved was clearly addressed to a predominantly non-English audience, for at one point the speaker interrupts his argument to say, 'You Englishmen who have become my brethren in the faith – if by any chance some of you are here listening to me – observe how God predestined Gregory to be your Apostle.'[12] Clearly then, neither the speaker nor the main part of his audience were English; and from the tone of his other remarks, the speaker expected ignorance and opposition from most of his audience.[13] Who was he and who were his audience?

For a long time I thought that the words I have quoted might just have been appropriate in a sermon preached by Eadmer in Scotland, when he was bishop-elect of St Andrews in 1120. But I did not then know that the piece belonged to the earliest portion of Eadmer's manuscript, which was completed by 1116. Since Eadmer never held a position of public responsibility before this date, the sermon cannot have been preached by him.[14] So we return to the more natural interpretation of the words as coming from a foreigner in high position, speaking to an audience in which there might be a few, but not many, Englishmen. When we remember that, apart from this sermon, Eadmer's manuscript

---

[11] For details, see A. Gasquet and E. Bishop, *The Bosworth Psalter*, London, 1908, pp. 33–4, 84, 104–6. The feast on 3 September is among the early twelfth-century additions to the calendar in MS. Arundel 155. The older date, on the basis of evidence now lost, presumably preserved the date of Gregory's ordination to the priesthood; the new one was certainly the date on which he became pope, which could easily be worked out from the data provided by Bede.

[12] *Eia fratres – forte enim aliqui de gente illa haec me dicentem presentes auscultant, – eia, inquam, vos Angli, fratres nobis in Christiana fide effecti, vobis a deo predestinatum et missum beatum Gregorium pro apostolo suscepistis.* Wilmart, 1935, pp. 212–13.

[13] Wilmart, 1935, p. 212: *Qui igitur eum (Gregorium) praevium ad caelestia sequi desiderant, ducatus ipsius primordia venerari non abnuant. Nam qui ea sua devotione amplecti nolunt, ipsi sibi testes sunt quod eum ductorem habere refugiunt. Hoc quoniam humana consuetudine et ex divina historia satis patet, plura inde ducere supervacuum existimavimus. Quid etiam ex his colligi possit inferre nolo, ne, si dixero, illos qui eo duce niti renuunt, eo cuius vice functus est niti duce subterfugere, et iccirco Christi qui eum suis ovibus ducem instituit nolle ordinationi adquiescere, videar nimis aliena multorum voluntati proponere.* [14] For details, see below, pp. 417–18.

contains only his own works and his report of another sermon of Anselm, the likelihood that Anselm was the preacher of this sermon also is very high indeed.[15] Moreover, there is a date when it would have been peculiarly appropriate: at the beginning of September 1101.

To understand the significance of this date, it is necessary first to remember that the country had recently been invaded by Robert of Normandy, and Henry I had been saved largely by the exertions of Anselm. As soon as Robert withdrew, Henry I held a great meeting with all his main supporters at Windsor at the beginning of September. As usual on such occasions, several important privileges and charters were issued, and two are especially important in connection with this sermon, for they are the first (and perhaps only) known charters to be dated on *the feast of the Ordination of St Gregory*. The first of these charters set up a bishopric in the city of Bath; the second completed the setting up of a new bishopric at Norwich.[16] Anselm and a large part of the Norman baronage witnessed them both.

If I am right in thinking that the sermon preserved by Eadmer was delivered by Anselm on this occasion, Anselm was associating himself with an Anglo-Saxon restoration at a significant moment in his archiepiscopal career. He had returned to England from his long exile, and with Henry I securely on the throne, he at last looked forward to some years of creative activity. Everything that he believed to be true about the vast area of responsibility of the church of Canterbury had its origin in Gregory the Great. So restoring the old feast could be looked on as a foundation for future action. The change of date, from the obscure day of Gregory's Ordination to the day which marked the beginning of his papal reign, was also appropriate: from an English point of view, his most important action as pope had been the mission of Augustine, which inaugurated the see and primacy of Canterbury. Looked at in this light, this sermon fits precisely into the pattern of Anselm's policy as archbishop.

---

[15] As a further indication of Anselm's authorship, it may also be mentioned that the sermon introduces one of Anselm's favourite images of a complete man as a four-square stone. See *Memorials*, pp. 146–7, 195, 305, 314–16, for other examples of the use of this image.

[16] For the charters, see *Regesta* ii, nos. 544, 547; and for the occasion, see *HN*, p. 131.

2   *Alexander's reports*

For reasons which will appear later, Eadmer ceased to be the recorder of Anselm's words in about the year 1100.[17] His place was taken during the next nine years by Alexander, a Canterbury monk of whom we know little except that he accompanied Anselm during his second exile. Although he was not as talented a reporter as Eadmer, he seems to have been equally assiduous, and the records he has left are even more extensive than those of Eadmer and had a much wider circulation in the Middle Ages.

In the first place, he has left a collection of twenty-one sermons or fragments of sermons preached on various unspecified occasions. He put this collection together between 1116 and 1120 at the request of Anselm's nephew, also called Anselm, who during these years was papal legate in Normandy and asked Alexander for a copy of the reports which he was known to have kept. In sending the young Anselm this body of material, Alexander complained that he could send only a small part of what he had collected, because some unauthorized person had carried off the remainder of his material. Nevertheless, he was able to send reports of twenty-one sermons, or parts of sermons, to Anselm's nephew, and these form a valuable addition to our knowledge of Anselm's spoken words.[18] They lack the intimacy of Eadmer, and preserve much less of the characteristic turns of phrase with which Eadmer enlivened his work, but they supplement our knowledge in a variety of ways. They show that the similes and parables reported by Eadmer were used on several occasions and in various contexts.[19] A comparison with Alexander confirms the authority of Eadmer's reports, but it also shows that there is more art in Eadmer than appears on the surface. This is clear when we compare a report of the same sermon by Eadmer and Alexander: Eadmer has preserved the repetitions and ejaculations of the spoken word which Alexander lost; Eadmer is sometimes less clear in doctrine, but more lively in detail; and he has not scrupled to add to the end of his report words that no doubt came from Anselm's lips, but could not possibly have belonged to the original sermon.

---

[17] See below, pp. 411–14.
[18] For these reports, see *Memorials*, pp. 19–30, 105– 95, 269–70.
[19] For a clear example of varied repetition, see *Memorials*, pp. 31–4, 271–91.

Alexander's reports are important because they preserve a great deal of material which seems to have had little interest for Eadmer. Eadmer found his satisfaction in the similes and parables with which Anselm's talk abounded; he says nothing about an equally ubiquitous form of Anselmian discourse – the endless divisions and subdivisions of a subject, to which Alexander's reports, no less than Anselm's written works, bear witness. The whole range of Anselm's writings testifies to his interest in verbal analysis, and from Alexander we know that this was a feature of his conversation as well as of his more formal speculations.

3   The reporter of Anselm's parables

What happened to the remainder of Alexander's material? Were there any other reports of Anselm's spoken words at Canterbury? Strictly, we do not know. But there is reason to suspect that the transcriber and purloiner of whose activity Alexander complained was none other than the most famous historian of the period in England, William of Malmesbury. The evidence of his activity as a transcriber, and almost certainly also a remover of letters of Anselm from the Canterbury archives during the years between 1115 and 1120 is set out below. There is also evidence that he listened to Alexander's reminiscences of things heard and seen during Anselm's exile, for he includes two distorted versions of Alexander's anecdotes in his *Historia Regum*, which was completed in 1120.[20]

Whether or not the suspicion that William of Malmesbury was the purloiner of whom Alexander complained is justified, it is certain that a large amount of the reported talk of Anselm, and that which had by far the greatest success, comes from a collection of material which was abstracted from Canterbury by some collector who put it in circulation within about twenty years of Anselm's death. The title of the collection varied, but it was always associated with the name of Anselm; and in the course of time the title given to the whole collection became stabilized as *Liber de Similitudinibus*, which sufficiently covered the greater part of its contents. Under this title it had an immense success in the later Middle Ages. The two earliest manuscripts date from about 1130; but the work was

---

[20] For an account of William of Malmesbury's dealings with Anselm's letters, see below, pp. 402–3, 470–3. For two stories about Gregory VII, which are found both in Alexander's *Dicta* and in William of Malmesbury, see *Memorials*, pp. 212–14, and *GR*, ii, pp. 322–4.

not widely known until the thirteenth century, when the growing interest in Anselm's theology, and in the minute analysis of the powers of the soul with which the *De Similitudinibus* abounds, gave it a very wide circulation. In the fourteenth century, alone among the records of Anselm's informal talk, it is almost always included in the increasingly common general collections of his works.[21]

The popularity of this work in the late Middle Ages reflects the increasing interest in Anselm's thought among theologians, but it also shows that much of the interest was concentrated on those parts of his thought which were not to be found in his formal treatises, and sometimes not at all in his authentic works. We do not know how the *De Similitudinibus* was first introduced into university circles, but it was already established academically in the mid-thirteenth century, and Thomas Aquinas cites it under Anselm's name almost as often as the *Cur Deus Homo*. Once established it kept its place in the canon of Anselm's writings. Like Eadmer's treatise on the Conception of the Virgin, which had a similar history, it owed its success partly to the widespread desire for complete collections of the works (or supposed works) of important authors, and partly to the relevance of the subject-matter to the controversies of the fourteenth and fifteenth centuries. For a variety of reasons, therefore, the *De Similitudinibus*, after an obscure start, reached a wide audience with the status of a genuine work of Anselm – which in substance it was, though Anselm himself had never seen it.

When Alexander was quite forgotten, and Eadmer remembered, if at all, only as the writer of a not very widely read biography, these fragments conveyed to a later age most of what it knew of Anselm's talk. Late medieval scholars were not interested in the circumstances or graces of Anselm's talk, nor in the names of its reporters.

---

[21] For the text of the *De Similitudinibus*, and a discussion of its nature, author, and sources, see *Memorials*, pp. 4–18, 37–104. At the time when those pages were written, neither Fr Schmitt nor I was aware of the extent of William of Malmesbury's involvement in the transcription and (as now seems to me likely) abstraction from Canterbury of items of Anselm's correspondence. The whole question of the compilation of the *De Similitudinibus* remains extremely complicated, but several features in the textual history of the work – such as its dissemination from a centre other than Canterbury – would be explained if its compilation was associated with the collection of Anselmian materials which William of Malmesbury evidently possessed. It should, however, be noted that the distribution of early manuscripts of the *De Similitudinibus* does not point to Malmesbury as the centre from which this work gradually won a place for itself among Anselm's collected works. On this point, see *Memorials*, pp. 15–18.

They wished only to have what was useful for their purposes, and the *De Similitudinibus* served them well. In its 192 chapters it contained crumbs which even Aquinas thought worth picking up. To live a posthumous life in this fossilized form was a curious fate for talk which had once been so vivid and new; but a record which links Anselm's great treatises with his table-talk and daily discourses is valuable, and the record cannot be left without an illustration of its subject matter.

Let us take as our point of departure Anselm's speculations about the soul. This was a subject to which he often returned, and about which he said things which never got into his formal treatises:

In the soul [he explained] there are three natures: Reason, Will and Appetite. By reason the soul is allied to the angels, by appetite to the beasts, by will to both. Will holds a middle place between Reason and Appetite, inclining now to Reason, now to Appetite. When it turns to Reason, it is imbued with those things which are rational and spiritual; when it turns to Appetite, it is imbued with things carnal and irrational. So, according to the operation of his Will, a man is either rational and spiritual or carnal and animal.[22]

Thus begins one of the sections of the *Dicta Anselmi*. Since the same distinction is also found elsewhere in Alexander's record of Anselm's talk, it seems clear that this question was occupying Anselm's mind during his last years. But thirty years earlier, when he was prior of Bec, Anselm had said something very similar to Guibert of Nogent, who years later remembered what had been said:

He taught me [Guibert wrote in his Autobiography] that there was a threefold or fourfold division of the spirit, and he treated the operation of the whole interior mystery under these heads: Desire, Will, Reason, Intellect. What many, including myself, regarded as a unity, he resolved into distinct parts and showed that the first two parts were not identical unless joined to the third or fourth.[23]

It must be admitted that Guibert's report is not as clear as one could wish. But it provides clear proof that, in talking to the young monk whose first steps in philosophy he was guiding in about 1075, he was already making the point that the Will is poised between Desire and Reason, which is more fully developed in talk recorded in the *Dicta* thirty years later.

That the soul was composed of parts, and that, being made in the

---

[22] *Memorials*, p. 174; and cf. p. 308.   [23] Guibert, *De Vita Sua*, PL 156, col. 874.

likeness of God, these parts should be three in number, was an ancient doctrine. But Anselm departed from the form in which this division was most commonly found in the authors of the early Middle Ages from the time of St Augustine to St Bernard. These authors followed a Platonic tradition in dividing the soul into three parts: Memory, Reason, and Will. In giving an independent status to Appetite or Desire, Anselm foreshadows a less intellectualist approach to the problem of the soul. It is no more than a hint, but it marks a deviation from an accepted mode of thought, and it evidently caught the attention of his audience.

If we may judge from other fragments of his talk, the faculty of the soul to which he devoted the most minute attention was the will. On this subject he was remarkably copious, and the first forty chapters of the *De Similitudinibus* are entirely occupied with an analysis, in which ninety modes of self-will are distinguished under the three main divisions of *delectatio* (thirty-one modes), *exaltatio* (fifteen modes), and *curiositas* (forty-four modes).[24]

Carrying our inquiry a step further, we have a record of words which he spoke to the monks of Arras as he passed through on his second journey to Rome in 1103. It will be remembered that he had much to think about; not least the papal letter which he had received but not opened in England for fear of the chaos that its contents might cause. But he was always ready for discussion on matters of deeper importance, and in Arras he had a conversation which had aroused the interest of one member of his audience, who wrote to ask him to write down the main heads of his argument. Anselm, continuing his leisurely journey, had reached Bec, where he opened the papal letter, and settled down to pass the summer months and avoid the heat of an Italian summer. In his leisure hours he wrote a summary of his argument to his correspondent in Arras:

You ask me to recall to you by letter the three modes of pride of which I spoke to you, because you have forgotten two of them. I said there are three modes: (1) in judging, as when a man thinks of himself more highly than he ought to think; (2) in willing, as when a man wishes to be treated otherwise than as he ought to be; and (3) in action, as when a man treats himself better than he ought to do. Of these modes, the last (in action alone) is the least blameworthy because it is in ignorance; the second (in willing) is worse; but the first (in

---

[24] For these sub-divisions see *Memorials*, pp. 41–50.

judging) is worst of all because then a man wrongly thinks he is right. These (1, 2, 3) are the simple modes of pride, but they can be combined into three double modes,(1 + 2, 2 + 3, 1 + 3); or into one triple mode (1 + 2 + 3). Thus there are seven modes; three single, three double, and one triple. . . May God who has given me understanding to distinguish the features of Pride and Humility, give me grace to avoid the first of these and embrace the second. Greet my lord and friend the bishop of Arras. [25]

These were the subjects which he talked about as he passed from one religious community to another on his way to Rome – certainly more congenial to him than the wretched business which was taking him there – and everywhere he found friends and listeners to whom this kind of talk came as something new and worth remembering. They were experiencing the stirring of a new spirit of analytical inquiry, and it was Alexander's great virtue as a reporter of Anselm's talk that he should have preserved notes on this kind of talk, while Eadmer, even in the days when he was the privileged reporter, should have preserved only the similes with which Anselm illustrated his reflections on the human will and the activity of the soul. Nevertheless, both he and Alexander deserve a high place among those who preserved the memory of the essential features of Anselm's personality. Despite his one-sidedness, Eadmer's contribution to the preservation of Anselm's memory is so much greater than any other that he requires a chapter to himself. But before we go on to Eadmer, we may consider the last great service which Anselm's pupils and admirers performed in collecting his letters for posterity.

II THE COLLECTORS OF ANSELM'S LETTERS[26]

Alongside the friends and disciples who preserved records of Anselm's conversations and sermons, those who collected his letters deserve an honourable place, if only because they preserved more of Anselm's written words than all the rest put together. The bulk of his surviving letters is about twice that of all his other writings, and most of them would probably have been lost but for the efforts of these collectors. Bulk of course is not everything. We could better spare all Anselm's letters than the *Proslogion* or the

---

[25] *Ep.* 285 (iii, 75).
[26] In the following pages I shall place in a general setting and summarize the conclusions for which the evidence is given in greater detail in the Appendix (pp. 458–81) and in the literature there cited.

Prayers and *Meditations*. Nevertheless, the letters provide an essential body of material for understanding the development of his mind and aims, his conception of the religious life, and his attitudes to the political problems of his later years. At every stage in his career, they help us to identify the subjects to which he attached most importance.

In giving credit to Anselm's disciples for the collection of his letters, I am going against the opinion of several notable scholars who have argued that Anselm himself was responsible for collecting his letters, and they have pointed to two manuscripts, the first, **N**, made in about 1092, and the other, **L**, made (as they would say) between 1105 and 1109, as the collections which he himself made of the letters which he wished to preserve for posterity. They have then gone on to argue that the letters which are preserved, and (even more important) the omission of certain letters in **L** provide trustworthy evidence of the picture of himself which he wished to hand down to posterity.

If this were true, the precise contents of these manuscripts would have important consequences for our understanding of his mind and personality. Consequently, though the mechanics of the preservation of these documents is the subject of our inquiry, it has repercussions for our interpretation of his character and aims. Broadly speaking, the conclusion which we reach will support one of two divergent views of his personality. If we are persuaded that he himself directed the making of these volumes, and especially of **L**, we shall portray him as a man of political shrewdness and calculation, who gathered, or omitted, letters with a view to omitting some traits, either in himself or in his cause, which would be in some way detrimental. On the other hand, if we conclude that the collections were made by his admirers using imperfectly preserved materials, then he will appear as a man who did little or nothing to preserve an image of himself for posterity.

Nevertheless, even if the second of these two views is correct – as I believe it to be – we must not fall into the error of thinking that he attached no importance to his letters. All of them, even the most intimate, are public statements of a religious ideal. As we have already seen, he often wrote letters which on the surface are intimately addressed to a single person, but are intended to be read by others. Moreover, Anselm did not forget the letters he had written. On one occasion, some thirty years after writing a letter to a novice at Cluny, he urged another novice at Canterbury 'to find and read' it.[27] On other occasions, he copied large passages from earlier letters in later ones. He certainly had no objection to his letters being collected and read, and there is reason to think that he was himself collecting his letters in the years between about 1085 and 1093. Moreover, it may be argued that, if he expected a monk to be able to find a letter which he had written to someone else thirty years earlier, this implies that his letters had already been collected under his direction. The first of these points will be dealt with presently; as for the second, it will suffice to say that the phrase which he used in advising the Canterbury novice to read his earlier letter does not imply that he would find it in any existing collection. The letter in question was in fact to be found among the materials which he had left at Canterbury when he went into exile, and he might well have expected it to be fairly easily discoverable.

We must not, however, attach too much importance to the question we are now investigating. If we find, as I believe we shall, that Anselm, after an initial interest in collecting his letters before he left Bec, either changed his mind or had no time for continuing his work of collection, we shall save him from the imputation of shaping his image for posterity. But in the end the value of his letters lies, not in the manner of their preservation, but in their contents, in their revelation of his aims, his friendships and his religious ideals. Nevertheless, the manner of their preservation has some importance for understanding his attitude to his own writings and the contribution which his disciples made to the preservation of his memory. As a first step in our inquiry, we must understand the state of his correspondence during his lifetime, and the stages in the process whereby this body of material was collected into the volumes which contain the bulk of his surviving letters.

As an aid to understanding what we are doing, there are some general features of letter collections which first need to be understood.

I   General problems of letter collecting

Collections of letters at all times present complicated problems which are always more or less the same. First, even if the writer himself makes a collection of his own letters, he seldom has the copies which he sent to the addressees. What he generally has are

---

[27]   *Ep.* 336 (iii, 103): *Consulo tibi ut quaeras epistolam quam ego feci domino Lanzoni quando novitius erat.* The letter referred to is *Ep.* 37 (i, 29).

fair copies, or more often drafts, or even several different drafts, of the documents which he had actually dispatched. Occasionally letter writers will have kept a register of their letters. But even then the texts thus preserved are not always the same as those which were dispatched: they are often revised texts containing what, on further reflection, the writer would have liked to have sent. There were indeed several medieval authors who did just this: they kept copies of letters and then revised them for publication. But there is clear evidence that Anselm did not keep any such register of his letters before 1100. So, for most of his life, he was not a careful preserver of his letters. Consequently, anyone, whether himself or some other person, who wished to make a collection of his letters before 1100, had to collect the material from drafts and fair copies at Bec or Canterbury, or from their recipients.

The evidence for this state of affairs is of various kinds, and belongs to different periods of his life. To begin with, we have a letter which Anselm wrote in about 1085 to the monks of Bec at the priory of Conflans, in which he mentions that he is waiting for the letters which he had asked their prior, Maurice, to return to him. Then, another letter of 1092 shows that he was still waiting for some of these letters.[28] So we start with clear evidence that during his years at Bec, despite the value he attached to several of his letters, Anselm had no complete collection of them in his possession.

Then later, when he was archbishop, we have decisive evidence that, in the years from 1093 to 1100, he was similarly negligent in preserving his letters, for the later collectors of his letters at Canterbury could find no more than about half of the letters which had been preserved by their recipients. After 1100, however, whether as a result of his experience of more business-like systems of preservation at Lyons and Rome, or for some other reason, it is clear that the preservation of his letters was much more thoroughly undertaken: the relative completeness of the archiepiscopal letters in the Canterbury manuscript, **L**, provides eloquent testimony to a change of practice after this date. The important question which remains to be resolved concerns the nature of the change: did it simply mean that more care was taken after 1100 to preserve drafts or copies of letters than previously, or did it mean that the letters which he sent out, together with some of those which he received, were copied into an official Register under Anselm's immediate supervision? As I have said, this is more than a technical question: if

[28] See *Epp.* 104 (ii, 14) and 147 (ii, 51).

397

the work of compilation was done under Anselm's supervision, he would seem deliberately to have omitted some letters, and these omissions might suggest that he rejected them because he thought that they would for one reason or another be detrimental either to his own reputation or to the causes which he wished to promote.

It is important not to take too rigid a view of this matter. Until very recently, no one making a collection of letters for whatever purpose would aim at including everything. Even if Anselm were making his own collection, he would certainly have omitted some, perhaps many, letters as unimportant. The only question we are here considering is whether he currently made the collection which has survived in the Canterbury manuscript **L** as has been alleged. Only if the answer to this question is 'Yes', need we bother about the reasons for the omission of letters which may simply not have been available to collectors at a later date.

In what follows, and in the Appendix which will deal with these questions in greater detail, I shall examine the evidence, which – as I believe – shows quite conclusively that, with the exception of a single manuscript for which Anselm was *not* responsible, his letters were preserved during his whole lifetime, both before and after 1100, only in drafts and bundles of individual copies in the archives of Bec and Canterbury; and that the work of collecting them into volumes was a memorial exercise, undertaken after his death by his disciples and admirers.

2   *Two central manuscripts*

I turn first to the two manuscripts, **N** and **L**, which have been claimed to be collections made under Anselm's personal direction. Of these two, **N** contains only his letters as prior and abbot of Bec, and **L** contains a collection of his letters throughout the whole period from 1070 to 1107.

It may be noted to begin with that the pre-1093 letters in **L** have a character, both in text and arrangement, strikingly different from the same texts in **N**. Consequently, if Anselm was responsible for **L**, he had forgotten, or chose to neglect, the work he had earlier done in **N**. In fact, as I shall hope to show, he was responsible for neither of them, and the divergence between the early letters in the two manuscripts is intelligible on grounds which have nothing to do with Anselm's responsibility for either of them.

We may begin with **N**, which contains only letters of Anselm's years as prior and abbot of Bec. It is generally agreed that the manuscript can be dated shortly after 1092; and, since we know that Anselm was collecting his letters at this time, there is a *prima facie* case for believing that a manuscript containing a collection of his letters at this early date is likely to represent his own work. Indeed, it is almost certain that whoever made the collection, whether Anselm or someone else, was using materials which Anselm had brought with him from Bec or had collected while he was staying at Westminster with Gilbert Crispin in the Autumn of 1092.

Despite these congruities, however, there are very strong reasons for thinking that **N** was made without Anselm's knowledge or supervision. The texts are poor, and several of them are drafts of letters of which the full texts later existed at Canterbury and were used for the main collection of his letters in **L**. Moreover, **N** omits the letters to his former pupil Maurice, which Anselm had been trying to retrieve before he was archbishop, and which he must in the end have succeeded in retrieving, for they were certainly at Canterbury when **L** was compiled.

It would appear, therefore, that **N** was compiled while Anselm was still engaged in his ultimately successful attempt to recover his letters from Maurice. Moreover, this state of incompleteness is borne out by the confused order in which **N** presents the letters: apart from the broad division between the letters of his priorate and those of his abbacy, the order is chaotic, and the scribe in his haste has copied one letter twice. Further, although the materials from which **N** was made were at later at Canterbury, and were found there by William of Malmesbury during the years from 1120 to 1123, when he made his own copies of them, William clearly had no knowledge of the existence of **N**, which seems never to have been at Canterbury, and was never part of Anselm's literary archive.

The most plausible conclusion to be drawn from these scattered data is that **N** was an unauthorized copy of materials in Anselm's possession made during the months in 1092–93 when he was at Westminster, or at latest during his early months as archbishop of Canterbury. If it seems surprising that a copy of material in Anselm's possession should have been made without his knowledge, we know from other evidence that it was not uncommon for Anselm's admirers to make unauthorized copies of his writings, and – though he objected – he could do nothing to prevent it.[29]

I now turn to **L**, which has been thought to have been compiled

---

[29] On this, see the evidence cited below, p. 463, n.

under Anselm's personal supervision between about 1103 and 1109. It contains most of Anselm's surviving letters as archbishop, as well as a fairly full collection of his earlier letters as prior and abbot of Bec. It was written at Canterbury and belonged to the cathedral library at Canterbury, but there are several reasons for thinking that it was not in existence before 1120–23.

In the first place, as Dom Wilmart who first studied it in detail rightly remarked, it has a striking similarity with another Canterbury manuscript of the early 1120s.[30] More important, William of Malmesbury, who searched for Anselmian materials at Canterbury during these years and made copies of what he found, clearly did not know of its existence, which would have been very surprising indeed if Anselm had been known to have been responsible for its compilation. William made a very extensive search for Anselmian material, but the only collection of Anselm's letters in a single volume which he found were those which Eadmer had copied into his *Historia Novorum* between 1009 and 1114. Apart from these, he found a large number of uncollected letters. He subsequently copied, or directed other scribes to copy, these letters into volumes which are central to our whole inquiry. To understand them we must first examine their background.

3 The importance of William of Malmesbury's initiative

We have already seen that William of Malmesbury's accounts of his visits to Canterbury in search of historical materials during the years 1120–23 provide important evidence for the 'finding' of the primatial forgeries at Canterbury during these years. These accounts are equally important for what they tell us about the state of Anselm's letters. Three manuscripts, **MFD**, have survived, and another now lost is known to have existed, into which William, or those who worked for him, transcribed the material which he found. They experimented in various ways of organizing this material. In one of the manuscripts derived from William's discoveries (**M**), some of Anselm's letters are in total confusion, but others are arranged according to the persons or classes of person to whom they were addressed. In two others (**DE**), these same letters are arranged in a roughly chronological order; and in the manuscript now lost, the papal documents were extracted to form a

[30] See below, p. 476n.

volume by themselves. It is clear from these varied attempts to arrange Anselm's letters in different kinds of intelligible order, that William himself had found them at Canterbury in no order at all.

To attempt to arrange the considerable body of material which he collected, and to transcribe the resulting collection in one or more volumes, would have taken many months, and I believe that it could only have been done by removing some of the material from Canterbury to Malmesbury. Indeed, it is clear that the three volumes of William's collection which still exist, as well as the lost volume, were not made in Canterbury: two – **M** and the lost collection of papal letters – were almost certainly made in Malmesbury; and the other two – **FD** – though not themselves from Malmesbury, were probably also copied from material at Malmesbury.

This dispersal of Anselm's letters in William of Malmesbury's copies does not necessarily mean that these materials were removed without the consent of the Canterbury monks. Indeed, there are good reasons for thinking that, when the final collection **L** was made at Canterbury between – as I judge – about 1125 and 1130, it was made with the help of William of Malmesbury and of the materials he had collected and arranged in the ways I have described. So it is likely that William remained on terms of friendly co-operation with the monks of Canterbury, and he probably returned at least some of the materials which he had removed during his researches of the early 1120s. The result was that these letters, which had first been arranged by William of Malmesbury, were also available to the collectors at Canterbury who were responsible for **L**. But, in addition to these letters, it is clear that many other letters came to light during the years after William's researches, and these too were added to the collection in **L** up to the very end, while it was being transcribed. It follows from this that **L** is to be regarded as the latest stage in a long process of collection and arrangement, which begins with the selected texts transcribed into Eadmer's *Historia Novorum* between 1109 and 1114, continues through the discoveries and copies made by William of Malmesbury from 1120 to about 1123, and reaches its climax in **L**, which incorporated William's discoveries and added several more items which he had missed. The result is that **L** is the most complete collection of Anselm's archiepiscopal letters.

L is not, however, the most complete collection of the letters of Anselm's earlier years at Bec or of his early archiepiscopal years from 1093 to 1100. For these letters we must look to Bec, and we must begin by understanding the changing state of affairs at both Canterbury and Bec in the 1120s.

4 The final collections of Canterbury and Bec

When William of Malmesbury began making his collection of Anselmian materials, Anselm's main friends and disciples were scattered. Eadmer was in Normandy with Anselm's successor, Archbishop Ralph, from 1116 to 1119, and then in Scotland for much of 1120 attempting in vain to reduce the see of St Andrews to dependence on Canterbury. Boso had returned to Bec after Anselm's death, and the young Anselm, the archbishop's nephew, had also left Canterbury at about the same time and was in Normandy acting as papal legate from 1116 to about 1120.

During these years also, Anselm's reputation was at a low ebb among the monks at Canterbury on account of his failure to defend their primatial rights. In these circumstances, Anselm's letters, and the fragments of his unfinished works and reports of his talk, seem to have lain neglected until William of Malmesbury, who was to become one of Anselm's most devoted admirers, began investigating them. I have briefly outlined the results of these investigations. But then, on the heels of William of Malmesbury's initiative, the situation of Anselm's earlier disciples changed. Eadmer returned to Canterbury permanently in 1121 and later became precentor with authority over the library and the copying of manuscripts. In 1122 also the young Anselm became abbot of Bury St Edmunds, and soon afterwards Boso became abbot of Bec. These changes brought Anselm's disciples into positions of authority at the two centres of his life's work, and the work of collecting Anselm's letters, initiated by William of Malmesbury, could at last go ahead with fresh vigour both at Canterbury and at Bec. The manuscripts of his letters, which still survive from Canterbury, Malmesbury, and Bury St Edmunds, and the great collection formed at Bec, perhaps under Boso's initiative, and certainly during his years as abbot, now destroyed but preserved in three copies, become intelligible when they are seen as inter-related efforts to salvage the scattered remains of his letters and drafts of his unfinished works. The manuscripts, **MDF** from Malmesbury, **LP** at Canterbury, the ancestor of **VCE** at Bec, are the witnesses to this activity. The climax of the whole endeavour was the Bec manuscript from which **VCE** were copied, and the Canterbury manuscript **L** with its copy **P**.

There is still much to be done to fill in the details of this combined effort, but the cumulative evidence suffices to show that the joint efforts of Anselm's admirers at Canterbury and Bec during the 1120s produced the collections of Anselm's letters which saved them from destruction. They came just in time to perform this essential service, for interest in Anselm's letters became very dim in the next generation, and it is likely that most of his letters would have disappeared if they had not been collected while his memory was still bright. The central features of the whole process are, first, the pioneering researches of William of Malmesbury, then the collaboration in exchanging texts between Malmesbury, Canterbury and Bec, which made possible the formation of the volumes which belonged to one or other of these three monasteries. These main stages were accompanied by continuing discoveries of new letters at Canterbury, which were added to **L** up to the very end, to the extent of requiring supplementary quires to contain the most recently discovered material.

The existence of these collections provides a happy ending to the drama of Anselm's fluctuating relationship with the communities of both Bec and Canterbury, and adds a new name to the list of Anselm's disciples in William of Malmesbury. These years also provided a happier ending to Eadmer's career than had seemed likely in 1120. Although he returned to Canterbury in 1121 as a defeated politician, his return to his monastic origins enabled him to assist the process of giving permanent form to the hitherto confused and perishable remains of Anselm's letters. This was only the last of his services to Anselm's memory, and we may now turn to review his contribution as a whole.

CHAPTER 17

EADMER AND ANSELM

I THE DEVELOPMENT OF A DISCIPLE

1 The happy years

Nearly everything that can be known about Anselm's life and the development of his thought and devotion comes either from his own writings or from those of Eadmer. A few exceptions must be made. Gilbert Crispin's *Life* of Herluin, the founder of Bec, supplies some important details about Lanfranc's influence on the growth of the monastery, and hence of the scene that met Anselm on his arrival in 1059. Then, some forty years later, our knowledge of Anselm's preaching and conversation would be much poorer without the reports of the Canterbury monk Alexander and the compiler of the *De Similitudinibus*. In addition, the letters of Lanfranc and of Urban II and Paschal II, which were preserved at Canterbury among Anselm's correspondence, also make a substantial contribution to our knowledge of his aims as archbishop. But, when all allowances have been made for other sources, it remains true that, apart from Anselm's own writings, which are only accidentally autobiographical, Eadmer contributes more than all the others put together to our knowledge of Anselm. He was not only Anselm's daily companion and most assiduous reporter of his words and actions from 1093 onwards, but he had also heard Anselm's own account of many incidents in his life going back to the days before he had left Aosta. There was a happy time when Anselm had even approved Eadmer's writing a record of all that he had seen and heard. Sadly, this approval was withdrawn, and then the reporting ceased during Anselm's lifetime; but, by a stratagem, the record survived, and Eadmer completed it after Anselm's death. We shall come to these incidents presently.

In addition to this, Eadmer has another claim to our attention. To understand Anselm in his contemporary setting, it is necessary to know what influence he had on his contemporaries. In a man who was pre-eminently a teacher and talker, as well as a writer of some of the most original theological and devotional works of the Middle Ages, the normal place to look for the record of his influence would be in the writings of his pupils. But here, with the exception of Eadmer, the records – in comparison with the power of the originating impulse – are disappointing. Boso, who was intellectually the brightest of his pupils, wrote nothing. Guibert of Nogent, who owed much to Anselm, wrote nothing which followed Anselm's main lines of thought; on the contrary he followed the rival model of Anselm of Laon. Honorius Augustodunensis also, having experienced the initial impulse of Anselm at Canterbury, followed other models for the rest of his life. Gilbert Crispin and Ralph remained faithful to the lines of theological argument and meditation which they had learnt from Anselm, but they were too fully engaged in the task of ruling monastic communities to leave a lasting mark as authors.[1] Among all Anselm's devotees, Eadmer alone made writing his life's work, and left works of lasting importance which are thoroughly Anselmian in inspiration.

They have received less attention than they deserve. Only the *Historia Novorum in Anglia* and, at a lower level, the *Vita Anselmi* have appealed to historians. The *Historia Novorum* has always been recognized as the first piece of large-scale historical writing in England after Bede. Much more dimly, the *Vita Anselmi* has been recognized as the first intimate contemporary biography since Asser's *Life* of King Alfred. In addition, students of doctrine have more recently come to recognize Eadmer as the writer of the first treatise outlining a doctrine of the Immaculate Conception of the Virgin Mary. But he also wrote lives of saints, prayers, meditations, and accounts of relics, which have scarcely been known to exist, much less read. They have had the misfortune to belong to what are generally reckoned to be different compartments of knowledge, but their interrelations need to be closely studied if Eadmer's life and his association with Anselm are to be understood. Only a brief outline of these various sides of Eadmer's mind can be attempted here, but it must always be remembered that his association with Anselm, and the influence of the one on the other, are associated with a large background of saints' *Lives*, and a tradition of devotional works, much of which lay in deep obscurity until Dom Wilmart, the great investigator of medieval spirituality, rescued large parts of this literature from oblivion. In brief, to understand

[1] See above, pp. 371–6.

the Anselm whom Eadmer preserved for posterity, we must also understand Eadmer's gifts and limitations, and the traditions which he embodied.

This is not easy: no one wrote a biography of Eadmer as he wrote one of Anselm. We must rely almost exclusively on what he casually let fall about himself in the course of writings devoted to other subjects. Fortunately he was much given to reminiscence, and it is this which makes possible the task of understanding him and of extending our understanding of Anselm through him.

He was nearly thirty years younger than Anselm, born a few years before the Norman Conquest, and brought up from infancy in the monastic community of the cathedral church at Canterbury. Since he tells us that he was a small boy in 1070–71 and adolescent in 1079, and since he was old enough in 1067 to remember the arrangement of the old church of Canterbury which was burnt that year, we cannot be far wrong in placing the date of his birth about 1060. He was about twenty when he met Anselm during his first visit to Canterbury in 1079. As usual, Anselm talked chiefly to the young men, and Eadmer at once became his devoted admirer. This was not uncommon: Boso and Guibert of Nogent, and doubtless many others, were similarly captivated by Anselm's talk at about the same age. But it is significant that the basis of Eadmer's admiration differed from theirs: they found in Anselm an elucidator of difficult doctrines and a stimulus to intellectual inquiry; Eadmer found him a foreigner who, unlike all the other too numerous foreigners around him, understood and defended Old English piety. Other English monks were to make the same discovery about Anselm, but only Eadmer linked Anselm's continuing influence with his own past, and made the combination the foundation of all that he was to do afterwards.

Of Eadmer's family, our only certain knowledge is that he had a nephew, a sister's son, with the Norman name of Haimo, who was a monk at Christ Church Canterbury in about 1115. About fifteen years later, we find another relative called Henry, a man of some substance, living near Canterbury as a tenant of the monastery. It seems also very likely that his mother was the poor woman to whom Lanfranc paid the considerable pension of thirty shillings a year, about which Eadmer tells a touching story.[2]

---

[2] *HN*, pp. 13–14. Knowles, 1940, p. 109, first suggested that the widow in this story might well be Eadmer's mother, and this is very likely, for it is hard to see how Eadmer could otherwise have known all the details which he gives.

These scanty facts about his family background suggest that he came from a family of English gentry, closely associated with the church of Canterbury, and probably impoverished, certainly reduced in status, by the Conquest. This background dominated all his thoughts and feelings: pride of race, the grievances of the conquered, and the love of Canterbury, all combined to produce a sense of indignation and nostalgia in writing of the present and the past. He nursed his memories and cherished a secret sense of superiority while he watched the downfall of his nation. Writing fifty years after the Conquest about the systematic rejection of Englishmen for ecclesiastical appointments, Eadmer wrote:

Their nationality was their downfall. If they were English, no virtue was enough for their promotion; if they were foreigners, the mere appearance of virtue, vouched for by their friends, was sufficient for them to be judged worthy of the highest honour.[3]

Nearly sixty years after the Conquest he wrote in similar vein to the monks of Glastonbury, who claimed that they possessed the body of St Dunstan, which they had filched from Canterbury:

I was not a little confounded to hear such a foolish and even laughable story, especially as it is said to have been invented by Englishmen. Alas, why did you not consult some foreigner – one of those experienced and knowledgeable men from beyond the sea – who would have invented some likely lie on such an important matter, which you could have bought?[4]

These are the feelings of the oppressed, and though Eadmer did not often express them, they never died. The long friendship with Anselm did not extinguish the sense of grievance. Nor did it diminish his enduring nostalgia for the past. It simply gave a new content to these emotions, and brought a new hope for the survival of the insular tradition.

A feeling of resentment is in itself of no great interest and of no creative power. But to this was added a sense of community, concentrated in the well-being of the church of Canterbury. This gave a direction and driving force to what might have been only a barren grievance. Lanfranc had done much to preserve the lands and greatness of Canterbury: but, as we have seen, there was much more to be done to preserve the traditions of the monastery, which Lanfranc in almost every sphere save the primacy had threatened and diminished. The task of reviving and preserving these

[3] *HN*, p. 224.   [4] *PL* 159, col. 803B.

traditions called for more research into archival material than had been necessary in any previous generation. The rights of Canterbury, especially with regard to York, required much turning over of chronicles, papal privileges and records of episcopal professions, in the hope of extracting from them what was eagerly believed, indeed *known* to be true, but scarcely capable of documentary proof. The threat to liturgical observances and devotional habits called for an intense effort to recall and set down in writing their credentials in saints' lives and records of miracles. These were matters which had scarcely needed to be examined, still less defended, before the Conquest. But now the effort of recall was the only path to survival. Osbern, also under Anselm's inspiration, had first responded to this challenge; and there are signs that, even by 1093 when his permanent association with Anselm began, Eadmer had come to think that he could do better.

The survival of the threatened tradition depended on research, which began in recollection, and ended in creation. Eadmer was well equipped for both. From an early age he had been (as he himself says) deeply interested in all that passed under his eyes, especially in all that concerned ecclesiastical usage. He had also been an eager listener to the traditions of the community which the memory of the older monks could carry back at first hand to the days of Cnut, and at second hand to those of King Edgar in the mid-tenth century. For these tales he had an astonishingly retentive memory. The recollection of them remained with him undimmed until old age, and the fragments which came casually from his pen give us our best – almost our only – insight into the life of the monastic community at Canterbury during the hundred years before the Conquest.

We know that between 1089 and 1093 Osbern had chosen Eadmer as his confederate in their secret search for relics, and he may have marked him as his successor in restoring the past. It is likely that also during these years Eadmer wrote his first work – a *Life* of St Wilfrid, whose body had lain beneath the high altar of the old church at Canterbury. The work gave Eadmer his first chance to express all his feelings about Britain and its past, the 'other world' set in the midst of the sea, filled with every kind of earthly and saintly riches, which made it a target for the cupidity – the *caeca dominatrix animi cupiditas* – of its neighbours. Hence, all its woes; hence too the driving into exile or martyrdom of its saints –

Mellitus, Justus, Wilfrid, Dunstan, Edmund and Elphege – all saints whose lives were illuminated by miracles from birth to death. Eadmer infuses a life and colour into these scenes which Osbern, who wrote in an ornate Ciceronian Latin, could not match. By contrast, Eadmer's style is always familiar; the speeches which he puts into the mouths of his characters flow with natural ease.

These qualities were to have a new use when Anselm chose him as the most intimate member of his household. This position brought him sixteen years of journeyings more extensive and protracted than those of any Englishman known to us since St Wilfrid himself. In Anselm's company, he made two journeys to Rome, spent three years at Lyons and two months at Cluny, visited southern Italy, saw the Normans in action at the siege of Capua, and observed the relations of Greeks and Latins at the Council of Bari. In these travels he made a fleeting acquaintance with all the chief ecclesiastical personalities in Europe: Urban II, Paschal II, Hugh abbot of Cluny, Hugh archbishop of Lyons, Guy archbishop of Vienne (later Calixtus II), to mention only the most outstanding. It was a wonderful experience for a Canterbury monk whose mind had hitherto dwelt exclusively on subjects of local concern to his own monastery, and who had probably never stepped outside the county of Kent since he was born. Eadmer's enlargement is conspicuous in all that he wrote during these years.

Yet even in the midst of these scenes it was to Canterbury that his mind instinctively reverted. For instance, the Council of Bari was one of the great ecclesiastical occasions of Urban II's pontificate, and Eadmer describes the scene with his customary vividness. He sat at Anselm's feet, and took in his surroundings with relish. What especially caught his eye may be gathered from his own words:

Since it was always my custom from infancy to give diligent attention and to commit to memory whatever novelty presented itself, especially in ecclesiastical affairs, I looked discreetly round the Council spread out before me, noticing the seating arrangements and the method of conducting business, perhaps with more curiosity than wisdom, as one who had never seen anything like it before. And while I looked, I saw the archbishop of Benevento, whom I already knew well, wearing a cope more precious than that of anyone else present; for the pope was presiding not in a cope but in a chasuble with a pallium on top of it. As I looked at the archbishop's cope, and saw that it outshone all others, I remembered some words which I had heard as a boy from the older members of our church, the worthy Edwy, Blackman, Farman, and others. They had been accustomed to say that, when they were scarcely more than boys, Queen Emma had enriched the church with an arm of the blessed apostle Bartholomew.[5]

The story they had told him was that Queen Emma had bought the arm of St Bartholomew from the archbishop of Benevento, and had given it to Canterbury. To the purchase price Archbishop Aethelnoth had added a precious cope richly embroidered with gold, which had been taken back to Benevento. Eadmer tells this tale at great length, and concludes:

When I saw the archbishop of Benevento thus adorned with a cope outshining all others, I felt quite sure that it was the one about which I had formerly heard, and was not a little pleased. I pointed it out to Anselm and told him what I had heard as a boy. When the Council was finished, I approached the archbishop of Benevento, and in the midst of friendly talk I began to speak about his cope and asked him where he got it from, speaking as if I knew nothing about it. He told me the whole story and related how his church had obtained it from Canterbury, just as I have described.[6]

Eadmer wrote on many more important subjects than this, but on none that was more to his taste. What made the incident peculiarly satisfying was that it took place when Anselm and Eadmer were further from Canterbury than in any of their travels: they were sitting in Bari in November 1098 at the junction of the Greek and Roman worlds; and the finest object in view had come from Canterbury in the days before the Conquest. Eadmer could feel that he had the world at his feet. It was too good to last.

2 The fall

From Bari Anselm and Eadmer went in the pope's entourage to Rome, where Eadmer had the further experience of sitting at the tomb of St Peter with Anselm among the cardinals; and from Rome they went to Lyons. Here they remained with Archbishop Hugh for about eighteen months from May 1099 to September 1100, awaiting the moment when they could return to England. Apart from a visit to Cluny and probably to other monasteries where Anselm preached and Eadmer wrote a record of his words, they both had leisure for literary work. The only work of Anselm's which can be definitely ascribed to these months is his last and most carefully organized meditation *On Human Redemption*, in which

[5] *HN*, p. 107.   [6] *HN*, pp. 107–10.

the argument of *Cur Deus Homo* was recast in the form of a meditation. But it is also likely that he gave final form to his speech at the Council of Bari to produce his work on the Procession of the Holy Spirit; and perhaps he also wrote or drafted his *De Conceptu Virginali et de Originali Peccato*, as an appendix to *Cur Deus Homo*.

As for Eadmer, he too had plenty to occupy him. For seven years, he had been an assiduous recorder of all that he saw and heard. His most important notes concerned Anselm's recollections of his past life, going back to his childhood in Aosta, and his flight from home; his early days at Bec, his visionary experiences and early friendships. In addition to these monastic scenes, Eadmer had notes on Anselm's election as archbishop at Gloucester in March 1093, on his consecration at Canterbury in December, on his interviews with the king at Hastings in 1094, at Rockingham in 1095, and at Winchester in 1097, to mention only the occasions about which Eadmer has left the fullest reports.

In making these notes, it is likely that he had no clear idea of the final form they would take. He wanted to record everything that he could learn about Anselm, either from his recollections of his past, or from his many conversations. But he also had notes on great occasions at which he had been present, and of miraculous events observed by others, all written with a lively awareness of the importance of small details for conveying a vivid impression of the scene. One of his greatest merits is that he did not see events as others saw them, and this was one reason why his vignettes did not fit easily into any known literary form. He seems not yet to have been sure whether he was writing a saint's *Life* which could stand beside those of Dunstan, Wilfrid and Elphege in the Canterbury lectionary, or simply an account of a remarkable friend and teacher. He was aware, and no doubt regretted, that Anselm had never quite produced an absolutely convincing miracle to which he could testify without a shadow of doubt. Others indeed, Baldwin the head of Anselm's household among them, had seen miracles, and Eadmer duly put them into his record. But he himself seemed only to see the trembling of the veil between nature and the supernatural, sufficiently wonderful to one who was writing about a master and friend who had captivated his imagination and devotion, but not quite on a level with the flashes of unearthly power which he had been able to record in his *Life* of St Wilfrid.

We must return to this puzzle later in assessing Eadmer's credentials as a biographer. For the present, it is enough to record that while Anselm was occupied with preaching at Cluny and other monasteries which they visited, and in writing his *Meditation on Human Redemption*, Eadmer too had much to do in thinking about and writing up his notes. He must have had quite a pile of sketches of events in various stages of preparation, on scraps of parchment, on wax tablets, on loose quires almost in book form. He had perhaps by now decided to make *two* works out of his accumulated notes: one on Anselm's *Life*; the other on the public events which he had witnessed. But he was chiefly engaged on the *Life* of Anselm, and when Anselm asked to see what he was doing, he was both apprehensive and pleased. The story may be told in his own words, for, after keeping it to himself for nearly twenty years, he was finally persuaded – or rather ordered – by Anselm's successor, Archbishop Ralph, to tell the world about it, and the grief which it had caused him. His account runs as follows:

When I had first taken in hand this work [he is referring to his *Vita Anselmi*] and had already transcribed on to parchment a great part of what I had drafted on wax tablets, Father Anselm one day called me to him privately and asked what it was that I had drafted and transcribed. And when I showed that I would rather keep silent than speak, he ordered me either to show him what I had written, or to give up and concentrate on other things. Now, since I had often shown him similar things which I had written, and had received his help in correcting them when I had got things in the wrong order, I gladly showed him what I had written, hoping for his corrections. Nor was I deceived in my expectation, for he corrected some things, struck out others, changed some, approved others. I was filled with joy to have my record supported by so great an authority. Indeed, I was bursting with pride. But, a few days later he called me to him, and ordered me to destroy the quires in which I had gathered the whole work together, judging himself unworthy of any such literary monument for posterity. I was utterly confounded. I did not dare to disobey him flatly; but I could not face the destruction of a work on which I had spent so much time. So I obeyed him in the letter by destroying the quires on which the work was written, having first transcribed the contents on to other quires. Indeed, my action was not without the sin of disobedience, for I obeyed otherwise than I knew he intended. Wherefore, I beg anyone who reads these words, if my work has given any pleasure, to pray for me in this and all my other sins, lest their weight makes it impossible for me to come to him whose life and acts I have in some sort set forth.[7]

Recalling this incident was the most painful duty that Eadmer had ever to face. He kept it as a secret for nearly twenty years, before

[7] *VA* II, lxxii, pp. 150–1.

he finally confessed his great act of disobedience to Anselm's successor, Archbishop Ralph. Ralph ordered him to record it in the *Vita Anselmi*, which Eadmer had by this time brought to completion; and this is how we come to know about it. But, although Eadmer's subterfuge saved the *Life* from destruction, it left his work – and even his life – in ruins. Anselm lived for another nine years, and during this time Eadmer had to give up all the recording of events, which had been the most creative part of his life for the previous seven years. Both *Life* and *History* lay without another word being added to them until after Anselm's death. Worse still, he was henceforth excluded from Anselm's confidence. Harsh, even inhumanly harsh, one may think; but everything we know of Anselm has shown that his soft words were compatible with – indeed are only intelligible when associated with – complete singleness of purpose. One can only suppose that if Eadmer had at once thrown all his notes on the fire, their relationship would have continued as before. But Eadmer did not destroy what he had written. Anselm was probably aware of this, or at least knew that he could not rely on Eadmer's obedience, and the result was exile from the particular Eden in which they had been living.

How do we know this? Quite simply we know it from the state of both the *Vita Anselmi* and the *Historia Novorum*. Both these works still exist in the fair copy of them which Eadmer made in the years immediately after Anselm's death. In this manuscript, the *Vita Anselmi*, down to the year of Anselm's death in 1109, fills five quires, each of sixteen pages. Four of these five contain the events down to 1100, and they are filled with what Anselm had told him about his early life, followed by detailed reports of Anselm's words and actions on various occasions down to the year 1100. By contrast, the nine years of Anselm's life after this date occupy just one quire, with no single report in similar detail, until we come to Anselm's death-bed, which occupies nearly half of the whole quire.

Similarly, the *Historia Novorum*, in which the public events as contrasted with the private events of the biography were recorded, undergoes a comparable change after 1100. Whereas the previous seven years are filled with detailed accounts of meetings and discussions in which Anselm took part, the period from 1100 to 1109 has only the bleakest outline of his movements with several long gaps. The change, however, is less noticeable in the *History* than in the *Life* because, after 1100, Eadmer filled his *History* with official documents. To put the matter statistically: whereas, the

History of the years from 1093 to 1100 contains only four documents, there are thirty-nine for the years 1101 to 1109. In brief, the last nine years contain a quite different kind of record.

So the two works survived the crisis of 1100, but their character was completely changed: in the *Life* all personal talk dries up after 1100; in the *History* likewise, Eadmer seems to have had very little knowledge of Anselm's intentions and no talk which he could report. The only really lively incident recalls a characteristic rebuke when Eadmer was chagrined at obtaining only a very small fragment of a bone of St Prisca; and the only meeting reported at some length was with the pope in 1103, when Anselm said nothing, on the strange ground (as Eadmer reports) that he did not wish to give the impression that anyone save Christ alone was the door of the sheep-fold.[8]

It would seem, therefore, that during the nine years after 1100, Eadmer was excluded from Anselm's confidence, unable to make any record of the passing scene, and equally unable to work on the material which he had earlier collected.

3 Patching up the past

After two years of failing health, Anselm died at Canterbury on 21 April 1109. His death meant that after the long journeyings of the last sixteen years Eadmer was back in his monastery. At this point in his life, it might have seemed that Anselm had both made and ruined his life. In 1093, he had taken him out of the monastic community at the moment when he was ready to take over from Osbern the task of defending and reviving the ancient pieties of the community. Then, after seven wonderful years of new experience and stimulation, there had been eight more, still as Anselm's constant companion, but without his confidence, and with only an obscure role as his chaplain. Now, in 1109, he was back in the community without an office, but with time and – at last – freedom to finish his two books of history and biography.

No doubt, during the previous nine years, he had often thought about the ways in which he might continue the interrupted work. So far as the *Life* was concerned, there was not much he could do beyond sketching Anselm's later years and making as much as possible of a few miracles and Anselm's death-bed scene, which had been marked by further signs of sanctity – the miraculous

---

[8] For the first of these incidents, see *VA* II, lv; for the second, *HN*, pp. 152–3.

enlargement of his stone coffin, an empty phial of balsam providing sufficient for Anselm's embalming. On the question which had long hung in the balance, whether his biography could become a saint's *Life* capable of taking its place among the *Lives* of the Canterbury saints, Eadmer's mind was now finally clear: it was to be a saint's *Life*. But the flow of miracles did not continue. The members of the Canterbury community seemed no longer interested in Anselm, and Eadmer had to bring his work to an end without much satisfaction.

With regard to his *History*, here too he had come to a decision: during the last nine years he had discovered a theme, which he explained in his Preface, written – like all prefaces – after he had finished his work:

The principle intention of this work is to describe the causes of the discord that arose between Anselm and the kings of England, which led to his long exiles from the kingdom. The cause of these exiles is the novelty [*nova res*] of our time, which came into existence at the time when the Normans began to reign in England. From the time when William of Normandy subjugated the land by force of arms, Anselm alone became a bishop or abbot without first becoming the king's man [i.e. doing homage] and being invested with his bishopric or abbacy by receiving his pastoral staff from the king's hand. The only other exceptions were two bishops, Ernost and Gundulf [both bishops of Rochester and therefore exempted from this practice].

The theme Eadmer had discovered was a brilliant solution to his problem of knitting together the letters and records which, of necessity, had taken the place of the earlier accounts of Anselm's talk and meetings. Moreover, it was a theme which could serve to give coherence to Anselm's policy as archbishop; and it had the further merit of taking up once more his old theme that all the evils in England came from foreigners who had subjugated the land.

Eadmer was not the first – and certainly not the last – historian to discover the value of a theme which gave coherence and dignity to his story, and made it intelligible to his readers, at the small expense of a little distortion. He did not need to distort it much: it was simply a matter of importing into past events principles which had not been in the minds of the actors. A few small adjustments, no more. He could even claim with truth that Anselm had not received his pastoral staff from the king's unaided hands: the bishops had pressed his resisting fingers round the shaft, and he did not think it necessary to explain that Anselm had no objection at that time to the principle of royal investiture. He was further from the truth when he claimed that Anselm had not done homage to the king, for his own words show that this was not true.[9] But fortunately Eadmer was not a vigorous reviser of the material he had collected in Rufus's reign, and since he had little to say about the later years, the new formula provided a convenient frame into which Anselm's actions might be fitted.

By 1114 both works had been completed down to the time of Anselm's death, with brief supplements on later events. He was even able to end the *History* on a note of modest success. Anselm's last reported act had been to send to Thomas, the recently nominated elected archbishop of York, a letter threatening him with excommunication if he assumed his office without a profession of obedience to Canterbury. Eadmer duly copied this letter into his *History* and added a few pages describing the events which led to Archbishop Thomas's profession of obedience to Canterbury at the royal court at Christmas 1109, after the scrutiny of the same documents that had been produced in 1072.

So now at last the profession of obedience to Canterbury by an archbishop of York, which had eluded all Anselm's efforts, was achieved almost without a struggle by means of the old alliance between king and bishops. On this relatively cheerful note, and with some further optimistic reports of the success of Anselm's legislation against married clergy, Eadmer was able to bring his *History* if not to a triumphant, at least to a respectable close.[10]

4 The road to disaster

Eadmer had no sooner put the last touches to his two works in 1114, than the archbishop of York died, and was replaced by Thurstan, a man of similar background to his predecessor in the royal service, but of entirely different character and outlook: an early example of a royal servant who became an ardent upholder of the rights of his see as archbishop. In the same year, after a vacancy of five years, a new archbishop of Canterbury was at last appointed to succeed Anselm.

---

[9] *HN*, p. 41: *pro usu terrae homo regis factus est*; and cf. pp. 267–8.
[10] *HN* p. 214: the work originally ended at the bottom of this page with the quotation from Luke xiv, 24, recalling the *sortilegium* at Anselm's consecration, which had been reported earlier (p. 43). The additions on pp. 214–16 were written in 1119. The further additions of Books V and VI are later still.

The archbishop of York at once announced his determination to fight against the primacy of Canterbury, and the stage was set for the next stage in the conflict, which within six years was to lead to the irremediable collapse of the effective primacy over the whole of the British Isles, which Anselm had been prepared to defend at all costs.

Ralph, the new archbishop of Canterbury, was not by nature a fighter, but he was a Benedictine monk from the circle of Lanfranc and Anselm, and his eight years as archbishop were dominated by his struggle for the Canterbury primacy over York. With Eadmer as his main adviser, he spent four years abroad in pursuit of an objective which became ever more chimerical. They were years of growing despair. The archbishop seems to have kept out of England largely to avoid having to consecrate the archbishop of York without a profession of obedience, but travelling with him to Rome no longer brought meetings with fresh minds and thrilling scenes of ancient splendour. Gradually the truth became plain that, barring some spectacular deliverance, Canterbury's case had outlasted the vision with which it began, and the prospects were increasingly dark.

These were the conditions in which Eadmer was abroad with Archbishop Ralph for nearly three years from 1116 to 1119. Early in 1119 ill-health forced him to leave the archbishop in Normandy and return to Canterbury. He seems to have had a chilly reception. A new generation of monks was growing up which looked back with admiration to the strong and successful administration of Lanfranc, and deplored the weaknesses of Anselm and his successor in asserting the rights of Canterbury. In self-defence, Eadmer took up his literary work yet again, but with ever-decreasing hope. To the *Life of Anselm* he could add only two miracles of men saved from drowning by invoking Anselm's aid, and his enforced confession of his disobeying Anselm's command to destroy the whole thing. As for the *History,* he added in some confusion the news that the long-lost proofs of papal confirmation of the primacy had been found after an intensive search in 1120.

Then, at almost the same time, a new opportunity of striking an independent blow for the church of Canterbury presented itself: Alexander I of Scotland invited Eadmer to become bishop of St Andrews. Lanfranc had already prepared the ground in Scotland by colonizing the abbey of Dunfermline with Canterbury monks, and it seems to have been as a result of this far-sighted initiative that Eadmer appeared as a suitable candidate for the bishopric. To Eadmer it must have seemed a sign from heaven that all was not lost. A foothold in Scotland would have out-flanked York and kept the primacy in existence until better days. In this spirit Eadmer set out for Scotland, determined to defend Canterbury on a new battlefield. He demanded that he should be consecrated as bishop of St Andrews, not at York as was customary, but at Canterbury as the mother-church of Britain. No one took him seriously, and the struggle was a short one. Within six months he had relinquished his ring and staff without consecration, and he was back in Canterbury early in 1121, a defeated man.

Everything that he had fought for and hoped for seemed at this moment in ruins. The primacy, as Lanfranc and Anselm, and as Eadmer too with most of the other monks of Canterbury, had envisaged it and worked for it, was now hopelessly lost. The *Historia Novorum* had drained away into a thin trickle of insignificant events. The *Vita Anselmi* had failed to ripen into the complete record of a personality which had captured his loyalty and admiration at their first meeting forty years earlier, without succeeding in winning an acknowledged place as the record of another Canterbury saint. When he got back to Canterbury from the failure of his Scottish adventure, Eadmer's career, after all its visions of glory, had reached its lowest point.

When in the early months of 1121 Eadmer returned to Canterbury, a defeated and discredited man, Archbishop Ralph was already ill, and he died on 20 October 1122. He was Eadmer's last patron, and Eadmer played no further part in public events. The new archbishop, not a Benedictine monk but an Augustinian canon, played the last Canterbury card by producing the forgeries at the papal court; but they came too late to save anything from the ruins of the primacy. One by one the causes for which Eadmer had worked and fought were being lost. He seemed to have reached the end of the road.He brought his *Historia Novorum* to an abrupt and feeble end, and settled down after so many active years to be an obscure member of a defeated community.

5   The years of recovery

Then, all unexpectedly, he had a new burst of productive life. It is probable that he became precentor of the monastery, the first important office he had ever held in the community.[11] This office would have given him the general supervision of the library, the duty of supervising the writing of new books, and of providing the necessary texts for the divine Office, and more particularly for the veneration of those long neglected saints for whom the new church and the expanding calendar of saints made ample provision. This was work for which he was well fitted, and during these last years he went back to the task of providing texts for the commemoration of the ancient Canterbury saints. He wrote a *Life* of an early archbishop of Canterbury, St Breguin, and a number of works to commemorate the relics of the church, for use at the appropriate times in the liturgical year. His mind turned incessantly to the past, and his description of the old church with many details about former members of the community comes from this period of his life, when the new and greatly extended choir of the cathedral, begun under Anselm, was at last reaching completion.[12]

On 4 May 1130, the new choir was consecrated in the presence of the kings of England and Scotland. The old English saints were now sumptuously housed. The active primacy, for which Anselm and Eadmer had struggled for so long, had been irretrievably lost. But the old glory had returned after all, with Anselm firmly established among the local saints. During his last years, Eadmer was able to provide the necessary texts and recollections for re-establishing the past in the consciousness of the monks of Canterbury. In his new-found serenity, incidents of his life with Anselm, such as his discovery of the identity of his guardian angel, came back to his mind, and after all his disappointments he was able to add a supplementary book of posthumous miracles to his *Life* of Anselm.

This final addition at last brought Anselm's *Life* into line with

---

[11] The only definite evidence for Eadmer's precentorship appears to be Gervase of Canterbury, *Historical Works*, ed. W. Stubbs, *RS*, ii, 1880, p. 374. Gervase was Eadmer's successor as the historiographer of the community at Canterbury. Although he was writing about sixty years after Eadmer's death, he is likely to have been right on such a point. Besides this evidence, the general scope of Eadmer's renewed burst of activity as a writer is consistent with the duties of precentor.

[12] According to Lanfranc's *Constitutions*, p. 82, the precentor had charge of all the books of the monastery in addition to his general responsibility for the chants and lessons in the choir. For Eadmer's writings of this period, which are associated with the veneration of the Canterbury saints, see below; and for the place of the relics of the saints in the new choir, see the plan on p. 327. The provision of a chapel of the archangel Gabriel, whom Eadmer believed to be his guardian angel, at the south-east of the new crypt which was dedicated in 1130 may be a reflection of Eadmer's influence.

the *Lives and Miracles* of the other Canterbury saints. In the new and splendid lectionary, which was made during these years, Anselm took his place alongside St Dunstan and St Wilfrid. Only fragments of this great lectionary now survive, but we know that six volumes were needed for the saints of the whole year, and the fragments that remain bear the marks of the finest period of Canterbury book-production; they embrace the main objects of Eadmer's devotion, and their completion would have formed a fitting end to his career.[13]

In the midst of this new outburst of literary activity, Eadmer composed meditative prayers in the style of Anselm, and used a typically Anselmian argument to support the recently revived Old English devotion to the Immaculate Conception of St Mary. Moreover, if my argument about the date of the compilation of the great Canterbury collection of Anselm's letters is correct, Eadmer as precentor, no less than as Anselm's closest companion throughout his years as archbishop and recipient of his earliest recollections of his years at Bec, must have had some share in the compilation of this memorial to Anselm's memory. In every way, Eadmer in his last years had cause to become reconciled with the failures of his middle years, as he recalled the most fruitful years of his life with Anselm. His mind seems to have returned increasingly to these years, as we shall see when we come to consider his last works.

His mood became gentler in his old age, and though he did not at once, or possibly ever while his strength lasted, give up all hope of getting back his bishopric of St Andrews on terms consistent with what he believed to be the just rights of Canterbury, he could confess that his zeal for the claims of Canterbury had in some ways been indiscreet. It is noteworthy that in one of his last works he no longer referred to Anselm as *primas totius Britanniae* – the proud title which had justified his own attempt to subject the see of St Andrews to Canterbury – but simply as *primas totius regni*

---

[13] N. R. Ker was responsible for identifying fragments of this large lectionary in BL MSS Cotton Nero C vii, Harleian 315, and 624, and Canterbury Cathedral MS E.42. The fragments in Harleian 315 contain a text of *VA* which must have been written soon after 1123. The lectionary also contained Eadmer's work on the miracles associated with the relics of St Ouen, with a continuation in a different hand written after 1128. So the whole enterprise offers evidence of Eadmer's activity between 1123 and 1130, when the main Canterbury MS of Anselm's letters (L, for which see below, pp. 473–7) was also compiled. Furthermore, it seems likely that John of Salisbury used this copy when he made his abbreviation of *VA* for the canonization process in 1163, for he refers the reader who wishes to know more to the *grandia volumina* from which he made his abstract. See *PL* 190, col. 1,038; Biffi, 1988, p. 116.

Anglorum. Even this was more than could be sustained in an increasingly hostile world, but it shows his happily contracting horizon. Already, as early as 1121, shortly after his return from Scotland, he had written to the monks of Glastonbury, urging them

to restrain the forwardness and insolence of those young men who open their mouths solely that they may appear to know, and who give free rein to whatever their loquacity may suggest, thinking themselves great when others in their simplicity will listen to them. I know there have been people like this – perhaps I was one of them – so I can easily believe that now also there are men such as I formerly was. But now I am an old man with white hair, and many things which in my youth I thought important, I now hold of no account.[14]

It is impossible to be certain of the date of Eadmer's death. He was commemorated at Canterbury on 13 January, but as to the year we are very much in the dark. It has been argued that he lived until about 1144, but this suggestion was based on a series of improbable conjectures about the composition of the *Historia Novorum* and cannot be maintained. The discovery of a continuation of Eadmer's treatise on the miracles of St Ouen, however, has given a more trustworthy *terminus post quem* for the date of his death. Since this continuation refers to Prior Elmer it cannot be earlier than 1128. Yet if Eadmer was responsible for this addition to his earlier work, he had ceased to supervise his writings with his customary care, for it is written in a very poor hand.[15]

Eadmer may have lived for some years after 1128, but he was no longer active. His own manuscript of his works, which testifies to the activity of half a lifetime, had been brought to a close. His claim to the bishopric of St Andrews, maintained for some years after his return to Canterbury, had been relinquished. Peace had been restored between Canterbury and the king of Scotland. Eadmer's successor had at last been consecrated. Over much of the field of conflict in which Eadmer had been engaged, the last years of Henry I's reign were a period of peace. Superficially, Eadmer had failed in his practical policies, but the links with the Anglo-Saxon past which he had worked to maintain had been strengthened beyond all expectation. Meanwhile those who were themselves part of pre-Conquest England were sliding quietly from the scene. Among them Eadmer disappeared almost without remark.

[14] *Memorials of St Dunstan,* p. 421.
[15] I may add here that the great Canterbury collection of Anselm's letters (**L**) also ends in miscellaneous addenda. If it too belonged to Eadmer's time as precentor, the state of its final pages could be another indication of his failing powers.

II EADMER'S 'ANSELM': FROM INTIMATE PORTRAIT TO SAINT'S 'LIFE'

I The intimate portrait

I have already mentioned that four of the five quires in Eadmer's manuscript, which contain his *Life of Anselm*, were already in existence substantially in the form in which we now have them in 1100, and that nearly everything of biographical value in the whole work is in these four quires.[16]

Of the post-1100 additions, by far the most interesting is the preface. First, it describes the relationship between the *Life* and the *History*: the latter, it says, contains an account of Anselm's relations with the kings of England, which any contemporary could have known about; but the *Life* tells of Anselm's *privata conversatio, qualitas morum*, and *exhibitio miraculorum*, in this order. With the exception of the miracles, for which Eadmer seems not to have had the seeing eye, the subject of the work was private history, below the surface of public events.

This distinction between public and private events is something new. We find no similar distinction, for example, between Bede's *History* and his *Life of St Cuthbert*: both these works deal with the same kind of events, and a large part of the events in both concerns supernatural interventions in human affairs. Eadmer's distinction between public and private events was symptomatic of a distinction which Anselm had done much to develop. His prayers and meditations were an example of private devotion breaking away from a long tradition of predominantly corporate prayer. His theological method was based on introspective meditation, which presupposed, but did not mention, the great body of publicly approved doctrine. Eadmer echoes this division in his distinction between the private and public events of Anselm's life.

In Anselm, he had a subject ideally suited for a new kind of intimate biographical treatment. But Eadmer's peculiar talents also made a contribution in bringing to his subject an ususual visual clarity in his descriptions and an intimate knowledge of his subject. To these qualities, he was later to add an appreciation of Anselm's place in the line of Canterbury saints. All these elements were necessary for producing the work as we now have it; but his intimate knowledge of Anselm laid the foundation for everything of

---

[16] For a detailed description of the manuscript, see Southern 1963, pp. 367–74.

greatest value in the work. The conviction that Anselm belonged to the great roll of saints emerged more slowly.

The title which he gave the work – *Vita et Conversatio* – contains a hint of the new intimacy of his point of view; but in itself it was not new. It had often been used in earlier saints' *Lives*, but the *conversatio* which these *Lives* described was not private: it referred to the rule of life which they followed, and normally this was a corporate rule. In the Benedictine Rule itself, and generally in Benedictine writers, the word *conversatio* embraced the whole discipline of a regular religious community. Then, in his Preface, Eadmer added the word *privata*, and in this addition he announced a personal and intimate view, which only those who lived in the friendship of Anselm could experience. This *privata conversatio* did not consist merely of spoken words: it referred to a whole discipline of life. But with Anselm, whose thoughts easily found expression in talk, *privata conversatio* was often quite simply conversation. We may remember the very earliest report of Anselm by an eye-witness, Gundulf, who became a monk at Bec only a year before Anselm. When he later spoke to his friends about his early years at Bec, he recalled that, when they were together, Anselm would talk, while he – Gundulf – would be moved to tears. Here we see both sides of Anselm's *conversatio*: his spoken words reflected his spiritual *conversatio* and the combination of the two moved Gundulf to tears. In a few words this sums up the whole quality of Anselm's life as it appeared to his friends: his words came straight from an inner experience, which they perfectly expressed.

Gundulf was the first to have this experience. Some fifteen years later, Eadmer at Canterbury and Guibert of Nogent at Flay had similar experiences: Anselm's talk brought a new light into their lives – the light of someone who had experienced the spiritual world which they sought. That was why not only Eadmer, but also the other reporters whose work I have outlined above, made Anselm's talk a central part of their record: they were not following a convention, they were recording a unique experience. After 1093 Eadmer heard Anselm talk on very many occasions, and until 1100 it is Anselm's talk that gives Eadmer's biography its distinction and substance.

It can be proved that in some of his reports Eadmer put together words which he had heard on several different occasions,[17] and even

---

[17] For a clear example of this, see *Memorials*, pp. 271–91, and above, p. 385.

when he recorded words spoken on a single occasion, many of the words he used were doubtless his own. But this is only to say that there is more art in Eadmer than appears on the surface. No one who reads the biography can doubt that Eadmer's chief claim to fame as a biographer lies in his mastery of the art of recording the spoken word in a vivid and natural way. This is a difficult art at any time, but it was especially difficult in Eadmer's day, when authors commonly used direct speech, not as a vehicle for the sentiments of the speaker, but as a rhetorical embellishment, to convey the writer's own interpretation of events. This kind of rhetorical speech, authorized by antiquity, can be exemplified everywhere in the writings of Eadmer's contemporaries. The reader is not deceived: he knows that the speeches are a rhetorical device, and judges them accordingly. Eadmer was doing something quite different: the words he reports give the impression, and were intended to give the impression, that it is Anselm who speaks. This was more than a technique of writing. It was the stirring of a new sense of personality.

The report of talk and the quoting of private letters must have a large place in any intimate biography. It is only in this way that we can learn more of a man than events and his published works can tell us. Anselm was an ideal subject for this treatment. His early letters come nearer to our idea of private correspondence than those of any of his contemporaries, much nearer even than those of Abelard and Heloise. And yet, as we have seen, Anselm did not look on the letters which reveal his most intimate thoughts and sentiments as 'private' in the sense that they were only for the recipient: they were expressions of an intimacy that all could share if they shared his life of religion. Therefore, he wished them to have a wide circulation. They were private in coming from his inner experience; public in seeking to provoke in others a religious life which all could share. It was in understanding this relationship between Anselm's words and his experience that Eadmer made his main contribution to the art of biography.

The novelty of his procedure can be judged by comparing Eadmer's biography of Anselm with the contemporary biography of Wulfstan, bishop of Worcester, by William of Malmesbury. In this biography, William writes:

I have not related the words which were, or may have been, spoken from time to time, being anxious in all things not to jeopardize the truth. It is the mark of an idle man to dispense words when deeds may suffice – unless indeed there are some words which require a brief mention because of their special splendour.[18]

Here William takes it for granted that the value of words reported by the historian lies in their 'special splendour', that is, their rhetorical excellence, not in their revelation of the nature of the speaker. Similarly, in another contemporary *Life*, that of St Stephen of Grandmont, we find a similar eschewing of reported speech as outside the scope of biography. And this is especially striking because Stephen, like Anselm, was an influential talker, whose disciples retained the memory of his sayings. His biographer sacrificed them unwillingly. But he sacrificed them nevertheless in obedience to a principle:

I pass over in silence the things that he taught his disciples when he spoke to them about the observances of religion, the formation of morals, and whatever pertains to the salvation of souls. Such things are written in his *Sententiae*. I speak of the most evident marks of his sanctity. It is to these *things* that credit should be given rather than *words*. For who knows the thoughts of Man except God, who 'fashioneth all the hearts of them and understandeth all their works'?[19]

While Eadmer's contemporaries thus hesitated to record talk as the most genuine record of their subject, Eadmer took the plunge: 'It seems to me impossible to obtain a full understanding of Anselm's manner of life if only his actions are described, and nothing is said of how he appeared in his talk.'[20]

The taste for psychological elaboration became very widespread in the course of the twelfth century, and left a deep mark on the literature of the period. Everyone began to feel the need to infuse a passionate inner life into the characters of literature, and to elaborate the thoughts and words of historical characters. Those who revised earlier saints' *Lives* in the late twelfth century tried to repair the omission of the inner thoughts and motives of their subjects by inventing suitable words to put in those subjects' mouths. Peter of Blois's elaboration of the ancient *Life* of St Guthlac of Crowland is a good example of what could be done by this kind of literary elaboration. Indeed, Eadmer himself had already used his facility in recording talk in giving his *Life* of St Wilfrid a modern look. But in writing of Anselm he had a subject

[18] *Vita Wulfstani*, ed. R. R. Darlington, *R.Hist. Soc., Camden 3rd Series*, 1928, p. 2.
[19] *Vita S. Stephani Grandimontensis*, c. 25, *PL* 204, col. 1,019.   [20] *VA* I, xxi.

whose talk he had heard and which he aimed at reproducing in a lifelike way. I do not think that this can be said of any other contemporary biography.

2   *The saint's* Life

There can be little doubt that from an early date Eadmer hoped that he was writing the *Life* of a saint. But here he had a difficulty. He had already written one *Life* of a Canterbury saint, whose body lay (or was thought to lie) at Canterbury. But Wilfrid's life, like those of all other early saints, was bathed from birth to death in supernatural events. In these *Lives*, the miraculous was not merely an addition to ordinary life; it *was* their ordinary life. Miracles on the scale of the past could not indeed be expected in the eleventh century; but it was still widely expected that miracles would be numerous wherever there was sanctity. Anselm came to Canterbury already with some reputation as a man to whom and through whom miracles happened, and Eadmer had seen what he believed to be a miracle in 1093 when the growth of a fire at Winchester had been arrested after Anselm, at Baldwin's bidding, had stretched out his hand to halt it.[21] This gave him his first miracle to record on English soil.

From this time, therefore, the model of earlier saints may have been in Eadmer's mind. And yet, it was all very different from the old days when the miraculous had beeen part of daily experience. It was not until 1098, when he was in the village of Liberi in southern Italy, that Eadmer saw another occurrence which could reasonably be thought miraculous. The peasants were desperately seeking a suitable place to dig a well; Anselm, on being appealed to, directed them to dig in an unlikely place, and after several days' work the living water broke forth among the rocks.[22] As compared with the ancient saints, it was not much. Others were more fortunate or less scrupulous, and Eadmer was glad to report what they told him, but he could not see what they saw.

It is necessary to emphasize this peculiarity of Eadmer's experience and vision because it did much to determine the kind of biography he wrote. There was a matter-of-factness about both Baldwin's and Alexander's manner of telling a story which is absent from Eadmer's narratives. We have only to compare Alexander's account of the curing of the blind man at Lyons with Eadmer's

[21] See *VA* II, ii, and above, p. 241.   [22] *VA*, II, xxxi, pp. 107–9.

account of the cure of a mad woman on the road to Cluny to see the difference. Alexander's account leaves no shadow of doubt: a blind man begins making an uproar; Anselm sends to find out the reason; Alexander reports; Anselm tells the man to come forward; he makes the sign of the Cross and splashes holy water on the man's eyes; the man goes away seeing with perfect clarity.

Eadmer's method is quite different. He reports events with much circumstantial detail, but with a striking failure to see the decisive event: he and Anselm are riding towards Cluny; a clerk approaches and asks Anselm to cure his mad sister; Anselm turns a deaf ear to his tearful entreaties and rides on; the man persists; Anselm still repels him. Then they come to the crowd holding the mad and gesticulating woman. The crowd seizes Anselm's reins, begging him to put his hands on her; still he refuses; they swear at him; at last he relents, makes the sign of the Cross and rides quickly away, drawing his cowl over his head weeping, leaving his companions. This was the way Eadmer told a story, with much lifelike detail but slow in coming to the point. And after all, he cannot say whether the woman was cured. He can only speak from hearsay. He believed what he had heard, but he had seen no cure. This was not the way to tell a miracle story; but it is the way things happen in real life.[23]

Eadmer would no doubt have liked to write a work bristling with conventional miracles, and he filled most of the few pages not occupied by official letters from 1100 to 1109 with miraculous banalities. But even in these pages he preserved the scrupulosity of vision which prevented his seeing the miracles which others saw. One of the very few definitely miraculous events which he himself experienced was the supernatural supply of balsam and enlargement of the sarcophagus after Anselm's death. But no flood of miracles at the tomb followed to testify to Anselm's sanctity, and Eadmer had to bring his work to an end without any wealth of posthumous miraculous events. Then, between 1109 and 1114, two small miracles were reported, and these he added, together with his own confession of disobedience to Anselm's order for the destruction of the work. This was the state of the work when Eadmer went abroad in 1116. When he returned to Canterbury in 1119, he began, as we have seen, to make additions to his *History*; but he does not appear to have made any further additions to the *Life* until after the death of Archbishop Ralph in October 1122.

By this time, the question whether Anselm was to be treated as a

[23] See *VA*, II, xlii, p. 120.

saint or not was becoming increasingly urgent.The number of those friends, in Eadmer's words, 'whose love for Anselm still burned brightly' was gradually diminishing. More disconcertingly, the number of those who thought of him as a great failure was growing. On the other hand, though painfully slowly, the number of recorded miracles was growing too. Eadmer decided that the time had come to add an appendix of miracles which would bring Anselm's *Life* into line with those of Dunstan and Oswald. He was now in the last phase of his life: precentor, responsible for the service books, the last of those who remembered the community of pre-Conquest days. If Anselm was ever to join the great line of Canterbury saints, now was the moment.

The book of *Miracles* which Eadmer now added to the *Life* was his last tribute to Anselm. Although fourteen years had passed since Anselm's death, he still had very few miracles to record: a few visions, some cures by means of Anselm's girdle, a final miracle of the extinction of a fire at Bury St Edmunds, written down as it came to hand: it was not much. The doubts of the young monks at Canterbury about Anselm's spiritual powers were easily intelligible; among them there were detractors who thought that Eadmer had written too much and proved too little. But slowly the tide was turning. Anselm's tomb was becoming a place of resort for those who sought his counsel and aid as the latest of the Canterbury saints. In adding the appendix of miracles, and including Anselm's *Life* in the great new Canterbury Lectionary of about 1125, Eadmer had done everything in his power to perpetuate the veneration of his master.[24] If anything more was to be added, it could not be by him. He may have meant it literally when he said that his trembling fingers forced him to lay down his pen; he could do no more. He had done what he could to give Anselm a place among the Canterbury saints.

III   IN ANSELM'S FOOTSTEPS

1   *The area of successful imitation*

Anselm's talk always had the power to excite his listeners, but the only part of the wide area of his speculative and devotional innovations to which his pupils found it possible to make a lasting contribution was in their *Prayers* and *Meditations*. The reason for

[24] See *VA*, pp. 152–71; and, for the manuscripts, pp. xxii–xxiv. These supplementary pages had almost no circulation outside Canterbury.

this is not hard to find. In his theology, Anselm had perfected a method of rigorous argument to which contributions could be made only by minds of comparable clarity and force, and could only safely be made when these qualities were combined with a clear grasp of the lines of orthodox development, which is a rare combination indeed. Then, in the other area in which Anselm had made a distinctive mark – in his letters of friendship – there are several signs, even in his lifetime, that Anselm's language was open to too many misunderstandings to be imitated.[25] But in his *Meditations* and *Prayers* he struck a vein which attracted many imitators. Indeed, the chief defect was that it was too easy to imitate: that is to say, to imitate the style without the austerity and concentration of mind without which Anselm's style would seem sugary, almost at times childish.[26] His best imitators were those who, without Anselm's peculiar ferocity, had at least a cause to promote greater than their own excesses of sentiment. To later generations, their work appeared indistinguishable from that of Anselm himself.

The prayers and meditations of Anselm's friends have a place in his biography as evidence of the enlargement of expression that Anselm brought to those who knew him – especially, it would seem, to those in England who had known the deprivations of the Conquest. There are several signs that pre-Conquest monastic communities contained men who were seeking to express themselves in new ways. But they were cramped by the limitations of their environment, and later by the repression of the new aristocracy, which replaced the old quite as ruthlessly in the monasteries as in the world. It was only in the visual arts that Anglo-Saxon freedom of expression persisted, accompanied at least for a generation by an atrophy of the written word. It was here that Anselm brought new life in introducing his friends to new methods of discourse.

Among these successful imitators, Eadmer has a high, and perhaps the highest, place chiefly because he was always more than an imitator: he was a man with a cause – the revival of Canterbury's

---

[25] It is perhaps an indication of Anselm's realization of this fact that (if my account of his letter-collection is correct) he never resumed the work of collecting his early letters after his breach with the monks of Bec in 1093, though he may have had some part in arranging the drafts in the Bec archives in 1105. (See below, p. 465.)

[26] I quote here the word used to me by Eduard Fraenkel commenting on the contrast between the seriousness of the matter and the 'childishness' of his style in his early letters.

past greatness. Although, like all the others, he lacked Anselm's clarity of intellectual perception and his ruthlessness of self-examination, he had a sense of the past, an observant eye, and an interest in himself and others, greater perhaps than Anselm's. Without Anselm, he would have been a local hagiographer, filling gaps in the record of the Old English saints, displaying a remarkable talent for imaginative historical reconstructions, and an unwearied curiosity about all that concerned the church of Canterbury. Anselm opened to him a new world of devotional expression; he gave him a subject – or rather two subjects: Anselm himself in his relations with those around him, and the role of the saints; above all, of the Virgin Mary in the process of Redemption. As we know, the first of these subjects was rudely snatched away in mid-career. But the second came to life again as soon as Eadmer was once more settled at Canterbury with a role in his monastic community.

2 *Eadmer's* Prayers *and* Meditations

Besides his portrait of Anselm, Eadmer wrote four *Prayers* and *Meditations*, which provide the best evidence of the revival of Anselm's influence on him as soon as his public life (for which he was even less fitted than Anselm himself) was finished, and all his thoughts were again directed to the cycle of prayer in the ancient community. It is perhaps not an accident that they are the only writings to which Eadmer took care to attach his name: they are expressions of his own inner life and of his return to Anselm after the disasters of the fourteen years since Anselm's death. The first is the only one which may have been written in Anselm's lifetime. The others all belong to Eadmer's last years, when he was no longer involved in the wider ambitions of Canterbury, and could review his years with Anselm in calm, perhaps sentimental contemplation, but also with a certain new independence of outlook. The personal emphasis of their titles in his manuscript is unmistakable, and I give their full titles in the notes. In the order in which they appear in his own manuscript, they are:

I 'ON THE EXCELLENCE OF THE BLESSED VIRGIN MARY'[27]
This is the earliest of his devotional works, perhaps written in Anselm's lifetime, and its title alone would suffice to declare its

---

[27] CCCC MS 371, pp. 190–212, with the title, *Consideratio Edmeri peccatoris et pauperis Dei de excellentia gloriosissimae Virginis Matris Dei.* (*PL* 159, cols. 557–80.)

dependence on Anselm's more famous prayers. Its form and title are remarkable as expressions of the affective piety of which Anselm was the chief initiator, and many of its phrases show distinctly the influence of the language of Anselm's prayers:

Excitemus ergo mentam nostram fratres mei, et enitamur, quantum possumus, ut in celsitudinem tantae Virginis attendamus.

Or again:

Erigite, obsecro, fratres mei, erigite aciem mentis vestrae ad contemplandam tam miram divinae dignationis operationem, tam ineffabilem et stupendam omni seculo huius mulieris gratiam et exaltationem.[28]

Sentences such as these indicate the spirit of the work. It was a meditation written in the personal and effusive manner which Anselm had made familiar in his *Prayers*. But though the language and the appeal for mental elevation are Anselmian, the audience and method of argument are different. The audience is the whole community of the monks of Canterbury: Anselm by contrast prays in the privacy of his chamber. Eadmer indulges in historical rhapsody: Anselm engages in fervent introspection. Yet, both in language and thought, there are some striking similarities. Eadmer attempts to prove the *necessity* of events in Mary's life, as Anselm proves the *necessity* of the Incarnation itself. They both attempt to show that historical events are intelligible as the necessary consequences of the divine plan of salvation. Indeed, so Anselmian did the tone and content of Eadmer's prayers appear to later generations that they were commonly accepted as genuine works of Anselm throughout the Middle Ages, and indeed almost to our own day.

II   AN APPEAL TO ST PETER[29]

This long meditation transposes Anselm's manner of self-examination into a series of historical ruminations on the events in Peter's life. It is a development of Anselm's much earlier, and much more anguished, prayer, from which it is derived in manner, but from which it deviates widely in spirit. Instead of Anselm's sharp and painful self-examination, Eadmer reflects on each incident in Peter's life with peaceful loquacity and warmth of feeling. The

---

[28] *PL* 159, cols. 558D, 564A; cf. Anselm, *Or.* 7, Schmitt, iii, p. 18
[29] CCCC MS 371, pp. 425–40: *Scriptum Edmeri peccatoris ad commovendam super se misericordiam beati Petri ianitoris caelestis.* For the text, see Wilmart, 1935, pp. 192–205.

result shows how Anselm's manner of elaboration could be adopted by an observant historically minded follower, and this freedom of development in a multitude of different modes was the secret of the success of Anselm's prayers in all their later and variously diluted forms.

III   EADMER'S GUARDIAN ANGEL

In his last years, Eadmer's thoughts naturally often returned to his years with Anselm. One of his recollections went back to the time of their exile – perhaps to those months in Lyons when he and Anselm had their fatal talk about the future of Eadmer's reports on Anselm's words and works. This is what Eadmer recalled:[30]

Being far from my native soil and from my compatriots and friends, I often sat and turned over in my mind many things, some of them transitory and temporal, and some – but more rarely – eternal. At times, the enormity of my sins overcame me, and I sighed with confusion and wonder at the long-suffering patience and goodness of God. I seemed to see Him deputing some good guardian to defend me from the attacks of evil demons . . . Meditating often about this, I desired greatly to know the name of my guardian, so that when possible I could honour him with some act of devotion. One night I fell asleep and saw someone standing by me saying that my prayer was heard and that I might know without doubt that the name I desired to know was – Gabriel!

IV   EADMER ON THE IMMACULATE CONCEPTION[31]

The cause which prompted Eadmer's most important meditation was the doctrine of the Immaculate Conception of the Virgin Mary. It appealed to Eadmer in the first place because it was one of the Anglo-Saxon festivals which Lanfranc had thrown out of the Canterbury calendar, and which Anselm could not, on theological grounds, support. But where Anselm was silent, Eadmer spoke, and succeeded beyond all expectation.

The case has a special importance in providing a study in dependence and independence: the breach between Anselm and Eadmer which diminished the *Vita Anselmi* was in one sense intensified, and in another healed, in Eadmer's greatest *Meditation*:

---

[30] *Insipida quaedam divinae dispensationis consideratio ab Eadmero magno peccatore de beatissimo Gabriele archangelo.* For the text, see Wilmart, 1935, pp. 371–9.

[31] CCCC MS 371, pp. 395–415, *De Conceptione Sanctae Mariae editum ab Eadmero monacho magno peccatore.* The work was later commonly attributed to Anselm (e.g. in *PL* 159, cols. 301–18), not only in the Middle Ages but until H. Thurston and T. Slater in their edition, Freiburg i. Br., 1904, based on Eadmer's own MS, finally established Eadmer's authorship.

it advocated a doctrine towards which Anselm pointed, but from which he had drawn back. Indeed, when we review the whole course of Eadmer's relationship to Anselm, there is a strange appropriateness in this situation: Eadmer here followed Anselm in method, and went beyond him in doctrine; in going along the same road, he reached a destination of which Anselm disapproved. It might be an allegory of the whole of Eadmer's complicated discipleship.

It would take us far beyond the scope of this study to examine the substance of Eadmer's argument in detail; but its outline, the historical situation which provoked it, and its entirely unpredictable success, must at least be sketched.

Like the two prayers to St Peter and to Eadmer's guardian angel, it belongs to the last years of his life, when his ambitions as a fighter for the rights of the church of Canterbury had collapsed, and he was turning his mind increasingly to meditation, prayer, and his duties as precentor. This change of direction took his mind back to the Anglo-Saxon devotions, which it had been Anselm's first and most successful contribution to the welfare of the Canterbury community to support. To use his own words, he looked back

to those former times when the feast of the Conception of St Mary, the Mother of God, was more widely celebrated, particularly by those in whom a pure simplicity and humble devotion to God was strong. But afterwards, greater knowledge and a more searching examination had puffed up the minds of some, so that the simplicity of the poor was despised, and the celebration of the feast was done away with and utterly destroyed as lacking all reason.[32]

'The men', he said, 'who brought about this abolition were men of great authority, abounding in riches and able to give a reason for what they did.' He does not mention Lanfranc by name, but Lanfranc's name must have been in his mind when he wrote those words. Perhaps he also felt just that degree of triumph that a devoted disciple can allow himself, that even Anselm with all his remarkable talents had failed to see the light on this subject. And now, despite all the failures of the past years, he felt strong enough to break new ground in defending, with new arguments based on methods learnt from Anselm, the simplicity of the past against the reasoning of the present. So at the very end of his life, when so much else that he had defended in Anselm's name was going to destruction, he was discovering an Anselmian manner of defending

[32] *PL* 159, col. 301.

theologically the hitherto mute instincts which had shaped the piety of the Anglo-Saxon Church.

Most of Eadmer's devotional works had only a local significance, but in writing about the Immaculate Conception, he was engaged on a more momentous adventure than he knew. He thought he was defending a local devotion; he was actually at the beginning of an international event. There was a greater future in store for his treatise and for the cause which it advocated, than he could have foreseen.

Everywhere the atmosphere was now more favourable to this revival than it had been before. Monks in other churches were seeking to revive their ancient pieties at Westminster, Ramsey, and at Bury St Edmunds where Anselm's nephew was now abbot. Among other symptoms of the revival, the re-appearance of the feast of Mary's Conception, on 8 December, was becoming a conspicuous feature in the calendars of several ancient English monasteries. It does not appear that Eadmer's treatise had any immediate influence on this revival. Probably at first the growing collections of miracle stories were more important. Among these, there was a story about a miraculous appearance of the Virgin Mary to Elsi, abbot of Ramsey, during a storm at sea in about 1085: Mary promised to save the ship, and in return had charged Elsi with the task of spreading the observance of the feast of her Conception. 'Elsi' was not a name likely to inspire confidence in the Norman world, and the story was given a better patron when it was recast as an encyclical letter purporting to have been written by Archbishop Anselm exhorting his fellow bishops to promote the observance of the feast. It is not known who thought of this mild deceit, but it turned out to be a master-stroke. Both the letter and Eadmer's treatise grew in fame; both acquired the name of Anselm, and both were frequently quoted in support of the feast of the Immaculate Conception in the later Middle Ages.[33]

The circulation of such stories was the easiest of all ways of winning adherents to a cause, but Eadmer chose a different and much more Anselmian way of defending the celebration of the feast on theological grounds. His main argument followed a line of reasoning which Anselm had been responsible for introducing. It may be briefly paraphrased thus:

---

[33] The letter about Elsi's vision is to be found, but without Anselm's name, in *PL* 159, cols. 323–6.

Everything that God does, is done in the best possible way: that is to say: the means chosen must be those that best correspond to the excellence of the end. Christ, therefore, must have been born in the way that best corresponded to the supreme excellence of the event. From this it followed that it was necessary that he should be born of a Virgin; necessary also that this Virgin should be sinless; (necessary too, if this were possible, that she herself should have been conceived without sin). Since it was *fitting* for God to meet these conditions, it was *necessary* that they should be met. (Therefore it was necessary that Mary should have been conceived without sin.)

This argument from congruity had been developed in Anselm's *Cur Deus Homo* to explain why no other mode of redemption than the sacrifice of the Son was compatible with God's perfection.[34] To this Eadmer added, that no other mode of birth was compatible with the source of Christ's human perfection than the Immaculate Conception of the sinless Mary.

Anselm in fact, as we know, and as Eadmer must have known, would not have approved: he held that no one, not even the Virgin Mary, could be exempt from Original Sin without destroying the strict necessity for the Incarnation. Eadmer himself had expressed this opinion in his earlier *Meditation* on the excellence of the Virgin Mary. But by the late 1120s, Eadmer had changed his mind, and this new *Meditation* was the result. Among his works it is the one which more than any other illustrates the full complexity of Eadmer's mind and achievement: it contributed to the restoration of the ancient practices of the Canterbury community; it provided the first theological expression of a local devotion which was to sweep through Europe; it carried one stage further the work of Anselm; and under Anselm's name, it became a notable landmark in the history of the medieval Church. Although the world called it Anselm's, it was – all unwittingly – Eadmer's greatest contribution to the spread of Anselm's fame.

By a curious accident of history, which may be recalled as an appendix to the final union of Anselm and Eadmer, we can observe the process of assimilation at an important moment in history. In about 1320, the Oxford Carmelite John Baconthorpe described the doctrine of Mary's Immaculate Conception as a 'fantastic kind of heresy'. But then he records that he found a book – in fact Eadmer's – ascribed to Anselm:

---

[34] See especially *CDH* I, xii; Book II elaborates the argument.

I found that Anselm, in a treatise entitled *De Conceptione B.V.M.*, which I discovered in the house of the Franciscans at Cambridge and later also in Paris in an ordinary stationer's, holds that she did not contract Original Sin.[35]

By the 1320s, therefore, Eadmer's book was beginning to have a wide circulation, not under the name of an obscure monk, but under the name of a theologian whose views and methods of argument were at last beginning to arouse widespread discussion and agreement. This association of Anselm's name in support of the disputed doctrine must have led many besides John Baconthorpe to have second thoughts. In 1328 a provincial council in London under Archbishop Simon Meopham, evidently on the strength of this work, quoted the authority of Anselm in ordering the feast of the Conception to be observed in all churches throughout the province of Canterbury.[36] A century later, in 1438, the Council of Basel, in decreeing the obligatory observance of the feast, prescribed portions of Eadmer's work under Anselm's name, to be read at Matins.[37]

It is a fitting end to the complicated story of the relations between Anselm and Eadmer, indeed of the influence which Anselm had on his disciples, that the one work of Eadmer's which survived to achieve a European influence – strongly marked though it was by Anselm's influence – should have have arrived at a conclusion which was the opposite of Anselm's. And further, that though it contradicted Anselm on an important point, it owed its success to the belief that it had been written by Anselm himself. The ambiguities in the whole development illustrate one of the permanent features of Anselm's influence: although he was the most lucid and decisive of writers, and knew exactly what he meant, he cast over every subject an iridescence filled with contradictory possibilities.

---

[35] Quoted by I. Brady, *Franciscan Studies*, 15, 1955, p. 196n.

[36] D. Wilkins, *Concilia Magnae Britanniae et Hiberniae*, 1737, II, 552.

[37] The decree was passed on 17 September 1438, largely under Spanish pressure. John of Segovia composed the Office with passages from Eadmer's *De Conceptione*, attributed of course to Anselm. See *DTC* vii, pp. 112–13.

CHAPTER 18

A BACKWARD GLANCE

I ANSELM IN HIS TIME: BETWEEN TWO WORLDS

The preceding chapters have traced Anselm's development in prayer, meditation, friendship, philosophy, and theology, and in theological controversy; in his position as archbishop; in his work for the monastic community at Canterbury; in the records of his sermons and informal talk, and in the collecting of his letters; and finally in his relations with his biographer, who was also his companion, disciple, reporter, and – at a significant moment – rebel.

Broadly speaking, from the time of his arrival at Bec in 1059, we have found three threads running through Anselm's whole development. First, there was the influence of Lanfranc, who provided his intellectual tools and in whose footsteps he followed at every stage in his career. Second, there was the consistent personal style of thought and sentiment, largely based on his total immersion in the language and thought of St Augustine, which had formed his mind before he wrote any of his surviving works. These influences provided the inspiration for his earliest *Prayers* and letters, and for the meditations which culminated in the *Proslogion*.

Then, thirdly, in the period after 1078, there were the years of diversification under new influences from the world outside the monastery. The number of priories of Bec had grown as a result of the increasing prosperity of the families associated with its endowment, and this enlarged the area of Anselm's pastoral responsibility. His area of theological inquiry had also been extended under the hostile impulse of Roscelin, and of the arguments of the Jews which Gilbert Crispin had told him about, and of the teaching of the school of Laon as reported to him by Boso. These influences contributed to the second period of Anselm's theology from the completion of the *Proslogion* in 1078 to that of the *Cur Deus Homo* in 1098.

437

Then finally, the situation in which he found himself as archbishop of Canterbury led him to define his view of local religious traditions; and the new Hildebrandine system of Church government, as represented especially by Hugh of Lyons, forced him into an uneasy balance between a broadly federal Church embodied in the primatial claim of his church at Canterbury, and the centralized ecclesiastical organization associated especially with Gregory VII, which was gradually gaining widespread assent.

Without doubt, Lanfranc was the essential provoker of Anselm's growth, not only in giving him stability when he most needed a firm direction, but also by leaving Bec and giving him freedom to develop in his own way after four years of intense absorption in Benedictine discipline and Augustinian thought. The responsibility for training a new generation of monks, which he inherited from Lanfranc, gave Anselm a group of young men eager to hear his thoughts. The early removal of some of his closest friends from Bec to Canterbury was immediately responsible for his earliest flow of letters, which opened a new phase of his life culminating in the great meditations of the *Monologion* and *Proslogion*.

A similar process of enlargement followed his election as abbot in 1078: a widening of his theological interests to embrace the connection between will and action; a widening also of his monastic activity in his responsibility for the religious life of small communities of monks, as well as widows and recluses, attached to Bec. Finally his confrontation with Roscelin and his removal to Canterbury brought him a new – in itself unwelcome, but in its results enlarging – experience of the growing controversies of the time.

His responsibilities for preserving the rights of Canterbury and the discipline of the wider Church were the first real check to the natural course of his development. But in some ways the archbishopric gave him new opportunities for the work he liked best and was best equipped to undertake. There was nothing he did better than giving a monastic community freedom to develop in its own way under his benign direction, and his sympathetic guidance of the Canterbury community with its rich and strange devotional resources left a profound mark on its later development. In the course of this work, there arose a complicated and fruitful mingling of his own devotional innovations with the pieties of the Old English Church, and it was not an accident that the pupils and friends of these last days at Canterbury became the most active preservers and continuators of his devotional writings and methods.

By contrast, however, the work of administration was always a burden to him. He did not do it well because he had no instinctive sense of what was possible in ordinary affairs. His political actions display a single-minded and dedicated scholar dealing as well as he could with problems that had no clearly defined place in his monastically oriented world-view. His contacts with Hugh of Lyons, and the papal theorists whom Hugh represented, brought him into contact with, and in some degree committed him to adopting, a new way of organizing the Church in relation to the external world; but it was an ideal which he never absorbed into his own thought. Only the community at Canterbury, as a living witness to a great monastic past, gained his full allegiance. On its behalf, he devoted his full strength to the task of maintaining its primatial claims, and this turned out to be a fruitless exercise because it ran counter to the main European development of his day.

His ineffectiveness as an administrator did not arise from scholarly vagueness, but from the depths of his convictions. The thoughts and aims of worldly men puzzled him without arousing his interest. He simply could not understand how men who believed in Heaven and Hell could be so obtuse as to prefer earthly gain at the expense of eternal happiness. His world as archbishop was filled with such men, and in dealing with them he was doomed to failure, for he could not enter into their calculations, even to frustrate them. But naturally, when a man of his integrity and self-abnegation acts on a public stage, his actions are often unexpected, and sometimes produce greater practical results than the policies of more aggressive politicians. His two long exiles are a case in point: they achieved nothing, but they provided an example for the most successful exile in medieval history – that of Thomas Becket. But, so far as Anselm was concerned, his periods of exile had no clear aim, and whatever results they had were accidental.

It is mistaken to measure the results against some large aim and ask how far this aim was achieved. The only practical aim for which he felt a personal responsibility was the maintenance of monastic life in its fullest measure of religious dedication in the communities at Bec and Canterbury, and in all other places to which his influence could reach. In this task, which extended and invigorated him, he met with disappointments. The criticism and hostility which he aroused in leaving Bec caused him much pain, and was probably one of the causes of the more subdued tone of his later letters of friendship. At Canterbury, the criticism he incurred for his long absences, and for his failure to safeguard the rights of the community to the full extent that he would have wished, and perhaps the knowledge that Eadmer had not obeyed his command to destroy his *Life*, all cast a shadow on his later years. But, within the limits of truth and justice and of his own limited competence in practical affairs, he thought that he had done all that he could.

His frequently declared wish to be rid of these duties is to be taken literally. He did not like or wish for public notice. Nevertheless, the positions which he had accepted under pressure brought new opportunities for doing some of those things which he wished to do: they broadened his theological vision, and enlarged the scope of his meditations by introducing him to new problems. His responsibilities as abbot, then as archbishop, gave him opportunities for shaping the lives of men and women in monastic communities other than his own; his conflict with Roscelin and the growing controversies with the Jews and in the schools gave a new direction to his greatest theological work; his monastic friends at Canterbury enlarged the scope and influence of his devotional innovations and gave him a small group of new disciples, among them his biographer and historian, who were the recorders of his talks and sermons, and the main preservers of his letters.

Running through all periods of his life after 1059, his relations with friends and pupils, in one sense extraordinarily warm, and yet governed by a rigid discipline and aim, provided a practical demonstration of a union which could only be consummated in Heaven. Pupils and friends were essential for eliciting his thoughts, but none of them, whether at Canterbury or Bec, could sustain his method of theological reasoning at a sufficiently high level of excellence or vigour to establish a continuing tradition after his death. Indeed, it is doubtful whether his lonely and introspective method could in any circumstances have become the source of a continuing tradition. In his pupils' manner of writing, and in the subjects they wrote about, we can trace the continuance of an Anselmian school of monastic writers at Bec and Canterbury through the first half of the twelfth century.[1] But their similarity is in style and subject matter, rather than in the uncompromising

---

[1] For this tradition at Canterbury, see above, pp. 322–9; and Leclercq, 1953, 45–117, 141–73.

search for precision which characterized all Anselm's thought. After those who had known him had died, the thread of his continuing influence ceased, only to be renewed intermittently when circumstances favoured a return to his manner of thought.

The scholars and religious leaders who were mainly influential in shaping the contemporary world were men with different abilities, working in circumstances favourable to the exercise of widely diffused influence in many parts of Europe. Anselm of Laon among his contemporaries, and St Bernard, Hugh of St Victor, and Abelard, whose work was just beginning when Anselm died, all had pupils who made contributions of major importance in the later development of European religious thought and life. As Cistercians or schoolmen they all belonged to influential and expanding groups with well-defined aims in the contemporary world. The greater monastic cohesion of Cîteaux, the greater impetus of intellectual effort in the schools, the more robust eloquence of St Bernard, the more vigorous and communicable dialectic of Abelard, all helped to ensure that their thoughts and their pupils had an immediate influence which cannot be claimed for Anselm.

It had been clear from an early stage in his career that Anselm's influence would be of slow and selective growth. It was part of his character that, penetrating though his influence on individuals might be, he would never be a dynamic leader in his generation. The two vital forces in reshaping the thought and government of Europe in his day – scholastic thought and the ever-broadening consequences of the Hildebrandine reform movement – were both quite alien to him in method and outlook. It was all the more important therefore that he should have had a few sympathetic followers who could preserve his memory and his works as an inspiration in a more distant future.

In any attempt to define his position in the sequence of major European figures, the old saw about his being the 'last of the Fathers and the first of the Scholastics' has a certain fascination. It stimulates by vexing: he is neither the one nor the other. He is a representative of that intermediate period between the Patristic and scholastic centuries, which may best be called the 'Benedictine centuries'. These centuries, in the thinness of their intellectual tradition and the singleness of their purpose, were wholly distinct from the world of the Fathers, whose thoughts were shaped by the great amalgamation of cultures of the ancient world, which Christianity gradually conquered. And they were equally distinct from the elaborately organizing period of thought and government from the twelfth century onwards.

There is in Anselm neither the richness of content and breadth of vision of the Fathers, nor the accumulation of materials into large organized bodies of thought and practice, which characterize the scholastic centuries. He was not concerned with the organization of large masses of material, nor with the creation of new processes of law or government, which were the great achievements of the schools of the twelfth and thirteenth centuries. His method was solitary and peaceful contemplation, and his thought grew, not by the confrontation of opposites, but by meditating on the meaning of concepts. He aimed at rigour of construction linked with intensity of vision.

Yet he was like later scholastic theologians in one respect: he had a single method for describing the whole of reality. The slight and fragmentary appearance of his works, and their absence of any claim to completeness, conceal their essential unity. In later theological writers, their system is on the surface: they work down from God to the Angels, from the Angels to Man, from the Fall to the Sacraments. In Anselm the system is implicit; though not visible at first sight, it is there. His place in relation to scholasticism is like that of Descartes in relation to the scientific movement from Newton to our own day. Descartes, in the view of Newton and his successors, was wrong in most of his detailed scientific concepts, but he anticipated them in seeking a single method to describe the whole of the physical universe. This is what Anselm did with the intelligible universe of the Christian faith. He gave his whole life to answering the fundamental questions: what kind of universe, what kind of God, what kind of behaviour is appropriate to a Creation which required its Creator to be put to death on the Cross?

Whatever judgement may be passed on Anselm's system, or on his recorded words and actions, they had a unique power to stimulate those whom he met, and they retain this power unimpaired to the present day. There is nothing in Anselm which is simply ordinary. Even in those fields where his response is most fully conditioned by his circumstances and by the thoughts of those around him – as for instance in all that concerned the primacy of Canterbury – he brought a sharper definition of the ideal to bear on practical action. This sharpness of mental images was not fortunate for his work as an ecclesiastical statesman, but for a contemplative theologian it is the one thing needful, and it made Anselm an effortless innovator. He founded no school, and the immediate future turned against his methods and ideas; but he touched the thought, the piety and the politics of the time at every important point, and gave new images and new lines of thought to those who came under his influence.

His capacity to stimulate pupils, which was most conspicuous throughout his whole life, was disappointing in its tangible results. Pupils were stirred into activity by his large and perceptive spirit, and the writings of two or three of them – Eadmer pre-eminently, and Gilbert Crispin and Ralph of Rochester and Battle in some notable works – combine originality with real force. But it was not through them that Anselm influenced the future. His theological influence has been gently pervasive, and occasionally awakening; his personal qualities have always found admirers; but in the area of his most persistent influence, in private prayer and devotion, his genuine work quickly became submerged in a sea of diluted imitations, some of which had virtues of their own; but none preserved the agony or intensity of Anselm's early productions.

His pupils left no sharply defined impress on the future, but they helped to keep his influence alive by collecting his letters and the records of his sermons and conversations, and to these materials they added their own more commonplace, though not negligible, appendices. In all these activities Eadmer took a leading part, and – most important of all – he left a record of Anselm's personality which gives unity to the widely different branches of his work, and would suffice to keep his memory fresh even if all else had disappeared.

II   THE UNITY OF ANSELM'S LIFE AND THOUGHT

If there is one quality which stamped Anselm's thoughts more than another, it was the intensity which came from concentrated meditation. He wrote about everything as from a visionary centre. When he wrote about God, he wrote from the experience of God's existence, even though that experience was no more, to begin with, than the experience of understanding the word 'God'. His whole argument grew from this understanding: intelligible only as absolute being, the word guaranteed the existence of that for which it stood and laid down the lines of further discovery.

In shaping this argument, he stood alone. Yet there was nothing he sought less than originality or individuality. If he removed authority from his arguments, it was not to replace it with his own views: quite the contrary, it was to install authority so deep in the foundations that it was out of sight and beyond dispute. The conclusions he sought to establish were those already authoritatively declared. It was the peculiarity of his system that reason neither went beyond authority nor fell short of it; the spheres of reason and faith were identical. Faith did not cease because its tenets were established by reason, nor did reason add certainty to faith. It only added clarity.

In several respects, his qualities are those of a mathematician; if mathematics is nothing but a series of tautologies in which every conclusion is contained in the premiss, the same may be said of Anselm's arguments. For example, in his argument for the existence of God, God's existence turns out not to be the end of the argument, but the necessary prerequisite for the beginning, even for understanding what it means – or how meaningless it is – to say that there is no God. A true understanding of the word and its implications is necessary even for our capacity to think at all. Anselm's attitude to the arguments by which he established the necessity for any dogmatic truth, such as the necessary manner of God's existence, or the necessary manner of Christ's redemption of mankind, is similar to that of a mathematician who discovers the proof of a theorem which he already knows in practice to be true, but seeks to prove also in principle.

Yet at the time when Anselm wrote, mathematics was a dead language, soon indeed to be revived, but not in Anselm's lifetime. From the contemporary practitioners of the art he could have got no hint of the type of reasoning which alone would satisfy him. He learnt his method in introspection in the silent rigours of his early days at Bec.

From a general point of view, the time could scarcely have been less propitious for a mind such as Anselm's. It was a time ripe for scholasticism – that is, for the gathering together of the results of past thought, re-appraising them, and putting together systematically the redefined truths of the past. This was work which was just beginning to be undertaken in the second half of the eleventh century, most notably in the schools of northern France. But Anselm, in his three-year journey through France as a young man, did not even stop to mix with the students of the schools which were beginning to reshape the thought of Europe.

444

This is itself a somewhat astonishing fact. When Lanfranc had made his way through the areas of Burgundy, Touraine, and Le Mans to Normandy thirty years earlier, the schools of these regions had been much less highly developed than they were when Anselm made the same journey. Yet Lanfranc had seen something of their importance, and had become a notable figure in them before he gave up everything to become a monk at Bec. But Anselm never showed any interest in the work of systematically excerpting and comparing ancient texts which led to the scholastic reorganization of knowledge during the next two hundred years.

Instead, he chose, or rather allowed others to choose for him, the monastic life. The form of monastic life which he passively accepted was not as elaborate as that at Cluny, but it was sufficiently elaborate to be unsuited to profound theological speculation. In the first place it allowed too little time for study; secondly, it did not normally provide a questioning, eager, and ever-changing audience of fresh minds. But above all, it was directed to other ends than rigorous intellectual activity. The heavy burden of repetition, the sustained effort of attention demanded by the requirements of the divine office, the interruptions of study and sleep at uncomfortable hours, the responsibilities of communal discipline, and the administration of large, widely separated estates – all these conditions encouraged the type of intellectual labour which could be taken up or put down like a piece of knitting: it discouraged prolonged efforts of intense concentration which could not easily be discontinued and taken up again without an effort.

That Anselm felt these restraints, and that he was worried by the pull of conflicting obligations, is certain.[2] That he overcame them was due in the first place to his natural intensity of mind, which allowed him to absorb what he read without feeling the need for detailed dependence on authorities. This faculty allowed him to pursue his meditations without constant reference to a large scholarly apparatus. He did not quote Augustine because he did not need to: he stood in his shoes. As for the stimulation of an audience, he found it not in a classroom nor in debate, but in colloquies with one or two like-minded young men to whom he talked with unrestrained freedom: he talked with Gundulf, his contemporary as a monk, in the first place, and then with an unending stream of new listeners – for it seems that he always did most of the talking.

[2] See *VA* I, xix, pp. 29–30.

So it came about that in the midst of an exacting routine of monastic offices, he could develop the modes of meditation and dialogue, which were the two forms in which he thought and wrote most naturally. For thought developed along these lines, the immediate circumstances of his life were unexpectedly favourable. During his first twenty years at Bec he had few administrative responsibilities; he had a library rich in the works of Augustine; above all, he had the constant stimulus of young minds. Even at Canterbury, he left administration largely to others; and if he then had less opportunity for attracting new pupils, the best of his old ones, Boso, could still be summoned from Bec to help him. He benefited too from his periods of exile: they freed him from business and allowed time for meditation.

His preferred stimulus was the presence of young minds, and his dialogues are a tribute to his debt. His *dicta* about the young are some of the best which Eadmer preserved. His educational theories – if his genial similes can bear so pompous a description – resemble those of a much later, or much earlier, time. On no issue was he more remote from his own age than in his opposition to the insensate brutality with which monastic teachers, no doubt imitating the rest of the world in this, treated the children under their care. His similes of the growing tree which requires freedom for growth rather than restraint, and of the goldsmith who works by gentle pressure and a discreet evocation of the desired shape, rather than by heavy hammer-blows, belong to a train of thought which only found full expression in the romantic theories of the nineteenth century. And the answer which he gave to those who asked him why he devoted more attention to adolescents than to children or adults, looks as far back into the past as these similes look forward into the future. He answered that the wax of youth was alone fit to take a new impression, being neither so soft as to lose, nor so hard as to repel, the imprint of the seal. This is a simile which Plato had already used with a rather different application, in his *Theaetetus*:

I would have you imagine, then, that there exists in the mind a block of wax, which is of different size and nature in different men; harder, moister, and having more or less of purity in one than in another . . . This block of wax is the gift of Memory, the mother of the Muses. When we wish to remember anything which we have seen, or heard, or thought in our own minds, we hold up the wax to our perceptions and thoughts, and the wax receives their impression as from a seal. We remember and know what is imprinted as long as the image lasts; but when the image is effaced, or fails to 'take', then we forget and no longer know.[3]

Anselm cannot have known this or any other passage in the *Theaetetus*, and there is no evidence that he had read even the one dialogue of Plato, the *Timaeus*, which in part at least was widely available in Latin and which Lanfranc knew well.[4] But an innate similarity of mind between Anselm and Plato led him to some of the same thoughts and images. Besides, Plato was here describing the process of meditation which was the fundamental process of all Anselm's thought. So the two minds met, not just in imagery but in their processes of thought. No doubt, the *Dialogues* of Plato have a dramatic force, a width of interest, and a breath of the busy world which is lacking in those of Anselm. But in his determination to leave no objection unanswered, and to answer each question in his own words and in his own way, Anselm comes nearer to the great master of philosophic dialogue than any other medieval writer.

III   ANSELM NO HUMANIST

As the great monasteries became increasingly wealthy and important pillars of society, their priors and abbots and the abler monks, with all their administrative duties, had less time for the choir, and still less for meditation. There were many in Anselm's time who discerned the ill effect of this development on religious exercises of all kinds; and we might expect that Anselm, who could see such consequences as well as anyone, would have encouraged monks to seek the simpler forms of monastic life which provided more favourable conditions for the kind of meditative spirituality which he had developed. But this is not what we find. As he made progress in his religious life, he came to think that such calculations of better or worse led away from the essential task of self-abasement in the presence of God. Although his charming style, his mildness, the warmth of his expressions of friendship, may seem to speak of his humanity, he was no humanist. What then was he? In attempting to answer this question, it will be useful to examine three stages in his practice and theory of self-abasement.

---

[3] *VA* I, xi. *Theaetetus*, 191 c–d. I have slightly modified the translation in *The Dialogues of Plato*, translated by B. Jowett, 4th ed., Oxford, 1953, iii, pp. 294–5.

[4] See Gibson, 1971, pp. 435–50, for Lanfranc's discussion of a passage in the *Timaeus* mentioned by Augustine.

First, he took great pains to argue against those among his friends who desired to move from an over-elaborate form of monastic life to something simpler. This was one of the growing concerns of spiritually gifted monks, to whom the weight of accumulated customs and business, and the wealth which was necessary to sustain this over-elaborate form of monastic life, appeared as hindrances to their spiritual growth. But Anselm did not encourage them. To one discontented monk, he wrote:

Whoever takes the vows of monastic life must study with the whole of his mind to root himself lovingly in whatever monastery he may have made his profession, unless it is such that it forces him unwillingly to do evil. Let him refuse to pass judgement on the manners of others, and on the customs of the place even if they seem useless, provided that they are not against the divine commands. Let him rejoice at finding himself at last where he can remain for the whole of his life, not unwillingly but voluntarily; let him drive away all thought of removal so that he may quietly give himself up to performing the exercises of a pious life. And if it seems to him that his spiritual fervour could achieve greater and more useful ends than the institutions of his present monastery allow, let him believe that he is either deceived in thinking that those things are greater which in fact are equal or inferior, or in supposing that he could accomplish what is above his power; or at least let him believe that he does not deserve what he desires.[5]

This may seem an argument for monastic conservatism. But it is nothing of the kind. It is an argument about self-abnegation in the midst of uncongenial elaborations of outward things. To desire simplicity is good; to endure elaboration as a matter of obedience is better.

Then, secondly, his *Prayers* and *Meditations* seem to offer individuals a new measure of freedom. These are his words:

The purpose of the prayers and meditations which follow is to excite the mind of the reader either to the love or fear of God, or to self-examination. They are not, therefore, to be read in a tumult, but quietly; not cursorily or quickly, but slowly and with intense and thoughtful meditation. Nor should the reader trouble about reading the whole of any of them, but only so much as (with God's help) he feels to be satisfying or useful in stirring up his spirit to pray. Nor is it necessary for him to start at the beginning, but wherever he pleases . . .[6]

This is freedom indeed, far removed from the injunction in the Benedictine Rule that books were to be read *per ordinem ex integro*,

[5] *Ep.* 37 (i, 29). Eadmer quoted the greater part of this letter in *VA* I, xx; and Anselm advised a novice at Canterbury to find and read it. (See above, p. 396.)
[6] *Orationes sive Meditationes, Prologus*, Schmitt, iii, p. 3.

from beginning to end. There is a large liberty in Anselm's words, and this liberty is the same for all – for women as well as men, for those in the midst of secular cares as much as for monks in the midst of their religious routine.

But if we examine the contents of the *Prayers* rather than the manner of using them, it turns out that the freedom he advocates is only the prelude to a greater rigour of self-abasement. His prayers are introspective religious exercises which begin by stimulating anxiety as a prelude to a rigorous discipline of the will. The introspection is simply the beginning of the road to self-contempt, and only accidentally a journey of self-discovery. Least of all is it an invitation to discover the grandeur of human powers. In the whole of Anselm's writings there is no place for joy in 'Man's unconquerable mind'. There is a paradox here, for the idea of God which he found in his mind at the beginning of the *Proslogion* is of greater value than all other human discoveries put together. But, then, the idea of God is not arrived at by human ingenuity or effort: it is found by clearing the debris of the everyday world from the mind, and finding what God has placed there. So here, as everywhere, Anselm's thought begins with the rejection of self, and freedom in the manner of prayer holds out no promise of enlarged individual liberty: it is simply a prelude to a more thorough self-abasement through self-knowledge.

This brings us to the third and most complete expression of the need for self-rejection, which is found in Anselm's recasting of the central exercise of the religious life as described by St Benedict in the chapter of the Rule devoted to the Twelve Steps of Humility. Characteristically, St Benedict sets out these steps in a rather haphazard fashion. They start with the fear of the Lord and then survey the world, looking now in one direction, now in another, from this central point. Their sequence is as follows:

1 fear the Lord;
2 renounce self-will;
3 obey your superior;
4 bear injuries patiently;
5 confess your evil thoughts;
6 be content with insignificance;
7 believe that you are vile;
8 do nothing out of the ordinary;
9 be silent;
10 do not laugh;

11 speak little and quietly;

12 be humble in act and thought.[7]

Thus the Rule gently guides the members of the community towards perfection along a series of stepping stones, not systematically arranged, but following an order which might in practice be different for every individual within the community. Yet, although all the exercises require individual exertion, the presence of the community is necessary for nearly all of them.

But now consider the Steps of Humility as Anselm recast them in his teaching. Of course, we must understand that he did not intend his steps to *replace* the steps of the Rule; only to supplement them. But the change of stance and aim which he introduces is very striking. The calm unsystematic flow of experience in the Rule is replaced by a rigidly logical sequence of stages by which an individual may approach perfection. In Anselm's progress, no step can come in a different order: every earlier step comes necessarily before the next, and they all take place within the individual soul. The community might just as well not exist except as a source of potentially hostile criticism, which is to be used for the soul's health in further self-abasement. What Anselm describes is an interior development which takes place as a result of an intense effort of introspection, bringing a constantly unfolding self-rejection. The steps towards this end, which Anselm sets out, are these:

1 know yourself to be contemptible;

2 be grieved by this knowledge;

3 confess that you are contemptible;

4 persuade others to think you are contemptible;

5 allow others to treat you with contempt;

6 be content to be so treated;

7 rejoice to be so treated.

Whoever reaches this height of humility lives in clear unclouded light, in inviolable serenity, free from all storms.[8]

As often in Anselm, one might think that there is an element of mental sickness in this love of contempt. Indeed, Anselm might say, since the soul is sick, how can it be otherwise? But then, we might reply, it is like a worm luxuriating in its lacerations under the harrow. But here we would be mistaken. The harrow is all within. Just as we found in Anselm's experience of friendship, that the final

---

[7] *Reg. S. Ben.*, c. vii.

[8] See *Memorials*, pp. 81, 110–16, 308–9, for different versions of reports of Anselm's words on this subject, all of them however retaining the same framework.

state of 'loving' refers not to an emotion but to the state of the will, so here the progressive stages of self-humiliation are not to be thought of as states of feeling, but as states of being which bring the soul to freedom and light in the presence of God.

These seven steps of humility may also throw some light on the perplexing question of the crisis in his relations with Eadmer in 1100 which led to Eadmer's act of disobedience, and to his apparently lasting exclusion from the intimacy which he had formerly enjoyed. I have described the blighting effect of this incident, and I imagine it will be generally thought that Anselm's reaction was exaggerated, even harmful, and that Eadmer did, if not the right thing, at least something humanly excusable, in resorting to the subterfuge of transcribing what he had written before obeying Anselm's command to destroy.

But in the light of Anselm's seven steps of humility, the incident has a different message. In encouraging Eadmer to record his reminiscences of his past, Anselm too had fallen into the trap of desiring to be well thought of in the world. If Eadmer had thrown the whole thing into the fire at once, all would have been well. But he didn't, and Anselm could not trust him again. Harsh, indeed, and inhuman by any ordinary standards, but intelligible in view of the final end of 'rejoicing in being despised'.

Further, in judging this incident in its theological setting, we may also remember that Anselm had recently written in his *Cur Deus Homo* that it would be better that the whole universe should perish than that anyone should take one single glance contrary to the will of God.[9] Of course Anselm did not confuse his command with the will of God: yet in this world, and in the monastic order, the abbot's will, unless evil in itself, was to be obeyed as the will of God. Anselm no doubt thought he had himself been weak in allowing Eadmer to hear and write so much; but once he saw, perhaps with some natural pleasure, that it was leading to the glorification of himself, he must have wondered on which of his seven steps of humility he was standing. Looked on in this light, it is easy to understand his determination to order the destruction of the whole work; and, in this same context, we can understand that it was Eadmer's duty as a monk to obey absolutely.

Still, no one can avoid an uneasy feeling that Anselm was here caught in the net of this world, and that he should either have allowed nature to take its course and Eadmer's *Life* to survive, or

[9] See above, pp. 216–18.

insisted more rigorously on demonstrable destruction. Undoubtedly Eadmer believed he was in grave sin in his disobedience; and as
we know, he did not confess it for twenty years. Sensibly enough,
Anselm's successor, Archbishop Ralph, condoned the disobedience, and Eadmer went on to propagate the work which he had
been ordered to destroy, and to complete it with a special section of
miracles as a fully authenticated saint's *Life*. In its final form, it was
no longer a work of memoirs of a saintly friend; it was at last, what
Eadmer had no doubt always hoped, and what perhaps Anselm
feared, it would become: the latest of the long list of Canterbury
saints' *Lives*.

This is perhaps the most disturbing incident in Anselm's life. So
far as it is known to us, he seems to have gone either too far, or not
far enough; to have been severe without being effective; to have
spoilt Eadmer's work, indeed to have seriously injured his life,
without achieving the result he aimed at. It is easy to be critical
about such a sensitive subject for which we have only one side of the
story. But the main elements of the story are clear, and no one can
understand Anselm's life without coming to a provisional understanding of what the incident meant to him within the context of his
seven steps of humility.

IV ANSELM AND ETERNITY

Leaving on one side the personal problems of the incident, what we
can say with some confidence is that it reflects the dilemma of
Anselm's general position in monastic history. The whole tendency
of his teaching and example was to foster individual spiritual
exercises, inquiries, discussions, and meditations within the
monastery. In doing this, he was moving away from the corporate
spirit of the old monasticism into the age of individuality. Yet, his
aim was not to promote individuality, but rather to destroy its main
manifestation in the consciousness of Man's independent powers in
relation to God. Consequently, despite all his cultivation of the
individual, the medicine he prescribed was the absolute renunciation of self. What St Francis was later to symbolize in throwing off
all his clothes, Anselm expresses in the final act of interior
nakedness: rejoicing in contempt.

Although, therefore, Anselm seems on the surface to be
promoting the movement towards individuality which characterized much of the piety of the later Middle Ages, his intention was

the opposite. He looked inwards, was horrified by what he saw, and urged the need to turn away from the self to God. His view of liberty as a state of inability to make the wrong decision, of liberty therefore in perfect submission to the divine will, is a consequence of his view of the need to reject every symptom of self-esteem.

This programme of looking inwards in order to see, not the self, but God, is the method of the *Proslogion*. The argument proves the presence of God within the 'chamber of the mind' which understands the meaning of the word 'God'. Whoever understands the word is on the road to the experience which will only be complete in eternal life. The outline is already in the mind, but the searcher is not, or not yet, enlarged by this experience: it remains only the faintest outline of the experience of eternity.

A similar situation is outlined in the *Cur Deus Homo*. Anselm removed from the universe that lawful power which the Devil, the destroyer of law and order, had been thought to exercise over mankind. He substituted the power of the God-Man, at once Creator and the Created within the system, as the sole source of the redemptive process. For one moment of time, that which is beyond the system is within it as the source of its re-creation, drawing everything to God. This change of emphasis may seem to enlarge the scope of humanity in the universe, and Abelard and Robert Grosseteste later interpreted Anselm's argument in ways that greatly enlarged its human potentialities.[10] But, for Anselm, the only enlargement was in the sovereignty of God: human nature contributed nothing to its redemption.

We have observed a similar feature in Anselm's ideal of friendship, which seems on the surface to be filled with human sensibility and warmth. So it is. But with this proviso: in anything approaching its full warmth, Anselm's friendship is available only to those who have made, or are about to make, the complete surrender of themselves to monastic discipline. Ardent and passionate though it is in appearance, it comes with that stamp of renunciation upon it, which makes it fit for eternity. In brief, here too the appearance of human enlargement is illusory unless viewed from a stand-point beyond this world.

So too in politics. The only cause to which Anselm could devote

[10] For Abelard, see above, pp. 210–11; for Grosseteste, see R.W.Southern, 1986, pp. 219–25, and D. J. Ungar, 'Robert Grosseteste and the reasons for the Incarnation', *Franciscan Studies*, 16, 1956, 1–3.

himself whole-heartedly came from the association of the monastic community with the saints. In safeguarding their rights, Anselm was not thinking, though no doubt many members of the community were thinking, of their corporate grandeur. Still less was he thinking of his own grandeur. He was thinking only of his unalterable duty as archbishop to protect the rights of the saints to whom lands, customs and a primatial position at Canterbury had been given forever: he feared, as he declared, to appear before the divine Judge unless he had punished those who in his time as archbishop had infringed the primatial jurisdiction committed to his care.[11]

Everything in Anselm's view of the world is both intensely personal, and yet forms part of a whole which embraces both time and eternity. The things of this world contain what we might call intimations of eternity. But this is too weak a phrase to describe Anselm's thought. The relationships of individuals in friendship, or of communities in rights and jurisdictions, were more than symbolically related to eternity: they were an integral part of the eternal order of truth, love and justice, and yet they retained their full earthly reality.

There was nothing of which this was more true than friendship as he described it in his letters, and practised it in his monastic talk. Friendship is perfected in Heaven; but it can be remarkably fully experienced on earth, where it exists in a state of warfare with the world. In this respect, Anselm's friendships belonged to the ancient heroic world in which friends risked their lives for each other in the midst of deadly dangers. The analogy is not as far-fetched as it may seem. We have Anselm's own words: 'Dearest, you have enlisted in the army of Christ, in which it is necessary, not only to drive off the enemy by violence, but also to use some cunning in doing so'; and, in another letter, 'Do not fear to become a knight in the service of so great a king, for he will be with you in every danger'.[12] The virtues which Anselm everywhere insists on in his friends are also those of military life: absolute obedience, abandonment of self, unwavering commitment. The warfare is

---

[11] The memory of this fear was preserved by the monks of Canterbury and reported to John of Salisbury when he wrote his abridgement of Eadmer's *Vita Anselmi* more than fifty years after Anselm's death. See *PL* 199, col. 1035, and Biffi 1988, p. 106. In itself this would not be good evidence; but it is borne out by Anselm's last letter, written shortly before his death, to the archbishop of York. See above, pp. 343–4.

[12] *Epp.* 37 (i, 29), 38 (i, 30); 117 (ii, 19).

spiritual, but its characteristics are those of real war at its most heroic.

But here too there is a problem. If the warfare in which Anselm and his friends were engaged was so serious, it might seem that the sterner language of discipline and harsh duty, which we know he could use to those who had fallen away, would at all times have been more appropriate than the soft language of kisses. Why did he not use the harsh language which he knew well how to use to those who had fallen away?

I think the answer is that he wrote from the standpoint of one who had already gained the victory over doubt and disobedience. With the exception of his logical text-book, *De Grammatico*, he wrote nothing until the victory had been gained, and thereafter he wrote always from the position of an achieved victory. Those who have dedicated themselves to the militia of monastic obedience are already victors, if only they remain steadfast. That is why he wrote so despairingly to Gunhilda, with whom he had exchanged vows of fidelity to the service of Christ.[13] She had fled from a victorious field, and he wanted to say that she had only to return to ensure victory. Beneath all the harshness of his description of her position, there is something like the pleading of a lover.

We see here why the older monasticism had not encouraged intimate friendships or emotions, or for that matter thoughts, of such intensity. Such experiences broke up the solidarity of the community in its daily grind along the road to salvation. Anselm would not have thought of himself or his friends as having escaped from this daily corporate struggle: but they could also stand above it. His aim in his letters of friendship was to encourage endurance, and at the same time to celebrate a victory.

This habitual stance of writing from a position of achieved victory which needs only persistence for its completion helps to explain why political action was the least satisfactory part of Anselm's work. To ensure success, political problems require to be viewed from the level of political action. The advocate of political action may identify the goal which he seeks to promote with eternal justice; but he must plan and act on the level of this world, planning and choosing the means most likely to lead to the desired end. Anselm always resisted a descent to this level. His natural element was inner activity, and the ends which he sought

[13] See above, pp. 262–4.

455

were those which could be reached only from within. Ultimately he was concerned only with the task of building up the necessary number of souls to complete the kingdom of Heaven. When this number had been completed – probably at no very distant date – this world's history would come to an end and all would be rolled up in eternity.

Apart from this end, no political programme had any interest for him. He did not identify himself with any organizational programme, except in the few letters in which he used borrowed phrases which never became part of his general discourse.[14] He had no plan for a better future for this world. In politics, he would have been content for organizations to stay as they were, but he was bound by obedience to carry out legitimate decrees imposed by papal authority. He was also bound by his office as abbot, and then as archbishop, to safeguard the gifts to God and the saints made by benefactors to the churches of which he had reluctantly become the embodiment. These gifts of saints now in Heaven were inviolable offerings, already part of a supernatural order, not subject to diminution, even by the pope. As for papal decrees, they too were part of a supernatural order, and he would have wished them also, once made, to remain unchanged. If Paschal II was willing to change what Urban II had decreed, it was not for him to object. But he did object when Paschal II appeared to wish to diminish rights granted by Gregory I, which he as archbishop was responsible for safeguarding. Although earthly, these rights were part of the kingdom of Heaven, and on them he could not compromise.

More generally, in viewing every problem *sub specie aeternitatis*, he shared with all thinkers of a Platonic tendency their difficulty in separating the world from God, and one individual from another. In philosophy, he was an extreme idealist, attaching an unqualified existence to general concepts. As he told Roscelin, 'Anyone who does not understand how many men are one man in species, cannot understand how, in the most secret and sublime nature of God, several Persons, each being perfect God, can be one God.'[15] He seems here to think that the same logic which applies to the relations between the Persons in the Trinity and to arguments about the Unity of God applies also to the relations between one man and the rest of the human race. If he had lived in a time of more intense theological controversy, words like these would have come

[14] See above, p. 288n.
[15] *Ep. de Incarn. Verbi*, c. 1 (Schmitt, ii, p. 10). See above, p. 179.

under severe scrutiny. At one moment, Roscelin seemed to threaten him with the need to explain himself on this point. But despite this hostile intrusion, Anselm could evolve his theological explanations in peace, using images which he thought suggestive, without having them torn to pieces in debate.

His instruments of thought were very simple, much simpler than they would have been a generation later. He took words very seriously: they were the doorway to the kingdom of essences to which the believer, unless blinded by the things of this world, had the key. Hence he pushed his analysis of words with relentless activity. He was fortunate in living before the discovery of the full range of Aristotle's logical works; the complexity of the problems they raised could only have been a hindrance to him. But the price he paid for his freedom was a certain philosophical naivety. Likewise it may perhaps be claimed that a share of philosophical naivety is as much an aid to understanding his thoughts as it would be a hindrance in understanding the thoughts of St Augustine or St Thomas Aquinas.

St Augustine's writings are full of a long philosophical tradition; those of Aquinas are monuments of technical proficiency in a highly complex art. Augustine and Aquinas both lived in a world in which the world outside Christendom was seen to be much larger than than the world of Christians; and the literature which an apologist had to command in order to succeed was enormous. The age of Anselm was by comparison an age of innocence. His thoughts are those of the cloister, round which the raging winds of controversy were beginning to be heard, but had not yet penetrated. He could think in the cloister in peace, best of all perhaps – as his friends suspected – in exile. By the end of his life, he was already old-fashioned; but his best thoughts are above fashion, and they can be taken up at any time and found to be as fresh as ever.

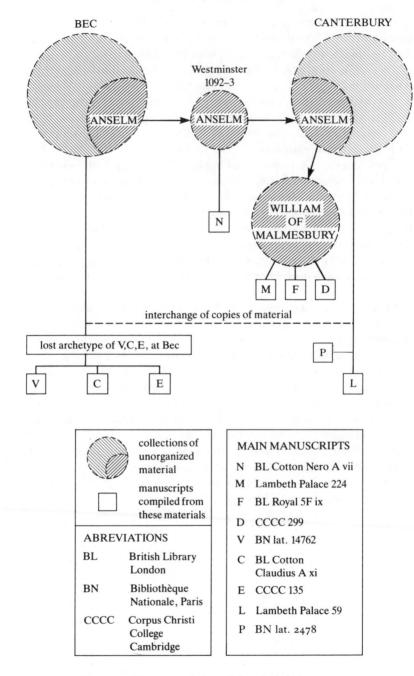

Figure 2 The transmission of Anselm's letters

APPENDIX TOWARDS A HISTORY OF ANSELM'S LETTERS

It will be convenient to begin with a list of the main manuscripts and the symbols used by Dom Schmitt in his edition, by which they will be referred to in what follows. With the exception of **N** all the MSS in the list contain letters of all dates from 1070 to 1109 in varying numbers and arrangements.

N London BL MS Cotton Nero A vii, probably 1092–1100: the earliest MS of Anselm's letters containing only those of his priorate and abbacy at Bec; perhaps from Rochester.

L London Lambeth Palace MS 59, from Christ Church Canterbury; c 1125–30. For the date, see below. The main collection of Anselm's letters from 1070 to 1109.

P Paris BN MS lat. 2478: a copy of **L** made before its final additions.

M Lambeth Palace MS 224: a partial copy made by William of Malmesbury of material which had been gathered by him at Canterbury probably in 1120–22, and selectively copied in this MS not long afterwards.

F London BL Royal MS 5 F ix: another copy of William of Malmesbury's material, containing more texts with a different arrangement. Date: probably second quarter of twelfth century, provenance unknown.

D Cambridge, Corpus Christi College, MS 299: another copy of the same body of material, with a few texts not in **M** or **F** and with an arrangement similar to that of **F**: c 1200.

V Paris BN MS lat 14762, thirteenth century.

C London BL MS Cotton Claudius A xi: thirteenth century.

E Cambridge Corpus Christi College MS 135: second quarter of twelfth century, from Bury St Edmunds.

This group of MSS (**VCE**) goes back to a lost MS made at Bec, probably shortly before **L** was completed. Of these three MSS, **V** is the closest to the lost exemplar.

459

II   THE PROBLEMS AND THEIR IMPORTANCE

There are several reasons why a history of the transmission of Anselm's correspondence will one day be written, and why it is important; there are several reasons also why it cannot yet be written as fully as will be possible in future. With regard to its importance, it will clarify Anselm's own attitude and that of his disciples to his correspondence, and it will show who the collectors were, and what were their aims. Some of these problems – in particular his own part in making the collection – can, I think, be solved at once. Other problems, in particular the date and personalities involved in making the main collections, and the date when they made them, can probably be solved in their main outline. But there are questions about the roles of his various disciples which cannot yet be fully settled, because though the material exists in remarkable abundance, and though the main stages in making the collection are fairly clear, there are many details which at present elude explanation. The interpretation of these details calls for a vast number of minute observations, and an intimate knowledge of the manuscripts. The observations which follow are very incomplete, and I have no doubt that they will require correction and completion at many points, but I think they will suffice for some purposes, and they may save others a certain amount of labour, and perhaps some errors.

Indeed, it was the appearance of important errors of interpretation which caused me to take up again work which I had abandoned fifty-five years ago on learning that Dom Schmitt intended to include the letters in his then projected edition of Anselm's *Works*. Dom Schmitt, with whom I worked in great harmony, made an error (as I believed, he came to agree[1]) about the date of **L**, which has led other scholars to some false conclusions. I mentioned this mistake in a footnote in the first edition of this book. But a footnote is never enough and the error grew, first in the hands of Norman Cantor, then of Walter Fröhlich, and then in the very full and detailed elaborations of Sally Vaughn on the same theme. I have replied to these elaborations in an article in *Albion*, to which Vaughn has replied.[2] But obviously much more is needed to

---

[1] See our joint note in *Memorials*, 1969, p. 333; but Dr Fröhlich has pointed out to me that Fr Schmitt repeated his earlier view in the *Prolegomena* to his edition, published in 1968, p. 239.

[2] See Cantor 1958, pp. 169–70; Fröhlich 1984, pp. 58–71; Vaughn 1987, pp. 132, 135, 137–8, 139–40. 225, 293–4, 295n., 297; Southern and Vaughn 1988, pp. 192–220.

complete the picture, and I shall try here in a preliminary way to supply an outline of what I believe to be the essential features of the case.

What I aim to do here is simply to set out the main elements of what I believe to be the correct solution to the problem of the compilation of Anselm's letter-collection, leaving it for others to test and elaborate or modify my conclusions. But first, it is necessary to make it clear that in approaching any letter-collection, there are a number of questions to be asked, and it is only when they have all been answered that we can understand the collection in detail. Of these questions the most important are these: from what materials was it made? For what purpose was it made, and on what principle are the letters selected and arranged? Who made it and when? It is with a view towards a full answer to these questions that I add this Appendix of observations made over many years, and ask indulgence for errors which have no doubt crept into such a miscellaneous assortment of details.

III   ANSELM'S LETTERS AS PRIOR AND ABBOT OF BEC

With regard to the question of who made it, our starting point must be Anselm's intention in collecting his letters from correspondents during the years between 1085 and 1092. The fact that he should have had to do this, whatever his intentions may have been, tells us something about his failure to preserve copies of letters which he thought important. We know that he had kept some letters, because he used the contents of one of them on several later occasions, and advised a monastic novice to read it. Moreover, many of his letters were written with considerable stylistic care, and many of them contained instructions and reflections on the monastic life which he thought important. So it is strange that he did not take more care in their preservation than he seems to have done. Nevertheless, the fact seems undeniable that he had no adequate system for their preservation.

His realization of this fact seems to have come to him during his later years as abbot, probably in about 1086, when we find him trying to get one of his closest early pupils, a monk called Maurice, to return letters which were in his keeping.[3] Whether the letters which Anselm refers to had all been written to Maurice, or whether Maurice had been Anselm's secretary and custodian of his letters,

---

[3] See above, p. 397.

does not appear. Possibly both. In either case, it seems clear that Maurice had been careless, for Anselm was still trying to get back his letters to him in 1092.

In one respect Maurice's carelessness is our gain, for Anselm's two letters which attest Maurice's failure to return them provides the only evidence we have that Anselm ever intended to collect his letters. They also show that he had not got very far by 1092. Nevertheless, even if he had received no letters from Maurice, Anselm certainly had some drafts, fair copies and original texts of his letters in his possession by 1092. We know this from the letter written while he was at Westminster in the autumn of 1092 to the prior of Bec, asking for the letters which Maurice had failed to send him.[4] And when we find a manuscript, **N**, which cannot be much later than this date, which contains letters from 1070 to 1092, but none later, we can feel fairly confident that this manuscript has some connection with Anselm's activity in collecting his letters at this date. But we can feel even more confident that this manuscript was not made under Anselm's supervision. The reasons for this conclusion are these:

1 Apart from dividing the letters into those which belong to Anselm's priorate and those of his abbacy, the order of letters within these divisions, while showing some attempt at a chronological sequence, is chaotic.

2 **N** omits some twenty early letters which appear in later collections made at Bec and Canterbury, described below. It is true that the last quire of the manuscript is lost. But since some of the missing letters belonged to Anselm's priorate, they were clearly omitted because they were not available to the compiler of **N**.

3 Among the missing letters are all those which Anselm wrote to Maurice, with the exception of a draft of one, and the text of another which was written to several other monks besides Maurice. Of these, the draft may have been in Anselm's possession, and Anselm could have received the letter sent to several monks from one of its other recipients.[5]

4 Several of the letters which are found in **N** in imperfect drafts of

---

[4] See above, pp. 186, 189.
[5] The letters to Maurice in **N** are *Epp.* 51 (to others besides Maurice) and 97 (in draft). **N** omits eight other letters (*Epp.* 42, 43, 47, 60, 64, 69, 74, 79) addressed to Maurice alone, which formed part of the final collection made at Canterbury.

abbreviated texts, were later in better texts in the Canterbury archives, and were then incorporated in **L** to which we shall come presently.

5 **N** does not seem to have been preserved at Canterbury among the rest of Anselm's literary remains, for it was not used by the compiler(s) of **L**, which is certainly a Canterbury compilation. Moreover, although William of Malmesbury (for whose activity, see below) knew several texts which are in **N**, he does not quote them from **N** nor in the order in which they are found in **N**.

In brief, we can be sure that Anselm himself was not responsible for such an incomplete, disordered and textually defective collection of his letters. It is much more likely to have been the work of an unauthorized admirer, who had access to his literary baggage – a form of poaching about which Anselm complained more than once.[6]

N was almost certainly written in England, probably by a monk with Canterbury connections, but more likely of Rochester than Canterbury itself. The reasons for thinking this are:

1 The collection of Anselm's letters in **N** from an early date, and perhaps in its original conception, was bound up with a collection of Lanfranc's letters, which could only have been found at Canterbury.

2 The drafts and copies from which the Anselmian part of **N** was compiled were at Canterbury in about 1120, when (as we shall see) William of Malmesbury used the same material, without having access to **N**.

3 The contents of **N** correspond to a manuscript in the library at Rochester in 1202, and the likelihood is that **N** is this manuscript.

To sum up: the compiler of **N** had access to Anselm's materials in an imperfect state, before he had finished making his collection of drafts and copies, and there are no signs that he ever resumed it. **N** therefore stands alone as a monument of this incomplete attempt, and it will be convenient to list the contents of **N** and compare them with the later contents of the collections made at Bec (**VCE**) and Canterbury (**LP**).

---

[6] See **De Veritate**, Pref.: *a quibusdam festinantibus . . . transcripti antequam perfecti essent.;* **De Incarn. Verbi***: quidam fratres me nesciente transcripserunt atque aliis legendam tradiderunt.* And for further illicit transcriptions, see *Epp.* 250 (iii, 60); 253 (iv, 15).

1 The contents of **N**

I Letters of Anselm's priorate: 1, 3, 4–8, 16, 38, 14–15, 12–13, 11, 17–18, 20–22, 29, 23, 25, 28, 24, 32–4, 36, 35, 6(again), 51, 50, 44, 41, 40, 38–9, 66, 45, 2, 61, 49, 58, 68, 46, 26, 59, 27, 48, 54–6, 71, 57, 76, 62, 67, 37, 78, 53, 80–85, 65, 86–7;

II Letters of Anselm's abbacy: 89(draft), 90–95, 117, 99, 101, 97 (draft), 100, 103, 106, 108, 110–111, 105, 114–15, 98, 104, 116, 107, 118–9, 109, 122, 133 (incomplete: here the MS ends).

Arranging these contents in the order of Schmitt's edition, this gives us the following:

I: 1–8, 11–18, 20–29, 32–41, 44–46, 48–51, 53–59, 61–2, 65–8, 71, 76, 78, 80–87,

II: 89 (draft), 90–95, 97 (draft), 98–101, 103–111, 114–119, 122, 133. . .

2 Pre-archiepiscopal letters in **V**

If we compare this list with the contents of the final compilation made at Bec, represented best by **V**, we find two attempts at collecting the letters of Anselm's priorate and abbacy. The first runs as follows:

Extracts from 1, 3, 4; then full texts of 5–6, 8–9, 16–17, 20–22, 25, 28, 30–31, 35, 37–8, 44–5, 49–51, 53, 59–61, 65. Here, in the middle of 65, the sequence stops abruptly.

A second sequence now begins, which is divided, as in **N**, into two series, containing respectively the letters of the priorate and of the abbacy. These two series run thus:

I Letters of Anselm's priorate: 1–8, 11–17, 20–22, 25, 28–51, 53–86;

II Letters of Anselm's abbacy: 89–94, 96–101, 103–106, 109, 116–117, 110–115, 118–122, 102, 125–7, 129–134, 136–144, 146–147; followed later by 123 and 124 with a contemporary note, *Duae istae epistolae in superioribus scribi debuissent.*

A glance at this list will suffice to show, first that **V** contains two attempts at making a collection of Anselm's early letters, of which the second is much more complete than **N**, and (even more important) that it achieved a chronological order which modern scholarship can scarcely improve. This suggests that whoever arranged this collection was familiar with the circumstances at Bec during the years after 1070, and the question arises whether Anselm himself had any part in this arrangement. I think this is possible, for he spent several months at Bec in 1105, and he could have taken an interest in arranging his letters in the monastic archives. This can be no more than a possibility, for there were other monks at Bec who would have known enough about the circumstances of those years to perform the task. Nevertheless, it is an attractive possibility that Anselm himself was responsible for this arrangement. But even if he was responsible for arranging the pre-archiepiscopal material, he could not have been responsible for the later part of the collection in **V**, for (as we shall see) this owed much to collaboration with a collector at Canterbury in the 1120s.

3 Pre-archiepiscopal letters in **L**

The pre-archiepiscopal letters in **L** run thus:

> 1, 3, 2, 12, 4–11, 13–17, 19–25, 28–43, 61, 44–51, 58, 68, 53, 60, 54, 66–7, 59, 69–71, 62, 55–7, 72–86, 89–94, 96–101, 103–6, 109, 116–7, 110–15, 118–22, 102, 125, 128–34, 136–44, 146–7, 107– 8, 149, 153–4. Letters 52, 87, 95, 135 are omitted from this sequence, but appear later among the letters for 1106.

If this list is examined, it will be seen that, with regard to the order of letters, a chronological order has generally been achieved which is very much better than **N**, but not as good as **V**.[7] With regard to contents, **L** omits the following letters which are in **V**: 63, 64, 65, 123, 124, 126, and 127, as well as 52, 87, 95, and 135, which only became available to the compiler of **L** at a late stage in the composition of the collection. By contrast, however, **L** contains several that are not in **V**, namely: 9, 10, 19, 23, 24, 52, 87, 95, 107, 108, 128, 135.

The only conclusion that at present can be drawn from these differences is that the two main collections **V** and **L** do not represent a single concerted effort, but must be seen as two separate, but – as we shall see in their archiepiscopal collections – interlocking attempts to make a complete collection of Anselm's surviving correspondence.

To sum up so far, it is obvious that both **L** and **V** are more complete than **N**, and that the arrangement in both achieves a much more successful chronological order than **N**. But there is no

---

[7] If we compare the contents of **N** with **L**, the following are omitted in **N** which are included in **L**: 9, 10, 19, 42–43, 47, 52, 59 (full text), 60, 69–70, 72–75, 77, 79, 96, 97 (full text),102, 112–113, 120–121, 123–132, 134–144, 146–7. But **L** omits the following which are in **N**: 18, 26, 27, 65.

organic development either from **N** to **V**, or from **N** to **L**, or from **V** to **L**.

IV ANSELM'S ARCHIEPISCOPAL CORRESPONDENCE

1 Preserving the letters

By far the greater part of Anselm's surviving correspondence comes from the last sixteen years of his life when he was archbishop of Canterbury. Whereas only 147 letters survive from the period 1070 to 1093, more than twice that number survive from the sixteen years from 1093 to 1109. There is of course nothing surprising about this: the increase in business and the need to preserve some important documents would sufficiently account for the survival of a larger number of letters.

But there is a further distinction to be made: only sixty-three letters have survived from the eight years 1093 to 1100; but two hundred and sixty from the eight years 1101 to 1109.

Further: of the sixty-four surviving letters of 1093 to 1100, only thirty-two were preserved by Anselm or his officials; the others were preserved by their recipients, notably the monks of Bec. By contrast, the letters of the later years from 1100 to 1109 were preserved almost exclusively by Anselm or his officials at Canterbury. So for Anselm's first eight years as archbishop no more letters are preserved than for a comparable period before he was archbishop, and of these he himself preserved only about half. From this we may conclude that his business habits remained as primitive during his early years at Canterbury as they had been in his years at Bec, but changed substantially after 1100, perhaps as a result of his first exile, which brought him into contact with the wider administration of the Church at the papal Curia, and in the household of the papal legate Archbishop Hugh of Lyons.

Moreover, after 1100, he was engaged in negotiations which lasted for several years, and he had good reason for keeping many more letters. No doubt a full explanation of the change would require several other factors to be taken into account, but this may suffice for our present purpose.

2 The manner of their preservation

Another and more profound problem now arises. Although after 1100 Anselm began preserving many more letters than in the past, this does not mean that they were kept in any systematic order. Still less does it mean that they were transcribed into a volume, to serve as a permanent record of important doctrines or great events. In all discussion about letter-collections, it is essential to understand the great difference between *preservation* and *collection into codices*. The former is an archival (if archival is not too grand a word) business, and may mean no more than putting drafts and copies of outgoing letters, together with incoming correspondence, into bundles and cupboards, where they may lie in confusion for many years. Preservation requires no more than this, and this would be the normal state of any medieval office, as is abundantly shown in many later medieval pictures. But collecting these same letters, and arranging them in orderly fashion in a volume, requires patience, scholarship, and the sustained effort necessary for reducing an inchoate jumble of material to order in a carefully written volume.

This second task is the one which chiefly concerns us, for it is only in this collected form that any of Anselm's letters, apart from a handful of charters, have survived. To understand the amount of work and outlay involved in collecting letters into volumes, it is necessary to remember the miscellaneous nature of the material in its uncollected state: preliminary drafts; fair copies of letters sent out; the 'originals' of letters received. If this material was not kept in an orderly form (and there are many indications that it was not) the difficulties of putting it in order after the lapse of about twenty years were considerable.

We have already seen that Anselm's earlier intention of making a collection of his letters as prior and abbot of Bec resulted in a muddled and incomplete collection of letters in all states from drafts to final copies, which was finally deposited at Canterbury. In addition to this collection, the monks at Bec had also kept many of the pre-1093 letters which were never sent to Anselm, and therefore never came to Canterbury.

A precisely similar situation arose after 1093. Anselm's staff at Canterbury kept some drafts of letters sent out; the monks of Bec kept several letters from Anselm of which his staff either kept no copy, or lost the copies they kept. Equally, other recipients kept letters which they received which were either not kept by Anselm's staff, or were kept and lost. It was only after 1100 that Canterbury became the repository of by far the greater part of Anselm's surviving correspondence.

So much for the mechanics of the survival of the letters. We must now examine the process of collecting these dispersed materials into volumes.

3 The collecting of the letters into volumes

I DID ANSELM MAKE A COLLECTION OF HIS
ARCHIEPISCOPAL LETTERS?

The question now arises whether Anselm ever formed or carried out any plan for collecting his archiepiscopal correspondence, such as he had perhaps planned but failed to do with his earlier letters. The main evidence is a letter of Anselm to a Canterbury scribe, Thidericus, written from Lyons in about 1105, in reply to a request for a copy of a letter (or letters) which Henry I had written to the pope. To this Anselm replied: *non intelligo utile esse si serventur*. We know from an earlier letter of Anselm that Thidericus was a scribe (whether also a monk is not clear) who was employed in making copies of Anselm's works, and the letter I have quoted has been interpreted as an indication that he was also employed by Anselm to make a collection of his letters, and it is further argued that the collection which he made was in fact the Canterbury manuscript **L**.

I have argued at some length elsewhere, first, that even if he was making such a collection, it cannot be **L**, which was certainly not in existence at Canterbury in 1120, and shows every sign of having been compiled from uncollected letters and drafts between about 1123 and 1130; second, that the letter to Thidericus will not bear the weight of the conjecture which has been based upon it. It is of course true that the community at Canterbury was intensely interested in the outcome of the three-cornered negotiations between the pope, the archbishop, and the king, over investiture and homage, and Thidericus may well have been collecting documents bearing on this issue. But that Anselm in Lyons should have employed Thidericus in Canterbury as his personal assistant in compiling a definitive collection of his letters, instructing him to leave out some and include others, is in the highest degree unlikely. As for the suggestion that **L** is the very manuscript which Thidericus was employed in making under Anselm's direction, the evidence about its existence and structure given below points decisively to a date between about 1123 and 1130.[8]

---

[8] See Southern 1988, pp. 194–200, for the evidence about the role of Thidericus, or Theodore, at Canterbury.

II HOW WERE THE EXISTING COLLECTIONS MADE?

I shall come to the evidence of **L** presently. But first I shall describe the steps which were taken by Anselm's disciples and admirers to collect his letters during the years after his death. From this inquiry the conclusion will emerge that the main body of his correspondence was collected during the decade 1120 to 1130 by monks at Canterbury and Bec, with some powerful assistance from the historian and scholar, William of Malmesbury. I shall try to show in some detail how they went about their task.

Before approaching this problem, a further problem needs a brief mention. Quite apart from the problem of assembling all the remaining drafts, copies, and originals, it was necessary for anyone intending to make a volume of letters to decide how they should be arranged when assembled. There was a choice between four main possibilities, and we shall find that three of the four were tried in the process of producing the manuscripts of Anselm's letters which now survive. The first method is to weave the letters into a narrative of the events which provoked them. The second is to arrange the letters by subject matter; the third, to arrange them by correspondents; the fourth, to arrange them chronologically. All but one of these methods were tried with Anselm's letters.

Eadmer began the process by inserting forty-two letters from Anselm's correspondence in his *Historia Novorum*. This method had the advantage over all others that it placed the letters in the context in which they were written or received. But it could never have embraced more than a small part of the whole bulk of Anselm's letters.[9]

Another arrangement which could accommodate many more letters was to arrange them by subject matter or by correspondents. Of these two possibilities, the former was excluded by the great variety of subjects, which defied classification. Arrangement by correspondents was more attractive and easier. It also appealed to a deeply ingrained hierarchical instinct, to start with popes, then emperors or kings, and so on down the social scale. This was tried in one manuscript (see **F** below); but there were too many correspondents of uncertain status to be satisfactory below the top level of society, as we can see from the only manuscript in which it was tried.

---

[9] Eadmer inserted the following letters to or from Anselm in his *Historia Novorum*: *Epp.* 154, 171, 201, 206, 216*, 222, 224*, 226*, 282*, 283*, 303, 305*, 308, 310*, 353, 365*, 367*, 368, 369, 397, 398*, 401, 422, 430, 441, 442*, 443–5, 451, 452, 455, 456*, 470*, 472. Those marked with an asterisk are not in **L**.

APPENDIX

The fourth possibility, and the best if it can be achieved, is chronological arrangement. This is often impossible even for a well-informed collector, and it can never be achieved with complete success. But it was possible in Anselm's case, because several of those who made the collections had been close to him in his life-time and knew the circumstances referred to in most letters. So, in the end, a chronological arrangement was the method which was adopted in all the main manuscripts. Inevitably mistakes were made; and new letters kept turning up which upset the chronology. Yet, despite the mistakes and difficulties, the surviving manuscripts prove that the collection was made by men who were sufficiently familiar with the events to make a fairly reliable chronological arrangement possible. So the questions which now arise are: who were these men, and when and where did they make their collections, and how successful were they?

4   The collectors of the letters

I.   EADMER, 1109–1115
We must begin with Eadmer. As we have seen, in about 1100 Anselm had forbidden him to continue to collect notes on his conversation, but after Anselm's death he completed his *Vita Anselmi* and filled out his *Historia Novorum* by adding the complete texts of forty-two letters listed above.[10] He did this between 1109 and 1115, and it represented the first step in collecting into a single volume Anselm's letters as archbishop. It was a small step indeed, but the prelude to all that followed.

II.   WILLIAM OF MALMESBURY, 1120–1123
During the years 1115 to 1119, Eadmer was once more absent from Canterbury in the company of Anselm's successor, Archbishop Ralph. But during these years and for several years afterwards, William of Malmesbury was busy collecting material for two separate histories: the first, his *Gesta Regum*; the second, his *Gesta Pontificum*. In preparing these works, he visited monasteries with records which could contribute to his work – among them, naturally, the cathedral monastery of Canterbury. Here he found Eadmer's *Historia Novorum* and *Vita Anselmi*, as well as the

---

[10] For the letters quoted in Eadmer's *Historia Novorum*, see the edition of M. Rule, 1882, pp. 38, 46, 76, 91, 128, 134–6, 139, 149–51, 154–7, 160–62, 163, 167, 169–71, 173–79, 184–86, 191, 195–6, 199–206, 216.

collection of sayings of Anselm compiled by Alexander.[11] We are not here concerned with the use he made of Alexander's *Dicta Anselmi*, but only with his use of Eadmer's *Historia Novorum*, and more particularly with the evidence it gave him that a large body of Anselm's correspondence had survived. In his *Gesta Regum*, he used Eadmer's *Historia Novorum* extensively, transcribing several of the letters which Eadmer had included in this work. Then, in his *Gesta Pontificum*, which was finished slightly later than the *Gesta Regum*, he mentions the great abundance of Anselm's correspondence which lay at Canterbury.[12] He still referred readers who wished to read Anselm's letters to Eadmer's *Historia Novorum*, but he seems also to have become an enthusiastic student of Anselm's works, and thoroughly imbued with a realization of the importance of the Anselmian material which he had found at Canterbury. As a result of this enthusiasm, in addition to the letters mentioned or quoted in his two *Histories*, he collected a mass of Anselmian correspondence, which has survived in different arrangements in three separate volumes, as well as in a further volume of papal letters which he refers to, but which is now lost. The manuscripts (**MFD**) in which this material has survived may now be briefly described.

M. A considerable part of this manuscript is written in William of Malmesbury's own hand, and it is the most important of the three manuscripts in which his collection has survived. It contains just over two hundred letters of Anselm in two distinct series:

I. Folios 121v.–155 contain 104 letters of Anselm from all periods of his life at Bec and Canterbury in no discernible order. Some of these texts are unique: for instance, they include an

---

[11] For William of Malmesbury's visits to Canterbury, see R. M. Thomson, 1987, p. 73. For his quotations from Anselm's letters taken from Eadmer's *Historia Novorum*, see *GR*, ii, pp. 489–92. For Alexander's complaint about the loss of records of Anselm's *Dicta*, see above, p. 389.

[12] The following is William of Malmesbury's account of the surviving material, *GP*, p. 113: *Epistolarum seriem, quae in immensum porrigitur, apostoli ad regem et Anselmum, et Anselmi ad regem, et regis ad Anselmum, hic non placuit intexere. Volentibus legere liber Edmeri copiam faciet, quas ideo vir ille apposuit ut nullus eum mendacii carperet et ipse invictum robur dictorum assumeret. Effluebat enim otio, utpote solius Anselmi gestis enucleandi intentus. Ego maius opus moveo et in multorum gesta conor, ideoque necessaria tantum libans, fastidio lectorum mederi meditor.* In addition to the manuscripts described below, William's treatise *De laudibus et miraculis sanctae Mariae*, with its Anselmian overtones and its account of a story which he had heard from the Canterbury monk Alexander who had heard it from Anselm, may also have had its origin during his visits to Canterbury in the years 1120–23. See the edition by J. M. Canal in *Claretanium*, viii, Rome, 1968, especially pp. 116–20, 157–9, 192.

otherwise unknown draft of Anselm's *Epistola de Incarnatione Verbi*, which is probably the draft sent to Anselm from Bec during the autumn of 1092. Other early letters in **M** show a close connection with those in **N**, though it is clear that he did not copy **N**, for not only is the order of letters in **M** quite different from that in **N**, but also **M** has letters which are not in **N**.

II. On f.155, this first sequence of letters ends, and is followed by a new sequence, also of about 105 letters, which occupy folios 155–172. All the letters in this section belong to the period after 1093. Most of them are also found in the later Canterbury compilation, **L**, but a few are unique. All the texts in **M** are greatly abbreviated and generally treated with a freedom which is characteristic of William's treatment of all his texts. But there is also one important new feature: he attempts to organize the letters according to their *recipients*. Thus, instead of the total disorder of the first sequence, we have a new and (for Anselm's letters) unique form of organization. For example, the last sixty letters of this second section are arranged in the following sequences:

fol. 162v–165: *Letters to or from Queen Matilda*: 288, 317, 320, 321, 329, 346, 347, 384, 385, 406;

fol. 165v–9: *Letters to or from the monks or administrators of Canterbury during Anselm's exile*: 330, 286, 289, 292, 293, 291, 299, 312, 311, 313, 314, 316, 327, 336, 328, 332, 333, 349, 355, 356, 357, 364, 374, 380, 431;

fol. 169v–71: *Letters mainly to Norman or French monks or clergy*: 468, 421, 407, 345, 343, 302, 335, 285, 298, 375, 383, 434, 418, 410;

fol. 171v: *Letters to nuns*: 403, 405, 414, 420.

Another important indication that William had already gone some way towards organizing the material he had collected at Canterbury is the way in which the texts of papal letters are treated: in **M** we find only the addresses, followed by the note: *Require in decretis pontificum*. Clearly, therefore, he had already sorted out the papal letters to make a separate collection in a volume which has not survived.

Then there is another indication that **M** does not contain all the material he had collected from the Canterbury archives: the other two manuscripts (**F** and **D**) which preserve copies of much of the material which we find in **M**, also have letters of Anselm which are not in **M**, but show similar editorial characteristics to those in **M**. Most important of all, instead of the arrangement of letters according to correspondents which we find in **M** and **D**, **F** has the letters arranged in a chronological order which is identical with that later adopted in the final Canterbury collection in **L**.

I have already quoted the arrangement of the last sixty letters in **M**; here are the last sixty in **F**:

319, 321, 329, 332–3, 343, 336, 345–7, 349–50, 353, 355–7, 361, 391, 364, 372, 374–5, (368), 380, 383, 382, 384–5, 387–90, 403–7, 410, 283, 413–4, 418–21, 430, 397, 422, 425, 431, 434, 443, 445, (222–3), 467–8, 471–2.

These letters in **F** are also in the great Canterbury manuscript **L**. But there is one important difference: although the order of letters is the same in both manuscripts, **L** has letters that are not in **F**. This observation has important consequences for understanding the development of the collection as a whole. It shows that the attempt to arrange the letters of the archiepiscopate in chronological order, of which there is no trace in **M**, has already begun in **M**'s companion volume **F**, and that it is continued and expanded in **L**. It is too early to say that this shows some degree of co-operation between William of Malmesbury and the Canterbury compiler of **L**, but this seems the simplest explanation of a congruity which could not have come about by chance.

Whatever the truth may be on that point, we may begin to envisage a development in the process of collection and arrangement. During the years immediately following William of Malmesbury's search for Anselmian material in the Canterbury archives in *c* 1120–23, an increasing number of letters was gradually assembled and arranged in a roughly chronological order, and this process finally led to the compilation of **L**, to which we must now turn.

III.   THE GREAT CANTERBURY COLLECTION: L, *c* 1123–1130

The process which finally produced **L** seems to have occupied several years of no doubt often desultory activity. And even when **L** was thought to have been completed, a few new discoveries were made which called for additions on supplementary quires, sometimes with indications pointing out where they would have been placed if they had been discovered earlier. There is much that still remains unclear about the process, but the evidence points to the co-operation of several helpers probably over several years in the task of collection and arrangement.

The way in which the volume was made up has caused some confusion in earlier discussion; so I must first explain that the main body of the letter-collection in **L** is written on twenty quires, each of eight leaves with the exception of quire no.7, which has only seven. The twenty quires therefore end on f. 159v., and not on f. 160v. as they would have done if all the quires had had eight leaves. When the scribe reached the end of the twentieth quire, he was in the middle of letter 469, and he had only two more letters (471 and 472) to copy. So (presumably to save parchment), instead of starting a quite fresh quire, he wrote letters 471 and 472 on the blank leaf of an old quire which already contained miscellaneous Anselmian material on fols. 2 onwards, but still had some vacant spaces in addition to the blank leaf at the beginning. The blank leaf at the beginning was sufficient to accommodate the two letters 471 and 472. These were the last letters of Anselm's life, and they brought the whole collection to a natural conclusion.

But then new letters came to hand. The first of them was a letter (*Ep.* 193), written to the pope in 1095, shortly after Anselm had received his pallium. The strange feature is that though it had not been available at Canterbury for the compiler of **L**, it is found in its correct position in the group of manuscripts **VCE**, which are the descendants of an original collection at Bec. A possible reason for this might be that it had been carried to the pope at the Council of Claremont by Boso, who (it may be remembered) became ill on his mission and had to retire to Bec to recuperate.[13] I make this suggestion only tentatively; but if it is confirmed by further research, it would be one sign that, at this late stage in the compilation of **L**, there was co-operation between Bec and Canterbury, which led to an exchange of material between the two monasteries in the later stages of the formation of the letter-collections which were made at both places in the late 1120s.

Then, after the addition of *Ep.* 193, further new letters came to hand at Canterbury, and they too were added in vacant spaces in this additional quire, and – to accommodate further oddments – two further quires of Anselmian *Miscellanea* were added to **L** at this late stage in its development.[14] The result of these additions was

---

[13] For Boso's mission and illness, see above p. 202n.
[14] For a description of the Anselmian miscellany on these last folios of **L**, see *Memorials*, pp. 333–352, and F. S. Schmitt, 1936.

that **L** finally contained the following main block of letters of Anselm's archiepiscopate:

156–8, 160–2, 180, 182, 185–89, 191–2, 194, 196–99, 206, 210, 213, 211, 214, 222–3, 227, 170–1, 217–8, 228, 219, 220, 229–38, 240–41, 203, 242, 244, 243, 245–54, 256–9, 201, 260–77, 474, 278– 81, 285–90, 292–6, 291, 297–302, 306, 308–9, 312, 311, 313–4, 316–25, 354, 326–8, 307, 303, 334, 329, 332–3, 335, 336, 315, 338–47, 349–50, 353, 355–8, 360, 359, 361, 391–2, 364, 368–72, 374–8, 52, 135, 95, 87, 379–81, 383, 382, 384–90, 395, 394, 393, 399–400, 396, 403–10, 283, 412, 401–2, 413–21, 430, 397, 422–9, 431–6, 443–5, 441, 446–50, 455, 451–2, 461–9, 471–2.

This concluded the collection in its earliest form. But then, various additions were made at different times on the supplementary quires, as follows:

193, 411, then the Conciliar decrees of Anselm's Council of 1102, followed by a joint letter of Anselm and Thomas Archbishop of York relating to the Council; then, 331, 212, 255, 202, 200, 440, 207, 471 (for a second time, but this time incomplete at the beginning), 472, 469, 475. It will be observed that these new additions come from every period of Anselm's years as archbishop, and testify to the confusion in which his literary remains had lain for nearly twenty years.

It is apparent from these facts that the whole process of producing **L** with all its additions must have occupied several years, no doubt with gaps and a good deal of uncertainty about the exact contents of the manuscript, which led for instance to the duplication of *Ep.* 471. But then some reader or reviser knew the correct position of some of the newly found letters, and added notes indicating where they would have come if they had been available earlier.

I shall now sum up the results of this inquiry so far.

The starting point for collecting Anselm's letters into volumes cannot have been earlier than 1120, when William of Malmesbury's collection of material, and his indications of the state of the material in his *Gesta Regum* and *Gesta Pontificum*, provide decisive evidence of the confusion of Anselm's literary remains at this date.

We must then allow some time to elapse between William of Malmesbury's gathering of material and the new activity at Canterbury, which owed something to his example. Altogether, therefore, a date between about 1123 and 1130 would seem to be the most likely limits for the production of **L** with its various supplements; and this, I may add, confirms Wilmart's original observations about the date of the handwriting of the main body of **L**.[15]

A full description of the make-up of this very complicated volume would require much more expert treatment than I can give it. Nevertheless, the details I have given will suffice to illustrate the difficulties that faced the compilers of the collection, and the extent of their success. In the first place, it may seem incredible that the process of merely finding the letters should have given so much trouble. But the manuscript provides ample evidence that new discoveries were being made even while the manuscript was being written. It also bears witness to the difficulties of arranging letters in chronological order after a lapse of twenty years. The degree of success of the compilers of **L** may be judged by reading the sequence of numbers quoted above, and remembering that the numbers represent Fr Schmitt's attempt to arrive at a chronological order. If we ignore minor displacements and late discoveries, it will be seen at once that the compilers of **L** succeeded reasonably well.

IV.   THE GREAT BEC COLLECTION: **V** (*c* 1125)

It only remains to say something about the collection which was made at Bec during the period when **L** was being compiled. I have already mentioned that the collection of Anselm's pre-1093 letters at Bec was superior in numbers and arrangement to the collection at Canterbury from which **L** was compiled. It seems that, during the years when **L** was being put together at Canterbury, a parallel process of compilation was in progress at Bec. I have associated the new impulse at Canterbury with two monks who were both devoted to Anselm: Eadmer and William of Malmesbury. The destruction of Bec's medieval library makes it impossible to speak with any assurance about the instigator of the parallel work of compilation at Bec, but one possibly significant fact may be mentioned: Boso, who spent several years with Anselm at Canterbury between 1094 and 1097, and again between 1106 and 1109, became abbot of Bec in 1124.

The manuscript **V** which I am about to describe can best be understood as a copy of a now lost Bec manuscript, which contained

---

[15] See Wilmart 1931, p. 39: 'je le daterais vers 1120'; perhaps, he adds, in the same hand as MS BL Cotton Cleopatra E I, also of the early 1120s.

drafts and letters in the archives at Bec, which were partly unknown at Canterbury; but also incorporated material of the archiepiscopal years from Canterbury. Meanwhile, some material from Bec would seem to have been incorporated in **L** at a late date in its compilation – a date which we may notionally place between about 1125 and 1130. Whether the making of the Bec manuscript was directly associated with Boso's election as abbot of Bec in 1124 it is impossible to say; but the evidence of **V**, which we have reason to think closely follows its Bec exemplar, would be consistent with such a suggestion.

Despite the disappearance of the Bec manuscript of Anselm's letters, which certainly existed in the mid-twelfth century, when it was recorded in the library catalogue of Bec, we can get a good idea of its contents from three surviving copies, **V**, **C** and **E**, which are listed above. Of these manuscripts, the most interesting is **V**, which admirably preserves some curious features which seem to come from its archetype. In particular, it shows that several attempts were made to organize the material before a satisfactory arrangement was finally achieved. For example, **V** starts with two attempts at collecting Anselm's pre-archiepiscopal letters as listed above (p. 464). These letters are then followed by two sequences of letters of the period after 1093. These sequences are:

(I.) 148–52, 155–164; then, after a small gap: 165–7, 170, 172–6, 209, 178–180. This sequence is separated from the next sequence by the insertion of two early letters, 123 and 124, with the note that they should have been included among the series of Anselm's abbacy. After this insertion, the second series of archiepiscopal letters begins, and this occupies the remainder of the manuscript:

(II.) 156–8, 160–2, 180, 182, 185–89, 191–3, 197, 199, 210, 212, 213, 211, 222–3, 227, 218, 220, 231, 233, 236, 238, 240, 203, 242, 244, 243, 247, 249–50, 252, 257–8, 260, 262, 264, 268, 271–2, 276, 474, 278, 280–1, 285–6, 289, 293–6, 291, 297–9, 301–2, 308, 312, 311, 313–4, 317–23, 327, 332–5, 343–5, 347, 355, 391, 364, 368, 374–5, 378, 52, 95, 380, 382, 384–7, 389–90, 403–7, 410, 283, 413–18, 420–21, 397, 425, 427, 429, 431, 433–6, 443, 446, 450, 455, 451–2, 468, 472, 193, 212, 205.

The first and most striking feature of this list is the great wealth of material for the years 1093–1100 that is lacking in the Canterbury manuscript, **L**. As I have mentioned above, **L** has only twenty-three of the sixty-five surviving letters of the years 1093–1100; for the same period, **V** has forty-four. We can be sure that these were letters which had been preserved at Bec, where they seem to have been kept in two batches, the first ending with Anselm's conse-cration as archbishop when he formally ceased to be abbot of Bec, and the second with his successor's benediction as abbot, for this distinction was carefully noted in the Bec exemplar from which **V** was copied. These letters are **V**'s most important contribution to Anselm's surviving correspondence.

For the period after 1100, however, the compiler at Bec was almost completely dependent on material from Canterbury. We can deduce this mainly from the fact that whereas the above series (I) is entirely independent of Canterbury, the series (II) not only reproduces the letters in **L**, but does so in the same order as **L** – but with many gaps. In short, just as **F** contains the same sequence as **L** with a great many gaps, so **V** has the same sequence as **L**, also with gaps, but fewer gaps than **F**. In short, **V** appears to be a copy of the material at Canterbury at a later stage in its formation than **M** and **F**, but earlier than the final copy in **L**.

In order to understand the relationship between the process of collecting and arranging Anselm's letters, and the recording of these stages in surviving volumes, it is important to recognize that the scribe of the archetype of **V** used the material at Canterbury at an earlier stage of development than **L**. This is apparent partly from the gaps in **V**; partly from texts in which **V** has variants (e.g. in the witnesses in *Ep.* 318) which show that the archetype of **V** could not have been copied from **L**, but probably came from the original of which both manuscripts are independent copies; partly also from the appearance in **V** of three letters (*Epp.* 193, 212, 205) which are not in **L** in its original state. Consequently, while recognizing the general congruity of **V** and **L**, it is necessary also to take account of their differences.

With regard to the point in the development of the Canterbury collection at which material for the archetype of **V** was provided, it may be mentioned that whereas the material collected by William of Malmesbury appears to have contained about one third of the archiepiscopal letters in **L**, the collection in **V** represents about two-thirds of **L** during the same period, substantially in the same order as in **L**. Anyone who wishes to know which letters in **L** are *not* in **V** has an easy way of finding out: the first hundred and one letters in

Book IV of Migne's reprint of Gerberon's edition of Anselm's *Works* are the letters which are in **?**, the copy of **L**, but *not* in **V**. By contrast, nearly all the letters in Gerberon's Book III, from number 43 to 188, are in **V**.

This means that the collector of the archetype of **V** at Bec owed nearly 150 of his archiepiscopal letters to the compilers of **L** at Canterbury. But, scattered among these letters in **L**, there are about another hundred letters which are not in **V**. It may of course be suggested that the compiler at Bec intentionally omitted these letters for one reason or another. But, when we consider the internal evidence in **L**, which makes it clear that new letters were being discovered while **L** was being written, the more likely explanation for the omission of so many letters in the Bec manuscript is that they had not yet come to light. All this will seem very complicated; but the complications do no more than reflect the difficulties of making volumes containing a very large number of letters preserved in drafts and copies which needed to be discovered at Bec, Canterbury, and – after William of Malmesbury's intervention – at Malmesbury also, with only intermittent and imperfect communication between these three centres.

V   TRANSMISSION OF THE COLLECTION

These three collections, associated respectively with William of Malmesbury's visits to Canterbury in or about 1120, with a collector at Bec *c* 1125, and one or more collectors at Canterbury from about 1123 to 1130, represent the main efforts during the Middle Ages to collect and transmit Anselm's letters in the form of a permanent collection. They testify to Anselm's continuing influence among his disciples for a generation after his death.

But it must finally be added that Anselm's letters never became an integral part of his works, and very few copies of the collection were made after 1150. The political events which they recorded soon lost their interest, and the spirituality which they expressed soon appeared too rarefied to compete with the spirituality expressed in the letters of St Bernard, which continued to have a vast circulation throughout the Middle Ages.

Small groups of selected letters of Anselm had more success than the complete collection, and the earliest printed edition of Anselm's Works (Nuremberg, 1491) contains a small selection of *Epistolae*

Hortatoriae (*Epp.* 101, 112, 121, 168, and a few others) which had circulated in German manuscripts among Anselm's Collected Works in the late Middle Ages. The edition of J. Picard in 1612 first made the letters a regular part of Anselm's Works. Picard was a canon of St Victor in Paris, and therefore made **V** the basis of his edition, with the consequent omission of many letters. The next editor, G. Gerberon, who was a monk of St Germain in Paris, had access to the manuscript **P**, which was a copy of **L**, from which he gathered most of the letters printed in his Book IV. Consequently, Book III in Gerberon represents the contents of **V**, which Gerberon took over from his predecessor Picard; and his Book IV represents the additional material in **L** as preserved in its early copy **P**. His edition of 1675, therefore, however irrationally arranged, was the first reasonably complete edition of the letters, to which Dom F. S. Schmitt (1938–61) added the further fragments (some of them of very great interest) which he and Dom Wilmart had found in the additional pages of **L** and other English manuscripts.

VI SUMMARY

To sum up the results of this discussion: a clear distinction must first be made between the processes of preservation and collection. Preservation took place mainly at Bec and Canterbury, and probably resulted in a confused collection of packets of letters, rather than a well-arranged body of material. The process of collection and arrangement in volumes intended for future readers probably began about 1120, with the search for material at Canterbury by William of Malmesbury, which was continued and completed during the next ten years, with Eadmer probably playing an important part. A parallel effort at Bec during the same period may be associated with the election of Anselm's close friend Boso as abbot. These various initiatives resulted in three main collections at Malmesbury, **M**, Bec, **V**, and Canterbury, **L**. An examination of the contents of these and their associated manuscripts shows that new letters were being discovered throughout the whole period when the main collections were in course of production, and that more was still being found while **L** was being transcribed, and even after it had been thought to be complete. The whole process of discovery, arrangement, transcription and final correction was probably spread out between 1120 and 1130.

Looking back to the period of Anselm's lifetime, the process of preservation was especially important at Bec during the first eight years of Anselm's archiepiscopate, and in Canterbury after Anselm's return from his first exile in 1100. The letters of 1093–5 at Bec, and of 1100 to 1109 at Canterbury, were never combined in a single series until Dom Schmitt's edition.[16]

---

[16] See above (p. 257n.) for Schmitt's omission of the almost certainly genuine *Ep.* iii, 159. With more reason, but some inconsistency, he also omitted a brief letter which he had printed from MS Trinity College Cambridge, MS 35, in *RB*, 1931, 224–238.

INDEX

Abelard, Peter, his alternative solution to the problem *Cur Deus Homo*, 210–11, 453

Adam, a servant of Anselm, 245

Adela, countess of Blois, sister of Henry I, meets Anselm at Laigle, July 1105, 300

Adelaide, daughter of William the Conqueror, earliest recipient of Anselm's *Prayers*, 92–3, 99

Aelfheah, *see* Elphege

Aelsi, abbot of Ramsey, *see* Elsi

Aethelnoth, archbishop of Canterbury (1030–8), 410

Agnes, Empress (widow of Henry III), 92, 99

Alan Niger, brother and successor of Alan Rufus, 263

Alan Rufus, lord of Richmond, 261–2

Alcuin, his contribution to private prayer, 96–7

Alexander I, king of Scotland, invites Eadmer to become bishop of St Andrews, 417

Alexander II, Pope (1061–73): orders Lanfranc to continue monastic establishment at Canterbury, 308–9; his quotation of forged privilege of Boniface IV, 309, 353, 356

Alexander, monk of Canterbury: his membership of Anselm's household, 244, 368; his reports of Anselm's sayings and sermons, 389–90; perhaps responsible for improvement in keeping Anselm's letters after 1100, 244; some of his materials removed from Canterbury, 389

Alfred, King, his prayer book, 95–6, 99

alter orbis, 270

anonymous reporter of Anselm's sayings (possibly Alexander or Boso), 390–4

Ansellus, *see* Anselm of Laon

Anselm, bishop of Aosta (d. 1026), 8

Anselm, nephew of St Anselm, monk of Chiusa: brought to Canterbury by Anselm, 10; papal legate in Normandy (1116–20), Abbot of Bury St Edmunds (1122–48), 402; asks for copy of his uncle's sermons, 389; perhaps associated with collection of Anselm's letters, 402; advocate of the Feast of the Immaculate Conception, 434

Anselm (Anseau) of Laon, master of school of Laon, 4, 203–4

ANSELM, St, *see also* CANTERBURY, **EADMER, LANFRANC**

CAREER, xxvi–xxix

PERSONAL CHARACTERISTICS

administrative incompetence, 181–4, 439

anxiety, 19, 243

confrontations, not part of his method, 175–9

horror of worldly advancement, 168–70, 183, 189–90

ignorance of canon law texts, 265–8

interest in medicine, 171

knowledge of classics (esp. Horace), 61, 236

lack of moderation, 348–51

opposed to Crusade, 169–70, 172

personal magnetism, 182, 184

soft in manner; severe in substance, 182–3

talk, importance of, in his life, 118–20, 382–4, 393–4

visionary experiences, 6, 67

DEBT TO LANFRANC

commitment to monastic life, 15, 29–32

introduction to logic, 44–6, 50, 59–65

483

ANSELM, St, (*cont.*)
stimulus of great issues, 29–30, 52–3
the problem of Truth and Justice, 41–
2, 316
use of essential books, 53–9
familiarity with Aristotle, 48–50, 62–5
familiarity with Augustine, 55–9
stimulus of Lanfranc's departure, 65–
6, 230
Anselm's recognition of his debt,
59–62
growing apart, 60, 65–6
Anselm's silence on Eucharistic
dispute, 45–6
Lanfranc's criticism of *Monologion*,
119–21
his help in crises at Bec, 183–4
a model of an archbishop, 230–2,
236–7
defence of the Canterbury primacy,
230–35
DEBTS to:
Aristotle's *Categories*, 62–5; *De
Interpretatione*, 65
Augustine, 71–82, 117–18, 120–2, 129
Berengar, 46–7
Bible, 69–71, 161–2, 172
Hugh of Lyons, 285–9
Seneca (?), 129n
THEMES AND CONCEPTS
beauty, 212–13
belief, 123–5
Bible, 69–71, 172
cogitatio, 78–9, 129–31
definitions, importance of, 129–30,
173
education, 446–7
experience of things believed, 178–9
faith seeking understanding, 125–7,
134–5
feudal imagery, 214–16, 221–7
'fittingness', 180–1, 201–2
freedom and obedience, 167–70, 172–
4, 217–20, 254–5, 277–8, 380
friendship, 118–19, 138–9, 141–7,
155–61, 165, 232, 453
general substances, existence of, 179
honour, 200, 221–7
intellectus, 131
introspection, 104–5, 116, 121, 450
justice and mercy, 213–16
libertas ecclesiae, 276, 284–9
local traditions, 315–16, 319, 322–3,
330–31, 453–4

meditatio, 77–80, 120–3, 129–31,
134–5
monastic life, 146–7, 161–5, 182,
452–5
monastic vows, 168–70, 260–4
obedience, *see* freedom
papal authority, 255, 258–9, 336
punishment, necessity of, 220–1
rectitude, truth and justice, 41–2, 65,
172, 214
Redemption, the only means of, 206–
7; its universality, 211–16; grounds
of acceptance, 214–15
royal authority, 250–5
sapientia, 131
self-abasement, 99, 450–1
truth and justice, 41, 65, 172
words and the things they stand for,
73–7
COMPARISONS AND CONTRASTS,
with:
Abelard, 210–11
Augustine, 71–86, 457
Descartes, 442
Lanfranc, 65–6, 228, 310–19
Newman, 217–18, 380
WORKS, commented on:
Cur Deus Homo, 197–227, 264, 279–80
De Casu Diaboli, 65n., 172–4
*De Conceptu Virginali et de Originali
Peccato*, 411
De Grammatico, 62–5, 125, 370
De Libertate Arbitrii, 65n., 172–4
De Processione Sancti Spiritus, 279,
411
De Veritate, 42, 65n., 172–4
Epistola de Incarnatione Verbi, 177–81
Monologion, 116–27
Proslogion, 116–18, 127–37, 147
PRAYERS AND MEDITATIONS
the collection as a whole, 91–112
Prol. 111, 448
Med. 2, 104–5, 350
3, 410–11
Or. 1, 111
3, 46, 111
4, 110
5–7, 106–9
8, 85, 93
9, 93, 101–3
10, 11, 93
13, 85, 93
14, 93n., 110–11, 186
16, 85, 93

LETTERS

The collection as a whole: importance attached to his letters by Anselm, 146–7, 395–6; his attempt to collect them, 186, 397, 461–2; abandoned, 399, 462–3; state of his letters in his life-time, 396–8; collection made by William of Malmesbury, c 1120, 400–1, 470–3; collection later made at Canterbury, 401, 473–5; collection made at Bec at about this time, 402, 476–9; final conflation of these collections, 401–2, 479–81

Individual letters commented on:

Ep 4 (i,4), 144
  5 (i,5), 144–5
  10 (iv,121), 92–3, 104
  16 (i,14), 145–6, 154
  17 (i,15), 168–70, 222
  20 (i,16), 369
  28 (i,20), 107
  30 (i,22), 312
  37 (i,29), 396, 448, 454
  57 (i,48), 60–2
  65 (i,56), 256
  77 (i,68), 71–2
  89 (ii,1), 183–4, 271, 331–2
  109 (ii,17), 286n.
  117 (ii,19), 169–70, 454
  130 (ii,26), 145–6
  136 (ii,41), 176–7
  147 (ii,51), 111n., 186, 189
  149 (iii,2), 318
  152 (iii,5), 318
  156 (iii,7), 184
  161–2 (iii,12, 13), 254–5, 257
  165 (iii,16), 160, 232
  168–9 (not in PL), 262–4, 455
  175 (iii,23), 337
  176 (iii,24), 250, 271, 286n.
  177 (not in PL), 251
  182 (iii,29), 321
  183 (iv,105), 228, 265
  190 (not in PL), 251
  191 (iii,35), 252, 269, 273
  192 (iii,36), 269
  195 (iii,85), 252
  198 (iv,116), 338–9
  206 (iii,166), 228, 253, 279
  210 (iv,40), 287
  214 (iv,2), 336
  222–223 (iii,44–5), 295
  235 (iv,9) et al., 288
  253–254 (iv,15; iv,113) et al., 348–9
  257 (iii,62), 152
  268 (iii,67), 7
  281 (iii,74), 295–6
  285 (iii,75), 393–4
  303 (iii,169), 342
  305 (HN, p.155), 297–8
  311 (iii,90), 299
  321 (iii,97), 289
  353 (iii,171), 299–300
  397 (iv,77), 302–3
  405 (iii,127), 165
  451 (iii,152), 332, 343
  452 (iii,153), 332
  465 (iv,97), 345
  iii, 159 (not in Schmitt), 257–8
Ep. de sacramentis ecclesiae (Schmitt,ii, p. 240), 174

SIMILITUDES
castle and countryside, 223
honour, of God and feudal lord, 225–6
king and tenants, 224–5
lord, tenant and fruit-tree, 222–3
mother and daughters, 219–20
universal order and feudal relationships, 226–7

Anselmid family, 8–9
Aosta, 3, 5–7
Aquinas, Thomas, his quotations of Anselm, 370
Aristotle
  Categories: diffusion in the eleventh century, 48; influence on Eucharistic controversy, 44; Anselm's joke about 'opposites' stems from, 61–2; Anselm's comments on, 62–5;
  De Interpretatione, Anselm's reference to in CDH, 65
Arnost, monk of Bec, later bishop of Rochester, 313, 415
Aspres-sur-Buech, Anselm at, 241
Augustine, St: in relation to Anselm, 71–86, 117–18, 120–1, 457; in relation to Lanfranc, 37, 55–8; on friendship, 140n.; on sodomy, 152 n.

Baconthorpe, John, and the Immaculate Conception, 435–6
Baldwin of Tournai: his career before becoming a monk of Bec, 241; Anselm makes him his main man of business, 241; his forceful and

Baldwin of Tournai (*cont.*)
   credulous character, 241–2; his later
   gossip about Anselm, 261n.
Bangor, bishopric established 1092, 337
Bari, Council (1098), Anselm at, 279,
   409–10
Barlow, F., on William II's sources of
   income, 187n.
Bartholomew, St, relic of, at
   Canterbury, 410
Basel, Council of (1438), Anselm quoted
   as authority for Immaculate
   Conception, 436
Battle, Anselm responsible for
   promotion of Prior Henry to abbacy
   of, 322
Beaumont family, patrons of Bec, 92n.
Bec, monastery of (*see also* **ANSELM**,
   Boso, **LANFRANC**: growth of
   community, 68, 184–5; foundation
   of priories, 166n., 185; hostile
   critics of Anselm at, 191–3;
   Anselm's relations with, after
   resignation, 249–50
Bede, main source of Canterbury's claim
   to primacy, 354, 358
Benedict, St, *Rule* of: on twelve steps of
   Humility, 449–50; on abbatial
   elections, 192
Berengar of Tours: his doctrine of the
   Eucharist, 44–7; his grammatical
   argument, 46–7; Anselm's
   comparable argument, 47;
   contrasted with Lanfranc's, 47–51;
   his condemnation in 1050, 26; and
   in 1059, 24n., 26; his complaint that
   Lanfranc misrepresented his
   retraction, 27; conclusion to be
   drawn from this complaint, 27–8
Bianchini, Joseph, 96n.
Bischoff, Dr Bernard, 34
Bishop, Edmund, on post-Conquest
   revival of Anglo-Saxon cults, 316n.
Boethius on Aristotle's *Categories*, 61n.
Böhmer, H., on 'Lanfranc' forgeries,
   352
Boniface IV, Pope (608–15), forged
   privilege of, for monastic
   community at Canterbury, 309,
   353–4, 356
Boniface V, Pope (619–25), privilege of,
   with forged grant of primacy to
   Canterbury, 353, 361
Boso, monk and abbot of Bec: his arrival

at Bec, 202; his essential
   contribution to Anselm's *Cur Deus
   Homo*, 203–5, 220; his role in
   Anselm's life, 202–3, 244–5, 367–8,
   371; his mission on Anselm's behalf
   to the Council of Clermont, 202–3;
   possible role in the collection of
   Anselm's letters, 402, 476; perhaps
   responsible for Anselm's
   Similitudines, 383; and for two
   additions to *VA*, 245
Boswell, J., on homosexuality in Anselm
   and his contemporaries, 148–52
Bregwine, archbishop of Canterbury,
   Eadmer writes *Life* of, 419
Brooke, Z.N., 24n., 36
Burchard, archbishop of Vienne, 8
Burchard, bishop of Worms, his
   Decretum, on reconsecration of
   altars, 258n.; on sodomy, 150n.
Burgundius, Anselm's brother-in-law, 9
Burgundy, kingdom of, 7–8; duchy of,
   11–12
Bury St Edmunds, abbey of: the young
   Anselm becomes abbot, 402;
   possessed MS of Anselm's letter-
   collection, 459

Caen, abbey of St Stephen, founded as
   penance for Duke William's
   marriage, 24; Lanfranc the first
   abbot, 24
canonica dicta, 72
CANTERBURY, cathedral of Christ
   Church
Monastic community and its buildings
   under Lanfranc, 308–18
   under Anselm, 272, 321–9
Preservation of Anselm's writings at,
   370, 399–400, 468–9, 473–6
Primacy of
   under Lanfranc, 330, 340, 352–7
   under Anselm, 330–3; 335–5
   under Ralph, 357–8, 416–18
   the resort to forgery, 359–63
   see also **ANSELM, EADMER,
   LANFRANC**
Priors of
   Henry, 144, 168, 313–14
   Ernulf, 322–3
   Conrad, 323–5
Canterbury, St Augustine's abbey, 359
Cassian, John, on friendship, 139–40
celibacy, clerical, 25, 248–51

Cerne, abbot of, 252
Chaise-Dieu, monastery of, 289
Charlemagne, his scheme of daily
    prayer, 96, 99
Chester, monastery of St Werburgh,
    167n, 188n; see Hugh, earl of
Chiusa, monastery of St Michael at, 10
Clermont, see COUNCILS
Cluny, 12; visited by Anselm, 280;
    Anselm's sermon at, 385-6;
    influence of the architecture of
    Cluny on Canterbury, 325
Cnut, King of Denmark, 237
Conflans, priory of Bec, 110
Conrad, prior of Christ Church,
    Canterbury, 323, 325
Conversatio, the meaning of the word,
    423
COUNCILS
    Papal
        1050, at Vercelli, 26
        1059, after Easter, in Rome, 22-8,
            256
        1078, in Rome, 349n.
        1095, at Clermont, 202, 252
        1098, Oct., in Bari, 279
        1099, after Easter, in Rome, 28n.,
            280-1; decrees on homage and
            investiture, 281-4, 292-4, 295, 299,
            302-3, 305-6;
        1148, in Rheims, 280-1
    English Primatial
        under Lanfranc, in 1072, 1075, 1078,
            1080, 1085, 236-7
        under Anselm: his refusal to hold a
            council without royal assent, 269; in
            1102, 348-50; in 1108, 350-1
Crispin, Gilbert, monk of Bec and abbot
    of Westminster: brought to England
    by Lanfranc, 314; Anselm visits him
    at Westminster in 1086, 167; and in
    1092-3, 192, 198; his discussions
    with Jews contribute to Anselm's
    CDH, 198-202; he is the source of
    one of Anselm's rare quotations of
    canon law, 257; perhaps regarded
    himself as Anselm's theological
    heir, 372; his Vita Herlvini, 29n.,
    39n
Crispin, Miles, 26, 29n.

Descartes, 131, 136, 442
Devil, rights of: their importance in pre-
    Anselmian soteriology, 207-8;

    rejected by Anselm, 208-9
Dublin, bishopric of, subjected to
    Canterbury by Lanfranc, 338
Dunfermline, abbey of, colonized by
    Lanfranc with monks of
    Canterbury, 417
Duns Scotus, John, Anselm's
    outstanding medieval heir, 370
Dunstan, archbishop of Canterbury
    (959-88), his importance in the
    Canterbury tradition, 310

EADMER
    CAREER
    Born, c 1060, 406
    probably descended from family of
        local Kentish gentry, 406-7
    child oblate of Christ Church,
        Canterbury, 406
    enthusiasm for Old English past,
        406-10
    interest in all things heard or seen in
        childhood, 319-20
    first meeting with Anselm, 1079, 42,
        166n., 316, 319
    secret search for Canterbury relics, c
        1090, 318
    chosen by Anselm as his companion,
        1093, 318-21
    his role in Anselm's household, 242-4
    reputedly nominated by Urban II as
        Anselm's adviser, 243
    keeps records of all he saw and heard
        with Anselm, 1093-1100, 243-4,
        247-9, 275-6, 368, 409-12
    ordered by Anselm to destroy these
        records, 412
    his disobedience and its results,
        413-14
    reports two sermons of Anselm, 385-8
    completes his record after Anselm's
        death, 1109-14, 414-16
    serves in household of Archbishop
        Ralph, 1114-20, 417
    offered bishopric of St Andrews in
        Scotland, 1120, 417-18
    ejected after attempting to assert
        authority of Canterbury, 418
    spends last years in literary and
        liturgical activity, 418-21
    precentor, 419n.
    death, c 1130, 421
    WORKS
    Historia Novorum, its fullness and

EADMER (*cont.*)
vivacity of detail, 1093–1100, 247–8; discovery of overall theme causes distortions, 248, 415–16; change of character after 1100, 413–16; originally ended in 1109 with victory over York, 416; later supplement records setbacks, leading to 'Lanfranc' forgeries, 359–60; finally ends with death of Archbishop Ralph, 416–18

Vita Anselmi: its great merit in reporting Anselm's talk, 422–6; meagre on miracles, 426–7; miracles slowly accumulate to make a *liber miraculorum*, 427–8; John of Salisbury's abbreviation of, xxix, 347

Other works, inspired by Anselm and Canterbury: *Life* of St Wilfrid, 408; of St Breguin, 419; *Prayers* in Anselm's manner, 430–2; *De Conceptione sanctae Mariae*, 432–6

education of children, monastic, 184, 311, 446
Elmer, prior of Christ Church, Canterbury, 369
Elphege, St, archbishop of Canterbury (1006–12): Anselm's argument in support of his sanctity, 42, 316, 330; Osbern's *Life* of, 317; incorrupt body of, 323
Elsi, abbot of Ramsey, and the Immaculate Conception, 434
Ermenberga, Anselm's mother, 7
Ernost, *see* Arnost
Ernulf, prior of Christ Church, Canterbury: appointed by Anselm, 322–3, 325; his interest in the Anglo-Saxon past, 322
Ethelbert, King (d. 616), 309
Eucharistic dispute, 25–8, 43–53
Eulalia, abbess of Shaftesbury, 265

Fécamp, abbey of, problem of reconsecrating altar at, 257–8
Folceraldus, cousin of Anselm, 9
Francis, St, a point of contact with Anselm, 452
Fröhlich, Dr W., 460n.

Gaunilo, monk of Marmoutiers, his criticism of the *Proslogion*, 113

Gerard, bishop of Hereford (1096–1100), archbishop of York (1100–8), 341
Gervase of Canterbury, 419n.
Gibson, Dr Margaret: on Lanfranc's scholastic achievement, 16; rejects view that Lanfranc's strength lay in dialectic, 18; on his *Commentary on St Paul*, 42; on the question of Lanfranc's presence at the Roman Council of 1059, 27; on the 'Lanfranc' forgeries, 352n.
Gilbert Crispin, *see* Crispin
Gloucester, royal council at (1093), 189–91
Godrich of Finchale, 93n.
Gottschalk of Orbaix, 40
Gratian, *Decretum*: on reconsecration of altars, 258n.; on sodomy, 152
Gregory I, the Great, Pope (590–604), 123; importance of his *Regula Pastoralis*, 234–5; renewal of Feast of Gregory's *Ordination* by Anselm, 235, 386–8
Gregory III, Pope (731–41), forged primatial grant to Canterbury, 353, 361
Gregory VII, Pope (1073–85), 4–5; decree of 1078 on investitures and episcopal elections, 191, 265–6; relations with Hugh of Lyons, 282–3, 285–6
Grosseteste, Robert, studied Anselm's works, 370, 453
Guibert of Nogent, reporter of Anselm's talk, 119, 165, 382–3, 392
Guigo of Chartreuse, Anselm's sermon on eternal life falsely attributed to, 386
Gundulf, Anselm's father, 7
Gundulf, monk of Bec, bishop of Rochester (1077–1108), 31; the recipient of Anselms *Prayers to the B.V.M.*, 107: reporter of Anselm's talk, 119; recipient of Anselm's letters, 144–7
Gunhilda, daughter of King Harold: wears veil at Wilton but takes no vows, 262; abducted by Count Alan Rufus, 262; Anselm begs her to return, 263–4; her friendship with Anselm, 262–4
Guy, archbishop of Vienne (1090–1121, later Pope Calixtus II): talks with

Anselm, 383; papal legate to England, 1100–1, 336

Haimo and Rainaldus, Anselm's relatives, 9, 155–6
Henry I, king of England (1100–35): relations with Anselm, 289–307; coronation, 290; his charter of liberties, 290–1; supported by Anselm against his elder brother Robert, 290–3; exiles Anselm, 296–8; threatened with excommunication by Anselm, 298–301; completes conquest of Normandy, 301; makes peace with Anselm, 301–2; obtains modification of papal prohibition of homage of clergy, 302–3; thereafter gives Anselm only lukewarm support, 344
Henry, prior of Christ Church, Canterbury, 313; recipient of Anselm's letters, 144, 168, 315; plans to visit Italy, 168; becomes abbot of Battle, 322
Herbert Losinga, bishop of Norwich (1090–1119), 237
Herluin, founder of Bec, 183
Hermann of Tournai, reports details of Anselm's life, 241n., 261
hermit, Anselm considers becoming a, 31
Hervey, bishop of Bangor (1092–1109), 337
Hildebert, archbishop of Tours, on Lanfranc, 17
homosexuality, see Boswell, sodomy
Honorius, Pope (625–38), privilege with forged primatial grant to Canterbury, 353, 361
Honorius Augustodunensis: his connection with Canterbury, 378; makes use of Anselm's sermon on Joys of Heaven, 377; and of Anselm on freewill, 377–8; and on heinousness of sin, 379–80; essentially a magpie, 380–1
honor, concept of: in CDH, 224–7; in Magna Carta, 226
Horace, Anselm's quotation from, 232n.
hospital, Anselm considers founding a, 31
Hugh, abbot of Cluny (1049–1109), his talks with Anselm, 383

Hugh, bishop of Die (1073–83) and archbishop of Lyons (1083–1106): his importance as agent of Hildebrandine policy, 277–8, 285–6; threatens Norman prelates with excommunication, 286; his excessive zeal rebuked by Gregory VII, 282; early relations with Anselm, 250, 286; Anselm's long visits, May 1099 – August 1100, 278; December 1103 – May 1105, 298–300; his influence on Anselm, 278, 286–9; counsels acceptance of compromise in 1106, 303
Hugh, earl of Chester, 188n.
Hugh of St Victor: his lectures in Paris, 34; on meditation, 122
Hugh the Chanter, of York, chronicler of the primatial issue, 334n.; his account of Anselm's consecration, 341n.; his account of the final debacle of Canterbury's claim to primatial authority, 361
Humbert, cardinal: leader of attack on Berengar in 1059, 26; his death in 1061, 24, 26
Humbert Whitehands, count of Savoy, 8–9
Hunt, R.W., 49n.
Huygens, R.B.C., 45
Hyginus, Pope (c 139–42), letter attributed to, 257, 258

Immaculate Conception, Feast of, 10, 432–6
indagatio, 122–3
investiture dispute, its place in Anselm's life, 232–4, 264–6
Ivo, bishop of Chartres (1090–1115): on reconsecrating altars, 258; on investitures, 282; on sodomy, 152

Jerome, St, on Galatians, 41
Jerusalem, Anselm's view of, 170
Jews, role of, in CDH, 198–202
John XII, Pope (955–63), letter to Archbishop Dunstan with forged primatial addition, 353
John, abbot of Fécamp, his Prayers and Meditations, 92
John of Salisbury: abridges Eadmer's Vita Anselmi, 454; his account of Council of Rheims, 1148, 28n.

Ker, N.R., 38n., 420n.
kissing, in political and religious life, 153–4

Laigle, Anselm and Henry meet at, July 1105, 300
Lambert, abbot of St Bertin, sayings of Anselm attributed to, 383

LANFRANC, Archbishop
CAREER
legal career at Pavia, 17
teacher of logic and rhetoric in schools of N. France, 17–18, 39–41;
monk and prior of Bec, 14, 28–30, 32–8, 40–3, 53–9; fame of his school at Bec, 20, 29–30; builds up library at Bec, 53–9; annotation of MSS, 36–8; his excellence as a teacher, 29–30, 39–43; teaching progresses from logic and rhetoric to theology, 20–1, 35–5; chief adviser to Duke William of Normandy, 20–4; Nicholas II's recognition of his importance, 19–24, 32; his intervention in Eucharistic controversy, 24, 26–8; his use of dialectic in this controversy, 47–50; his use of equipollent propositions, 50–2
abbot of St Stephen, Rouen, 28
archbishop of Canterbury, 28; directed by Pope Alexander II to retain monastic community, 308–10; his problems with the monks and their solution, 310–29; takes monks from Caen and Bec, 313–14; reorganizes monastic community, 309–15, 326; hostile to Old English saints and traditions, 310–15; persuaded by Anselm to honour St Elphege, 316–17; his defence of the primacy, 334n., 340, 355–6
WORKS
Commentary on St Paul, 33–5, 40–3; its development, 33–5; a possible influence on Anselm, 42
De Corpore et Sanguine Domini: date of composition, 43–3; its dialectical argument, 47–8; its use of Aristotle's *Categories*, 48–50; its use of equipollent propositions, 50–2
LOST WORKS:
Quaestiones Lanfranci(?), 18n. i
De Dialectica(?), 18n.

Lanfranc, nephew of archbishop, grounds of his hostility to Anselm, 184, 192
Leo IX, Pope, decree against sodomy, 150n.
Levison, W., on 'Lanfranc' forgeries, 352n., 353n.
Liberi, Anselm completes *CDH* at, 279
libertas ecclesiae and the growth of corporate liberties, 277–8
Liebermann, F., on Hugh of Lyons, 285
Limerick, Anselm and bishopric of, 339
Llandaff, Anselm consecrates bishop of, 338
Lucca, bishop of, his protest at Vatican Council, 1099, 280–1
Lyons, Anselm at, 279, 280, 286–8, 297–300

Macdonald, A.J.: on date of Lanfranc's anti-Berengarian treatise, 44n.; on date of 'Lanfranc' forgeries, 352
McIntyre, J., on *Cur Deus Homo*, 221
Magna Carta, 226
Malcolm III, king of Scotland, 1058–93: his visit to his daughter Matilda at Wilton, 1093, 260–1; breach with William Rufus, 261; killed 1093, 262
Malmesbury, *see* William of,

MANUSCRIPTS (in addition to those listed on pp. 36–8, 458–9)
ADMONT,
Stiftsbibliothek 289; 112
BERNE
Bibl. publ. 334: 34–5
CAMBRIDGE
Corpus Christi College, 371: 385–8, 422, 430–3
Trinity College, B.16.44: 24n.; 32n.; 54n.; 256
EVREUX,
Bibl. municipale, 96: 111n.
HEREFORD
Cathedral, O.1.vi: 257n.
LONDON
BL, Arundel 155, 387n.
Cotton Nero C vii, 420n.
Harleian 315 (and related fragments), 420n.
Harleian 624, 420n.
OXFORD
Bodleian Library, Digby 158, 257n.

D'Orville 45, 96n., 98–9
Rawlinson, A 392, 110n.
St John's College 165, 109n.
PARIS
Bnl. 16,713, 245n.
J. Picard's lost MS, 257n.
VATICAN
Reginensis 499, 66n.

Manzikert, battle of, 169
Marcigny, Cluniac priory of, 10
Mary the Virgin, St: Anselm's *Prayers* to, 106–9; *see also* Immaculate Conception
Matilda, Countess of Tuscany: meets Anselm, 111; recipient of Anselm's *Prayers*, 111–12; Anselm urges her to take the veil on her death-bed, 163
Matilda, daughter of Malcolm III of Scotland, queen of England (1100–1118): Anselm attempts to force her to return to monastic life, 260–2; reluctantly performs marriage ceremony with Henry I, 262n.
Matilda of Flanders, the importance of her marriage to William the Conqueror, 21
Matthew, D., on endowments of Norman monasteries in England, 185n.
Maurice, monk of Bec, fails to return Anselm's letters, 461–2
Maurilius, archbishop of Rouen: his *Prayer* to St Peter, 98–9; advises Anselm to become a monk, 31; and to accept the abbacy of Bec, 183; and archbishopric of Canterbury, 267
Meditation, its significance in the Benedictine Rule, 94–5, *see also* **ANSELM**
Meopham, Simon, archbishop of Canterbury (1327–31), quotes Anselm as authority for Immaculate Conception, 436
monasteries and lay benefactors, 95–7
Montclos, J. de, on Lanfranc's absence at the Council of 1059, 27–8; on the date of Lanfranc's Eucharistic treatise, 44n.
Montgomery, Arnulf of, friend and devotee of Anselm, 338
Moses, monk of Canterbury, runaway

monk, befriended by Anselm, 157–8
Murchertach, high king of Ireland, 339

Newman, Cardinal, uses an image drawn from Anselm, 217–18, 380
Nicholas, St: Anselm's prayer to, 93n., 110–11; miracles of, 17; translation to Bec of relic of, 110–11
Nicholas II, Pope (Dec. 1058–61): election and policy as Pope, 19–24; attitude to the Normans, 19–21; letter to Lanfranc, 20–4, 32–3; activity in 1059, 22–3; legitimation of Duke William's marriage, 25
Norman, a chaplain of Anselm, 245–6

Odilo, abbot of Cluny, 3
Ordericus Vitalis: on Anselm, 66; on the elaboration of monastic offices, 45
Osbern, Anselm's pupil who died young, 145
Osbern, monk of Canterbury: sent by Lanfranc to Anselm at Bec for 'correction', 315; their union of souls, 157; Anselm's influence on, 315–18; Osbern's role in restoring the Anglo-Saxon past, 317–18; his *Life* of St Dunstan, 317; and of St Elphege, 317; his secret search for relics of St Ouen, 318; his pleas to Anselm to accept the archbishopric, 318
Osmund, bishop of Salisbury (1078–99), 237–8, 260
Ouen, St, relics of, at Canterbury, 318

Pächt, O., 112n.
Paschal II, Pope, 4, 290; Anselm's first letter to, 287; his changing position on homage, 294–8; his refusal to support Anselm's primatial claims, 341–2
Peter, St, pre-Anselmian *Prayer* to, 97; Anselm's *Prayer* to, 101–2; Eadmer's *Prayer* to, 431–2
Picard, J., editor of Anselm's works, 257n.
Plato: *Timaeus*, 57n., 134; *Theaetetus*, 446–7
Praeiectus, St, Anselm's anecdote about, 346

Radulfus of Laon, *see* Ralph
Rainaldus, relative of Anselm, 9

Ralph, monk of Bec: brought to Canterbury by Lanfranc, 373; prior of Rochester, abbot of Battle, 373n.; writes *Prayers* and *Meditations* in Anselm's style, long accepted as Anselm's, 372–6

Ralph, Master of Laon and brother of Master Anselm, his doctrine of Redemption refuted in *Cur Deus Homo*, 204–11

Ralph d'Escures, bishop of Rochester (1108–1114), archbishop of Canterbury (1114–22): employs Eadmer in his household, 1114–20, 417; writes a long defence of the Canterbury primacy to the pope without mentioning the papal privileges, 358; dies, 418

Regino of Prüm, on sodomy, 150n.

Regularis Concordia, Lanfranc's neglect of, 310–11

Richard of Clare, abbot of Ely, 292

Richeza, Anselm's sister, 7, 9–10

Robert, abbot of Bury St Edmunds, 292

Robert, count of Meulan, excommunicated by Paschal II, 299

Robert, duke of Normandy: consents to Anselm's removal from Bec to Canterbury, 267; invades England 1101, 293; is actively opposed by Anselm, 293; Anselm gives him no support when Henry invades Normandy 1106, 301

Robert of Melun, Master, on the importance of the spoken word, 334

Robert of Tombelaine, on the *Song of Songs*, 154

Rockingham, council of, Feb. 1095, 269

Rodulfus, *see* Ralph

Roger, bishop of Salisbury, his marriage, 349

Roscelin: his imputation of heresy to Anselm, 123, 175–80; his importance in Anselm's development, 203

Russell, Bertrand, enthusiastically accepts the ontological argument, 128

saints, 'resting-places' of, 319

St Andrews, bishopric of, 417–18, 421

St Davids, bishopric of, 337

St Neots, priory of Bec, 166n.

St Werburgh's abbey, Chester, foundation of, 188

Samson, bishop of Worcester (1096–1112), rebukes Anselm's intransigence on Canterbury's primacy, 345–6

Savoy, counts of, connection with Anselm's family, 8–9

Schmitt, Dom F.S., 257n., 460n.

Schulz, F., 17n.

Seneca, *Quaestiones Naturales*, a possible source of Anselm's argument on God's existence, 129

Sergius I, Pope (687–701), privilege with forged passage recognizing the primacy of Canterbury, 353, 361

servitium debitum, a feudal image in *CDH*, 224–5

Shaftesbury, nuns of, Anselm's letters to, 228, 265

Sigebert of Gembloux, on Lanfranc, 17, 40

sodomy: in canon law, 149–50, 152; Anselm's legislation against, 152; Anselm's extreme repugnance to, 153

Stephen, St, Anselm's *Prayer* to, 93

Stephen of Grandmont, *Life* of, compared with *VA*, 425

Textus Roffensis, 322n.

Theaetetus of Plato, 446–7

Theobald, archbishop of Canterbury (1138–61), his household, 239, 306

Theodoric, a German pupil of Lanfranc, 44n.

Thidericus, a Canterbury scribe, 468

Thomas I, archbishop of York (1070–1100): Lanfranc's letter to, 140–1; submits, but only for his own lifetime, to the primacy of Canterbury, 340–1

Thomas II, archbishop of York (1108–1114), resists Anselm's claim to primacy, 343–4

Thomas Becket, St, archbishop of Canterbury (1162–70): his household, 240; forged charter of liberties for Canterbury distributed to, 362–3; his exile compared with Anselm's, 439

Thurstan, archbishop of York (1114–40), successfully revives primacy dispute, 416–7

Urban II, Pope (1088–99):
acknowledged in Normandy, 1088,
268; accepted by William Rufus,
1095, 269; holds Council at
Clermont, 1095, 202–3, 255;
summons Anselm to Rome, 1098,
279; with Anselm at Bari, 1098,
279; and at Rome, Easter 1099, 280;
decrees against lay investiture and
clerical homage, 280–4; death, 287

Vaughn, S.: on Anselm's aim in
collecting his letters, 460; on the
meaning of Anselm's instructions to
monks of Bec about friendship, 160;
on the date of *Ep*.147, 189n.; on
Anselm's desire to be archbishop,
190n.; on Anselm's abilities as an
administrator, 184n.; on the reason
for Anselm's threat to
excommunicate Henry I in 1106,
301; on Anselm's relations with
Queen Matilda, 262n.
Vienne, visited by Anselm, 280; *see also*
Guy, archbishop

Walter, cardinal-archbishop of Albano,
papal legate: brings Anselm his
pallium, 270; disagrees with Anselm
about legality of his election, 269;
and about their jointly summoning
a Council, 272–3
Walter Giffard, chancellor of Henry I
and bishop of Winchester, 291
Waterford, bishopric of, 339
Westminster Abbey, *see* Crispin, Gilbert
William I, duke of Normandy and king
of England: his stature as a ruler, 4–
5; his collaboration with Lanfranc,
20–4; problem of his marriage, 21–
4; importance of Lanfranc in its
solution, 25

William II, king of England: his
ecclesiastical claims, 250, 252–3; his
military aims and activity, 251–3;
his policy respected by Anselm,
250–3, 273; threats to territorial
rights of Canterbury the main cause
of Anselm's active opposition, 270–
2; William's recognition of Urban
II, 269; Anselm pleads against his
excommunication by Urban II, 279;
his death, 289
William of Corbeil, archbishop of
Canterbury (1123–36), 418
William of Jumièges, on Duke William's
marriage, 25n.
William of Malmesbury: on Osbern,
317; on Eadmer, 247; on the church
at Canterbury, 324–3; collects
Anselm's letters and other works,
400–2, 470–3; removes some of
these materials from Canterbury to
Malmesbury, 390–4; reports
discovery of the 'Lanfranc'
forgeries, 360; assumes that
Lanfranc used these texts in 1072,
360
William of Warelwast, royal messenger
and later bishop of Exeter, 246–8, 304
Willis, R., 325n., 326–7
Wilmart, Dom André, 91n., 109n.,
251n., 476
Wilton, nunnery of, 260–4
Windsor, a sermon to royal court at, 3
Sept 1101, 386–8
Wulfstan, St, bishop of Worcester,
William of Malmesbury's *Life* of,
compared with *VA*, 424–5

York, archbishops of, and primacy of
Canterbury, 339–44, 359–61; *see
also* Thomas I, Thomas II,
Thurstan